TEXAS BLUES

John and Robin Dickson Series in Texas Music

Sponsored by the Center for Texas Music History

Texas State University–San Marcos

GARY HARTMAN & GREGG ANDREWS,

General Editors

TEXAS BLUES

The Rise of a Contemporary Sound

ALAN GOVENAR

TEXAS A&M UNIVERSITY PRESS College Station

Unidentified men, n.d. Photograph found in Dallas.
Courtesy Texas African American Photography Archive.

Manufactured in China by
Everbest Printing Co.through
Four Colour Imports

This paper meets the requirements of
ANSI/NISO z39.48-1992 (Permanence of Paper).
Binding materials have been chosen for durability.

Library of Congress Cataloging-in-Publication Data
Govenar, Alan B., 1952–
Texas blues : the rise of a contemporary sound / Alan Govenar.
p. cm. — (The John and Robin Dickson series in Texas music)
Includes bibliographical references (p.) and index.
ISBN-13: 978-1-58544-605-6 (cloth : alk. paper)
ISBN-10: 1-58544-605-X (cloth : alk. paper)
1. Blues musicians—Texas—Interviews. 2. Blues (Music)—
Texas—History and criticism. I. Title.
ML394.G68 2008
781.64309764—dc22
2007039152

Publication of this book is supported in part by a generous grant from the Summerlee Foundation, Dallas, Texas.

CONTENTS

FOREWORD Paul Oliver

Well, the Blues come to Texas, lopin' like a mule,
You take a high-brown woman, man, she's hard to fool
You can never tell what a woman's got on her mind,
Man, you can't tell—what a woman's got on her mind
You might think she's crazy 'bout you, she's leavin' you all the time . . .

These words[1] were sung by Blind Lemon Jefferson on the very first secular recording that he made, entitled "Got the Blues." It was recorded in March 1926 and it was backed by "Long Lonesome Blues" when it was issued on Paramount 12354. Blind Lemon, who came from the rural region of Wortham, Texas, is considered to be the first male folk blues singer on record, and is regarded by many as being the finest of his time. This accolade, however, also goes to Charley Patton from the Mississippi Delta among some enthusiasts; he too was recorded by Paramount, but some three years later. There has been much writing on the Mississippi blues, and many enthusiasts would argue that blues emanated from the Delta—no, not the delta of the river, but a flatland region in the north of the state.[2]

So when Jefferson sang in the opening couplet, "the blues came to Texas, lopin' like a mule," what did he mean? Did he mean that the blues as a music came rapidly to Texas from somewhere else, as rapidly and as disturbing as the loping mule? Or did he refer to the blues as a state of mind, of depression, or melancholy—or of frustration, in this case? This we might assume from the second line, and the duplicity of the woman to whom he refers in the subsequent verses appears to confirm it. But still the question remains: did the blues, as a song and music form, come to Texas from elsewhere, or did it originate there?

Some collectors and writers on the blues argue that

1. Blind Lemon Jefferson, vocal with guitar, Chicago, March 1926. *Got the Blues*, Paramount 12354.

2. William Barlow, *Looking Up at Down: The Emergence of Blues Culture* (Philadelphia: Temple University Press, 1989), pp. 26–55 and Robert Palmer, *Deep Blues* (New York: Viking, 1981).

(TOP)
BLIND LEMON JEFFERSON, CHICAGO, MARCH 1928, "PINEY WOODS MONEY MAMA," PARAMOUNT 12650–A.
(BOTTOM)
BLIND LEMON JEFFERSON, CHICAGO, JUNE 1928, "LOW DOWN MOJO BLUES," PARAMOUNT 12680–B.

(LEFT) BLIND LEMON JEFFERSON, "SUNSHINE SPECIAL," CHICAGO, OCTOBER 1927, PARAMOUNT 12593.
(RIGHT) BLIND LEMON JEFFERSON, "LONESOME HOUSE BLUES," CHICAGO, OCTOBER 1927, PARAMOUNT 12593.

its origins lie in Mississippi and that it filtered, or was brought by migrant workers, to Texas. The couplet song termed "Dink Blues" is regarded as having been heard sung by a woman who came with a "boatload of women" to Texas in 1899 from Memphis, Tennessee,[3] the inference being that she brought the song with her. But she was brought to join workers in a Texas levee camp and she may have well picked up the song in Texas.

Archeologist Charles Peabody, excavating in the Delta in 1901,[4] noted the songs of his Clarksdale workmen, including a few blues verses, four years before Howard Odum collected some there.[5] These were the earliest to be gathered in Mississippi, whereas blues verses were heard in Texas in the late nineteenth century. W. H. Thomas, an early president of the Texas Folklore Society, noted the years in which he collected them. One song was "Jack O' Diamonds," which was later recorded by Blind Lemon Jefferson. Another was an early "Railroad Blues."

I got the blues, but I haven't got the fare
I got the blues, but I haven't got the fare,
I got the blues, but I'm too damned mean to cry.
Oh, where was you when the rollin' mill burned down?
On the levee camp about fifteen miles from town[6]

Gates Thomas, the brother of William Thomas, also collected proto-blues in those early years, several of a couplet and refrain line form, the first being heard in 1886.

The old hen cackle, she cackle in the corn
The next time she cackle, she cackle in the barn.
Well, the old hen cackle, she sholy gwain to lay[7]

The last that he noted was collected in 1906, which was a sixteen-verse blues on the subject of the cotton pest, "The Boll Weevil."

The first time I seen him he was settin' on a square
Well, the next time I seen him, he was a-crawlin' everywhere
Just a huntin' him a home, Babe, just a-huntin' him a home[8]

Many other examples of early Texas proto-blues and blues could be cited, some being included in *On the Trail of the Negro Folk Songs* by Dorothy Scarborough, who was from Waco. Her book was published in 1925 and included items noted in the previous fifteen years.[9] It is clear that these were all from folk-song collections—in other words, they were collected for their value as additions to the folk songs that had been gathered, or they were new variants of songs already collected. The collectors were creating anthologies of folk song and seldom referred to the singers themselves, or the instruments they played. Gates Thomas's variant of "Don't Love-a Nobody" was one that he secured in 1893 "from a Negro cook in Sherman, who was a fairly good self-taught musician and did a little adapting on his own, playing his results on an organ."[10] But this identified source was a rare exception, and even so, he did not name the musician, or where the organ was situated and played.

3. John A. Lomax and Alan Lomax, *American Ballads and Folk Songs* (New York: MacMillan, 1934), p. 193.

4. Charles Peabody, "Notes on Negro Music," *Journal of American Folklore* (1903), No. 16, pp. 145–52.

5. Barlow, p. 47.

6. William H. Thomas, "Some Comments on Folk Songs of the Negro, and their Economic Interpretation," Texas Folklore Society brochure, pp. 3–13.

7. Gates Thomas, "Six Negro Folk Songs from the Colorado Valley," in Mody Boatwright, et al., *Texas Folk and Folklore* (Dallas, Texas: Southern Methodist University Press, 1934).

8. Gates Thomas, "South Texas Negro Work Songs; Collected and Uncollected Songs Secured 1887–1905" in J. Frank Dobie, ed., *Rainbow in the Morning* (Publications of the Texas Folklore Society, No. V).

9. Dorothy Scarbrough, *On the Trail of Negro Folk Songs* (Cambridge, Massachusetts: Harvard University Press, 1925).

10. Thomas in J. Frank Dobie.

For blues enthusiasts there are many questions that arise from these noted blues. How widely were they distributed? Who were the singers, and where did they live or work? What were the circumstances in which they performed: on the street? in bars and clubs? Were they members of small groups or were they solo performers? We may like to know whether they made a living out of their playing—or were they all performing for pleasure or simply releasing their feelings? What did they think of the blues as experience and as music? Who did they hear and admire? What did they know of music elsewhere. . . . ?

And who were the blues singers and players who never did record, but who enjoyed local reputations as performers? These and many more queries come to mind as we listen.

Our knowledge of the singers, what instruments they played, and how these were essential to the nature of blues music is very much conditioned by recordings. Fortunately, Jefferson was recorded in 1926 and many times thereafter until his tragic death in 1929. And there were many others, such as Henry Thomas "Ragtime Texas," Will Day, and "Little Hat" Jones; as well as women singers, such as Gertrude Perkins, Lillian Glinn, and Hattie Burleson; and pianists like Alex Moore, and later, Black Boy Shine and Andy Boy, some of them recorded in Chicago or New York, but several others by the field units of companies that visited Dallas, or occasionally, San Antonio. Yet there are many about whom we know little, or nothing. What personal information that we have on the lives, careers, contacts, and experiences of some of the singers was only acquired in the late 1950s and after, as the listening audience for blues grew internationally. What was learned was largely gained in the northern cities, since the racial segregation that was still being imposed in the South was a major deterrent.

As we have seen, there is evidence of blues in Texas at a very early date, and it may well have developed in the state. Moreover, it persisted for the whole of the twentieth century and many of the major singers and musicians, such as Mance Lipscomb, Alex Moore, Sippie Wallace, T-Bone Walker, and Lightnin' Hopkins, are Texans. T-Bone Walker and Gatemouth Brown were to be heard in the post-World War II years. And of course there were many others: some well-known from their recordings, others active but recording little, while still others were supporting musicians who played for jazz groups or the early phases of rock music. They came from many parts of East Texas, some moving to the cities while others became known on the West Coast and other destinations. Meanwhile, with the founding of record companies in the state, such as Don Robey's Peacock label in Houston, several blues singers from other states established themselves in Texas.

All of this is why this book, *Texas Blues: The Rise of a Contemporary Sound*, is so important, for its author, Alan Govenar, has spent many years seeking the blues singers and musicians of all generations, in order that he could interview them, photograph them, and obtain in their own words not only their life stories as blues artists but also the meaning and value of the blues to them. Here readers will find the answers to many of the questions that have been mentioned above. Significantly, the fascinating story becomes clear—the development of the blues in Texas over the century that followed the period when those first blues lyrics were collected.

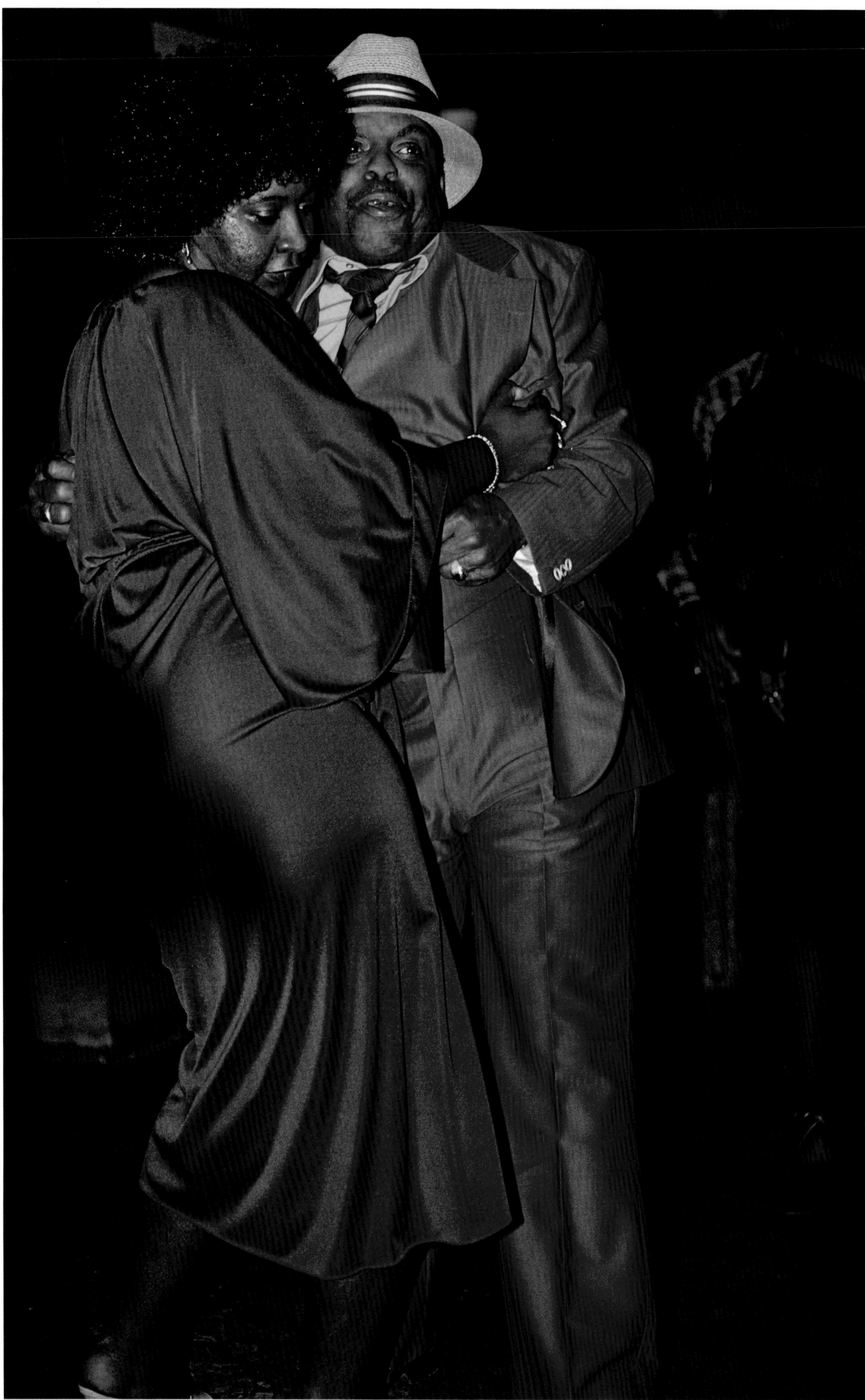

ACKNOWLEDGMENTS

In making this book I have been helped by many people. Foremost, I am grateful to the blues artists who inspired this work. This volume is dedicated to these musicians and to the memory of those whom I heard but never met.

I am also thankful to the researchers and collectors who made their work available to me: Don O, Bill Fountain, Akin Babatunde, Chuck Nevitt, and Tim Schuller in Dallas: Sumter Bruton in Fort Worth; L. E. McCullough, Tari Owens, Clifford Antone, Susan Antone, and John Wheat in Austin; Lorenzo Thomas, Meta Welborn, Lanny Steele, Tracy Hart, Benny Joseph, Robert Turner, Johnny Copeland, Milton Larkin, Arnett Cobb, and Joe Hughes in Houston; Dick Shurman in Chicago; David Evans in Memphis; Tom Mazzolini, Chris Strachwitz, Pat Monaco, and Les Blank in the San Francisco Bay area; Esther Crayton and Vida Lee Walker in Los Angeles; Michael P. Smith in New Orleans; Paul Oliver, Valerie Wilmer, Roger Armstrong, Ray Topping, and Bruce Bastin in England; Hans Ekstang, Erik Lindahl, and Tommy Löfgren in Sweden; Francis Hofstein in France; Jan Donkers, Hans Kramer, and Marcel Vos in The Netherlands.

My documentation of Texas blues was supported in part by Documentary Arts, Dallas Museum of Art, National Endowment for the Arts, Texas Commission on the Arts, and City of Dallas Office of Cultural Affairs.

The concept of this book coalesced during the summer of 1987, when I toured the major European blues and jazz festivals writing travel articles. Transportation was provided by Delta Air Lines, KLM, FinnAir, and Eurail to Denmark, Finland, Sweden, France, Switzerland, England, and The Netherlands. Though many of the people I met during these weeks of travel do not figure directly in this book, their fascination with the subject helped me to clarify my point of view and to better understand the cross-cultural appeal of blues. I extend my appreciation to these individuals and to the organizers of the Copenhagen Jazz Festival, Pori Jazz Festival, North Sea Jazz Festival, Grande Parade du Jazz, and Montreux Jazz Festival, who provided me generous hospitality and thoughtful dialogue.

In the creation of this book, Jay Brakefield assisted with research, transcription, and copyediting, challenging me with e-mails and questions that often yielded fresh perspectives. Alan Hatchett and Kevin Grossman aided me in the organization and editing of thousands of photographs I made and gathered over the last two decades and then worked diligently with me to scan and process the final images for publication.

My wife, Kaleta Doolin, whom I met in 1988, a few months after the publication of my book *Meeting the Blues*, has shared in my passion for music and life, offering suggestions, insights, and humor as my work on this book progressed. My daughter Breea accompanied me on many of my early blues journeys when she was growing up and remains steadfast in her encouragement. My son Alex had an uncanny ear for the Texas sound as a child and continues to engage me in an ongoing conversation about music, from the roots of blues to "scratch" and underground hip-hop.

Alan Govenar

DANCERS, LONGHORN BALLROOM, DALLAS, 1984.
PHOTOGRAPH BY ALAN GOVENAR.

SHOTGUN HOUSE, DALLAS, 1920s.
COURTESY TEXAS/DALLAS HISTORY AND ARCHIVES DIVISION,
DALLAS PUBLIC LIBRARY.

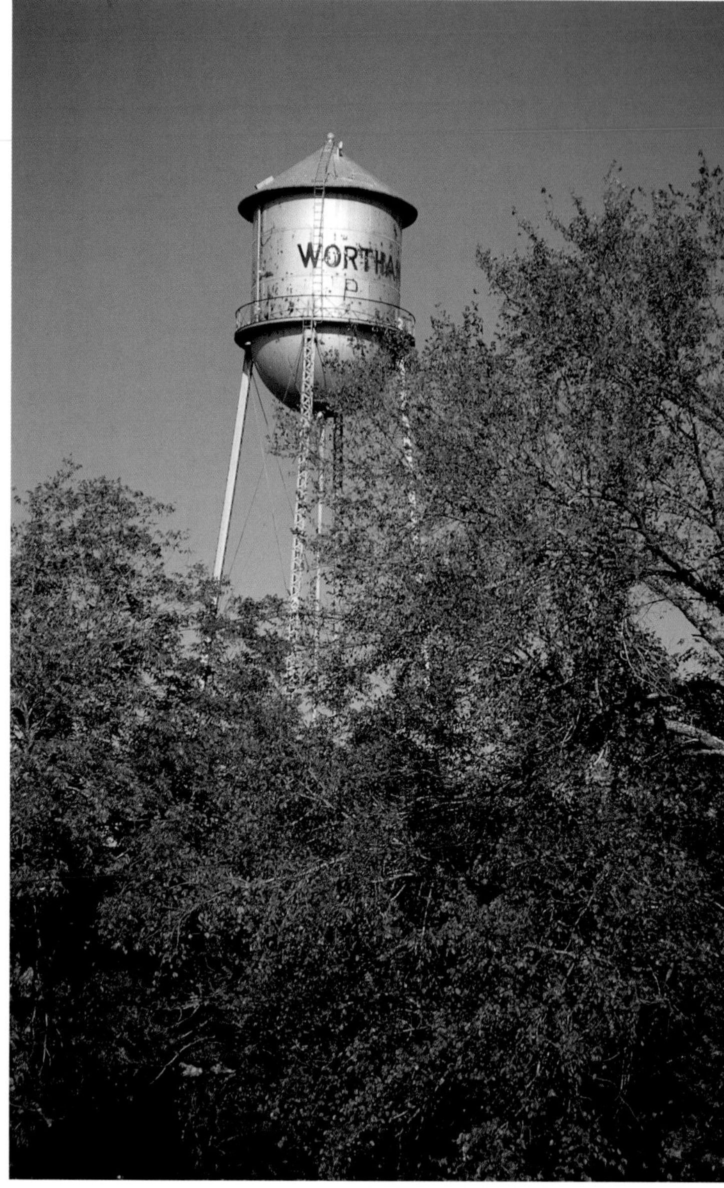

FREESTONE COUNTY, 1987.
PHOTOGRAPH BY ALAN GOVENAR.

PROLOGUE

1987

On Highway 75, in Freestone County southeast of Dallas, Depression-era shotgun houses scattered along the roadside appear deserted. An old black woman, wearing a long, dark skirt, trudges out of the shadows; two children carelessly slam a screen door, and it becomes clear that people still live inside.

Quince Cox, a cemetery caretaker in Wortham, Texas, leans forward on his John Deere tractor with a whirring mower blade. As I walk toward him, he idles the engine and lowers his sweat-stained felt hat into his lap. I tell him I'm looking for the grave of Blind Lemon Jefferson, and he explains he's eighty-three years old and knows "just about everything about Blind Lemon." Then he points across a gravel path to the old "Negro" burying ground.

"Anyone over the age of sixty," he says in a hoarse voice, "remembers that day well." He recalls with sudden clarity Blind Lemon's funeral in 1929, his body brought back from Chicago, where he had died tragically. He continues, "Two or three hundred people came, black and white, to watch his coffin lowered in the ground, but not too many people come through these days talking about Blind Lemon."

To find Blind Lemon Jefferson's grave, you have to ask somebody. The marker, at the far end of the Wortham cemetery on Highway 14, is easy to miss. There are no road signs leading the way. The cemetery itself is on an unmarked dirt road, and the gravestone is an unmarked concrete slab, occupying roughly one square foot of ground. A plaque placed by the Texas State Historical Association in 1967 identifies the grave. Someone has left a wreath of plastic flowers.

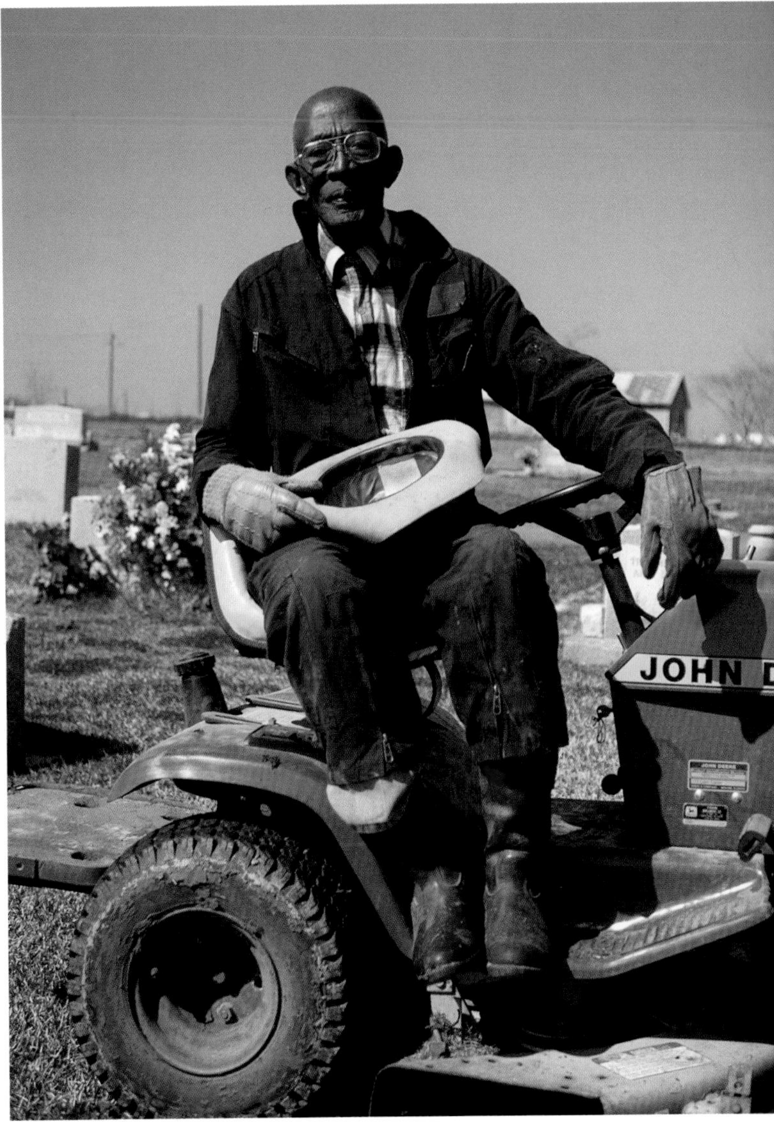

QUINCE COX, WORTHAM, 1987.
PHOTOGRAPH BY ALAN GOVENAR.

The history surrounding the short but influential recording career of Blind Lemon Jefferson has been well established. However, the details of his personal life remain obscured by legend and a lack of solid documentation. There is only one known photograph of Blind Lemon, a publicity still that was reproduced as a graphic in advertisements for his records.

I had hoped to find out more information in Wortham, but the cemetery caretaker doesn't remember much

(LEFT) BLIND LEMON JEFFERSON'S GRAVE, WORTHAM, 1987. PHOTOGRAPH BY ALAN GOVENAR.
(RIGHT) BLIND LEMON JEFFERSON, CA. 1927.

more than the funeral. He does suggest, however, that I talk to Bertha and Mamie Williams, who live in the country near where Blind Lemon was born and knew him as a young boy. After listening to the directions carefully, I find the house without any problem, but when I knock on the door there is no answer. I hear a television and knock again. As I start to leave, a stoop-shouldered woman comes to the door with a cane. I try to explain that Quince Cox has told me about her, but she has difficulty hearing me.

"What?!" she calls out in frustration, apparently not understanding what I am saying, and I repeat, "Do you remember Blind Lemon Jefferson?"

"Who?" she replies, still confused, but then a smile comes to her face. In a deep voice she says, "Why, he's been dead for nearly fifty years," and closes the door in my face, saying, "Thank you."

As I drive off, I realize the absurdity of what I am doing. The search for new stories about Blind Lemon was motivated in part by my interest in the Swedish blues magazine *Jefferson*, named for the legendary singer. In *Jefferson*, a caricature of Blind Lemon, modeled after his publicity still, appears on the inside back cover with a blurb that changes each month. In the cartoon, editor Tommy Löfgren puts words in Blind Lemon's mouth

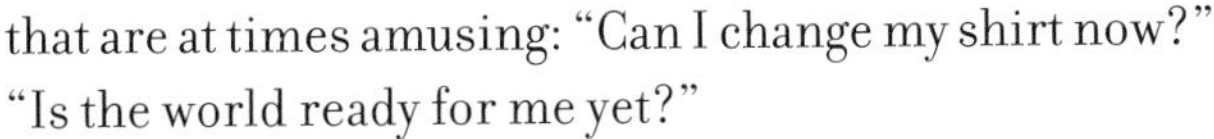

(TOP LEFT) BLIND LEMON JEFFERSON CARTOON, *JEFFERSON* MAGAZINE, NO. 100 (SUMMER 1993).
(TOP RIGHT) WORTHAM, 1997. PHOTOGRAPH BY ALAN GOVENAR.
(BOTTOM) BLIND LEMON JEFFERSON'S GRAVESTONE, WORTHAM, 1997. PHOTOGRAPH BY ALAN GOVENAR

that are at times amusing: "Can I change my shirt now?" "Is the world ready for me yet?"

The paradox of Blind Lemon Jefferson's local obscurity and the international interest in his career is nowhere more evident than in these cartoons. Despite the neglect he suffered in Texas, Jefferson is celebrated abroad as a seminal figure in the history of blues music. Texas blues itself continued to suffer the same paradox until recently. It, too, had been neglected in its own back yard and, consequently, had not been well documented as a regional style.

1997

A small group of concerned citizens in Wortham raises the funds to erect a pink granite headstone for Blind Lemon Jefferson, engraved with his birth and death dates and the epitaph: "See That My Grave Is Kept Clean." The first Blind Lemon Jefferson Blues Festival is held in Wortham, Texas, on September 13, 1997.

1999

On a hot, jet-lagged November morning, the city of Dakar, Senegal, is overwhelming. Piedmont blues songster John Dee Holeman and I get into an un-aircondi-

tioned taxi and head for the *banlieues* to see Barou Sall, whom I had recorded the day before. Sall played the *hoddu*, a five-stringed plucked lute. His instrument had been handmade by a friend of his father's in the 1920s. I had recorded him in my hotel room with his small ensemble (including Lumam Sy, bass *hoddu;* Yella Diop, singer; and Djiby Daillo, *djeube* drum) and had wanted to buy an instrument from him. The *hoddu* he brought to me was also made by his father's friend, but Sall had installed an electric pickup in its body in the 1970s. When I looked at this rusty piece of metal apparatus and taped red wire embedded in the top of the instrument, I wasn't impressed, but the next morning I remember its sound. Holeman, who was invited to Dakar with me by Le Centre Culturel Français, says he thinks this *hoddu* might be what I'm looking for. I had come to Senegal looking for the origins of the blues, but instead I found an instrument that probably had more to do with the roots of the American banjo. Holeman had watched Sall tune the instrument and felt he could do the same.

The *banlieues* of Dakar are more like villages than suburbs, interconnected by unpaved streets; dust billows into the air as the ox-carts, beat-up cars, and garishly painted, overcrowded buses bump along. Merchants display their wares on the side of the road, and people carry waterjugs, stacks of clothes, boxes, mattresses, and platters of fruit balanced on their heads.

In a small, shaded room, Sall sits with his family—his wife, his father, his two children, and one of his cousins. No one says a word, except for his elder son, who has been our escort and who wants only a telephone card in exchange for his help. I look again at the instrument, and hand it to Holeman, who tunes it to an open G and begins to finger-pick a banjo tune. He was right. This is the instrument I was looking for. "The Pulaar," Sall's son explains, "are a country people—this is the instrument of the shepherds—the cattle herders . . . but now, many have moved to the city looking for work."

The apparent parallels between the Pulaar in Senegal and the plight of African Americans in Texas and elsewhere in the South astonish me, instilling a feeling that I have made an important connection, one which at that point I was intellectually incapable of expressing. I pay

DAKAR, SENEGAL, 1999. PHOTOGRAPHS BY ALAN GOVENAR.

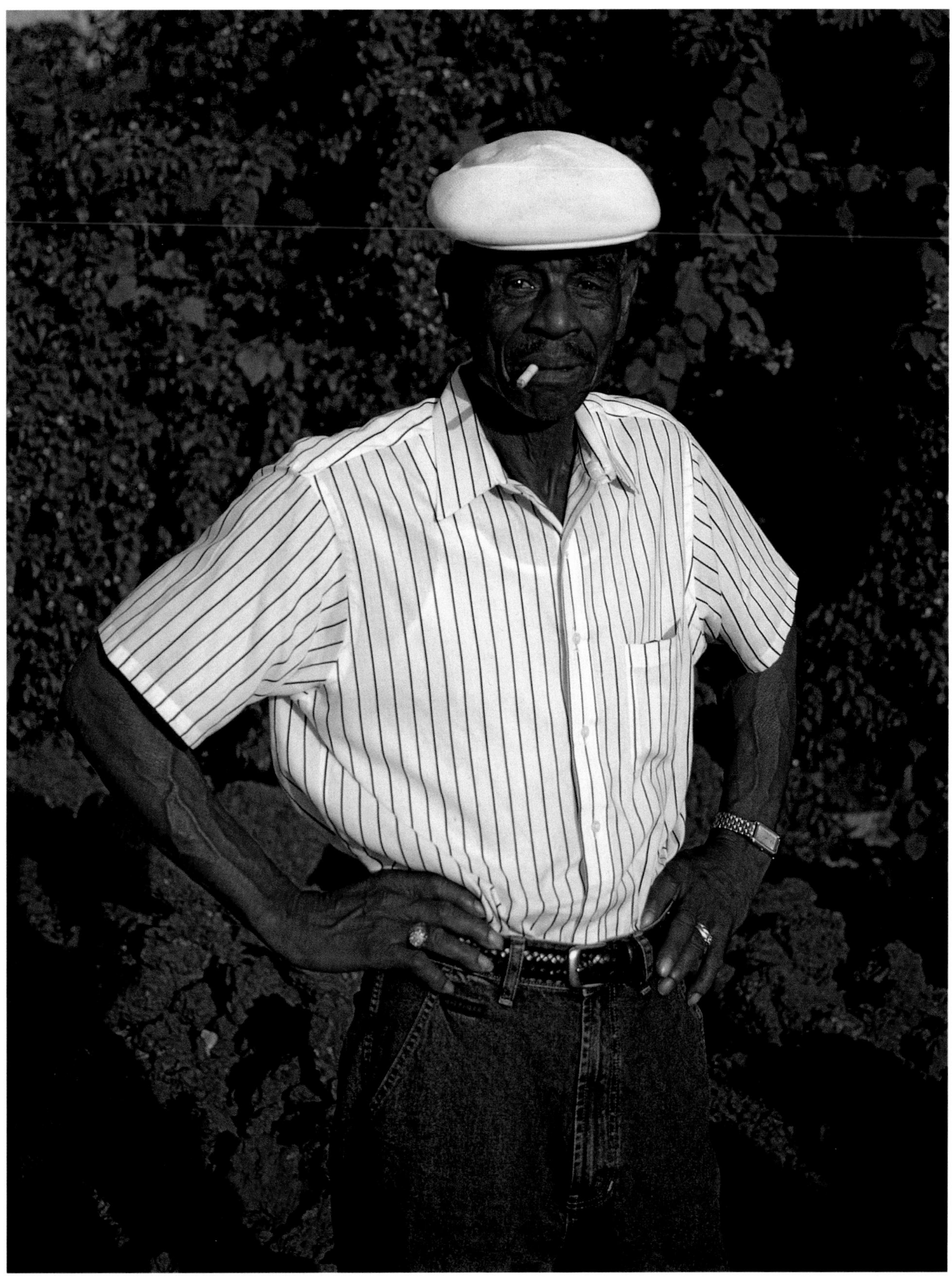

JOHN DEE HOLEMAN, DAKAR, SENEGAL, 1999. PHOTOGRAPH BY ALAN GOVENAR.

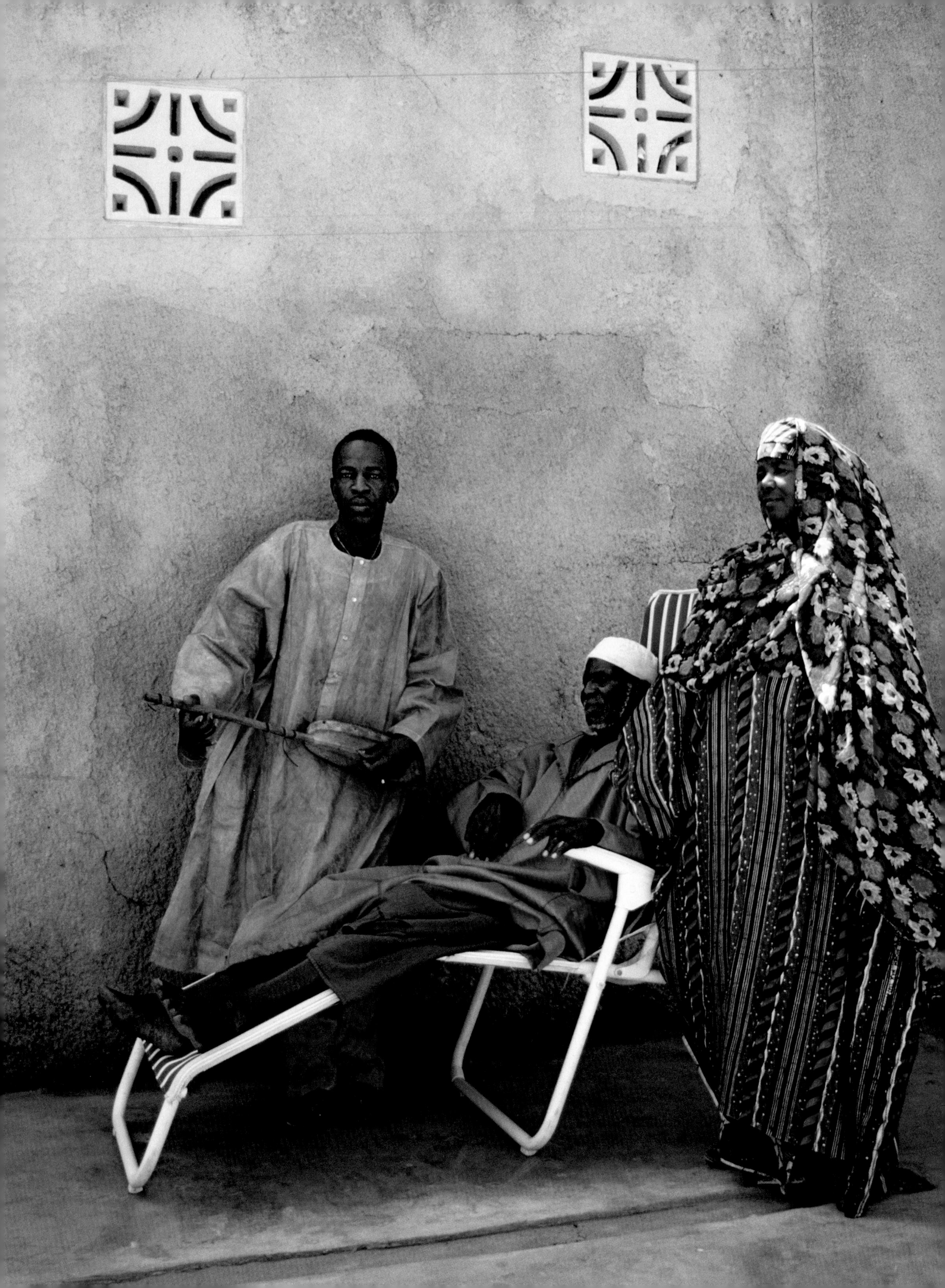

Sall for the instrument, photograph him and his family, shake hands, and leave.

As we drive back to our hotel in Dakar, I close my eyes. The humidity steams from the pavement and the sun swelters through the layers of haze. The sidewalks are jammed with beggars and hustlers, hawking everything from African masks to plastic toys—open palms and jarring faces, the deformed, the maimed, and the indigent—those for whom eye contact is an invitation to come closer, to ask, to plead, to explain why and where and ultimately how much is needed to get through another day. These are haunting vestiges of the slave trade and the punishing years of Western colonization.

Like others before me, I scour the littered cultural horizon of West Africa for the foundation of the blues, but I am starting to learn something I didn't expect. I sense the music in the people I see, and I hear sounds that wail in my imagination. It had never occurred to me that in West Africa I might find the roots, not only of the blues, but of country music as well.

2003

On a Wednesday morning in early October, I drive to Centerville, Texas, with the French psychoanalyst and blues aficionado Francis Hofstein and his wife Nicole, to record Clyde Langford, a blues singer I had read about in a newspaper article and interviewed on the telephone. We listen to the recordings of Barou Sall and his ensemble. The morning fog is so dense that the landscape is muted and barely visible a hundred feet ahead.

Arriving at FM 1119, the road on which Clyde lives, I can't find his house. I call him on my cell phone and he tells me he's seen me drive past twice. Finally, we get settled. Clyde pulls out his acoustic guitar at around 10:30 and plays until about 2:00 P.M., refusing to take a break. At first, I don't know what to think of his guitar; the body is beat up, and he seems to flail the strings with his metal thumb pick as if he were playing a banjo. The bridge of the guitar is loose, and the vibration of the bass strings has a strange distortion.

Clyde learned the rudiments of guitar from Joel Hopkins, elder brother of Sam "Lightnin,'" but he was clearly influenced by country music as much as by blues. Growing up, he loved to listen to the radio and tried to imitate what he heard, adding his own distinct interpretation. He never played much in public, preferring

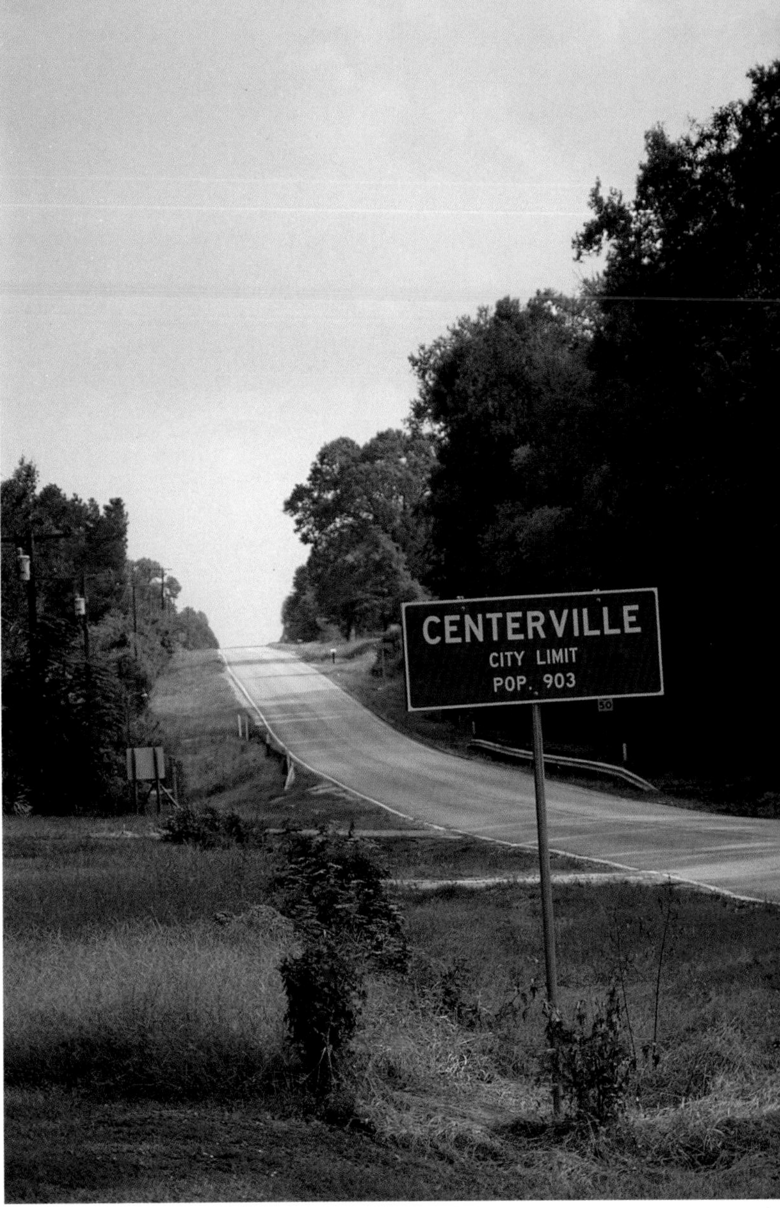

(ABOVE) CENTERVILLE, 2003. PHOTOGRAPH BY ALAN GOVENAR.

(OPPOSITE) BAROU SALL WITH HIS WIFE AND FATHER, DAKAR, SENEGAL, 1999. PHOTOGRAPH BY ALAN GOVENAR.

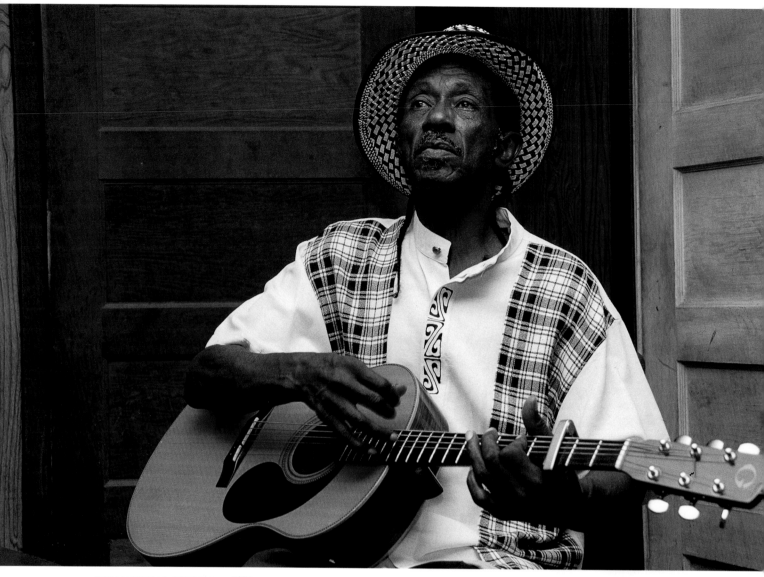

CLYDE LANGFORD, CENTERVILLE, 2003.
PHOTOGRAPH BY ALAN GOVENAR.

THE SLAVE HOUSE AND THE DOOR OF NO RETURN, GOREE ISLAND, SENEGAL, 1999. PHOTOGRAPH BY ALAN GOVENAR.

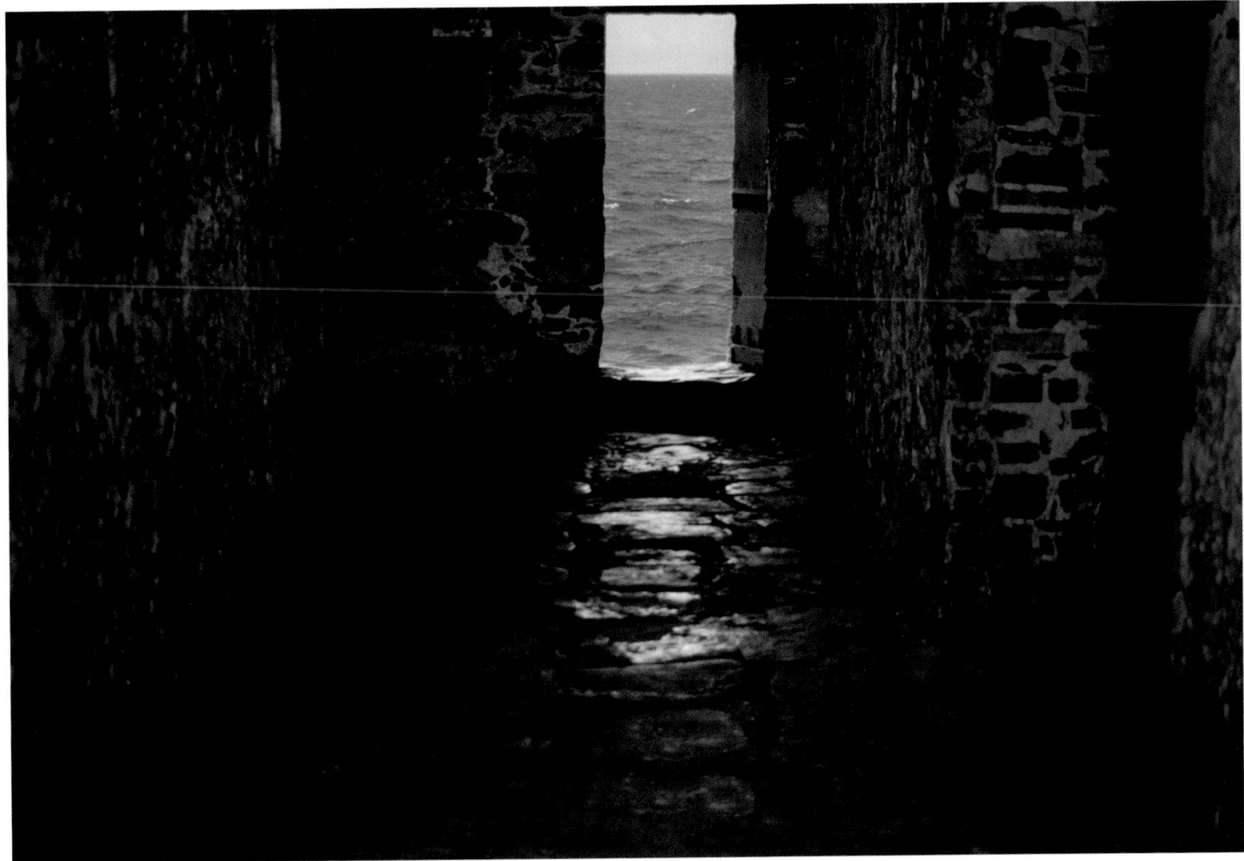

THE DOOR OF NO RETURN, GOREE ISLAND, SENEGAL, 1999.
PHOTOGRAPH BY ALAN GOVENAR.

instead to keep a day job and to entertain himself, his family, and friends at an occasional dance in town.

Francis, Nicole, and I are surprised; here is a country blues singer who reminds us of the music of Barou Sall we listened to that morning in the car. The sun starts to break apart the low-slung clouds, and by mid-afternoon the fog burns away.

About a month later, after editing the recordings, I am still uncertain about the fidelity of Clyde's guitar and decide to go back to Centerville to record him again with a different instrument. Finally, after listening to these new recordings, I realize that changing guitars does not significantly alter his playing. While the vibrato of his guitar is unusual, it seems to perpetuate an African quality in the way in which he combines buzzing and the distortion of tonal sounds.

WORTHAM, 2007. PHOTOGRAPH BY ALAN GOVENAR.

BACK TO WORK

When I started *Living Texas Blues* in 1984, the task was immense, and when it was published a year later by the Dallas Museum of Art, I felt my work was just beginning.

WORTHAM, 2007. PHOTOGRAPH BY ALAN GOVENAR.

My passion for Texas blues was propelled by my appreciation for the music itself, but I was also motivated by the need to know more. My research led me in various directions that resulted in five books—*Living Texas Blues* (1985), *Meeting the Blues* (1988), *The Early Years of Rhythm and Blues* (1991), *Juneteenth Texas* (coedited with Francis Abernethy and Patrick Mullen, 1996), and *Deep Ellum and Central Track* (coauthored with Jay Brakefield, 1998)—and a new musical, *Blind Lemon Blues* (cocreated with Akin Babatunde, 2004).[1]

Now, as I begin rethinking *Meeting the Blues,* I feel more prepared, but not necessarily more certain. Going to West Africa may not have yielded definitive evidence or conclusions, but travel to Senegal and to Goree Island, to the Door of No Return, did make me more acutely aware of the connections between African and African American music.

1. The world premiere of *Blind Lemon Blues* was presented at the Forum Meyrin in Geneva, Switzerland, February 27–28, 2004, and as the opening of the Festival de L'Imaginaire at the Maison des Cultures du Monde in Paris, France, March 3–8, 2004. *Blind Lemon Blues* was featured as part of the *Works & Process* series at the Guggenheim Museum in New York City, February 11–12, 2007, and had its off-Broadway premiere at the York Theatre, February 15–25, 2007, followed by performances in nine cities in Belgium and the Netherlands as part of the World Music Theatre Festival, March 10–25, 2007. *Blind Lemon Blues* was an outgrowth of *Blind Lemon: Prince of Country Blues,* also written with Akin Babatunde. *Blind Lemon: Prince of Country Blues* was presented in two workshop productions (June 4, 1998, Open Dialogue VIII, National Conference of the Association of American Cultures, Dallas, Texas; and May 27–June 12, 1999, Majestic Theatre, Dallas, Texas) and in its premiere at the Addison Water Tower Theatre (May 24–June 16, 2001, Leon Rabin Award for Best New Play or Musical).

INTRODUCTION

The extent to which the "memory" of Africa informed the origins of the blues varies from place to place in the American South.[1] Legal importation of slaves from Africa to the United States was officially outlawed in 1808, although illegal trafficking continued up to the Civil War. George Howe (1890) reported that the last slave ship arrived in the United States in 1859, but it remains unclear how many African, Caribbean, Mexican, and other slaves were transported by professional "touts," or "blind" customs inspectors, or through the Republic of Texas, which during its existence, from 1836 to 1845, cultivated a slave-based economy.

Historian Randolph B. Campbell writes that the "rate of growth accelerated rapidly during the 1840s and 1850s. The rich soil of Texas held much of the future of slavery."

> The census of 1850 reported 58,161 slaves, 27.4 percent of the 212,292 people in Texas, and the census of 1860 enumerated 181,566 bondsmen, 30.2 percent of the total population. Slaves were increasing more rapidly than the population as a whole. The great majority of slaves in Texas came with their owners from the older slave states. Sizable numbers, however, came through the domestic slave trade. New Orleans was the center of this trade in the Deep South, but there were slave dealers in Galveston and Houston, too. A few slaves, perhaps as many as 2,000 between 1835 and 1865, came through the illegal African trade.[2]

Campbell goes on to suggest that most of these illegal African slaves were concentrated in East Texas, in counties that already had the greatest number of slaves. The most solid evidence of this exists in voter registration records from 1867, when African Americans were asked for the first time to identify their birthplaces and more than 200 said they were from Africa.[3]

It is difficult to assess the extent to which these Afri-

1. Gerhard Kubik, *Africa and the Blues* (Jackson: University Press of Mississippi, 1999), 47.

2. Randolph B. Campbell, "Slavery," in *The New Handbook of Texas*, vol. 5 (Austin: Texas State Historical Association, 1996), 1081–83.

3. Randolph B. Campbell, *An Empire for Slavery: The Peculiar Institution in Texas, 1821–1865* (Baton Rouge: Louisiana State University Press, 1989).

"A TYPICAL TEXAS COTTON FIELD AT PICKING TIME," KEYSTONE STEREOVIEW, N.D.

COURTESY TEXAS AFRICAN AMERICAN PHOTOGRAPH ARCHIVE.

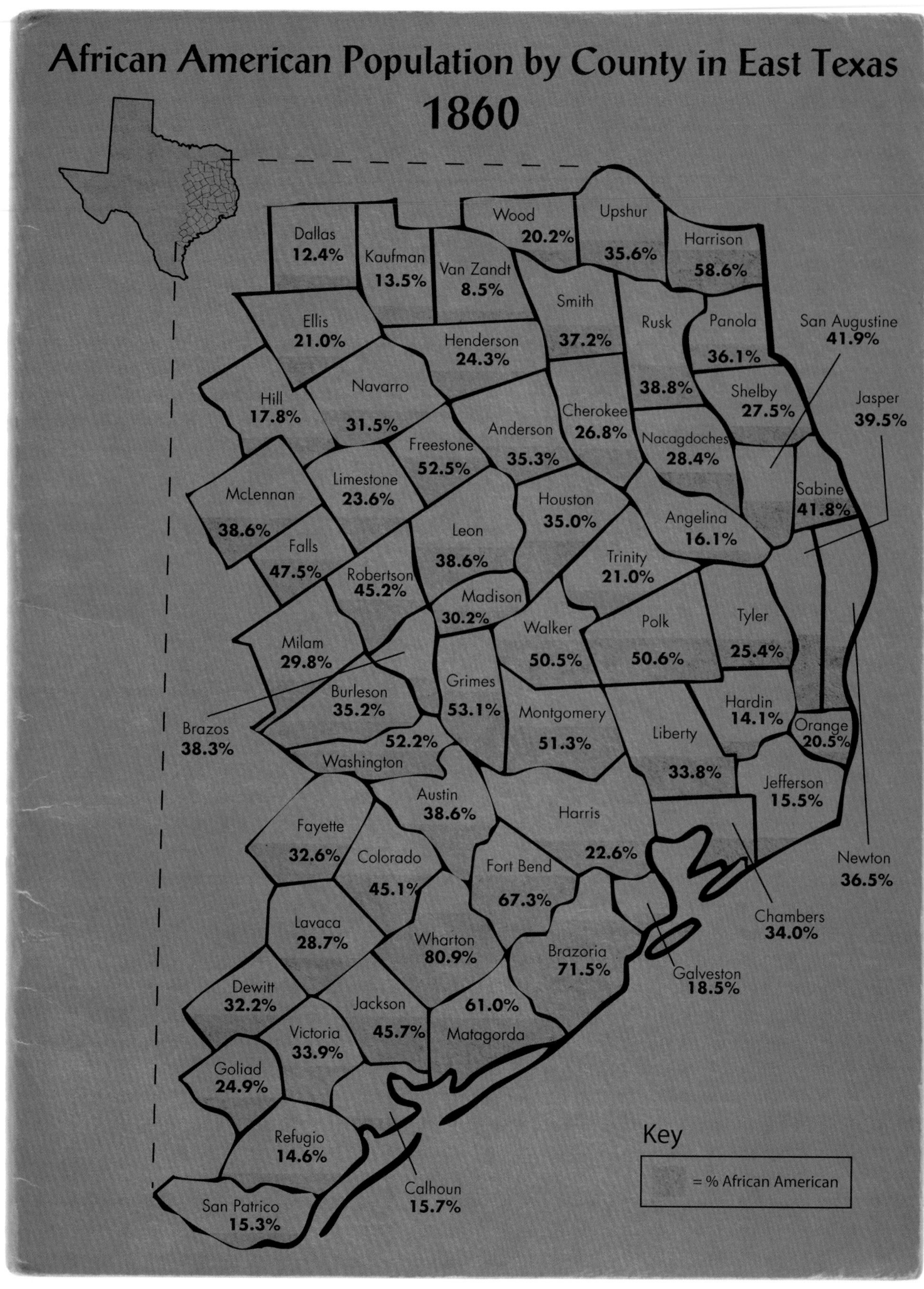

OUTLINE OF EAST TEXAS COUNTIES IN 1860 BY TERRY G. JORDAN.

STATISTICAL DATA BY RANDOLPH B. CAMPBELL AND RICHARD G. LOWE.

"HAPPY LITTLE TOM [PLAYING A HOMEMADE AFRICAN FIDDLE], PHOTOGRAPHED IN 1861, NEAR CHARLESTON, SOUTH CAROLINA," STEREOVIEW, N.D. COURTESY TEXAS AFRICAN AMERICAN PHOTOGRAPHY ARCHIVE.

cans who were brought to Texas illegally as slaves before the Civil War affected the growth of African American culture during the years of Reconstruction. Ultimately, questions related to their musical traditions remain largely unanswered: What instruments did they play? What songs and musical traditions were passed from this generation to the next? Did these Africans influence the development of a Texas style of blues?

SLAVE NARRATIVES

Documentary evidence of the musical traditions of nineteenth-century African slaves and ex-slaves is limited. However, over the last decades, research into the narratives collected from ex-slaves during the 1930s by the Federal Writers' Project of the Works Progress Administration (WPA) has brought forth new perspectives on the early history of black music in America.

John Minton, in reviewing the accounts of more than 600 former slaves in Texas, compiled in more than 6,000 pages of typescript, elucidates the context of musical instruments made and played during the years of slavery, focusing on the fiddle, or violin. While Minton demonstrates the predominance of the fiddle among Texas slaves, he also cites the presence of the banjo, "windjammer" (concertina), accordion, and guitar.

Minton states, "There can be little doubt that the facility with which enslaved Africans in the New World adopted, and adapted to, the European violin is attributable in large part to the prevalence of fiddles of various types throughout sub-Saharan Africa. And, in fact, many of the fiddles played by American blacks weren't European at all. Reports of homemade fiddles . . . are commonplace, and while descriptions are often scanty, it only makes sense that these ostensibly unorthodox items at least partly perpetuated African traditions rather than merely imitating the European counterparts."[4] This is also probably true of the banjo, which also has African counterparts and antecedents.

Musicologists and folklorists generally concur that the plucked lutes of the Senegambia region of the West African savannah, especially the *xalam*, *hoddu*, and *gam-*

4. John Minton, "West African Fiddles in Deep East Texas," in *Juneteenth Texas: Essays in African American Folklore*, edited by Francis E. Abernethy, Patrick B. Mullen, and Alan B. Govenar (Denton: University of North Texas Press, 1996), 295.

"TELL ME DAT YOU LUB ME DARLIN' DINA," STEREOVIEW, N.D.
COURTESY TEXAS AFRICAN AMERICAN PHOTOGRAPHY ARCHIVE.

bere, seem to prefigure the banjo in the American South.[5] Gerhard Kubik points out that these instruments were probably remembered by African Americans in the late eighteenth and early nineteenth centuries, and that their use as accompaniment for intrafamily song traditions, or the story songs of *griots* (tradition-bearers) or *xalamkat* (*xalam* players), may have been a factor in the development of blues. Moreover, some of these songs in West Africa, specifically "Baba ol'odo" and "Ma d'enia," have an AAB form in a structure comparable to that of early blues and preserve "an older pattern of pentatonic pitch patterns."[6]

The references to music in the WPA narratives are generally brief and lacking in detail, though they are highly suggestive. Harre Quarles, age ninety-six, who was born in Missouri and migrated to Madisonville, Texas, exclaimed, "Massa tell us we're free on Juneteenth. I made a fiddle out of a gourd before freedom and learns to play it. I played for dances after I's free."[7] Apparently, for Quarles, playing this African-styled instrument was symbolic of his newfound freedom. Juneteenth, mentioned by Quarles, is still celebrated today and commemorates June 19, 1865, when U.S. General Gordon Granger, the newly appointed overseer of Texas, landed at Galveston and read his military orders, proclaiming the emancipation of slaves in the state.

Emma Weeks of Austin spoke in passing of a banjo picker called "Joe Slick," who had been brought directly from Africa, but she didn't know anything more about the instrument or the repertory of music he played.[8] Simpson Campbell, born in 1860 in Harrison County, Texas, recalled: "On Saturday night you'd hear them fiddles and banjos playin' and the darkies singing. All the music gadgets was homemade. The banjos was made of round pieces of wood civered [covered] with sheepskin and strung with cat-gut strings. One of the oldest fiddlers of slavery time teached my brother Flint to play the fiddle."[9]

Campbell's description of the banjo concurs with that given by Litt Young, born in 1850, in Vicksburg, Missis-

5. Cecilia Conway, *African Banjo Echoes in Appalachia: A Study of Folk Traditions* (Knoxville: University of Tennessee Press, 1995), 26–29.

6. Kubik, *Africa and the Blues*, 46.

7. George P. Rawick, *The American Slave: A Composite Autobiography*, series 1, vol. 5, *Texas Narratives, Part 3*, 223.

8. Minton, "West African Fiddles in Deep East Texas," 300.

9. Rawick, *American Slave*, suppl., series 2, vol. 3, *Texas Narratives, Part 2*, 614.

BAROU SALL PLAYING THE *HODDU*, DAKAR, SENEGAL, 1999. PHOTOGRAPH BY ALAN GOVENAR.

BOUKOUNTA N'DAIYE PLAYING THE *XALAM*, DAKAR, SENEGAL, 1999. PHOTOGRAPH BY ALAN GOVENAR.

sippi. Young was "refugeed" by his owner to Harrison County, Texas, where his enslavement continued. After emancipation, Young found work as a sawmill hand and tie cutter during the construction of the Texas & Pacific railroad from Marshall to Texarkana. In his WPA narrative, Young said that when he was a slave, "Us have small dances Saturday nights and ring plays and banjo and fiddle playin' and knockin' bones. There was fiddles made from gourds and banjos from sheep hides."[10]

Both Campbell and Young mentioned that the banjos they saw and heard were covered with sheep hides, and were played along with fiddles at dances and "ring plays." Although these dances and ring plays are not described in detail, the presence of the ring play has been well documented throughout the antebellum South. In recent times, Bessie Jones, of the Georgia Sea Islands, described the nature of these plays to folklorist Bess Lomax Hawes: "One gets in the middle of the ring and they all clap and sing . . . and it go on until you get to each one . . . each player, then having a turn in the middle," where each player is encouraged to show off, through strutting, teasing, flirting, wiggling, or other individualized dance steps.[11] The ring play, like other forms of African and African American responsive style, involves a high degree of overlap between individual voices and physical movement.[12]

Eighty-five-year-old Campbell Davis, a native of Harrison County, remembered the music of the fiddle and banjo, but he, too, did not once elaborate on the specifics of parties during which those instruments were played.

> Sometimes dey have parties Saturday night and couples git on de floor and have music of de fiddle and banjo. I only remembers one ring play:
>
> *Hop light, li'l lady*
> *The cake's all dough*
> *Don't mind de weather*
> *Jus' so the wind don't blow*"[13]

10. Rawick, *American Slave*, series 1, vol. 5, *Texas Narratives, Part 4*, 228.

11. Bessie Jones and Bess Lomax Hawes, *Step It Down: Games, Plays, Songs and Stories from the Afro-American Heritage* (Athens: University of Georgia Press, 1972), 58.

12. Roger D. Abrahams, *Singing the Master: The Emergence of African American Culture in the Plantation South* (New York: Pantheon Books, 1992), 103–6.

13. Rawick, *American Slave*, series 1, vol. 4, *Texas Narratives, Part 1*, 286.

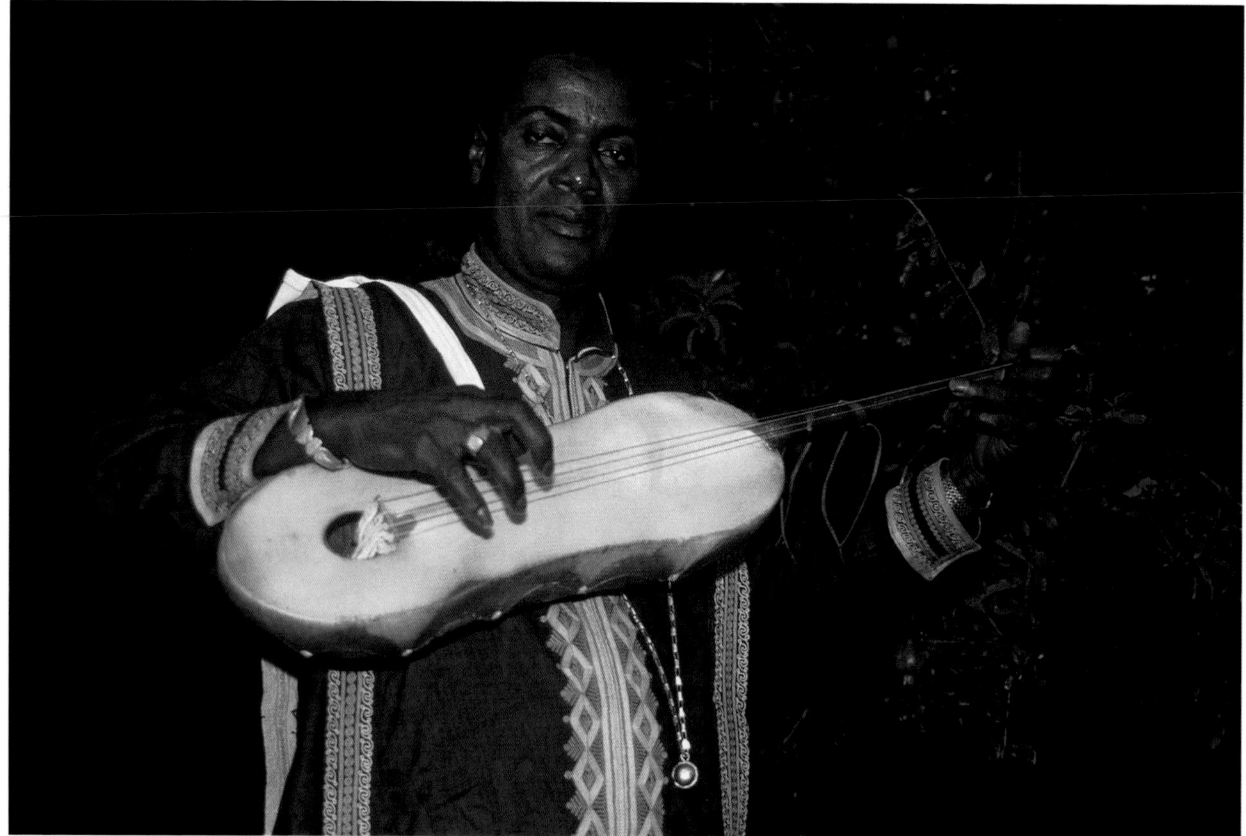

MASIREN DRAME PLAYING THE *GAMBERE*, DAKAR, SENEGAL, 1999. PHOTOGRAPH BY ALAN GOVENAR.

Agatha Babino, a resident of Beaumont, Texas, who was born around 1850 near Carenco, Louisiana, remembered, "We have a dance outdoors sometime. Somebody play fiddle and banjo. We dance de reel and quadrille and a buck dance."[14] Eighty-two-year-old Chris Franklin, another resident of Beaumont (originally from Bossier Parish, Louisiana), went into greater detail about the occasions on which music was played and people danced:

> De white folks 'low [allow] dem to have de frolic with de fiddle or banjo or windjammer. Dey dances out on de grass, forty or fifty niggers . . . barefoot as de goose. It jes' de habit of de times, 'cause dey all have shoes. Sometimes dey call de jig dance and some dem sho' dance it, too. The prompter call, "All git ready." Den he holler, "All balance," and den he sing out, "Swing your pardner," and dey done it. Den he say, "First man hand off to de right," and dere dey goes. Or he say, "All promenade," and dey goes in de circle. One thing dey calls, "Bird in de cage." Three joins hands round de gal in de center and dey dance dat way awhile.[15]

Both Babino's and Franklin's accounts are descriptive of Anglo-European square dances, though Babino's passing reference to "a buck dance" implies a more African-rooted style.

FROM BANJO TO GUITAR

The repertory of African American "square dance" music continued in East Texas at least until the late 1920s, when Henry "Ragtime" Thomas was recorded. Thomas is an important link to understanding the transition from banjo to guitar in the development of a Texas blues style. He played an ostensibly "banjo repertoire" of dance tunes on the guitar, in addition to experimenting with early forms of blues.

Thomas, born around 1874 in Big Sandy (Upshur

14. Ibid., 38.
15. Ibid., 58.

"TEXAS EASY STREET BLUES," VOCALION RECORDS 1197, HENRY "RAGTIME TEXAS" THOMAS RACE AD, N.D. COURTESY DOCUMENTARY ARTS.

W.B. MANSFIELD FAMILY ALBUM, PHOTOGRAPH BY PHILIP H. ROSE & JUSTUS ZAHN, GALVESTON, TEXAS, CA. 1887, COURTESY TEXAS AFRICAN AMERICAN PHOTOGRAPHY ARCHIVE.

County), Texas, was one of nine children born to freed slaves. He left home as a teenager to hobo around East Texas as an itinerant musician and singer, not only performing with a guitar, but sometimes accompanying himself on harmonica and quills (panpipes).

WPA narratives attest to the presence of quills among Texas slaves as an instrument often paired with the fiddle. Minton points out that the term *quills* was "applied both to panpipes and, less frequently, to homemade fifes, both easily fashioned from East Texas' abundant cane or reeds, though green willow was sometimes used for the latter."[16] Bill Homer (born 1850) recalled the typical dance band as "de fiddle an' de quill." "W'at am de quill? I's splain, dey am made fo'm de willow stick w'en de sap am up. Yous take de stick an' poun's on de bahk til it am loose, den slips de bahk off. Aftah dat, slit de wood in one end, an' down one side. Put holes in de bahk, an' den put de bahk on de stick. De quill am

16. Minton, "West African Fiddles in Deep East Texas," 300.

den ready to play lak de flute. Some ob de niggers larn to be good quill players."[17] Henry Thomas was a very talented guitarist and quill player himself, as demonstrated in his earliest recordings for Vocalion in 1927 in Chicago. In this session (October 27) Thomas recorded two square dance tunes, "The Fox and the Hounds" and "The Little Red Caboose," one "rag ditty" entitled "Bob McKinney," and one blues, "Red River Blues." In his subsequent sessions, Thomas showed his versatility, performing a diverse repertoire that continued to include square dance tunes, blues, gospel, and rag ditties, as well as "coon songs" and minstrel-influenced material.

Thomas's recordings offer a glimpse of the legacy of nineteenth-century folk and popular song traditions, though as Stephen Calt writes, "Their documentary value is uncertain, for the extent to which he was representative of his age can only be surmised. In assessing the value of Thomas's music from a documentary standpoint one must distinguish between characteristics that seemingly reflected his era, that seemingly resulted from his given repertoire or career orientation, and that reflected individualities and idiosyncrasies."[18]

Although Thomas was the only songster of his generation in Texas to be recorded, he exemplifies a larger tradition. "Lines and verses that Henry Thomas sings are reported from Mississippi in 1906 and from Georgia in 1904," Mack McCormick explained in his 1974 liner notes to a reissue of Thomas's recordings. "Portions of his blues repertoire were known at an early date in Paducah, Kentucky, and in Mobile, Alabama. He shared much, not only with Charley Patton, but with William Moore in Virginia."[19]

Some of Thomas's songs, however, are firmly grounded in his Texas roots. His voice has an East Texas intonation that identifies him with local tradition. In "Don't Ease Me In" he sings, "Got these Texas blues, I got the Texas blues. . . . Says, I looked down Main, Old Ellum too" [referring to the Deep Ellum area of Dallas]. And in his monologue "Railroadin' Some," he calls out the train stops he passed through en route to Kansas City, St. Louis, and Chicago, and then again, on his way back to East Texas: "Change cars on the T.P.! [Texas & Pacific Railroad] / Leaving Fort Worth, Texas! Going through Dallas! Hello, Terrell! Grand Saline! Silver Lake! Mineola! Tyler! Longview! Jefferson! Marshall! Little Sandy! Big Sandy! And double back to Fort Worth!"

Thomas spent the formative years of his career playing for country dances, and apparently the tempo and syncopation of his songs earned him the nickname "Ragtime Texas." However, it is likely that when he was recorded during the years 1927–29, his producer at Vocalion sampled his repertoire and encouraged him to perform representative pieces that the company thought might sell the best. The resulting recordings over this two-year period include one ballad, one monologue, two gospel songs, four composites (with elements of ballads, blues, square dance calls, rag ditties, and other musical fragments), five "reels," and ten blues.

In many ways, the scope of Thomas's repertoire typified that of the African American songsters of his generation, most of whom were itinerant like him. He was eclectic in his instrumentation, singing, and other vocal effects, and was likely influenced not only by folk and popular song styles, but by the humming, wordless moaning, and overlapping call-and-response shouting of field hollers and work songs.[20] This was also true of Thomas's contemporaries, for whom there are some recordings and limited anecdotal evidence.

Mance Lipscomb (1895–1976), a country blues songster in Navasota, recalled that his father, Charles, was a fiddler, and that an uncle, George, played banjo. Even Blind Lemon Jefferson (1893–1929) was known to play at country dances in Couchman (near Wortham) and the other farming communities and small towns close by.

Hobart Carter, a native of Wortham, said that Jefferson performed at "breakdowns" and that he was sometimes accompanied by a fiddler named Lorenzo Ross. "They had a hallelujah time. We had our suppers and things. Saturday nights and things like that. All through

17. Rawick, *American Slave*, suppl., series 2, vol. 5, *Texas Narratives, Part 4*, 1788.

18. Stephen Calt, "Texas Worried Blues," Yazoo 1080/1 (1989).

19. Mack McCormick, "Biography of Henry Thomas: Our Deepest Look at Roots," Herwin 209 (1974).

20. For example, the antecedents of Thomas's song "Don't Ease Me In," McCormick noted (ibid.), "can still be heard in the flat fields among the Brazos River where the farms of the state prison system lie, some of them crowded now by the sprawling edge of Houston suburbs. The convicts turn out to work the fields by hand labor methods that exist practically nowhere else and to learn the redundant song phrases "Don't Ease Me In" and "All night long" with the multiple meanings that gave them special significance in prisons where women never came and where the lights in the dormitories were never turned out."

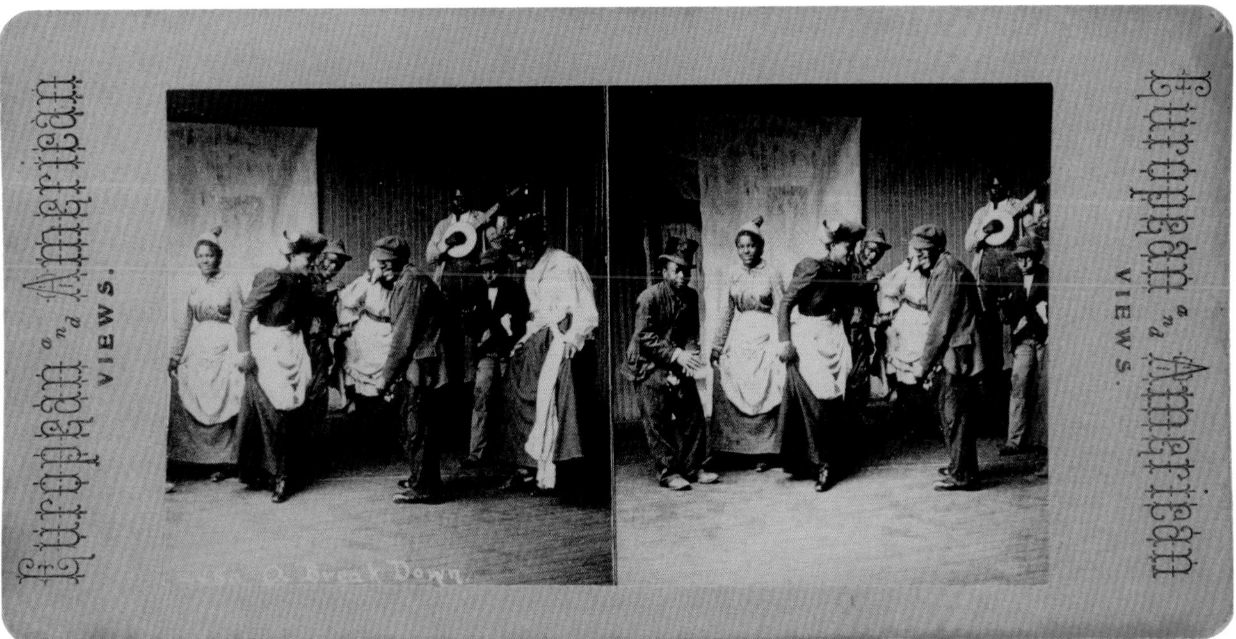

"A BREAKDOWN," EUROPEAN AND AMERICAN VIEWS, STEREOVIEW, N.D. COURTESY TEXAS AFRICAN AMERICAN PHOTOGRAPHY ARCHIVE.

the winter, we'd have some cold nights and some rainy nights. We had plenty of chock houses at that time. You get some sugar, put it in a crock. Let it set three days and get to drinking it. Chock houses were everywhere at that time."[21]

The term *breakdown* had been in use since the early nineteenth century and referred to the customary dance among slaves in the South. Roger D. Abrahams posits that it may have come from the harvest season itself, for the act of cutting the ear from the stalk was called "breaking down the corn." "*Breakdown* enters vernacular American English as a reference to the kind of dance associated with slave holidays. Almost certainly this usage achieved its primary meaning from the *breaking down* or *away* that occurred at the end of many slave dance routines, such as 'Patting Juba,' in which one dancer asserted himself or herself with such astonishing virtuosity that everyone else began to watch, to pat along, and to lend encouragement."[22]

Quince Cox, a longtime friend of Carter's, recalled,

BLIND LEMMON JEFFERSON, "YO YO BLUES," PARAMOUNT RACE AD, *CHICAGO DEFENDER*, 1929. COURTESY DOCUMENTARY ARTS

21. Hobart Carter, interview by Alan Govenar, June 7, 1999.

22. Abrahams, *Singing the Master*, 102. It is interesting to note that the phrase *breaking down* was used in a similar way in the 1980s to describe the movement in break dancing.

BLIND LEMON JEFFERSON, "RAMBLER BLUES," PARAMOUNT RACE AD, *CHICAGO DEFENDER*, DECEMBER 3, 1927. COURTESY DOCUMENTARY ARTS.

T-BONE WALKER, "I GOT THE BLUES," IMPERIAL 5193.

"Lemon played anything he had to play. And he played pretty good, too. What did we call them songs? Reels. . . . He could play anything you asked him to play."[23] In addition to dance tunes, Cox said Jefferson sometimes "howled" or "squealed" when he performed in public. "You hear one of them around a wolf or a possum or a coon or something on the track, he could do that good, too. Sure would . . . oh yeah, he'd squeal just like a dog. Make it sound good, too."[24]

Clearly, Jefferson was heavily influenced by the music and sounds he heard growing up, and the breadth of his more than eighty recordings during the period from 1926 to his untimely death in 1929 attests to his prowess as a tradition-bearer and innovator. Possibly, Henry Thomas played in Wortham or in some of the places that Jefferson himself frequented. However, regardless of whether or not they ever interacted, by the time Jefferson recorded in 1926, nearly two years before Thomas was discovered by recording scouts, his repertoire had apparently become almost exclusively blues (though he did record two religious songs, using a pseudonym).[25] How and when Jefferson—and Thomas, for that matter—began to play blues is open to speculation, and while they recorded blues, the extent to which they continued to play other styles of music is unknown.

One factor in the development of blues may have

23. Quince Cox, interview by Alan Govenar, Wortham, Texas, June 7, 1999.

24. Quince Cox, interview by David Evans and Luigi Monge, Wortham, Texas, March 18, 1999.

25. Alan B. Govenar and Jay F. Brakefield, *Deep Ellum and Central Track: Where the Black and White Worlds of Dallas Converged* (Denton: University of North Texas Press, 1998).

OLD FIDDLERS CONTEST, FORT WORTH, TEXAS, APRIL 13, 1901. PHOTOGRAPH BY C.L. SWARTZ, COURTESY FORT WORTH MUSEUM OF SCIENCE AND HISTORY.

BLIND LEMON JEFFERSON, "WORRIED BLUES," PARAMOUNT RECORDS, BLIND LEMON JEFFERSON RACE AD, *CHICAGO DEFENDER,* MAY 19, 1928. COURTESY DOCUMENTARY ARTS.

been the increased availability of guitars. Notably, the 1894 Sears, Roebuck & Co. catalog had a section for musical instruments and paraphernalia, including published music. All eight guitars offered for sale—ranging in price from $4.50 to $26.00—were gut-strung (strings made from animal intestines). Steel-string guitars appeared in the catalog sometime after 1897, by 1900 at the latest.

There are no interviews with Henry Thomas or Blind Lemon Jefferson in which they explain why they wanted to play the guitar. Still, it seems plausible that the first generation of African Americans born out of slavery associated the banjo and fiddle, which were both common in East Texas, with the suffering of parents or grandparents. Buying a guitar or any musical instrument was nearly impossible during slavery, and in this way, the acquisition of a guitar may have been symbolic of freedom, autonomy, or leisure. Moreover, the guitar is more expressive than the banjo, with more melodic, harmonic, and percussive possibilities. The notes on the guitar can be held or bent longer, echoing the emotion of the singer or evoking its own voice as a response to humming or wordless moaning.

Blues music expresses the hardships of newly freed black Americans. The freedoms offered by Reconstruction were hard-won: racism, Jim Crow laws, and the Ku Klux Klan were major obstacles to African Americans' economic independence and self-determination. Still, leisure was vitally new and served as a catalyst in the development of the blues, even under the most desolate circumstances. Early blues answered the need for a release from everyday life.

The blues is intensely personal music; it identifies with the feelings of the listener—suffering and hope, economic failure, the breakup of the family, the desire

BAPTISM IN THE RIVER, N.D. COURTESY INSTITUTE OF TEXAN CULTURES.

to escape reality through wandering, love, and sex. In this way, blues is somewhat different from African songs, which usually concern the lives and works of gods, the social unit (the tribe or community), and nature. With its emphasis on the experience of the individual and his or her successes and trials on earth, blues reflects Western concepts. Yet, as a musical form, the blues shows little Western influence. The traditional three-line, twelve-bar, AAB verse form of the blues arises from no apparent Western source, although some blues does incorporate Anglo-American ballad forms, which have six-, ten- or sixteen-bar structures. Early blues drew on the sources available at the time of its creation: field hollers and shouts, which it most closely resembles melodically; songster ballads, from which it borrowed some imagery and guitar patterns; and church music, which trained the voices and ears of black children. These, with the exception of the ballad, were the descendants of African percussive rhythms, syncopation, and call-and-response singing.

Although blues drew from the religious music of both African and Western cultures, it was often considered sinful by the church. Blues singers were often stereotyped as "backsliders" in their own communities. In many areas blues was known as the devil's music.

As historian Larry Levine points, blues blended the sacred and the secular. Like the spirituals and folktales of the nineteenth century, blues was a plea for release, a mix of despair, hope, and humor that had a cathartic effect upon the listener. The blues singer had an expressive role that mirrored the power of the preacher, and because of this power, blues was both embraced and rejected by the black community and the church.

The spiritual power of the blues is often associated with worldly pleasures that, for some, made the music sinful. In Texas, blues musician Li'l Son Jackson explained to British blues aficionado Paul Oliver: "If a man hurt within and he sing a church song, then he's askin' God for help . . . if a man sing the blues it's more or less out of himself. . . . He's not askin' no one for help. And he's really not really clingin' to no one. But he's expressin' how he feel. He's expressin' to someone and that fact makes it a sin . . . you're tryin' to get your feelin's over to the next person through the blues, and that's what make it a sin."[26]

Given the lack of centralized bureaucracy in the black American church, the relationship between the blues

26. Paul Oliver, *Conversation with the Blues* (New York, 1965), 165.

singer and the community varied from place to place. Rarely were blues singers completely ostracized. They lived on the edge of what was acceptable, and derived their livelihood by performing at juke joints, house parties, and country dances.

EARLY WRITTEN REFERENCES

The earliest written reference to what might be considered blues music in Texas was made in 1890 by Gates Thomas, who recalled a song entitled "Nobody There" with the following single stanza:

> *"That you, Nigger man, knockin' at my door?*
> *Hear me tell you, Nigger man, nobody there."*[27]

Thomas did not indicate whether the singing was accompanied by an instrument, but as David Evans points out, Thomas did print a pentatonic tune containing the tonic, flatted third, fourth, fifth and flatted seventh tones, all of which combine in a manner that makes it ostensibly a blues tune. In the early 1900s Thomas published other song texts that he had collected from blacks in South Texas. Some of these included verses that had been noted by other writers in various areas of the South. The song "Baby Take a Look at Me," for example, was transcribed by both Thomas and Charles Peabody in Mississippi. And "Alabama Bound" and "C. C. Rider" are variants of blues songs that Jelly Roll Morton recounted in New Orleans.

The diffusion of these early songs suggests that many African American musicians were itinerant and that blues was part of an oral tradition that developed in different areas of the South. But the documentation of this tradition in the writing of Gates Thomas is scant. By all accounts, the blues was widespread in the early 1900s. Thousands of blacks during this period were looking for work and escape from all-too-prevalent racism.

Blues musicians were often migrant workers, following the crop harvests, lumber camps, and boomtowns. Some settled down and labored as sharecroppers, leasing small tracts of land controlled by white landowners. Others continued in their search, roving from town to town, working odd jobs in the growing urban centers—Dallas, Houston, Shreveport, and Atlanta—cities whose black immigrant populations were crowded together into segregated neighborhoods of shotgun shacks and pasteboard houses.

"DALLAS BLUES" SHEET MUSIC, 1912. COURTESY DON O.

Far more thorough than Thomas was Howard W. Odum, who conducted fieldwork in Lafayette County, Mississippi, and Newton County, Georgia, between 1905 and 1908. Of the 115 song texts Odum collected and printed in "Folk Song and Folk Poetry as Found in the Secular Songs of the Southern Negroes,"[28] roughly half were what he called "blues" or "field blues," songs that he felt "reflected the secular life and mental image of the Negro." Odum was not familiar with the term *blues* as designating a kind of song, even though two of his texts use this word. In song 11, the singer repeats the line, "I got the blues, but I'm too damn mean to cry." While this lyric is evocative, Odum did not explain its meaning or the musical context of its usage.

27. For more information, see Gates Thomas, "South Texas Negro Work-Songs: Collected and Uncollected," in *Rainbow in the Morning*, ed. J. Frank Dobie (Hatsboro, Pa., 1965): 154–80.

28. Howard W. Odum, "Folk Song and Folk Poetry as Found in the Secular Songs of the Southern Negroes," *Journal of American Folk-Lore*, 24 (July–September 1911): 255–94, 351–96

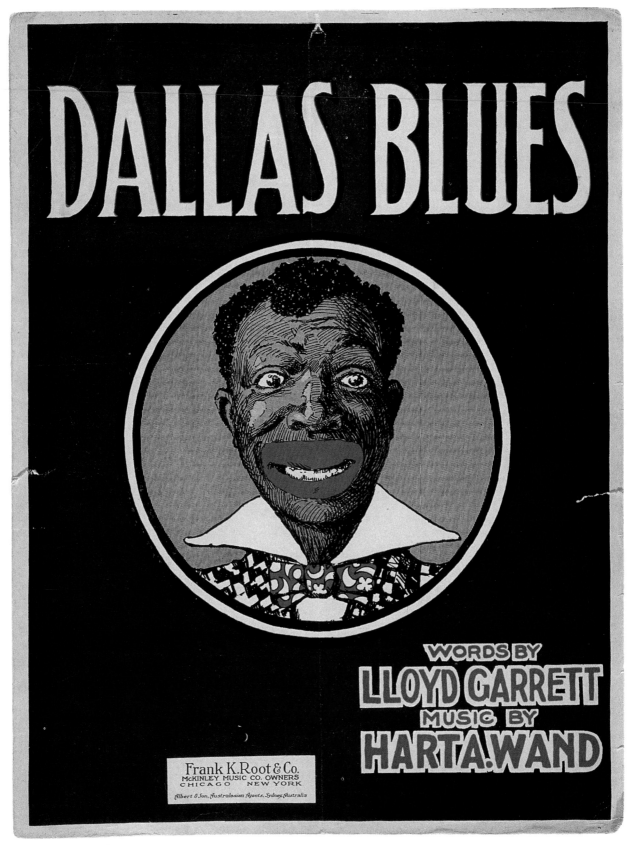

"DALLAS BLUES" SHEET MUSIC, 1918. COURTESY DON O.

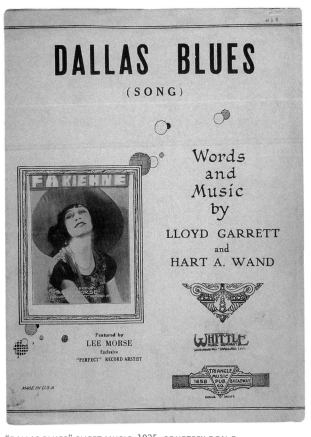

"DALLAS BLUES" SHEET MUSIC, 1925. COURTESY DON O.

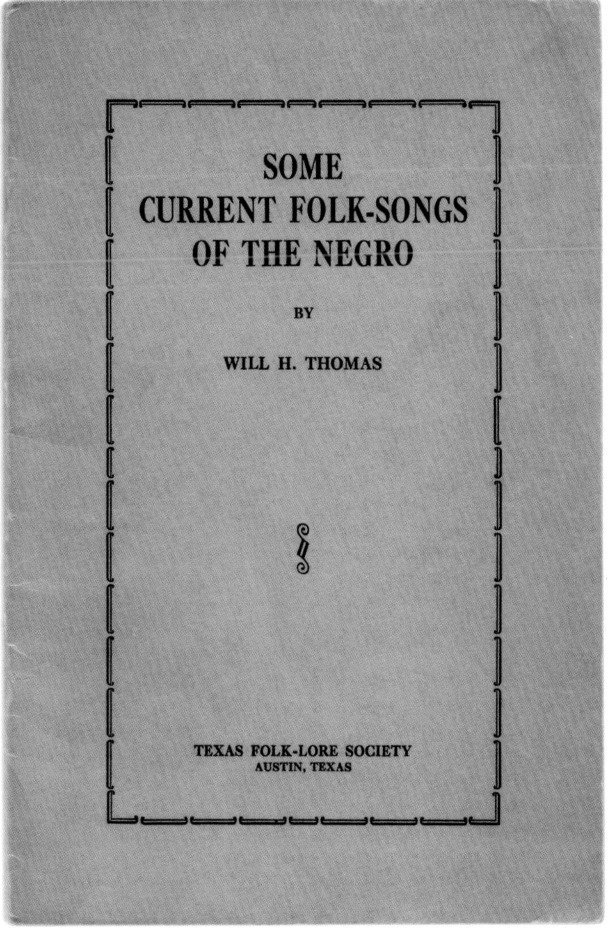

SOME CURRENT FOLK-SONGS OF THE NEGRO, BY WILL H. THOMAS, 1912, PUBLISHED BY THE TEXAS FOLK-LORE SOCIETY, AUSTIN, 1936. COURTESY TEXAS AFRICAN AMERICAN PHOTOGRAPHY ARCHIVE.

DEEP ROOTS

The use of the word *blues* to describe a mood or feeling dates back at least to the early 1600s. According to the *Oxford English Dictionary*, *blues* is a shortened version of *blue devils*, which meant "a baleful demon." By the late 1700s, *blue devils* had come to mean "melancholy." According to some sources, *blue devils* also was a reference to apparitions seen by people suffering from delirium tremens. So, without making too much of it, the blues early on seems to have been associated with both alcohol and the devil.

In the nineteenth century, music historian Samuel Charters points out, "it [the term *blues*] was a common expression in the United States, though there was some confusion as to exactly what it meant to be 'blue.' In 1824, 'in a fit of the blues' meant a 'depression of spirits.' In 1853, a Boston newspaper, the *Yankee Blade*, recommended a humorous novel '. . . to all who are afflicted with the blues, or ennui.' . . . In the 1850s, it meant boredom. By the 1880s it meant unhappiness: 'Come to me when you have the blues.' The word was used occasionally in song titles, but as a slang expression, without reference to any Negro musical style. By 1910, the term 'blues' was heard everywhere, and there was an expectant moment while the term and the music that was to be called 'the blues' became more and more popular."[29]

The first published blues was an instrumental piece, entitled "Dallas Blues," by an Oklahoma City musician, Hart Wand, who overheard a black porter whistling a tune as Wand practiced his violin. One afternoon, according to Charters, the porter said, as he listened

29. Samuel B. Charters, *The Country Blues* (New York: Da Capo, 1975), 34.

leaning on his broom, "That gives me the blues to go back to Dallas."[30] The phrase stayed in Wand's mind, and he had a young pianist friend, Anabelle Robbins, arrange the tune, which he self-published in March 1912, and sold around town for ten cents a copy. While the original arrangement of "Dallas Blues" is essentially a melodic composition, it does have a twelve-bar structure, in three four-part phrases, very similar to later blues patterning.

Wand's "Dallas Blues" was followed by Arthur Seal's "Baby Seal's Blues," published in August 1912, and W. C. Handy's "Memphis Blues," in September 1912. That same year, Will H. Thomas, Gates Thomas's brother and an English professor at the Agricultural and Mechanical College of Texas, published a short essay entitled *Some Current Folk-Songs of the Negro and Their Economic Interpretation.* This publication, the first produced by the Texas Folklore Society, contained several songs and the sections of others that Thomas recalled hearing sung by "colored semi-rural proletarians" on his farm about two years earlier. One song was called "The Railroad Blues" and began with lyrics that are suggestive of a traditional blues structure, though Thomas's transcription seems fragmented: "I got the blues, but I haven't got the fare, I got the blues, but I haven't got the fare, I got the blues, but I'm too damn mean to cry."[31]

Thomas, not fully understanding the significance of "The Railroad Blues," commented that it was the only song in his collection in which he "detected insincerity." Moreover, he concluded: "Now the Negro may have periods of despondency, but I have never been able to detect them. . . . The Negro then sings because he is losing his economic foothold. This economic insecurity has interfered with those two primal necessities—work and love—and you will notice that the thoughts in these songs cluster around these two ideas."[32] Overall, Thomas's view of Negro blues and Negro folk songs in general was shaped by his own political and economic views and failed to explore the music on its own terms.

PRECONCEPTIONS AND ETHNOCENTRISM

The major problem with early accounts of blues is that they were often limited by the collectors' preconceptions about the nature of "Negro life." The Thomases were ethnocentric, and they edited the texts they collected to make them "better," overlooking the integrity of the texts and music as they were actually performed. Perhaps the most glaring example of this ethnocentric approach is Walter Prescott Webb's report of his meeting with a young singer named Floyd Canada in a Beeville, Texas, pool hall in 1915. Webb wrote that Canada, with guitar, banjo, and harmonica accompaniment, sang a song to the tune of "Dallas Blues" that ran to a length of eighty stanzas of four lines each, rhyming in couplets. From what is known about blues today, however, the song collected by Webb seems absurd. It is likely that Webb, believing the songs to be incomplete, simply reconstructed the true texts by combining two AB stanzas to make the quatrains, and pulled together several blues with the same or similar tunes to generate a text that, if correct, is the longest blues ever recorded. In any event, it is clear that Webb recognized the importance of what he collected. He called the song "The African Iliad" because he believed that it told the "whole story of the modern Negro; what the Negro held to be of the highest importance . . . his desires and aims, his love and hate, his ethical and chivalrous ideas."

THE FIELDWORK AND LEGACY OF JOHN A. LOMAX

John A. Lomax, who was conducting fieldwork in Texas at roughly the same time as Webb, was far more analytical than his contemporaries. He nurtured a lifelong interest in African American life and music.

In his autobiography, *Adventures of a Ballad Hunter,* Lomax recounted his early contact with African Americans in Bosque County. When he was eight years old, he was churning butter when

> the sound of the grindstone reached me. I rushed to the back yard, where under a mulberry tree by the smokehouse, a handsome black boy was turning the sandstone slab as my father pressed down an axe on its whirling surface. . . .
>
> So, I met Nat Blythe, and a three-year friendship began. He was eighteen, I was nine. Nat was an infant when his mother died. She left him a bond

30. Ibid. Reportedly, the first printing of "Dallas Blues" sold out in a week; the second sold almost as fast; and finally, Wand sent the third edition to the copyright office, where it was entered September 12, 1912.

31. Will H. Thomas, *Some Current Folk-Songs of the Negro and Their Economic Interpretation* (Austin, 1912), 1–13.

32. Ibid., 5, 9.

> servant to Colonel Blythe until he was twenty-one. That same day at noon, I found Nat resting under the mulberry tree studying a Webster's blue-backed spelling book. He was as far as "ba-be-bi-bo." He became my first pupil.[33]

Lomax recalled that he tutored Blythe "three or four hours a day" that summer, and he continued over the next three years. "At the end of the final term . . . he was through the fifth reader, he had studied history and geography and arithmetic, and he could write a good letter."[34]

From Blythe, Lomax said he learned his "sense of rhythm." Blythe "danced rather than walked. When he slapped his big friendly hands against his thighs they almost sang a tune. If he stopped chanting . . . and kept on patting, you forgot the song and listened absorbed to the speaking rhythm of his hands."[35]

This early fascination continued throughout Lomax's life, from collecting ballads along the Texas Gulf Coast "district, where Negroes are thicker than mustang grapes," to his folk collecting trips with his son Alan to the Mississippi Delta and Louisiana, where ultimately they found Huddie Ledbetter, better known as Leadbelly.[36]

Through their discovery of Leadbelly, the Lomaxes were able to demonstrate that the traditional music was very much alive in America. Challenging the ballad scholars Francis J. Child and Cecil Sharp, Benjamin Filene points out, "they [John and Alan] dismissed notions that an authentic folk song must be hundreds of years old and that only fragments of true American folk culture survived in contemporary society. The Lomaxes depicted a much more robust folk tradition. They argued that traditional American music remained vibrant, creative and essential to American life."[37]

Alan Lomax urged Americans to "fight the tendency . . . to begin to regard [folk] culture as static—to leave out of consideration its living quality (present and past)." In a lecture to the Progressive Education Association in 1940, he expressed his desire to convince his audience that "there is, was and will be something here that is in American folk music to be looked into; and that there is enough to go around for a long, long time."[38]

Despite John Lomax's quest for "authenticity" in American folk music, he was limited by the prevailing academic views and interpretations of his time. Before conducting extensive fieldwork among African Americans, he observed in a 1917 article in *The Nation:*

> . . . .there surely exists no merrier-hearted race than the Negro, especially in his natural home, the warm climate of the South. The Negro's laugh may sometimes speak the empty mind, but at the same

LIGHTNIN' AND HIS GROUP SINGING, DARRINGTON STATE FARM, SANDY POINT, TEXAS, APRIL, 1934. PHOTOGRAPH BY JOHN A. LOMAX. COURTESY LIBRARY OF CONGRESS.

33. John A. Lomax, *Adventures of a Ballad Hunter* (New York: Macmillan, 1947), 9.

34. Ibid.

35. Ibid., 11.

36. Charles Wolfe and Kip Lornell, *The Life and Legend of Leadbelly* (New York: HarperCollins, 1992), 113–14.

37. Benjamin Filene, *Romancing the Folk: Public Memory and American Roots Music* (Chapel Hill: University of North Carolina Press, 2000), 55.

38. Ibid.

PRISON ROAD GANG, SOUTHERN U.S., 1934.

PHOTOGRAPH BY ALAN LOMAX. COURTESY LIBRARY OF CONGRESS.

BLIND LEMON JEFFERSON, "PENITENTIARY BLUES," PARAMOUNT RECORDS RACE AD, *CHICAGO DEFENDER, SEPTEMBER 15,* 1928.

COURTESY DOCUMENTARY ARTS.

> time it reveals a nature upon which trouble and want sit but lightly. . . . It is credible, at least, that the Negro's self-pity is based on feelings of race inferiority—a feeling of which he may well be only sub-consciously aware. . . . And it seems further credible that he has come to lump the troubles for which he himself is largely to blame along with the inevitable hardships of his situation until he has grown to regard himself as the victim of hard luck, generally abused by everybody; and, at least in many instances, he seems not averse to nursing his gloom a little.[39]

Even into the 1930s, Lomax's daughter, Bess Lomax Hawes, recalls, her father "had a theory that, in the prisons, he might be able to find some vestiges of slavery songs because he regarded the prison system as being akin to slavery." He discovered that his theory was wrong, and "he found that a new repertory had been developed, and he, being a responsible guy, went and recorded it. And he thought it was beautiful. . . . He didn't think very much about genres. He thought about poetry. He quoted blues lines all the time, even if he didn't fully understand they were blues. He loved poetry."[40]

Despite the limitations of Lomax's capacity to fully interpret the music he collected, Hawes characterizes her father as a progressive thinker.

> He was a grass-roots populist for most of his life. . . . Father would, every election day, go around and pick up anybody who worked for us, any black person that worked for us, and any others that he knew. And we would get a big carload and go down to the polls.

39. John A. Lomax, "Self-Pity in Negro Folk-Songs," *The Nation* 105 (July–December 1917): 141–45.

40. Bess Lomax Hawes, interview by Alan Govenar, April 30, 2004.

BANDWAGON, BONHAM, TEXAS, CA. 1910–1915.
PHOTOGRAPH BY ERWIN E. SMITH. COURTESY LIBRARY OF CONGRESS.

> He would make everybody get out and go up there and vote. . . . It was sort of a *noblesse oblige* feeling that he had. That's why he took every black person he knew to vote. He knew if he didn't do it, they wouldn't go on their own. And he knew that they would be abused if they did. So, it was his job to see to it that they got there and they voted. I remember one time someone complained. They didn't want to vote for anybody, and he said, "Well, just go ahead and vote anyway because it's your duty as a citizen."[41]

Lomax was born in 1867, and while his attitudes toward African Americans may have been influenced by the relatively progressive period of Reconstruction that he experienced as a child, he lived most of his adult life during an intensely racist period in the history of the United States. Hawes remembers that when Lomax started recording blacks outside of the prison system, he was often ridiculed. "It was very difficult at that time in the South for a white person to sit on a black person's front porch and record. He got threatened a number of times."[42] In many ways, social pressures forced Lomax to accept, or at least acknowledge, the same ambivalence about black people that was common to most white Americans during the early years of the twentieth century.

In describing Leadbelly, Lomax often emphasized that "Leadbelly had served time in a Texas penitentiary for murder . . . he was the type known as killer and had a career of violence the record of which is a black epic of horrifics." Still, he thought of Leadbelly as singing with "absolute sincerity." In publicizing Leadbelly's New York debut for a hotel luncheon for University of Texas alumni, Lomax wrote, "I've heard his songs a hundred

41. Ibid.
42. Ibid.

UNIDENTIFIED GROUP OF MUSICANS, N.D. COURTESY TEXAS AFRICAN AMERICAN PHOTOGRAPHY ARCHIVE.

times, but I always get a thrill. To me, his music is real music."[43]

Clearly, by the end of his life, Lomax's perspective had expanded, though he had some difficulty accepting that Leadbelly himself had become urbane and had aspirations and ambitions of his own. "He talked about how Leadbelly couldn't manage his life very well, that he was constantly getting into trouble," Hawes says. "And he would try to help him to not get into trouble by giving him a reasonable salary, which he did, from his point of view, and finding him the best places to stay that he could find back then. I keep saying that people never saw Father in the terms in which he lived. They're seeing him in the terms in which they live . . . they judge him by the standards of the present rather than seeing him as a person of his own time."[44]

Lomax's representation of Leadbelly and of African American musicians in general resonated, as Filene suggests, with a "current of primitivism that ran through early twentieth century modernism. Avant-garde writers, artists, and intellectuals used the 'primitive' as a source of imagery, metaphors, and behavior patterns that fulfilled personal longings and enabled cultural critiques." From Picasso and the cubists, who were inspired by the stark geometries of African sculptures, to Joseph Conrad, whose description of a journey down the Congo River signified his exploration of the darkest depths of the human soul, the primitive became a symbol among artists and intellectuals alike that could "encompass violence, sex, irrationality, and, at the same time, noble innocence and childlike naiveté."[45]

The most significant contribution of John and Alan Lomax was their pursuit of living traditions through active fieldwork and recordings of the folk songs they collected. As early as 1933, John Lomax was appointed honorary curator of the Archive of Folksong at the Library of Congress, and over the next decade, he traveled around Texas and elsewhere in the South to record spirituals, field shouts and hollers, prison work songs, and blues. John Lomax's books, edited with Alan Lomax—*Negro Songs as Sung by Lead Belly* (1936) *Our Singing Country* (1941), and *Folk Songs, U.S.A.* (1947)—and his autobiography *Adventures of a Ballad Hunter* (1947) are enduring documents of the social and cultural context in which the blues evolved.

THE INFLUENCE OF BLIND LEMON JEFFERSON

With the growth of the recording industry during the 1920s, the audience for blues expanded within black communities nationwide. Demographic studies, for

43. Filene, *Romancing the Folk*, 59.

44. Bess Lomax Hawes, interview by Alan Govenar, April 30, 2004.

45. Filene, *Romancing the Folk*, 63.

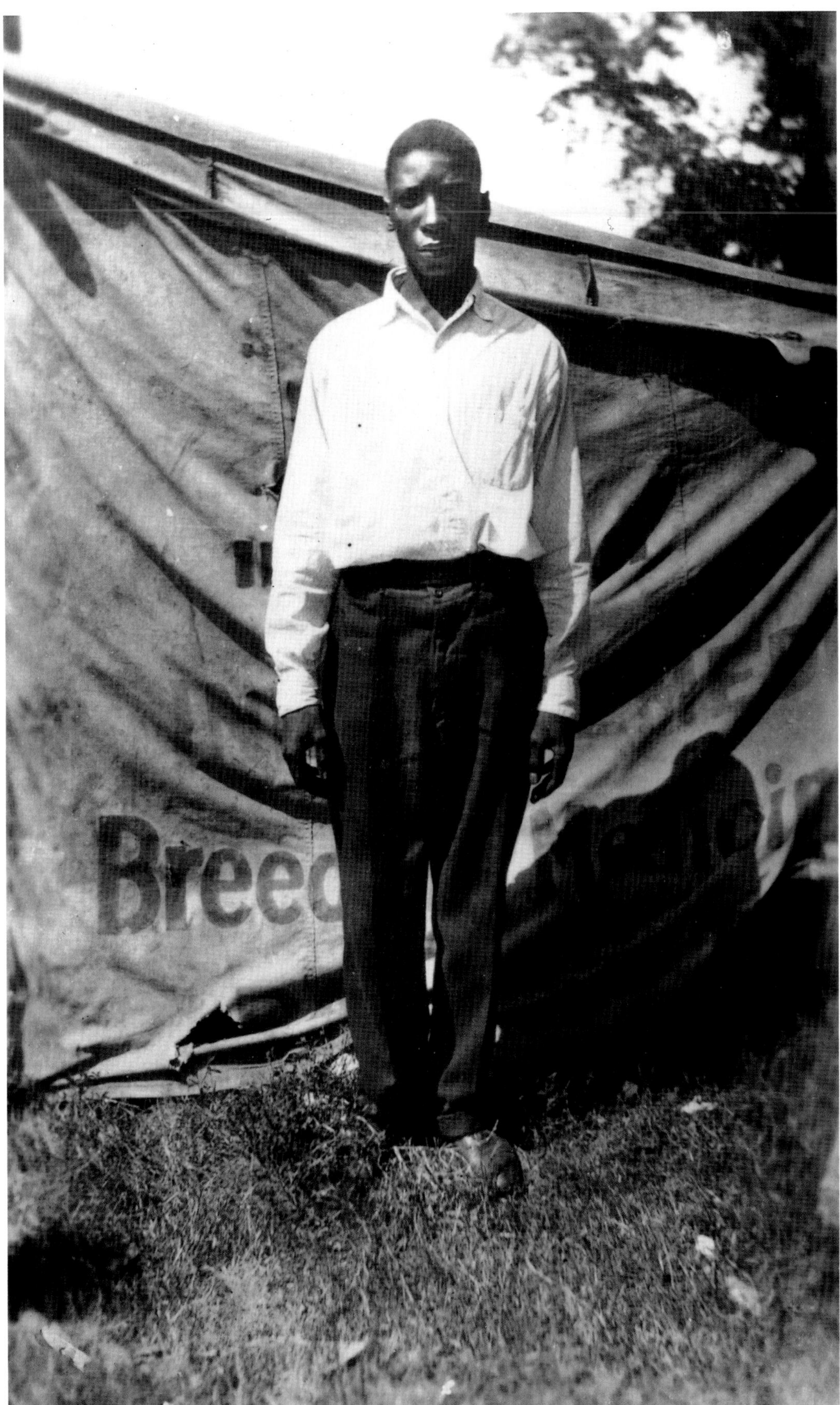

T-BONE WALKER, ASSISTANT IN DR. BREEDING'S TOURING MEDICINE SHOW, 1920s. COURTESY HELEN OAKLEY DANCE.

example, indicate that Blind Lemon Jefferson's records sold thousands of copies to blacks across the South and the urban North. But in Dallas, Jefferson was known primarily as a street singer who performed daily with a tin cup at the corner of Elm Street and Central Track.

Despite his limited commercial success in Dallas, Blind Lemon Jefferson did have a great influence on the development of Texas blues and blues in general. He was the first guitar-playing bluesman to attract a national audience and thereby was a catalyst for the recording of hundreds of blues singers, male and female, black and white. Jefferson had a singular approach to creating his blues, and was extraordinarily virtuosic in performance, as evidenced by the breadth of the poetic art of his lyrics, his subject matter, two-octave vocal range, and innovative guitar styling. In some of his songs, he uses essentially the same melodic and guitar parts with every stanza. Others have little repetition of melodic or guitar figures, presenting instead, as David Evans points out, "something new at every turn. Some are highly rhythmic and dance-related. In others Jefferson breaks time or displays a highly flexible approach to tempo . . . the striking of long, sustained notes on the guitar, mandolin-like tremolos, and even silent spaces during his singing, all of which have the effect of shifting the vocal line."[46]

Evans believes that Jefferson "is more in the mainstream of influence on contemporary blues guitar" than the legendary Robert Johnson, who is often credited with synthesizing "much that had gone before in blues and pointed the way to the future of this music." Jefferson was actually doing "many of these same things ten years before Johnson."[47]

THE IMPORTANCE OF T-BONE WALKER

Jefferson's profound impact on the development of blues is probably most apparent in the music of Aaron "T-Bone" Walker, who, "beginning in the early 1940s, influenced virtually every electric blues guitarist who ever played lead guitar in a band."[48] Walker's debt to Jefferson is apparent in one of Walker's early recordings, made in Dallas in December 1929, just weeks before Jefferson's untimely death in Chicago. In "Wichita Falls Blues," Walker sings a variant of the opening stanza of one of Jefferson's first big hits, "Long Lonesome Blues."

Moreover, Walker adopted Jefferson's style of holding the guitar almost perpendicular to the chest. With this approach, contemporary guitarist Duke Robillard, a disciple of T-Bone Walker, explained, "when you hold the guitar out from yourself, like he did, against your chest, your hand just rests on the strings and it seems good."[49]

Walker applied the innovations he learned from Jefferson to his own playing, but also integrated the swing and jump blues of the regional or Territory jazz bands of the 1920s and 1930s. In the Territory jazz bands that toured the Southwest, the guitar was primarily used as a rhythm instrument to underlie the voice and horn sections. The introduction of the electric guitar occurred first in these bands and was pioneered by Eddie Durham of San Marcos, and Charlie Christian, of Bonham. By using electric amplification, jazz guitarists were able to sustain notes and increase the resonance and volume of their sound. Christian is often credited with teaching Walker about the electric guitar and its potential as a solo instrument.

In the rhythm and blues of T-Bone Walker, the electric guitar assumed a role that superseded the saxophone, the predominant solo instrument in swing jazz. The interplay between the saxophone and the guitar remained important in rhythm and blues, but the relationship between the instruments was transformed. The rhythm and blues band sound became tighter and depended on the interplay of the electric guitar with the horn section, piano, and drums.

After moving to Los Angeles in the early 1940s, Walker radically changed his approach, playing electric guitar in a call-and-response style with a big band. But he continued to carry forward Jefferson's legacy by improvising staccato melodic lines, lightning-fast single-note runs, harmonic substitutions, and flexible rhythms. Surely, as Evans suggests, "if T-Bone is the father of modern lead guitar in the blues and its deriva-

46. David Evans, "Musical Innovation in the Blues of Blind Lemon Jefferson," *Black Music Research Journal* 20, no. 1 (spring 2000): 88–89.

47. Ibid., 97–98.

48. Evans, "Musical Innovation in the Blues of Blind Lemon Jefferson," 98.

49. Helen O. Dance, *Stormy Monday: The T-Bone Walker Story* (Baton Rouge: Louisiana State University Press, 1987), 240.

50. Evans, "Musical Innovation in the Blues of Blind Lemon Jefferson," 100.

JIMMIE RODGERS, CA. 1929.

BILL NEELY, AUSTIN, 1984. PHOTOGRAPH BY ALAN GOVENAR.

tive genre, rock 'n' roll (its 'baby,' to quote a popular catch phrase and song), then Blind Lemon Jefferson is its godfather."[50]

In Texas, blues developed a unique character that resulted not only from the introduction of the electric guitar, but also from the cross-pollination of musical styles—itself a consequence of the migratory patterns of blacks—as well as the impact of the recording industry and mass media commercialization. Not only is the black population of Texas less concentrated than that of other states in the South, but blues music in Texas also evolved in proximity to other important musical traditions: the rural Anglo, the Cajun and Creole, the Hispanic, and the Eastern and Central European.

WHITE CROSSOVER

The white crossover to blues in Texas began in the nineteenth century when black fiddlers, banjo players, and guitar songsters performed at white country dances. Eddie Durham recalled in interviews that his father was a fiddler who played jigs and reels as well as blues. Mance Lipcomb's father was a fiddler, and his uncle was a banjo player; Gatemouth Brown's father played fiddle and guitar.

White musicians were exposed to blues at country dances and minstrel shows and among black workers in the fields, road gangs, turpentine camps, and railroad yards. Country singer Bill Neely said that he first heard blues when he picked cotton in Collin County north of Dallas in the 1920s, but he learned to play blues by listening to Jimmie Rodgers.

"Jimmie Rodgers was a bluesman," Bill Neely said. "A lot of those songs Jimmie Rodgers didn't write. He got them from the blacks he heard when he was growing

51. Bill Neely, interview by Alan Govenar, August 10, 1984.

up in Mississippi and when he worked as a brakeman on the railroad."[51]

The influence of blues and jazz is also apparent in the western swing bands of Bob Wills and Milton Brown, in which the horn sections of the Territory jazz bands were imitated and developed through an evolving instrumentation that included the steel guitar. In addition, blues and jazz influenced Mexican American and Tejano, as well as Anglo-European, popular music.

The emphasis in this book is upon modern and contemporary performers, and consequently, the text primarily focuses on rhythm and blues. The phrase *rhythm and blues* was introduced in 1949 by *Billboard* magazine. It was a substitute name for a chart that been headed until then "Top 15 Best Selling Race Records." The phrase *race records* had been in use since 1920, when the success of an Okeh record, "Crazy Blues," by Mamie Smith, motivated other record labels to record black female vocalists, many of whom would later be regarded as the "classic blues singers." In time, the term *race* became a catchall for any type of black recording—blues, jazz, folk, pop, big band. After World War II the connotations of *race* seemed offensive, and *rhythm and blues* came into use.

Rhythm and blues is different musically from the blues that had preceded it. As music historian Arnold Shaw suggests, "If the blues was trouble music and urban blues adjustment song, then rhythm and blues was good-time dance music. If the blues was loneliness and self-expression song, and urban blues nostalgia and growing music, then rhythm and blues was group and joy music. If the country bluesman wailed and the urban bluesman sang, the rhythm and bluesman shouted."[52]

Rhythm and blues was a response to a new environment, to the realities of inner-city ghettos and urban migration. One of the most important sources of rhythm and blues was gospel music, which imbued it with a vital repertoire, form, and style. In rhythm and blues, the patterning of early country blues was eclipsed by the musical forms of gospel and pop songs. If it was rhythm and blues that gave rise to what record producer Sam Phillips and disc jockey Alan Freed called rock 'n' roll, rock 'n' roll spelled the demise of rhythm and blues until the mid-1960s, when The Rolling Stones, The Beatles, and other English groups appeared in America and brought recognition to their African American musical mentors. British rock 'n' roll refocused popular attention on the great black bluesmen by recording their songs and helping to promote their performances.

In the 1970s rhythm and blues was again eclipsed by popular music in America, but foreign interest grew. With the rise of British and European record labels and the international festival circuit, black American blues performers gained a new and vital forum for preserving and advancing their music. The audience abroad has saved blues from extinction and continues today to provide an arena where older and younger musicians, both black and white, are able to launch their careers. Stevie Ray Vaughan, for example, began to attract international attention after a 1982 performance at the Montreux International Jazz Festival in Switzerland. Among European audiences, blues, like jazz, is appreciated as an art form, intellectually and emotionally.

Since the 1980s there has been a steady resurgence of enthusiasm for blues in America. The Chicago Blues Festival attracts hundreds of thousands of people every year. Blues festivals are held throughout the United States, and blues performers are recognized through the annual Grammy and W. C. Handy awards. Blues "tourism" has become popular throughout the South, especially in Mississippi, Louisiana, and Texas, where Blind Lemon Jefferson is now recognized on an automobile license plate. Within this context, Texas blues musicians have achieved unprecedented prominence.

My intent in this book is to republish the accounts of all the musicians represented in my earlier books and supplement them with corrected information and additional oral histories collected from others. Since 1981, I have interviewed and photographed more than 100 Texas blues artists, and I have traveled throughout Texas, to several major American cities, and to cities and festivals abroad: Chicago, New Orleans, Oakland, San Francisco, London, Copenhagen, Helsinki, Stockholm, The Hague, Amsterdam, Paris, Nice, and Montreux. I traveled from neighborhood clubs to backcountry roads, to international festivals and concerts, to libraries and to the streets themselves in search of insights into Texas blues.

52. Arnold Shaw, *Honkers and Shouters: The Golden Years of Rhythm and Blues* (New York: Collier Books, 1978), 240.

During each interview session the questions were essentially the same. I asked each musician to talk about his or her early years, training, influences, key recordings, anecdotes, instruments and instrumentation, performance style, audience response, and the meaning of the blues on a personal level and in the context of American culture. In assembling this book, I transcribed my interviews and also drew on the work of other researchers and collectors, including Jay Brakefield, Allan Turner, Tary Owens, Chuck Nevitt, Tim Schuller, Bill Fountain, Don Ottensman (Don O), Tom Mazzolini, Dick Shurman, and Tommy Löfgren. Where I have used other people's work, I have credited them accordingly.

The result lies somewhere between history and personal chronicle. The sense of time within the oral histories is more associative than linear, and the point of view varies with the perspective of the speakers. Each of the musicians has a separate story, and there are many instances where contradictory accounts are told by and about the same musicians.

In presenting a variety of perspectives, the lack of a single style that distinguishes Texas blues from that found elsewhere in the South becomes apparent. However, even if the attempt does more to underscore than to clarify its complexity as a regional, or more accurately, multiregional, music, the definitive history of Texas blues can be established only through the consideration of different oral accounts, discography, and photographic documentation.

The photography in this book comes from a variety of sources, including historical collections and the work of contemporary photographers. The majority of the photographs represent my own work over more than two decades, focusing on black community life in Austin, San Antonio, Houston, Dallas, and rural East Texas. To supplement my work I have selected from archival photographs of the Texas African American Photography Archive (which I cofounded with Kaleta Doolin), as well as from the portfolios of other photographers, including Benny Joseph (Houston), Susan Antone (Austin), Valerie Wilmer (London), Michael P. Smith (New Orleans), Patricia Monaco (San Francisco), and Hans Ekestang and Erik Lindahl (Stockholm). The interplay between oral accounts and photography creates a series of portraits wherein the musicians emerge as individuals and performers. These portraits articulate the emotive and visual power of the blues experience.

EAST TEXAS

"PLOWING IN THE CUT-OVER LAND," NEAR MARSHALL, TEXAS, 1939.
PHOTOGRAPH BY RUSSELL LEE. COURTESY LIBRARY OF CONGRESS.

OSCEOLA MAYS

December 13, 1909–April 20, 2004; interview, 1981

Osceola Mays was born Nell Douglas in Waskom, Texas, east of Marshall. She adopted the name Osceola after an American Indian visited her family home and she asked to be named for him. Her parents were sharecropper farmers, like many other African Americans in East Texas, who eked out a living cultivating and selling cotton. In 1936 she married Clarence Mays, who was also a sharecropper, but when the crops failed in 1945, the family moved to Dallas. Clarence took a job in a dry-cleaning business, and Osceola worked as a nanny and domestic. Over the years, she preserved the oral traditions of her childhood, singing a cappella spirituals and reciting poems that she composed, in addition to recalling those that her grandmother, Laura Walker, and her mother, Azalean Douglas, had taught.

"PEOPLE ON THE MAIN STREET ON SATURDAY MORNING," SAN AUGUSTINE, 1943. PHOTOGRAPH BY JOHN VACHON. COURTESY LIBRARY OF CONGRESS.

"FAMILY WITH SUPPLIES IN A WAGON, READY TO LEAVE FOR THE FARM," SAN AUGUSTINE, 1939. PHOTOGRAPH BY RUSSELL LEE. COURTESY LIBRARY OF CONGRESS.

Blues was a music Osceola remembered hearing at an early age. "When I was a girl on the farm," she said, "I could hear them men in the fields, going through the woods singing blues. 'You never miss your water until your well is gone dry. / You never miss your baby till she says good-bye.'" Some of her most vivid memories were of Blind Lemon Jefferson, whose recordings she first heard at the height of his career in the late 1920s.

As she was growing up, Osceola's feelings toward blues were shaped by her mother and by her grandmother, who was ten years old when the Emancipation Proclamation was signed to end slavery. "My grandmother and mother told me, 'Don't sing the blues,' and I never sang any around them. Tradition, I guess, old people thought it was wrong to sing songs that wasn't allowed in the church. And they call them blues, and you don't call the church songs blues. Old people in the old days thought the blues was just terrible, terrible, but some truth was in those songs. They said, 'That's the devil's work. Just leave it alone. That's the devil's work. I don't want to hear you sing those songs.' And I couldn't sing them. I grew out where I just didn't. I believed it was the devil's work."

As she got older, Osceola continued to listen to blues, but also remained active in the Baptist church. "I

OSCEOLA MAYS, DALLAS, 1983. PHOTOGRAPH BY ALAN GOVENAR.

haven't stopped listening to the blues," she said. "I still hear them on these programs on television. Well, some of those blues tell things real true."

In many ways, Osceola's memories of early blues are representative of the attitudes of three generations of African Americans, who migrated away from the cotton fields of East Texas to the cities of Dallas and Houston. Blues was a music that was born during her grandmother's generation and flourished during her own and her mother's lifetimes on the periphery of African Ameri-

OSCEOLA MAYS, DALLAS, 1983. PHOTOGRAPH BY ALAN GOVENAR.

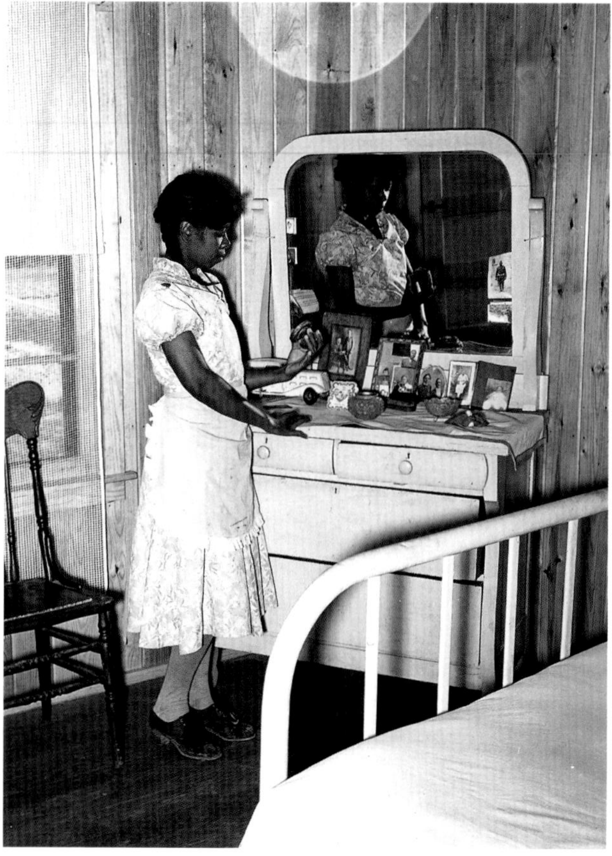

"SABINE FARMS, A FARM SECURITY ADMINISTRATION PROJECT FOR NEGROES, BEDROOM OF CLIENT'S HOME," NEAR MARSHALL, TEXAS, 1939. PHOTOGRAPH BY RUSSELL LEE. COURTESY LIBRARY OF CONGRESS

can community life. Blues expressed the sorrows and joys of three generations of African Americans in East Texas and demonstrated the enduring strength of the oral tradition.

I was fourteen or fifteen when I heard those blues records, heard them on my cousin's record player. Ben William had one. They played them and I'd hear them. Blind Lemon Jefferson, Bessie Smith. She was a woman's blues singer. She sang "Back water risin,' comin' in my windows and doors, and my house fell down, I can't live there no more."

I loved to hear Blind Lemon Jefferson. One song he sang I remember.

I was standin' on the courthouse square one day
One dime was all I had
Everybody gets in hard luck some time
Say I'm broke and ain't got a dime
but everybody gets in hard luck some time
Do you want your friend to be bad like Jesse James?
Take two six-shooters and rob some passenger train
Oh, one dime was all I had
One dime was all I had
The woman I love is five feet from the ground
She's a tailor-made woman
She ain't no hand-me-down
One dime was all I had
Ain't but one thing that give a woman the blues
When she don't have no bottom on her last pair of shoes
The blues ain't nothing but a good man feeling bad
Blues is the worst thing that a good man ever had.

(OPPOSITE) OSCEOLA MAYS, MAISON DES CULTURES DU MONDE, PARIS, FRANCE, 1989. PHOTOGRAPH BY ALAN GOVENAR.

MAISON DES CULTURES DU MONDE
direction Chérif Khaznadar
MINISTÈRE DE LA CULTURE, DE LA COMMUNICATION,
DES GRANDS TRAVAUX ET DU BICENTENAIRE / ALLIANCE FRANÇAISE
TEXAS IN PARIS
COWBOYS SONGS, BLUES, SPIRITUALS
JOHN BURRUS
BILL NEELY
OSCEOLA MAYS
5-22 DEC 1989
U.S.A.
45 44 72 30
101, BD RASPAIL

JOHN T. SAMPLES SR.

(January 10, 1898–January 13, 1998; interview, 1992)

MOTHER AND CHILD, NACOGDOCHES COUNTY, 1943. PHOTOGRAPH BY JOHN VACHON. COURTESY LIBRARY OF CONGRESS.

On the porch swing in front of his white frame house in Liberty, Texas, south of Kilgore, John Samples rocks back and forth, strumming his guitar and singing to himself in the morning heat as a soft September breeze rustles the cottonwood tree overhead. The arthritis in his hands belies the clarity of the stories his fingers tell as he works to pick the strings of his guitar.

(OPPOSITE) JOHN T. SAMPLES, LIBERTY, 1993, PHOTOGRAPH BY ALAN GOVENAR.

I grew up on a farm. My daddy raised cows, horses, hogs, chickens, cotton, and corn. John and Ella I. Samples were my parents. But my mother passed away when I was four. I just barely remember her. And my father lived until he was fifty-eight. I'm living longer than any of my people. I'm ninety-five years old, born January 10, 1898.

I remember my grandmother. My grandfather died before I was big enough to know him. My grandmother's name was Charlotte Samples, and she had three kids by my granddaddy, two sons and one daughter. But she was married before to a Muckelroy and also had three kids by the Muckelroy husband.

Both of my grandmothers were born in slavery time. My mother's mother was a slave, and I don't remember her husband. He died before I was big enough to know him. Both of my grandmothers were widows. My daddy's mother told me about slavery, how they used to sell them for about fifteen hundred dollars on up and how they had to pick cotton and chop cotton from sunup to sundown. I heard my grandmother sing. Oh, she'd sing different songs, old songs back there, "Nearer My God To Thee," songs like that, "Glory Hallelujah."

I've been playing the guitar ever since I was five years old. My daddy brought me a guitar when he saw I was going to play. A cousin of mine, Nora Day, taught me some notes on the guitar, but mostly I taught myself. I started to play and I've been playing ever since. I just enjoy it. I've got arthritis in my fingers now and can hardly play, but the guitar is my pastime. I do it when I'm sitting around my house. I play guitar, piano, and French harp. My daddy was the best French harp player in the country around here.

I played a little blues when I was growing up. I just picked it up, played whatever I could, and finally learned to play pretty good. There were a few blues singers around, fellas playing guitar. I had two good friends who played blues, Tommy Austin and Sam Tiyeaski. Sam was half-Spanish, half-Indian. They were real good, and I

learned a few songs from them. Jesse Atkins sang the blues, and John Henry Blackman and Josh Henderson.

I worked on the farm until I was twenty-one years old. Then I got married to Ruby King and I moved to Sweetwater, where I went to work at Davis Drugs as a porter, delivering medicine. With Ruby, I had six children; two are dead, Cecil and Espinola. Resie lives in New York City, Ruth is in California now, and Charlie and Clara Bell are still in Sweetwater.

I organized my own little band in 1927 in Sweetwater, and I had a bass violin player and a ukulele player, and I played the guitar and we would sing. Noel Bennett played the ukulele and piano and Titus Blacksley played the bass violin. We called ourselves Poison, Antidote and Prevention. I was "Poison" and Bennett was "Antidote" and Titus was "Prevention." We had a bad band, I'm telling you. We played for house parties, for the two colored cafes in town, and for dances out on the ranch for white people. We played "Darkness on the Delta," "I Never Had a Chance," "In Shady Green Pastures," and other popular songs and some blues, what we called West Texas Blues. It had a kind of country sound. We played around for dances, and one thing led to another and my boss finally carried us to Lubbock, and we played at the Retail Druggist Convention. He gave us one of the best times I ever had.

I used to know several yodeling songs. I just had that voice. I didn't have to learn it. I could just do it. I could do that when I was a kid. And I played for Jimmie Rodgers. He came to Sweetwater when I was there. I played his songs and he offered me a job. I was at Davis Drugs and the music store was right across the street. And they all knew I could play and sing, you know. I could play his songs. I heard them on the Victrola. So, the fellas who worked with me came and carried me over to where he was singing. And I sang his songs and played them for him. Oh, he got more kick out of that. I could sing good as he could back in them days. I could yodel just like him.

Around 1930, my bass violin player passed away and that kind of broke up my band. He got sick and died, and the other fella, he went to preaching. I had the band for about five years, and then I continued playing by myself. I moved back to Kilgore during the oil boom in 1931, I believe it was. I went to work at the Longhorn Drug Company, delivering medicine, cooking in the kitchen, cleaning the store. I did everything around there they wanted me to do. I went all over town. I worked for Mr. Scotty Lucas until he passed and Mr. Cline and Mr. Beaty bought the store out. I worked for more than twenty years for Mr. Beaty and Mr. Cline, two of the nicest people I ever worked for in my entire life. I worked there forty-two years and I retired there eight years ago. Everybody was so nice to me.

During the oil boom in Kilgore there were more people than I had ever saw in one place. There were so many people in Kilgore during the oil boom it would take you all day to drive to Longview and back to Kilgore. Traffic was that heavy. I played at residences, homes. People would give little parties and dances and they'd get me to play for them.

A lot of black people around Kilgore had a lot of land. They owned farms during the oil boom. A lot of them got ahold of lots of money. We got a little money. Our land was on the west edge of the oil field. We got a few oil wells, but they didn't last too long. The man said when he drilled them we were on the west edge of the field. They lasted four or five years, and that was about it.

I married Flossie Mae Timms, who was part Chickasaw Indian, around 1938 in Kilgore and had four children by her, John Junior, Bobby, Lena Mae, and Emma Lee. I taught John and Bobby to play guitar when they were seven or eight, and they're still playing.

I've always used a pick to play my guitar, a straight pick and a thumb pick. I make my own straight picks. I take the top off a milk jar and just trim it down, and it makes a good pick. I play the bass with my thumb pick and I take a round pick and slip it on my pointing finger. And when I don't use my thumb pick or finger pick, I use a straight pick to strum the guitar.

I play church songs: "Down at the Cross," "Jesus Keep Me near the Cross," "Jesus on the Main Line," "Someone Cares." I'm a member of the Mount Pleasant C.M.E. Church and I sing there. And I play popular songs, a few blues. I can play anything I ever picked up but the fiddle. I can't play a violin. I wrote several little songs. I imagine about a few. I just sang them to myself. "It's a Lovely Life Living by Myself," "You're Always Telling Me to Wait until You Call—I Wait and Wait and Wait and You Don't Call at All," and "I Fell in Love When I First Saw You." Some of the songs I play I heard when I was growing up. Nora Day taught me how to play "Nobody's Business," and a friend of mine in Longview, Dollar Bill they called him, taught me "Hesitatin' Blues." "Daddy

Double Do Love You" I learned from Tommy Austin and Sam Tiyeaski. My daddy played "Hen Cackle," "Listen to the Mockingbird," "Beautiful Lady in Blue," and "God Be with You till We Meet Again."

I never heard anybody play just like my daddy. He used to take a wide-mouth beer glass and play his harp inside of the glass to give it a different tone. And I learned it from him.

I figured someday I might get to record some of them songs I like to play. I always wanted to do that. I always wanted to record some songs. My motto, I think, is be honest, live your best, and the best will come back to you.

I keep my farm mowed down with my tractor. Last year I planted peas, but the deer ate up most of them. So this year I didn't plant any.

I play the guitar and the French harp and it just relaxes me. I forget about all my worries. I live by myself. I have an old black dog named Jo Boy, and I play my music for company.

JOHN T. SAMPLES, LIBERTY, 1993.
PHOTOGRAPH BY ALAN GOVENAR.

MANCE LIPSCOMB

April 9, 1895–January 30, 1976; interview by Jay Brakefield and Allan Turner, 1972

Mance Lipscomb was part of a songster tradition that began in the nineteenth century and involved a variety of styles common to both blacks and whites in the South. Lipscomb's repertoire included country blues as well as ballads, rags, dance pieces (breakdowns, waltzes, two-steps, reels), and popular sacred and secular songs. He finger-picked an acoustic guitar and sometimes used a pocketknife for a slide.

As a young boy, Lipscomb played guitar accompaniment for his father, Charles, who was a fiddler at country dances in Navasota and elsewhere in Grimes County. His father disappeared one night when Mance was eleven and never returned home.

At sixteen Mance Lipscomb began working as a sharecropper on a 20-acre plot of Brazos River bottom land, which he farmed for the next forty-three years to support his family. In 1954 he was put in charge of a 200-acre farm, but he refused to work for a salary instead of a crop, and he quit. He took a job as a truck driver and later worked as a lawn-mowing contractor until August 1960, when he was discovered by researchers Mack McCormick and Chris Strachwitz. A local man called Peg Leg had told them about Lipscomb, who played music as a sideline and often performed at Saturday night suppers.

On the basis of that first meeting, Strachwitz decided to start his own label and record Lipscomb. Strachwitz named his label Arhoolie, and he released the first Mance Lipscomb album later that year, and with its success, he launched an extensive series of Texas blues recordings, featuring new material and reissue albums of Lightnin' Hopkins, Juke Boy Bonner, Black Ace, Li'l Son Jackson, Alex Moore, Bill Neely, Mercy Dee, Big Mama Thornton, and others.

In his mid-sixties, Mance Lipscomb became popular with the largely white folk revival audience and made his living from music for the first time in his life. He was in demand at festivals and college clubs and coffeehouses. California filmmaker Les Blank made a documentary about Lipscomb, *A Well-Spent Life.* Each August, the film is shown at a blues festival in his honor held in Navasota.

We knew we were on the route to Dallas, but we didn't let other people know where we was going. It's anywhere we thought; first thing, we'd put them off, so they wouldn't follow us, you know. And that was our alibi. When we got to Dallas, we hung around where we could hear Blind Lemon [Jefferson] sing and play. Not only me and Son, there were hundreds of people up and down that [Central] Track. They went for that, country people, a lot of town people.

So that's where I got acquainted with him, 1917.

He hung out round the track. Deep Ellum, the street called Deep Elm. You cross Deep Ellum and turn, go down the track. Central Track run right through Ellum. They moved Blind Lemon out of town, forbid him right in town, but the law would let him stay out of town. He was a big loud songster, and he'd have all that gang of people gathering around him so fast, and wouldn't cluster in town. A certain distance away and they would allow him to play and sing. That he wouldn't bother anybody. Some of them went for it, some of them didn't like it.

They gave him privilege to play in a certain district in Dallas, and they call that "on the Track." Right beside the place where he stood round there under a big old shade tree, call it a standpoint, right off the railroad track. And people started coming in there, from nine thirty until six o'clock that evening, then he would go home because it was getting dark and somebody carried him home.

It made his living. I don't know how much money he made, but he made his living that way. He was a big stout fella, husky fella, loud voice. And he played dance songs and never did much church song. I ain't never known him to play a church song. He's a bluesman.

He had a tin cup wired on the neck of his guitar. And when you pass to give him something, why he'd thank

MANCE LIPSCOMB, NAVASOTA, CA. 1960.

PHOTOGRAPH BY CHRIS STRACHWITZ. COURTESY ARHOOLIE RECORDS.

you. But he would never take no pennies. You could drop a penny in there and he'd know the sound. He'd take and throw it away.

Well, I liked Blind Lemon Jefferson's playing and his kind of blues. He had double notes in his music.

Oh, oh, I don't got no mama now.
Deedle deedle deedle dee du du
Oh, oh, I don't like no mama now.
Deedle deedle deedle dee dee du

Well, that's not no time there. That's just like you in the field, ain't got no instrument at all. You just in the field workin,' and if you ain't got no time at all, you just got your mind made up, you singin' to pass time. Just like you think if you sing, the sun go down quicker or the days go shorter. But when you get out to sing something in a mood with time, one, two, three, that's what music is made out of.

I never did go and interfere with him. He was a big, husky fella. I was a country guy, you know. And I stood my ground with him, but I could hear all he was doing, and see what he's doing. I didn't want to approach him, that I was paying attention to him just because I was going to try to learn how to play. I know he wouldn't have liked it. That's the reason I was staying my distance from him. Now, he didn't care about how many people come near him who wasn't playing guitar. But somebody who was standing around there listening and trying to figure out what he's doing and how to play maybe like him or something, you know that didn't go so well with him. A lot of people would ask him "How do you play so-and-so?" But I would never ask him nothin.' I just stayed quiet and listened to him. And when I got ready to leave I didn't say hello or goodbye.

We'd see him when we come to Dallas. We got through with our crops, somewhere long about September or August. And October and November, up until the next year, we'd have cotton to pick in Dallas. And we wouldn't be up there the whole season, just went out there for emergency, pick up a little Christmas money, maybe come a flood, or drought or something at home. We get fifteen or twenty-five, thirty dollars, well, we rich, you know. Then, we come back home to Navasota.

There [in Navasota] what you call a club now, we called them Saturday night dances, dance all night, all night long. I had three crews to interpretate with. The first crew was at eight o'clock. I played a hour for them. They had everything in full bloom. Long about twelve o'clock, here another crew come in there. Fresh crew! I fan them out, play all night till four o'clock in the morning, sometimes till eleven o'clock on Sunday, setting right in one chair.

Now when I get to playin' I go out of the bounds of reason because when I start, I don't like to stop. As long as it look like they payin' attention to me, I can play all night for them.

See, I play straight time. Straight, straight strictly time. I will play that there split time, well, I ain't gettin' nowhere because that's the way I learnt. Once you learnt, son, and been at it as long as me, you can't veer from it. You feel it, and you know how you learnt, and then when you start, gonna start right. Gonna start, with a certain speed, and different chords.

See, I know every chord that I wanna make, and puttin' in music. I play, oh about three-fifty say, and when I play those three-fifty songs, listen to me, it's a lot of different sounds coming out of that guitar. But I never break my time, what you call rhythm. Three or four things you can call it. Rhythm, time, and the beat. All of it's the same thing.

Say, for instance, you say, "Well I can beat you from here to the highway." Well, you got a certain—you ain't got no gait. You got a certain limit of time. You could beat me here to the highway. You gonna run fast and try to beat me there. If you run slow, you can't beat me there. But that's what you call time, and then break your time, well can keep up and do something with that time. But if you start off slow, and then run fast, well that's not no time. You done broke time.

Well, [if] you go out there, say, "I'm goin' try to run from here to the road in ten minutes," you know it [got] a ten-minute limit. So you say I'm gonna run here, out to the road in three minutes, you speedin' up. You got to speed up because you done took some of them minutes away from there. See, that's what you call time.

You done heard me play over in Austin. Whenever I start a song, I keep it a real beat where I can tap my foot and you can pat your foot. Now you find music, it's not got no rhythm, that's time; ain't got no beat, that's time, and all things like that. If it ain't got the right rhythm or right time, and right beat, it's some bad music coming up there.

You can get in the good pattin' your foot or shakin' yourself or just settin' down, you can get in the motion.

MANCE LIPSCOMB WITH HIS WIFE, ELNORA, AND LARRY KIRBO, AUSTIN, 1974. PHOTOGRAPH BY ALAN POGUE.

You're shakin' yourself because you got that time and motion. But that's the same thing, that motion, that you just leaned yourself thisaway. You're motionin.'

And then if you ain't motionin' you can take your foot and tap there. That's what you call rhythm and time, all right, comin' out of your foot. Then in the motion of your body. That's rhythm and time. It comes out that way.

It matches up a whole lot of ways, but it ain't but one thing. You got straight time, beat, rhythm, and motion, all four of them things is the same thing, and gait right in there alongside of them. But once you go too fast, then jump over and go too slow, you broke down your time. [There] is no regular time there. Good music is time. It's not no good music if it's untimely.

You change music when you playing different songs. You can play a hundred songs in E sound, but they the same song. Lightnin' Hopkins a E man, E and a little A, only type he try to play. He can play E chord good as he want to. And everything he going to play, that have any kind of sense to it, he going to play in E. And maybe sometime in A.

That rascal can sing, though. He can play them songs that he mix them up so bad you'll think he singing five thousand songs. But you know many songs he singin'? Don't y'all tell him because I might see him and he'd kill me. He's singin' two songs out of five thousand. But see here, I'll show what key he's in. If you get him out of this key here, he ain't no good at all. That's E.

Say "Play a C chord," that's a change in a song. He don't know how to mix his fingers up there. "Play a D chord." That's changin' song. You just as good as him in that. Anybody can make a D chord as good as him. But he going to run you crazy with E stuff, and A.

I can play five hundred songs in E, but I ain't playing nothing but one song. But if I change and put the song from E to C, G, F, B, sharps and sevenths, I'm playing different songs. You get the song by sounds of the ear, you can listen to them.

I first met Lightnin' in 1938, I believe. In Galveston. My sister and brother, who is a twin to my baby sister, they live in Galveston for thirty-five or forty years. I call them Coon and Pie, Willy and Little are their real names. And Pie got some kids, my nieces and nephews. So I go to Galveston very often when I felt like it to see them.

My brother, he run around and he loved to drink, says, "Let's go out and hear Lightnin' Hopkins."

I said, "He's here?"

He said, "Yeah, he's here."

I said, "I wonder what you have to pay to go in and hear him."

He say, "Oh, it's a dollar. I'll pay your way in."

See, I didn't have much money in them days. I said, "Well, if you'll pay my way, I'll go out and hear him."

So I went out. He [Lightnin'] had heard of me, but he didn't know me. I went to the place where he was playing, I believe it was on Thirty-Third Street in Galveston. They had the house loaded up.

I sat down right by him. I didn't say nothing to him and he didn't say nothing to me because there were too many people for us to get to talking and knowing one another. And I didn't want him to know me no how. So, I sat, catched on to what he was doing.

He had an electric guitar, you know, that plug in. He had his boots on, had one of his legs down in his boot, the other one was down here, had nice clothes on. He made a lot of money. They were paying him somewhere long about one hundred dollars a night. That was real good money in them times.

Well, his sister was there. He had a sister standing there and looking at what he was doing. She's a tall woman. And she looked there at me and I'm setting beside him. Somebody told her who I was, and she told her brother, Lightnin.' She says, "Brother? You got to play this guitar. You settin' beside a famous man."

He looked around at me, said, "Who's, what famous man? I ain't scared of nobody."

She says, "You liable to be scared of this man. Do you know who he is?"

He said, "No, I don't know who he is, and damn if I care."

And she said, "Well, you gonna know him?"

He says, "How am I gonna know him?"

She says, "Because people are going to want him to play a song."

Lightnin' says, "Who the hell is this man you talkin' about?"

She says, "That's Mance Lipscomb."

He jumped up out of his chair and shook hands with me. Said, "I'm sorry I said that about you. I'm gonna let you play a number."

I said, "No, I don't want to play. You gettin' paid."

He says, "Yeah, but the people gonna want you to play."

So I refused to play for him, and a boy from my home town here in Navasota, raised up with me, he said, "Lightnin,' I'll give you a dollar to let Mance play his 'Bumblebee.'"

And Lightnin' couldn't play it. He got mad when they asked him to let me play "Bumblebee," because he knew he couldn't play it. So he said, "You oughta be walkin' while you're talkin.' I ain't gonna loan Mance my guitar."

The man says, "Well, I know you ain't gonna loan it to him, but I'll rent it."

"I ain't gonna rent it to him. Now when I get through playing here tonight, if Mance wants to go home and stay all night with me, I'll let him go home with me."

I said, "No, I'm right across the street here with my sister." So, that's the first time I seen him. We remained good friends from then on.

Lightnin' comes from Centerville, he stayed out from Centerville, and drifted in over to Conroe. From Conroe he went in the direction of Houston, and in Houston he got a big name because he was a good songster.

I'm glad the young people are catching up about what the music is. They know music now, but six or seven years ago they didn't know nothin.' Say, "Aw, play me some rock 'n' roll." Half the majority is going with rock 'n' roll now. You know who's doing it. The teenagers. But people get above teenagers, eighteen, nineteen, twenty, on up, they want to hear that solid music, something you can remember. The best rock 'n' roll is related to the blues, got blues in it.

I don't try to criticize nobody's music because everybody doing their own thing. Now, understand what I'm talking about. There's plenty of people who can play something I cannot play. Why? They're doing their number. They doing their thing. But I can do some things a whole lot more than other fellas can do because I'm playing all kind of chords in music. Ever since I been here I been playing different sounds and music.

SAM "LIGHTNIN'" HOPKINS

March 15, 1912–January 30, 1982; interview by Les Blank, 1968 (courtesy Les Blank and Flower Films)

THE HOUSE WHERE SAM "LIGHTNIN'" HOPKINS LIVED WITH HIS MOTHER IN THE EARLY 1950S, CENTERVILLE, 2008. PHOTOGRAPH BY ALAN GOVENAR.

The music of Sam "Lightnin'" Hopkins is firmly rooted in the Texas blues tradition. He embodied the music's transition from rural East Texas to Houston. Hopkins grew up hearing the blues in Centerville, midway between Dallas and Houston, and the surrounding area. He learned to play the guitar from his brother John Henry. But in 1920 the young Sam Hopkins heard Blind Lemon Jefferson at a Baptist church social in Buffalo, Texas. In a story Hopkins often told, he tried to play along, but Jefferson was displeased and shouted, "Boy, you got to play it right!" When Jefferson realized that the other musician was an eight-year-old boy, though, he hoisted the child onto the bed of a truck and let him play.

From that day on, Hopkins devoted himself to the blues, performing on the streets of Crockett and other area towns and in cafes and beer joints. He sometimes traveled to Houston to play, and he moved there in the late 1940s. Hopkins developed a distinctive guitar style that was influenced by Jefferson and by other musicians, such as the very popular Lonnie Johnson. Most of Hopkins's best recordings feature just him and his guitar, but after he moved to Houston, he often performed with other musicians playing drums, piano, harmonica, bass, and guitar.

Hopkins did not begin recording until 1946, when Lola Cullen of Aladdin Records, talent-hunting in Houston, picked him up, along with pianist "Thunder" Smith, and brought the two to Los Angeles. She left behind Hopkins's aging cousin, the vocalist Alger "Texas" Alexander. It was on this trip that Hopkins apparently got his nickname, though he told various stories of its origin over the years. Those initial sides were later reissued by Pathé Marconi in France.

A year later, in 1947, Hopkins began recording for Bill Quinn's Houston-based Gold Star label. Over the next two years, he produced his finest work. In these recordings, Hopkins established his mastery as a down-home guitar stylist and singer who could improvise lyrics as

RICHMOND, 1960S, PHOTOGRAPH BY CHRIS STRACHWITZ. COURTESY ARHOOLIE RECORDS.

"BLUE DEVIL BLUES," OKEH RECORDS 1094, TEXAS ALEXANDER RACE AD, N.D. COURTESY DOCUMENTARY ARTS.

he sang. According to Chris Strachwitz, whose Arhoolie label later reissued the Gold Star sides, "Can't Be Successful" was composed on the spot when Hopkins discovered that his wife had already collected his payment from Quinn and that it wasn't enough.

The success of these recordings launched Hopkins's career and led to numerous opportunities for recording with Gold Star, Jax/Sittin' In With, and Herald. Although most of his recordings were made with acoustic guitar, he demonstrated his creative dexterity on the electric guitar in his 1954 Herald sessions, which resulted in twenty-six superb sides. They were later rereleased on the Diving Duck label in the Netherlands.

By 1959, when Strachwitz met him in a Houston juke joint, Hopkins's commercial recording career had begun to wane. That meeting inspired Strachwitz, a Silesian immigrant teaching German in a California high school, to record Hopkins. Along with other blues musicians, Hopkins benefited from the folk/blues boom of the 1960s and came to the attention of other collectors and researchers, such as Mack McCormick, Sam Charters, and Paul Oliver. In 1969 Hopkins was the subject of a documentary film, *The Blues Accordin' to Lightnin' Hopkins,* by Les Blank and Skip Gerson. Until his death in 1982, Hopkins performed across the nation and around the world, though he often turned down gigs because he hated to fly. Dozens of his recordings were issued on revival labels, such as Prestige/Bluesville, Candid, Sonet, and Diving Duck. Of these, the Arhoolie, Prestige/Bluesville, and Diving Duck are the most consistent. Many of the others are marred by low-end production and the inescapable fact that after years of hard living and heavy drinking, Hopkins had lost the vitality of his early years.

In 2002, on the twentieth anniversary of his death, Hopkins was remembered with the unveiling of a statue on Camp Street in Crockett, where he often played when it was the heart of the town's black commercial and social life.

The blues is something that is hard to get acquainted with. Just like death. The blues dwell with you every day and everywhere. You can have the blues about being broke, about your girl being gone. You can have the

SAM "LIGHTNIN'" HOPKINS, 1960s. PHOTOGRAPH BY LES BLANK. COURTESY FLOWER FILMS.

blues so many different ways till it's hard to explain. But whenever you get a sad feeling, you can tell the whole rotten world you got nothing but the blues.

It don't make any difference. If you're a hundred years old, you get the blues. The blues dwell with you. When you born in this world, you born with the blues. Upset is the blues. Worry is the blues.

Up in Centerville, people working in the fields picking cotton day in and day out. Yeah, they got the blues. You just work it off and make yourself feel good somehow. You got to do something, like they work in the field. Okay, could be another field over there. Could be someone at that field that you like to be working with, you know. And if you can't work with them, you got the blues real bad and first thing you know, you done jumped that rope.

The blues come by what you love, and you always love something. You have the blues by anything. You can have a car and wake up in the morning and have a flat. You get to walking and nobody helps you; you ain't got nothing like the blues. You gonna walk until you find somebody who says they'll try to help you. Trouble is the blues.

When I first started hoboing, I taken a freight train to be my friend
When I first started hoboing, I taken a freight train to be my friend
Yeah, you know that train is gone,
I just standing there wondering, would it ever come back again

The blues come from small shotgun houses, narrow streets, poor vision, poor upkeep, and what have you. It did not come from the brick homes. It did not come from the mansions. I think blues is nothing but a whole lot of soul. When I say soul, it's just something that's given to you. You feel it. You can't say what it means, you just feel it. And when you feel it, you play it, if you are a musician.

When people have the blues, it's something like this. Let's say you setting down right now thinking. You be thinking about something. You got the blues on your mind. Now, like you have a girlfriend and she leaves you. You get the blues. It means you lost her and are having a whole lot of trouble. And that's when you start singing from your soul.

I know a man that had a woman he loved. If he didn't love her, he would never have went crazy. That's in Austin. They put him in the crazy house. He stayed there a long time, but he never did get over her. He loved that woman, but he found that woman doing wrong.

Cried all night, cried all night for her
Because any way I'm looking, ain't gonna cry no more
Going away this summer, going away this summer
And I won't be back no more
If I don't find my woman, I won't be back at all

I ain't too fast to love. You know what I mean? I'm just passing by, babe. Just hit you and go. Good bye, good God bless you. That falling in love gonna cause something else. I ain't going to fall in love with nothing, ain't joking you either. There's too much going on, man. See, that's the reason I can make it like I do. I don't love nothing.

I tell you what. I'd rather love a dog that goes up this street than fall in love with a woman. You know why? Because that dog is gonna like me if I feed him. Hell, I can go up there and feed a damn woman till she falls out, and that son-of-a-gun get up and shoot me in my back for another man. No, she don't love me. Bull corn, love don't come like that.

Do you think I'd love you? Just put me to be the woman. Me and you gonna be man and wife. I'm gonna love you and trap you for somebody else up there. Is that love? Hell, no, that's hate.

Let me tell you something. This world is so wicked and wild. If you ain't got somebody to stay with you like I got, just keep away because, partner, they ain't doing nothing but laying every day for you. They laying for you. They got it figured out when they see you coming.

You know what? Me and my first wife were together fourteen years and I never seen her naked in my life. Wasn't nothing wrong with her and I know it. She told me that it was something that she was born with, to never get naked with no man, regardless to whom, husband or anyone else. You understand me? I don't be lying. We were together, but she was never showing me, just like you get up here and pull your clothes off naked. "You get it under the covers. You can pull off anything and you still won't see me naked." And she never walked in front of me naked in her life. Now, I'm not lying to you. My daughter's in Crockett. Her name's Annie Mae.

I've been married seven times and I'm gonna marry seven more, I think. I'm gonna try. That little old girl you see me with now, that's the last one. Glory Be, she's in Santa Monica right now. A big used-to-be. You know that song I made about "Glory Be"? That was my wife too. You heard that song about Katie Mae? That was my wife too, and I ain't lying. You heard a song about Ida Mae? That was my wife, too. I'm not bull corn.

You know, Ida Mae's a good girl
Folks say she don't run around at night
Yeah, you know, Ida Mae's a good girl
Folks say she don't run around at night
Yeah, you know, you can bet your last dollar
Oh, Ida Mae will treat you right
Yeah, you know, I tried to give that woman everything in the world she needs
That's why she don't do nothing, man, but lay up in the bed and read
I called her, Ida Mae. Oh, Ida Mae
Ida Mae, Oh, Ida Mae
Oh, don't you hear me?
You know I bought a radio, even bought an electric fan
She just said, "I'm gonna lay here and read and God knows I ain't gonna have no other man
Makes me feel so good, till I don't know what to do
Yes, I save every dollar Po' Lightnin' makes
And I got to bring it home to you

You heard that song about Mary? That was my wife, too. Now, I'll tell you what. There's a song about practically every wife I ever had. When I play guitar, I play it from my heart and soul. I play my own music. And I just keep it up because the blues is something people can't get rid of. And if you ever have the blues, remember what I tell you. You'll always hear this in your heart. That's the blues. Now, I want to tell you what you've done.

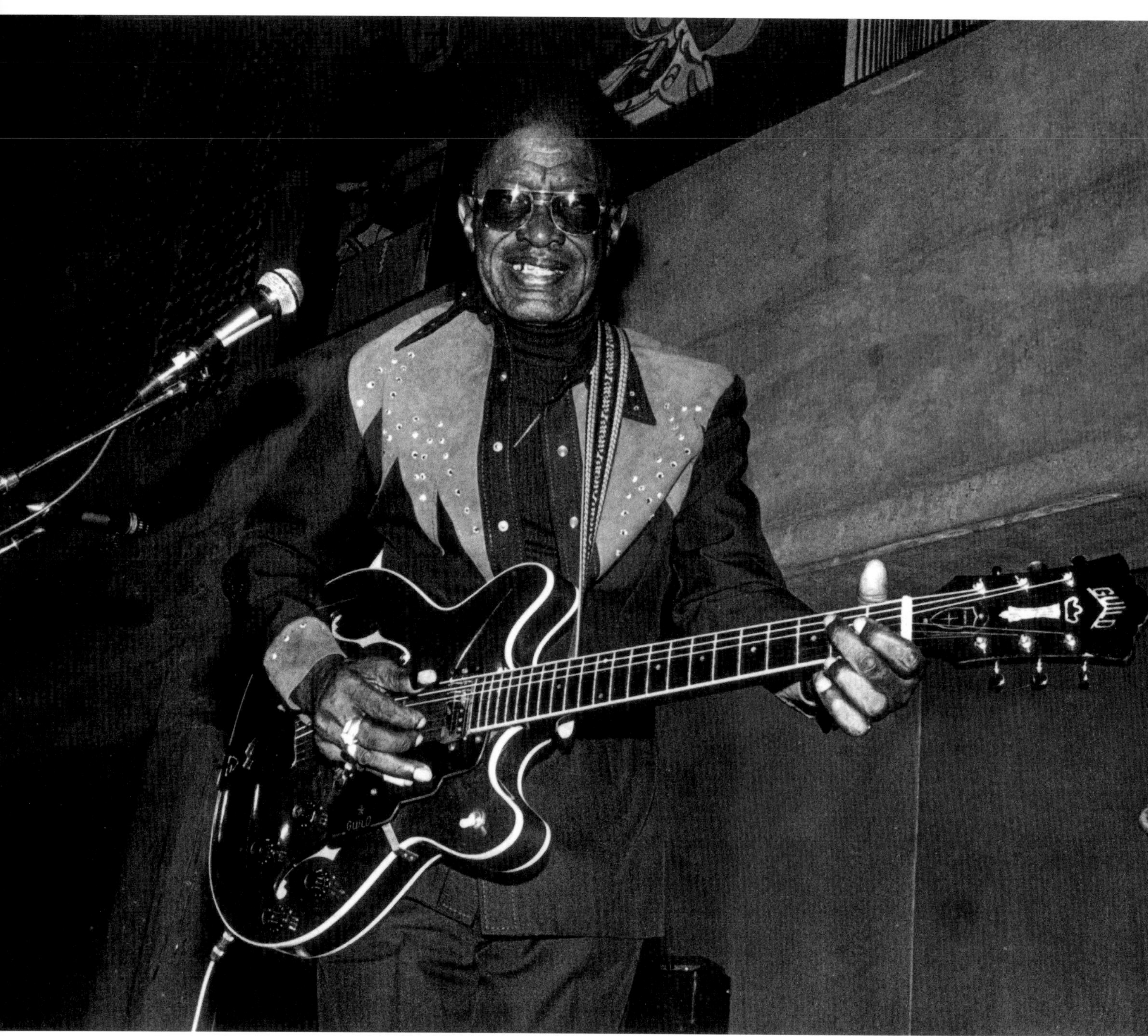

SAM "LIGHTNIN'" HOPKINS, SWEDEN, 1972.

PHOTOGRAPH BY ERIK LINDAHL. COURTESY TOMMY LÖFGREN.

That woman named Mary, she going to stay out all night long
That woman named Mary, she would go and stay out all night long
Well, you know, she wouldn't come back to the house until Po' Lightnin' and his blues was gone
Know you got another man, Mary, that's why you treat me so unkind
I know you got another man, Mary, that's why you treat me so unkind
You know the blues gonna dwell with you, I can't get these blues off of my mind

I say, if I had wings as an angel, I'd tell you why I'd fly. I'd fly to the heart of Antoinette and that's where I'd give up to die. That's the last one I put out about the wife because that's her. And you know what I mean? I've got to say something about them no-good girls.

Tell me, pretty baby, why you do me this way
You know the sun is gonna shine in my back door one day
Come on and go home with me
Come on, pretty baby, and go home with me
I'll make you happy in the morning as a pretty woman can be

Now, they'll make you buy divorce, if you're not married to her. Just stay with her six months and she'll file on you to get a divorce. Yeah, that's true. You might just as well not marry because you gonna pay the same thing for the divorce. Just live with her. But I guess I don't know. I don't know what they are doing. Do you? I sure don't. But if she call down there and tell them people downtown you been with her better than six months, you got to buy a divorce. You don't believe me? You call down there to the city of Houston and see. Just call down there. You are automatically married to that woman at six months. And I know it's true. But I'm glad that I ain't got them kind of things to do, you know. See, because every time I get ready to go, I just throw the divorce money up on the table and the paper's already signed. I'm gone. I done bought about seven divorces. I love these women. You know what I mean? But if they make me mad, I'm gone. Goodbye, honey, because there's another somewhere else, just like the saying goes, "For the flower that blooms, there's another of a different color." White flowers, blue flowers, I can pick any kind I want. And if I got a blue one that makes me mad, I go get me a red one. I kind of like to pick my flowers, and if I get hot, I pick a good one. Ah, yeah, baby, I'd be hiding. I've caught many rabbits in them little kind of wildflowers.

COTTON PICKERS WEIGHING IN, 1920s.
COURTESY ARCHIVES DIVISION, TEXAS STATE LIBRARY, AUSTIN.

You know, I've always liked little girls, all of my life. I used to pass by their houses. I knew she was in there and I'd peep through that window. She'd be there snoring and I tip-toed to the window just to see how sweet she snored. She made me feel like jumping through the keyhole in her door. Well, that's my song. I tip-toe to the window, baby. And let me whisper in your ear. I got something to tell you. I don't want your daddy to hear. Boy, she had a mean old daddy. He didn't like me and the fact is, I didn't like him. I just loved his daughter and I didn't care nothing about him. But he didn't want me nowhere around because I guess I wasn't fit for his daughter. She was pretty and I was ugly. You take pretty and ugly and you can't put that together, not and make it match. They were real bright and I'm dark. I guess he wanted her to have a yellow man.

Man, I've been places in Louisiana where I tell you I couldn't go in because of my color. I got to be your color. It's true. They used to go in there and break up them joints because it was dignified. They didn't want no dark-skinned person to come in there. You know, the world's been entangled ever since I knowed it was a world. But it didn't make any difference because I didn't have to go in there because I've got some of the prettiest blue women on God's earth.

SAM "LIGHTNIN'" HOPKINS MEMORIAL (DETAIL) BY JIM JEFFRIES, CROCKETT, 2008. PHOTOGRAPH BY ALAN GOVENAR.

I tell you what, if you be here on Sunday, go up to this church and I'll show you some of the prettiest dark women that ever walked. I want to show you some pretty colored women. What the hell do I want to fall out by the bright-ass women? Shit, you know I'm not color-struck no kind of way. I ain't joking. I go to church and I set there and let them pass by me. And I say, "Y'all look nice today." And when church is over, I say, "Baby, I want to speak with you, if your husband don't get mad." I dig in my little deal. I just wait till the day for church and I know I'm gonna get some pretty women. Man, these people are trying to save their soul from hell.

I'm no preacher and I don't promise you that I tell the truth all the time, but I tell you what I promise you. When I go to church, you know that I'm up to something. I'm either up the right or up the wrong. You believe that. Now, I don't call it wrong if a man does what it takes to find him a good woman. You know what I mean, kind of take a little snitch on his wife. And if she catches me, I'm just as humble as a crawfish. I'll back up with my paws up. You know, just don't want too much punishment. But ain't a man in the world don't want extra. You know what, I got four tires on the ground and I got a spare in the back. Well, the way I keep my women is, if one put me down that spare gonna pick me up, baby. And I never worry about no one, nothing.

When I play a guitar I play it from my heart and soul. This is a gift I got. And the other people who hear my music from records and things, they try to say the words that I say about that because they heard me say it. But when they get with me to play it, they cannot play it because they wasn't cut out for it. This is a gift to me from God. And I been playing a guitar since I was eight years old. I played with the most famous man that I thought was in this world, Blind Lemon Jefferson. And I'm right here to track him on down because I can play his music, but here's where I might have done ruined myself. If I'd a been the man to try to play like Blind Lemon Jefferson, I wouldn't have been myself. And you take a man that try to play like me, he ain't himself. He's just trying something.

But you take me, I play my own music and I ain't found nobody play like me but my two brothers, and they dead and gone. And right now, I don't find nobody pick a guitar like I do. I play it different. I teach people. But they start out and what they be trying to do they have to change it because they cannot play the kind of music I play. They change it and make something else out of it.

There's good players in this world that change just a little bit, but some runs I make they just can't make. But you can tell they just near about to it. But it takes a whole lot.

Well, I seen people play it but I didn't talent after them. I picked up the guitar and played with what's in my mind. And from that day to this it's been always like that. And when I sing a song, it's near about just like the guitar talks. I make that guitar almost say what I say. It's so near to it, you can tell what it says. That's just like that beautiful "Trouble in Mind." I'm not lying. I don't find nobody that plays like that. Now, Billy [Bizor] on the harmonica is coming close, but you watch when me and him play it together. You watch the changes and you watch what my guitar does, and you watch what his harp gets off from saying. It's exactly the word that my guitar does. I want you to pay attention.

I can just sit down with guitar players and I can show you the difference. I can show you. I know you got pretty nice hearing. I want you to listen at me and the man playing the same song and see where you can tell the difference.

It's nice [playing with other people] if you just want to have a little jump and enjoy something. You just soon boom along with them. But when it come down to business, these people really want to hear music. They ask me, "Stop them people." I've been asked that many many times. "Please play by yourself. We can't get to understanding when them people up there. Some going one way and some going the other."

And you know that you can't just make somebody do something when they going wrong all the time. It's true. I just take my guitar and play by myself. I love to play with a drum and a harmonica. But you take a guitar player that's gonna play with you, he gonna throw you off. Now, I tell you. I recorded; I had a band behind me for that hit song about "Backdoor Friend." I had a piano, drum, bass, and harmonica. But I had to take them off that. I made a hit with it. They never could do it, so I did it by myself. Whenever you gonna do something right, you near about have to get by yourself. That's just the way that guitar playing goes. I love a guitar.

When I go cut albums, I cut twelve songs in an hour and fifteen minutes. I wouldn't be that long, but I have them play it back so I can see my own mistakes. If I see I made a mistake in that song, I straighten it out. It's seldom I make a mistake in that song when I'm by myself. Now I made a mistake about "Just like little red ants, some coming and some going." That's what I should have said, but sometimes you get your words tied up, twisted around. I do.

Practically most songs I play I been playing before that, and they ask for it. The new songs, I got mostly on record. They have to be released and then they know more about what they ask me. They still like "Rocky Mountain," "Pretty Girl," "Short Haired Woman," and different songs they like. I like them too, "Trouble in Mind," "Oh, My Baby, Take Me Back," "Mr. Charlie," old songs.

"Mr. Charlie," that's mine. Just about every song I play is mine. Nobody didn't write it up.

Guy give me an idea because it's true. He could not talk. He'd have to pat himself to get his words out, thump his fingers, trying to tell you something.

I ask my mama, "What is it?"

She said, "He stutters. He trying to say it."

It looked pitiful to me. It look like it hurt him. Couldn't get his word out. So, I thought about "Mr. Charlie." And the boy did leave and he went to Mr. Charlie and here's what made me say, Mr. Charlie say, "If you can't talk it boy, sing it."

Well that was down to the last, because he was trying to tell Mr. Charlie that he wanted a home and the other little fraction of things I put there myself. And I say, Mr. Charlie say, "If you can't talk it, sing it."

Now, you take a man that stutters. You know, John Lee Hooker, he stutters. Y'all know he does. But put him to singing and see if he stutters. He don't stutter when he sings. He sings it. That's the reason I figured Mr. Charlie say, "Just sing it if you can't talk it."

I don't know what makes a man stutter. They say don't tickle a baby because it'll make him stutter. Maybe they tickled him when he was little. I ain't joking. You think I'm jivin.' Maybe somebody tickled John Lee when he was a baby.

He cannot just talk a conversation with you without jabbering. And that other boy that I'm talking about, it would take him a half a minute to get a word out. But if you want him to sing, he would rear back and sing you a tune. That's the way we would do it. I'd holler, "Sing it." And he'd holler, "Your mama want you to come home." Sure enough, Mama done sent him. But if he tried to say "Mama want me to come home," he get to thumpin' and he couldn't get it to come out.

FRANK ROBINSON

June 24, 1930– ; interview, 2002

FRANK ROBINSON, CROCKETT, 2002.
PHOTOGRAPH BY ALAN GOVENAR.

I was born on Highway 7 west of Crockett, in a place they call Snow Hill. Don't too many people live there anymore, but it used to be quite a community. I left there as a kid and we moved to the farm. And I did farm work until my mother died in 1941, and I was living across the loop on 287 North and we moved from across the loop, inside of the loop. And that's where I grew up at and went to the Ralph Bunche School.

My dad's name was Walter Robinson. He was a farmer, and he was a carpenter. He loved to bull ride and bronc ride. He played guitar. He played fiddle. He played harmonica. And he had a second guitar and bass fiddle, piano. And they would play all that harmonica during the time that they were playing. Back then, they called it a call and a sit. And they would start to playing the guitars and fiddling, and one would be singing. And the words are kind of like talking. In words, he'd be telling them what to do, and they'd be doing whatever he said. They'd just dance like that till late in the night. Oh, they called some of it barrelhouse; they called some of it stark [stop] time. And they called it country blues, and that's about all I know about it.

Back then, they had country breakdowns every weekend, when we was living in a large house then on the farm. And they would put a table across the door and they would set it up with home brew and moonshine and stuff like that. They'd get to playing and dancing, and they'd last all night long. I couldn't play at all back in them days, but I loved the music.

My dad knew Blind Lemon, but I didn't. My dad had his records. Sure did. I loved his music. I remember quite a few of them, but it's been years since I tried to do any of them. He used to sing one, "Crawling Baby Blues," I believe was the name of it, and then he sung another one I liked, "See That My Grave Is Kept Clean." It started, "One kind favor that I ask of you, please see that my grave be kept clean." I used to sing that one quite a bit. And I had decided to start back to playing his style because there was a guy come here once from overseas, and they was interested in that type of music. So I said, "I believe I'll get back up on it." Of course, there wasn't too many people over here interested, but I liked it, and I said, "Well, whenever I go over there, I'll just play some of it." And so, I've had that on my mind for a long time.

I have a brother. He's in Arizona now. He's two years older than I am. My name's Frank, and his name was Jesse. [Our father would] dress us like cowboys and make us get on the floor and dance, and the people would laugh at us. He would give us nickels and dimes, and we'd clown right. And I just grew up liking the music. He had a lot of Blind Lemon Jefferson records, and we had one of those upright turntables, you have to wind it with a crank, crank it up and it would play two or three records, and then you've got to crank it again. I'd get up in the chair, and I'd keep it wound up. I loved Blind Lemon Jefferson. My daddy, he started preaching about '36, and he give me his guitar and I didn't know one string from the other. But I remembered the tunes what I had been hearing him play, you know. But however, I taken the guitar and tied some strings round the neck just like a bridle on a horse, and I got straddle. I would ride around the house and hit them strings and tell him to get up. And I tore my guitar up, riding it for a stick horse. And about the time I felt like I was large enough to play a song, this boy that married one of my younger sisters, somebody give him a guitar. Me and him was about the same age, and he couldn't play, and I couldn't either, so he come play with me, and he left the guitar off at my house. And I'd play on it and play on it, and he never would take it home, so one day my daddy told me to ask him did he want to sell it. Every once in a while my daddy would take it and tune it and play it, and that made me more interested. So I asked him, but his mother told him, said I could keep it and play it, but she didn't want him to sell it. So, two or three weeks later, he come play with me one day and he took it home, and I was lonesome. I had done got used to it then. And I wanted me a guitar, but I wasn't able to buy one. And I went to work on a farm in Latexo, and the boss man, he married a young lady and she was a guitar picker. But after he married her, he didn't want her to get out and play no more, so he asked her to give it up, and she did. They had an old bunkhouse out in the back. The hung the guitar on a nail out in the bunkhouse. That's where I'd eat my lunch every day at twelve. And I couldn't get through eating fast enough before I'd go and get the guitar and play the rest of my time. Then, I'd hang it up and go back to work. They seen me playing it every day, at least trying to play it, and one day he walked out there and say, "You like that guitar, don't you?" I said, "I sure do." He say, "You want to buy it?" I said, "I'm not able to buy it." He say, "Well, when you go home this evening, you take it with you and ask your daddy can you buy it.

If he say you can buy it, well, I'll fix it to where you can pay for it." So I brought it home and I told Daddy what he said. He say, "Well, it's a good guitar." Say, "If he fix it where you can pay for it, you go ahead and get it." I went back and I told him what my daddy said, and he said, "Well, I'll tell you what." I was making a dollar a day, ten hours. He said, "If you make a full week, you can pay a dollar, you can pay two dollars, or three dollars, just whatever you feel like you can get by on, that's what you pay, until you get it paid for." So I took him up on it. Back then, the hustling type of children, we would sell rubber and scrap iron and pecans, berries, just anything that was a nickel or a quarter in them days, that's where we'd be. And before the winter set in, I had done paid for my guitar. And I started playing hard. Everywhere I'd go, I'd have my guitar around my neck. And there was quite a few retired people in the neighborhood at that time that had played in their younger days, but they done give it up. And they'd be glad for me to drop by. I got used to them, and I'd go from one house to another with that guitar, just catching whatever I could.

Well, there were two brothers come from Tyler, Leo Roberts and Beachie Roberts. They were both retired. But they had been playing music for years. Leo married my neighbor, and I'd walk right by his house every evening, going down to some of the rest of them, and I didn't know he was a musician. And one day he called me, and he said, "You want to learn how to play that guitar?" I said, "I sure do." He said, "Well, if you come down here about two nights out of the week, I'll teach you how to play it." So I picked Tuesdays and Thursdays. I'd go down there and he'd get the guitar, and I'd be playing second for him. And he finally got me to where I could follow him, then he got his brother and another friend we had uptown there on the square, and we all got us a group together, and we started to going different places, schoolhouses and so forth. After he taught me three or four chords, well, I got to where I could listen to a record and find it by myself.

I started sawmilling after I left the farm, and I sawmilled far and near, all the way from Willis, and here in Crockett, and Kennard and just wherever they had a sawmill. I was just an all-around hand on a sawmill switch, and wherever they put me, I was good at it. Matter of fact, they gave me an over-average rating everywhere I went. And I sawmilled for years. I left home and I traveled all out through the West, New Mexico and Arizona, stayed for a long time.

In '61, I come back to Crockett. I taught a couple of guys how to play second guitar, and we started playing in a band. It wasn't but a very few weeks before we were getting calls from one club, beer joint club. People would always tell me, said, from the looks of the traffic, said they would think B. B. King's playing here tonight. I had a lot of fans back in them days. We played Palestine, Lufkin, Trinity, here in Crockett and Kennard, just wherever they'd call us. They had a place on the Trinity County line they called the Eight Ball. It was real popular back in them days. We'd play there through the week and on weekends, leave one place and go to the other. We'd travel. We was once playing four nights a week plus sometimes in the daytime. And wasn't much time for sleeping back then, but we was young and it didn't bother us too much. We had a good time. And during that time, Lightnin' [Hopkins] was playing one place or another down in Houston. Well, I had some friends down there. We'd go down there and we'd listen to Lightnin' and we'd come back and play. So one of the men that I was playing for said, "You think we can get Lightnin' up here?" I said, "I'm pretty sure if you get in touch with him and make some arrangements, he'll come." And so they did, and Lightnin,' they made a deal and he'd meet us up here every Friday evening and Saturday evening, and we'd all get together and have a good time and get ready for that night. And we played like that for a long time. So I was playing at a large place down at Trinity County at that time. Charity Barnes was running the place, and I was renting from her. And Lightnin,' he'd come up there and play. She was booking a lot of bands back in them days. And we just had something going all the time. And it was a lot of fun. So, that's just the way we was carrying on back then.

Oh, I met Lightnin' when I was quite a kid, I guess, seven or eight years old. My uncle was running around with him. And he had a daughter, whose name is Annie Mae Box. We grew up together, and he would always come and visit. My uncle, Clyde Robinson, he couldn't play, but he loved guitar music, so whenever a guitar picker would come to town, he would always bring them by the house. My family loved to hear guitar music, and I grew up knowing him. And after I got to be a teenager, then I would go to Houston, where he was playing at, and we would get together down there. Matter of fact, where I was staying, you could walk out in the yard and listen at him. You were just that close to where he was playing, that café was.

Well, they [my uncle and Lightnin'] drank and gambled together, but my uncle, he couldn't play. He could sing, but he couldn't play at all. And my daddy tried to learn him, but he was a fast type. He didn't have time to learn how to play no guitar, but he just loved to hear anybody else play it.

Lightnin' was over six feet tall, dark, and thin build, and deep voice. He was real friendly, but he liked to drink, and when he'd get to drinking, well, he was quite outspoken. You know, whatever he had to say, well, he didn't have any trouble saying it. Sometimes, he'd start confusing, on account of him speaking up, you know, so bold. But other than that, he was really nice. Me and him, we talked. He said never a hard word to me the whole time I knowed him. And I looked up to him just like I did my daddy and my uncle, surely.

Lightnin' used to joke a lot. I mean, he had some little short jokes he'd tell when he was fixing to play. I was thinking about it not too long ago. But it had been so long since I heard them till all I remember is some of the words, and I couldn't even put enough of it together to tell how it went. But I said I might run across—of course, he recorded quite a few of them. I might have some of them, but I ain't played them yet. I said I'm going to look through them and see if I can run across any of them jokes that he used to tell.

When I was a teenager, I played with Lightnin' sometimes—he would sing and I would play. And then, I would play second, but he had a drummer, but he didn't carry no bass man with him at that time. He was playing electrics. He had a hollow-bodied Gibson at that time, great big guitar. Only places I went with him were Trinity and Lufkin.

Of course, we went to Arizona one year on a truck together, but when we got out there, he went one way and we went the other one, and I didn't see him no more until I come back to Houston in the Fifties. I heard that record "Short-Haired Woman." We called him Sam; we didn't know nothing about Lightnin' in them days. My uncle said, "That's Sam Hopkins singing that song." And he said, "I'm going to see if I can find that record." They had a program out of Nashville, they called it "The Inner Groove," I believe. John R. was the deejay at that time. And I don't know where my uncle found the record at, but he come in one week and brought it. And we started playing the record. I got my guitar and I said, "I'm going to see if I can learn to play Lightnin's style," and I did.

Back in them days, the same man that taught me my chords, he loved baseball. And so they bought us all suits and we would go from town to town, and wherever we could get a game at, well, we'd play them. And I'd carry my guitar. And the only tune I could hit—all my friends that was older than I was, they loved Lightnin' style, and I learned to hit that tune he was singing, "It's Lonesome in Your Home When the One You Love Is Gone." And I could kick it just like I'd been kicking it for years, but I couldn't go all the way through with it. And they just had me just playing that little: "Just play it again." I said, "Well, I'm going to have to try to learn that all the way through, since that's all they want me to play." And so I started from then, learning, practicing Lightnin' tunes.

I played first base and was pitching. We called ourselves the Crockett Sluggers. It wasn't a league team. Them two brothers out of Tyler, they loved baseball, and one of them had a big truck. We'd go from town to town and just see who we could get to play us. Other people, they got their team together, and they'd be waiting on us. Sometimes, they would come to us. And would have parties afterwards. They would have little cafes, but they didn't have legal beer, you know. They had chock [homemade liquor]. Sure. We would go over there, and we'd start playing and dancing, and we had a lot of players back then that could play old-time music, but none of them play Lightnin's style.

Well, Lightnin's style, it was just something he put together himself, I guess. He didn't play like nobody I'd ever heard because some of the tunes that they always told me him and Blind Lemon played together, well, Blind Lemon used the chords, but he didn't sing nothing like Lightnin' Hopkins. Sometimes they would sing the same song, but Lightnin' would always change it up, fix it like he wanted. Blind Lemon had a big voice. He really did. He could get deep with his some of his tunes.

It never crossed my mind to ask him how he got the name Lightnin.' But the reason why I didn't ask him,

I just figured for myself, I said, You know, he used to could move his fingers so fast and play so fast till I just figured somebody called him Lightnin' because he could move his hands so fast, you know. But it never crossed my mind to ask him why they give him that name. But it was up on in the Forties, I guess, when they started calling him that. But we always called him Sam, and he called himself Po' Sam. A lot of songs he sang, he says, "This was what Po' Sam going to do."

He was always fighting and going to jail, and he stayed in quite a bit of trouble.

I wasn't there at the time, but I'd always hear about him starting fights at the dice game.

Lightnin'? Oh, I never knowed him to cut nobody. But one guy hit him in the head with a stick of firewood. Well, they was gambling on the ground, you know. And so he had one guy there, he was paying him. Ever time the fire'd go out, he'd go out there and gather up some limbs and so forth and keep the fire going, you know. They was only shooting a dime, shooting a dime and betting. And so Lightnin' got a little in the head. This guy told the man to go and get some more wood and put on the fire. And Lightnin' told him he didn't have to go get no wood and put on the fire if he didn't want to. And so the man said, "I'll go get it myself." And he went out there and he come back with a limb in his hand, and he hit Lightnin' 'cross the head with his limb. Well, it knocked him down. When he got up, he went and asked them, "How did the game come out?" And one of Lightnin's brothers was there at the time, and he had a pistol. And that's one reason Lightnin' spoke like he did, because he was expecting his brother to kind of back him up. But his brother didn't do nothing. So he told his brother, "You're going to have to get rid of that pistol," because if he didn't, he was going to get somebody killed. And they used to tell about how that happened. And another time—that was before he started staying over here, back in Centerville. A friend of mine told me that [they] locked him up and he had his guitar with him. He got to playing, and he played the guitar so, till they just opened the door and turned him a-loose. He come on out.

It was real bad around here. Matter of fact, a lot of places we'd go, and white folks that knew us, they'd come around and cops would come and escort them right back. They wouldn't let them mix at all back then. I know one guy, he was a great big white man, I guess he weighed a little over three hundred, but he's tall, and this little slim guy, he was drinking pretty heavy, and he kept a-telling him to come out from over there, but he just kept right on talking. And he come got him and stood him up, and the guy wouldn't run, but he was walking and looking back. And he was trying to make him run; he just kept kicking him; I guess fifty foot, he was still kicking him. He never did run. I said to myself, if I wasn't going to hit him, I believe I'd run away from him. He wouldn't kick me that many times, not just stand there. But he never did come back over there. And a lot of times, they'd ask to come over there. I had a friend, he live out there now, he was quite a dancer, and whenever he'd get on the floor—well, they had a window; they could look through that window and see what we were doing—and so he told them, said, "We want to go over there and watch them." But them patrols wouldn't let them come over at all. But it would be five or six in the window at all times; one bunch would leave and another bunch would come to the window, but they wouldn't allow them to come over.

I didn't really know nothing about them [Ku Klux Klan] gangs like that when I was growing up. It's just that if you went somewhere, I mean, sometimes, they just, I'd say, meddle for the fun of it, because if there was four or five of us walking—we walked just about everywhere we went back then, if we didn't catch a ride with somebody—and if we had to walk by them, before we got by them, somebody in the bunch would hit one or the other of us. And just like I said, they wouldn't get to hit us over once or twice, because we were good about running. And then they passed a lick or two, but then they couldn't hardly catch us no more.

Lightnin' talked about it [the way people treated him], and he talked about him being so outspoken and bringing a lot of it on himself. I remember once, me and him and Annie Mae was talking, and he said, "I was kind of overbearing." Said, "A lot of people done messed with me," and said, "If you messed with me back in them days, I was bad about doing something about it." And he told me he went to the pen, but if he did, it was while I was gone up north, because when I come back, he told me, said, "I've been to the pen."

When Frankie Lee [Sims] showed up around here, he knew a lot of Lightnin,' chords and runs, so I'd watch him, and it wasn't long before I was playing Lightnin's style. I knew Frankie Lee well, but he was living in Dallas. About every two weeks, he'd come down here and spend a couple of weeks with us. And all the time he was playing, I'd be watching him. And wasn't long before I was playing his music. And whenever me and my band would go out, they played their own style, them two brothers did. But they didn't ever play nothing that was on the jukeboxes at that time. They just played the records that was popular back in their day. Didn't too many of the school kids really like it. So I started to playing Frankie Lee tunes and John Lee Hooker and all like that. They would cut up so when I would start to playing, till they finally told me, said, "Seem like they enjoyed your way of playing better than they do ours." Well, after we done played awhile, they was already old, and one of them began to get kind of sickly, we stopped playing.

I had another friend down at Kennard a couple of years younger than I am. He had been playing with some of his friends down there, and he was doing pretty good. So I visited, and I asked him about us getting together, rehearsing songs. And he got one of his cousins, and we started out all over again. It wasn't long before we were playing again. We really got them going then.

Then, another family moved into the neighborhood, and there was one guy, he stayed at my house more than he did at home. So I asked him how would he like to learn to play bass for me. He said he'd love it, said, "Teach me." And at that time, there was a café in the neighborhood, right across there about three hundred yards, and I started teaching him. People found out we was rehearsing over there; we'd have a crowd just like we was playing for a dance every time we rehearsed. And in about three weeks, he was bassing good enough that we started going to clubs, and it just went on. We played, got started in from one place to another, and we played from the Sixties on up until '81. And they began to get better and better, and they wanted to try things for themselves on their own. So we all scattered up, and I took a truck-driving job, after we all busted up. I drove a truck a long time, and this recorder, out of Austin, come through, and he stopped at an antique place there on Goliad downtown, looking around at antiques, and he asked the owner, said, "Do you know anybody around here that play the blues?" She said, "I know two men." Say, "Can they play?" Say, "Yeah, because they used to play here. This was a joint before we turned it into an antique store." Say, "They played here for years. They's real good." He say, "Well, you get in touch with them, and I'll be back through here in about two weeks, and have them to meet me. I'd sure like to talk with them." So they called me and told me about it. I say, "Well, when he come back, you call me, and we'll meet him up here." It was Tary Owens, out of Austin, and we met, and he said, "Let's go over to your house and play some. Listen to some of your music." So we did, and he said, "How would y'all like to [go to] Austin and play in a club, and then next day, we'll record some." And so, we taken him up on that. And wasn't long before they [Tary and his associates] said, "Would y'all be interested in going to Holland, overseas, and playing over there?" Said, "Well, wherever we've played at, we're willing to travel." So it was a friend of mine that I taught. They nicknamed him "Guitar Curtis." His name was Curtis Colter. He was quite a—he liked to cut monkeyshines while he was playing. And so, we went over—we played in Austin, then we went to Holland and played and come on back. And they had a blues festival in Navasota, Texas. We went up there and we played, and after that, well, we decided we would start back to playing some. It had been five or six years since we done any playing at all. But we started back to playing around then, and a friend of mine have a place out on Highway 7, we'd go out there and get a crowd, and we'd play. And we just kept that up. They would call us to go somewhere. And that's how we got started back to playing. So I've been picking round ever since.

CLYDE LANGFORD

(June 6, 1934– ; interview, 2003)

CLYDE LANGFORD, CENTERVILLE, 2003, PHOTOGRAPH BY ALAN GOVENAR.

Lightnin' Hopkins's older brother, Joel, taught me when I was thirteen years old. He was a guitar picker, and he was sweet on my grandmother that lived with us. And he found out some kind of way that I was interested in learning to play a guitar. And that was a sure way he could get a chance to be around her. Over there, every day that, you know, he could, showing me how to play a guitar. And in the evening time, I'd get out of school, and things like that. Joel was part of my mama's daddy's people. Not really close cousin, but maybe a fourth cousin, somewhere like that.

The way I pick the guitar is unique to me. I use a metal thumb pick. I down strum with the thumb pick, all down strokes. That sets the rhythm. It's a kind of percussion. Then I make my upper strokes with my fingers, my pointing finger or the next two. I pick part with my fingernails and part with the tip ends, the meat part of my fingers. I don't use the little finger. Mostly, I tune to an open G. It's somewhat like a banjo. I have no idea why I play that way. I just picked it up. It's possible that I got some of it from country music and applied it to the blues. What makes it blues is bending the notes, and chokin' part of the neck. It's kind of hard to explain. It makes a chokin' sound. It's like you're chokin' someone with your hands around their neck and they're makin' a chokin' sound.

I've lived my whole life near around Centerville. I grew up in the country. We moved up in town the same year I started playing a guitar. I was thirteen years old. My mother's name was Helen Blayton Langford. My daddy was Fred Langford.

Both my mama and daddy picked cotton. I swore once I got grown I never wanted to see another cotton field. They got paid a dollar for each hundred pounds they picked. I started going out there with them when I was about five or six. There's a difference between pulling cotton and picking cotton. We pulled cotton. Picking cotton—you take that cotton out of the burr; pulling cotton, you get the burr and all. You pull the whole thing off. You can realize a little money pullin' cotton, but you hardly make anything from pickin' it. When I was about twelve or fourteen years old, I could pull anywhere to one thousand to twelve hundred pounds in a day. I could get three hundred to five hundred pounds on an average.

Daddy, he dug water wells, hand-dug water wells. My mama, she was a seamstress. She made skirts and dresses for women and girls. My mama was churchgoing. Daddy wasn't. Mama went to the Baptist church. She sang church songs.

Daddy went along with me playing blues because they discovered I loved it, but Mama, she didn't really go for it. In fact, she just couldn't stand the sounds of those strings when Lightnin' Hopkins would get down on that little E. She say she reckoned she don't suppose she could stand him because he was kin to her. Now that's her daddy's people. Those Hopkinses. And Joel, she didn't go for him because he was sweet on her mother, and she said he was sorry and wouldn't work. [Joel] would mow around in some of these white people's yards and make a little money to buy some whiskey and get that guitar and get about half drunk and act the fool. She couldn't stand him.

Yeah, I used to play for house parties round in the country on down out of Centerville, down below Middleton, store, little old country with the flat woods we called it. Well, that's just the kind of country community deal between Centerville and Midway. Midway is a little town south of Centerville.

At these house parties, people just served drinks and danced and things of that sort.

People made their own liquor. They had Charleston and Black Bottom, jitterbug, tap dance, slow drag, round dance, and things of that sort.

My great uncle, Peter Lacey, played fiddle just around in the country at little house parties. Mostly, I guess he played mostly what I'd call country and western music, and maybe few blues. Every time I heard him, he'd be playing by himself. He didn't make his own fiddle. I'm thinkin' his brother, Dr. Lacey, gave him his fiddle. Dr. Lacey was white, and Peter Lacey's mother was black. They never married. They lived together—in and out, in and out. Dr. Lacey had a white family, too.

Yeah, I remember hearing about Blind Lemon Jefferson. That's who Lightnin' Hopkins tried to imitate. No, I never heard one of his records. Lightnin' used to talk about Blind Lemon all the time. Well, he just said he wanted to be like him and things like that, and he was at an "association" one year in Buffalo, Texas, and he had a little old guitar. Blind Lemon was playing and he was picking his guitar along with him. And the people couldn't see him, said he was so little, and Blind Lemon picked him up and stood him on the back of a pickup where people could see him. And he used to like to talk about how Blind Lemon would make a note and he would make a note, and Blind Lemon would tell him, "Well, boy, that's my note. You keep that up, you'll be a good guitar picker one day."

Now, I used to play with Lightnin' [and] his brother. Joel and Lightnin,' they didn't play nothing alike. I learned to play Joel's style, but my preferable was Lightnin's style, so I just shifted from Joel's style to Lightnin's. Well, Lightnin's was more, to my notion, of a meaning, more a blues meaning. Joel's was kind of betwixt and between blues and country and western. However, I couldn't understand that for a long time, but one day, I realized why. Because, you see, a lot of people think that blacks had blues in their system ever since there's been blacks, but no. No, blacks, once they was brought from overseas, well, they was taught by whites to play what the whites played, which was country and western. But now before the whites taught them that, they didn't know nothing but African language and songs and the beat of those drums and things of that sort. And so, you know, of course, the whites, they wasn't going to go for that, and so they taught them to play country and western. But now, like me, in my day, coming up, I started off playing the blues, following in Joel's footsteps. But now, before we moved to town, I didn't know, really, nothing about blues. All I knew was country and western and not playing but singing. I used to try to imitate Gene Autry, Roy Acuff, Smoky Mountain Boys, Roy Rogers, and those three guys, I used to try to imitate, you know, singing. But I hadn't started trying to play no music. But now, when I started learning when we moved to town, and I started playing the blues, singing the blues, well I kind of got away from the country and western. That was the way that went.

When I was coming up, I kept a couple of guys with me. Sometimes I'd have three guys, another guy on a guitar, one on a set of drums. We was always playing out of town, like in Marlin or Temple, well, places a little closer, like Fairfield, Palestine, Oakwood, sometimes in Crockett, that's about thirty-three miles east of Centerville. Matter of fact, I used to play on KIVY over there when I was about sixteen or seventeen years old, every Sunday morning.

That's right. At a radio station over in Crockett. It was just a little old local broadcasting system at the time, and different ones that wanted to perform, you could go over there, and they would let you perform—sing, play music, dance, or if you had anything to sell, you could broadcast it [for the people who lived in the country around there]. Oh, they'd sell stuff like homemade candy—candy made out of peanuts, peanut brittle, syrup. Matter of fact, my manager, Bob Green, he sold a lot of syrup over there, ribbon cane syrup, and sweet potatoes, tomatoes, just different things like that. He'd broadcast it and let people know what days he was going to have a supply of stuff at his home and how to get there. And then they would know what day to go to Crockett to pick up something.

Oh, we didn't play too long. Couple or three numbers, and that was it. Oh, let me see. I believe "Long, Leany Mama" and "Poison Ivy," "How Much More Longer." Just different numbers. You know, I can't even really think of them. When I get my rig and start playing, all them numbers just brighten up or just picture up on my brain system, or just brighten up.

I never did play music all the time. I've worked the sawmill where they saw logs and make lumber to build houses and things of that sort. I've also worked pipelining, laying pipe and just things of that sort. Oh, I installed septic tanks. And of course, while I was in the United States Air Force, I was a supply helper. That was my position, a supply helper. I was in the Air Force part of '54, '55, '56. It was fantastic. It was very educational and a lot of fun. There was some things that went on that weren't really soothing to me, but I made exceptions for that, you know. I mean, I don't believe I would have been where I am today, which ain't too far, if I hadn't gone in. They teach you discipline. I mean, it's a good deal for young people to get into.

Lightnin' Hopkins didn't have no schooling. And he got his education just through being around, mingling with people, associating with people, talking to people, and things of that sort. He respected what little education he had. I mean, he weren't too fast to get up and speak a word because he knew that he didn't know too much and it would probably be the wrong thing. A lot of times you could ask him something, and he would just look at you through them big old black shades and wouldn't say a word, wouldn't give you no kind of answer. You'd ask him three or four different times; sometimes he'd give you an answer, sometimes he wouldn't. But you know, what I can gather, he was just afraid that he probably would say something and it would be the wrong thing.

I started playing music with Lightnin' when . . . oh,

CLYDE LANGFORD AND KATIE MAE BUCKNER, CENTERVILLE, 2003. PHOTOGRAPH BY ALAN GOVENAR.

let me see. All right, I was about between twenty-three and twenty-five. That was right after I had gotten out of the United States Air Force. [Lightnin' had already started making records by then.] He'd always have one or two guys with him, one on the French harp and one on a piano or on a set of drums, more or less. Sometimes, he'd play and have one more guitar picker with him. And that was me, every once in a while.

I've got a Honda 500, and then my baby's this Fender. Matter of fact, that Fender was a gift to me from Tim Duffy from North Carolina. He made me a present of that guitar in 2000. The Honda is an acoustic guitar, but it has a pickup. It can be electric, too.

I had an electric guitar when I played with Lightnin.' He was playing electric. I think his was a Gibson. Mine was a Supro. I got it in San Francisco, California. That was while I was stationed at Edwards Air Force Base, on Mojave Desert. It was a pretty nice guitar. Pretty nice.

When I went around with Lightnin,' oh, well, that was in Houston: Dowling, Fifth Ward, some rough places sometimes that I wouldn't dare to go now. But I was young and drinking, and I didn't have enough forethoughts to fear the danger that could possibly occur, or the malfunctions while I was there playing.

You had a kind of jittery feeling because all eyes would be on you when you'd walk in with your rig, your musical instrument. All eyes was on you and things like that. Well, guys would envy you because you was a musicianer and maybe one of their lady friends would come up and sit in your lap or something or make an attempt to come stand behind you, you were sitting in the chair playing your musical instrument, put their arms around you. And then their boyfriends would want to start some static or something like that. You'd run into stuff like that all the time.

They'd start off jitterbugging, then before they got through, it would be tap dancing or doing the Charleston, or the Black Bottom, things like that. They kind of mixed it up.

Billy Bizor blew harmonica with Lightnin.' He was a big old yellow-skinned fellow with a great big huge black mole on his face. Billy Bizor. And then Lightnin' had a guy on drums, oh, they called him Spider [Kilpatrick]. Of course, he had other guys that would play with him sometimes, whenever old Spider and Billy Bizor would be out of pocket. It was always some other guy that he could pick up, you know, to perform with him just for a bottle of wine. Things like that.

Well, now, back, I'd say right after I came out of the United States Air Force, latter part of 1956, Lightnin' pretty much played, it would be for blacks. But he started next, I believe, year or so, maybe two or three years later, he got to the place where he wouldn't play, it was hard to get him to play for any blacks. He mostly played for whites. He said he could make more money, said the whites would pay him much more money than the blacks would. And then you was very unlikely to have any fights or any misunderstandings playing for whites than what you would if you was playing for blacks. Say, you playing for blacks, you going to always get ready, somebody's going to start something if nothing but bust a whiskey bottle upside the wall or something.

I didn't play a long time with Lightnin.' I just went and played about a week and a half, maybe two weeks at the longest, every night, in Houston, and that was it. I never played with him anymore. Oh, whenever he'd come to Centerville, he'd stop by my house and we'd play together, you know, like that. He'd drive up in that Cadillac convertible. Lightnin' loved that convertible. Now he was partial to Cadillacs also. Maybe pink or an old dingy-colored red, some kind of old loud, flashy color.

I'd listen to Lightnin' Hopkins. But I'd also listen to old man T-Bone Walker, John Lee Hooker. John Lee Hooker, now that was one of them. What did he put out, "Boogie Chillen"? Old John Lee Hooker. Yes, sir.

Listen, I loved T-Bone Walker. I loved T-Bone Walker. I never did meet him. I loved his music. That music, T-Bone Walker. That old man was true poison with that guitar. "Stormy Monday" is all right. "Late in the Evening."

What keeps me going? Well, I don't know, but my guitar, I think about it more than I do anything. I'm more partial to it, I guess, than anything. And then, everybody around this little town is so sweet to me, and you know, things like that. I couldn't ask for a better place to live. They're just always encouraging me, you know, about my music and things like that.

Well, the blues can be a number of things. A lot of people tell you blues is just one thing, but blues can be a number of things. Blues is something in equivalence to a spirit. And then, too, blues is something that you make out of it whatever you feel happy. Blues is something strange, something that's unlike anything else. And it's so different from any other type of music. The real blues. You see, you've got people that's playing blues they call blues is not really blues. And it's people singing and playing, going through the motions of that. But it's so much different from any other kind. And some blues has a meaning to it. Some blues doesn't even have a meaning. You just feel it, singing and playing it. The music sound good, the singing sound good, but there's no meaning to it. I try my best to let it be a meaning to whatever I play and sing. [Musically] you got [chords] E, F, G, A, B, D. I don't read music. Just play by ear.

Me and my wife, the wife I had, we lived together about eighteen to twenty years. She died at a young age. All my kids are grown. The baby, she'll be twenty-nine the first of October. I've got two girls and five boys. The oldest one is Clyde Jr. The next one is Delingo. The next one is Banza Orna. The baby boy, we call him Frank for short, but his name is LaFrankieton. The girl, we call her for short Lena, but her name is Pasqualina. Oh, I better include these other kids because they'll think I'm denying them. Danny Wayne. Then this other girl is Linda Varnice. She's outside; I didn't raise her, but it might hurt her feelings if she's not included. I made up them boys' names. Now, Pasqualina, that's an Italian name, a Dago name. Pasqualina in Italian means Easter.

Well, I'm not married now. I've got a lady, Katie Mae Buckner, that lives with me.

Lightnin' had a Katie Mae. He sure did. But she was a different Katie Mae. Now, her man friend here years back and Lightnin' like to got into about this Katie Mae here. He was singing that number about Katie Mae and her man friend said, "Look." Said, "You ain't only one got a Katie Mae. I got a Katie Mae, too." My Katie Mae is past seventy-three, and I'll get wound up on that guitar, and the way she moves, you'd swear that she wasn't but about twenty-five years old. She's more energetic and super than any daughter or granddaughter she got. And she pushes me a lot in my music.

Now this might sound crazy, but it's the gospel truth. I've been with Katie Mae for a long time. Now, let me see, back in the Fifties, we was tight. We was dating. And then, she decided to leave Centerville and go to Fort Worth and live with one of her cousins and go to work up there. And so many years, and then it wound around. She came back to Centerville, had kids. She and her old man had kids. They grew up grown. I got married to another girl. Kids grew up. And my wife died. And then, her old man died. And bless my soul, we got right back where we started. Right back where we started. And, well, I guess that was what I would consider a dent that had been made or produced back that was considered as nonremovable. You've probably heard about making a dent that you can't move. So I think that's what happened there.

Right now, here in Centerville, we're getting ready to put up an opera house. Matter of fact, I named it. Leon County Opera House. Now, we're going to have a meeting this evening at seven o'clock, at the county courthouse. It's been several blacks invited, but I'm the only black who will be there. It'll be just a courthouse full of whites. I'm the only black there. And they asked me, said, "Does this offend you, you being the only black?" "No, my goodness. It sure doesn't. It doesn't offend me at all." But once we get it going, I'll guarantee you they'll be more black people round out of the Trinity River bottom and Brazos bottom than you can stir with a stick, once we get it going. Now, I'm one of the members, and I'm the sergeant at arms. That's my position. And they voted me in as that. You know, we had a big meeting last Tuesday. Matter of fact, it ought to come out in the paper this evening for Wednesday, for tomorrow.

I don't know just how soon we're going to get started building this opera. But we got the ground all ready, and it's going to be called the Leon County Opera House. And we've started bulldozing the land off, and then we're getting prepared for the sixteenth of August [2003]. That's going to be our opera opening day. But now, I don't know whether I'll even play. I'm not a hundred percent sure whether I'm going to play or not, but I'm determined to be there. I'd better be there. I'm one of the members.

There's some, since they found out about this opera house, trying to learn blues. They want me to teach them, but I'm afraid I can't. They kind of waited a little late in the day. Now, these guys, black people that's trying to learn to play a guitar, they's right smart older than I am. I'm sixty-nine, and they's up seventy-five, seventy-eight, seventy-nine years old. I think they might have waited a little late in the day, because I know if was going to learn to play one, I don't think I'd want to start now.

HENRY QUALLS

July 8, 1934–December 7, 2003; interview, 2003

HENRY QUALLS, ENNIS, 2003, PHOTOGRAPH BY DON O.

I was born here in Texas, right out from Terrell. My parents were farmers, sharecroppers. Randall Qualls and Scotty Qualls. Shit, man, ain't nothing easy about growing up around here. Aw, shoot, like I say, farming and all that sort of thing.

Somehow or other I got started in music when I was maybe thirteen or fourteen years old or something like that. I made my first guitar with my hands. Back in those days, people would buy apples, and that's what I made it out of, an apple box. You know what catgut strings are? That's what I used for my strings. And I took the baling wire and made my frets out of it. And it was a hell of a job, but I done it with my own hands. That's the first one I ever had. Didn't have no money to buy one, so I just made me one. I'd looked at them and seen how they had them made, and so I made it. See what I mean?

Oh, I ain't played nothing but the blues. That's all I ever played. It's the blues.

It's how you grew up and how your people grew up and understood it. There's other people trying to take the blues away, but they can't because it's the foundation of the music, the world. So I don't even try to explain it to them; I just let them talk. But I play it, learnt myself and all that stuff.

My folks played; all of them played. My grandmother had fourteen children. She come out of Louisiana. See, my grandfather passed away, and she married this other man. His name was Jim Wyatt, just like Wyatt's Cafeteria. See, people don't know all this stuff, but I know about it. And we had this land where they did sharecropping up there in Mesquite. And you know where they fly those little airplanes? Okay, if you're coming down towards Terrell, it's right on your left there. It had a school for black people, church house and all like that. And we wasn't allowed on the other side of the highway. That was way before they built Interstate 20 through there. And that's where that man, he was a white man, and he split the land up with my people. Well, they couldn't read and write, so they beat them out of the land, see what I mean?

Now, when my brother was living, we went downtown and tried to get our land back, but they had signed it over, put an "X" on it, see? And so they signed it over to them, so shoot. Then he passed away, and me and my cousins, we went down there, but we couldn't do nothing. Of course, we didn't have no lawyer or nothing, so shoot. We just lost it, like we did everything else in Louisiana, because you don't know no better, you see. Dumb, deaf, crippled, and blind. What you get thataway, you can't go nowhere. My aunt, she was living out there, and when she knowed anything, they told her that she had to move off of their land, and so that's what she had to do.

My grandmother was a church singer. She didn't play. But all my aunties and uncles played. They had fiddles and guitars, pianos and stuff like that. I don't know, it's hard to explain it, but they couldn't play real good, but they could play, you know, keep some sort of rhythm going, tunes. . . . they sung the blues. I was surrounded by it. But they all split up some, went to California and all different places. Some stayed in Louisiana. They never did go to New York, though. Most of them went west and east, split up.

I got a many kinfolk buried out there in the West. Lots of them buried there, whole graveyard, look like. I had one of my first cousins had twenty-five children. And they all buried out there in—some of them are buried in Abilene, and some are on up in Colorado City. And up in what you call, where they got that oil at. Yeah, Odessa.

Well, when I started playing [music], I was just playing, me and my cousins, aunties, and them, you know, playing. We played church songs, blues, some what you call country and western. Heard them on the radio. And there was this white man we knew, too. We knew him because we all grew up in the country. It wasn't back then like it is today. That's where I got the copy of making that instrument. Because he had a real one [guitar]. Nobody had any money. Shit, they didn't have none; I didn't. Nobody, so I thought I'd get me a copy. I saw how they were made, and so I just made me one. So, we'd get together and play, and I'd play theirs sometimes and so forth. And so, that's the way it went.

Times were hard. You wake up in the morning, you ain't got nothing to eat, then you got to hustle it. Run a rabbit; that's what we did. We didn't have no gun, man, we'd hunt with the dogs. They'd go catch it and bring it in to us, wouldn't eat it, either, unless we told them. Now, we tell them to eat, they'd eat it. But now, that was some good dogs, too, back in those days. So these dogs don't know nothing about no hunting no more. It sounds funny, but they don't.

See, back then, whenever it rained, that's what we were wanting to see. We knew then we didn't have to go to work; we'd go hunting. Everybody hunted together. Everybody had a pretty good dog or two and bring them booger. And like I say, they'd kill them rabbits, but they'd bring them right back to us, you see. But now, you got to be a good one training them boogers, because, see, the people feed them too much. And back then, you feed them scraps; that's what we called it. And didn't feed them nothing raw; we'd cook it in a wash pot and then feed it to them. We'd burn that fur from off it; burn it. Wouldn't feed them that. Oh, it's a long old story, long one.

I was born and raised in the country. I hate in town. I come up there and play music, but when I get through, I'm ready to come back, back home. I know where everything's at in my house. So, as time rolls on, and I bought my house and paid for it, and had it remodeled; in fact, I just had my fireplace chimney remodeled here the other day. Cost me a thousand bucks. And of course I burn that propane gas. And so, I just love the country. I don't know what I'd do if I had to live in town, or in the city, I just don't know. I just love being in the country. I've been around.

T-Bone Walker, I used to see him play in Dallas. Meet him, too. Yeah, but see, he used to play there going down there towards the Fair Park. He played there all the time. I've never known him to play in Terrell. Aw, shoot, that booger could play it all, I know. Yeah. Li'l Son Jackson, them, all would be there. Yeah, Li'l Son Jackson, and you know his name? Shorty Atkins, but his name was W. B., but everybody called him Shorty. All of them dead now, of course, but we'd go there and listen to them, you know. They was playing up there in Dallas. At them places where they sold that beer and stuff. Back then, you could buy beer in quarts, them big ones, and set the table up. That's what they called it.

I got my first electric guitar at Montgomery Ward's in 1959. Bought it on credit. I still got it, too. I got two of them. It was an Airline. No telling what they were; I got two of them. Aw, they're sort of reddish and black. But they sound better than these new ones.

Ain't no telling when I got my first acoustic, after I made one, because they come after I started playing. People just gave me some. Aw shoot, after I got my electric, we all up in Rockwall, Oklahoma. You know where Lawton is? That was the longest trip I made, back in the old days. We played at the military base up there.

We got together and made us a band. Five or six of them. Sax and trumpets and, let's see what else we had. It was two or three of them playing. I had bass, too. Oh, yeah, you know you got to have them drums. See, what I did, I went up there at Montgomery Ward, and I bought my guitar and my amp and a set up drums and a microphone. I never will forget it. And that's what we used, see. We didn't make no records.

We made up some songs, yeah. But even at that, I done forgot what we used to play, that been so long. Back then, I was much younger. Like I say, we was picking that cotton land. Built Lake Tawakoni. State hospital. We done a whole lot of different varieties of work. Whatever come along, we done it.

I guess God keeps me going. Lots of places in God. A whole lot. So I raised all these children, man, I had to work doing something. We'd play music at night, work in the daytime. Shit. Now, I don't have to do nothing, really, unless I want to; you know what I mean.

I just play whenever they call me. Still playing with Hash Brown. Yeah, he can play. He come from Connecticut. We supposed to went back up in Arkansas, but they never did tell me, so I don't know whether they went or what. See, we went to Fort Worth and give that show. And that's when they told me, but I ain't never heard nothing else from them. I don't know what they're going to do. Or did.

My music hasn't really changed. I won't be playing like these other people. Don't even try it. I can do it, though, but I don't like it. But I can play it. Hash plays it a whole lot. I usually let him and his band play. I just sit back and listen at it. But I don't really care that much about it. I forget all them guys' names that plays with us, but on them CDs.

Oh, man, when we went to Europe, I didn't want to come back. I really didn't. If it wasn't for my family, I wouldn't have came back. I'd have stayed because the people wanted me to stay over there. But I couldn't do it because all my hookup is in here, see, in Texas. But we got a chance to tour nearly all the countries, but not all, of course. It ain't nothing like it is here.

But I tell you, the biggest crowd I played for was in Chicago [at the Chicago Blues Festival]. I got the pictures of it and got the literature and all on that. The biggest crowd I ever played for. Six hundred thousand, man. And you couldn't walk. Of course, they rode me around up there in a golf thing, you know what I mean, me and Hash Brown. But we were the only ones went.

We didn't need no band. Just me and him. And we set them out of there, too. We heard a many, many band play. But they didn't play what we were playing. And we got the headline in the newspapers, sure. That's the biggest one. Even in Europe and all of them, it was big, too, over there, but not like that one. Man, six hundred thousand. Boy! That's a lots of people. There's a bunch of bands. I done forgot how many played. And there's where I met Lowell Fulson and Charles Brown. And now all of them dead, you see? That was the first time I ever met them. That was special there.

And we went out to California. Pee Wee Crayton was out there playing, too. California. We was up Long Beach. We were out on the *Queen Mary*.

Blues is the blues. B. B. and them, and what you call them, is supposed to come to Dallas pretty soon and play. B. B. and Bobby Bland. Yeah, they're supposed to be in Dallas pretty soon, raising some sort of funds; something about some children. They've had B. B. on television. Man, he say he gonna raise that money. That booger can play now. But see, he say he can't play what I play. I say, "Well, I can't play what you play, either."

Anyway, he's been to Terrell playing. That's when I first met him. He wrecked that bus down here, and he was playing down here in Terrell. That's been a long time ago, though. Yeah, he had a wreck in it. Somebody ran into it. It stayed down there a long time. He finally come and got it.

Yeah. I think about [spiritual things], too, a whole lot. But I'm turning women away. I am. "Get away from me!" An old gal jumped on my back and broke my back and two ribs. Me and Hash went up to his daddy's and mother's. We had to do some playing up there. And, man, I couldn't hardly get around. I ain't joking. But I could play. Yeah, this old gal jumped on me, clowning, and rode me down, man. Could have killed me.

Young woman, about twenty-something, I guess. A white girl. See, she wasn't supposed to be up on that stage. This man had this big stage built, and supposed to have had plenty security, too. But the security guard thought she was some sort of musician. But she wasn't. And she was full of that cocaine and wine, whiskey, whatever. I left my guitar up on the stage because somebody wanted to use it. Another band was supposed to play, too. When I got ready to come off, see, had them steps up there; I'm talking about four feet high. She jumped and rode me down off them steps plumb to the ground. And hurt me.

HENRY QUALLS, ENNIS, 2003, PHOTOGRAPH BY DON O.

I didn't go to the hospital; I should have. It happened down here in the country. It was on the outside, this blues festival we have every year, out in the country here. That woman like to killed me. So finally, a bunch of them got her up off me and picked me up.

I still play my old guitar, too. Yeah, I still got it. I've put out three or four records. Most of them I do the writing. Oh, man, I can't tell you all that. Most of it is from my life, things I feel.

UNIDENTIFIED DISK JOCKEY, TYLER, EARLY 1960S.
PHOTOGRAPH BY CURTIS HUMPHREY. COURTESY TEXAS AFRICAN AMERICAN PHOTOGRAPHY ARCHIVE.

K. M. WILLIAMS

October 19, 1956– ;
interview by Bill Fountain, 2004

FREDDY KING.

It's about soul and feeling. On the diddleybow, you don't have any placements like you do on the guitar. So all you have is what you hear. It's an African instrument. A one-string instrument. It came over with the slaves; part of our cultural heritage. Again, it's just a two-by-four with nails on each end. I used a piece of an old clock and an ink pen to bridge it up here.

My first guitar lesson came from a traveling bluesman [many believe to be Elmore James]. "You want to learn how to play the guitar?" he asked, "Yes sir," I replied.

So he sets me down, of course the guitar is too big for me. I was feeling the music. I guess he could tell I was feeling it. He said, okay, go like this. He taught me that, and that was my lesson. I worked on that lesson for years. I guess I'm still working on it. He was the one. He passed it on to me. I was a little kid. When you're a little kid, you don't know. But I guess as I grew up it stayed in my mind the whole time. Then I put the guitar down when I got to be a teenager. I did the normal teenage things. Then when I graduated from high school, me and my buddies went off to the military. I spent six years in the United States Navy. I went overseas and stuff like that.

K. M. WILLIAMS, WORTHAM, 2004.

I had been to church all my life, but I didn't know anything about being converted or born again. I had a conversion experience in my last year of the service. I got saved. I was always musically inclined, but it seemed like I gained the ability to compose. Like all my musical abilities. The things I used to struggle at, I didn't struggle with that anymore. It started coming to me and then I could write songs, compose songs. But I really didn't understand where I was going or why. So I thought maybe I was supposed to be a musician at church, you know, maybe that was my gift. And I did play in choirs and church for about fifteen years. I backed quartets, choirs, preachers. And in between those I did blues gigs, jazz gigs. But my thing has always been the blues, regardless of what I'm playing. I don't care what kind of music I tried to play, it sounded like blues.

FREDDY KING, *JUST PICKIN'*,
MODERN BLUES RECORDINGS MBLP-721.

FREDDY KING SINGS,
MODERN BLUES RECORDINGS MBLP-722.

So I gained this ability to write and compose. Then I went through some life issues. I lost my wife. I lost my family. I have lost everything that I've had. I've lost my home. I lost my job. I lost my wife. I lost my kids. So that right there has an extreme effect on you. Life crisis situations. And that really brought out me playing the blues and getting out there and performing for the public. I had played for the public before, but I wasn't pushed. Now it was like I had something I had to get out of me. I had to tell people what I was feeling so it might help somebody else. But at the same time I was being called into the ministry. So I was going through both. I was getting called into the ministry at the same time I was getting a calling for the blues. For me, it's all been the same. That's why my records have both the country blues and the spiritual sounds. To me, I don't see a difference.

There is no difference between the spiritual and the blues. It's all telling the truth. I'm talking about God one minute and then you mistreated me the next. Okay, well, that's not a lie. That's a part of the blues, so it's still the truth. 1995, 1996. I was still living in Cleveland. I had gone out to jams and the local Cleveland blues scene.

Then, I formed a blues band, K. M. Williams & the Blues Train, in 1997. The band opened for people like Robert Jr. Lockwood, Little Milton, The Holmes Brothers, and The Five Blind Boys of Alabama. I did that until 1999. I was also self-employed at the time, working as a subcontractor. Selling roofs, selling windows and doors. Going through a divorce, so I was basically doing anything I could to survive. I was literally playing blues to eat, and I'm not joking. If it wasn't for the blues, I would not have eaten. So I would never ever deny the blues. It's been good to me, it saved my life. I guess I got pretty down on my luck. Then the Spirit moved me to move back to Texas. I moved back and was staying with my brother. I decided to see what I could do here. I started frequenting the Coffee Haus. The first place I went to was the Coffee Haus.

I took this guitar; this is the only guitar I had left. I had a little bitty PA system I plugged into. That's how I got my first gigs here. Then I had an opportunity to make a demo tape. Next thing you know Don O [from the Dallas-based KNON radio station] heard it. I went on his show and introduced myself; next thing you know, I was on the radio. Then the next thing you know, he says, you should make your own CD. So I bought a little portable two-track. I wrote some songs. I had some songs I wrote five or six years ago. Some of the songs I had had in my head a long time. I went ahead and committed them to tape. To me, they didn't sound like much. They sounded like they always do. Nothing special. And that was *The Reverend of Texas Country Blues*.

ELECTRIFYING THE BLUES

AARON "T-BONE" WALKER, PUBLICITY PHOTOGRAPH. COURTESY HELEN OAKLEY DANCE.

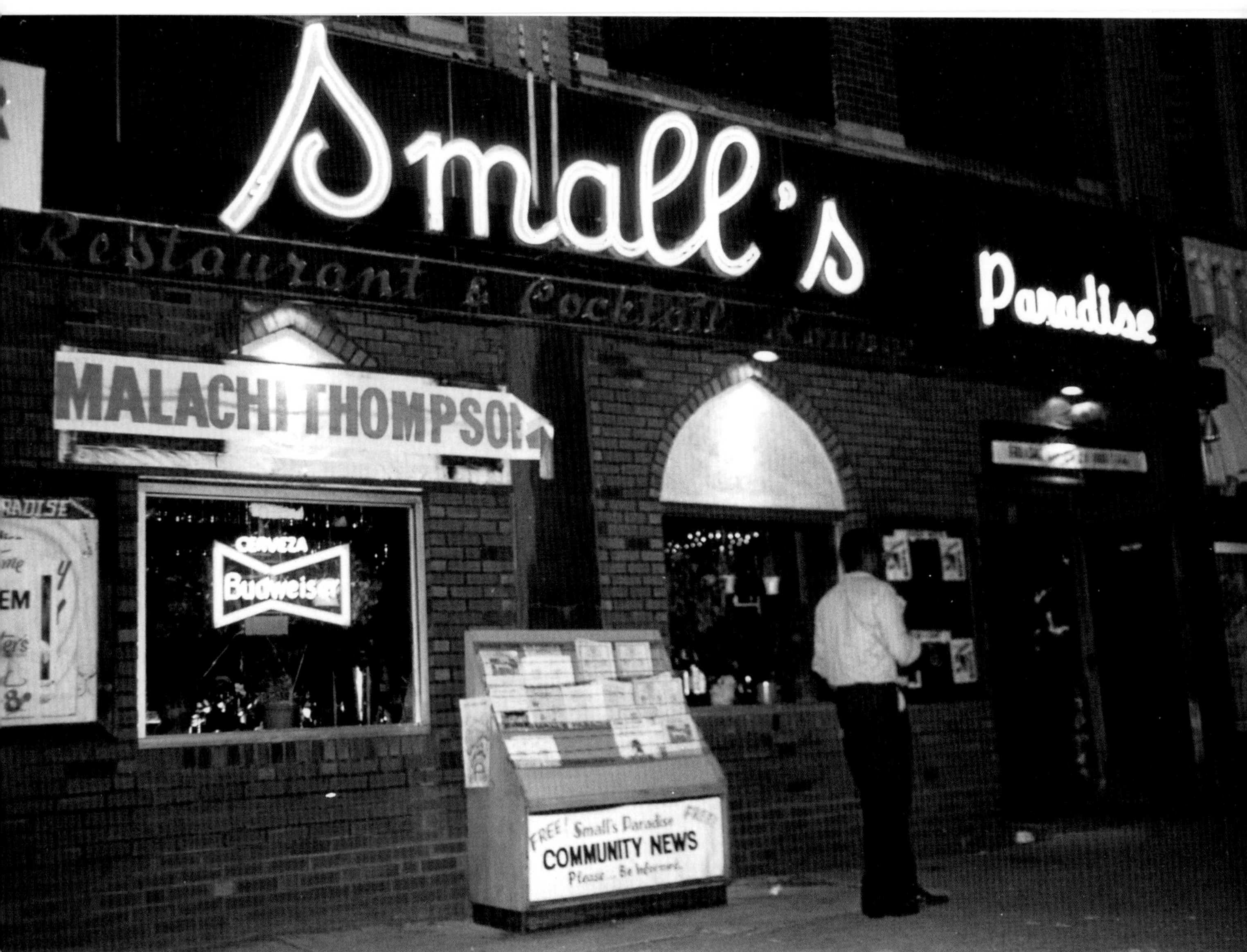

"Looking for Eddie Durham,"
Small's Paradise, Harlem, 1985.
Photograph by Alan Govenar.

INTRODUCTION

The advent of the amplified electric guitar in the 1930s allowed guitarists to be heard in a band setting and helped propel the instrument from the rhythm section to a lead role. Amplification also allowed players to sustain notes and to create a greater variety of tones and effects. Musicians working in Texas were in the forefront of the transformation of the guitar. Among them were Bob Dunn, steel guitarist with Milton Brown's Fort Worth–based western swing band, and three African American musicians: Eddie Durham, Charlie Christian, and Aaron "T-Bone" Walker.

Durham experimented first with a metal pie plate, which he inserted into the body of his acoustic guitar to create an amplified, though nonelectric, sound. The first electric amplification was accomplished by placing a pickup in the body of the guitar or under the strings. Essentially, a pickup is an electromagnetic transducer, or in simpler terms, a bar magnet wrapped with wire that picks up the vibration of the magnetized string and conveys it to an amplifier.

Durham had a considerable impact as an innovator and arranger who played both trombone and guitar. Dunn also played trombone, but became interested in the steel guitar and the possibilities of electric amplification after seeing "a black guy playing a steel guitar with a homemade pickup." Christian was a richly talented musician who, like Walker, played the Gibson ES-150 guitar, which was manufactured with an electric pickup and introduced in 1936. While Christian was known primarily as a jazz stylist, Walker did much to create the modern electric blues sound. Walker was a charismatic performer who played the electric guitar as a lead instrument and inspired countless young musicians to take up the instrument and start careers of their own.

The careers of Dunn, Christian, and Walker have been well documented, while Durham has received relatively little attention in works about blues and jazz. The following oral history with Durham elucidates his importance as an innovator in the role of the electric guitar.

EDDIE DURHAM

August 19, 1906–March 6, 1987; interview, 1984

My father was a fiddler, and all his six brothers played instruments. I was born August 19, 1906, in San Marcos, Texas. My oldest brother bought me a guitar when I was ten years old, and I've been in bands since I was in the fourth grade.

The first band I played in was The Durham Brothers Orchestra, where I played guitar and later trombone, the two instruments I stayed with all my life. I left The Durham Brothers Orchestra in the early 1920s and went on the road with the 101 Wild West Ranch Show band. It was with this rodeo and circus band that I started doing arranging. In 1926 I met Edgar [Puddin' Head] Battle, who was leading a group called The Dixie Ramblers, and in 1928 when that band broke up I went with Walter Page and the Blue Devils. Oran "Hot Lips" Page [a trumpet player in the band] was from Texas, as was Buster Smith on alto saxophone and clarinet. They also had Bill [Count] Basie on piano, and Jim Rushing was the singer.

In Kansas City I met and after a while joined Benny Moten. Kansas City was full of musicians in those years, Lester Young, Charlie Parker, Herschel Evans, Bill Basie, Buddy Tate, Mary Lou Williams, and Buck Clayton were all there. I was playing guitar and sometimes trombone. But with those big bands you couldn't hear the guitar. So I tried different ways to amplify the sound.

EDDIE DURHAM, GUITARIST FOR LESTER YOUNG'S KANSAS CITY SIX, 1940. COURTESY EDDIE DURHAM.

I made a resonator with a tin pan. It was back in the early 1930s. I'd carve out the inside of an acoustic guitar and put the resonator down inside there. It was the size of a breakfast plate. I'd put something around the guitar to hold it. And when I hit the strings, the pie pan would ring and shoot out the sound. I didn't have to do that for long because I ran up on a National. It had a resonator in it. It was used as a steel guitar with a bar. I removed the bridge and put an acoustic type bridge on it, because the other bridge held the strings up too high.

When I was with The Jimmie Lunceford Orchestra there was one microphone that was used by the singer, but when I played my solo, Lunceford would bring that microphone right up to my guitar. He was crazy about that resonator.

Then I tried converting radio and phonograph amplifiers, and even drilled into the body of the guitar. With that rig I used to blow out the lights in a lot of places. They weren't really up on electricity like they are now, no fuses.

Later after D'Armand came out with a pickup, I was one of the first people to use it. I made an attachment where I could play into the sound system. If I wanted to I could be all over the joint. I couldn't play rhythm because it was too loud. I just played solos.

In the spring of 1937 Charlie Christian came to hear me play in Oklahoma City. I was with Jimmie Lunceford, and we were there for about a month. During the day we sometimes jammed at a pool hall owned by Jimmy Rushing's father. And one day Charlie showed up with an old beat-up guitar that had cost him five dollars. He had big eyes to sound like a saxophone, and I showed him how by using down strokes he could get a sharper tone, and how if you use the up stroke you get a more legato sound, which the horns couldn't get. With

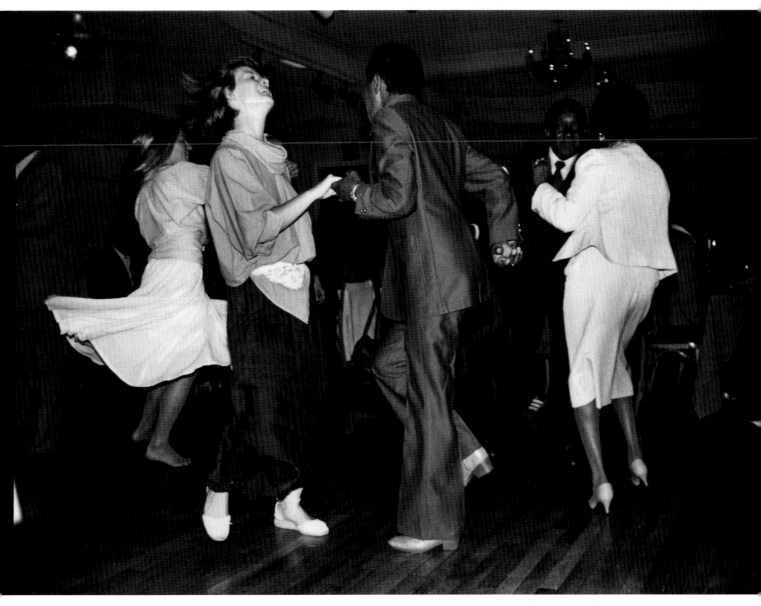

BIG BAND BLUES AT SMALL'S PARADISE, FEATURING EDDIE DURHAM, HARLEM, 1985. PHOTOGRAPH BY ALAN GOVENAR.

no legato the sound is more like a horn, but it takes an awful fast wrist to play the down stroke.

Well, I never saw a fellow learn so fast, nor have I ever seen anyone rise to the top so quickly. It wasn't long before Charlie Christian was a star with the Benny Goodman band. He could play those long, single-string lines in a full range, using all the strings. But he only got to play with Benny Goodman for a little more than two years. He had tuberculosis and died in 1942.

I played with just about every guitar I could get my hands on, Nationals, Epiphones, Gibsons, Danelectros and others. I even rigged up my own vibrato arm, before they made them on guitars. I took a clothes hanger and

bent it and hooked it on my finger. The bridges were swinging bridges. They weren't stationary in those days, and they had an apron-like tailpiece. The strings kept the apron in place, and I hooked the other end of the wire to the apron. When you shook the wire, the bridge would move and you had a vibrato. Most of the time I used it with chords.

Before World War II, I did arrangements for Glenn Miller, Jan Savitt, Ina Ray Hutton, and Artie Shaw. I even had my own big band that featured Buster Smith on saxophone. In 1941 I took over an all-woman band, The International Sweethearts of Rhythm out of Piney Woods, Mississippi.

It's hard for me to remember all the bands and arrangements I wrote. I didn't play too much in the 1950s and 1960s, though I did get involved in the Harlem Blues and Jazz band, and played in all sorts of combinations with Sammy Price, Kelly Owens, Hal Austin, Jerry Potter, Frank Foster, and more musicians than I can count.

KID "LIPS" HACKETTE, "WORLD'S GREATEST FLASH DRUMMER," FEATURED WITH THE EDDIE DURHAM BAND, 1944. COURTESY METROPOLITAN RESEARCH CENTER, HOUSTON PUBLIC LIBRARY.

(OPPOSITE)
EDDIE DURHAM, ZURICH, SWITZERLAND, CA. 1982, PHOTOGRAPH BY MARCO ANDREA FRANGI. COURTESY EDDIE DURHAM.

ROBERT LEE DUNN

February 5, 1908–May 27, 1971

MILTON AND HIS BROWNIES (WITH BOB DUNN ON STEEL GUITAR), *PIONEER WESTERN SWING BAND, 1935–36*, MCA 1509.

Robert Lee "Bob" Dunn was born in Fort Gibson, Oklahoma, the oldest of four children. His father, Silas Dunn, played at traditional country hoedowns, but Bob's most profound early influence was a group of Hawaiian entertainers he heard in a stage show in Kusa, Oklahoma. Bob took correspondence lessons on the steel guitar from Walter Kolomuku, and in 1927 he joined a touring troupe called The Panhandle Cowboys and Indians, which traveled from the Midwest to the Texas-Mexico border. In the early 1930s, Dunn replaced Wanna Coffman in Milton Brown's Musical Brownies, and stayed with the group until Brown's death in 1936. Dunn's first recordings for Decca with Brown are considered to be some of the earliest electric steel guitar recordings. Years later, fiddler Jimmy Thomason, who played with Dunn in Cliff Bruner's Texas Wanderers, recalled in an interview with researcher Gary Ginell that Dunn had told him how the amplification of the steel guitar originated: "It happened when Dunn was working on the Boardwalk at Coney Island in New York. Bob was up there playing steel guitar, standard guitar, and trombone. . . . And while he was doing this, he ran into this black guy who was playing these blues licks. Well, this just knocked Bob out and he got this guy to show him how he was doing it. Just as they were getting acquainted, this guy up and ran off. And Bob followed him all the way to New Orleans before he found him again."[1]

Unfortunately, Dunn did not remember the name of the performer who showed him his electric pickup, nor did he ever explain exactly how this first pickup was made. Dunn was a master stylist who admired the trombonist Jack Teagarden. Dunn took a similar jazz approach in his soloing and used horn-like phrasing.

After serving in World War II, Dunn earned a degree in music from the Southern College of Fine Arts and opened a music store in Houston, which he operated until his death.

Charles Edward Christian was born in Bonham, in northeast Texas, but grew up in Oklahoma City, where he served as a "lead boy" for his father, Clarence, a blind guitarist. Charlie took up music early, first playing the

1. Cary Ginell, *Milton Brown and the Founding of Western Swing* (Urbana: University of Illinois Press), 108–9.

CHARLIE CHRISTIAN

July 29, 1916–March 2, 1942

ukulele, then the guitar. He dropped out of school in the ninth or tenth grade and played on the streets and in clubs around the Oklahoma City business district called Deep Deuce, which was remarkably similar to Dallas's Deep Ellum. T-Bone Walker recalled that in the 1920s he and Christian, who were both talented dancers, often performed together outdoors in Oklahoma City, switching off on bass and guitar and then dancing together. During this time, reports have him (Christian) playing in dance halls with a microphone between his knees so his solos could be heard.

In 1936 Christian was among local musicians who accepted an offer to play in Dallas in conjunction with the Texas Centennial. These performances took place in various venues in Dallas. Bassist Milt Hinton recalled seeing Christian playing in a North Dallas dance hall, with a microphone attached to his guitar with rubber bands so he could be heard. Christian then hit the road with a succession of bands. It is uncertain when he began playing electric guitar, but apparently he was doing so by 1937. Eddie Durham may have played a role in helping Christian develop his single-string style, though his account of teaching Christian in 1937 is suspect.

CHARLIE CHRISTIAN WITH BENNY GOODMAN, NEW YORK, CA.1940.

In August 1939 the Columbia A&R man John Hammond heard Christian in Oklahoma City and got him an audition with Benny Goodman, the clarinetist and bandleader who was also Hammond's brother-in-law. Christian joined Goodman's band and remained with him, performing and recording prolifically for the rest of his short life. An easygoing man, Christian apparently was comfortable as one of the first black musicians in a white band, and he won the *Down Beat* poll as favorite jazz guitarist three years running.

Christian was an amazingly fluid guitarist and has been characterized as a "scratch improviser," one of those rare musicians who creates a new solo whenever he plays rather than relying on variations of his own stock of riffs and phrases. In the early 1940s he jammed with avant-garde musicians such as Dizzy Gillespie and was in the forefront of the emerging bebop movement that revolutionized jazz.

Aaron "T-Bone" Walker was born in Linden, in East Texas, and moved with his mother to Dallas when he was two. He stayed there and in Fort Worth, where his wife's family lived. His earliest memories were of his mother

(OPPOSITE)
CHARLIE CHRISTIAN, NEW YORK, 1940.
COURTESY INSTITUTE OF JAZZ STUDIES.

AARON "T-BONE" WALKER

May 28, 1910–March 16, 1975

AARON "T-BONE" WALKER, GUITARIST WITH THE MILTON LARKIN ORCHESTRA, RHUMBOOGIE, CLUB, CHICAGO, 1942. COURTESY METROPOLITAN RESEARCH CENTER, HOUSTON PUBLIC LIBRARY "singing the blues as she would sit alone in the evenings in our place in Texas." He made his first guitar from a cigar box. Then his stepfather, Marco Washington, a string-band musician, bought him a banjo. As a child, Walker often performed on the streets of Dallas, solo or with his stepfather's string band. In his younger days, Walker was known primarily for his tenor banjo playing, singing, and the acrobatic dancing that contributed to his showmanship after he became a star.

Walker's family knew Blind Lemon Jefferson, and the guitarist said he became a "lead boy" for the bluesman. Reminiscing in a 1947 article in *Record Changer* magazine, Walker said, "I used to lead [Jefferson] around, playing and passing the cup, take him from one beer joint to another. I liked hearing him play. He would sing like nobody's business. He was a friend of my father's. People used to crowd around him so you couldn't see him."[2]

In addition to Jefferson, Walker was influenced by the boogie-woogie piano and singing he heard at a Holy Ghost church in Dallas, as well as by the classic blues-women Ma Rainey and Ida Cox. Walker's favorite singer was Leroy Carr, whom he recalled in an interview with Arnold Shaw: "I just loved him. I never met him, but he made a record of 'In the Evening When the Sun Goes Down.' When I heard that one, it was dramatic—that was it."[3]

While he was living in Dallas in 1929, Walker's two recordings for the Columbia label under the name Oak Cliff T-Bone, "Trinity River Blues" and "Wichita Falls Blues," had limited success. Walker had not yet achieved his signature guitar style; in fact, his playing is barely audible on these sides, obscured by a more dominant second guitar, probably that of bluesman Willie Reed, and by the piano of Doug Finnell. Walker achieved fame after he moved to California and recorded "I Gotta Break, Baby," and "Mean Old World" for the Capitol label in 1942. The popularity of these songs established Walker as an instrumentalist and singer and sparked the beginning of West Coast blues recording.

Between 1942 and 1974, T-Bone Walker recorded prolifically, appearing on more than two dozen labels and working with the top blues and jazz performers of his day in America and Europe. Despite the acclaim he received from his fellow musicians, none of his records from the 1950s on made the *Billboard* charts. His greatest commercial success came from his 1947 recording

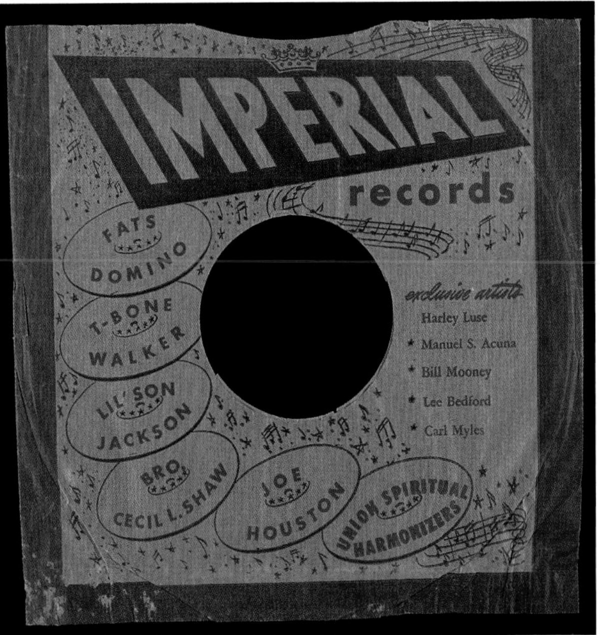

T-BONE WALKER, IMPERIAL RECORD SLEEVE. COURTESY TEXAS AFRICAN AMERICAN PHOTOGRAPHY ARCHIVE.

T-BONE WALKER WITH MARL YOUNG'S ORCHESTRA, "SAIL ON BOOGIE," RHUMBOOGIE M-33-1.

2. Jane Greenough, "T-Bone Blues: T-Bone Walker's Story in His Own Words," *Record Changer* (October 1947), 5–6, 12.

3. Arnold Shaw, *Honkers and Shouters: The Golden Years of Rhythm and Blues* (New York: Collier Books, 1978), 114.

T-BONE WALKER WITH MARL YOUNG'S ORCHESTRA, "IM STILL IN LOVE WITH YOU," RHUMBOOGIE M-33-2.
T-BONE WALKER, "GET THESE BLUES OFF ME," IMPERIAL IM-385.
T-BONE WALKER, "LONG LOST LOVER BLUES," CAPITAL 57-7002 3.
T-BONE WALKER, "TEEN AGE BABY," IMPERIAL IM-740.

of "Stormy Monday." Like those of his contemporaries, his career was eclipsed by the introduction of rhythm-and-blues-based rock 'n' roll.

Walker combined his other influences with the music of the Territory jazz bands of the 1920s and 1930s to create the modern sound. Fort Worth guitarist and music historian Sumter Bruton says that Walker also incorporated jazz chords learned from Charlie Christian—specifically, ninth, thirteenth, diminished and augmented chords. Virtually all blues rhythm guitarists now employ ninth chords when backing the lead player and singer, so T-Bone Walker could be said to have invented the contemporary blues sound that many players and listeners take for granted.[4]

The impact of Walker's playing on other musicians is hard to overestimate. He could hardly play a note that didn't swing, and his tone was luminous. Walker's playing affected any number of musicians in the same way that to Leroy Carr's playing affected him. When they heard T-Bone, that was it. Walker's career is well documented in Helen Oakley Dance's 1987 biography, though the book does not fully establish the extent of his importance as a musician and mentor. The accounts of musicians in this book, however, attest to his profound influence in Texas.

4. Interview with Sumter Bruton by Jay Brakefield, May 12, 2004.

DALLAS

ELM STREET THEATERS AT NIGHT, DALLAS, 1925. COURTESY TEXAS/ DALLAS HISTORY AND ARCHIVES DIVISION DALLAS PUBLIC LIBRARY

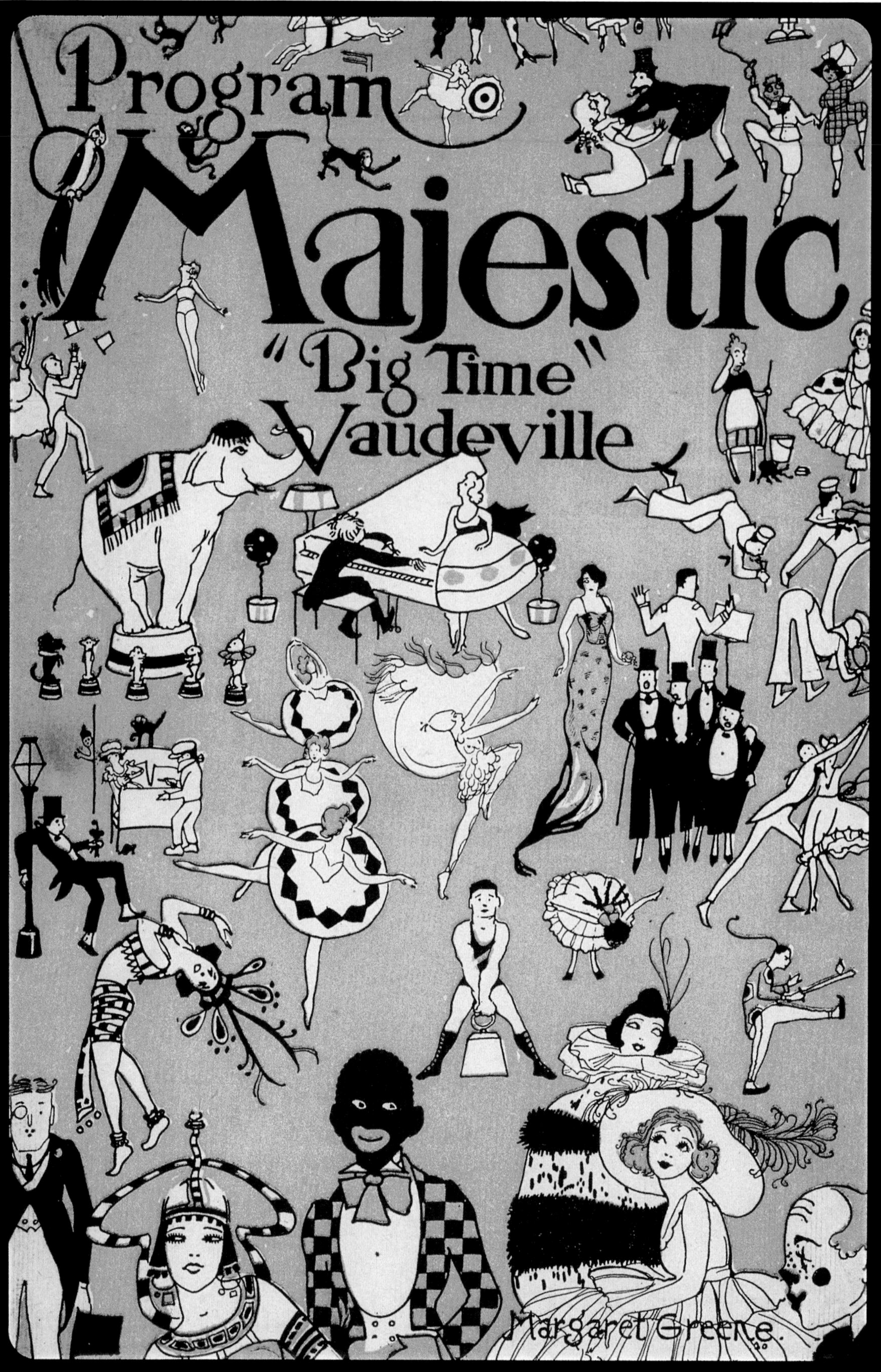
Program
Majestic
"Big Time"
Vaudeville
Margaret Greene.

INTRODUCTION

The number of African slaves in Dallas County was relatively small, growing from 207 in 1850 to 1,074 in 1860. During the Civil War, the number of slaves in the county increased significantly as slaveholders from elsewhere in the South tried to harbor their slaves in Texas. After the war, freed slaves established seven known freedman communities in Dallas County. The primary settlement, known as Freedmantown, was northeast of the city limits. The freed slaves buried their dead in a cemetery that was neglected and nearly forgotten, then unearthed by the widening of Lemmon Avenue and Central Expressway in the 1980s. More than a decade later it became the site of the Freedman's Cemetery Memorial.

Although Freedman's Cemetery was officially closed in July 1907, there is some anecdotal evidence that burials continued beyond that date. Dr. Robert Prince Jr., whose great-grandfather was Dock Rowen, one of the original trustees of the cemetery, says that his mother talked about seeing burials as late as the 1920s. Others, including attorney and former judge Louis Bedford, who grew up near the cemetery, recall that by the 1930s children liked to play on its grounds.

By then, the name of the African American community surrounding the cemetery had changed from Freedmantown to North Dallas. When this change occurred is not entirely clear, although it appears to have happened by the time of World War One.The legendary blues pianist Alex Moore used both names; he often referred to his birthplace in his songs as "Freedmantown, North Dallas." While this name distinction appears arbitrary, it may also be indicative of social stratification within the matrix of community life. The heart of this black community was the intersection of Hall Street and Thomas Avenue, and the streets were lined with cafes, drugstores, theaters, shoeshine stands, and other small businesses. The daily life of blacks thrived in this area until the building of Central Expressway spelled its demise, and people dispersed because of overcrowding.

DEEP ELLUM

The coming of the railroads in the early 1870s created the jobs that drew African Americans to Dallas from rural Texas and elsewhere, a process that intensified when the boll weevil ravaged the East Texas cotton fields in the 1890s. In Dallas the railroads also created a new business district about a mile east of the original Dallas

MAJESTIC THEATER, BIG TIME VAUDEVILLE PROGRAM BOOK, DALLAS, AUGUST 29, 1920. COURTESY TEXAS AFRICAN AMERICAN PHOTOGRAPHY ARCHIVE.

town square. In the early 1900s many European immigrants, primarily Russian and Polish Jews, established shops along the stretch of Elm Street near its crossing with the Houston & Texas Central Railroad track. This area came to be known as Deep Ellum—"Deep," apparently, because of its distance from downtown, and "Ellum" reflecting the way blacks, and perhaps some newly arrived Europeans, pronounced "Elm." Black businesses sprang up along the section of track connecting Deep Ellum and Freedmantown/North Dallas. Officially named Central Avenue, this strip became better known as Central Track or Central Tracks. A few black-owned businesses were located on the north side of Elm near the crossing.

Blacks also shopped in the white-owned businesses along Elm, where they received better treatment than in downtown establishments. In an era when most banks were off-limits to African Americans, the Jewish-owned pawnshops on Elm were a source of quick cash. When Dallas-raised bluesman Aaron "T-Bone" Walker sang, "It's a mighty funny world where a man's got to pawn his shoes," he may well have had in mind such Elm Street establishments as Honest Joe's and Good Old Dave's.

Thus, the Deep Ellum/Central Track area in the early twentieth century was a richly diverse cultural matrix. A visitor might well have seen day laborers being picked up for a trip to the cotton fields of Collin County or being dropped off at the end of the day. People patronized pawnshops, grocery stores, tailor shops, new and secondhand clothing stores, shoeshine stands, cafes, dance halls, and sporting houses. J. H. Owens, known as "Old Ironsides," evoked the ambiance in a 1937 column in the black weekly *Dallas Gazette:* "Down on Deep Ellum in Dallas, where Central Avenue empties into Elm Street is where Ethiopia stretches forth her hands. It is the one spot in the city that needs no daylight savings time because there is no bedtime, and working hours have no limits. The only place recorded on earth where business, religion, hoodooism and gambling and stealing go on without friction . . . last Saturday a prophet held the best audience in this 'Madison Square Garden' in announcing that Jesus Christ would come to Dallas in person in 1939. At the same time a pickpocket was lifting a week's wages from another guy's pocket, who stood open mouthed to hear the prophecy."

In the prosperous 1920s black entertainment flourished in Deep Ellum, which the *Dallas Morning News* called, in a 1925 article, "The Darkies' Playground." Theaters offered minstrel shows and vaudeville as well as movies. The grandest of the theaters were the Park and the Ella B. Moore, owned by former vaudevillians Chintz and Ella B. Moore. People could kick up their heels at the Green Parrot and Tip Top dance halls and in the elegant ballroom at the Pythian Temple, designed by black architect William Sidney Pittman. Gambling and drinking, though illegal, were popular activities, and music was everywhere. Some of the finest musicians of the day played in the theaters, cafes, and steamy joints and on the streets of Deep Ellum and Central Track.

The best known and most imitated street performer was Blind Lemon Jefferson, who followed Central Track north to Elm Street each morning with a walking stick and a guitar slung over his shoulder, and performed for enthusiastic crowds near the corner of Elm and Central. Around 1912 Huddie Ledbetter, better known as Leadbelly, met Blind Lemon Jefferson in Deep Ellum. Together, they played on the streets and in the nightspots, such as the Big Four, where Leadbelly remembered, "The women would come running, Lawd have mercy! They'd hug and kiss us so much we could hardly play."

A black businessman named R. T. Ashford owned a large shoeshine stand and record store at the corner where Jefferson played, and in the mid-1920s—possibly on the basis of reports to Ashford by an employee, boogie-woogie pianist Sam Price—a Paramount Record Company executive invited Jefferson to come to Chicago and make "race" records. The records were a huge success, and Jefferson returned to Chicago often. Between 1926 and his untimely death in 1929, Blind Lemon was the biggest selling down-home blues singer in the United States.

In addition to Blind Lemon Jefferson and Leadbelly, other important musicians in Deep Ellum included blues guitar stylists Lonnie Johnson, Little Hat Jones, Texas Alexander, and Funny Papa Smith; jazz guitarist Eddie Durham; and horn players Hot Lips Page, Buster Smith, Budd and Keg Johnson, Herschel Evans, and Buddy Tate. There were classic blues singers, such as Jewell Nelson, Bobbie Cadillac, Emma Wright, Lillian Glinn, and Bessie Tucker, and numerous barrelhouse piano players, including Jesse Crump, Alex Moore, Sam Price, and Doug Finnell. The major blues and jazz per-

ALPHONSO TRENT'S ADOLPHUS HOTEL ORCHESTRA, WFAA RADIO, DALLAS, 1920S. COURTESY TEXAS AFRICAN AMERICAN PHOTOGRAPHY ARCHIVE.

formers of the day, from Bessie Smith and Ma Rainey to Alphonso Trent and Benny Moten, always stopped in Dallas on the black TOBA (Theater Owners Booking Association) tours, and played in the Central Track area.

In the 1920s Dallas became a recording center. Ironically, Blind Lemon Jefferson never recorded there—he went to Paramount's studios in Chicago. However, other "race" labels held regular sessions in Dallas. Okeh, Vocalion, Brunswick, Columbia, and RCA Victor sent scouts and engineers to record local artists once or twice a year. Engineers came into the city, set up their equipment in a hotel room, and put the word out. Itinerant musicians found their way to Dallas, among them the legendary Robert Johnson, who recorded there in 1937. With the Great Depression of the 1930s race recording declined, but the Dallas–Fort Worth area remained a center of musical activity, featuring blues, jazz, country, and western swing. One of the best known black groups of this period was Coley Jones and The Dallas String Band, which variously included one or two violins, two guitars, mandolin, string bass, clarinet, and trumpet. The Dallas String Band performed at dances, picnics, and shows for white and black audiences, and often serenaded on the streets or outside the Moores' theaters. The bass player for Coley Jones was Marco Washington, who had led a string band that included his stepson, Aaron "T-Bone" Walker, as a child musician and dancer.

In the 1940s the railroad tracks on Central Avenue in Dallas were torn up to make room for Central Expressway, which was built in the 1950s. R. L. Thornton Expressway followed in the 1960s. These changes choked Deep Ellum off from downtown, and the remaining street life died. Deep Ellum became a warehouse district with industrial suppliers and repair shops.

Nonetheless, blues and jazz continued to flourish in the black communities of Dallas. The Rose Ballroom, opened by T. H. Smith in March 1942 and reopened as the Rose Room in April 1943, became a showplace for the best of the local and nationally known blues artists. T-Bone Walker, on his frequent returns to Dallas, performed at the Rose Room, as did Big Joe Turner, Pee Wee Crayton, Lowell Fulson, King Kolax, Red Calhoun, Buster Smith, Eddie Vinson, and Jimmy "T-99" Nelson. The Rose Room was renamed the Empire Room in 1951 and continued to feature the most popular rhythm and blues

DEEP ELLUM, DALLAS, 1922. COURTESY TEXAS/DALLAS HISTORY AND ARCHIVES DIVISION DALLAS PUBLIC LIBRARY.

artists of the day: Zuzu Bollin, Li'l Son Jackson, Clarence "Nappy Chin" Evans, Mercy Baby, Frankie Lee Sims, and Smokey Hogg. Both Sims and Hogg performed often in Dallas and were recorded at the Sellers studio on Commerce Street for the Blue Bonnet label in the late 1940s. (Hogg had actually recorded his first session in Dallas for Decca in 1937.) In "Goin' Back Home" Hogg sings about Deep Ellum and refers to Frankie Lee Sims's "Lucy Mae Blues," which Sims himself had cut for Blue Bonnet.

From the late 1940s to the early 1960s some of the most important blues recordings in Dallas were made at the Sellers studio. The facility was used by a variety of small, independent labels, including Blue Bonnet, Talent, Star Talent and Atco.[1] Featured performers included Frankie Lee Sims, Rattlesnake Cooper, Willie Lane, Sonny Boy Davis, ZuZu Bollin, Royal Earl and The Swingin' Kools, Ray Sharpe and the Blue Whalers, Finney-Mo, and Louis Howard and The Red Hearts.

By the late 1960s and early 1970s numerous white bands were experimenting with blues, including musicians such as Steve Miller, Boz Scaggs, Jimmie and Stevie Ray Vaughan, and Denny Freeman. Moreover, there was a wide array of black groups. Freddie King and Al "TNT" Braggs were active, as were Cal Valentine, Big Bo and His Twisting Arrows (led by nightclub owner Willie "Big Bo" Thomas), Z. Z. Hill, R. L. Griffin, and Johnnie Taylor. Many of these musicians were eventually forced to leave the Dallas area to better their careers. With the growing popularity of disco and rock, there were fewer opportunities for live performances, radio airplay, and recording.

The popularity of blues waxes and wanes, and it seems that every few years a new generation of fans discovers this vital and important music. Recently, 2003 was the "Year of the Blues" nationally, bringing a flood of recordings and documentaries. Many seminal performers have died over the years, including Stevie Ray Vaughan, Johnny Copeland, Little Joe Blue, Albert Collins, Al Braggs, ZuZu Bollin, and Robert Ealey (who once operated Fort Worth's famous Blue Bird club). Some of the deceased were older musicians who came out of retirement and enjoyed second careers in the 1980s. These included pianist Alex Moore, who in 1987 became the first blues performer from Texas to win a National Heritage Fellowship from the National Endowment for the Arts; bandleader and arranger Henry "Buster" Smith; and drummer Herbie Cowens.[2] Saxophone and piano player and vocalist Big Al Dupree continued to perform regularly at Dallas's Balcony Club up to his death in 2003, playing standards and some blues material. In spite of economic downturns and changes in nightlife habits, live blues persists in Dallas and Fort Worth.

1. In 1949 Jesse and Louise Erickson, the owners of Louise's Record Shop at 3313 Oakland in Dallas, began their Talent (later to become Star Talent) label. The Ericksons recorded Rattlesnake Cooper (Talent 180 and 181), Sonny Boy Davis (Talent 178 and 179), and Willie Lane (Talent 167 and 168, 171 and 172), among others (including the legendary New Orleans piano player Roy "Professor Longhair" Byrd).

2. In 1981 I formed a band that included Henry "Buster" Smith (bass), Boston Smith (piano), Herbie Cowens (drums), Benny Arredondo (trumpet), and James Clay (saxophone and flute) for the Downtown Dallas Traditional Music Festival, held on the campus of El Centro College. I called the band "The Heat Waves of Swing" in honor of one of Buster Smith's bands by the same name. Over the years, I enlarged the band for the Dallas Folk Festival, which I founded and produced (1983–84, 1986, 1988, and 1991). I included local and nationally known musicians such as David "Fathead" Newman (saxophone), Big Al Dupree, (piano and saxophone), and Shirley McFatter (vocalist).

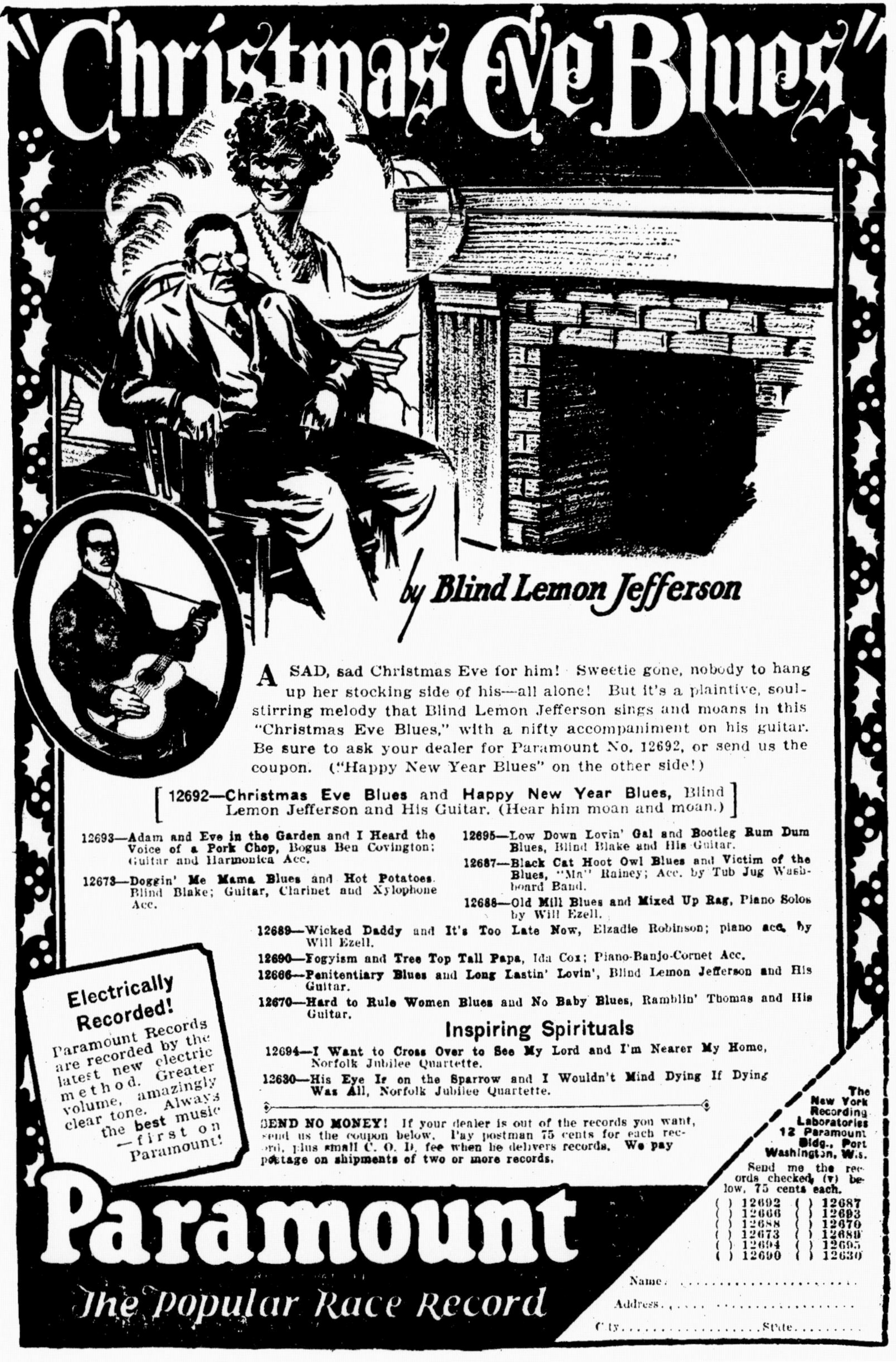

BLIND LEMON JEFFERSON *"CHRISTMAS EVE BLUES"*

PARAMOUNT RECORDS, RACE AD, *CHICAGO DEFENDER*, 1928.

COURTESY DOCUMENTARY ARTS.

Jay Brakefield, a Dallas writer and copyeditor, began exploring the Dallas blues scene in the late 1980s.[3] In 1997 Brakefield met Joanna Iz and Patti Coghill at a blues festival. "They said they were going to start a blues magazine in Dallas, and I replied, 'I'm a writer; call me and I'll write for you.' I gave them a card and promptly forgot about the encounter. Somebody's always starting a magazine. To my surprise, they did start a magazine, *Southwest Blues.* Seven years later, they're still putting it out every month while working other jobs to pay the rent, and I'm still writing for them."[4]

Southwest Blues primarily covers the blues scene in Dallas–Fort Worth, but also announces blues shows in other cities around Texas and publishes interviews with contemporary blues artists. Brakefield believes the Dallas blues scene may be underrated: "Austin has the reputation as the 'Live Music Capital of the World,' but Austin musicians drive to Dallas for gigs because they pay better. Not that anyone's getting rich. Clubs come and go, and the club scene itself goes through cycles. But on most nights, the dedicated blues fan can find live music somewhere in the sprawling metro area. A number of clubs have open-mic jams where anyone with the courage to risk making a fool of himself or herself can get up and play or sing. Generally, the aspiring performer signs up with the musician running the jam, then waits to be called onstage."

According to Brakefield, the "jam guru in Dallas is Brian 'Hash Brown' Calway, who moved to Dallas from Connecticut in the early 1980s."

> A talented guitar and harmonica player and singer, Hash Brown is adept at getting the best out of the jammers, many of whom are regulars. In addition to talented amateurs, many professionals stop by the jams on their nights off. Mississippi-born blues veteran Sam Myers, who once played with such giants as Elmore James, hit the jams when he was not on the road singing and playing harp with Anson and the Rockets. Myers was a deep bluesman, and the tone of the music changed when he took the stage. Jams can be pedestrian when the chemistry isn't right, but magic can happen, too. Several years ago, the blind Canadian slide guitarist Jeff Healey sat in at a Hash Brown jam, pulling fiery sounds from the electric instrument he plays flat on his lap like a steel guitar. Myers, who was legally blind, was in the house and joined Healey for a song.

Despite the popularity of a tee-shirt that proclaims "No white, no black, just blues," Brakefield adds, "there are black and white blues scenes in the Dallas area." Dallas is still a segregated city. Some audiences in South Dallas, Deep Ellum, and the Lower Greenville Avenue area are mixed, but there is still a sense that integration, though legislated, remains a civic goal more than a living reality. However, "there is considerable crossover," Brakefield points out. "Myers and other black musicians and fans turn up at predominantly white clubs, and whites venture into black South Dallas to play and perform, and they are still warmly received."

While the audience for blues has become predominantly white in the club scene of contemporary Dallas, R. L. Griffin's Blues Palace No. 2 in South Dallas has weekly blues shows, featuring himself, Tutu Jones, and a host of other African American musicians. Despite its location in what is perceived by some as a "dangerous part of town," the Blues Palace offers lighted and attended parking, and the club is hospitable to all. Most notably, it is about the only black-owned blues club in Dallas–Fort Worth that has a racially mixed audience of varied ages and socioeconomic demographics.

The word *community* may be overused, but there "really is," Brakefield says, a "blues community in Dallas-Fort Worth that draws people together by their love of the music. *Southwest Blues* and Dallas community-sponsored radio station KNON-FM help keep the music alive." There are a couple of small local record labels, including Richard Chalk's Top Cat and Dallas Blues Society Records, though Chuck Nevitt, owner of the latter, says he's not taking on any more projects because CD burners and downloading have made it economically unfeasible. Although there is no formal

3. I met Jay Brakefield when he covered the funeral of Alexander H. Moore Sr., for the *Dallas Morning News* in 1989. I had been asked to deliver a eulogy for Moore and was later interviewed by Brakefield. After several meetings, I asked Brakefield to collaborate with me on a book about Deep Ellum, a project that culminated in the publication of *Deep Ellum and Central Track: Where the Black and White Worlds of Dallas Converged* (Denton: University of North Texas Press, 1996).

4. Interview with Jay Brakefield by Alan Govenar, April 28, 2004. Quotations from Brakefield in the following paragraphs are also drawn from this interview.

blues "society," the magazine and an online discussion group, NorthTexasBlues@yahoogroups.com, help keep people in touch with each other and inform them of what's going on.

Documentary Arts, a Dallas-based non-profit organization, has been a catalyst for the recognition of blues in Dallas and around the state. It has organized the Dallas Folk Festival; developed concerts and stage shows for the Dallas Museum of Art, Amon Carter Museum, Benson & Hedges Blues (Dallas and New York), the Blues sur Seine Festival of the Maison des Cultures du Monde, and Banlieues Blues (France); and produced numerous films, videos, and radio series.[5] Documentary Arts has also developed a small label, which has released archival and contemporary recordings of Alex Moore, Alfred "Snuff" Johnson, Bill Neely, Osceola Mays, Clyde Langford, John T. Samples, and a compilation of black East Texas harmonica players and their songs.

Brakefield maintains, "For the more than forty years that I've been a blues fan, I've heard the same arguments and discussions over whether the music is being compromised or diluted by mixing with rock and other forms and over whether it will survive. But new people seem to discover the blues every few years, and it doesn't seem likely to die out anytime soon."

5. I founded Documentary Arts in 1985 to present new perspectives on historical issues and diverse cultures. See www.docarts.com for a complete listing of films, videos, radio features, and audio recordings.

HUDDIE "LEADBELLY" LEDBETTER

January 29, 1889–December 6, 1949

HUDDIE "LEADBELLY" LEDBETTER WITH HIS WIFE, MARTHA PROMISE, NEW YORK, 1935, PHOTOGRAPH BY ALAN LOMAX. COURTESY OF LIBRARY OF CONGRESS.

By the time Huddie Ledbetter reached Dallas in the early 1900s, he had already earned a reputation as a hardworking farmhand and cotton picker, a ladies' man, a gambler, and a singer who played windjammer (concertina), guitar, mandolin, harmonica, and piano.

Ledbetter, better known as Leadbelly, had come to Dallas from Shreveport, where he had rollicked in the black nightlife of Fannin Street. By then he had developed a highly rhythmic guitar style, influenced by the bass figures of barrelhouse blues piano. In Dallas Leadbelly found his way to Deep Ellum, which was much like Fannin Street in Shreveport. It was the place where hobos invariably landed and where African American, Hispanic, and white cotton pickers were picked up for transport to the cotton fields of Collin County, to the north.

On the crowded sidewalks of Deep Ellum and Central Avenue around 1912, Leadbelly met Blind Lemon Jefferson. They played together on the street and at house parties. Jefferson taught Leadbelly to play single-string runs on the guitar, though in his later recordings he seemed to prefer the heavy strumming he learned from barrelhouse pianists and from the Mexicans who sold him a twelve-string guitar.

In 1917 Leadbelly and Blind Lemon Jefferson parted ways; Leadbelly had killed a man over a woman and had been sentenced to thirty years at Huntsville Prison Farm. There he worked six years at hard labor, then tried to escape. Leadbelly's ability to improvise songs won him his release in 1925. Governor Pat Neff pardoned him because of a song Leadbelly had composed at a chance meeting while the governor was inspecting the prison:

Nineteen hundred and twenty-three
The judge took my liberty away from me,
Left my wife wringin' her hands and cryin,'
"Lawd have mercy on this man of mine."
I am your servant to compose this song.
Please, Governor Neff, let me go back home.
I know my wife will jump and shout,
Train rolls up, I come stepping out.
Please, Honorable Governor, be good and kind.
If I don't get a pardon, will you cut my time?
Had you, Governor Neff, like you got me,
Wake up in the morning and I'd set you free.

HUDDIE "LEADBELLY" LEDBETTER AT RUTGERS UNIVERSITY, NEWARK, 1944. COURTESY INSTITUTE OF JAZZ STUDIES.

After his release from Huntsville, Leadbelly returned to the Caddo Lake area of Louisiana, where he had grown up, and resumed his life as a musician. In 1930 he was arrested again, convicted of assault, and sentenced to ten years in the Louisiana State Prison in Angola. In 1934 he met John Lomax, who was doing fieldwork at the prison, collecting work songs, shouts, ballads, spirituals, and blues. Among the songs Lomax collected was another plea for a pardon, which he delivered personally to Governor O. K. Allen. The governor freed Leadbelly that year.

For a brief period after his release from Angola Prison, Leadbelly worked as Lomax's chauffeur. Lomax became Leadbelly's manager and arranged an extensive tour of white colleges and concert halls. The two men traveled the Northeast together. While on a concert tour, Leadbelly met Martha Promise. They later married, and he decided not to return to the South. Instead, the couple settled in New York City, where Leadbelly sang at political rallies and at folk music revivals and concerts. He appeared on programs with Josh White, Sonny Terry, Brownie McGhee, Woody Guthrie, Burl Ives, and the Almanac Singers.

Leadbelly's life and music represented a remarkable journey, from his hardscrabble beginnings and early experience playing at country dances to the left-leaning folk movement of the 1940s. He recorded alone and with folk groups and jazz ensembles. Though he is perhaps best described as a songster, he was a powerful blues singer, and all his music has a strong blues sensibility.

"GOODNIGHT, IRENE," WORDS AND MUSIC BY HUDDIE LEDBETTER AND JOHN LOMAX. INTRODUCED AND FEATURED BY THE WEAVERS AND GORDON JENKINS ON DECCA RECORDS. SHEET MUSIC BY SPENCER MUSIC CORPORATION, NEW YORK (1950)

HERBERT COWENS

May 24, 1904–January 23, 1993; interview, 1984

Herbert Cowens came from a musical family. Two brothers played drums, one sister was a dancer, and two others were singers. Cowens started as a shoeshine boy, and with the money he earned at street dancing, he bought his first set of drums. He played with local jazz bands, including The Satisfied Five, which he quit in 1926. In 1927 he left Dallas with Cleo Mitchell's Shake Your Feet Company. From 1927 to 1980 Cowens lived in New York City and worked in vaudeville, Broadway shows, and musicals. He also played for several notable bandleaders, including Eubie Blake, Fats Waller, Stuff Smith, and Fletcher Henderson. In addition, Cowens led his own band, The Kat and the Kittens, and made annual overseas USO tours to the Far East, Japan, Europe, and the Mediterranean. Cowens married Rubye Houston of Dallas in 1936.

When I was a youngster I had quite a few brothers and sisters, and it was a little rough at times. We were living in a place called Frogtown in the 2500 block of Cochran Street in what was then called North Dallas. So, when we went to and back from school, we had to cross McKinney Avenue. And in so doing, the white kids would throw rocks and we'd have to fight to get to where we were going. We'd have to fight to get to school and we'd have to fight to get home. But as far as grown-ups were concerned, we never had any trouble.

There were thirteen kids altogether, though I lost a baby brother in my younger days and I lost a sister. We all went to Booker T. Washington and then to Dallas Colored High School. In school we didn't have any instruments. So we had to march out to the beat of a drum. A young man before me played the drum, but he gave it up and I took it over, just beating the drum for them to march up and down the stairs. And after that, I started listening more to the drummer at the movies. He was named Jesse Atkins, and he was one of the greatest. Every time I'd go to the movies, I would sit there near the drummer, and it just came on me that I should be a drummer. And that's the way it started. I must have been about twelve or thirteen.

When I got into high school I worked as a "blackjack." I shined shoes, and with the extra money I earned I would buy a piece of drum. Of course, I got quite a few lickings, but I took the lickings and kept on buying the drums.

I worked two different shine parlors, and if I didn't like one, I was privileged to go on. I worked one on Main Street and one on Elm around the corner. And I also worked in another little place at Harwood and Elm. That was where the cowboys used to come in for the weekend.

In high school I started a little band called The Rainbow Jazz Band. We were just schoolkids, and we got a few jobs around Texas. It was a great thing to see, these five young guys trying to make a living. We had to walk just about everywhere.

Two of my brothers were also drummers, Alvis Vernon Cowens and Cardin Augustus Cowens. And I had two sisters who went into the business. I should say three. Beatrice was a singer, Louise was a singer, and Lorraine was a dancer.

We used to go the live shows at the Park Theatre. The first time I went, I must have been about ten years old because I went there with my father. (My father's name was Fred Douglas Cowens, and my oldest brother was named after him, Fred Douglas Cowens Jr.) We went to the Park Theatre to see a blues singer by the name of Ida Cox. They had different shows every week. Ida Cox, Bessie Smith, Ma Rainey. The Theater Owners Booking Association brought in shows one after the other. Dan James was in charge of the Park Theatre.

What I remember about Deep Ellum is the way the train passed right down Central Avenue. I liked going down there to walk by the hotel where all the musicians congregated and to listen to them talk. That was at the Delmonico Hotel, right at Swiss and Pacific. I saw Blind Lemon Jefferson at the Delmonico Hotel the first time, and the second time I saw him, he was crossing Central Avenue going over there to Fat Jack's, which was the movie house. I couldn't understand how Blind Lemon could play so good and still not see. He was wonderful, but I didn't ever talk to him. I just seen him go back and forth. I didn't know he couldn't see until I saw one guy help him across the street one day. That's the only time I knew he was blind. He'd start to playing and put his hat down and it wouldn't be long before it would be full.

Another group I remember was led by Coley Jones. He had what we call a string band. He had four pieces,

(OPPOSITE) HERBERT COWENS, DALLAS, 1926.
COURTESY HERBERT AND RUBYE COWENS COLLECTION, TEXAS AFRICAN AMERICAN PHOTOGRAPHY ARCHIVE.

HERBERT COWENS, BUCK AND BUBBLES SHOW, NEW YORK, 1930s. COURTESY HERBERT AND RUBYE COWENS COLLECTION, TEXAS AFRICAN AMERICAN PHOTOGRAPHY ARCHIVE.

and they would play anyplace that they could pass the hat. Everybody knew him. He not only played there out in the village under your window, he'd take his group and play in the drugstores downtown and out in Dallas. Most of what he played were blues.

I used to play in front of the Tip Top Tailors every Saturday. We played out in front and people would come out to hear the music and go have clothes made. Most of the time, I'd be with Frenchie. He was a trumpet player, and he had a band with three or four pieces in it, trombone, saxophone, trumpet, and drums. We played any kind of music that we knew at the time. Frenchie was a kind of heavyset fellow and he could blow his horn. They say you could hear it from Elm Street to far North Dallas. His real name was Polite Christian. I don't how he spelled it, but he was from New Orleans.

I met Buster Smith in front of Tip Top Tailors. He used to come to hear the band play. He was about my age, and he'd talk to me, and I would talk to him about music.

We used to go dancing on Central Avenue. They used to call it down on the Track. There was a skating rink that they turned into a dance place. They called it the Skating Rink at first and then they changed it to the Rink when they started the dancing.

Sometimes we'd go by the Green Parrot that was on Elm Street right beside McMillan's Cafe They had music at the Green Parrot, but I was too young to get up close to really see anything about the musicians and so forth.

R. T. Ashford had a shine parlor on the Track near the corner of Elm, and he sold records. He had three daughters that worked in there with him. Sammy Price worked at Ashford's. I was raised with Sammy. He lived across Leonard Street from where I lived. He lived on the west side of Leonard, and I lived on the east side. Sammy and I grew up together. We knew each other in Dallas and got to know each other again in New York. Sammy went on the road, and I left Dallas in 1927 with one of them TOBA shows, and when we got to Kansas City it closed. So then I was there and didn't have no job and didn't know anybody. But I got with a circus and worked with the circus for a while, and eventually I made my way to New York.

HERBERT COWENS, "THE KAT AND THE KITTENS," 1930s. COURTESY HERBERT AND RUBYE COWENS COLLECTION, TEXAS AFRICAN AMERICAN PHOTOGRAPHY ARCHIVE.

ALEXANDER H. MOORE SR.

November 22, 1899–January 20, 1989; interview, 1984

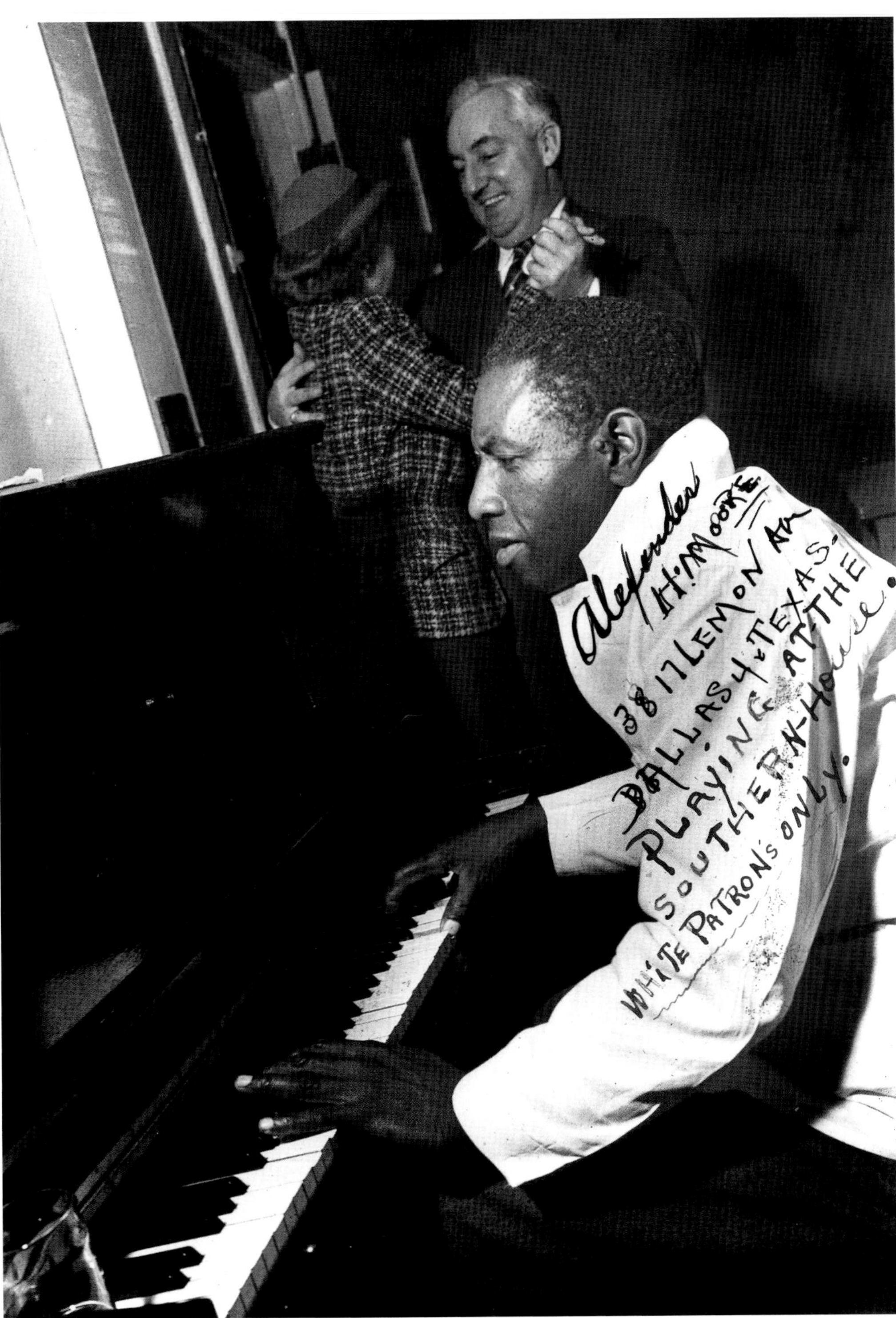

ALEX MOORE (DISHWASHER) PLAYING AT THE SOUTHERN HOUSE, "WHITE PATRONS ONLY," 1947. COURTESY ALEX MOORE AND DOCUMENTARY ARTS.

Alex Moore played a distinctive style of blues piano that brought together elements of boogie-woogie with ragtime and stride. Characteristic of boogie-woogie is the use of recurring bass patterns that lay the foundation rhythmically and harmonically for the sometimes short melodic passages. Similarly, ragtime and stride piano depend on repetitive bass patterns, though the rhythms are often broken, incorporating more complex harmonies. Together, these styles encourage spontaneity and improvisation in performance. They also retain African characteristics through the use of slurring up and down to a note, vibrato, call-and-response patterning, and syncopation.

In Texas the recordings of Alex Moore, Robert Shaw, Lavada Durst, R. T. Williams (Grey Ghost), and Walter Price exhibit stylistic similarities, such as recurring bass patterns and complex harmonies, but the rhythm and articulation of their songs vary greatly.

When I was first listening to blues music, a lot of colored cats played the piano. There were more piano players in North Dallas than anywhere in the United States. I could call them all, they'd be glad to have their name called off: Joe Curtis, Fred Curtis, Frank Ridge, Lovey Bookman, and see, the first washboard playin' I ever heard was a boy named Ben Nofsinger. That was around 1919, 1920.

ALEX MOORE WITH BLUES PROMOTER AND CLUB OWNER GEORGE PARKER, GREEN PARROT, DALLAS, 1984. PHOTOGRAPH BY ALAN GOVENAR.

I was deliverin' groceries in white folks' houses, well, they had pianos too. I'd always hit one note, and then sometime when I was in my teens, that's when I would try to play. Some of them people didn't care if I fooled around on that piano.

At that time people would herd cattle on foot from North Dallas through Hall Street and go clean out to Lamar [Street]—cattle, cows, sheep. I don't know what they did with them horses, but I remember the cattle, the Armstrong Packing Company. One day they brought a herd of horses through North Dallas, and my boss bought me a horse to deliver groceries, and a wagon. Then my job extended out further, clear out to Greenville [Avenue]. I got to see more pianos, trying to learn the piano. Around in 1920, '21, I got to hittin' on them pretty good, and come back to North Dallas and fool around up and down them alleys and streets and chock joints and such as that.

There were some kind of piano players. They played blues and boogie, that's all. 'Course, you take Jeff Garden, he was up in that little more classier playing, ragtime. That's what they played, blues and ragtime. Blind Bennie was ragtime. Bobby Bryant was a good ragtime player. K. D. Johnson, we called him Forty-Nine. He recorded with Bessie Tucker. He went up to Nashville, Tennessee, and they recorded him there.

The blues songs I heard didn't have no name. I had a cousin that played piano, while I was playin' marbles. They danced and sang, doin' the belly rub, while she just played the piano. Dave Buckner, that was one of the first ones I heard after her. He was playin' a bass drum and one of those bazookas [homemade wind instruments] and a piano all at the same time. You take Luther Smith, Leroy Maloney, Jess Maloney, he could hit those keys and play like mad.

Chris [Strachwitz] and Paul Oliver named the songs they recorded, all but one, "Blue Bloomer Blues." They'd ask, "What was that?" and I'd say, "You name them." All of them but "Blue Bloomer Blues." That's what they call flowers in Germany. Women wear bloomers.

Women winkin' and twinkin' at me
Some of them in that key
Women winkin' and wigglin' at me
Some other men I see

Find out and sit beside of one
And scratch her on her knee
Said, she couldn't go home with me, Daddy
I got to stay by myself
Said, she couldn't go home with me, Daddy
I got to stay by myself
I ask if she give me cab fare
And she say, "Yeah, and anything else."
I said, "Baby, Baby, Baby"
Will you give me what Mama did
when I was three months old
Will you give what Mama did
when I was three months old
I'll have to make you some sugar, dear
I can't stay at the same household
Hey, she pulled off them blue bloomers
and begin to whine and frown
She pulled off them blue bloomers
and begin to whine and frown
Yes, she pulled off her blue bloomers
and begin to whine and frown
I says, "Sorry, sorry, Judge."
She let her milk come down

My style of playing has changed a lot over the years. That's why they want to send me out of the country [to European festivals]. They say, "Alex, you don't play piano like the rest of them." Most of my songs I make up when I sit down to go play. I never do practice. I go play dominoes every day. That's all I do. I don't ever play piano at this house, maybe once or twice a month. That's because I play dominoes more than I play piano. The music is always here when I get ready. I just go and sit down at that piano and play it.

ABOVE LEFT: ALEX MOORE PLAYING DOMINOES AT THE MARTIN LUTHER KING JR. RECREATION CENTER, DALLAS, 1984, PHOTOGRAPH BY ALAN GOVENAR.

ABOVE RIGHT: JUNETEENTH PARADE, THOMAS AVENUE AT HALL STREET, DALLAS, JUNE 19, 1947. PHOTOGRAPH BY ALEX MOORE.

BELOW RIGHT: ALEX MOORE AT HOME, DALLAS, 1984, PHOTOGRAPH BY ALAN GOVENAR.

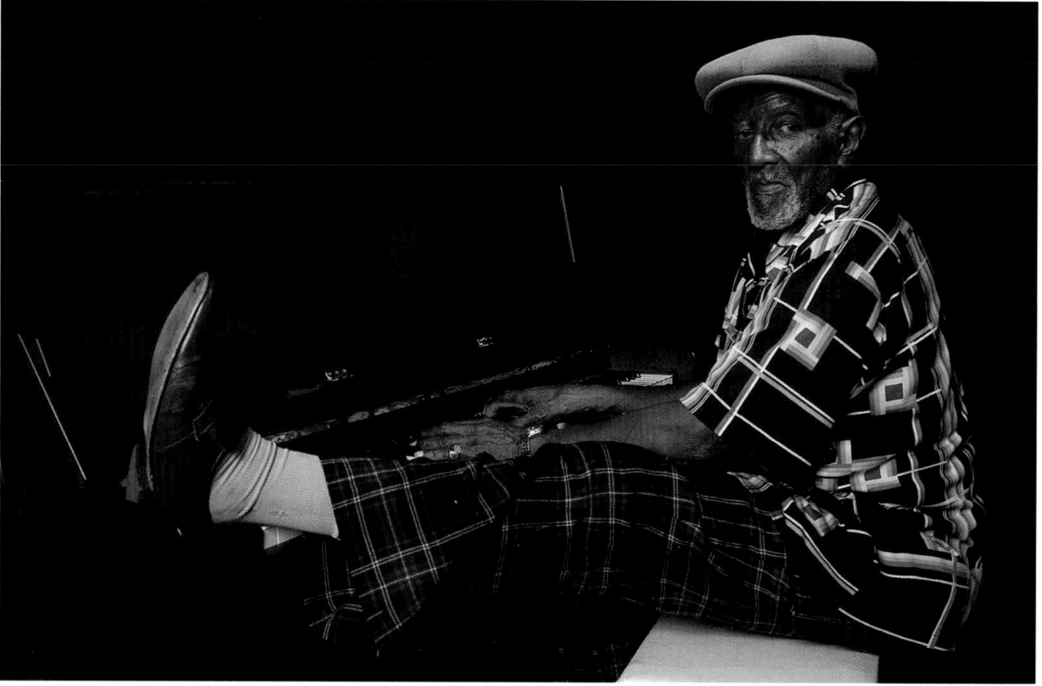

ALEX MOORE, OAK CLIFF, TEXAS, 1988. PHOTOGRAPH BY ALAN GOVENAR.

That piano kind of plays itself. That's what I'm talking about. That's why nobody can play with me. They can't write that stuff, blues, boogie, ragtime, that's me. I've always said that if I don't improve every night, then you don't owe me nothing, but they always paid me.

Good-lookin' baby
Be my sweet little wife
Come live with me
Be my sweet little wife
You can drink and smoke, pretty mama
If you like that kind of life
My house is warm
Why, my gas is on
My rent is paid
I'll get you a maid
Come live me with me, baby
When I was a little boy
I used to run out in the back yard
And chase rainbows
When I was a little boy
I used to run out in the back yard
and chase rainbows
Now that I got to be a man
You see me standin' on the corner
Chasin' pantyhose
Love you, baby
Want you for myself
Love you, pretty baby,
Want you for myself
Goin' to buy me an automobile
With lights on it for you
And nobody else
You see I'm crazy

[*Stops playing.*] Nobody else does that but Alex.

White man get the blues
Take it to the river
and jump in and drown
Black man get the blues
Take a rockin' chair
to the river and set down

BIG BO THOMAS

June 20, 1926– ; interview by Alan Govenar and Jay Brakefield, 2003

I was born in Forney, Texas. My mother's name was Gladys Pratt. And my father's name was Willie Thomas. He was a sharecropper. And I stayed on the farm till I was twelve years old, and then I come to Dallas. My mother and father separated, and he come to Dallas, and I came with him. I grew up in East Dallas. I lived on Hill Avenue, down off of Hill Avenue. Way back in there, on the Eastside.

I went to public school in Forney, Texas, and then I went to Booker T. Washington High School. I didn't finish. I went to the eleventh grade, man, and I left and went in the army.

My grandfather played guitar. His name was Manuel Thomas. He played the blues, too. He played like Howlin' Wolf and them. Yeah, Blind Lemon, he played all that kind of stuff. Grandpa used to say he went to Bishop College years ago. His parents were slaves. A man knocked on my door about fifteen years ago and said, "You've got twenty-five acres of land." I said, "I ain't got no land nowhere." He said, "In Southeast Texas." I remember my grandpa said he had twenty-five acres. I didn't know it was the truth. He said, "You've got to sign this, man. We're going to drill for a gas well." I said, "Well, listen, where?" He said, "Well, your great-grandparents were slaves. The land was given to them. The government gave them 150 acres, but he just got 25 because he was a stepchild."

BIG BO THOMAS (LEFT) AND UNIDENTIFIED MAN, DALLAS, TEXAS, EARLY 1970s. COURTESY TEXAS AFRICAN AMERICAN PHOTOGRAPHY ARCHIVE.

I played saxophone. Tenor. I was fifteen years old when I started playing the saxophone. I went to music school. I took music from a private teacher. Mrs. Madam Pratt. Her husband used to be the principal of Booker T. Washington. His name was Mr. James Pratt. I took lessons from Madam Pratt for five years. She was a graduate of Boston Conservatory. She was a nice person. She tried to get me to take voice.

See, I copied off of Louis Jordan, playing my saxophone. I went to the Harlem Theater there on Ellum Street. And my first wife was asking me, "Why don't you buy you a horn, Bo?" That's before I went in the army and tried to blow like Louis Jordan. I got my horn, but I

GRAND OPENING OF THE ROSE ROOM, RED CALHOUN AND HIS ROYAL SWING KINGS, DALLAS, APRIL 1, 1943, DALLAS EXPRESS ADVERTISEMENT. COURTESY DALLAS BLUES SOCIETY.

JIMMY BELL AND THE BOMBSHELLS, ROSE ROOM, DALLAS, 1940s. COURTESY TEXAS AFRICAN AMERICAN PHOTOGRAPHY ARCHIVE.

went to music school, and I played things Louis Jordan played, and I played after Illinois Jacquet. We played lots of jazz, man, everybody: Stan Getz, Sonny Rollins. We played all kinds of music, but I had to stop playing the progressive jazz and start playing the blues because wasn't no money in it. I had all the crowd in Dallas, see. And so, all the jazz artists would come and sit in with me. Like Fathead Newman was doing that. And James Clay. There was some bad musicians, see, used to play around here with me. And Claude Johnson. And Leroy Cooper. He was with Ray Charles. He used to play with me.

Well, I started playing music in 1947 when I got out of the army. I had been in the army band, too. I went overseas, in the Netherlands. And we had a band on the post. We played in town. I went to the South Pacific, the Philippine Islands. I was under General MacArthur. I played some music. Sure, I played music there. I played some music everywhere. I played music in town. We'd have shows in the city of Manila.

Everybody started calling me Bo when I came to Dallas, so I said that was catching to the ear, it was more easy and catching to the ear. And when I started my dance band, everybody started calling me Bo. That's how I got the name Big Bo.

I first started out with a band—I first had a seventeen-piece band, and I couldn't get no jobs, so I cut on down to Big Bo and His Satisfied Four. And I went on from there for years, for about five years, and I changed it to Big Bo and His Satisfied Six. And then back in 1960, I started booking all them stars and recording and cut a record called "Big Bo's Twist" and the "Hully Gully," in the twist days. And it made a big one. That was Motown Records. And I started booking all them stars, superstars, such as Tina Turner, Johnnie Taylor, Al Green. I'm the first one ever brought him here to Dallas. And Sam and Dave, O. V. Wright, Little Junior Parker. And Buddy Ace and Billy Preston and Lowell Fulson. T-Bone Walker. Charles Brown. I booked them. I played with Nat "King" Cole, man.

I played with Li'l Son Jackson, back in 1947. He wrote this number R. L. [Griffin] sings, and Aretha Franklin put it—"Rock Me, Baby," "rock me all night long." We went out to play one night on the nineteenth of June, went to Mexia, and we had a packed house there. Well, he come out and said, "I ain't going to pay nobody tonight." He didn't pay me my money. So the next night, he come by to get me, and I left. I didn't go with him. And I went on my own. And I had to call him up. I got so big, man, I always have had one of the best bands in Dallas, and one of the biggest names to ever hit this city.

I had two bands. I was so popular, I had two bands right here in the city of Dallas. Big Bo No. 1 and Big Bo No. 2. And they would have a crowd everywhere they go, and I'd have one, too. And what I would do, I would take my horn and go over there and play one or two numbers and come back to my main band, see. That's what I done, man. And when I started booking them stars—I'm the first one that brought Tyrone Davis to Dallas.

I started my own record label in 1960. It was called Gayshel. I named the record company after my daughter. Her name was Gayle. And I used the first three letters. And my son was named Sheldon. And I used four letters of his name. I was living out there in NorthPark across Inwood Road and Lovers Lane. I'm the first one that ever moved out there when all the civil rights come in. And I moved out there. What I done, when I was making all that money with the big time, I found a guy out there by the name of Blair Real Estate. I said, "Go out there, man, and tell all those white people about the black folks moving in." Well, you know, they didn't want to be around us too much back then, and they started running. And so that's how I happened to get my home out there up on Inwood Road and Lovers Lane, that's where I was living, up in there. And was the first black ever moved out there. And my daughter went to Thomas Jefferson, because you had to go to school in the neighborhood where you lived. And she finished SMU. I sent her to college; she got her master's. I made a lots of money, man, back in the Sixties. Early Sixties, I was making from $250,000 to $400,000 a year. That's right here in Dallas, making that kind of money, right there in North Dallas. I had three clubs. Zanzibar, the Peacock Bar, and the Empire Room. Three clubs, yeah, the leading clubs in Dallas, back then, for blacks.

AARON "T-BONE" WALKER GOLFING, DALLAS, LATE 1940s.
COURTESY MARION BUTTS.

I started my first club in 1959. It was called the Zanzibar. What I done, I used to play at the Zanzibar for a man named Mr. Ferguson. He was the first one ever advertised me. He was black. And you know, I'll tell you another somebody I played for: Jack Ruby. He used to own the Las Vegas Club. Oh, he was nice. He was a gangster. You know what he was. He was all right. He taught me what I know about the club business. That's when I went in the club business. I could play with him after hours. Matter of fact, in the early days, I'd work every night. That's how popular I was. Seven nights a week, and we'd play three matinees and four after-hours. When I started playing the blues, I took over Dallas, man. I was hotter than a firecracker. The Zanzibar was located at 2401 Thomas Avenue. It was near Thomas and Leonard.

DEEP ELLUM, DALLAS, LATE 1940s.
COURTESY TEXAS/DALLAS HISTORY AND ARCHIVES DIVISION
DALLAS PUBLIC LIBRARY.

Then I bought the Empire Room. Howard Lewis ran the Empire Room. He used to be the big time. He was leasing the club from this Mrs. Smith. She was a black woman who owned the place, and he was leasing it from her. So I bought it from her. I think it was about '65,

FRANKIE LEE SIMS, "HEY LITTLE GIRL," ACE RECORDS 527. FRANKIE LEE SIMS, "WALKING WITH FRANKIE," ACE RECORDS 527.

somewhere in there. But what Howard Lewis had done, he was sending people down to stage a fight. He was promoting all the big-name stars back then, see, but I put him out of business. He was pulling my placards down. I'd have three or four hundred placards made every week, and I had them all over town. That's how I got so big, man. The black people didn't know how to advertise. And then I went to radio, fifty to sixty spots a week on the radio, see. KNOK and KKDA, too.

I retired in 1971. And I haven't done anything with music since. I had plenty money, man. I made all the money that could be made here in Dallas if you was black. I was the leadingest man, one of the biggest names ever to hit this city. My name, I tell you what: Dr. Anderson used to be here, and me. It was in the *New York Times*. We made more money than any black man in this city in my day; see what I'm talking about? In one night, see. And I booked all them: Gladys Knight. All them people, there, I had all them people, man. The "Monkey Time" man, Major Lance. Billy Preston and all them people. Billy Preston got to be big. One time, he begged me for a job. He got stranded here, and I wouldn't give him no job. He said, "Man, let me play the organ with you, Bo. I want to play with you." I said, "No, man, I already got an organ player." He said, "Fred Lowery can't play no organ." And he said, "I will record with you." Now think about what I missed. He left and went and recorded "Nothing from Nothing," and they still playing it. And he say, "I told you, man." But I missed him. He wanted to record with me, and I wouldn't hire him. Lots of artists I missed. I'm the one that brought Tyrone Davis to Dallas, too. I first got the Zanzibar. I changed the name of the Zanzibar around to the Delmonico Ballroom.

Ooh, look here, man, it was so many people over there in old North Dallas. It be just like after a holiday or something like that. After people go to take all them presents they don't want back after Thanksgiving and Christmas. And that's the way it were. There were so many people in North Dallas, lots of clubs over there in North Dallas. But what I would do, everybody would be where I were. You had your project over there. You had all of the blacks over there. So many people over there, it's pitiful. See, you got them freeways through there now, what messed up everything for North Dallas. But now they got them beautiful homes and things there, Fox and Jacobs and all that stuff. They took over.

I recorded and produced records for a lot of people. Fred Lowery for Chess Records. R. L. Griffin, I started his career for him. I made him a superstar. I was the first one ever hired R. L. Griffin. He used to come with The Corvettes out of East Texas. I went down in East Texas and saw them playing all down there. I told him who I was, and he was so excited. I said, "Looky here, I want to give you a new place." He come to Dallas, he worked for my band, then he went back and got his family. And he was living out here in South Dallas out there on East Grand and Ervay, down in there, where it's real, real ratty. That's where he was living when I got him. I don't know where he lives now. The last time I seen him, he was living back up here in Oak Cliff.

I made about seven or eight or maybe ten records, man, myself. No vocals, man. I wasn't thinking about that back then. I made instrumentals, and they all was hits. I recorded seven different records myself, see. Yeah, Big Bo. See, what I done, I changed the name. I put out the "Big Bo's Twist" back in the twist days. And that was number one. That's when I went with Berry Gordy at Motown. Yeah, see, I recorded for Al Cline. He was an A&R person for Berry Gordy. And he come here, and he wanted to record me. He heard about me. And I put out the "Big Bo's Twist." Boy, and that record was everywhere. That was the only one I done for Motown. I quit him because he didn't give me my money. That record was number one everywhere, man.

I got the name Big Bo and The Twisting Arrows because of the fellow that leased this record here, "Big Bo's Twist," to Motown. I got my contract, and I was on Motown Records. That was a big label. And see, he had leased the record to Motown, "Big Bo's Twist" and "The Hully Gully." And so, when it came out, I didn't even know I was on Motown, see. I was in the hospital. I got shot, got hurt and everything. That was way back yonder. And I was in the hospital for six months. Fellow named Aaron Klein came in. He put me with Motown Records. He said, "Why your record didn't do no good, man. But I'm going to give you a hundred dollars." I needed some braces because, see, I got shot in the head and I was paralyzed from the hips down. But I did. I was shot in the head by a jealous woman when I was asleep. I was paralyzed from the gunshot wound, yeah. That's what's wrong with me now, walking. Of course, my vision got back on me, too. I was blind for six months, totally blind. Doctor said I'd never see again. That was before I really got in big times. Now my vision is kind of bad, but I'm doing all right. I have a maid who comes in and helps me.

I stayed in Parkland Hospital six months. When I came out of the hospital, they told me to make my doors larger for my wheelchair. And I went in and my band was going down because I wasn't there as leader, see. The last job, the last night they were going on, I had to go to work on crutches. And then I built my name, got back there. And my name was so big, it was on KBOX, KLIF, interviewing me, all them stations, not only the black stations. And old Buddy Harris; remember him, used to be here? I used to play for him every Monday at the Cavalcade of Blues at the Longhorn Ranch. I was playing out there long years ago, me and Nat "King" Cole. I played with Nat "King" Cole, on the same show. Muddy

TWO UNIDENTIFIED CHILDREN, ABE AND PAPPY'S, DALLAS, 1950S. COURTESY TEXAS AFRICAN AMERICAN PHOTOGRAPHY ARCHIVE.

Waters, Little Walter, and Jimmy Reed, long time ago. I played on shows with Fats Domino, all them.

The doctor said I never would be able to walk. But I did. They said I'd never play my horn. I made him a liar. I tried and tried and tried and tried. And they said they were going to help me. I stayed in Parkland six months. That was in 1960. It was tough. But back in 1954, I had acid thrown in my face. Another jealous woman. I was sleeping. And I recovered from that.

Now, B. B. King, he wanted me to go with him. I played behind B. B. King out there at the Longhorn when it first opened up. And Jimmy Reed and all of them. B. B. King begged me to go on the road with my band after I was in business. I booked B. B. King at one of my clubs, at the Empire Room, and he begged me, said, "Bo, come go with me on the road." He begged me, and I said no. He come four or five times. "I want your band to back me. Man, you got a good band." I said, "No, man, I'm making too much money. You couldn't pay me enough money." And B. B. King is still going. He got the whites, too. That's why he's so big, see. He wanted the

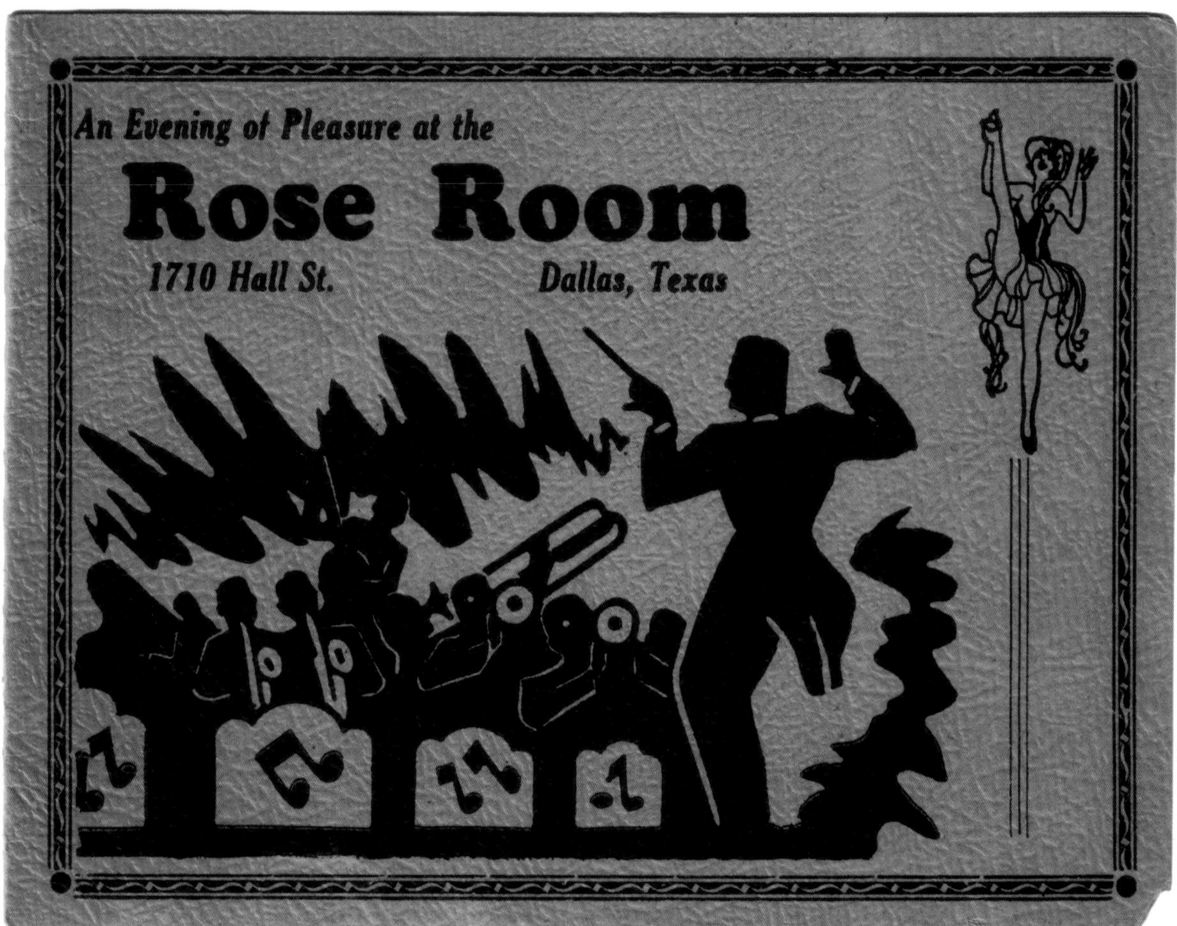

ROSE ROOM SOUVENIR PHOTO WALLET, 1940S. COURTESY TEXAS AFRICAN AMERICAN PHOTOGRAPHY ARCHIVE.

black field, but the white people, when they got him, that's when he made it. Ray Charles, the same thing, because it's more of y'all.

I'm going to tell you something about the race, too, what's happening here in a minute. You asked me how it was. Okay, I'm going to tell you how it was. All right. I used to play around in white clubs. And the boys was slipping around the corner with the white girls, too. We had all that stuff back then. And so, I had a bunch of white people coming over to the Zanzibar. And I had trouble with the police. Look here: "Say, boy. Where you meet all of them people, these white people coming in there?" That was in the Sixties. It happened right after Martin Luther King got killed. The same time. And he say, "Look, boy, where you meet all these white people?" And I said, "Look here, man, I'm a recording artist." "Don't get smart with me, boy." I say, "I'm a recording artist." "You getting smart?" "No, I'm not getting smart with you." "Where you meet all these white people?" And I say, "I'm a recording artist. They're playing my records on KLIF, every white station in town and every black station, every hour, two or three times an hour, they're playing my records. That's how I met them. And I used to play in white clubs." "Well, look here. You go back there, boy, and tell them white people to get up and get out of there. You don't want them in here."

The police said that to me. "You go back and tell them to get out of here." I said, "Look, I can't tell them that. They're free, man; that would be liable for a lawsuit." All right. They put me in the car, and they took me on out Pearl and went on over to Main Street. They took me down there. "Now what they doing down here for?" "Well, the chief want to talk to you." And when I got down there, they say, "This is Big Bo here. We going to put Big Bo in jail now or what?" He said, "No, the chief want to see him. I'll put him in jail when we get back." We went upstairs, and the chief said, "Look, Bo, we done told you. I'm the one told them guys what to tell you down there. And we don't want them white folks in there. They ain't nothing but a bunch of whores down there. And they're going to bring on trouble. And if you don't, boy, we're going to say you're bootlegging, we're going to say you're selling narcotics, we're going to say you're running a ring of prostitution, we're going to search everybody."

I said, "Okay." He said, "Don't get smart with me." I got a little smart, you know. "Don't you tell me that no more, boy. Get on out of here! And if you do it again, if you let them white folks in, and another thing: You can't have no black security no more. You got to pay." Wasn't but thirty dollars a night then. "We want three of our officers out there every night. And your black security, the only way they can work is they work under them." They sent three policemen. I had to pay them thirty dollars a night, every night. They had them out there where I wouldn't let the white folks in. Now that's what they told me, man. And that's what I had to do. Well, that's what I done. Aw, man, it was lots of racism in Dallas.

Don Robey [in Houston] and I done things together, and Rouseau, too. He had a buddy named Rouseau. And I played at his club. Man, I booked clubs; I booked stars, all down at Don Robey's place at the Bronze Peacock. I booked O. V. Wright, Joe Hinton. And I booked Buddy Ace. I booked all over Texas, Oklahoma, everywhere, man. I had things going here and things going there. I got so big I had to start going to the auditorium, and then I had to start going over to the State Fair Music Hall, and they made me have twenty policemen out there; that's what they do to black people when they're having fun. You have to pay the police to watch outside and everything. I had to pay twenty policemen. And I had so many people; I had Gladys Knight out there. She was playing in my club, but she was drawing so many people, I had to get a bigger place for her to play. . . . We had several out of the Fire Department, too, we had so many in there. "Look here, Bo, next time you come, we got to retire this here; we got too many people in here, Bo. The next time we come, we ain't going to give you no big ticket; we're going to put your black ass in jail." That's what they tell me. And Chess would press my records for me. And he done me crooked, too. My wife went up to California, and I had a record called "High Body" and he had put it up there, and I hadn't sent it up there. My wife said, "Bo, you got record number one up here in Los Angeles." I said, "I ain't sent no record out there." "Yes, it is." I said, "Well, tell the radio station man I said thank you, and who sent it?" He said, "Leonard Chess." See, that's what they were doing.

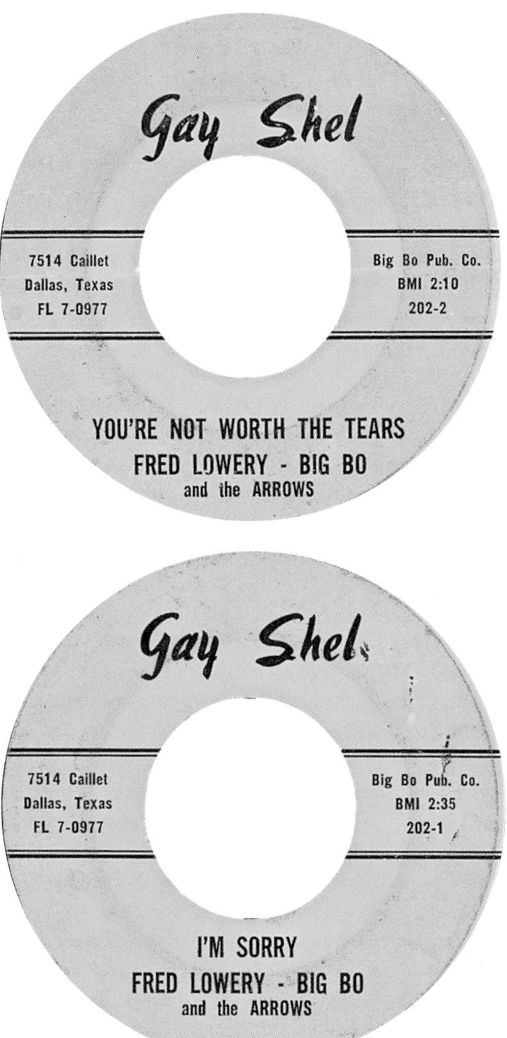

FRED LOWERY – BIG BO AND THE ARROWS, "YOU'RE NOT WORTH THE TEARS," GAY-SHEL 202-2. FRED LOWERY – BIG BO AND THE ARROWS, "I'M SORRY," GAY-SHEL 202-1.

What keeps you going is the right kind of food. I eat good now. I like ribs, beef, chicken. I eat all that stuff like that and I eat plenty of vegetables. See, I'm seventy-seven years old. Blues was my life, see. And another thing, it was good for me. Blues is nothing but just you sing what you feel. You make up songs as you go. It's a tough world out there.

WILLIE WILLIS

December 12, 1932–April 28, 2000; interview by Don O, 1998

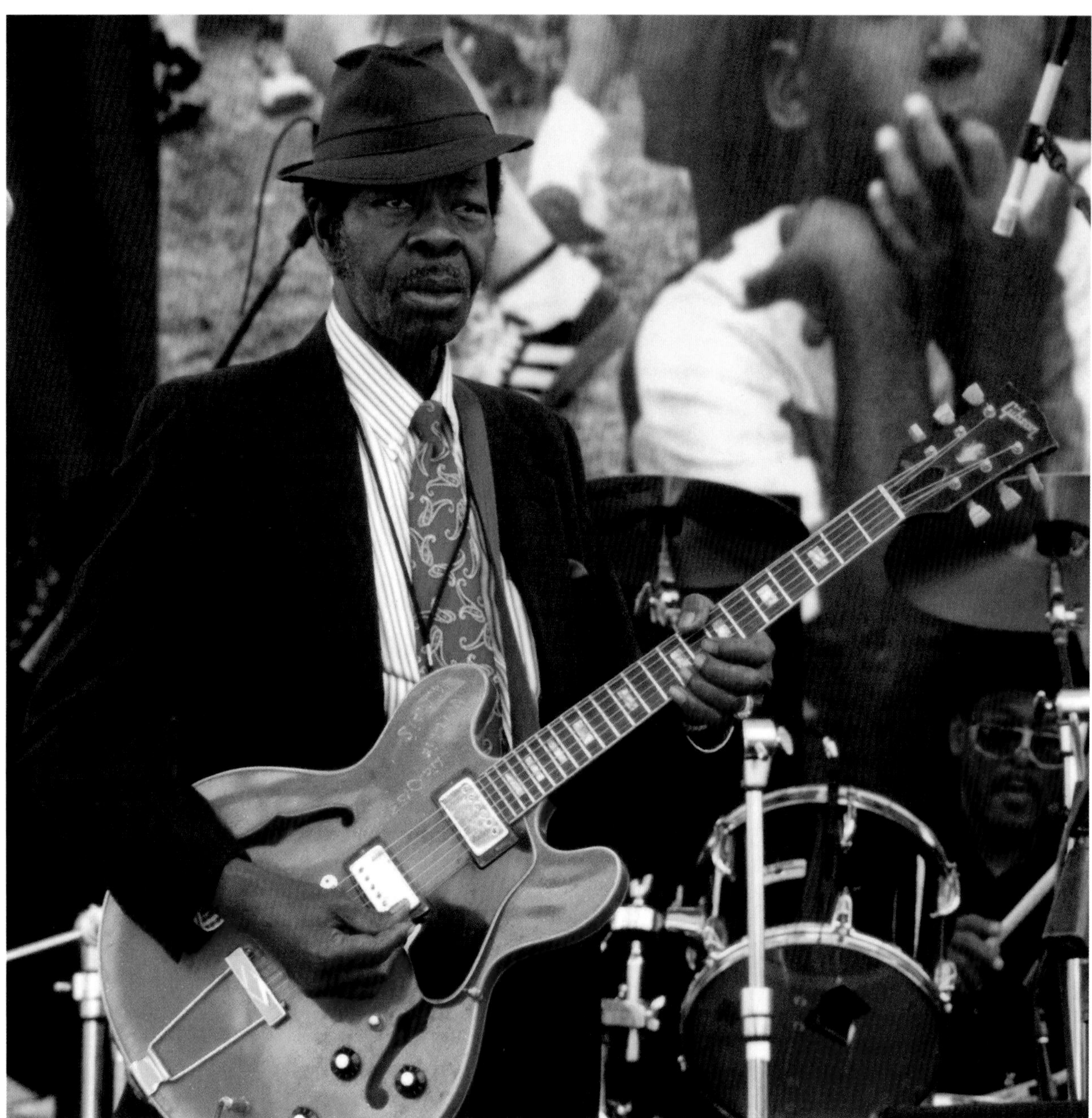

WILLIE WILLIS, DALLAS, CA. 1998.
PHOTOGRAPH BY DON O.

I'm from Fairfield, Texas. We had a big family of eleven. It was only my older sister and me that took up music, and she played for church all the time. My sister and my mom both wanted me to play with my sister in church. I came out wanting to play blues. I took the other side of it, so that was that.

I grew up listening to WSM in Nashville and John R's show on WLAC in Nashville. I was torn between two types of music at that time, hillbilly music and blues. Hank Williams Sr., was one guy then in the country field that I really loved. Not only was he a good songwriter and singer, he had one of the best country bands that has ever been. He had some great musicians. Louis Jordan was tops in the black music field back then.

The first blues song I learned how to play was an old John Lee Hooker song, came out in 1948, "Boogie Chillen." I started to carry my old guitar to school, sit out there at break time, and I'd have all the little girls gathered around me. I had all the peanut butter sandwiches I wanted to eat, if I trusted them! Anything I wanted, long as I played that one song. I was attracting so much attention out there my schoolteacher wrote a note to my mom. Not only did I get my behind tore up, I had to stop carrying my guitar. I was grounded, man! I missed all those peanut butter sandwiches! Those little girls just pulled up stakes and went on about their business.

Shortly after getting out of high school, me and another guy teamed up and were playing at a grocery store. We weren't playing nothing right. We were just hittin' a lick here and a lick there. It was a lot of fun.

Soon after that I went in the service and went over to Korea. I met a guy in the service named Grady Young. He was an incredible singer. Singing country music! He already played guitar. When I was in Seoul I bought a cheap guitar, something I wouldn't have to worry about when we would rotate back home. Grady was good on singing and covering himself while he sang, but he had no lead experience whatsoever. So that was my part. I wasn't much of a chord guy back then, but for notes I ran the guy crazy. Just about anything I heard I could play. He used me for the lead. We teamed up with some other guys—drums, piano, mandolin, bass—and played maybe four or five shows at the service club tent. They called us the Third Division Players. We were in the same division as Audie Murphy. Right up the road they had American Forces Radio. They heard us playing out there one day. The captain started letting us have a fifteen-minute show on Friday. We got so good they gave us thirty minutes. Then we went to playing for the officers' club, and just stayed busy. We busted up when our hitch was over, and I came back to Dallas and Fairfield.

I kind of laid low for a while. I went around to hear other players back here, but I was scared to get up there with most of them. They were bad back then. West Dallas and Central Tracks were terrible places. I got to meet guys like Li'l Son Jackson. I had the utmost admiration for him. I didn't like the way he played guitar, though. A lot of players used those clamps [capos] back then. I sure liked all his records, though.

I had about three things on my mind that I was going to try to do. Follow up with the guitar, or I had cousins with funeral homes and they wanted me to be a mortician, and I had my eye set on a barbers' course. First, I finished the course at Fairfield Barber College. The year I got my license, 1955, I came to Dallas for good. There was so much red tape in being a barber, there wasn't very much demand, and so I gave up on that. I could not handle working in that funeral home. My nerves just weren't that good. So there was another job I blowed. I went down to the Adolphus Hotel and ended up working there for nineteen years. I started as a dishwasher and ended up as the kitchen steward. Went from the bottom to the top. I was playing a little music on Sunday nights and sitting in with other bands. I teamed up with Frankie Lee Daniels. He had a daughter that played organ, and he played guitar. He had a lady vocalist and a male singer.

I got to see and play a lot of music around this time. Frankie Lee Sims, Jimmie Wilson, Bo Thomas, Peppermint Harris. I did a million shows with Lowell Fulson, T-Bone Walker, Johnnie Taylor, Joe Simon, Mercy Baby, a few with Albert King, and a whole lot of shows with Freddie King. Mercy Baby was an incredible singer and one of the best drummers that has ever been. He was playing drums for me over on Second Avenue at the Famous Door just before his wife killed him.

Around this time I started working on my own vocals. It takes a lot of self-confidence to convince yourself to sing. You have to satisfy yourself first, then you can improve yourself from there. The more you sing, the better you can control your voice. It takes at least as much work to learn how to sing right as it does to learn how to play right. Stage fright takes some time to get used to. I'd get butterflies in a minute.

WILLIE WILLIS, DALLAS, CA. 1998.
PHOTOGRAPH BY DON O.

I made one single record on the Ride label in 1956, an answer off of the original "Black Night," it's called "Good Black Night." I didn't get nothing out of it. I just wanted to get a record out there, that's all. Wrote that with Fats Washington.

My people were flabbergasted that I really did learn how to play. I went and played at my old high school after I had my record out, and everything changed around for me. Makes you feel good to go home and people have good things to say about ya. I carried my mom to the grocery one time, and to have her, when she used to whup my tail and make me put that guitar up, going around in the store, as she shopped, telling everyone in the store that I was her oldest son and a musician, that made me feel so good, that she finally had accepted it. She wanted me to go the other way, but I didn't.

I was playing down at the Prohibition Room way back before the West End boomed up down there. Before that I played at the Cave on Greenville and University, and St. Christopher's at Park Lane and Greenville. I was getting fifty to seventy-five dollars a night and working three or four nights a week, while working at the hotel, too. I was doing good. That was money back in them days.

In 1989 I cut an LP for Soul Staff Records called "Blues Food for the Soul." I wound up going overseas to Amsterdam, Holland, off that LP. They were selling 45s over there for five and six dollars a copy. They were gettin' twenty-five and thirty dollars for the LPs. I signed a whole lot of autographs over there. They were black-marketing my music over there making all the money and I wasn't getting none! I got thrown to the dogs on that one!

I made my last CD for Trix, "Down Home In Dallas," in 1994. We did that over at Audio Dallas here in town. I just got through cutting a bunch of new songs for Fedora Records in April. I've been listening to that tape over and over, and I think that's the best one I've done yet. We're also trying to work out a trip to Brazil right now.

Blues has taken hold fast. Faster than a lot of players realize. It's going to continue to get better. I tell you why. The people done got the feeling of it now, and they like what they feel. They gonna promote it to the highest. Used to be, there was only one or two places that were buying blues overseas. Now, they are selling it anywhere. The more they hear it, the more they like, the more they buy. The coverage and promotion is catching up to rap and the other stuff out there. I feel real good about where the blues is right now. There's too many people wanting to know if I'm tied up with a label right now. I'm getting all kind of feedback. It sure feels good.

I done struggled to take everything they can dish out to me. The good Lord let me live through it, and here I am. I learned how to get along with people, and I maintained that through the whole of my lifetime. When I first started playing I would get four dollars a night. All the other guys would drink back then. I never drank. They would spend that money, and all I had to pay for was some coffee or soda water. I just want everyone to know I am very grateful to the man up yonder for putting up with me this long. For Him, letting something decent and nice come out of this long music thing I've been dealing with.

LONGHORN BALLROOM, DALLAS, 1984.

PHOTOGRAPH BY ALAN GOVENAR.

VERNON GARRETT

January 18, 1933– ;
interview by Don O, 1998

From 1986 to 1998, Vernon Garrett called Dallas home, and he returns several times a year, often performing at R. L. Griffin's Blues Palace No. 2.

I was born in Omaha, Nebraska. I first became interested in music through the gospel singers who came through town when I was a little boy. Seeing them made me want to sing. In Sunday school every week Deacon Robinson would ask one of the children to sing a song to start the lesson. All the other kids were ashamed. Well, I wasn't and was always the first one to hold up my hand. That gave me a chance to sing just about every Sunday in Sunday school.

Other kids I went to school with at that time were from singing backgrounds. We would get together on the back steps at Tech High and harmonize. Eventually we formed our own little gospel group. That's how I first got started. We got pretty good and opened for some of the professional gospel groups who came through Omaha. I was fifteen at the time. The group broke up, and I joined another group called The Southern Wonders. Claude Jeter of The Swan Silvertones heard me when I opened for them and The Soul Stirrers. For a short time I was with The Swan Silvertones. Then I left and went into the service. I was aboard the USS *Sarsfield* in the Korean War. We worked all over the Atlantic and as far as Guam. We worked with the first U.S. atomic sub, the USS *Nautilus*, out of Key West, Florida. All around Cuba, Guantanamo Bay, where the rough waters are.

After I got out, guys I had known, like Lou Rawls and Sam Cooke, were recording. I stayed in Omaha for about three months after I got out of the service and joined a vocal group called The Mixers. We were starting to get pretty good, and I thought maybe they'd like to go to the West Coast and try to get something started out there. My sister was in Omaha on vacation and would take us back with her. They wouldn't go, but I did.

In Los Angeles the hot talent show at that time was run by Johnny Otis at the Club Oasis every Thursday night. Guys like Ted Taylor, Johnnie Taylor, Johnny Morrisette, all kinds of folks were competing in that show. The prizes were fifteen, twenty, and twenty-five dollars. When I first started appearing, I won. I won so much that comedian Leroy Skillet told me I should turn pro. I said, "How do you do that?" They ran a talent show on Wednesday and Thursday at a club called the Brass Rail. He started introducing me to do guest numbers instead of the talent show, and it began to grow from there. That's how I started singing on my own. From there I met a group called The Sliders. They needed a lead singer, and I joined their group. We became a very well-known group in L.A., along with The Hollywood Flames, The Penguins, The Fortunes, and other groups. We did a recording called "Love Is Like a Mountain" for George Garabinia. Gene Mumford hired away our tenor for Billy Ward and The Dominoes. That was the end of our group, and I was back on my own again.

I was working as a solo vocalist when I met my wife, Jewel. She wanted to sing with me, but I continued as a solo for a while. Finally, she went on a talent show and won second prize. That was my first chance to really hear her sing, and she handled it very well. That's when we became the team of Vernon and Jewel. We started working together in a little club in Compton, California, every weekend. People paid fifty cents to get in. I was playing drums and singing, and another guy was singing with us, King Solomon. They liked us so well I got off the drums and we really became a full-fledged team. Illinois Jacquet, the jazz saxophonist, owned the Network recording label and heard about us through his brother-in-law. He had his brother Russell put us under contract and take us in the studio. The first song we recorded was "You're Going to Be Paid for the Way You Treated Me."

The first place it was a hit was in San Francisco. Jewel's brother and sister were there, and they told us we needed to come up there because the record was doing well. We got us a little trailer, put it behind our car, and hit the highway. We had hooked up with a very good guitar player named Claude High who had been stranded down in Los Angeles. By the time we got to the Bay Area, he had our stuff down and fit with us just like a glove. We were a team. Times were tough at first. One time, we had barely enough gas to get across the Bay Bridge.

Jewel would steer while Claude and I pushed the car for a few blocks. Then we drove the last few blocks to arrive in front of the club. We went through some things there. It's funny when I think of it now. Jewel was a whiz on a sewing machine. She made her own gowns and kept me and Claude dressed.

Finally, we did a guest shot at Slim Jenkins's club in Oakland, and that was the beginning. Slim hired us for Friday and Saturday nights. He provided a lady on organ and drums, and paid us seventy-five dollars a night. He said if the crowd got better he'd give us a raise. Jewel, the guitar player, and I split it even, twenty-five dollars apiece. We had a full sound with that guitar player and the lady on the B3. People started coming, and he started booking us to open for the big road acts like Bobby Bland, Etta James, and other big acts. People liked us, and we were riding in Cadillacs and Lincoln Mercurys! Eventually, Kent Records heard us and put us under contract. That's where we made the male/female version of "Lonely Lonely Nights." We sold about 80,000 copies in Chicago alone. We did very well for several years together. We were so successful we even built our own thirty-two-unit apartment building.

Then Jewel got sick with breast cancer. She did well after the operation, but eventually the cancer spread to her lungs and she passed away. I was so despondent I stopped my career. I just drove back between L.A. and San Francisco and drank a lot. I wasn't broke, I wasn't looking for anything, I just didn't know what to do. I was back in San Francisco in the Pickwick Hotel downtown. I don't know if I was dreaming, had a vision, or what. I felt I was very much awake. It was my wife. I buried her in a turquoise blue gown, and there she was. She asked me what was I doing there when God gave me the talent to sing, and I knew that's what she wanted me to do. That was it. I went downstairs, checked out, got in my car, stayed on the highway for about an hour, cried, got myself together, and drove back into L.A.

That weekend I walked into a club where Charlie Green had a five-piece orchestra, and a guy was singing the very song my wife had sung on that talent show. I asked the piano player if I could sit in, and Charlie Green hired me that same night. That's when I started back to work. The return of Vernon Garrett, all by myself. Before that it had always been Vernon and Jewel. I was still under contract to Kent Records. They put me with Richard Parker and had him produce a session with me. Maxwell Davis did the production after that until Kent records went out of business. After that I did some on my own. I freelanced two albums with Jerry White. "Love Me Right" and "Johnnie Walker Red" did real well for me. He never paid me any royalties. Told me it didn't sell. Never even sent me a statement. I know "Stranger in My Bed" did well in Texas. I keep up with all the record shops, Mr. Blues and all the others, so I was familiar with how it was doing. There was no way for me to keep an account, so I stopped fooling with him.

Al Bell, longtime Stax producer, also had me on his ICA label. Monk Higgins found a song for me, "I'm at the Crossroads, I Got a Choice to Make," written by jazz guitarist Freddie Robinson. At the time I was at a crossroads myself. My girlfriend wanted to know if I was going to stay with her or go back to my new wife. I really liked that song. It took us about twelve hours to cut it, but when we were done we had a good record. It started happening in the last part of 1978 and went on into 1979 and it's still going on. That's the song most people know me by and the one they want to hear. It did great in Chicago, St. Louis, all over. Made the Top 20 in *Jet*. That was my biggest seller. I'm still working behind that record.

After moving to Dallas, I signed with Ichiban. There's more work here. In Los Angeles I was considered local, and it was pretty much L.A. and San Francisco. Dallas, Fort Worth, Tyler, Marshall, Oklahoma City, Austin, San Antonio, Midland are all in easy reach here. A lot of guys are working this circuit, so I came down here and checked it out for a couple of weeks and then called my wife and told her to start packing for Texas. I was here in Dallas from 1986 until January of 1998. I've been back in L.A. since then and am now in the process of moving back to Dallas. I leased a club out there from a TV star we all know, but she was very hard to work with. We were paying her $7,000 a month plus what we spent on liquor and entertainment. During the rainy season it was raining in the club! We had Little Milton in there, wall to wall, sold out completely, and we had to put buckets out to catch all the rain coming in the roof. She wouldn't fix the roof or kitchen or anything. I lost a lot of money and had to back out of that. Better to quit before it put us in the soup line.

So now I'm back on the road to work. My wife, Doris, sings in church and she joins me onstage sometimes.

She made her debut here in Dallas back in October at R. L.'s Blues Palace. My contract with Ichiban is about up. I have only done three albums in seven years so they are behind on producing me. I haven't been pushing them or anything. I haven't pursued another label because I have been very happy with what Ichiban has done for me with the European market. All the other companies I had been with, I had never made it across the water. They got me quite a lot of work in the European market, and that helped me a lot. I played a hotel chain in Switzerland for three months, the first time I ever went. Working seven nights a week in the winter. People would ski all day and then come down to the lounge and listen at the blues in the evening. I did three weeks of one-nighters in Italy. The greatest audience I have performed for was in Japan. They were singing my material! That was strange. They were really familiar with my music.

I consider myself a rhythm and blues, ballad, and blues singer. Back when I was doing talent shows I was doing Top 40 stuff. The only gospel I have recorded was that one with The Swans. I write every so often. When an idea comes to me I'll write a song, but mostly I depend on other songwriters. I haven't had much chance to record my own stuff yet. "Doors of My Heart" on Too Hip to Be Happy is one of mine.

The Moore Brothers have been my band for about eight years. They've been over to Europe with me, too. They're good guys. I first met them here in Dallas at the Cowboy Lounge. They had been playing gospel and weren't too familiar with the blues, but they were willing to learn. We were rehearsing four or five nights a week in the guitar player's garage. We got tickets from the police because the neighbors were trying to get us to stop. We kept at it, and finally they found out we were recording and on the radio. Now the yard is full of folks coming to hear us play! Now they're fans instead of enemies!

I'm looking forward to a few more years in the recording business. I'm alive and well, and the public can look forward to some good new material from me soon.

AL "TNT" BRAGGS

May 23, 1938–December 3, 2003; interview, 1987

AL "TNT" BRAGGS, PEACOCK RECORDS PUBLICITY PHOTOGRAPH, 1960S. COURTESY AL BRAGGS.

AL "TNT" BRAGGS, 1960S. COURTESY AL BRAGGS.

I started out playing hillbilly. I listened to Ernest Tubb, Hank Snow. I'm particularly fond of Lefty Frizzell. I'm a pretty good yodeler. I loved all the yodeling cowboys. When I was real young I used to get behind the radio and take the back off and sing through the radio like I was on the air. Then I'd get a broom and pretend I was playing the guitar.

My mom taught me how to sing spirituals. First she taught me how to sing the lead. Then she would switch and she would sing lead, and she taught me how to harmonize. From there I joined this spiritual group and I started singing spirituals. We idolized The Soul Stirrers, and that naturally meant Sam Cooke. After Sam Cooke, we started listening to Bobby Bland, B. B. King, and Little Junior Parker because we could get Duke records regular here, Houston, Texas, being somewhere down the street.

Don Robey owned the whole thing, Buffalo Booking Agency, Peacock Records, Duke, BackBeat, SureShot, Songbird. You know, he had an incredible array of spiritual singers, where he really got his business started. He had The Dixie Hummingbirds, The Five Blind Boys, The Mighty Clouds of Joy, all of the biggest. I could sing like them, but by this time I was more interested in blues.

All of my life I've been able to imitate people, and my songs were Bobby Bland, B. B. King, The Five Royals, some Drifters. I was working at the Golden Duck across from Pappy Dad's Barbecue. That's when North Dallas was hot. We had the State Theater and all that stuff, Pappy Dad's Barbecue. Thomas Avenue and Hall Street. This is when North Dallas was *the* part of town. The Green Parrot was in North Dallas. When I first heard about the Green Parrot, it was owned by George Parker, upstairs on the corner of Thomas and Hall.

I was playing for Elmore at the Golden Duck, after hours, and what Elmore would do was, whenever there would be an act in town at the auditorium or at the Longhorn [Ballroom], he would go by and get everybody to go by his club, all the entertainers, and have them make the announcement for whatever reason. And they would all come by, and he'd get me to sing these people's songs.

There was a big show in town, Jackie Wilson, Little Willie John, Sam Cooke, and they came over. Elmore [Harrington] wanted them to go on stage, but they wouldn't. So Elmore came over to me and said, "Al, start off with Little Willie John." I started off with Little Willie John's "You Better Leave My Kitten Alone." And then I did "Let's Go Steady" by Sam Cooke, and they wouldn't budge. They were standing over by a little round table set up for them with drinks, girls. Then I did Lloyd Price's "Have You Ever Had the Blues?" And every time I did a song, one of these guys would bump the other and laugh at it. "Hey, he really got you down." Then Elmore said, "Do 'Danny Boy'!" Jackie Wilson's "Danny Boy." Now I'm known for doing this song. All of my life I've been doing "Danny Boy." I started singing "Danny Boy," and in the middle of that song, Jackie Wilson jumped straight up, pulled me up from the keyboards, and said, "C'mon, we're going to sing this together."

After that, the owner backed me to form my own group. Al Braggs and The Organizers. Well, we played around town, was the house band at the Empire Room, all the clubs. Sometimes we'd play three gigs, a matinee on Sunday from three to seven. Then we'd have an hour to go and set up and hit it from eight to twelve. And then we'd have another hour to go set up again and play after hours from one to four. In two days, we'd do six gigs. That takes a toll, making big money, twenty-five or thirty dollars apiece.

By me playing at the after-hours places, Bobby would come by, him and B. B. And oh, I could sound just like Bobby, still can to this day. He'd come by, and I'd sing all his stuff. So one night he told me. He said, "How would you like to record?" And I said, "Fine."

He said, "Well, next time I come, I'm going to bring Don Robey" to the after-hours place where I played, the Golden Duck, for Elmore Harrington.

Sure enough, four or five months later—Bobby used to come about six times a year. Well, the next time Bobby came in, he brought Robey in. Here I am. Don D. Robey. This man is a legend. This is the man is the creator of Big Mama Thornton, "You Ain't Nothin' But a Hound Dog." There's where Johnny Ace was made. And all these spiritual singers. And Robey looked like a white boy all his life, and he took advantage of that. He didn't pretend to be white, but if you thought it, if you didn't know any better, you wouldn't know from him. He was shrewd.

So he came in and said, "Are you Al?"

I said, "Yeah."

He says, "Bobby told me that you sing good."

"Well, I try to."

"I'm going to be around for a while, and I want to hear you sing."

I said, "Okay."

So he sits down, and I go into it. I knew it was coming. I was really prepared for this. I did all of Bobby, B. B., I did everybody and showed him that I could do all kinds of stuff. Back then it was all right to copy somebody's style. So after the show, he comes up and says, "How would you like to record?"

"Hey, I'd love it."

He says, "I'll tell you what to do. You give me a time and you be down in Houston at such-and-such time and I'll record you."

When the time came, he said, "I'm going to Chicago and I'll come through Dallas and pick you up, and we'll go on to Chicago and I'll record you."

I couldn't believe it. During this time I also had the opportunity to go see Mr. Berry Gordy at Motown. This girl, Joyce Coleman, who worked at the Golden Duck, she had a direct contact with him. But I elected to go with Don Robey. Berry Gordy was not the man he is today. Robey had more going for him. He had all these big stars, Gatemouth Brown, Junior Parker. I wasn't going to turn this down.

AL "TNT" BRAGGS AND BOBBY "BLUE" BLAND, LONGHORN BALLROOM, DALLAS, 1984. PHOTOGRAPH BY ALAN GOVENAR.

Mr. Robey came to Dallas and had Mr. George Parker bring me to Love Field. I board the plane and we go to Chicago. When I get there, they put me with Big Willie Dixon, bass player, still playing that upright bass, and he is the producer of my first record in 1959. The tune they gave me, I didn't think fit me, and that's how I came up with "I Don't Think I Can Make It." On the other side was "An Angel." And that tune came out, and it took off immediately for me.

Then there's some talk about Bobby Bland and Junior Parker splitting up. And someone calls from New Orleans wanting to book Bobby Blue Bland. So Evelyn Johnson at the Buffalo Booking Agency tells him, "I'll tell you what I'll do. If you take a date on Al Braggs, then we'll give you a date on Bobby."

"Who? I don't know no Al Braggs."

She says, "Al Braggs is dynamite. He's going to turn flips. He dances, he sings, and he's dynamite. Tell you what: You take a date on Al Braggs and we'll give you a date on Bobby and Junior later on." Reluctantly, he takes the date and the man forgets my name. All he remembers is that I'm dynamite. So when I get to New Orleans to play the date, I got three days. I see "Mr. Dynamite. TNT from Dallas." This is on the marquee. I say, "Oh, somebody else is here from Dallas." Then I see, "Plus Miss TNT, the dancer." Oh, this is his wife. That's what I'm thinking.

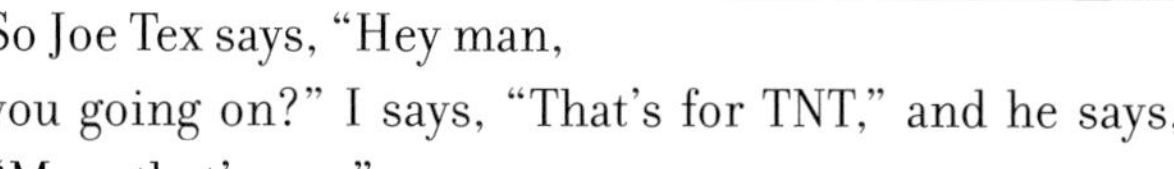

So on that same show was Joe Tex, Joe Hinton, Al Toussaint was the bandleader over the musicians. All the way up to show time I was looking for TNT from Dallas, and then I was introduced: "And now ladies and gentlemen a star from Dallas, TNT!" So Joe Tex says, "Hey man, you going on?" I says, "That's for TNT," and he says, "Man, that's you."

That's how I became TNT. I did "I Pity the Fool," and I turned a flip off the stage, I was almost falling, and just fell off into a split and just came up into something. I screamed, I crawled on the tables. And the next day the reviews said, "TNT is really TNT."

From there I went back to the company, and Don Robey said, "We'll have to do a record on that." And I guess a good year or two passed before I came up with the song "Take a Look at Me, I'm Doing the TNT." It became so popular, I liked it.

In 1961 Junior Parker and Bobby Bland were split up. When they split, the band went with Bobby, and they gave Junior another band. So they said, "Who do you want, Junior?" and he says, "Joe Hinton." And Bobby says, "Give me that kid out of Dallas." So they called me, and I got to join Bobby in Indianapolis.

One time, about a year later, we were in Chicago, and I wrote my first song for Bobby. I'm a night person and I always carry around a little tape recorder to get down my ideas. Well, our rooms were next to each other, and I get this idea around three in the morning, and I call Bobby and wake him up. I told him, "I've got this wonderful tune." He said, "Who is this?"

ABOVE: LONGHORN BALLROOM, DALLAS, 1984.
PHOTOGRAPH BY ALAN GOVENAR.

"This is Al."

"Boy, go to bed and call me in the morning."

"Oh, no, Blue. Just listen to it right now." So I sung it, beating on the table, "Love and affection, a heart so true. I'm yours for the asking. . . . When you need a good loving . . ."—all that.

Bobby says, "Okay, call me in the morning."

The next day it wasn't any better. Bobby just did not like the song. He says, "I hated it, Al, and calling me at three o'clock in the morning didn't help it none."

So I showed it to Don Robey, and he says, "How much do you want for it?" And I sold the song, which was named "Call on Me," for $300. Well, Robey immediately decided to name Bobby's new album *Call on Me*. That was a hard lesson. I sold the song, and that's all I got out of it. That was one of Bobby's biggest hits.

Then I wrote another song for Sam Cooke, but he died before he could record it. So Bobby says, "I'll record it," and he gave it to Joe Scott. He was the arranger, who coached and taught Bobby. Joe Scott says, "Mr. Robey, we need to add strings." And they did, and the song, "Share Your Love," came out in 1963.

One night we were playing the Regal Theater in Chicago, and Aretha Franklin said she loved the song. She would stand in the wings and listen to Bobby sing "Share Your Love." And Aretha Franklin called me over and said, "Can I record that record?" I thought she was kidding, and a year or two later, she did it. And when it came out, it really took off. But I never did receive any royalties for the song.

I stayed with Bobby until 1965, 1966, and then I went out on my own. He understood, but the company didn't like it. Bobby told me, "If you don't make it, you can always come back to me." But Don Robey, Evelyn Johnson, they didn't see it. So Evelyn says, "If you're going to go out and die, I may as well go out and book you." And she sent out a little flier and she didn't think anything was going to happen, and I got three months of dates.

Between 1959 and 1969 I had nine records released on Peacock. The last song I had was "I Like What You're Doing to Me." That came after "That's a Part of Loving

COMEDIAN HI-FI WHITE, LONGHORN BALLROOM, DALLAS, 1984. PHOTOGRAPH BY ALAN GOVENAR.

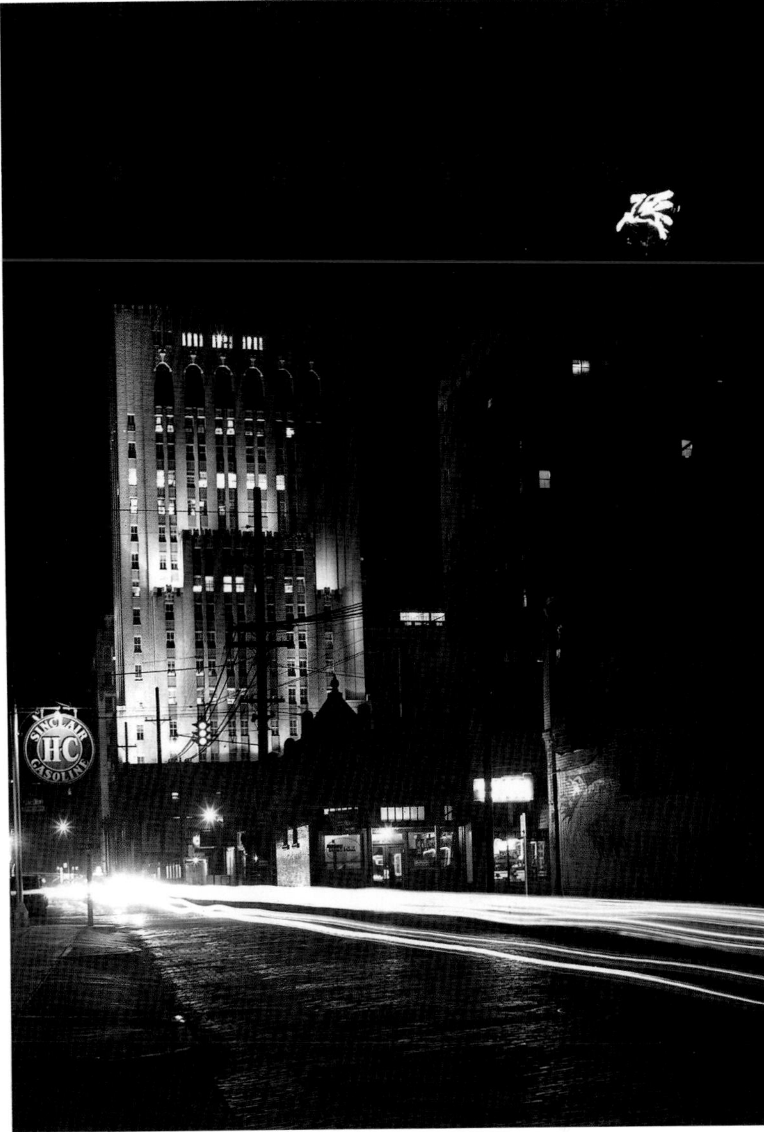

DALLAS, 1942, PHOTOGRAPH BY ARTHUR ROTHSTEIN. COURTESY LIBRARY OF CONGRESS.

You." I cut "Cigarettes and Coffee," "I Don't Think I'm Going to Make It," "We Belong Together," "The Earthquake," "Take a Look at Me, I'm Doing the TNT," "Joy to My Soul," "Chase Some Tomcat." Then I recorded about five or six that were never released. What hurt me so bad was that they took their time. If I got a release a year . . . the only ones that got good releases were Junior Parker and Bobby Bland. Junior was big; everything Elvis had was done first by Junior. Elvis's songs read like Junior Parker's, like "Train I Ride," "Drivin' Wheel," "Look on Yonder Wall," "Barefoot Rock."

Finally, I leave the company in 1969, and then I started working with Angus Wynne at his club called Soul City and with his company, Showco. So after a while, they asked me about "Share Your Love," and I told them that I never got any royalties. So they said they wanted to sue on my behalf, and won, but I didn't find out until I talked to Evelyn Johnson. They had to pay me all the back royalties.

Z. Z. HILL

September 30, 1935–April 27, 1984; interview by Jim O'Neal, June 26, 1982

(courtesy *Living Blues*)

Z. Z. HILL, DALLAS, MID-1970s. PHOTOGRAPH BY GEORGE KEATON. COURTESY TEXAS AFRICAN AMERICAN PHOTOGRAPHY ARCHIVE.

Beginning in 1982, Z. Z. Hill's "Down Home Blues" held a spot on the *Billboard* charts for ninety-two weeks. The success of this song, released on the Malaco label, signaled the resurgence of rhythm and blues and has become one of the best-selling blues ever. However, aside from the title cut, few of the songs are actually blues. Like Johnnie Taylor, Hill earned his reputation as a soul singer who performed to a disco beat for Columbia Records in the 1970s.

Born in Naples, Texas, Arzell "Z. Z." Hill began his career by singing in the choir at the Gethsemane Baptist Church and in a gospel quintet called The Spiritual Five. Following his graduation from high school in 1953, he moved to Dallas with an uncle. He continued to sing in local church choirs, though he also started working in small clubs, performing popular tunes by B. B. King and Bobby Bland. His debut single, "You Were Wrong," on M.H., a San Diego–based label founded by his older brother Matt Hill, made it to the *Billboard* pop charts for a week in 1964. Z. Z. then signed with the Kent label, and later recorded for Atlantic, United Artists, Malaco, and Columbia.

In an interview with Jim O'Neal in *Living Blues,* Hill identified Sam Cooke as his most important influence. For more than twenty years, Hill recorded as a soul singer on Kent, Columbia, and United Artists. In 1980, he signed with Malaco, and achieved his greatest commercial success. "It was a time for the blues to come back," Hill recalled, "after all that disco." The phenomenal sales of "Down Home Blues" was a testament to Hill's sensitivity to the evolving tastes of his audience and to the promotional prowess of Dave Clark at Malaco. In his next album, Hill proclaimed, "I'm a Blues Man," but his career ended unexpectedly a short time later. Z. Z. Hill died in April 1984 from a blood clot, the result of an auto accident two months earlier.

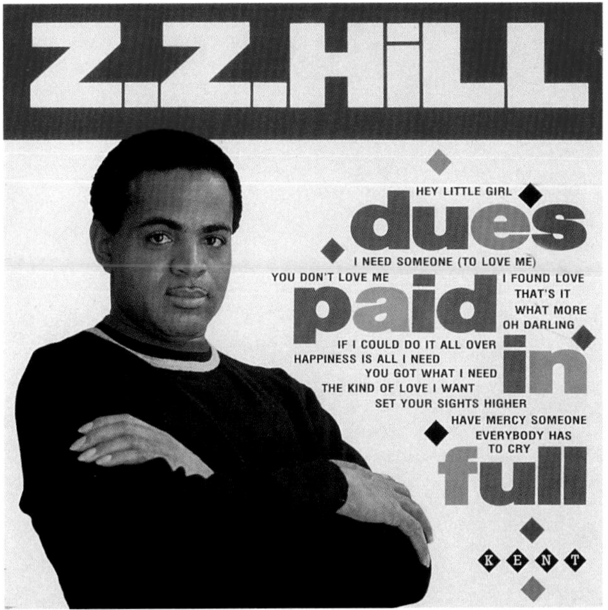

Z. Z. HILL, *DUES PAID IN FULL*. KENT 018.

BOBBY PATTERSON, DALLAS, 1960S.

COURTESY TEXAS AFRICAN AMERICAN PHOTOGRAPHY ARCHIVE.

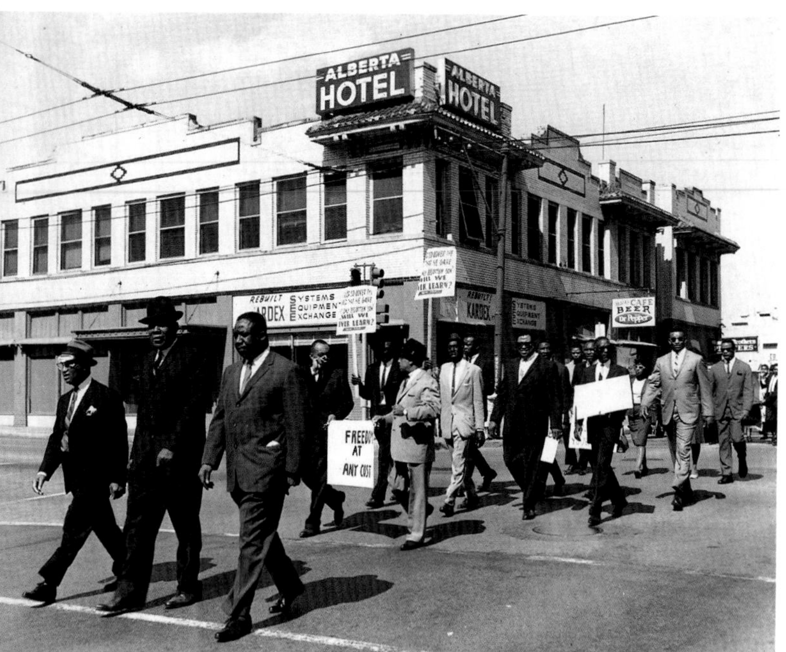

NAACP PICKET. FRONT ROW: (LEFT TO RIGHT), C. JACK CLARK, TRAVIS CLARK, ROOSEVELT JOHNSON; SECOND ROW: C. B. BUNKLEY, UNIDENTIFIED, GEORGE ALLEN; THIRD ROW: (RIGHT) TONY DAVIS, PETTIS NORMAN; FIFTH ROW: FRANK CLARK. DALLAS, 1965. COURTESY MARION BUTTS.

We got just about all of them [radio stations] across the country playing the blues. In all the major cities. Every city across the country is playing it but Dallas, Texas. My hometown! Dallas, Texas, and that's home for me.

I don't think they have anything personal against me, you know, as an artist, or even so to speak as to be a homeboy from Dallas. Because there was another group came out of Dallas and went solid gold. Yarbrough and Peoples, they're from Dallas. So I don't think it's just that. I really don't know what it is. I just think they refuse to play the blues.

I have always been labeled a blues singer: "Aw, he sing blues. Ha, ha, he sing the blues." You know? But I've always did a lot of contemporary stuff that wasn't blues, and a lot of ballads, and of course I wasn't too successful with it, doing those type of things. But I'm kinda versatile when it comes down to recording and singing, yeah. I did a little country and western, on the first album on Malaco. "I'm So Lonesome I Could Cry," by Hank Williams. But it just depends on what people like and what they can get into.

I like what the people like. I can get into what the people are into. If they really get into Z. Z. doing this or doing that, you know, I'm comfortable with it.

JOE "LITTLE JOE BLUE" VALERY

September 23, 1934–April 22, 1990; interview, 1987

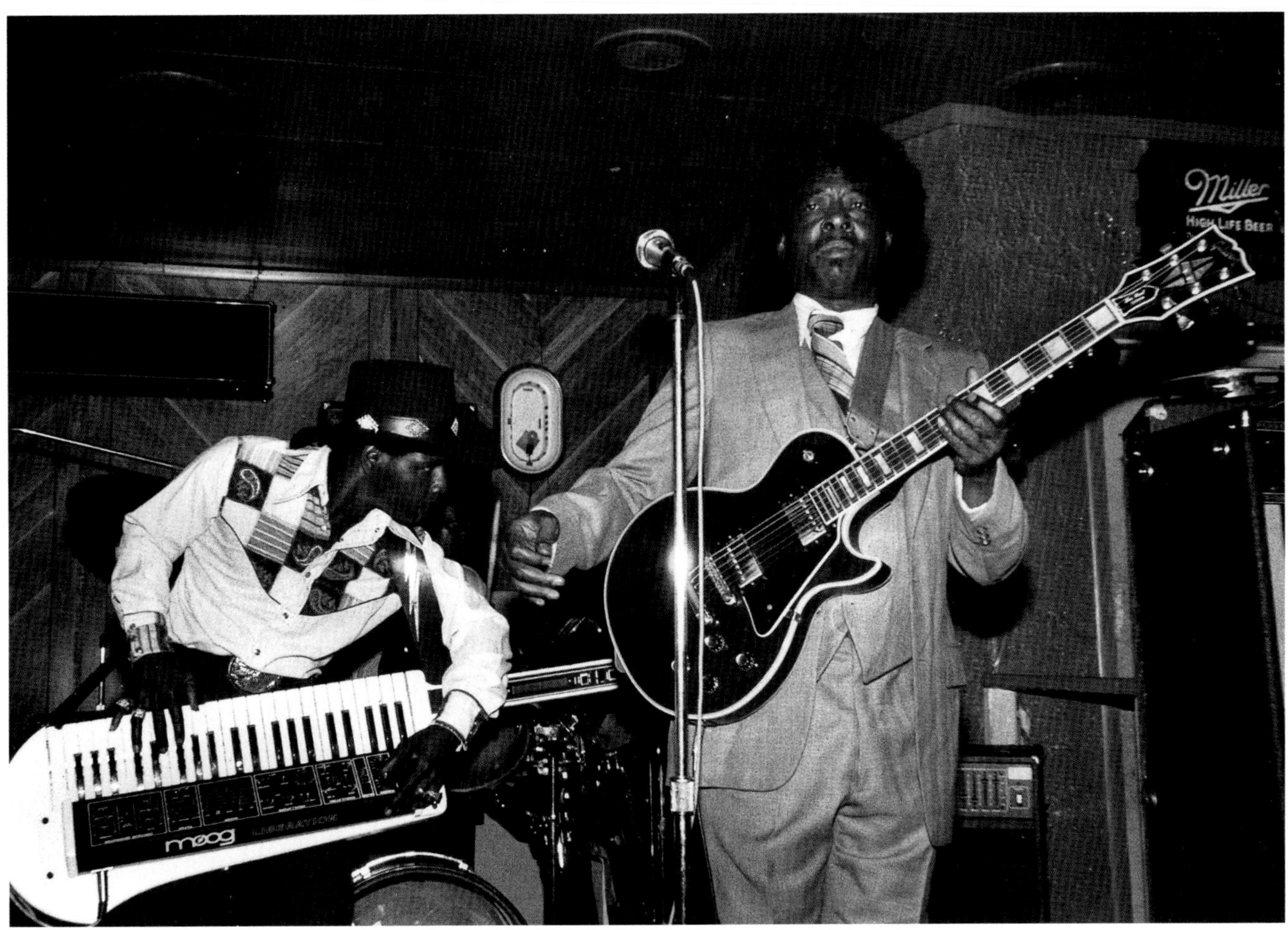

LITTLE WORLD AND LITTLE JOE BLUE, CLASSIC CLUB, OAK CLIFF, 1984.
PHOTOGRAPH BY ALAN GOVENAR.

LITTLE JOE BLUE, DALLAS, 1980s. PHOTOGRAPH BY GEORGE KEATON. COURTESY TEXAS AFRICAN AMERICAN PHOTOGRAPHY ARCHIVE.

The blues is something that happens in everyday life. To my idea, the blues is something simple. It doesn't have to be about a lady. Sometimes your boss man makes you mad and you have to feel it on the inside, but you can't quit it because otherwise you wouldn't have one [a job]. When your lady makes you mad and you know you can't live without her, that's the blues.

The way I sing a blues song, I have to feel it. When I play the blues, I just see what's happening. I don't write blues. If someone else makes it up, I can sing it. It needs to have a punch line. It has to have simple meanings to it, so that everybody can understand.

Sometimes blues songs have a repeating line. You give it in a certain way and then you come back. You may say, "Baby, I don't want a soul hangin' around my house when I'm not at home." You're kind of telling her. Then when you repeat it, "Baby, I don't want a soul hangin' around my house when I'm not at home," the emphasis is different. You're telling her like you really mean it. In the blues you need to set a foundation. You don't start at the top and then come down. You build a blues, and then you have punch line with a special phrasing. That's the story, like the song I sing, "I've been puttin' off talkin' to you, baby, about the things you do. I feel sooner or later, baby, it'll settle down to just me and you. But instead of slowin' down, you seem to be pickin' up speed. You used to tell me how you'd be back, but now you don't tell me how you feel. I wasn't born yesterday." That's the way it is. It builds up to a climax: "I wasn't born yesterday." In other words, she's doing all these things that you know she's changed, but she's not aware that you know.

Conditions started me singing the blues. I was always around a lot of singers. I was born in Vicksburg, Mississippi, across the river from Louisiana. A lot of blues singers would come through town. Jimmy Liggins, Lowell Fulson, T-Bone Walker, Howlin' Wolf, Muddy Waters, all of them used to come to our town to a place called the Green Lantern. I would take all my money that some people might spend on the movies, and I'd go to the dance for fifty cents. They wore nice suits, and a country boy like me didn't have no suits. So I watched them, and I always pictured myself doing that.

R. L. GRIFFIN

December 9, 1939– ; interview, 1987

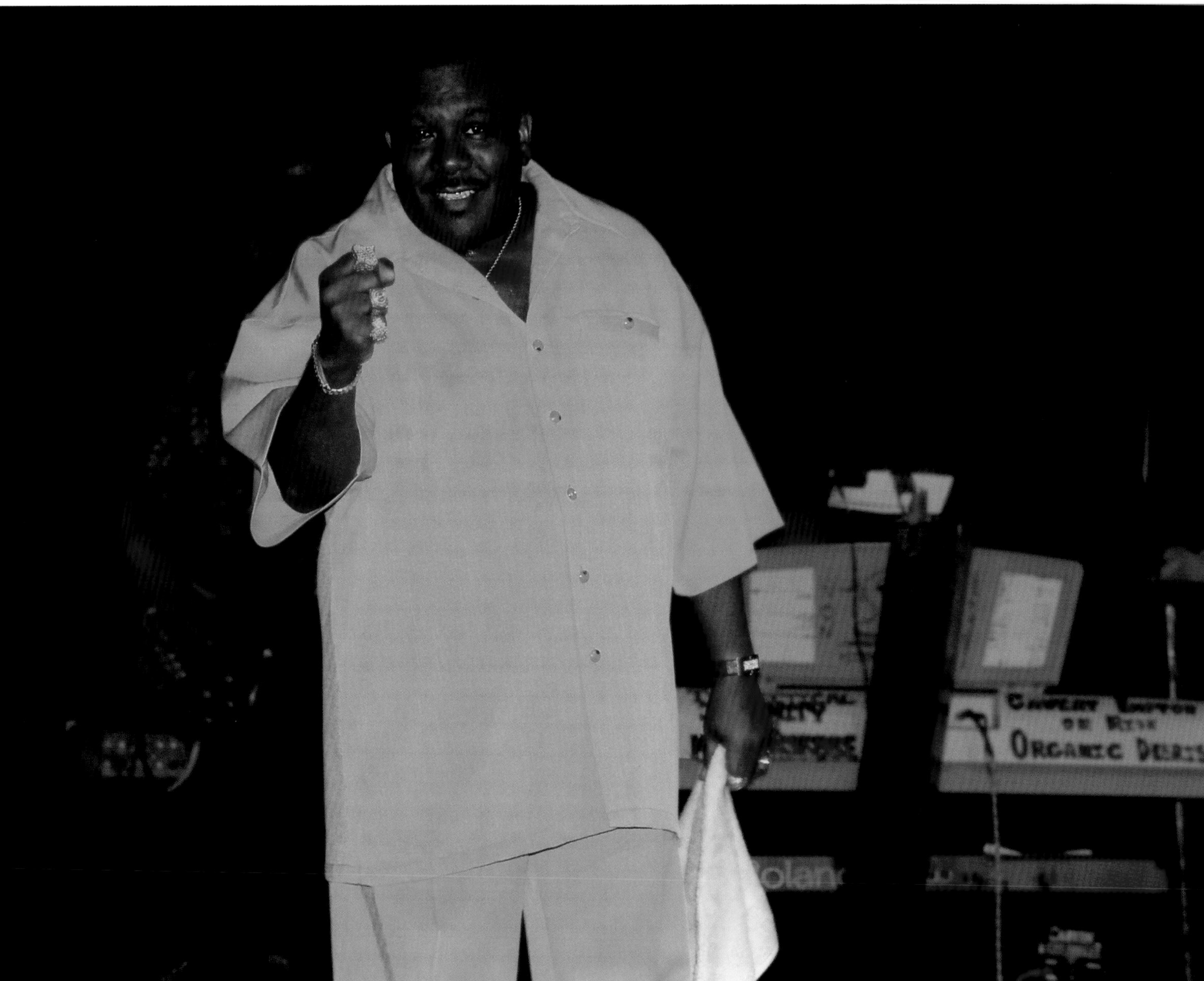

R. L. GRIFFIN, R. L'S BLUES PALACE NO. 2, DALLAS, 2007. PHOTOGRAPH BY ALAN GOVENAR.

R. L. Griffin has established himself as a blues recording artist, entertainer, and club owner. R. L.'s Blues Palace No. 2 has become the premier blues club in South Dallas, featuring local and nationally known performers, including Tutu Jones and Vernon Garrett. R. L. also has his own radio show on KKDA 730 AM. KKDA also broadcasts his live show from his club each Saturday night. He performed weekly at the Climax Club in Tyler from 1979 to 1986, and then appeared regularly at the Classic Club in Oak Cliff. In 1992 he toured to Amsterdam at the recommendation of Buddy Guy. He completed an album with Al Braggs and Earnest Davis called *I Got to Go On,* which also featured Smokin' Joe Kubek on lead guitar. Griffin also released a cassette called *I Want to Be Rich* that was released as a CD in England. In recent years, he has worked with Edward Holt on his Pinetop Blues Festival in Nacogdoches.

Everybody can understand the blues because there's a story. I was first introduced to the blues by my school director. Then I met a man by name of Freddie King and he really inspired me. I sang with Freddie King. We're both from East Texas. He was from Gilmer and I was born in Kilgore. We were what you'd call home boys.

I was the only one in my family who was a musician when I first started. I was in the school band at C. B. Dansby High School. My band director, Mr. Rufus B. Anderson, first got me started into music. When I first started I was a drummer. One day he had a program in the chapel and they got me to sing "Fever" by Little Willie John. I didn't know I could sing. From that day on I decided I wanted to be a singer.

The first band of my own was called The Corvettes. We were playing R&B music, the same kind of music James Brown was playing. I had an eight-piece band, almost an orchestra. We were doing a lot of James Brown, Ted Taylor, all those guys.

The blues in Dallas isn't really any different, though the people in East Texas seemed a little more into the music. In small places there wasn't as much pop music. More people were writing their own songs and singing blues.

I came to Dallas in 1965. I was on my way to Los Angeles and I had an uncle living here. See, I was a drummer at first before I was a singer. I stopped in Dallas and sat in with a group called Big Bo Thomas and The Twisting Arrows. They were the hottest group here, had been since the 1950s. When Bo heard me, he said he wanted me to join his group that had James Lynn Marsh, Fred Lowery, Don Williams. Not too long ago I got together with old guys. Bo Thomas was a legend, "The Big Bo Twist." He was good in his time and he can still blow that horn, tenor saxophone. He was known for his song "Cornbread."

In the 1970s I started playing with Freddie King after Big Bo Thomas kind of faded out. Freddie didn't have a band and he used mine. I was a stand-up singer then, starting to work on my own music.

When you start writing a blues song, it may be at night, and then on the next day you get another idea. Sometimes when you're having lots of problems, you know, you sit down and you put something together. You go to thinking. Well, you can't pay a bill, it gives you the blues. You have to put your mind together. You got to be able to write a hook line. You would start out with my baby and then you'd have go back to my baby, every verse, you repeat it. That's the form. Take the song:

Every day, every day I have the blues
Every day, every day I have the blues
When you see me worryin' it's you I hate you to lose
Nobody worry, nobody worry, nobody seem to care

It's telling the story over and over.

It's about life.

My favorite blues singer at the time I began singing was Bobby Bland. He was my admiration. Every time I heard that Bobby Bland had a new record, I would run and get that Bobby Bland tune. And when I sang the songs, people said that I really sounded like Bobby. In time I put together my own style, but I drew on others. A personal friend of mine was Z. Z. Hill, one of the top blues singers from Dallas. We were good friends. He came over to my house and I went over to his. He said to me once, "Whatever you do, Grif, keep your own style." And that's what I've been doing.

Z. Z. Hill's "Down Home Blues" in 1982 was a turning point. In the 1970s everybody was bypassing the blues, but now it's changed. Disco came by and went fast. The people who really loved the blues never stopped listening to it. "Down Home Blues" was a real inspiration. I made it into my coming-on song, followed by Bobby Bland's "Nothing You Can Do." When you do those songs, you always get the audience going. Now, the music trend is beginning to change on the radio. There's more of a white audience sticking with the blues.

When you're singing for a black audience you have to come up with one of the top songs, but with a white audience you can do your older songs. I think blacks are more up to date. They want to hear new material.

I started my own club, Blues Alley, in 1985. I had been working at the Classic Club in Oak Cliff when a couple of friends suggested it to me. I was doing such a good job of pulling people in for someone else. They told me, "Why don't you open your own club?" So I did, and it's going great. The audience for the blues is definitely coming back. Not too long ago I was in Tyler at the Climax Club and I drew two, three hundred people.

In Dallas these days there are several blues singers. Johnnie Taylor is probably the leading performer. He's had several hit records with the Malaco label. His song "Still Called the Blues" is one of his big records now. He's done four albums with Malaco. Johnnie's one of the best soul singers around. You just have to give to him, and he's got it.

Blues has a little different feeling than soul and is a little deeper, I think. The instrumentation might be the same, but the sound varies. I have a full show band, two guitars, keyboards, drummer, two horns [alto and tenor saxophones], and myself on vocals and harmonica. I was inspired to get into harmonica by Al "TNT" Braggs, who at one time was playing harmonica, too, and he told me, "C'mon and try it." So I started playing a little bit, and everybody kind of liked it. Now, I'm including it in one or two tunes during my show.

Some of the other blues singers in Dallas are Little Joe Blue, Charlie Roberson, and Ernie Johnson. Little Joe Blue is out in Los Angeles now, doing some recording. His newest is "Dirty Work," produced by Leon Haywood. Charlie Roberson also plays in and out of town. Last week he was in Midland, Houston, and back here on a show with Vernon Garrett and Barbara Lynn. Charlie's latest song is "Let Me Do Something for You." Ernie Johnson has a different style. He's a little more explosive. At one time, Ernie was with Stan's Records, and they released his last record, "In the Mood for the Blues."

Al Braggs is still active, but he's mostly doing writing. He's producing my new record and doing writing for a new Bobby Bland LP. The new song Al wrote for me is called "Bad Blues, Bad Blues." All you have to do is call Al, and he'll let you know exactly what he's doing. He always keeps some new songs.

I have three records out now on the Classic label, "Something on Your Mind," "It Doesn't Have to Be This Way," and "I Don't Think I'm Going to Make It." "Cry, Cry, Cry" is on a new label in Dallas called P&P Productions. Right now, I'm shopping around my new record. I'm feeling better than ever. I'm forty-five now, and I get plenty of rest. I'm up late when I perform, but I don't make a habit of it unnecessarily.

My approach to the blues is almost the same as it's always been. Now, you can do more in the studio, cut a whole LP with two musicians. The blues is what you put into it.

TUTU JONES AND R. L. GRIFFIN AT R. L.'S BLUES PALACE NO. 2, DALLAS, 2007.
PHOTOGRAPH BY ALAN GOVENAR.

ERNIE JOHNSON

Interview by Bill Fountain, 1999

I moved to Dallas, Texas. I first had a job working at Baylor Hospital. Can you imagine me working at Baylor Hospital? I was a porter. My brother and I, we were just working you know, coming out of Winnsboro, Louisiana. At an early age, I was in the cotton field working. I hauled cotton because I learned how to drive early. I hated picking. I hate the sticking in my fingers, aw, man. I used to sing a lot. Our radio, we only had one station that we could get late at night. About seven or eight o'clock, John R. came on from Nashville, Tennessee. They played all the good records, like we do at KKDA, like Clyde McPhatter, Dee Clark, Loyd Price, Ivory Joe Hunter [Johnson's cousin], Fats Domino. But when Sam Cooke came along, that was it.

ERNIE JOHNSON, DALLAS, CA. 1986. PHOTOGRAPH BY GEORGE KEATON. COURTESY TEXAS AFRICAN AMERICAN PHOTOGRAPHY ARCHIVE.

Until Bobby Bland came along and killed all of them. I just dropped them all for Bobby. Because I liked the big voice, and Bobby was so cool with his stuff, you know? I heard Bobby singing one evening, and man, I just stopped. It was just like a block. I said, who is this guy? "Further on Up the Road." Oh, man. Then he came out with "Little Boy Blue." This guy was singing, man. I guess after that I just wanted to sing. I saw my cousin come in that time, Ivory Joe, had this big suitcase full of money. Here we were out there working for fifty cents a day, a dollar a day. I said, oh, man, this is it. At that time I didn't know if I was ever going to make money singing. But I noticed all the kids would follow behind me when I started singing. I knew I must be doing something.

I knew I wanted to travel. I used to sit out. Winnsboro, Louisiana, is a small little city. Kind of a little small country town. You'd see a plane go over. Basically all you would ever see was a cropper, those planes that sprayed the crops. I'd be saying to myself, how and where can I get on that and get away. I'd see the birds fly by and I'd be saying man, I kind of wished I was a bird and could fly out of here. I got people in a lot of trouble. Seeing somebody get a whooping was my favorite thing. I'd set 'em up. My classmates, I got them in trouble. I'd do crazy things. I was liable to bring a spider in there and put it in the teacher's drawer. Who did that?! She'd whoop everybody in the classroom then. Back then everybody would get a whooping.

I came to Dallas in 1957. My brother and I. At the time, Johnnie Taylor was getting with The Soul Stirrers. I met Johnnie a long time ago. Johnnie and I got to be real close. My brother was killed in a car accident. I met Johnnie. I was moping and crying a lot. He said what's wrong, you know, and I told him. He said, well, I'm your big brother now. That happened way back. Even though we disappeared, got away from each other, I moved to Florida, I always had a relationship with him. His road manager, as he got rid of him, I ended up with him. So there was always a Johnnie thing involved.

My gospel stuff didn't last too long. When I came to Dallas, we messed around a little bit with gospel. But I could sing anything. I could yodel. I would do yodeling for country-western songs. People don't know that Little Richard was one of my favorite artists, too. Because of the soul. I probably liked him before I did Clyde McPhatter. I loved the way Clyde and the others had this attitude of singing. They were so good. For me to sing one of their songs, I didn't really realize it then, but I had to be singing. I could sing it like it was "A Lover's Question." I didn't realize it, but if you sang those tunes, you could sing.

JOHNNIE TAYLOR, DALLAS, CA. 1986. PHOTOGRAPH BY GEORGE KEATON. COURTESY TEXAS AFRICAN AMERICAN PHOTOGRAPHY ARCHIVE.

JOHNNIE TAYLOR, *WALL TO WALL*, MALACO 7431.

Dallas is one of the hardest cities in the world to get yourself together. I cut my first record in 1968. I was with a guy named Fats Washington. It happened so strange. Everybody says how do you tell the story the same way every time, I say because I'm not lying. It's easy to tell something and tell the truth. We were cutting the record with Fats and Lowell Fulson. He was cutting a record called "Too Soon." I got a vocal on that record. Lowell was a little out of it. I was singing it, and my part sounded better than his part because he was out of it. Dr. Larry T-Byrd Gordon, who was in my band The Soul Blenders at the time, was recording with him.

B. B. King called, and he was coming by to see Lowell and Fats. I went and picked him up. Brought him by the station. I was singing, you know, trying to get the music together for the band, so Lowell could sing when he came back. B. B. told Fats, why don't you cut that little boy there? Fats said, I think I will, because he was mad at Lowell. Fats sat there and wrote me a tune called "Loving You," just like that. It sounded like a song Bobby Bland had out at the time called "Ain't Nothing You Can Do"; same arrangement, same sound. T-Byrd arranged it. We called them ice cream changes because there wasn't nothing really happening. It ended up being a big record for me. People were buying it like crazy because they thought it was Bobby Bland. When Bobby came back to town, later on, Fats was playing the record in the back, way back, and Bobby was playing dominoes with Fats. Bobby said, "Fats, I don't remember doing that song." I was so happy because to me, Bobby Bland was like when I met Nancy Wilson. She was my sweetheart all through my life growing up. If I fooled with any girl or something, I would just close my eyes and there come Nancy. Oh man, I love that woman. I got to meet her, and I see how people are now when they meet me and they are trembling and shaking.

My band, The Soul Blenders, we worked with Freddie King. We backed Freddie on a lot of dates. Freddie just took me in like a brother. Talked crazy to me. Called me crazy names.

Guitar James and Miss Lavelle White had a show to do out in Greenville. Johnnie Taylor was supposed to be the headliner for the show. Johnnie didn't show up. Now we move into a star thing. Now James wanted to move into the co-star, Miss Lavelle was the star, so now they needed somebody to open the show. So I had never sung before on the blues side, but I knew songs like "Annie

Get Your Yo Yo," and some Sam Cooke, and for the band to play, I figured let me pick something simple. Not a lot of changes in it. I did "Annie Get Your Yo Yo," and people just ran.

Man, I called over to my job and fired my own self. I was working for the city of Dallas. I was working at White Rock Park at the time. I had got me a process [hair straightening] because I liked Bobby Bland's hairstyle. I had already got my hair all whooped down, whatever they call that stuff, it was process then, had my hair kind of laid like Bobby Bland because Bobby, to me, had one of the best hairstyles. I went back home, my brother and them were laughing, what are you doing, man? Hey, you can't work like that. I said, I'm already working, I'm a star. They said, man, you gonna starve to death.

The next record I cut was in 1969, just before I got ready to leave. It was "Your Precious Love." Fats died before he got back. He never did get to hear it. We worked out of Arkansas for a while. I stayed there for about a year. I had a television show down there. I was on TV here, on Channel 11 with Curtis Pierce. We had a thing called "Operation Soul." I was the coordinator for bringing in talent. That had to be around 1965, 1966.

I'd like to go in the studio and do a remix on "Party Time." I might cut a gospel album, I got enough to do it. I wish Johnnie could have been here with me because he would have been such a big influence on that.

I worked with Carlos Santana. Carlos and I did a tune, it just came out, called "Daughter of the Night." He is such a nice guy. I'm serious, the guy is for real. I had forgot about it. I got a call overseas. They said, "Ernie, I got the tape on you with Santana." I said, "What?" "The Daughter of the Night." I didn't even know the thing was out.

My thing is, basically, I like to write about what is really happening. Not necessarily to me. Most of my songs come from talking or tripping. Something you might say might give me a good title. That's all I really need. A good title. I can write about a dog laying on the sidewalk and make it sound good. You know, you can be singing a sad thing, but the way you phrase it, you can make it sound like it's happy. You can sing it with a minor or something where it sounds like it's sad.

I try to talk to the kids. Try to get them away. I wish I could get them all on a bus to Galveston or something. Let them know that it is a beautiful life. A lot of them are locked up. The parents are working. Don't have time.

CHARLIE ROBERSON, DALLAS, CA. 1986.
PHOTOGRAPH BY GEORGE KEATON. COURTESY TEXAS AFRICAN AMERICAN PHOTOGRAPHY ARCHIVE.

That's why I am the uncle of the whole United States. Uncle Ern. All over the world. Right now in Dallas, over a hundred-something kids "Uncle Ern" me. I was lucky to have a lot of uncles. These kids don't have that. I try to help them if I can. Try to give them some good advice. Stay in school. Don't be out bumming. When they are out of school, get a job.

My daddy was a hard worker. He was just a guy who could never sit down. I didn't inherit all that from him, but I am still active. I got a lot of energy from him. He'd walk, and we ran. That's how he'd walk. My godson was telling me, Pops, you walk too fast. He was running, I was walking. I looked back. I thought about me and Daddy. I'm glad I got the strength to do that.

ANSON FUNDERBURGH

November 15, 1954–   ; interview, 1987

ANSON AND THE ROCKETS, DALLAS, EARLY 1980s.

When I got my first guitar, it was a little old acoustic, and the woman I bought it from had a daughter who had a whole bunch of 45s. And in those 45s was "Hideaway" [by Freddie King], "Honky Tonk," "Sno Cone" by Albert Collins, some Jimmy Reed, "Big Boss Man," and a few of those kinds of things. That was a Roy Rogers, a little fake guitar. I was in grade school, six, seven, eight years old. I didn't know exactly what was goin' on, but I knew I liked it. It kind of hit my ear.

I've been playing in nightclubs since I was fifteen, fixin' to turn sixteen. I've had little bands on and off since grade school. I'll be thirty-three next month.

Boz Scaggs was from Plano, where I grew up, but I never really met him until the last two or three years. I never really saw him. I knew his brother.

Most of what I've acquired out of the music has been from records. I've seen Freddie King a lot, but I never saw Muddy Waters, though I did get to play with Lightnin' Hopkins at the Granada Theater. That was in 1976, 1977. That was fun. He was a grumpy old coot. I guess he had heard it all. I can imagine it feeling like it's a repeat. I know what it's like for me now. Sometimes I wonder what it would be like with another forty years tacked on. Lightnin' Hopkins, though, could really play. He was great, he played electric guitar, and had a band—drum, bass, him, myself, and Marc Benno.

In a way I'm more influenced by the Chicago sound, Muddy Waters, Magic Sam, Buddy Guy, B. B. [King]. I like that harmonica a lot; Little Walter. Robert Jr. Lockwood, Luther Tucker, they're all big influences, too. I kind of pulled something from everybody. I do what I do and go on. I don't think about it too much. [So much of the Chicago sound is the immediacy of the performance. It's a live sound.] Any time you use a harmonica you have to relate to what they did in Chicago.

Sam Myers is from Mississippi and played in Chicago. He really added a lot to my band. [Anson and The Rockets] was started about nine years ago, October 1978, with a basic harmonica, bass, drums, and lead guitar. We stayed with four pieces for about a year, and then we added a piano. The band has gone through a lot of personnel changes to get to where we are now, Sam Myers on harmonica and vocals, Randy Simmons on bass, Matt McCabe on piano, Marc Wilson on drums, and myself. We've been together since about 1986.

I met Sam Myers in Jackson, Mississippi. I was playing with the old band, and Sam was living there. So we were playing, and a guitar player that worked with Sam, named Pete Cushie, came up to us. He was a young white guy and told us about Sam Myers, and I said, "*The* Sam Myers?" I had a lot of his early records, but I didn't know that he was still alive. As it turned out, Sam didn't get a chance to come to see us that time, but the next time, he got up and played. I flipped over him, and I tried to get Hammond Scott from Blacktop Records [my label] in New Orleans to do a record with Sam, and finally he agreed. That's how the *My Love Is Here to Stay* album came about. The newest album, released this year, is called *Sins*. Sam plays on that, of course, though I did use a different band on *Love Is Here to Stay*. I didn't want it to sound like a Rockets album. It was for Sam. We did his tunes mostly, "My Love Is Here to Stay," "What's Wrong? What's Wrong?" "Poor Little Angel Child," some he had recorded before, but he redid them. A few were covers, a Little Walter tune.

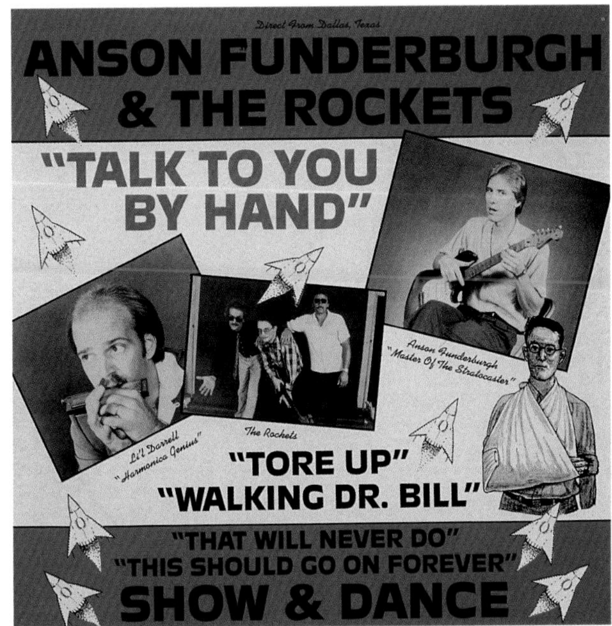

ANSON FUNDERBURGH & THE ROCKETS, KRAZY KAT 777.

Earl King wrote two songs for the new album, "A Man Needs His Lovin' All the Time" and "Leftovers." Sam Myers wrote three songs; one was a cover of "Sleepin' in the Ground," one of his early songs. I only wrote one of the tunes, an instrumental called "Chill Out," a tribute to Albert Collins. In putting together the album, I work as a kind of arranger to make the tunes sound a little different.

SAM MYERS, 1987. PHOTOGRAPH BY RANDY JENNINGS.

ANSON FUNDERBURGH, 1987.
PHOTOGRAPH BY RANDY JENNINGS.

ZUZU BOLLIN, "STAVIN' CHAIN," TORCH RECORDS, 6912-B.
ZUZU BOLLIN, "CRY, CRY, CRY," TORCH RECORDS, 6912-A.

Exciting New Guitar Wizard Looms On Dallas Musical Horizon

ZUZU BOLLIN, *TEXAS BLUESMAN*.
COURTESY DALLAS BLUES SOCIETY.

"ZUZU BOLLIN IS THE SENSATIONAL NEW GUITARIST WHO IS 'LAYING 'EM IN THE AISLES AROUND DALLAS,"
DALLAS EXPRESS, 1950S. COURTESY DALLAS BLUES SOCIETY.

I'm just now starting to develop my own style. I pulled some of what I do from various influences. Now, when people hear me, I hope they think, hope it sounds like me. I don't really want to sound like someone else. My biggest influences in my solo work were B. B. King, Freddie King, and Magic Sam.

The blues is something I really enjoy doing. I wouldn't know how to act without it. I've been doing it a long time. There was a time I mostly played black clubs. That was in the mid-1970s, with a group named Delta Road. I played all over South Dallas, on Metropolitan, the Jade Room, Forest Avenue, the Spider Lounge, and the New York Ballroom. The black people we played for loved us, most of the older blacks, because we did something special for them.

Sometimes you listen to the lyrics of the blues and you get tickled. It makes you feel good. It makes you happy. In this way, the blues is like country and western. It's about life. Sometimes you'll hear the lyrics and it will just make goose bumps go up on you. The blues is something that anybody can relate to if they really stop and listen. I see people out there who I think might not really understand what they're hearing, but they're tapping their foot. People like the beat. A lot of people who grew up on rock music are finally starting to figure out the roots. I had a hard time making it in Dallas for a long time. Austin had a lot more going for it, the early Antone's days, and there was another place where I used to hear Jimmie [Vaughan] in a group called Storm, and they used to pass the hat to pay the band. Times have not always been great. The blues can make you sad. It's a very emotional music. It moves people in one way or another. The blues is simple but very honest. It seems the more complicated you make it, the further it gets from the true sound.

MIKE MORGAN

November 30, 1959– ; interview by Bill Fountain, 2000

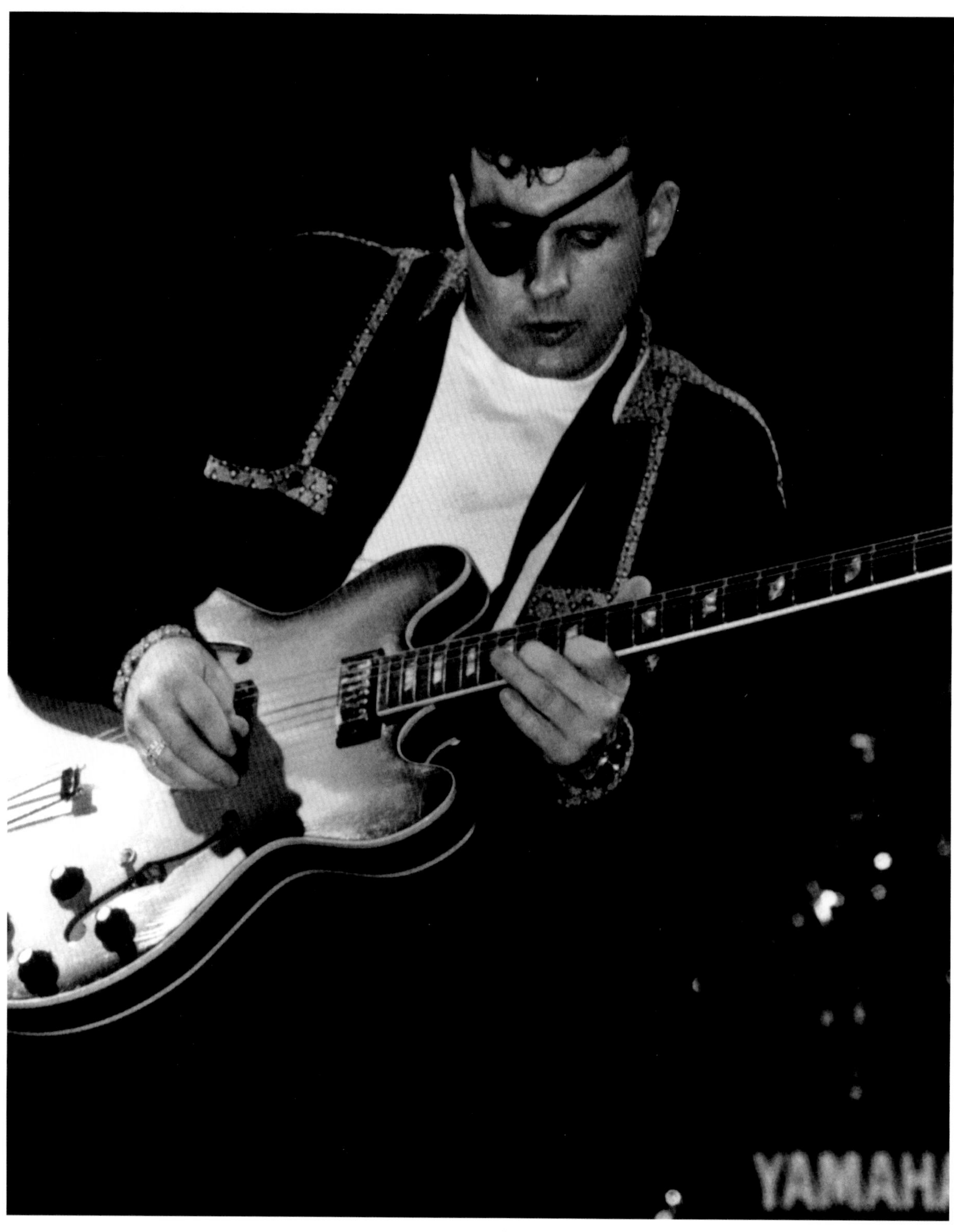

I started back about the time Stevie Ray's first record came out. I had played guitars on and off since I was a kid, but never really played. I had a couple of little garage bands in high school, but never anything serious till about 1986 when I started this. Hillsboro was not a big blues Mecca. It was just a small town where people listened to the Zoo [K102]. That's what I grew up listening to—Top 40 rock 'n' roll music. A guy turned me on to that Stevie record, and it sparked some kind of interest I hadn't had before. I had always had interest in it, just never had enough to push me to the next level.

In 1986 I moved up here to Dallas. Darrell Nulisch started singing with me. That was my first big break, getting an accomplished guy in the band. A guy people had heard of. It enabled us to make our first road trips to Memphis, Kansas City, and Jackson, Mississippi.

I really woodshedded for two years. Darrell was the one that said: "Here, just pick stacks of records." I was like: "Who's this Lazy Lester?" You know? "Little Walter, who is this?" I didn't know anything. All I knew was Anson [Funderburgh], The Thunderbirds, Ronnie Earl, and Stevie [Ray Vaughan]. I would take all these records and I made all these tapes. All these guys I had never even heard of. Then I said, "Hey this is pretty cool," and then I said, "Yeah this is real cool."

A lot of subtlety, that's what most of the older stuff is. Subtle coolness, which a lot of people don't get. A lot of musicians don't get. They are trying to play this stuff, they don't understand the subtle coolness, so, in my opinion, they don't get it. It doesn't work. That's really what it's all about. It's sometimes in your face, you know, I play in your face a lot but I know when to be subtle and I know what being subtle is. When you dig in and really listen to this stuff, you get it. You really begin to understand it when you cross that barrier.

I remember when it happened. At first when Darrell gave me this stuff, I said, "This is tired, man." Too much going on. There was nobody screaming or wailing. But then when you really listen, they are wailing. It's just wailing in a different way.

[Nulisch sang with Morgan for six months or so before getting an offer from Ronnie Earl.] There wasn't any doubt what to do at that point. I had only been playing a couple of years, and Ronnie already had three records out. So he went up there with him and did two records. [Later] I was out traveling without a record, so we were struggling. Then I found out about Lee McBee.

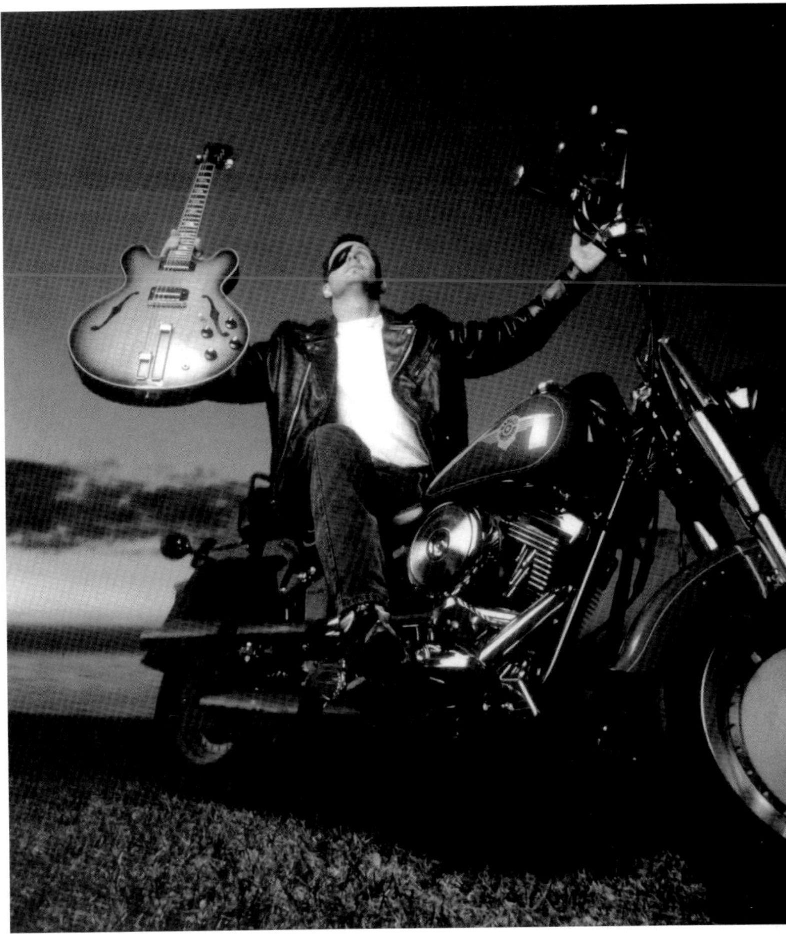

MIKE MORGAN, DALLAS, CA. 2002.

(OPPOSITE) MIKE MORGAN, DALLAS, CA. 2001.

[His band, Mike Morgan and The Crawl, includes McBee on harmonica, Johnny Bradley on bass, and Marc Wilson on drums.]

I used to drag my poor girlfriend, who had to work the next day, every Monday night to Dallas. Drive up and listen. I could name you a handful of songs I learned just sitting there watching him. Then, he [Anson] called me one day out of the clear blue and told me he talked to Blacktop. And that they were interested in hearing us. At that point, I had only been seriously playing a couple of years.

Blacktop was looking for a band that was out touring. They had some great records from some really cool, obscure guys, but they don't tour. But for the record company to make any money, you gotta go out and get your name out there. At least let people know that you have a record out. I was stunned. Honestly, I don't think I was ready to make a record at that point.

It's funny how I started off knowing nothing and thinking I really knew a lot. Here I start this band, got all this attention, I'm thinking, "Man, I'm the guy." But in the course of twelve years, I've humbled a whole lot. You don't learn it all. You never learn it all. You get out there and you realize, shoot, there are so many good guitar players that could cut my head off, you know, roll it down the alley. There's just no room to have a big head. I try to keep learning and hope somebody likes it.

Things have continually gotten better. As far as the way things are going, it's gotten a little bit better every year. Our acceptance, our crowd, you know, when you go out on the road, there's not so many nights where there's nobody there. People are waiting to see us, excited to see us. Part of that is from having so many records out.

We used to tour all the time. Since I've gotten a little older, I kinda lost my inclination to want to be gone. I mainly do it now when I have a record out.

I'm a huge motocross fan. I've done it ever since I was a kid. I'm just too old to make any money at it now.

MEMO "THE LONE WOLF" GONZALEZ

August 2, 1956– ; interview by Don O, 1993

As you walk up to the door you hear some great blues rattling the walls. You pay a small cover, way too little for the great sounds you've heard from outside. Inside it's dark, smoky, and packed. The dance floor is full, and folks are jumping around like their shoes are on fire. You can't quite see the stage for all the dancers, but you can hear the music better, and you know you're in the right place. Wailin' harp, great guitar, honking saxes, a driving rhythm section, and deep, heartfelt, soulful vocals. An original tune, too. Who are these guys? Welcome to a typical night with Memo Gonzalez and The Mistreaters.

Memo Gonzalez is a Dallas native. He's been into music since he could barely ride a bike. Not just blues. All kinds of music. He was first introduced to blues partly due to the remaining prejudices of the 1960s.

We lived in a predominantly Anglo area and I really didn't have many friends around home. Most of the white kids weren't allowed to play with us. That's just the way it was back then. When I started school, there were a few more Mexicans, but there were black kids, too. I became buddies with a number of them, and I used to ride my bike over to play with them. Their parents used to have rhythm and blues on the record player, and I got so I really liked that kind of music. I'd go home and my sister would be listening to rock 'n' roll and I enjoyed that, too. My dad liked that dentist office music. He even got mad when The Beatles came on the *Ed Sullivan Show.*

In elementary school, I took piano lessons and later started playing trumpet and coronet. I really preferred the low tones of the coronet to the high, shrill ones of the trumpet. I used to play hour after hour. My dad finally got tired of listening to it, and he went out and got me a mute to keep the noise down! By junior high I was in the marching band. Mr. Falkas was the traditional marching band director. He treated me like dirt because I was always trying to play those low-down blues licks I'd heard on the radio. He wanted nothing to do with R&B. He liked all that Doc Severinsen stuff. What a square. Fortunately for me, in the ninth grade the band was taken over by Mr. Watson, a black guy, and man, he turned my life around. He loved all that Grambling Marching Band stuff and even tried to get us into soul marching. That meant we got to learn all kinds of great soul tunes in school. I haven't played any Doc Severinsen stuff since.

I used to have classes with the son of Freddie King. He was a great guy. We used to talk music all the time. Freddie used to pick him up at school sometimes, and I was always knocking on the window and yelling, "Hey, Freddie!" Freddie used to scowl and tell me, "Just move away from the car, boy."

I played in the North Dallas High School band. We did all right, considering we were a small band from a racially mixed school. We pretty much kept up with them. But in my senior year at high school, I got in a fight and got stabbed in the back with a bayonet. It punctured a lung and just barely missed my heart. That kept me off my horn for a while, and that really discouraged me. The only course I made straight As in was music. I went through some really tough times, got messed up on drugs, and dropped out of school for a while.

That's when I picked up the bass guitar. I was listening to mostly rock 'n' roll around then. Hendrix, Led Zeppelin, that kind of stuff. I didn't have the blues stuff figured out, and I just plain didn't know how. I took a few lessons, and eventually I ran into Felix Reyes. I'd been doing sheet metal and welding work with my dad up until then. One day I was getting my bass out of the pawnshop, and Felix was getting his guitar out. He said he was starting a reggae band and needed a bass player. I said, "Cool, I've always wanted to learn reggae." We were called The Iraters, a big old twelve-piece reggae band! That lasted for a while, but eventually we got tired of it and me and Felix went back to our true love, R&B.

That led to the formation of a band called The Weebads. That band lasted for years with dozens of the area's best players rotating through. I was still playing bass until Ronnie Palmer came along. Dave Issacs, our drummer, really wanted to bring Ronnie in on bass because he had worked on the road with Steve Miller and Boz Scaggs. Fortunately, Felix didn't want to get rid of me and gave me six months to learn the harmonica. I learned from listening to records by James Cotton, Charlie Musselwhite, and Jimmy Reed. They're still my heroes, especially Cotton. I love Sam Myers, too. He's an encyclopedia. I wish someone would record him just talking about his adventures. He's a real treasure.

I'm not a Chicago-style harp player like Little Walter. I'm not a purist, never have been. I believe in injecting my own style into everything I do. We do some Clarence Carter stuff, and while I like Clarence Carter, I'm not going to sing it like he does. It's the same thing with the harmonica. I infuse my horn experience with my harp playing. I like it like that. I don't play a lot of harp because I don't feel like I have to play a lot of harp. I like to infuse my harp into the way a song is flowing. I don't want to dominate the song with a harp. Some musicians don't even consider the harp to be a real instrument because it's difficult to infuse it in with other things. But that's what I've always tried to do. Be a part of the music rather than a dominant instrument. Everybody should have solos, and I take my share, but I don't want to do songs completely dominated by harp.

The Weebads went through many transitions over the years. Breaking up, re-forming, changing members, but I was almost always with the band. One time, I worked with Jim Suhler in one of his early bands, The Road Hogs. I first started singing while working with Jim Suhler. I had written a few songs, but Felix used to sing my songs in The Weebads because I didn't really have the courage to stand out front and do it. Plus nobody ever really gave me the chance. Jim didn't have a lot of confidence in his vocal talents, even though he had a great singing voice. He wanted me to help him sing a few of my songs. That gave me some confidence, and I started writing even more songs. We kind of built each other up, both in songwriting and singing. Of course, he's a big hit today, touring with George Thorogood!

After the break-up of The Road Hogs, I got back together with Felix Reyes and re-formed The Weebads. We added Richard Hunter on bass and Ritchie Vasquez on drums, so we called the rhythm section 'the swinging Richards.' We were sounding great, too. Unfortunately, Felix found himself in a situation where he had to leave town all of a sudden. Johnny Moeller took over the guitar duties, and I wound up singing and fronting the band. I guess to make up for my discomfort out front, I just started moving around a lot, feeling the music, closing my eyes. That's how I still do it today. We played all over the Southeast, with Johnny Moeller doing the guitar work. Then came that fateful day at the Thunderbird Lounge when Darrell Nulisch walked in. I said, "Hey Darrell, check out our guitar player." He said, "Yeah!" and then he stole him from us! They went on to make a CD for Blacktop. Then we had Mike Flanigan until he decided he wanted to do his own thing. Then the "swinging Richards" went off and joined Killbilly. Richard Hunter's still with them, but Ritchie Vasquez is now playing drums for Cold Blue Steel. I still wanted to keep The Weebads going, so I got Hash Brown back into the band. He was actually one of the original members. Paul Size [now with the Red Devils in L.A.] was playing bass with us. Jason Moeller was doing drums. Paul and Jason made the move to Austin, so we got Terry Groff and Bobby Baranowski to replace them. That was a great musical combination. Hash Brown and Felix Reyes are my greatest mentors. Hash taught me a lot about playing harp.

The Weebads' regional touring brought my harp work to the attention of Austin record producer Eddie Stout of PeeWee Records. That led to solo appearances on PeeWee's *Texas Lovers* and *Texas Harmonica Rumble* LPs. It also led to a European tour in 1991 that included a stop in the mining town of Nikel, Russia. We were going to do a "Rock for Russia" benefit. This was back when the Soviet Union was falling apart. We weren't sure if we were going or if it was even safe to go until the last second. The KGB confiscated half the relief supplies we brought. Milk, orange juice, stuff we brought for the children. . . . They cleared out a floor for us in a sanitarium, and that was our hotel. The really bad ones were still on the floors above us. We had about eighty people and just one bathroom. It was terrible. . . . Everything was rationed. The food was horrible. We walked into a little store, and when we opened the door the funk almost knocked us to our knees. Darrell Nulisch started gagging. But the people in Russia were wonderful, and the crowds were so responsive. I signed autographs till my hand was cramped. They love rhythm and blues. They can identify with it. I went to a music school for little kids and we did a three-piece harp thing with Eddie Stout playing bass on this huge, stand-up, four-string, balalaika thing. We took supplies of milk to the school, and the kids were stuffing the cartons in their pockets to take home to their families. . . . Right across the border in Norway it's the land of plenty. It's so nice. Our rooms had heated bathroom floors. The rooms were clean and comfortable. Food was plentiful and delicious. Crystal-clear water. Just sixty miles away in Russia, it was just filth.

The Weebads eventually broke up for the last time. I got really tired of managing the band. It's a lot of headaches. Hustling gigs, keeping the band members happy, and all. I wanted to concentrate on writing and learning new songs. Little Ralph had just quit The Mistreaters after his wife had their baby girl. Steve Coronado asked me to join the band, and I haven't been this happy in a long time. It's great. We have Ray Jimenez on guitar, band leader Steven Coronado on sax, and have just added Chuck Flores on bass, and Joe Coronado on drums. We're going in the studio in August to do a demo tape. Hopefully we can find some backers to extend it to an album. Eddie Stout is also sending me a plane ticket to play the Utrecht Blues Festival in Holland. It's at a little town outside of Amsterdam. I'm not sure if I'll go or not. Depends on the money. We will be playing around here quite a bit, so come on out and we'll all get drunk and get tattooed!

WOMEN AT THE CLASSIC CLUB, OAK CLIFF, 1984.

PHOTOGRAPH BY ALAN GOVENAR.

ROBIN "TEXAS SLIM" SULLIVAN

July 26, 1963– ; interview by Don O, 1993

In 1993 Robin "Texas Slim" Sullivan was one of the hottest unsigned blues men in the Dallas–Fort Worth area. He had been thrilling area club audiences for over fourteen years, yet his only recording until then was a self-released demo made with one of his early bands, Blue Ice. Only about 100 copies were made. In 1992, Slim finally quit his day job, something prophesied in one of his first original songs, and pursued a music career full time with his new band, Texas Slim and The Gems. Slim's reputation soon began to spread outside of the Metroplex. He played a sold-out show in Cambridge, Massachusetts, and began to tour regularly through Kansas, Arkansas, and Tennessee.

The Gems broke up about 1995, and Slim joined local bar band Cold Blue Steel. He honed his chops even further and learned a lot about the business side of music from front man James Buck. His rhythm section, Kenny Stern and Bill Cornish, spent some time touring with Joe Kubek before rejoining Slim for the Texas Slim Blues Band in 1996.

I was born in 1963, the big year for Dallas. The Kennedy year. Born here at Baylor Hospital, I've been here all my life. My very first memory of hearing blues would have to be John Lee Hooker in about the eighth grade. Which is a major time in life, you know. It really influenced me. I was turned off by all the commercial music at that time, and just hearing it blew my mind. I knew that was The Stuff. It was just a record a friend had. I think the first blues record I bought was Lightnin' Hopkins.

I knew as early as fifth grade that I wanted to play music. My older brothers were playing around with it, and I had taken lessons off and on. I messed around with guitar, drums, and bass. I had played guitar since I was about seven years old and was playing mainly drums by the eighth grade. Hearing the blues made me want to play guitar more. I decided that same year to go to the Dallas Arts Magnet High School, so it was a potent time in my life. When I first started playing guitar I used to jam on a simple blues riff. I didn't even know it was blues, but it's what I played.

The first blues song I consciously tried to play was "Kansas City." I heard one of my brother's friends play it, and I liked that cool beat. I thought, "I can do that," so I was singing "Kansas City" when I was eight years old. I didn't even know it was blues until years later. My high school guitar teacher encouraged me to get into a working situation, so I joined a country and western band and played that predominantly through my high school years. It wasn't commercial rock. I was protesting that. I knew it wasn't a permanent situation. I spent all my spare time listening to blues. We played a lot of big gigs. We were on TV, *4 Country Reporter* it was back then. We were on *PM Magazine* back when that was local. We also played national TV on NBC, the Muscular Dystrophy Telethon at the Dallas Convention Center. I did "Johnny B. Goode" and played like a pretty hot little fifteen-year-old guitar player on a Stratocaster.

Once I turned sixteen and had wheels, around 1979, I started thinking I could have my own band. That's when I started my first blues band with two of my best friends. We called it Blue Ice. The original Blue Ice was Richard Pickerell on bass and Randy Ventrika on drums. The significance of those guys is they were my older brother's friends. They were older than me, and they had a big influence on the music I listened to. Randy was a great guitar player. He's really the one that got me kicked into electric guitar. He had an electric guitar, an amp, and a fuzz box, and we could go over to his garage and turn it up loud and nobody complained. In fact, the neighborhood kids would come by on their little scooters and stop and listen. That was when I was around nine or ten years old. He is the one who really started me playing. I saw him play and I said, "I've got to do that." He's a carpenter these days. He opted for the family life, lives out in the country, and is doing really well.

The first paying gig with Blue Ice was at Big Ralph's City Dump, Marsh Lane at Northwest Highway, which was in my neighborhood. It was a biker bar. I even tried to paint on a moustache to keep me out of trouble because I definitely wasn't old enough to be in there. That particular gig was also my first experience at playing blues for a not-so-friendly crowd. They did not want to hear blues. They wanted to hear Z. Z. Top. I was saying stuff like, "This next song is by Freddie King, but

I think Z. Z. Top did it one time!" I was a little scared. After I graduated high school, I went to college up at North Texas State [now the University of North Texas] in Denton, and I kept Blue Ice going. We played on campus a couple of times at Bruce Hall, which is the music dorm up there. Wild parties. Those were a real inspiration to me because all those other musicians were there. Those were great gigs that I was actually in control of. We played real blues, and everybody loved us.

Alex Moore was important to me even before I started Blue Ice. During the time I played country, I would mow anybody's lawn to afford to buy a new blues album. I'd mow lawns, then hit the record store. I was largely listening to country blues. That's when I bought all my Blind Blake, Blind Lemon Jefferson, Robert Johnson, and everything I could get my hands on. It was more available and cheaper back in the late Seventies. Blues was not popular back then. They were the cheapest records in the store. I was going, "Yeah! I can get John Lee Hooker and Lightnin' Hopkins records for a buck!" They thought they were scamming me, but I was scamming them! I became friends with Alex Moore because my mom worked at the library downtown. She knew I was interested in blues, because I was trying to mow the lawn two or three times a week. They had Alex booked on a Tuesday afternoon lunch program as a solo artist. I went down there, and after his performance I just couldn't get up. The auditorium cleared out, and Alex was still at the piano. I was still in my seat and just couldn't move. I thought to myself, "This is really something. I just have to meet this man. If I just get to shake his hand I'll be so honored." So I finally got up and went down there, and Alex didn't really have anybody else to talk to. He said, "You can take me home if you want to." So I said, "Sure!" We became friends that quick. He was so generous with his time, with what he knew, with the history he had lived. He was a proud man. When I was up in Denton I'd get these letters from him. Big envelopes marked all over—"Alex Moore, 1969 blues festival, International Arhoolie recording artist, piano player, Helsinki, Finland, 1969, Stuttgart, Germany," everyplace he'd been. The whole envelope would be completely marked with this incredibly detailed script work. I've still got those and treasure them.

Of course, the next thing I wanted to do was play with Alex. But people would tell me, "You can't play with him, man. Nobody can follow Alex!" Well, I thought I could, and I decided I had to try it. We got together the first time at my house. My mom had a piano. We invited him over on a Sunday afternoon. Fixed him dinner and everything. I first started trying to play with him, and he would go with this wild, quick, sudden change, and I would jump and try to be right there with him and land it a half-second late. Alex said, "Now wait a minute. When I make a mistake, you just keep on going right. I'll meet you at the end." So I said, "If you say you made a mistake, I'll just ignore what you're doing and I'll just play the straight twelve bar blues." So we tried it the first time. He went with his quick change and I didn't go with him. I just kept going. When it got to the turnaround at the end of the twelve bars, Alex was way off, and he comes back in and just nailed it! I couldn't believe it. He never was lost. He was just out there on his own planet! I learned how to play with Alex, and I did maybe five gigs with him. They were all duo gigs, just me and Alex. Very, very memorable. Somebody in this town has tapes of those, and I would do anything to get a copy!

I met Little Joe Blue in the days of the Nash Street House, around 1984. Another period of growth for me. I had moved back into Dallas from Denton and was beginning to get a little more mature; I was still just a kid! It was the same type of attraction as with Alex. When I first saw him I just had to meet him. When I did, we hit it off really big. He was very complimentary of everything I tried to do. He was so encouraging. He told me, "You've got it, you're good, stay with it, and don't ever stop." He meant a lot to me. I remember we played the Bronco Bowl with only about 300 people there. That place held about 2,500, so there was plenty of room. Joe and I went out into the audience and played and sang together. Another time we did a Sunday matinee at Poor David's, and he turned around and told me, "Now, Slim, I'm going to put this guitar over my head. You put yours behind your back and let's go get 'em!" So we proceeded to stroll through the audience and we got 'em! Him with that big Les Paul behind his head! I'll remember those gigs forever.

So many of the guys that are still around had an impact on my electrical style. I saw Anson Funderburgh for the first time when I was about sixteen. I know I wasn't old enough to be in the club. But it was in my neighborhood, I could ride my bike home. I just remember I was in awe of Anson. I still am. Joe Kubek, Jim Suhler, Hash Brown, Mike Morgan—basically we all

ROBIN "TEXAS SLIM" SULLIVAN, DALLAS, CA. 2001. PHOTOGRAPH BY DON O.

go way back in the struggle. I told Jim just the other day, "Keep happenin'! Every time something good happens for you it seems to rub off on me, too!" It's great to see Jim's band, Monkey Beat, taking off. Joe Kubek is killin' them everywhere. Mike used to come down and jam with us when we played at the old McKinney Station. He put my name in the acknowledgments when he put out his first CD on Blacktop. I asked him why, and he said it was because I always used to let him sit in. I was amazed. We're all kind of family. Me and Hash Brown are tight from way back. We know what it's like to live the blues.

My second band, The Texas Blues Experience, came about because I was trying to improve my booking status. I took on a full-time manager who really made some heavy demands, including the name change. I had taken the name Texas Slim just because I thought it was cool. It's like all those old records I've got. Those guys were dodging the labels by using different pseudonyms, and it's just a cool historical thing. I called Alex and said, "Hey, what do you think?" He thought it was the greatest thing in the world, so I've been Texas Slim ever since. I'm keeping it forever. I met drummer Kenny Stern in college at North Texas. John Bush, who was the conga player with Edie Brickell and The New Bohemians, was in The Texas Blues Experience. Yes, we were the only blues band with a conga player. Kenny is my drummer now. He's been with me most of the time since 1982. He just feels it when I'm going to make a move, and he's right there, *bam.* Just like that. That comes from years of being together. He went through the years with Little Joe Blue and has played with Kubek, Mike Morgan, Jim Suhler, the whole gang. I strongly rejected the name Texas Blues Experience. It was something that was forced on me. The whole promotion bit was kind of taken out of my hands, and I had no control. I was still young and learning. As soon as I lost the manager I lost the name. I liked Blue Ice, and I went back to it for a few years. Keyboard player Andy Comess came into the picture about 1986 when I got Blue Ice back together. His brother Aaron, who is now the drummer for The Spin Doctors, was our bass player in that period, 1986 to 1987. Basically, I was with them and Kenny until Snooky Duke came along. Blue Ice eventually folded because we were starving to death.

Basically, it was because we wanted to play real blues and be in control of our own music. We weren't making any money, and I wasn't doing very well with the booking. I was in a situation where I had a family and I had a lot of pressure to not be doing that type of thing. There were a lot of different things that caused it to fold.

Snooky Duke and the Roadrunners was a case of me just not being able to sit at home and not play. I walked into that gig. It was an every Sunday thing. I just wanted to play. I met Mouse Mayes and Guthrie Kinnard and Christian Brooks and thought they were great people and dynamite players. We did a lot of blues with Snooky Duke, mostly Stevie Ray stuff, real hard-edged stuff. I like that stuff, too. It was just a situation where I wasn't the boss. I didn't have any say over what we played or didn't play. I was kind of yearning to be back in my own situation. I stayed with it for about two years. Financially, it was a successful band. We worked a lot. When I finally did quit my day job I was still with Snooky Duke. I started Texas Slim and The Gems within one month after quitting my day job.

Now with The Gems, I have Kenny and Andy back. We've just added the best bass player I've played with in my life, Bill Cornish. His progress is so rapid we hope to have a studio date soon. I think by April we'll be in the studio. We just did a live DAT tape at Schooner's and may put some of that out as well. We have lots of people wanting tapes. We're on a mission and we're on a very positive track. We play a wide variety of blues. Hard-edged blues, traditional blues, blues so quiet you can hear people talking and glasses clink. Right now we've got about a dozen original songs. We want to eventually have three sets of originals so we can use the standards as fill-ins to mix things up. We are totally committed to blues. All kinds of blues, but blues. If you hear an R&B tune, you know that the next one is going to be more hard-core blues. We like to mix it up a bit to keep the people on the dance floor. The clubs expect that. That shuffle and dance beat helps us. Then we kick back into a slow blues and all the blues freaks light up and lean forward in their seats. You may even see some acoustic blues in future gigs. That's not gone away from my repertoire. I still have my acoustic songs. They relax me like no other music can. It's hard, when you're packing so much gear, to carry an acoustic guitar, too. I usually don't in the group situation, but I may try a solo gig just to get it out there.

This is the first band in which I've really played the regional circuit. We've played in Topeka, Kansas, at the Getaway. They book folks like Joe Kubek, The Crawl, and Little Jimmy King. It's a great spot. The Ritz in Wichita. I'm booked in Arkansas, mainly clubs in the six- to ten-hour driving range. We've played Huey's in Memphis. We went there once and found out Jay Sheffield, the M.C. of the W. C. Handy awards, books that club. We sent him a tape and he thought it was okay. He was a little hesitant to bring us in, but he booked us because Mike Morgan and Joe Kubek had said we are all right. He came up to us after our first set and said "Dynamite! Any time you are coming through, give us a call!" Our biggest show so far was up in Cambridge, Massachusetts, at Dan Aykroyd's club, House of Blues. We sold out two hours before show time and turned away 200 at the door, in the rain! We're already booked there again for Memorial Day weekend, doing two shows a night. They're opening up several more of those clubs nationwide so that may cause us to expand our circuit a bit!

I think right now things are really good for the blues. I heard John Lee Hooker is finally rich from the success of *The Healer*. Finally, after forty years he's getting rich! Buddy Guy's getting rich from *Damn Right I Got the Blues*. I see that as part of a trend. We actually have it a lot easier than them because they've broken down some of the barriers. Hopefully, I won't have to wait forty years before I get *the* record deal. There's a lot of major labels signing blues acts. The Red Devils are on Def American, which is Warner Brothers. MCA, Point Blank, Charisma, and Virgin are others. Robert Cray is on Mercury Polygram. Buddy Guy's Silvertone label is actually RCA. I see a lot of others that are probably going to jump in. The mainstream rock market has fragmented into so many different styles, how can you possibly keep up with them all? How do you tell pop from alternative from heavy metal from grunge from rap and whatever? They're all kind of coming into their own, and I see blues maybe standing on its own and becoming another mainstream thing. Selling consistent numbers of units and becoming just another piece of the pie. I think blues is big enough right now that I don't see why MTV doesn't do maybe a two-hour show each week just on blues. I can't believe it hasn't broken into that league by now. Major labels are the ones that control those markets, and with the number of big boys moving into blues, it just has to be a matter of time. If they're going to sing blues, they're going to have to promote them.

BNOIS KING

January 21, 1943– ; interview by Don O, 2000

BNOIS KING, DALLAS, CA. 2002. PHOTOGRAPH BY DON O.

There are plenty of blues bands with two guitarists, but blues bands with two lead guitarists are rare indeed. One such band is from right here in Dallas. Either Smokin' Joe Kubek or Bnois King could have a solo career in the blues world. Together, one plus one equals more than two. Between 1992 and 2000 they released one album on the Netherlands' Double Trouble label and five CDs on Bullseye Blues, toured all fifty states and many foreign counties, were nominated for W. C. Handy Awards, and held the number-one spot on the *Living Blues* Radio Poll. Whether either could have accomplished those things alone is debatable, but together they have made it look easy. There are no doubts in blues circles that they are still on their way up. The band released its newest CD, *Roadhouse Research*, on Blind Pig Records. It charted number one on the *Living Blues* Radio Poll in March 2003.

Joe and Bnois have distinctly different styles. Joe has a rapid-fire, staccato, blues machine-gun style, while Bnois has a smooth, fluid, flowing, jazzy style. They combine two of the most popular blues guitar styles ever to come out of Texas into a sound that is both old and new. Bnois King's vocals, discovered very late in his career, add another powerful dimension to the band. He brings together a smooth mix of Junior Parker's sound with a delivery and stage presence that is among the best in the business.

I was born in a little old town about thirty miles from Monroe, Louisiana, called Delhi. Music was always in my consciousness. I can't ever remember not beating, pickin,' or pullin' on something trying to get some sounds out. My grandmother was heavy into religion. She was sanctified, holy-fied, and everything else. There was always a lot of music around. She bought a guitar, I think with the intention of learning to play it herself, but she never did. I think I must have been around eight or nine years old when I discovered it and picked it up and started bamming and beating on it. I have seven brothers and two sisters, and not a one of them plays anything. My mother and grandmother couldn't play anything. I don't know where it came from. I never saw my dad. Maybe it came from him. I guess it mainly came from church, the radio, and watching people through the years. By the time I was about ten I was able to play a few things on it.

During this time Jimmy Reed, Chuck Berry, Fats Domino, all those people were pretty much Top 40. That's what I heard on the radio. We could pick up this real good radio station in Memphis where I heard a lot of Howlin' Wolf, Muddy Waters, John Lee Hooker, all those people. What really caught my attention, I didn't know what it was at the time, was jazz. I just knew it had a sound that I liked. I still don't know why it does. My parents thought I was crazy. It wasn't popular. I had to really turn the knobs to find it, but every now and then I'd find some.

My grandmother would take me into church, and that's where I first started to try to play behind people. I'd make a few sounds behind the people in church. Then one day I met a guy named Blind James. He played for a gospel group and actually knew how to play a guitar. That's when I found out I was tuning it wrong. He taught me how to do it right and taught me some chords. So I started to get a little bit better.

We didn't have a music teacher at our school, Boley High, until the last couple of years I was there. A guy named James Moody finally came from New Orleans when I was in eighth grade. He heard me messin' with my guitar. Turned out he had a band called The New Sounds which was a big band, twenty-piece orchestra. He heard me and took me under his wing. He played piano, but he was really a sax player. He started to teach me about music techniques and about the history of music. Where different stuff came from. The first time I heard names like Leadbelly was from him. He taught me about all these different people. He couldn't play guitar, but he would sit down and play something on the piano and I would learn it. All by ear. I learned my first jazz tune through him. One night he decided to put me in the band. That was right when Elvis Presley had made it big. It almost became mandatory for a band to have a guitar. He helped make a guitar a hot item, to the point if people didn't see a guitar in the band, they didn't want to see the band. Now he didn't want me to play my guitar, just stand there and hold it. This was the first gig I ever played, and it was at Grambling College. Paid me fifteen dollars. At the time I was working on a milk truck. I had to get up at two o'clock in the morning to deliver milk, and that was only paying fifteen dollars a week! So I said, "Hey! What's wrong with this picture?" All I was doing was holding my guitar, and I got a whole week's pay. I knew right then I wasn't going to run behind a milk truck getting chased by dogs anymore. That's when

I decided I needed to pursue music. I got really serious when I saw I could actually make some money.

When I started playing blues and got away from the church thing, my grandmother left Louisiana. I haven't seen her from that day to this. I don't know if she was just disappointed or what. It may not have had a thing to do with me, but being that age, that's what I thought, and I guess I still think that today. I went to a Catholic school my first two or three years, and she paid for that. She had high hopes for me. She wanted me to go to college. She did not want me to be a musician. She did not want that. She wanted me to amount to something else. In her mind, when I got serious about that guitar, I failed.

James Moody's band was comprised of a lot of instructors. Some were from Baton Rouge, some New Orleans, Grambling, Ruston, and neighboring areas. There were high school music teachers from Monroe and West Monroe that also had their own bands. They were all part of this one big band with James Moody. Naturally, I felt pretty intimidated in that band, so I eventually just quit and joined a bunch of street guys, like me, who were just playing by ear. They were called Jo Jo and The Night Creatures. I felt a lot more comfortable with them. That's how I got my experience on playing stuff like Jimmy Reed. That was popular, so that's what we did. James Brown was starting to get hot around then, so we added that. Just the contemporary music of that time. After doing that for a while I decided I needed to get out of Louisiana.

I had an aunt in Houston, so I made contact with her and she said, "Come on." I must have been about sixteen. Man, what I saw in Houston was frightening! At the time Albert Collins had a hot number out called "The Freeze." Joe Hughes was there, but I don't know if he had any records out or not. He had a band that could jump from playing Muddy Waters, Howlin Wolf, etc., to "Killer Joe" by Quincy Jones. It was a five-piece band with guitar, bass, keyboards, sax, and trumpet. I remember that band real well because I was so impressed with it. It was in the Third Ward at a club called the Club 500. All the old blues cats know about that club. It was the hot spot. That and the Club Matinee, which was in [the Fifth Ward]. The Eldorado Ballroom was right across the street from the Club 500. I saw folks like Joe, Clarence Hollimon, Wonder Boy Travis, and Melvin Sparks (he was monstrous!). I mean it was frightening. All of them were just head and shoulders over me, and I had an opportunity to sit and watch them play. I was in the clubs every night. I wasn't in Houston for more than a couple of months because I could see I needed to learn more. I went back to Monroe and decided to stay away from the city for a while until I got my stuff together.

One of my friends in Monroe was named Sonny Green. He played with a band called Little Melvin. He eventually moved on to Amarillo, Texas. Several months later he sent me a bus ticket. That's back when there was still a big Strategic Air Command base there. There were a whole lot of airmen and a whole lot of money in that town. There was a club called the High Hat Club, which was open all night every night. A band could play there seven nights a week and never have to move their equipment. At that time the club owner owned all the equipment anyway, so he could tell you what to do. We had a good band there. We did that for a few years, then Sonny and I moved to Wichita Falls. All this was during the 1960s, and the exact dates are kind of foggy. I was experimenting with all kind of stuff around then, so don't ask me the dates. They had a club there on Flood Street where everything happened seven nights a week. We never made a whole lot of money, but we got to play every night, pay the bills, and get our chops together. There was an Air Force base there, too, so there were plenty of people coming out.

I started getting pretty good around this time and started to meet some people. I actually went back to Houston and played a gig with Johnny "Guitar Watson." This was with a band and drummer named Dusty Rose. I played rhythm guitar. It was about a week-long engagement, then I went back to Wichita Falls. I also got to open up for Lou Rawls at the base up in Altus, Oklahoma. This was with a band called The Soul Enticers. We opened again for him down in Wichita Falls.

The 1970s showed up, and I kind of got frustrated with music. I got a day job at a car lot washing cars, airing the tires, and keeping the batteries charged. That was my gig for a couple of years. I didn't own a guitar back then, but I would go down to the music store almost every day and pick up one and play on my lunch break.

I got the itch again around 1974 or 1975 and bought me a guitar and amp. I finally had a car and a little money in the bank because I had been holding a regular job for a couple of years. I was in my early thirties, and that was the first car I ever owned! I picked up and moved to Denver for a while, but there wasn't much happening there. So I came back to Wichita Falls, hooked up with a couple of guys, and formed a trio. We called ourselves The Grand Wazoo. We ended up back in Colorado again! Still nothing going. I picked up a few little gigs playing jazz, but not enough to live on. So it was back to Wichita Falls and my day job.

About 1978 I went to a place in Fort Worth called the Aquarium. There was a band in there called Just Us. They were playing sort of a fusion/funk/jazz mix. I asked them if I could sit in, and they liked what they heard. They asked me to join the band, and I went off and thought about it for a while. Tommy Hopkins was the band leader. I went back to work in Wichita Falls, then one day it just hit me. I hopped on the phone and told them I was ready to move to Dallas. I had a 1974 Cutlass Supreme. I sold that and bought a 1969 station wagon, paid cash for it, threw everything I owned in the back, and drove to Dallas. That was in 1979. I drove directly to the Arandas Club in South Dallas, clothes and everything in the car, took my guitar and amp out, and played a gig. I was with that band for a couple of years playing nothing but black clubs in Dallas and Fort Worth. Sonny's Lounge, E.T.'s, the Arandas, and other clubs, mostly in South Dallas.

Then I met George Forms, who had a duo called One Plus One. It was piano and bass with a drum machine. Well, the piano player quit. They were playing a place called Smokey's, a barbecue place on Lemmon. The band set up in a little corner. Somebody told him about me and the fact that I knew chords. He came and talked to me, and that worked out for about three years. We mostly played South Dallas, too, but occasionally we'd do a gig at Mr. C's in the West End. I also did a gig with Big Joe Williams at the Fairmont. One Plus One opened, and they liked my playing well enough that they asked me if I'd like to back Big Joe in his big band. That was cool. The duo was paying well, but eventually my partner got a little greedy on me, so I quit.

I was back stumblin' around Dallas in the early 1980s, and I ran into a lady keyboard player, Kendra Holt. She started taking me around to all these places I had never seen. I remember the Prohibition Room was like a flashback. I thought the blues as I had known it was dead. No one was playing it in South Dallas. There was soul blues, like Z. Z. Hill, Tyrone Davis, Little Milton, and Denise LaSalle, but that was all you could hear. I didn't know anyone was still playing Jimmy Reed or Freddie King. I went back one night and sat in with Hash Brown or somebody. I didn't make a connection that night, but it felt good.

Later they were trying to start up Mother Blues again. I walked in that place one night and I saw this big guy. It was Joe Kubek. I didn't know him and he didn't know me. We just stood there and looked at each other. Somehow we ended up in the dressing room of the performers that night, and we still didn't speak. We also ended up onstage during the jam, and even played some together. Even though we never spoke, I remembered him because he could play. I left that night and didn't think about it again.

Then one night I went down to Poor David's Pub, and there was Joe Kubek. He came over and said, "Say, man, I remember you. You want to play a little bit?" That was the first time we ever spoke. When we got onstage together, it was immediately like I had been playing with the guy all my life. There was no clashing, no competition. Every time I would do something, he would do something that made me sound good. Every time he did something, I would do the same. It was just automatic. I had played with a lot of guitar players, but it always turned into a shooting match or a duel or just completely clashed. This was without any conversation about it. He told me "This gig don't pay much." (That was really stretching it! Sometimes we made two dollars!) "But why don't you come over here on Mondays and sit in with us." At the time he had Phil Campbell on drums and Paul Jenkins on bass. Bobby Chitwood would sit in from time to time, as would Paul Harrington. Occasionally, Sam Myers would join us.

I didn't really start singing until I was with Joe. I sang one or two songs a night when I was with One Plus One. It was always Jimmy Reed. I never saw myself as a singer. Every time I did, the house went wild, but I never put two and two together. It never added up. It was a joke to me. I was kidding. It was just a novelty. I never thought about singing seriously until I got with Kubek. Joe said, "Somebody is going to have to sing in this band." I told him I knew a couple of songs, but at that time I did not even own a single blues record. I rushed out and bought a whole bunch of records by folks like B. B. King, Albert Collins, Howlin' Wolf, Muddy Waters, Sonny Boy Williamson, John Lee Hooker, and Little Milton. That was my crash refresher course in the blues. Then I started learning the songs like "Buzz Me" that no one else was covering. I started going to the jam sessions to see what everyone else was singing. They were doing all the obvious songs like "The Thrill Is Gone," "Sweet Sixteen," and "Stormy Monday." I started learning all the obscure songs no one else was doing so that we would be different. Every Monday I would come in with a new song. That's how I became a singer. Before that I had never even considered it. It was there all along, I just didn't know it.

I had also never written an original song in my life. I had made up a few jazz riffs, but that was about it. I had never been on any recordings, either. Lyrics? I didn't ever think about singing, so why would I write any lyrics? That was foreign to me. Now that's one of my primary jobs.

Our first CD, *The Axe Man*, happened at Dallas Sound Lab. Marc Benno was in some kind of management position there, and he talked his boss into doing a blues record. We did it late at night, maybe it was two nights. I forgot all about it. I didn't think it would ever see the light of day. Next thing I know, it comes back on CD. All I know is they released it in Europe somehow. It came out just a few days before *Steppin' Out*, our first CD on Bullseye. I was totally surprised. I remember posing for the picture on the cover in Montgomery, Alabama. I don't know how they got that picture and got that on there. I haven't seen a nickel from that release. Joe hasn't either, I think. We bugged them for a while, to no avail. We called them, we had our lawyer call them. Ain't nothin' happenin' there.

One night Phil [Campbell] taped us on a little tape deck and sent it down to Antone's. They liked it and booked us. It was a Wednesday night or something, so few people showed up, but Clifford [Antone] liked us. They invited us back again. That's when we began to get the idea we had something going. We started playing little gigs in Ardmore, Longview, Shreveport, Abilene, local and regional touring. We thought we were really stretching out when we started playing places like Chattanooga, Tennessee, and Wichita, Kansas. Phil was doing all the booking. We finally figured out that the only way we were going to make a living was to go out on the road. Joe had expired around D-FW and I had, too. We'd played every little place around here. You couldn't hardly make thirty dollars a night, and it was getting worse and worse. We eventually ended up with an agent, and he got us farther down the road to places like Memphis. That's how the record deal came about. The club owner knew the folks at Bullseye, invited them down, and they signed us.

The only big city we haven't played is Milwaukee. I love playing Manny's Car Wash in New York City. Any night of the week there, we have a house full of folks that have our records, know who we are, and have been listening to us. It's always packed, and we are never there on a weekend. I like B. B. King's in L.A., the Zoo Bar in Lincoln, there's so many places. I wish I had my book so I could rattle them all off.

Charting number one on the *Living Blues* Radio Poll made me feel elated. They don't give that up real easy. That says something to me. At last people are starting to take us seriously. For a while, I don't think people thought we were going to last. I think the longevity and being consistent with what we do is important. We're not blues purists. We know that. We can't play pure blues. We can't. There's just too much stuff mixed in me, and Joe's got too much stuff mixed in him. We're not pure anything. I think a lot of people didn't take us seriously for a long time. That's kind of like a seal of approval. We are now approved blues guys.

On the stage we are a nondrinking band. Everybody knows that coming in. Joe and I have been through that and are lucky we lived through it. I've been sober ten years now. We don't tell guys not to drink, just don't drink around us or when you're working. No substance of any kind in the truck. Nothing onstage, and have a clear head at showtime. Those are the only rules. Some people just can't stick to those rules and can't understand why they're so important to us.

This business doesn't pay a lot of money, and you put a lot of miles on the road. People come along and think it's a picnic, and they find it is a hard, grueling job. It is hard work. When they see New York City for the first time, it's exciting. By the fourth or fifth time it's, "Oh no, New York City again!" After a while, it's just another gig. Some people just get the travel out of their system and they're ready to go. There's personality conflicts, too. When you're cooped up in a van with the same four people, day after day, if you can't get along, or at least respect each other, you have a real problem.

I told you I was late in my life when I got my driver's license. I was thirty-one years old. I needed my birth certificate to get it, so I called my mom and she got it for me. When it came back, it came back B. Noris King. I guess they couldn't understand her. Like I have an initial for my first name! That's what's on my passport. I'm stuck with that! Whenever I write a check or something that's how I have to sign my name! People at home know my real name. If they ever have to look at my license to do an obituary it's going to come up B. Noris. You have the real scoop, now.

I had an anxious feeling when I heard we were going to be playing Poor David's recently. I wanted us to do well there, since that's where we started. I was not expecting it to fill up and pack out like it did. It was totally beyond my expectations. I didn't think our fans would come out there to see us since we'd been playing the Blue Cat so much. They were there. A lot of the folks that did come out weren't Blue Cat people. I saw a lot of strange faces, but they knew about us. . . .

The only thing that could pull me off the road would be a real bad illness. If I had to do it on crutches, I'd do it. I'd have to be completely immobilized. If there is any way I can be rolled or pushed out there, I'm going. Johnny Copeland was the greatest inspiration to me of any human being. Here's a guy waiting on a heart transplant, and he was still playing gigs. He was uplifting other people in the hospital. You would think he would retire, but that never crossed his mind. How can it ever cross mine?

ANDREW "JUNIOR BOY" JONES

October 10, 1948– ; interview by Don O, 1998

ANDREW "JUNIOR BOY" JONES, CA. 1999. PHOTOGRAPH BY DON O.

Here's a great Dallas musician who has worked with Freddie King, Johnnie Taylor, Katie Webster, and other big-name blues stars. He has his own small, Dallas-based record label, GalexC Records, which is probably better known in England than in Dallas. For several years he has played guitar with one of the best-known blues men in the business, Charlie Musselwhite. He has recorded for several different labels, including RSO (on Freddie King's *Larger than Life* LP) and four albums for Alligator Records (three with Charlie, one with Katie Webster). Yet in his hometown of Dallas, few people outside of the tight-knit blues community have heard of Andrew "Junior Boy" Jones.

My grandmother gave me the nickname "Junior Boy." I've been Junior Boy ever since I can remember. I don't know why. I am a junior. My father is Andrew Jones Sr. People think Junior Boy is my real name. Bruce Iglauer [Alligator Records president] loves that name. He thinks it's real cool. Some people have a hard time calling me that, but it's cool. That's all I ever heard. Some people call me Andrew, some people call me Junior Boy. I guess I don't know who I am!

My uncle Adolphus Sneed is a sax player from the old school. He's about seventy-eight years old now. He was real popular around here. He had a big band with a full horn section, grand piano, the whole thing. They played the Wintergarden a lot. My mom was a singer with big bands, but she stopped singing after I was born.

I set up the GalexC label to record, mainly just for local exposure. The first thing we did was R. L. Griffin doing "Cry Cry Cry," Bobby Bland's old song, and "Gotta Be Foolin You," which I wrote. That's when I first tried my hand at producing. It was ironic because it was all R. L.'s money; he was the executive producer. Somehow the 45 got over to London and was a semi-hit. I got a letter from the editor of *Shades of Soul* magazine over there asking me about the record and wanting to do an interview. The way my label is spelled, GalexC, came about during the graphic arts setup for the label. It was supposed to be Galaxy, with the city of Dallas backed by a background of stars. The artist spelled it like that to be different. So I said why not, we'll just leave it that way, and that's how we registered it. Anyway, when the guys called me from England they were asking to speak to the president of "Galexk," that's how they were pronouncing it. I first told them they had the wrong number. Then I got to thinking about the funny spelling and said, "Wait a minute, I guess that *is* me!" I went on and gave the interview, and the record did well over there. It didn't play a big role for R. L. at that point, but it has helped him later on.

A friend of mine, Norman Darwin, from *Blues & Rhythm* magazine, asked Alligator if he could do an interview with me. We had been talking for a while, and I mentioned R. L. Griffin and my label, GalexC. His mouth flew open and he said, "Whoa! We got to start over." That thing brought around another opportunity where a label over there called Black Grape is talking about releasing R. L.'s latest album on CD. Al Braggs did some of the production work on that, too. We're finalizing the contract stuff right now. This year should be interesting for R. L. Griffin.

After working with R. L. for a while, I went back and worked for Johnnie Taylor again. He knew that I was going to leave at the end of 1987 because I wanted to join up with Tony Cole and Russell Jackson from B. B. King's band. They had a hot group out on the West Coast called Silent Partners. Tony had played with Bobby Bland, plus I had played with Freddie King, so we were sort of the new breed that had played with the legends. That gave us some legitimacy.

We were with Bon Ton West, which is Katie Webster's agency. I met Katie, and it was just a love affair, like brother and sister, right off the bat. She's still one of my favorite people. We worked with her for about a year. We did the *Swamp Boogie Queen* album with her on Alligator. After that, things weren't working out too well. The Silent Partners were a three-man operation, and the other two had been together since 1974. There were three votes, and I was always the odd man out. There was also the creative situation; other people were making the decisions. I had obligations here in Dallas, but I was living out in Sacramento. It just got to be too much.

Around this time we were doing sessions with different people, and one of those was with Charlie Musselwhite. Our band was hot. I hate to brag, but we were good, real good. We had the experience, having played with some of the best blues people of all time, so people were asking us to do session work. We were doing this Frankie Lee album and a Sonny Rhodes album out on the West Coast. I met Charlie on one of those sessions. We found we had a mutual friend in Little Joe Blue. He and Joe had been real tight back during their drinking days. We were sharing stories and we kind of hit it off. Then he asked the Silent Partners to back him up on a tour with John Lee Hooker. Hooker was the best man at his wedding, so he and Hooker are real tight. We were interested since Katie was over touring in Europe and we had the time. We were booked as a double bill, with us opening for Charlie, then backing his show. Midway through the tour, up in Saskatoon, Canada, the Silent Partners thing kind of came to a head. I had made my mind up to leave the tour, bring somebody else in, and go back to Texas. Charlie was not a part of our band, but he observed what was going on. He wanted to start his own backing band and asked me to be a part of it. I told him I was going to go back to Texas, cut some demos, and try it on my own. He told me, "Why don't you stick with me? I ain't never cut a demo in my life. I'll see you get all the exposure you need." A few months later he sent me the tickets, and we went off on tour to Australia. I've been with him for six years now.

When I started off, we had two different people than we have now. We had a good lady drummer from San Francisco, Linda Geiger. I felt we needed a little stronger drummer with more punch, so I suggested Tommy Hill, who I knew here in Dallas. We first brought him in to do a gig in Boston in 1988. I warned him that the intensity level was a little higher and that he'd have to do some real playing. Tommy said, "Yeah, yeah. I've been playing, too." I had gone over the show with him, so he knew the show mentally. By the end of that first show his hands were blistered and bleeding. The intensity is that high. He was busy. Not playing hard, but playing a lot. He wore gloves for a long time until he got used to what was going on. After he got into it, he was a big improvement for us. He is a very innovative drummer.

About two years ago we decided to replace the bass player, too. I knew Rudolph Parks from here in Dallas, so we brought him in. That didn't work out, so Charles [Musselwhite] started talking about bringing in Felton [Crews] from Chicago. After Charlie mentioned he had played with Miles Davis, that was it! Tommy also has a jazz background, so we knew it was going to be real exciting. It's been beautiful ever since. We just recorded our third album on Alligator. We've also been doing some stuff with Dan Aykroyd and his House of Blues label.

This will be my third time going to Australia with Charlie. We've been to Hawaii, New Zealand, Fiji, Japan, England, Germany, Poland, Holland, Sweden, Norway, Denmark, all over. We were supposed to do Scotland and Ireland this last tour, but something got messed up with the booking. When you go to Europe it gets unreal. They look at this music as a culture. They respect it. In Norway they even send kids to school to learn to play blues. They take it real serious.

We're on the road about nine months at a time. We haven't played here [in Dallas] in about two years. Hopefully, with this new album we'll be playing here soon. Junior Watson and Larry Taylor from Canned Heat are on the new one. The Five Blind Boys from Alabama with Charlie [Musselwhite]doing acoustic. There's a broad range of styles from the Forties up to today, which is the stuff I'm on. Charlie's trying to move up to the next level, like Bonnie Raitt, modern yet traditional. It's an interesting CD.

I am going to do something [in the studio] this year, hopefully with my sons, they're both players, and my friends, Tommy and Felton. There's going to be some blues. In fact, I've already got a blues track cut. It's going to be different stuff I like. I don't know how I'm going to market it or anything. It may be more hardcore blues. I'll do my rendition of "Hideaway," It's a little different from Freddie [King]. I like to beef it up a little. I've got some songs I've already written, and there's going to be a lot of original stuff. I want to do it with my kids because they know to do what Daddy says!

Aykroyd is talking about a *Blues Brothers* sequel, and he's interested in having Charlie in it. He likes the band a lot. He knows us all by name. He's a down-to-earth guy, kind of reminds me of Clark Kent. He showed us a good time up at his home in Kingston, Ontario.

I'd like to see the Dallas scene come around a little more. It is a little lax at the clubs. These young blues musicians like Randy McAllister don't get the support they should. I talked to Charlie last week, and I told him I was jamming with a guy that reminds me of a young Charles Musselwhite. He said, "Oh, yeah? Is he good-lookin' like me?" Randy is a fine young harp player. After being other places like Chicago, New York, the West Coast, you realize that people here don't take this music scene seriously. Musicians have something to say. I've been places where the musicians are maybe not as good as here, and people would come back and tell me about something I was doing. That impresses me when people really pay attention. I don't understand people who come out and have a beer and don't pay attention to the music. People are spilling their guts on stage. I was really appreciated out on the West Coast, but here I'm nothing. You have to leave town to make it and get the respect. It shouldn't be that way. I'm doing the exact same thing as I was doing here, yet out there people appreciate it more. They're showing videos of me in some clubs. It's not like I'm on some big head trip or something, but I like to be appreciated for what I do because I'm out there doing it for real. I'm not doing it for you to enjoy your beer. I just wish people were a little more appreciative here.

GREGG SMITH

February 7, 1951– ; interview by Don O, 1993

Gregg Smith is definitely a blues singer. At the end of his show he is always drenched in sweat. Not from doing somersaults or running around the stage. Just from singing. When Gregg Smith sings, you know it's coming from deep inside. You don't just hear it, you feel it. His album on the Ultrax label, *It's My Time*, couldn't have a more apt title. It should be his time. He has definitely paid his dues. Yet Gregg is another great Texas bluesman who is probably better known in Europe than in his own home state of Texas. Since this interview was done, Smith has toured extensively with Lucky Peterson, including several trips to Europe. His third album, *I'm Gonna Rock Ya*, was released on Ultrax records, distributed by Ichiban.

I was born in Honey Grove, Texas [about seventy miles northeast of Dallas]. My family was from that area, my grandfather, uncles, everybody was up there. Most of them are still there. My mother was a single parent, and she took care of us by running a little cafe and selling bootleg liquor on the side. They had a jukebox, and me and my brothers used to play that jukebox and dance and do the bebop to the jukebox.

I was amazed by the effect music would have on people. To see the reaction of grownups to my dancing and singing was great for me as a child. They rewarded us by tossing change at us, and that made it even more interesting. I was just three or four years old. My brothers were five and six. None of us were in school yet. I went on to school in Honey Grove for the first and second grade. Then my stepdaddy came into our life and we migrated to Albuquerque, New Mexico. I put together my first band there when I was about thirteen or fourteen years old. It was called The Soul Flames. We played teen centers, Job Corps centers, and the Elks Club. We got kicked out of the Elks Club! We had convinced the father of one of the band members, who was an Elk, to let us come and do a performance for them. It was going to be our first paying engagement. We thought we were a lot more polished than what we were. To us we sounded great. The only person who knew how to tune up in the band was the guitar player! I guess he was just kind of carrying the rest of us and hoping we would eventually develop an ear. I was singing a lot of James Brown stuff, Wilson Pickett, Otis Redding, Marvin Gaye, Solomon Burke, that kind of thing. It was like a ten- or twelve-piece band. Horns and everything! We used to walk around and drag instruments up and down the neighborhood with our little cases. We'd walk from house to house and play till the parents would run us off! We used to fight as much as rehearse.

I'll never forget that first gig at the Elks Club. We struck down on the first chord for "Papa's Got a Brand New Bag," and we were so badly out of tune that people just got up and started to leave instantly! The manager was rushing back there trying to stop us before all the customers were gone. By the time he got back there we had pretty much cleaned the house! . . . He came back there carrying a pair of pliers and walked up and slammed them down on top of the amplifier. We were all plugged into this one amp. It was the only one we had! He said, "Get your stuff, get outta here, and don't you come around here no more!" He gave us ten dollars, and we split it. It was about a dollar apiece. That kinda made us get our act together. We went back into rehearsals and practiced for five or six months. Then we entered a battle of the bands contest with an older gentleman, a grownup, who already had his own band, Doc Ren and the Purple Blues. We ended up winning the contest and were named best band in the city. We were doing soul stuff like "Tighten Up," "Funky Broadway," stuff like that. Winning that contest gave us the confidence to go ahead on.

We moved to Portland, Oregon, when I was about seventeen. I got into the community choir, the high school band, and joined a working band, The Antoine Brothers. We would play at a place called Cleo's Lounge. All the other guys were much older than me. They turned me on to the showmanship part of performing. Nolan Struck was the lead singer with the band, and by the time I graduated from high school he had moved back to Chicago. He invited me to come out there and work with him, and I took him up on it after I finished school. My mother really wanted me to go to college. I told her I'd just finished twelve years' worth of school and I didn't even want to think about another year of school right then! So I went on to Chicago and worked with Nolan. I'll never forget the first night I performed with him. We got off the gig about three-thirty or four in the morning. I was ready to turn in, and he said no, we were going to another club, have some breakfast, and then do another show! This was late Sunday night into Monday morning. So that's when I first got introduced into the Monday morning blues sessions in Chicago. We got to the place about six or seven Monday morning, and the place was packed. I couldn't believe it! McKinley Mitchell was there, Tyrone Davis, Johnny Dollar, and several others. I was amazed. Everybody was getting up and performing. Dancing was going on, food was going on. It was like a Saturday night! I had never seen anything like that. We played all over Chicago. I'll never forget one night outside of Pepper's Lounge. Me, Junior Wells, Buddy Guy, and Nolan Struck all standing around on the corner passing a bottle of Old Crow. Man, I thought I was poopin' in high cotton! That really inspired me. I got a great reaction from the crowds in Chicago, and I started feeling I could get on stage with guys like that and hold my own.

Then Uncle Sam sent me a draft letter. Back then, if you were in school, kept a full schedule, and kept your grades up, you didn't have to go. Around this same time, late August, my friends were telling me, "You didn't bring no clothes for a Chicago winter!" So my mother got her wish, and I went back to Oregon to go to college. I got some grant money and majored in music theory. I never finished that degree, but I'm just a few hours short. About this time I formed my own group, Gregg Smith and Shades of Brown. I had a lot of very strong players. The Wilson Pickett Band had come through there and broke up. Some of the band members teamed up with me. Willie Gresham was our awesome saxophonist. We would have a couple of days a week when we would have access to the rehearsal hall at the college arts center. Before we would even attempt to do a song, each player would have to break down their part on their instrument and then write out the music. This is how we would study. We broke songs down before we even began to play it. We'd analyze it, then we'd put it together and rehearse it. We were so tight from that disciplined approach. It taught us so much musically. We were opening for groups like Albert Collins in Oakland, Portland, all around the West Coast. I thought I was really on my way then. By the time I got to be about thirty-two, I was opening for folks like James Brown. I did three dates with James. I also began to do a lot of writing about that time.

By 1983 I began to feel I had outgrown being a local act in Oregon, so I picked up stakes and moved to Dallas. I had a lot of kinfolk in this region, being from Honey Grove. I also wanted to be more in the southern blues belt. I didn't have a car. I had sold my vehicle in Oregon, came down here, and started from scratch. Brought my publicity, bios, newspaper articles with me from back there. I immediately found out how good the musicians were at North Texas State [now the University of North Texas], and within a week or two I was up there recruiting band members. I put together a group of five musicians, and I used to catch the Trailways bus to Denton twice a week to rehearse. We got real tight, then I brought them over to South Dallas. I did my first blues gig here at the South Dallas Blues Festival in 1984 with Little Milton, Charlie Roberson, R. L. Griffin, Vernon Garrett, and myself. We got a lot of attention and got a good article written in *The Dallas Morning News* from that show. That later led to a gig at Boone's Club, where I met my wife. She was the bartender there. She had heard me down at the Dreamland Inn on Lamar and had told the club owner about me. He came down the next night and invited me to play at his place for a couple of months. That got me a little better known around town. A booking agent later introduced me to the Addison area, the Club Memphis out there, and we began to work up there quite a bit. Then I started working up and down Greenville Avenue. I think I pretty much worked every club that had live entertainment down there.

My album *The Texas Blues Wailer* was recorded live at the Rose Garden in 1985. Producer Phil York was a big help to me at this time. He had access to the equipment and put it all together. Helped me get the publicity packages out and everything. We're still real good friends. I'll always be indebted to him for his help. We pitched it to a label in Germany, but they were looking for something slightly different. So that recording really went nowhere. I used it mostly as a demo for clubs around the area, and it was a big plus having a professionally recorded demo cassette like that. I think some day we may still put that out.

Butch Bonner and I produced *Money Talks* in 1990, and it was distributed in the U.S through Ichiban. It was a finished product, and all they had to do was put it out. I went to Atlanta with Tommy Quon and his newest discovery, rap artist Vanilla Ice, to meet with John Abbey of Ichiban. They had previously expressed an interest in my product, but Tommy wanted to do a three-album package deal. So he said, "We'll let you have Gregg if you try Don Diego and Vanilla Ice." They signed the deal the same day, and we got a February 26, 1990, release date for all three projects. A month later, Ice had sold 50,000 to 60,000 copies, so they knew they had a hit rap record. Once that record went crazy, Tommy took that one from Ichiban and bumped it up to SBK. In the middle of all the negotiations and scrappin' for the Vanilla Ice dollars with Ichiban, *Money Talks* was abandoned in the middle of the sea with no paddle. That album still hasn't been promoted like it should have been. I think time will tell. It has the quality. It was done from the heart, and I think that comes across. I'm still getting airplay in a lot of different parts of the country, and it has been out since 1990. I licensed it to Prestige records in Europe which is distributed by Sony. *Money Talks* has been repackaged and renamed *Party Warrior* over in Europe. We added two songs that haven't been released over here yet, and the twelve-song CD package is doing quite well in the European market. One of the songs, "Lover's Hangover," was the number-one pick of the critics in *Blues and Soul* magazine in Europe [issue no. 619, August 25, 1992]. We've been talking about doing some touring over there this year, but nothing is set yet.

The trip to Italy came about through my hook-up with Ichiban. We took Trudy Lynn, Buster Benton, and Jerry McCain over with my band, Lazzar, for a six-week tour. We all met up in New York and flew over to Palermo, Sicily, and had a couple of days to rehearse together. We'd never met before, but Ichiban had sent us some tapes to work from earlier. I am so fortunate to have such a great band. They are fantastic players and are so disciplined. They can play behind anybody. We played our first show there in Palermo in front of a beautiful cathedral. The streets were packed with people. They kept getting closer and closer to the stage. Pushin' and pushin'! We usually try to electrify a crowd pretty good, but the promoters encouraged us not to incite the crowd too much. That was hard to do! They were afraid we'd make them riot or something. They love the blues over there. We toured a number of different resort towns all around the Mediterranean. Rode me around in a Mercedes! They had wine with every meal, breakfast, lunch, and dinner. The tables were always lined with all this great food, and we had our own personal waiters. After we finished each show, they'd give us each a bottle of wine to get on the bus with. We were practically winos by the time we came home! It was so beautiful over there. We played in one old city that had been dug up. They had a beautiful amphitheater stage. That's something, playing in an ancient amphitheater! They definitely didn't want us exciting the crowd too much in there. It was a great experience.

In 1992 I went into the studio for four and a half months to work on the *It's My Time* album for Tommy Quon's Dallas-based Ultrax label. The CD is just out. We have great plans for the *It's My Time* album but are just waiting for the proper time, financially, to push ahead with it. Tommy is a great gentleman. He believes in my talent and has invested in me quite extensively on this album. We'll be licensing it to Prestige as well. Right now I'm doing some booking work for the Venue Showroom, occasional appearances at the Longhorn Ballroom, and a few shows with Johnnie Taylor. Not too much touring. The main thing I'm working on right now is some bookings in Europe. I'm hoping to be headed back over there pretty soon.

TUTU JONES

September 9, 1966– ; interview, 2003

TUTU JONES, R. L.'S BLUES PALACE NO. 2, DALLAS, CA. 2004.

PHOTOGRAPH BY ALAN GOVENAR

I have to say life has been nice to me and taken me places and so forth. And this deal got me going, and I'm looking for more. I'm looking for more things to happen, and things are still trying to happen.

Music was in my genes. I was born with it. It comes from both sides, my dad and my mom. My mom's grandparents were musicians, too. I believe they played in churches and fish parties and stuff like that, you know, house parties during that time. So, my great-grandmother played the guitar, on my mom's side.

My great-grandmother on my mother's side played the banjo or ukulele. I call them all guitars. And then, my daddy's daddy, he messed around with the guitar a little bit. His name was Earl Jones Jr. He didn't really take it, to make nothing fancy out of it. They just loved to play and go out and play at fish parties and stuff like that and house parties, you know. But they'd always go out and see other entertainers, like John Lee Hooker and Muddy Waters, whoever came to town. I'm about the only one that's taken it [to a professional level]. Now, my daddy and my uncle and them, they kind of took it a little more seriously. They played the nightspots and this, that, and the other. My daddy, he kind of took it a little farther than my great-grandparents and things did, him and my uncle. But I'm the one that really took it even further.

My daddy's name is Johnny B. Jones Sr. My mom was named Albertha. Her maiden name was Clark.

My daddy had his band back in the Seventies, man. My daddy was a backup musician for people like Little Joe Blue and Ernie Johnson, Freddie King. All of them met back in the Sixties, like when Freddie and Johnnie Taylor and all of them first came to Dallas. My daddy was a young man then, and he played with a lot of guys like that, backing them up and traveling with them and so forth. And they all were good friends and running buddies. But after the Sixties, he kind of went out on his own, I believe, about '75 or '76. Before then, he had gotten his own little old band together, and then some guys started working with him.

My dad was a guitar player. He don't play it for a living no more. He might bang around or something, if he came around and saw my box [guitar] up in my house. I've been trying to get him to get back in it in so many ways. Sometime he feel like it and sometime he don't. I still can claim him as a guitar player. It's not that he can't do it. I believe he could if he would, just with somebody that's for real with him and get into it. He probably could play again, you know. He played electric. Me and him both played electric—acoustic guitars, too.

I started playing guitar when I was about four and a half years old or five, somewhere in there. But I did a lot of house jamming when I was that age, too. My uncle and them, they used to have a lot of house jams, you know. One of my uncles, my mother's oldest brother, had a big piano. I'll never forget. He had a great, big old piano in his living room. And he used to invite all the musicians over from time to time, and everybody would come by. My uncle, there wasn't hardly a day went by that he didn't play his piano and get something going.

My uncle was V. C. Clark. That was my mother's oldest brother. He played one of them big upright pianos that you saw during that time in the church—great, big old pianos, man, tall ones.

I'm from the south side. We stayed all over Dallas, but I originally grew up from the south side. I went to Old City Park, James Madison. I went to Gaston Middle School. I went from Old City Park School on back to Gaston, then to James Madison High School.

I started playing the drums, but that guitar thing had been in my blood. I already knew that I was going to probably be a guitar player, but this drum thing started out. So, in other words, me and my daddy both are just well-rounded musicians. We play some of everything, instruments. But anyway, the guitar and drums was our main axes. So, I started out playing drums, backing my uncle and them back in the Seventies, like '74 and '75 and on up.

We were playing clubs. I was playing these little juke joints and things, man, these beer taverns and things like that. That's where my uncle and them started out. Some of the places that we played, they stayed packed with people. Freddie King and all of them would come over and sit in when they weren't out of town. Places like the Red Fox, used to be on Harwood in South Dallas. That was a main beer joint and blues club there. I mean, everybody stopped by there. Anybody came through Dallas knew where it was at. My daddy and them met a lot of guys like Freddie [King]. And you had places like the Gold Room on Harwood. Sometimes you would have two places right across the street from one another or down the street from one another that were kickin' every weekend with some live entertainment. And they started Thursday, Friday, Saturday, Sunday. Four nights a week. That's when Dallas was really booming with the blues, from the Sixties to the Seventies. And probably way before then. I'm just counting the time that I came in on the scene. You had places like Gold Room, the Red Fox, and you had places like House of Jock. You know, Jock's came in the Seventies. We all hung out down at Jock's and played for old man Jacques down there. [His name is Jacques, but his bar is House of Jock.] And my uncle on my daddy's side once had a place down on Lamar in South Dallas, too, called, I think, H&W Blues Club. His name was Sonny Williams. That was my daddy's uncle. And we worked for him down there.

To me, Freddie King—when I was a little boy growing up, watching Freddie—Freddie King was just a normal country boy to me. But he was very, very businesslike and educated. He was a normal country boy who loved to play. He was really just everyday people to me. There was something about him that just worked like magic when he hit the stage. He was really a great influence for guys like myself coming up during that time. He also influenced Stevie Ray and Jimmie [Vaughan] when they were growing up and hanging out, watching him and other guys at Mother Blues. During that time, Freddie was still touring, but when he was at home, he would always play all the nightspots, come around and sit in.

Freddie even hit it more after whites and blacks really started together. But Freddie had done a lot of stuff up in Chicago, too, you know, before he got to Dallas. He had met a lot of blues players, like Muddy Waters, Hound Dog Taylor, Buddy Guy, John Lee Hooker, and Jimmy Reed. He had met a lot of them guys up there and got experience with the blues. He was another who had the blues born in his genes. You just can't go home, put on a record, and play the blues. This stuff's got to be in your blood. You got to come from a bloodline of it in order to make it feel right, in order to sing it. Anybody can go out there and pick up a guitar and start playing the blues. But you have to be born with this stuff. You have to be born and raised around it. For example, if you took a white guy like Stevie Ray. And they say, "Well, man, why does he sound so much like a black man?" You want to know why? He was raised around black folks, and it rubbed off on him. But he wasn't the first one to start that. What Stevie and I were doing, we were influenced by other great guys that was better than us, probably better than us and greater than us during that time, and they're the ones that started all of this stuff. So, I give all the glory to God, but I give all the most credit to guys like B. B. and Freddie and Albert and even my daddy. My daddy was part of that generation. My daddy was a motor scooter during that time he was playing. But anyway. We've all been influenced by somebody.

One thing that I liked about Stevie Ray Vaughan. He'd admit it. He'd say, "Man, if it wasn't for all the black guys that was born with this stuff and created this stuff, I don't know what I would sound like." He didn't like all that prejudice. And that was another reason why God blessed him so. Stevie was just an Oak Cliff–raised white guy who come up really admiring the black. And I admired his playing. I still love him to this day. I admire a lot of white players, because they admire the blacks. But to make a long story short, you have to really love the blues and be born in it. Now, you got more white guys now getting exposed to it than you did then. A lot of people say blues is really coming back, and I credit Z. Z. Hill and Stevie for helping to bring the blues back around.

I was working with R. L. Griffin before I stepped out solo career on this guitar thing. I always had played guitar and jams and around the house, but I never stepped out and started taking a professional concern about it until I went out solo. But anyway, when I was playing drums with R. L. Griffin and Z. Z. Hill, just before Z. Z. got back hot and started making his mark, the blues was just sitting on the back burner. And all this disco, rock, had the radio tied up, I guess it was just time for the blues to really come back. We were playing. Back during that time, the late Seventies and early Eighties, there wasn't a lot of blues bands playing that much, because disco had it so jammed up. But we was working, man, guys like me, R. L. Griffin, and maybe two to three other bands out of the Dallas area. But Z. Z. soon got his break again. It was just a blessing to go show that it was time for the blues to come back. The blues ain't gonna never die, I don't care what they say. I don't care how many musics come through here, how many music generations come through here. The blues ain't gonna never die. It's going to be here. It's something rooted in this world, and it's going to all be here. You can be rich or poor; you still can sing it. You can have some money today and broke tomorrow. Just anything. Blues comes in all kinds of shades of colors. But anyway, I credit Z. Z. Hill and Stevie Ray Vaughan, because they were just like

God sent them to bring this blues back in the door.

Oh, man, Z. Z. was one of the very guys that you can meet and you'll never forget him. He was good people. He was easy to work with. He wasn't hard to work for like a lot of guys I've met. He was a good guy that you can work for and you wouldn't be all crumbling and things when you worked with him, rehearsed with him. He was just a good guy all around. You couldn't beat him. I think what distinguished him was his not giving up, keeping the faith.

Well, Z. Z. kind of kept up with it. I think he kind of thought young, and by Z. Z. keeping up with the style was like keeping up with the young generation, which I do, too. I never get so far off into my own category that I can't understand people like my kids' music. So that kept Z. Z. going, motivated all those years, his faith and not giving up, keeping up with different styles of music, like I do. I like to listen to all different styles of music and try to keep up with what's going on the radio, on the FM or whatever, and you know I ain't gonna never leave the blues. And that's the way I record today. It's something about me that always keep that young generation rooted in my blues, so the young folks can dig it, not only just the older folks. When I sing my blues and play my blues, I be trying to get the younger generation to understand where they come from, because we have a lot of black generations, just basically like, "You playing the blues?" Say, "Well, this is where you come from." And to have to really sit down and listen to it to figure out where your background comes from. And B. B. said the same thing, said, "It makes me kind of angry when my own blacks don't really know where they come from." And the white audience, they just eating it up because they paying more attention. They get more off into it. That's the reason you see a lot of white acts playing the blues now. It started back in, probably, the Fifties or Sixties, when the whites really started getting off into the blues. I don't know how far back it started, but I'm just counting from my generation.

When I was coming up, we were listening to blues, but it was most like R&B. For example, like the Ohio Players and Earth, Wind and Fire, Rufus and Chaka Khan, these type of tunes. But when it all boiled down it, they still were singing the blues, but more soul and rhythm and blues, than it was blues.

See, I come from the soul. That's kind of the gospel. Both sides of my family come from the Baptist churches. That's the reason I have a lot of soul in my music, in my singing, in my playing, because I come from a Baptist family and we all come from that Baptist feel, just like Sam Cooke, Johnnie Taylor. And I grew up listening to cats like Johnnie Taylor, Sam Cooke, Otis Redding, O. V. Wright, Aretha Franklin, Bobby Womack, just to name a few: David Ruffin from The Temptations. And all these guys were a great influence on me. It was in their genes, too. It wasn't like they went to school for it and started writing it down. This stuff was just born in our genes, just come naturally.

I've been influenced by guys around me, like Johnnie Taylor. I worked with him and hung out with him. I was influenced singing-wise. I had also been influenced by Vernon Garrett and Little Milton. I worked with Little Milton, and I still do shows with him on and off. Their blues singing inspired me. I love to hear Little Milton sing the blues, him and Freddie King. When it came down to really singing the blues, it was Freddie King and Little Milton I loved to hear.

Today, you've got guys like myself and guys not even from Texas that's still trying to keep the Texas traditional blues going. I think what make Texas blues stand out is the root of it. It's the way you approach a song. If you get too far away from the blues and start trying to mix much of other things in there, you leave it. And what makes it Texas blues, like I say, is the guys from the plantation came to the city. That's what makes the blues, and you can't take it out of him. To me, it was a great sound to hear. Yeah, it was already just meant for me to be in. It was a great sound to hear when I was growing up, and most of the people my age, like thirty-six, thirty-seven years old, most of my classmates, are hip to the blues. Most of the guys I grew up with here in town, they was hip to the blues because their parents played it. And people played blues in South Dallas during that time like they'd never stop. Like on the weekend, people would crank their record players up and start hanging out. So most of the guys I went to school with, they grew up listening to the blues. They listened to blues and soul. During that time, rap was considered James Brown. James Brown was the funky rhythm and blues guy. So most of them rap people you hearing today got their ideas some kind of way. You know, history always repeats itself, but it comes toward you in a different way. That's the reason James Brown says, "All you copy-catters," you know. Because what these rappers are doing, James Brown was doing that back in the, what, Fifties and Sixties and Seventies. James Brown always sang like he was talking.

Yarbrough and Peoples, they're great. They are great friends of mine to this day. I met them years ago when they had "Don't Stop the Music" out, when they had their very first hit out, and they're still moving around today, touring, producing. . . . I know they're in the *Blind Lemon Blues* show [a new musical by Alan Govenar and Akin Babatunde].

I'm playing the Blind Lemon Jefferson Festival down there September the thirteenth; I'm headlining that festival. And then, I'm headlining the Dallas Black Chamber of Commerce Blues Festival up in Denton September the twentieth.

This is my first time playing Blind Lemon Festival [in Wortham]. I played the Denton Blues Festival with Ernest Johnson about two years ago. I'm looking forward to those festivals. I've been touring for the past two to three months. We've been steadily in and out, in and out, in and out; you know how that is. And I'm looking forward to playing there because I want to get down there. See, my mother is from Teague, Texas, and Freestone County and all back down in there. So I'm looking forward to getting down there because I might meet some of my people on my mama's side down there. And in Denton, Texas, I got, probably, some relatives up there going to school at North Texas, stuff like that. So I'm very interested in going up there.

I have an R&B band; we play rhythm and blues, blues, soul. I don't have certain guys playing. I just hire different guys; I keep a variety of guys playing. I don't have no certain members staying with me steady. I use a variety of band members. I put them together, send them a tape and rehearse them, and we go to work. I use horns on certain special gigs. But I usually keep a B3 [Hammond organ], a rhythm guitar player, bass and drums. And I add the horns in when I'm doing special gigs that they're paying enough to help bring a big package together. I use sax and trumpet. I usually use anywhere from three to four pieces and then myself.

My first recording was playing drums with Al Braggs. I did a lot of sessions with Al Braggs as a drummer back in the Eighties. Those were my first recordings. I did background recordings as a drummer, backing up other people with Al Braggs. I worked as a backup musician with Al Braggs, doing studio sessions for Big Ray Anderson and a whole lot of other guys.

I started my solo career in the early Nineties. I had my first record in '91. I did it on my own little budget. I didn't have a record company to pick me up during that time. So it didn't get publicized like I really wanted. So I re-recorded when I got with JSP, when I got with a record company.

Well, when I did my first solo recording with a record company, I was teamed up with some guys out of Dallas by the name of Junior and The Comets. It was a mixed band, white and black band. I was hanging out with them, playing with them for a while, because I had put my band down for a minute. And that was like in '91. I had put my band on hold for a minute because I wanted to scout it out and get some more publicity besides playing in the black joints. And I stared branching out, playing with some white guys. I remember Freddie King had made a big crossover working with the whites. And I wasn't prejudiced because my mom and dad didn't grow me up like that. I can easily get along with anybody. I don't care what color they are. Anyway, I wound up putting my band on the side for a minute during '91 and '92. I had a band called Tutu and The Right Time Show Band. I had a three-piece band; with myself, it was four. I was opening shows, too, when I first went solo. I was opening shows for Bobby Bland and others.

I was doing recording when I was with the group, L&C Show Band, which was backing up R. L. Griffin. We was backing up R. L., Z. Z., Ted Taylor, Al Greene, anybody that came through and needed a band in Dallas, and was on their way through here and going up to Wichita, Kansas, or whatever, on to Kansas City, Missouri. They called up R. L. and say, "Hey, man, we need to use your band." So, we was known for our great playing, and they'd hear about us for miles and miles away from home, you know. And we did a lot of traveling, too, all up in Oklahoma and Kansas City and this and that and the other. And so, after I left the group itself, The L&C Show Band, I went out on my own in '89, April of 1989, as a solo artist. I kept my band about three years at the most. So I decided to put my band on the side during '91 and '92.

I hooked up with this group called Junior and The Comets, this white group. We had two black guys and two white guys in it. Like I say, it wasn't no big thing for me to play with those white guys. Plus, I had seen a guy like Stevie Ray being around Freddie and them. They was getting along fine, and I thought, "Hey, man, I got good attitudes. I believe I can make a crossover, too." I thought about the things that Freddie went through. I said, "I know if Joe Blue and Freddie can get out here and get along, I can, too." So, anyway, I made a crossover. And I got with Junior and The Comics. We played together and started doing things here in the town. So, one night, we used to host this jam at a place called Schooner's. They've closed it down, now. I sure hate that, too; that was one of the best blues joints you can go to. Anyway, Don O from KNON was in there one Thursday night, and I was in there playing, and Don O thought it was a great thing for me to be recorded. So, after the break time, he came up and said "Hey, man, you know, you need to be recorded. Have you ever recorded?" And I said, "Yeah, I used to be a backup musician for Al Braggs. I used to do the backup recording with Al Braggs." And he said, "Well, man, you need to be on your own, doing your own thing." He told me the same thing Joe Blue told me back in '88. Joe Blue told me when we were playing at Bronco Bowl one night, he heard me fool around with his guitar, and he didn't know I could play guitar, but he knew my daddy played guitar. That's where that guitar thing came in. A lot of folks didn't know it, because I was sneaking off at jams and things, playing the guitar, not on professional jobs. Anyway, Don O said, "Man, you need to be standing out and fronting your own thing. I got a record company over in England, JSP Records. The owner, John Stedman, would love for you to send him something and see what you sound like." So anyway, about two three weeks or so passed, and I tried to get the package together, and I sent John Stedman a tape and, I think, a video, too, of me playing. And John Stedman thought it was great. He calls me back. My name is Johnny, but everybody know me by Tutu Jones. And John called me Johnny. He said, "Johnny, I believe you got something there, man. Would you like to front and produce your own recording? I'll put the money up front." I said, "Yeah." And so, that's how that came about. In other words, Don O set me up with JSP.

I have done one record with JSP. I didn't do others with JSP because I was trying to get record deals here before I got with JSP. I was trying labels like Alligator and they were turning me down. But I'm going to show you how the Lord was working with me. That's the reason I believe in God and I have faith in God. That's the reason I know my career's going to still go as long as I live. But anyway, to make a long story short, before JSP signed me, I was sending out demo tapes, pictures, and whatever I could, to get a record deal. These guys over here looked at me and said, "Yeah, our roster is stocked up, we're not signing nobody." The moment I signed with JSP, did my first recording, my recording came out in late spring of '94. About five months after my record was out, I was touring Europe for JSP. All the United States labels came running then. When I left JSP, I got with Bullseye, which is a Rounder label. I got with Bullseye, and I did two albums with them. And that's when my nominating stuff started coming in. Well, I did *Blue Texas Soul* with the Memphis Horns and some hometown guys for session musicians, some guys I grew up playing with. I had Ron Levin playing the organ and piano. So me and Ron Levin produced an album together, and the album became a good break for me. It was my first United States album, *Blue Texas Soul*, on the Bullseye label. I was nominated for a W. C. Handy Award, along with Little Milton, Johnnie Taylor, Johnny Adams and B. B. King. Ron told me, "Tutu, you got a great album." We let Papa Willie listen to it. Papa Willie is Willie Mitchell, who is a writer, producer, and arranger for Al Green. He helped write "Let's Stay Together" and all that. We let Papa hear a demo of it before we finished cutting everything. We cut the tracks and laid the foundation here, then we took it back to Memphis and did all the mixing. Anyway, Papa Willie said, "You got something, man," and Ron Levin, we were driving in Memphis, and he said, "Tutu, you're going to be nominated for this here, man." I said, "Well, I hope so." As soon as Bullseye got the masters and did all the printing up, five or six months later, I was nominated. That album gave me a lot of openings because I did "The Sky Is Crying" another way. I did it uptempo. Nobody ever did it that way. And that song is still getting airplay. Those albums are still getting a lot of airplay, helping me work; my first three albums. And I didn't have no idea. I just wanted to get out and a record going. But anyway, I've been blessed for them songs to just keep working for me. And as soon as I finished the Bullseye, that *Blue*

Texas Soul album, I did *Staying Power*. That was my last CD with Bullseye. And I produced that all by myself, and I used The Memphis Horns again on that.

I just finished a recording with Wanda King, Freddie King's daughter. She's doing it on her label. Me, Smokin' Joe Kubek, and Texas Slim are doing the guitar work on there. We all play on different tracks. I think track one starts with me. And I think the name of her album is *A Blues Point of View*, something like that. So, I just helped her with her album. And I'm trying to get my new live album out at this moment. Hopefully, I'll get it out sometime this year or next year. But in the meantime, I'm steady touring and playing the festivals and all the big bars at home.

My name Tutu came through my daddy. One day I was crawling and playing on the floor, and my mama and daddy were sitting there looking at me, and my daddy said, "We're going to have to give him a nickname because he looks like both of us. I tell you what, we'll just call him Tutu." So one Tu for him and one Tu for her. They had two kids together; that's me and my sister.

FREDDIE KING

September 3, 1934–December 28, 1976

Shortly after King's death, Tim Schuller (*Living Blues* no. 31 [1977]) wrote this appreciation of the musician:

Nobody expected to be writing obituaries for Freddie King yet. He looked too big and too strong to be anywhere near death, but on December 28, 1976, heart failure, a blood clot, and internal bleeding caused his death at Presbyterian Hospital in Dallas.

He was born September 3, 1934, and grew up in Gilmer, Texas. He received his first guitar lessons from his mother and from an uncle named Leon King, who died in 1945. He was sixteen when he and his mother moved to Chicago, where he almost immediately got work in a mill. His first jobs in a recording studio were on unissued Parrot sides by harmonica players Earl Payton and Little Sonny Cooper. In 1957 the El-Bee label released Freddie's first single ("Country Boy"/"That's What You Think"). He began gigging frequently and in 1958 quit work at the mill, surviving with ease on the cash he made playing clubs on the South and West sides. In 1960, he signed with the then-powerful King-Federal company.

This came about when Syl Johnson introduced Freddie to King-Federal A&R man Sonny Thompson. Soon after, King was in Cincinnati, recording the instrumental "Hideaway," a tune so popular that every bluesman with a band found it necessary to add it to his repertoire. Other successful recordings followed on Federal and though some were as dubious as "The Bossa Nova Watusi Twist" of 1962, his muscular guitar style was revealing its trajectory. [His songs that were issued on Federal 45s during this period are considered classics—"When Welfare Turns Its Back on You," "You're Barking Up the Wrong Tree," "She Put the Whammy on Me," "High Rise," "Some Other Day, Some Other Time," "Texas Oil," and "I'd Love to Make Love to You."]

King toured exhaustively during 1960–1963, and in 1963 moved to Dallas. He stayed with King-Federal until 1966, after which he signed with Atlantic and recorded two LP's for its Cotillion subsidiary. The label seemed bent on presenting him as a reinterpreter of standards, but his gut-level guitar playing wrenched new life from weathered classics like "Call It Stormy Monday" and "Ain't Nobody's Business If I Do," the latter of which always remained a staple in his act. Guitarists like Eric Clapton, themselves influential, revealed how their technique derived from Freddie's and he started to become known to a burgeoning rock audience. He was among the first performers to work the Fillmore in New York, and played there first in July 1971 on a bill that included Albert King, and, to the disgust of attending blues freaks, Mott the Hoople.

In 1971 King signed with Shelter Records, an association that yielded the albums *Getting Ready* and *Woman across the River.* He also played on the largely unloved Jimmy Rogers Shelter album, *Gold Tailed Bird.* Blues critics feared that Freddie's recordings were headed toward excessive pop flavor, and a later association with RSO proved they were not entirely incorrect. King's live gigs, though, remained blues despite what some regarded as excessive volume, and I for one thought he put on a satisfying show. I saw him work at many different places, including Cleveland's much mourned Smiling Dog Saloon, and his Saturday afternoon at the Ann Arbor Blues Festival of 1972 triggered some of the most intense crowd mania I've ever seen.

The last time I saw him was at the Tomorrow Club in Youngstown, Ohio. I arranged to meet him the next day at Robert Jr.Lockwood's for a brief interview. He was playing at the Agora in Cleveland and was staying with Lockwood, as he usually did when he played that city. When I finally got there, hours late, Robert had just put on the LP he recorded in Japan and was preparing to go to the state [liquor] store. King looked beat and was not overwhelmingly talkative . . . he obviously wanted to have conversation more than answer specific questions, so when Robert returned with the booze, I put the recorder away. I wish now that a more detailed interview had gone down, because two years and three days later, Freddie King was dead.

In a conversation with Bruce Iglauer in 1971 (*Living Blues* no. 31), Freddie King said:

Working in Chicago, that's where I first started playing in a band, but I been playing guitar since I was six. But I picked up the style between Lightnin' Hopkins and Muddy Waters, and B. B. King and T-Bone Walker. That's in-between style, that's the way I play, see. So I plays country and city.

It comes from the wrist, from the fingers here, and then I don't use any straight pick, I use two. I use fingerpicks, steel, on this, and a plastic pick on the thumb. And then I knock the tone down with the back of my hand. A lot of these rock groups, they hit wide open, whereas you see, I can hit it open. I can turn it all the way up to 10, and it still won't be too loud, see, because I can keep the sound down with the back of my hand like that.

I never played with a straight pick, man. I used to play with my fingers, and I met Jimmy Rogers and I seen he and Muddy Waters used those two picks, so they showed me how to. I used to use three, but then Eddie Taylor, he showed me how to get the speed out of it, see. He's fast, man, Eddie is. But in a way I'm fast in some things, you know.

In an interview in *Melody Maker* (December 18, 1977), King told Max Jones about a fight he once got into:

Freddie King's account of how he tackled a bouncer at a British club, who had punched one of his band members in the mouth was educative if humorous. This King has his tough moments. "So I hit the bouncer, the South Side way." Freddie's power-packed left demonstrated the blow. "He went down. Normally I don't enjoy fighting, but they hit one of my kids who I'd sent to get my money. So, I felt pretty mad. I told them, 'You three mothers together can't hurt me.' By now the kids were holding me and I told 'em, 'Turn me loose, there's no need to hold me back. I'm not rushing them; I'm going to let them come to me.'"

About Freddie King, Mike Leadbitter (*Blues Unlimited*, no. 110 [1974]) wrote:

Freddie, a musician's musician, has long been admired in France, but never really got the attention he deserved from blues enthusiasts at the time when he was really big and though he influenced several R&B guitarists of the era, it has only been in recent years that his Federal work has achieved collector status. Oddly enough, the probable reason for this is that he was just too popular, too commercial, too readily available, to suit our passion for the obscure.

Jimmie Vaughan, in an interview with Dan Forte (*guitar player* [July 1986]), recalled:

I had a black bald-headed manager, who had a station wagon and a trailer, and he booked me in all these black clubs in little bitty towns as Freddie King Jr. I would come out and play all of Freddie King's instrumentals. This guy just booked me because I could play Freddie King songs, and it was a novelty deal. All these black people would be waiting for "Freddie King Jr." and I'd come out, but play just like Freddie King. No singing—just "Hideaway," "The Stumble," "In the Open," and all the instrumentals.

I had those two instrumental albums he did on the King label (*Let's Hide Away and Dance Away* and *Freddie King Gives You a Bonanza of Instrumentals*). I used to know all those tunes. He was the greatest. He was from Dallas too, you know. Everything he played, it sounded like he'd sat down and figured it out beforehand. But actually, that's the way he played. That's the way you want to be; that's what style is all about. He kicked ass! He was such a great singer, everything about him. I'm totally from Freddie and B. B. King. I stole a lot things from B. B. and most of my lead stuff from Freddie.

WANDA KING

Interview, 2003

Uh-oh. My birth date? I wouldn't want to give the birth date, yeah. I was born in Chicago, Illinois. I can tell you this: I was born August the third. I won't give you the year. I'm the oldest, the first child of Freddie and Jessie King. Yeah. Freddie had moved from Gilmer. And you know what? There are conflicting dates. My Uncle Bennie said it was '49. And I remember my grandmother saying also it was '49. But someone else in the family said it was '50. So, I think the popular answer is 1949, he moved to Chicago from Gilmer, Texas.

Well, we were little kids when we moved here to Dallas, Texas. Chicago is rough. I do remember that, as being very cold in the winter. And we lived on a third-floor flat on the West Side of Chicago. And it was just a different environment, a very fast environment. I can recall my father going out at night, coming back in the morning, going to rehearsals. Now than I'm grown, I think about it, it must have been on the weekends, or during the week—actually on the weekdays. He would mention places like the Squeeze Club, Walter's Corner. I was very young, maybe five, six, and I still remember that. So, we moved to Dallas in '63. Actually, my mom left my father because he was enjoying the nightlife a little bit too much. And I put that information on my Web site, as a matter of fact, for Freddieking.com. I put a lot of information on there. Just tell me what you want to know. When I start talking about history, something will pop in my mind, and I'll begin to go in that direction, so if I leave off the path, pull me back in.

By the time we moved to Dallas, my mom had six kids. And my father was always a go-getter; he worked during the day. Now this was told to me, because I don't really remember this part of it. But it was told to me later on by my mom that he worked in a steel mill during the day, and he was underage. He was like sixteen, seventeen. And at night, he would hit the nightclubs and try to get the locals at that time—Muddy Waters, Howlin' Wolf, these guys—to let him play onstage or to get up there and play in the band. And finally, Howlin' Wolf, from what I remember him telling me, took a liking to him. And they became, really, friends for life. But he began allowing my father to actually come into the club, because the bouncer would have him leave the club once they realized he was too young. But Howlin' would let him stay, and eventually he started playing with the band. And he was able to get enough gig time to not work during the day. But the nightlife for a young kid in Chicago led to different things. My father began to gamble, and I guess carouse a little bit. And you can't do that when you have six kids and a wife. So, my mom just had enough of it, and plus, there were things happening because Chicago back then was such a hard life. There was probably gang violence and stuff going on. And my mom was just a country girl; she was also from Texas. She was from Centerville, Texas. It just so happened, her sister had moved to Chicago years earlier because she was much younger than them. And they had established a life in Chicago. They had married, and as a matter of fact, my mother's sister was married to my father's uncle. And that's how my mom met my father.

My mom had been a cheerleader in her high school, at Booker T. Washington in Dallas, Texas. Her maiden name was Jessie Burnett. And like I said, she was just a country girl, but apparently she enjoyed music because they stayed together until his death. But anyway, she left him, brought us all back to Dallas. I still remember all this: Santa Fe train, we came back to Dallas by train, moved in with my aunt, my mother's sister, and after six months, I think my father realized that my mom meant business. She wasn't coming back. And so, she had already had a little infighting with Sid Nathan, the owner of King Records. She pretty much was my father's backbone as far as the business part of it. When he didn't receive royalties, she would call up to Cincinnati and just chew out Sid Nathan. And I think he really respected her for that, because she had that kind of attitude. But anyway, we were here in Dallas, like six or seven months. She really didn't have any money, and it was hard for her to find jobs to support that many kids. So she contacted Sid Nathan and said, "Look, you owe Freddie money. I need it now because I got these kids to raise, blah, blah, blah, blah." Next thing you know, he sends her a big check, and my father and she talk it over, he decides to follow her to Dallas. And I think that move, of my father leaving Chicago, coming to Dallas, was the best thing he ever did, as far as—it created a whole different opportunity for him.

I grew up around music. I watched Howlin' Wolf, Magic Sam—these are people I just remember. I associate faces with names. My father would call Magic Sam "Magic." And Howlin' Wolf would come through. Muddy

(OPPOSITE) WANDA KING WITH TEXAS SLIM, DALLAS, CA. 2000. PHOTOGRAPH BY DON O.

Waters. And just a lot of people—Junior Lockwood. I just remember all these names and faces coming through when I was a kid. And my father was constantly bringing in music, bringing in a lot of music, because the King label—that guy Sid Nathan, he recorded everything. He had western people, Stanley Brothers. And because my father was on the label, he could bring all that stuff to the house, and I listened to all of it. But I particularly liked the blues. And then, my next favorite was jazz, of course. But all these people that I was early influenced by was part of the King family, the King record label.

My father had two personalities. He enjoyed playing poker, and he could drink. But he never brought that stuff home with him. So he was a different person, a father figure, with us. I think moving back to Dallas reacquainted him with his roots. Country boy goes to the city, you know, everything is so brand new, and it's sparkly and glittery and it's just exciting. And I think he had his fill for a moment and came back to Dallas, back to Texas, and he realized, it's okay to take it a little slow and slow it down a little bit. And from what I remember, I know that around '66, '67, I believe, he walked away from King. He didn't renew his contract. And it was tough. We had really a tough time during that time. He would do high school gigs, prom dances, whatever he could find to work. I always remember him working. He would hit that road and stay gone for maybe two or three months doing one-night stands on that Chitlin Circuit. He would come back with a bunch of money, pay the bills, head back out again. And I always realized we were doing pretty good because he would always—he got a new car every year. His favorite car at the time was a deuce-and-a-quarter Buick. If he was able to get a new car every year, I think he was doing pretty good. And that's pretty much the way he did. And then we moved up to Cadillac, and I said, "Oh, we're doing really good now," you know. I think he had every color, whatever hit his fancy that year, from midnight blue to a lime green. It wasn't quite lime green, but he had a Cadillac that was almost lime green. We had blue deuce-and-a-quarters, white on white, white and black. We had a beige one. I mean, we had everything but a red; I don't remember him having a red Buick or Cadillac.

Well, you know, if you read any history on my father, and due to the conversations I had with him after I grew up, with all our talks about the music, he was heavily influenced by [Lightnin'] Hopkins. You know, his style developed from acoustic. That was his first love because he didn't have an electric guitar until he moved to Chicago. Everything was acoustic. So he was heavily influenced by Hopkins, and one of his favorite musicians was Jordan, Louis Jordan. And he tried to mimic the notes that Jordan would play, note for note, by the fingers playing on the guitar. So he developed that style from that, and I think moving to Chicago allowed him to see a different, urban look from the guitar-playing style, because it became electrified. But I've always thought that his style was based on his acoustic playing. He did evolve that to the electric guitar and bending the strings, you know, playing with a pick.

As a matter of fact, it surprised me. I think I was like eighteen, I realized: he can play acoustic. He did a radio show with one of the local DJs, I think John Dillon, and he played "Sweet Home Chicago" and some other tune, acoustic. And I was shocked, because we didn't realize he had that ability. He did some acoustic on Leon Russell, on his recordings with Shelter.

In Dallas, my father played at Soul City; it was on Greenville Avenue back in the late sixties. I think it was the first place he met his future manager, Jack Calmes. Jack Calmes [pronounced Cal-mees] at the time was a teenager, and he had a band. He played at the Bridgeport. Now a lot of these are black venues. Jack Calmes was co-owner of Showco, the lighting production company for the concerts coming through. After my father passed, he went into a whole different [thing], just doing concert lighting and stuff. But let's see, he played at the Empire Room, which was the Ascot; before that, I think it was the Rose Room on Hall Street. It was just simply a little black club, a joint, but every major star went through there, including Ike and Tina Turner, Ray Charles. T-Bone. You name them, they've been there. They played that venue. They may know it as the Ascot, they might know it as the Rose Room, or they may know it as the Empire Room, but they played at Hall and Ross, right there at Hall and Ross.

My father knew T-Bone. You know, these guys respected each other. They recorded each other's music, they covered their music, and they respected their abilities. Now you had personality clashes. I won't get into any particulars, but you know, you had envy, musicians envying someone's popularity, but as far as the playing style and the music, I think they respected each other on a certain level.

When my father went to Europe, he was happily surprised; it was one of his earliest tours, I think it was late Sixties. He was overwhelmed and just shocked by the popularity of his music. And he and a few other black entertainers didn't know how popular their style was and the blues was over there. People like Eric Clapton and Jeff Beck and so many others, even—I was stunned to hear where Fleetwood Mac, the drummer, he even mentioned my father in an interview, you know, how he was influenced by him. Like wow! And these guys, they were young kids in Europe, buying his 45s. And I just recently saw a blues special on Channel 13 where Eric even talks about how he went out and bought a Freddie King 45. And on one side it had "Hideaway," and he was blown away by that. He flipped it over, and it had this whole new cool way of playing the guitar, bending strings on "Have You Ever Loved a Woman?" So, you know, these guys really pay respect to my father, and they show their popularity for him, but again, I think my father wasn't, like, stunned. He was happily surprised, but he had always, for some strange reason, had a white following, even on the U.S. side. I know that in Dallas, he would always have a few white young musicians or whoever, fans of blues, coming to the black clubs. And this was like taboo back in the Sixties, even Fifties, whatever, but he was part of the Sixties, but they would actually show up at the Ascot Room and Bridgeport. And when he was playing at Walter's Corner and Squeeze Club, these young white guys would show up with their girlfriends or whatever. So there was always a following of white youth for the blues.

Blues is not a color. It's not black; it's the emotion, it's a feeling. And anyone can feel it, and it's something about once it's there, you have to act on it. You want to be part of it, you know, you want to embrace it on some level. Even those who were afraid to venture out to the black clubs would go out and buy the music. And that's one thing I've always believed, you know, blues is just what it is. It just pulls you in. It doesn't matter who you are. If it's there in you, you're going to react to it. It's not sad, it's not happy, it's all over the place.

At one time I was pretty good at piano, but I moved away from that and focused on my writing music and singing. Well, actually, my brother and I, my late brother, Fred Jr., he formed a band, and I think he was in the fifth grade, fourth grade. And I was in the sixth grade. He formed a band, and I began to sing for the band, and we were actually performing and getting professional pay by the time I was in the seventh grade, and we were winning talent shows citywide and statewide. The only person that beat us out for the state title was Bobbie Humphreys, who became a famous jazz artist as an adult.

BOBBY "BLUE" BLAND WITH HIS BAND, LONGHORN BALLROOM, DALLAS, 1984. PHOTOGRAPH BY ALAN GOVENAR.

We did private parties in Dallas. As a matter of fact, I still remember playing for a state representative. We played for one of his kids' parties. We played for parties, store openings. Now that I look back on it, you know, we made pretty good money on the weekends, just for a couple of hours of performing. We would play for high school gigs. We were elementary kids, and we were playing high school gigs, sock hops. I went to Longfellow and then to Thomas Jefferson.

We were raised in North Dallas. My mom and dad bought property out in an area that was considered a white area of Dallas. So we were part of that early integration. We're talking about Inwood, Lovers Lane. As a matter of fact, right across the street was Highland Park, Greenway Park. And so, we were raised in an area that had very few blacks at the time we moved over there. And I went to a pretty much all-white school because that was the first year of integration. They had a quota system back then; only so many black kids could attend this year, whatever. But yeah, we were part of that particular decade, the Sixties, and there was integration.

I'm heavily influenced by my father's music, because he was all over the place with the blues. And I think that's why he was so popular, because he evolved from what he began with, the country-type style blues, to urban-style pop blues, and then he went to a rock blues. And I took all that I learned from him, and since I've always been a fan of jazz, I incorporate my style with what he did and add jazz to it. I don't think my father was ever a fan of jazz. I never heard him really talk about jazz, but I always loved jazz, even the earliest jazz music from the Thirties, Forties, whatever. Certain people pop out, like bebop. I like Billie Holiday, the fact that she sings off the note. I like that style. Julie London—I love her coolness when she sings; she's jazzy blues as well. And so, I incorporate those things I enjoy. And as far as my writing, I like the seriousness of the lyric of Nina Simone. Music for the moment, lyrics for the moment and the times that we live in, things that actually have value, as far as I'm concerned, make a statement about the life that I live. And so I don't think that it's "Oh, baby," you know, "My baby done done me wrong, and he done left me." I need to have more content.

I have a catalog of almost twenty-four songs. I'm on my twenty-third song as far as lyrics, and I'm trying to—as a matter of fact, that's what I was doing last week, trying to develop the bridge on that song so when I do bring the band together, I'll be able to say, "Look, I want you to do this, do that." So I guess I can say I have twenty-four songs. I recorded twelve, but only nine on the CD. I produced it. I wrote all the words. It took me about a year to put the music to the songs. I write poetry, and I'd already put a lot of stuff down on paper. So I began really nailing down the music part of it after I was laid off after 2002.

I worked telecommunications and computers for sixteen years, and that's a whole lot different. But when I first started working in telecommunications, it was supposed to be a short run. I was going to get back to the music because I had stepped away from music after my father died because it devastated me. It happened out of the blue; I wasn't prepared for it. So, I didn't sing. That was in '76.

What happened was that my father had ulcers. And like a lot of guys, they just don't take care, don't go to the doctor, don't do what they're supposed to do. But he would drink on those ulcers, and it became acute ulcers which bled. And it caused pancreatitis. So, he died of pancreatitis. But what led to it was the acute ulcers. See, now, if he had pancreatitis today, they would have been able to save him. But back in the Seventies, pancreatitis was deadly. It was like, "We can't do anything about it; we'll try, but we're not guaranteeing anything." So I guess it was just his time, but we weren't prepared for it, and we all tried to work through it as best we could. And the only way I could was just not to do music for a while. I had other personal things that was happening, and my family needed my attention.

The music's a very tough business. Even in the good times, it's tough, but you're not guaranteed to make any money. You can work every weekend and not make a lot of money at it because it's just—well, there was a stretch where you could. But for a female blues singer, it's even tougher. And the Eighties had rolled around to disco. They had completely stepped away from live music, almost completely. My brother stuck with it, and he was having a really tough time, struggling with it, because he couldn't find gigs because everybody was going to piped music. You know, no live band, just records, and eight-track. They didn't have live bands. All they had was the dancing and the disco ball and whatever.

I thought about getting back into the music, and I started doing private things, singing for weddings, going to gigs and maybe sitting in on a few songs. But after my brother passed in '91, I made a commitment. I said, As soon as I'm able to, I'm going to get back in this music, because it's what I want to do. Before I leave here, I want to leave here doing this music because I think it's what I was brought here to do. I think if you're meant to do it, you can't escape it. And that's where I am now; I'm doing music. And I still work every day because I've got to pay my bills.

It's the same type of work, you know. I've always been interested in computers. I build Web sites and stuff like that. So I still work, you know. I went to Brookhaven community college. Then I went to Richland and finished my two-year associate degree there. After that, I went on to UTA, University of Texas at Arlington. And I didn't complete my studies; I hate to say this, every time I say this: I'm like 20 or 30 hours from getting my degree. But I put time into college and did all that good stuff.

I'm going to start working on my Web site. I have a Web site already, wandaking.com. I'm trying to tap on every source of opportunity that I receive, and I'm trying to make sure that I don't waste the talent that the Lord gave me because I do feel that I have something to offer and leave to the world. If not that, I'll work hard at trying to make sure that my father's legacy continues. I've spent another five years struggling with a lot of these bootleggers, you know. And I've taken them to court. And I've won; I've beat them at their own game. My attorney said that the last figure was that they spent $265,000 on their attorneys, their experts, and I still beat them. They took me to the district—I guess they call it the district of the Supreme Court; it's in Louisiana. The circuit court? And I beat them again. So, you know, I tell anyone who has a beef, especially with the heirs of the late blues artists, where they've been ripped off, don't be afraid because these people have money. You find someone who will work on commission. You know, you got to do your own research. You got to present your case to the attorney so they can see, "There's a possibility I could beat this, because she got everything here, ready for me to take to court." And that's what I did. I went out and I got all the documentation. I did all the legwork. And I presented it to my attorney: "Here's what I have; can you sue them?" He said, "Yeah, hell, you've done all the work. You went and got all the copyright stuff." And I did everything; I try to have all bases covered. And when it's all said and done, I was able to beat them, but like I said, when people call me, I've had the family of a well-known jazz artist, and did some research, and he wrote some really good, famous songs. And his family called me and asked, "How can I sue so-and-so, so-and-so?" And I walked them through the steps: here's what you do.

FORT WORTH

ROY MILTON, FORT WORTH, 1940s.
PHOTOGRAPH BY CALVIN LITTLEJOHN.
COURTESY TEXAS AFRICAN AMERICAN
PHOTOGRAPHY ARCHIVE.

ELLA FITZGERALD, FORT WORTH, 1950S. PHOTOGRAPH BY CALVIN LITTLEJOHN. COURTESY TEXAS AFRICAN AMERICAN PHOTOGRAPHY ARCHIVE.

INTRODUCTION

Just as African Americans flowed into Dallas, they also migrated to Fort Worth and the surrounding areas of Tarrant County. During the Civil War, the slave population of Tarrant County more than doubled, from 700 to about 1,700. This growth was due partly to the importation of slaves from elsewhere in the South to Texas, where there had been relatively little fighting. Historian Alwyn Barr writes that slave owners were apparently confident that after the South won the Civil War, they would be able to reclaim their "property."[1]

After emancipation, however, about 60 percent of former slaves left Tarrant county, and by the time of the 1870 census the African American population had dropped to 672. About this exodus, historian Sonya Ramsey observed, "This was a time of great violence. . . . There were beatings, whippings, lynchings."[2]

By the 1880s the Texas & Pacific Railroad had expanded into Fort Worth, and the growing livestock market created jobs for cattle drivers, porters, janitors, and carpenters. African Americans accordingly began to migrate back to Fort Worth, and by the early 1900s a black middle class was emerging in Tarrant County. William "Gooseneck Bill" McDonald founded the Fraternal Bank & Trust Company in 1912. McDonald, a Republican activist and political leader, bought large tracts of land throughout Fort Worth and provided lots for blacks to build homes. African American communities grew up northeast of downtown, in a section of the city known as Hillside, and south of downtown, in the Rosedale neighborhood.

Ornette Coleman, the legendary blues and jazz performer and composer, was born in Fort Worth in 1930 and grew up in a small, wood-frame house at 309 Elm Street that backed up to the Santa Fe Railroad tracks in the Hillside area. Coleman's parents were extremely poor; his father was a cook, his mother a seamstress. In describing his life as a "poor black boy in a segregated city," Coleman said, "The south side was more wealthy territory. They had much better accommodations. Dewey [Redman, a saxophonist and close friend] had indoor plumbing down there. We had a honey pot."[3]

The "separate but equal" principle, upheld by the U.S. Supreme Court in *Plessy v. Ferguson* (1896), had legalized racial discrimination. Fort Worth, like Dallas and other cities throughout Texas, passed laws that restricted African Americans' access to public facilities and to virtually every conceivable place where whites

1. Alwyn Barr, *Black Texans: A History of African Americans in Texas, 1528–1995* (Norman: University of Oklahoma Press, 1973).

2. Quoted in Mitch Mitchell, Patrick McGhee, and Peyton D. Woodson, "Living History: Some of the African-American Communities in Tarrant County That Can Trace Their Roots Back to the Civil War Remain Intact," *Fort Worth Star-Telegram*, February 10, 2002.

3. Quoted in Chris Vaughn, "Jazz Visionary," *Fort Worth Star-Telegram*, November 23, 2003.

CHESTER THOMPSON, T-BONE WALKER, BOB COOPER, NEW JIM HOTEL, FORT WORTH, 1940s. COURTESY HELEN OAKLEY DANCE.

and blacks might have social contact. Civic change proceeded gradually, and many musicians, including Ornette Coleman, moved away from Texas as quickly as possible.

The center of African American cultural life in Fort Worth, as elsewhere, was the church. Coleman came from a musical family whose life revolved largely around spiritual and gospel music at the nearby Morning Chapel CME Church (where he was baptized) and Allen Chapel. The chapel, located at 116 Elm Street, was founded by five former slaves in 1865, and in the mid-1870s a one-room brick building was constructed that also served as Henry H. Butler School, Fort Worth's first private school for African Americans. In 1914 a sanctuary in the Tudor Gothic architectural style was completed; it was designed by William Sidney Pittman, the son-in-law of Booker T. Washington, who lived in Dallas and also designed the Pythian Temple in Deep Ellum.

Although Coleman recalled an active blues and jazz scene in Fort Worth, most recordings of African American music were made in Dallas. Growing up, Coleman and his friends gathered at the Grand Theater on Fabons Street in Fort Worth for talent shows featuring comedians, dancers, and other vaudeville performers. As he got older, Coleman began to perform with his half-brother James Jordan, Donnell Cole, Buster Turner, and Big Jay McNeely, and frequented the clubs and dance halls along Rosedale Street and Evans Avenue, which were much like those found in the Thomas and Hall section of Dallas. In Fort Worth, the Zanzibar club was nationally known for its retractable roof and touring shows, and the China Doll, the Paradise Inn, and the Zebra Lounge offered opportunities for the best of the young black musicians in Fort Worth, including John Carter, Bobby Simmons, King Curtis Ousley, Prince Lasha, Julius Hemphill, Ben Martin, and the tenor sax player and bandleader Red Connor.

Many of the touring TOBA shows that played in Dallas moved on to Fort Worth. In Dallas, the black musicians often stayed at the Powell Hotel, and in Fort Worth, they lodged at the Jim Hotel, located originally at 413 East Fifth Street. They performed at its College Inn. In its early years the College Inn hosted Cab Calloway, Louis Armstrong, Billie Holiday, Andy Kirk, and T-Bone Walker, and it later became a venue for Coleman, Ray Charles, and other musicians, both black and white, who performed and jammed there after hours. The legendary alto stylist Buster Smith was recorded on the Atlantic label in Fort Worth in 1959 at Clifford Herring Studio. That same year, Smith also accompanied Floyd Dixon at the Herring Studio for a release on the Mississippi-based Ace label.

MAUDE COOPER (BOB COOPER'S AUNT) AND T-BONE WALKER, NEW JIM HOTEL, FORT WORTH, 1940S. COURTESY HELEN OAKLEY DANCE.

In 1960 record producer Chris Strachwitz and British researcher Paul Oliver discovered Babe Karo Lemon Turner, a National steel guitar player who had released a single hit in the late 1930s called "Black Ace Blues." After a Fort Worth radio station started to use the song as its musical theme, Turner assumed the name "Black Ace" and kept this as his moniker for the remainder of his life. The recordings produced by Strachwitz for his Arhoolie label show the influence of Turner's mentor, Oscar "Buddy" Woods, and combine his impassioned and brooding blues vocals with what Scott Cooper of the *Santa Cruz Sentinel* has called his "Hawaii meets the Delta" slide guitar style.

By the late 1950s white musicians had begun to emulate and perform the blues of their black counterparts. To singer and blues aficionado Delbert McClinton, the musical environment in the Dallas–Fort Worth area was unique. Not only was there a long history of western swing, but also it was possible to hear Ray Price, Ornette Coleman, Cornell Dupree, Jimmy Reed, T-Bone Walker, Roger Miller, Bob Wills, and Doc Severinsen, all "comfortably co-existing within the same musical setting." There were weekly shows at the White Sands Supper Club and the Skyliner Ballroom in Fort Worth, and at the Empire Room (renamed the Ascot in the 1960s) and the Longhorn Ranch in Dallas. In addition, black bands often played at white fraternity parties and dances. This diversity, combined with the influences of rock 'n' roll, western swing, rockabilly, and soul that were heard live and on the radio, created a cultural context in which the cross-fertilization of musical styles occurred.

BOBBY SIMMONS (TRUMPET), KING CURTIS (ALTO SAXOPHONE), RED CONNOR (TENOR), UNIDENTIFIED BASS PLAYER, MID-1950s.
COURTESY CHRIS EVANS.

LITTLE RICHARD, DISK JOCKEY IN FORT WORTH, 1950s.
PHOTOGRAPH BY CALVIN LITTLEJOHN.
COURTESY TEXAS AFRICAN AMERICAN PHOTOGRAPHY ARCHIVE.

BLACK ACE, FORT WORTH, 1961.
PHOTOGRAPH BY CHRIS STRACHWITZ. COURTESY ARHOOLIE RECORDS.

In the 1970s and 1980s a new generation of musicians in Fort Worth came of age. Spurred on by the national success of Delbert McClinton, and energized on the local scene by saxophonist Johnny Reno and guitarist Sumter Bruton, the blues scene in Fort Worth centered on the Bluebird, operated by Robert Ealey. Bruton, who has mastered the T-Bone Walker style of playing, has also operated Record Town, a store that has become a Fort Worth institution and clearinghouse of information on recordings and on the local blues scene.[4]

In recent years, Bruton has continued to perform with pianist Mike Price in a band called Bruton and Price and The Swingmasters Revue. The band has included Ron Green on bass, Larry Reynolds on drums, and the legendary Buddy Ray on violin. Bruton relates:

> Buddy Ray was in his mid-70s when he recorded with us. He had played with Stuff Smith and Nat Cole, as well as with Bob Wills and other western swing bands. He was from Waco, and was the most soulful white player I ever worked with. He was a jazz player, but very blues oriented. I learned a lot from him. He had played guitar and tenor sax, too. Another band I play with is the Hank Hankshaw Band, or sometimes called just The Hankshaws. In that band, we play rhythm and blues and older country. Basically, I'm committed to the sound that probably starts with Charlie Christian and T-Bone and goes on from there. These days, there's not really much new happening in Fort Worth. The blues scene has gotten slow again. The blues has had its ups and downs. But the blues is not going away. There are a lot of great musicians out there. The blues started with a black audience, then it evolved into the white audiences, and now the white audience is getting old. There are a number of young black players coming onto the scene, but it's difficult to say who their audience will be.[5]

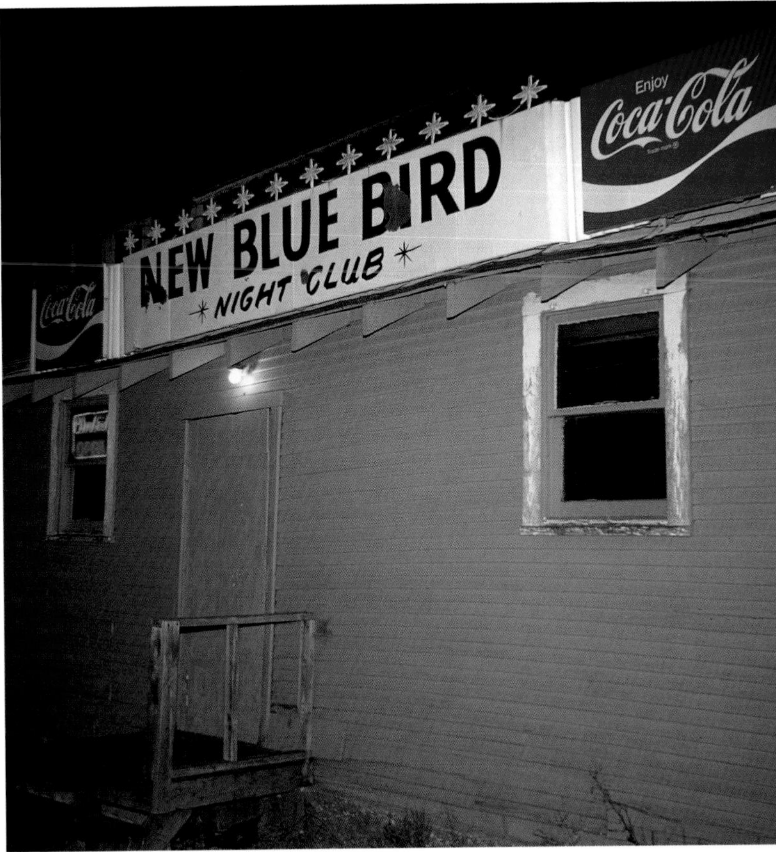

THE NEW BLUE BIRD, FORT WORTH, 1984.
PHOTOGRAPH BY ALAN GOVENAR

4. Record Town was opened in 1957 by Bruton's parents, Kathleen and Sumter Bruton, the latter of whom was himself a drummer.

5. Interview with Sumter Bruton by Alan Govenar, December 7, 2004.

ROBERT EALEY

December 6, 1924–March 7, 2001; interview, 1984

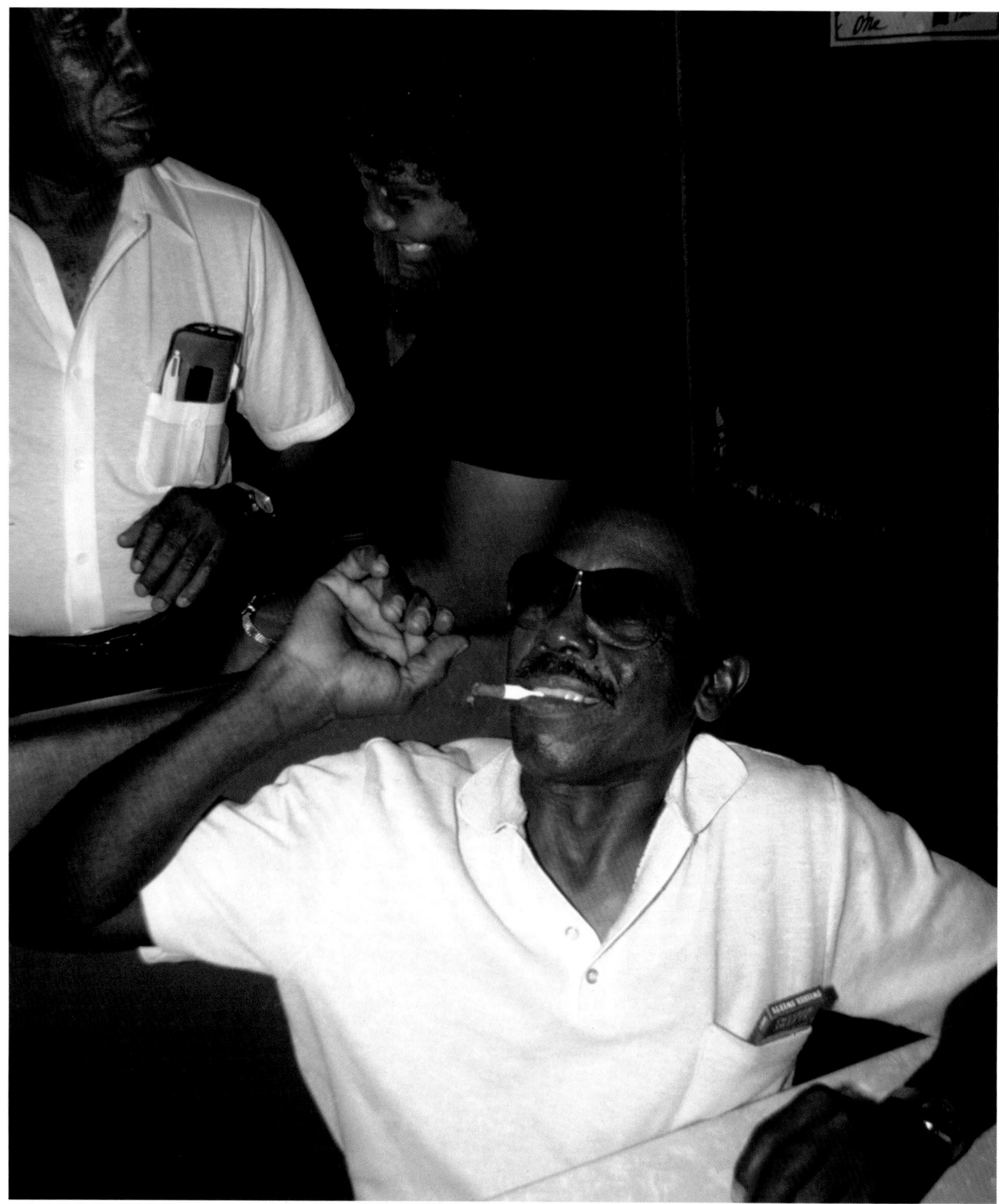

I've been playing the blues since I was about fifteen years old. I was a quartet singer in Texarkana. It was a church spiritual group, and I wanted to do something different. I was working for God, but I had to change over a little bit. My mama and daddy didn't want me to sing the blues. They wanted me stay with the good Lord. Well, I told them this, I said, "Look, Mama, I have to do something different."

And she said, "No, son, you sing this gospel. I don't want you singin' no blues."

I say, "What's the difference between singin' gospel or singin' blues?"

"Well, you serving the devil one place and you're serving God [in the other]."

I said, "Look here, I got to come up. I got to get grown one day and do what I want to do."

So she said, "Go ahead on."

I'm not doing anything different than I was doing. Fact of the matter is you're going to church and I'm singing the blues and I'll go to heaven quick as you will. God forgive you for some things.

My daddy went to one church and my mother went to another. Do you see what I'm saying? I wondered why they never went to church together. I couldn't figure it out, what was going on. Why couldn't they both go to the same church? And I still don't know why today. The way I feel, they must not have had the same God.

I remember one day a long time ago—I was twenty when I left home—I was singing to myself, and it was blues. But I sing church songs. But I used to listen to Lightnin' Hopkins, Li'l Son Jackson, Frankie Lee Sims, T-Bone Walker. He played the Bluebird not long before he died back home in California.

T-Bone was great, and he would sing the blues. He would upset the crowd the way he was on stage. And he was a singer.

I didn't start singing the blues professionally until I moved to Dallas. Then people got to liking me so well, coming more and more, and I got a big crowd. And that made me get on up in the world. When I moved over here to Fort Worth, I got with another band. We were The Boogie Chillen Boys. That made me famous, and I must have played at the Bluebird for another twenty or more years. And when Miss Mamie died, the owner, these white boys wanted me to get the Bluebird. I've had it for eight or nine years, and I got a lot of white folks coming out there.

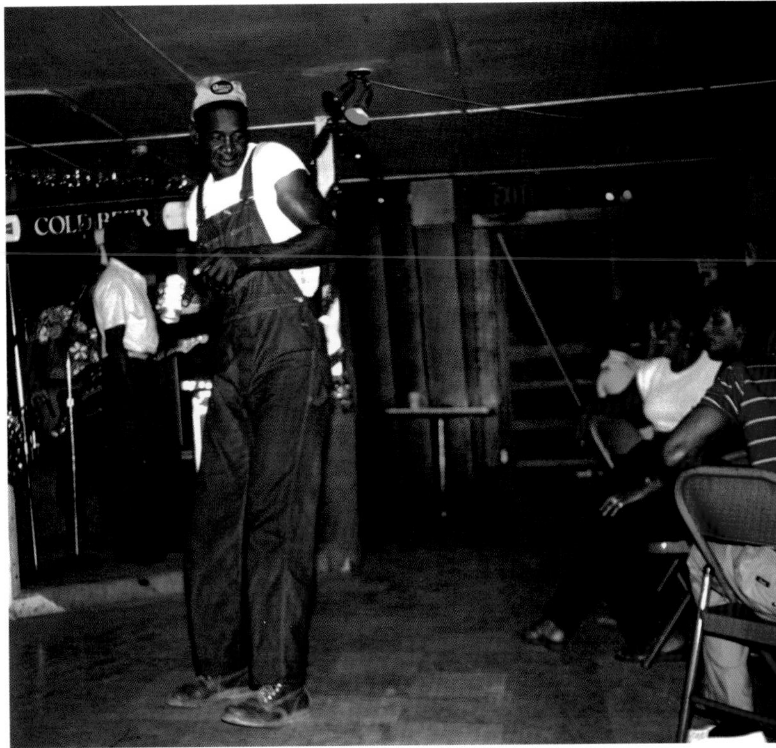

THE NEW BLUE BIRD, FORT WORTH, 1984.
PHOTOGRAPH BY ALAN GOVENAR.

OPPOSITE: ROBERT EALEY, THE NEW BLUE BIRD, FORT WORTH, 1984.
PHOTOGRAPH BY ALAN GOVENAR.

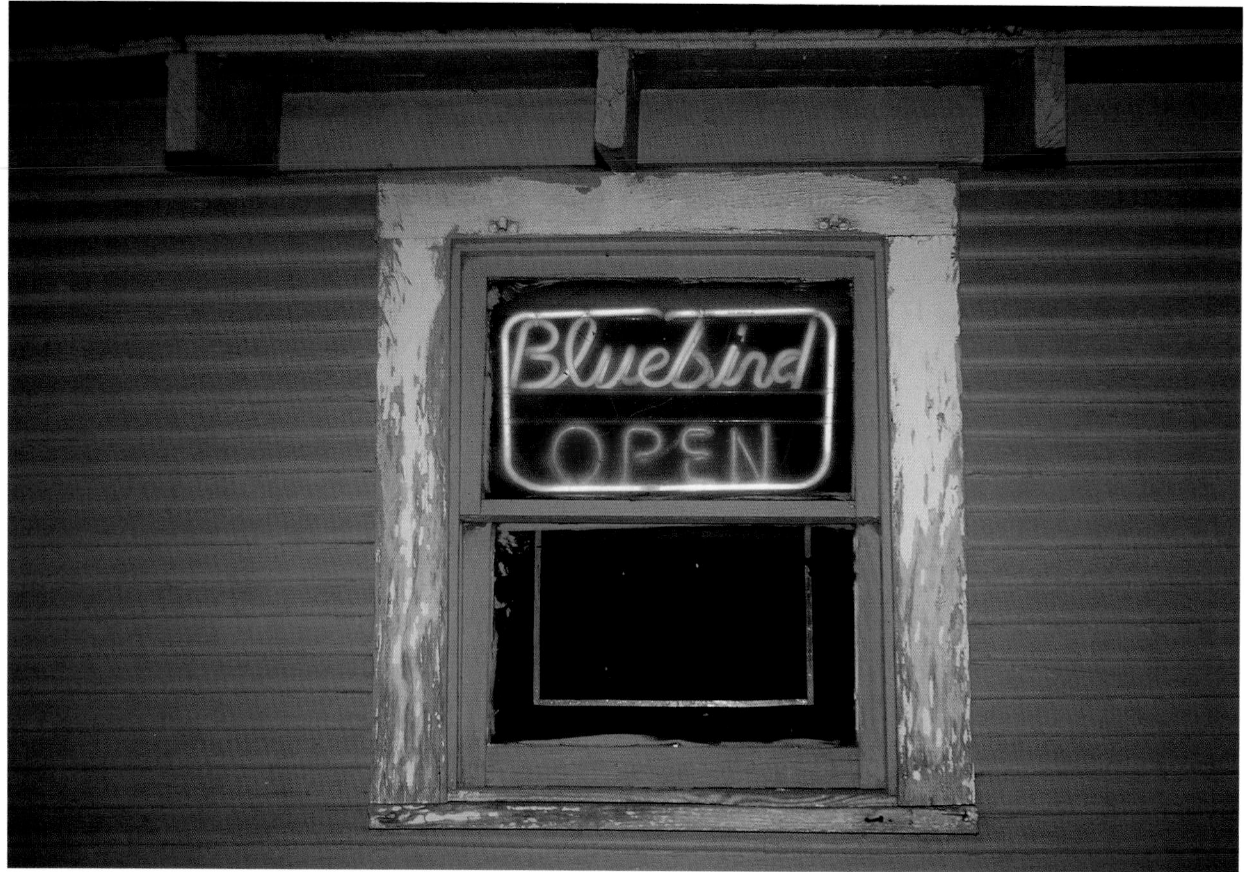

THE BLUEBIRD, FORT WORTH, 1983.
PHOTOGRAPH BY ALAN GOVENAR.

So when I first started out, I got with some white boys. They called me one day at the house. They say, "Robert, you want to come out and do something with us tonight?"

I say, "Where you all playin' at?"

He says, "At The Hop. We're just going to get something together."

I had been playing with another group for two months, and I quit. I got together with these white boys, and we practiced. Everybody was liking us. Then we left there and we got placed out of town. That's when the blues was coming back in, in the 1960s. We played Soap Creek Saloon on Sunday, and then Antone's on Monday [two Austin clubs], and everybody went wild over us. That was the band before The Juke Jumpers. We were called The Five Careless Lovers [with Sumter Bruton]. When we started out, it was three coloreds and the rest was white. And we had a ball, man. We really turned things out. White people started liking me. And they would rather hear me sing than anything else. They wouldn't come out to the club if I wasn't there. I was the king of blues.

Right now, they're still crazy about The Juke Jumpers. A lot of folks still say, "You could have kept Robert Ealey. You had a good thing going. But with Robert running the club, he couldn't go nowhere. He had to stay at the club." They travel all over the place.

A lot of people try to do away with the blues, but it don't work that way. As long as I'm in Fort Worth, the blues is going to stay here. And people are still crazy about the blues. There's something inside the blues that make people start wondering.

SUMTER BRUTON

October 31, 1944–   ; interview, 1987

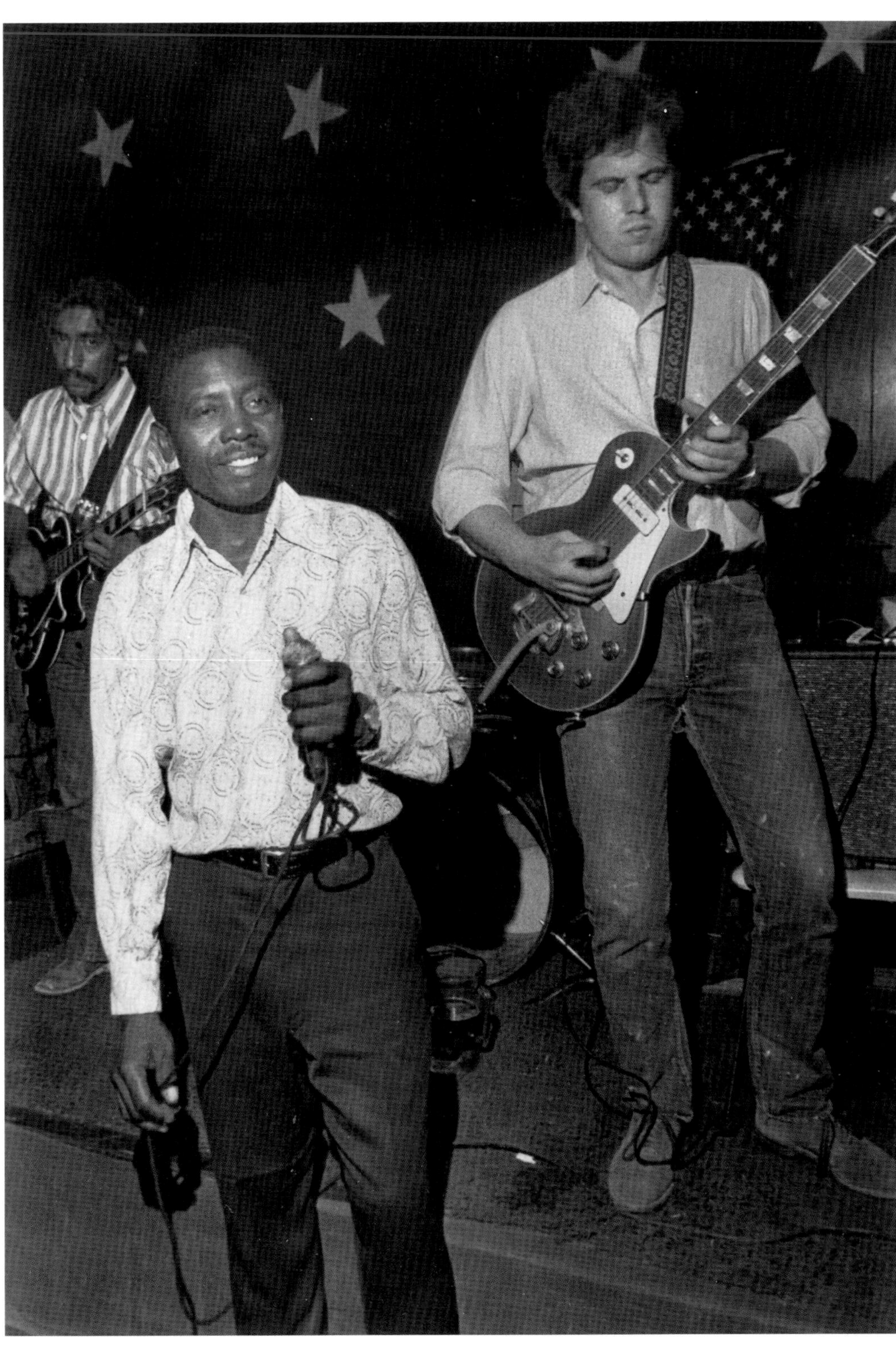

FREDDY CISNEROS, ROBERT EALEY, SUMTER BRUTON (L. TO R.), THE BLUEBIRD, FORT WORTH, 1971. COURTESY SUMTER BRUTON.

I'm originally from Fort Worth. My dad's from New Jersey, and we moved from there in 1948. I grew up listening to the music. My dad's a jazz drummer, been doing it for fifty-three years. He played in big bands when he was younger, but now he plays in five or six bands.

I started listening to the blues radio stations, KNOK in Dallas and Fort Worth, WLAC in Nashville, when I was a kid in '53, '54. I didn't start playing music until 1962 when I was in high school. I had been collecting records, but I wasn't playing. Then I went out to a frat rush party. I saw a band playing and thought I should do that, too.

The first band was a little group over at TCU [Texas Christian University], a few football players, a couple of frat guys. We played rhythm and blues. We played what was happening at the time, "Louie, Louie," all of that typical college stuff. Then in 1967 I got in my first full-time group with Robert Ealey. At first it was Robert Ealey, Ralph Owens, Johnny B, and me. You ask Johnny what it was, and he'll tell you Johnny B and The Tornados, and ask Robert Ealey and [he'll say] whatever he came up with at the time. We formed two bands together, Robert, me, Ralph [Owens] on piano, Mike Buck on drums, and Freddy Cisneros, which became The Five Careless Lovers in 1968. It was a mixed band, and we played The Hop and places on Camp Bowie, a lot of black clubs off Evans and out in the country. I can't remember the names, but we worked quite a bit, three or four nights a week.

The Bluebird opened originally as a barbecue stand around World War II, and the guy kept building onto it. It may have started in the 1930s, but in the 1940s it really started happening. Cecil Gant played there. T-Bone didn't come to the Bluebird until the time he sat in with Robert Ealey and The Five Careless Lovers.

The biggest rhythm and blues and jazz place in Fort Worth was the New Jim Hotel, opened up in the 1930s, first black hotel in Fort Worth. It had a barbershop, a restaurant open twenty-four hours a day, an after-hours club. T-Bone was in the house band there in the mid-1930s. There were pictures of T-Bone with Count Basie, Lena Horne, Charlie Christian.

Anyway, The Juke Jumpers didn't form until June of 1976. The original band was me and Jim Colgrove, Mike Buck, and Jack Newhouse. Buck went with The Thunderbirds after about three months. Then we got Mike Bartula, and Jack Newhouse left to join Stevie Ray Vaughan. So we got Jim Milan. In '79 we got Johnny Reno and after that Craig Simichek. He'd worked with other bands I'd been in. Johnny Reno left in 1983, '84 to form his Sax Maniacs. But he still plays with us every now and then.

We want to play that Texas R&B and a little rockabilly. Jim is into rockabilly, but I'm into R&B, Goree Carter, Duke/Peacock, Freedom, Macy's kind of stuff. So we put that together with a little jazz, rhythm and blues and rockabilly. We have that Texas swing style, and a little Louisiana, too. You go down the road about thirty miles from Port Arthur and you're to Lake Charles—T-Bone played Houston; he also played Lake Charles, Port Arthur, Beaumont, and Clifton [Chenier], he went the other way into Houston.

When we were playing in the late 1970s, the music was kind of dying out. They threw away all those Duke/Peacock 78s. The company had been sold, and, well, what are you going to do with them? But those albums are being reissued now. I've got a lot of the 78s, but the sound quality is better on the *Strutting at the Bronze Peacock* album reissued by Ace. And those 78s sounded good.

My guitar style comes out of that period, but includes everything from T-Bone to Charlie Christian, the Texas swing style, and, of course, people like Bob Wills. We have two guitars, two saxophones—tenor and alto, they can switch off—piano, and drums. We've done four albums now by ourselves and one with Robert Ealey. The first was *Panther City Blues* on Flying High records. The next was *Border Radio* on Amazing. That had Johnny Reno. And after that was *The Joint Is Jumpin,'* and the last one is *Jumper Cables* on the Varick label, which is part of Rounder.

I still like the same basic sound, and there are some other groups in Fort Worth getting into it. There's an interesting Spanish band these days out on the North Side. They're doing some James Brown soul stuff, but then they're doing Roy Milton, T-Bone, they're even covering some of our stuff. Their instrumentation varies, sax, two guitars, drums, but the bass player also doubles on sax, so one of the guitar players can play bass. The three brothers are the leaders: Steve Coronado, Joe Coronado, John Coronado; bass, drums, and guitar.

(OPPOSITE) AARON "T-BONE" WALKER (FIRST ROW, 2ND FROM LEFT), SUMTER BRUTON, (SECOND ROW, 3RD FROM LEFT), FORT WORTH, EARLY 1970S. COURTESY SUMTER BRUTON.

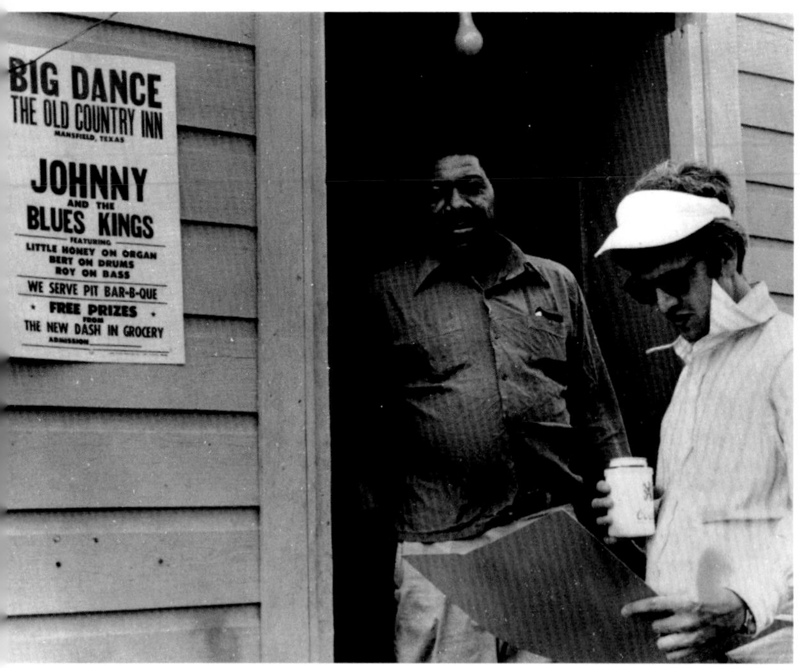

JOHNNY B AND SUMTER BRUTON, RENDON, TEXAS, EARLY 1970S. COURTESY SUMTER BRUTON.

THE JUKE JUMPERS LOGO. COURTESY SUMTER BRUTON.

Fort Worth has had some great ones. Finney Mo was one of those. His hit song was "My Baby's Gone." He was in his early fifties when he died. I have a bunch of tapes of him from KCHU, the station that was pre-KNON. He used to have a radio show he was on with Dave Liggins, Chops Arredondo, three guys from West Dallas who sat around and talked about the West Dallas days. And I heard Zuzu Bollin on the radio in those days. They say he's still around.

In the 1950s in Fort Worth there were Robert Ealey, Ray Sharpe, and C. L. Dupree was in town. Two of the best bands: Little Al and The HiFis and Lewis Howard and The Red Hots. Al had a pretty good-sized group, probably had three to five horns, conga player, piano. He had a lefthanded Fender guitar. He played all the frat parties. That was when the black bands played all the white frat parties. They did all over the South, the blues and soul music. Look at [the movie] *Animal House*, that's exactly the way it was, everybody doing the "Gator." There were a lot of wild shows. Lee and His Jolly Five. Aaron Watkins was a black booking agent in town, and he booked most of the frat gigs. You'd call him at four o'clock in the afternoon and say, "We need a band at eight." And he'd have a band there.

King Curtis left Fort Worth in the mid- to late Fifties, Ornette Coleman, Prince Lasha. The guy who taught all those guys to play was Red Connor. He was the legendary saxophone player of Fort Worth. In fact, my daddy even worked with him a couple of times out on Jacksboro Highway. Red Connor, he's dead. I don't know of any recordings he made other than some he did with Amos Milburn, who came through here and brought him to California where he did three sides with him. Red Connor was the guy that everyone talked about. He played in the 1930s and 1940s in lots of clubs. Back then they had clubs where the roof would roll back and you could dance under the stars.

In the 1950s the Duke/Peacock 1500 series was basically jazz with a boogie-woogie beat and a hot guitar, Gatemouth Brown. I'm forty-three, and in a way I'm not old enough to really know everything. You got to talk to the people who are in their fifties and sixties.

Delbert McClinton was one of the first bands I got to go see with a date. He was playing rhythm and blues. Delbert was one of the first white crossover bands I ever saw, but there were some others, maybe not as pure but the rockabilly bands, the western swing groups, also played blues, but with a different beat than a shuffle.

In Dallas at the time one of the best bands was Big Bo and The Arrows. They had an organ player, bass, drums, guitar, two or three horns. They made about seven or eight 45s, and they were all hits in this area. They got airplay on KNOK and CRZY. They were one of the hottest groups in the area in the 1950s and 1960s.

I always liked the blues, ever since I was three and four years old. I used get up in the middle of the night and play that Charlie Parker drumbeat with a *Down Beat* magazine rolled up. Charlie Parker was a great blues player as well as jazz. What you like in music has a lot to depend on your environment, what you get to listen to. I must of broken half my dad's 78s. I was just a little kid, and they break real easy.

I don't think my music is going to change a whole lot. I'm always trying to improve some, practicing, read better. I'm jazzy, blues, swing feel. I like chord changes, like the Houston Peacock sound. The Texas guitar is fluid, single string runs, and the way they bent the strings, the phrasing, ever since Blind Lemon Jefferson. Then there's that jazzy feeling, T-Bone Walker, Gatemouth Brown, and there's the influence of country, Bob Dunn [who played steel guitar with Milton Brown], and people like Lonnie Johnson and Eddie Lang, who wasn't from this area, but had a lot of influence here. They say some of the first guitar amps were made around Mineral Wells, for T-Bone and Gatemouth playing up in Fort Worth. And of course, there's the importance of the saxophone. Barney Kessel and others said, "Don't listen to guitar players, listen to saxophone players." You can play with a lot of interval jumps, a lot of feeling; it's harder.

THE JUKE JUMPERS, FORT WORTH, CA. 1978. COURTESY SUMTER BRUTON.

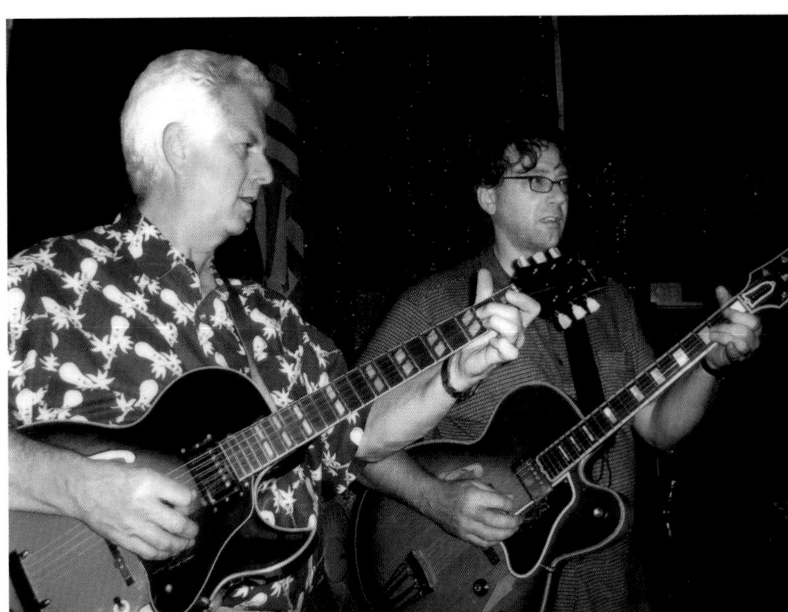

SUMTER BRUTON AND HASH BROWN, FORT WORTH, 2003. COURTESY SUMLER BRUTON.

RAY SHARPE

February 8, 1938–   ; interview, 2004

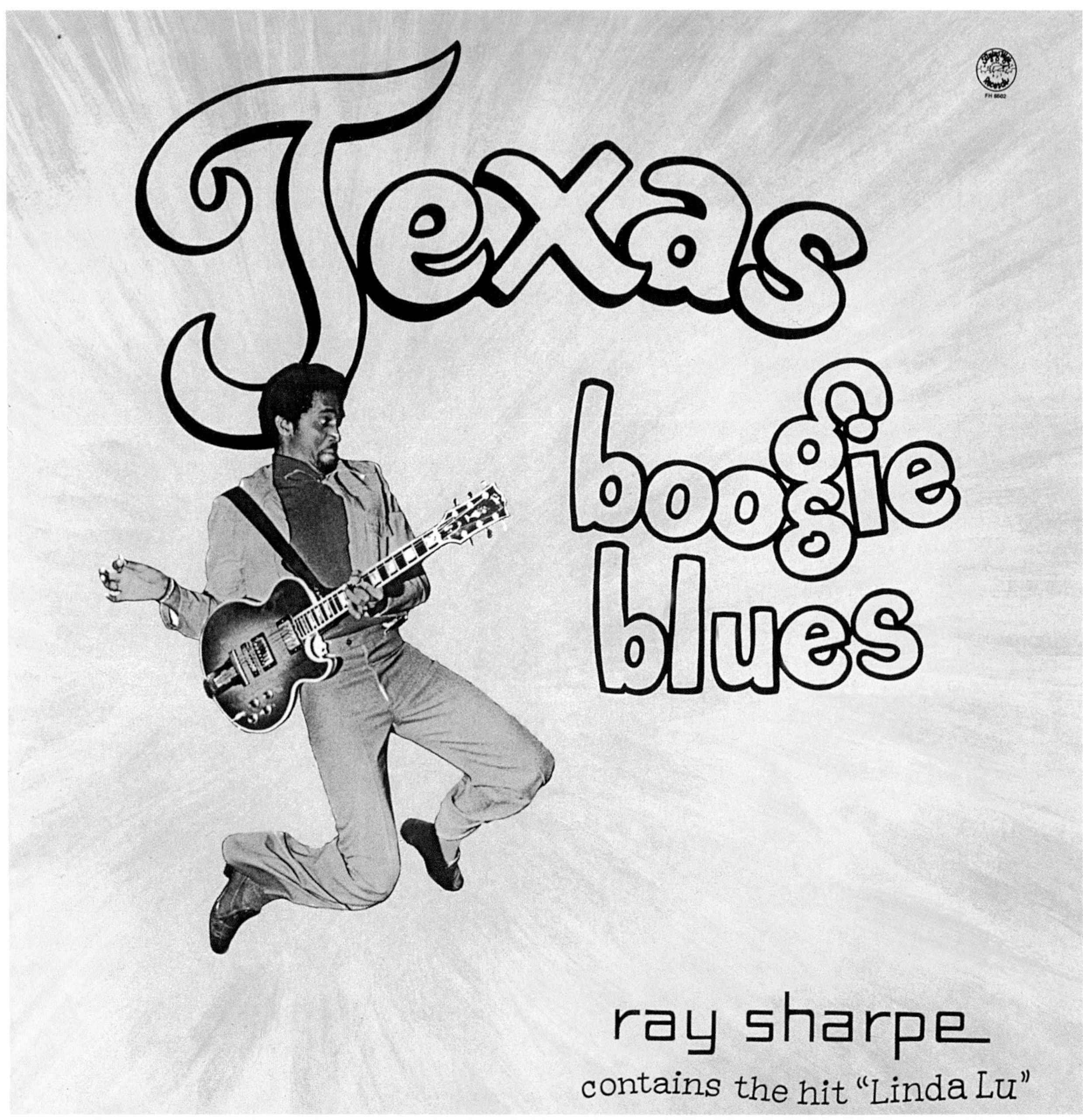

RAY SHARPE, "TEXAS BOOGIE BLUES,"
FLYING HIGH RECORDS, 1980.

I was born in Fort Worth. My mom, Dela Mae Sharpe, was from East Texas. She was from Marshall originally, and I'm not sure about my father. His name was Jesse Sharpe. I believe he could have been born in Palestine, but I'm not sure where his birthplace was. By the time I came along, they were separated, divorced and all that. I did get to know him. I mean, you know, I met him and got to know him, up to a point, anyway, up until about the time that I was ten years old and he was—nowadays you call it being an alcoholic, whatever, and he eventually lost his mind and had to be committed to a mental institution. His case was, I guess, assessed as so bad till he went to Rusk State Hospital. He stayed there until he was transferred in '62, '63, I believe. My mother had two nervous breakdowns, and she had to be committed to a mental hospital. She went to Terrell. And while she was there in Terrell, I got word that he had been transferred to Terrell from Rusk. And so I went to see him, but he didn't know me. My mother had her first nervous breakdown back in '57, I believe.

My mother was a cook. And initially, she used to do maid work, stuff like that, servants' quarters in rich families' homes. And by the time that I began to realize exactly what she was doing—around the age of four or five—she was working at a place called Lesley's Chicken Shack out on Camp Bowie, which was a franchise.

As a child, growing up, we didn't have electricity. But there were people across the street, neighbors, and up on either side of us. We lived in some little shotgun houses. There was a row of them in a section where there were nice houses, all on the same block, so people across the street—there were two families, and one family had some kids, some my age and some a lot older. And they had electricity, and they used to play their radio. They would have it out on the porch and everything. I would listen to it and hear some of the music that was being played. Oh, back then, it was Lucky Millinder, Buddy and Ella Johnson, big band sound, T-Bone Walker, Pee Wee Crayton, Ivory Joe Hunter. Boy, there was a number of them. Some of the names escape me at this point.

At the time, see, the radio stations served three different formats. And they had a format early in the morning which was rhythm and blues. And after the blues things went off, I think they played country music. And then after that, I believe they played Latino music. And then it was country again, and then they had the rhythm and blues thing late in the evening because I remember the deejay saying, they were calling this "Blues at Sundown." The show back then, the format for black R&B stuff was "Blues at Sunrise," and then in the late evening, it was "Blues at Sundown." They had several deejays that did the programming. And they had a lot of interesting music. Some of the artists—I remember these because these people used to come to Fort Worth on tour.

We had two stations. One was KWBC, and then one was KCNC. KCNC could have been the one because there was a disk jockey who was real known around here by the name of Jimmy Clemons, who is now deceased. He was not only a deejay, but he was a promoter; in other words, he brought shows. He brought some of the big shows into town, like Buddy and Ella Johnson and T-Bone and Pee Wee Crayton and Ivory Joe Hunter and people like that. They used to have their dances at a place called the Masonic Hall, which was also a temple for Masons. It was a great, huge hall, and I guess part of it sort of doubled as a place where they had the Masonic organization.

Listening to music back then, I was about six, seven, eight years old. And then my mother had serious health problems, and I went to stay with an aunt. Her name was Sarah Hayes. And I stayed with her from the time I was around ten to eleven, somewhere from the first through the fifth grade. My mother left where she was living in these little shotgun houses. My brother, who was somewhat of a little renegade, playing with some boys or something, caught the toilet—we had outdoor toilets, and it was a just a little wood hut, shack, or whatever you want to call it—and they somehow or another, playing with fire, caught the doggoned thing on fire. And though my mother told our rent man she would pay for the damage, he insisted that he didn't want her living there no more because of what my older brother had done.

His name was Joe Louis Sharpe. He was named after the boxer. My mother named me after a movie star, Edmond Lowe. My full name is Edmond Ray Sharpe. I guess Edmond was her favorite movie star.

In the immediate family, there were three, and then I had an older brother. By the time I was ten years old, my mother had remarried. And she had another son, and his name was Ladelle Eugene Ross. She became Ross then.

Back then, living in the community in which I lived, you just sort of never knew what was going on in the outside world, in the adult world. I mean, you'd hear talk, you'd hear your mother and older folks talking about various things.

Oh, Fort Worth was definitely racist back then, but I wasn't aware of it. The first time I became aware of anything that was racist, the way it was as far as blacks and whites were concerned, was in the late 1940s. During that period of time, I was living with my aunt, back in '48, '49; I was ten years old. So a lot of things I didn't hear about; I just became aware of it more or less after the fact because you'd hear about houses getting bombed over in Riverside. Of course, I lived on the south side, which is where I live now. I don't live too far from where my aunt lived. She's deceased now.

This racist thing, I first became aware of it when I was about nine years old, seven or eight, somewhere in there, and I was visiting my father. We used to go visit him on Sunday, and then we'd have dinner, my brother and my sister, which was just three of us then. I had a sister named Jean Esther Sharpe. We were there, and it was a duplex house. A family lived next door; they had about five or six kids. And one of their daughters, the oldest one, was coming somewhere—I don't know if she was coming from church. White boys used to ride up and down the street just kind of terrorizing people to some degree. And anyway, she was walking along this street by herself, up East Rosedale towards South Main Street, right here on the south side. Somehow or other, they knocked her down or chased her down and then literally ran over her with a car. She managed to be able to get up and get away from them. But I saw this with my own eyes around eight or nine years old, and it scared the hell out of me because I'd never seen anything like that, never heard anything like that. And it just isn't something that, you know, your mom and dad talked about, as a rule. But, I mean, it was there. And so they immediately got her to the hospital, and she lived through it and got past it. There was nothing to be done. Couldn't call the cops; if we did, they wasn't going to do anything.

I remember my mother taking me to the hospital, at John Peter Smith Hospital, what it's called now; used to be called City and County. . . . Some boy had been playing with some other boys on his street or whatever, and some white boys come along in a car and put a rope around his neck and drug him, you know, a short distance, and let him go. He come in the hospital all skinned up, you know, stuff like that, and his parents brought him to the hospital. So I witnessed this at nine, ten years old, during that time.

It was rather scary, considering that I wasn't exposed to being around whites. It's very limited. I remember going with my mother, going and getting on the bus to go somewhere. It's one of them things, when you get on the bus, you immediately go to the back, which is where you were supposed to go, and all that. And all the white people sit in the front. And if you get on and sit in the front, depending on the bus driver, well, you know, even if there wasn't any white people there, he'd make you get up and move, and all such stuff as that. Little by little, I became aware of it.

The first music I ever sung was country. But that's blues, too, you know. I mean, there's blues country and there's blues R&B, and my inspiration behind singing the country blues thing was a guy by the name of Jimmie Rodgers, who had been long since deceased. I heard his records. Yeah, there was a guy by the name of Kenny Sargent. He was on the radio station here; as I remember, the dial number was KCUL 1540, and he used to have an evening show that came on around six o'clock. It was on about two or three hours. And at one point during his career, he was a singer also. He'd sung with bands, and he used to play this big band music. But he'd mix it in with a lot of other stuff. And so I began to listen to it, to sift through the big stuff, so he can get to some of the other things I like. I remember him playing, the first time I ever heard Andy Griffith's "What It Was, Was Football" and "Grandma's Lye Soap." Those were a couple of routines that I later learned to sing. And I did the reciting of "What It Was" in the manner which he did it, as a youngster, because it was one of the first comedy-type things that I heard that made me laugh, and that I enjoyed. But he also played Jimmie Rodgers. And man, when he played him, I mean, it got my attention. The music was very simplistic, easy to listen to and easy to follow, or singing along with him, because there wasn't a lot of chord changes or music changes that you had to listen to and stuff like that. And Jimmie Rodgers, I bet if he had one blue yodel, he had about ten or twelve of them. "Texas Blue Yodel," and "Blue Yodel No. 1," "Blue Yodel No. 2," or whatever, but whatever he played, he used to talk about him. Of course, back then, you know, you wasn't really trying to get the history of the individual. And he used to mention, I guess, why he played him

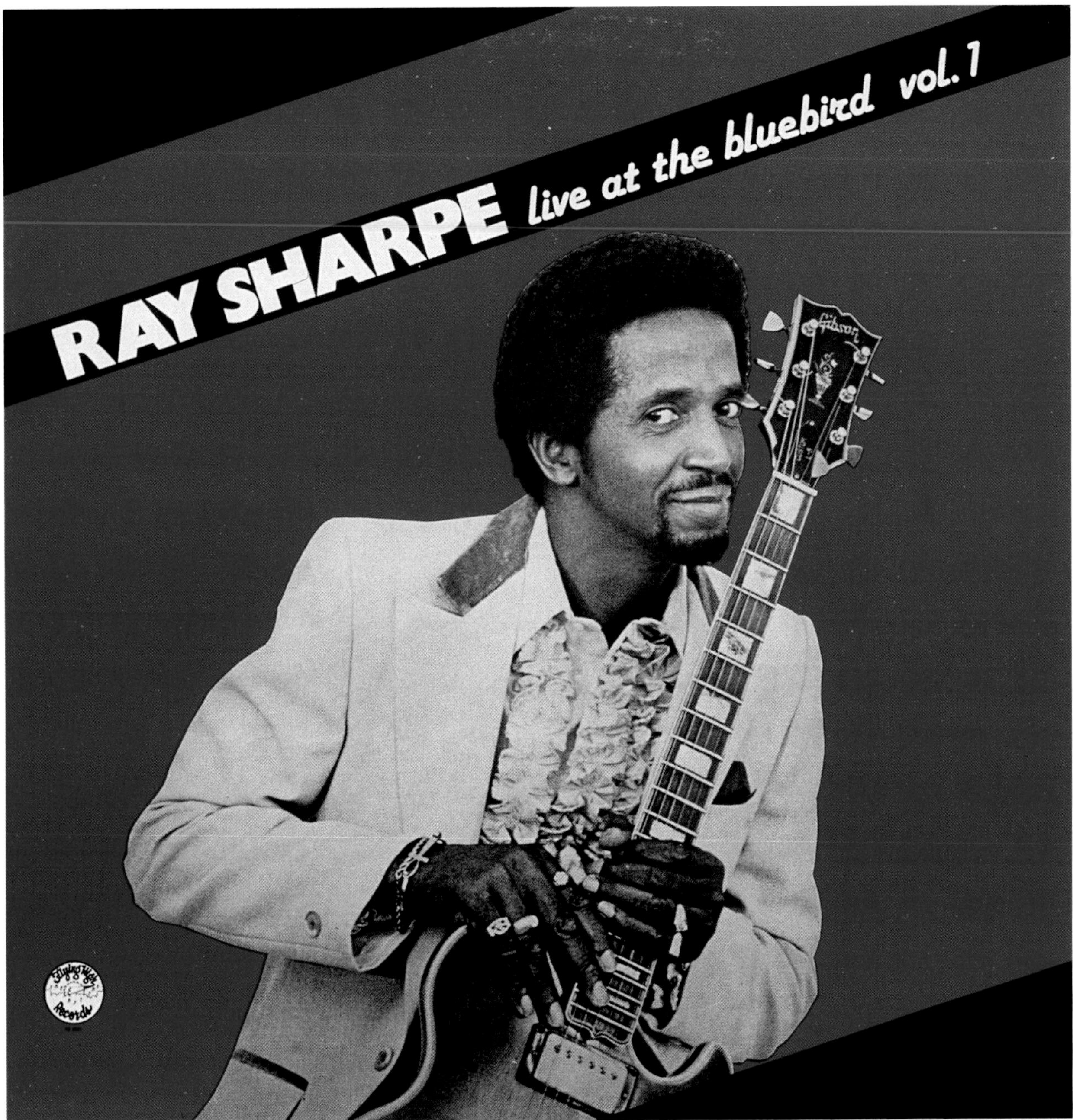

RAY SHARPE, *LIVE AT THE BLUEBIRD*, VOL. 1, FLYING HIGH RECORDS, 1982.

or whatever, and why he was a great admirer, but the mere fact that—it was literally love at first sight, listening to the guy, listening to his music, the way he played, the way he sang, the yodeling—and I began to emulate it, you know. I started doing it myself. I was doing this before I ever had a guitar. And so, those were the first songs that I sung.

I'm guesstimating I was around fifteen when I got a guitar. It was a Stella, just an old Stella guitar. I paid about fourteen dollars and fifty cents. Yeah, fourteen, fifteen; I was in the ninth grade. Yeah, I remember that now, because I used to work after school, fifty cents an evening, and help the janitor clean classrooms. I was at G. W. Carver at that time. I went to Terrell when I was in tenth grade. I went to G. W. Carver from the time I was in the sixth grade through the ninth grade.

First of all, when I got my guitar, I was trying to learn how to play. And basically, when you're learning how to play, you're playing open chords, so you're playing the kind of chords that country artists, for the most part—who are not lead players, who play accompaniment-type things, you know—that's what you're playing. So once I started doing that, man, I really lit into the Jimmie Rodgers stuff. And he had other things. He had something called "Frankie and Johnny," and oh, some other. The blue yodel is the one I liked. "Frankie and Johnny" was one I liked. "Frankie and Johnny" was the first song I ever sung, playing guitar.

I can yodel, still yodel. I do a song, one of my favorites, every now and then, called "Bojangles," where I will yodel. I don't always get the opportunity, it just depends on where I'm at and what kind of crowd it is. I'll just kinda sneak something like that in, depending on—if I'm going around to country joints or kind of an open-format club, then, that's one thing. But when you're playing blues joints, then, you're more or less formatted to do that, although a lot of R&B songs are country songs and a lot of country songs are R&B songs, so it just depends on the way they're done. But when I play country, I like to do it a little different. I've heard [blues] artists who've come along and will do some country songs, like Bobby Bland did "Today I Started Loving You Again." It was a Merle Haggard song, but he did it in such a funky way that it's blues, and it can be done in that manner. But generally, when I try to do some country, I like to do different stuff that has a kind of a spirited type of thing, something to get you in the mood or change the pace, something to grab your attention to, like "Bojangles." "Bojangles" is a song that a lot of people like, but maybe a lot of them don't request it. I used to get a lot of requests for it because I used to do it all the time. But it's a favorite. I first heard Sammy Davis Jr., doing it, and I thought it was his song. And lo and behold, I found out it was by Jerry Jeff Walker. And then The Nitty Gritty Dirt Band did a heck of a version, had a big hit on it. Of course, they did an up-tempo version of it.

Well, I literally got pushed out into it [performing]. I was playing and learning how to play, and then I started playing a few little blues tunes and stuff like that. My brother used to take me around because I was too young to get into these joints. He used to take me around to hear the blues bands play. And the first blues band I ever heard was a group called Boogie Chillen Boys, which had Robert Ealey, who's now deceased, and U. P. Wilson, who is from here. He's now in Paris, France. Yeah, he's in Paris now. He's been over there the last four years—he comes home periodically, so I understand. I have not seen him in, ooh, about four or five years. [Wilson died in 2004.] Robert Ealey passed about three, four years [ago].

So I used to go hear these guys play, and this was before I even learned how to play blues. I was just basically learning. This is when I started listening to a lot of R&B, and this was on KWBC. They had a disk jockey by the name of McNeil at the wheel, and he used to do the early-morning things, from around six o'clock to around nine or ten o'clock in the morning. You'd get a heavy dose of blues, from L'il Son Jackson to Frankie Lee Sims to some other blues artists. But these were, I guess you'd say, the ones out in the forefront. They were what we called the hot ones. They had other artists there doing it, I mean, records they were playing, blues, Pee Wee Crayton—oh, boy, memory gets lost on some of them. It's been so long. But anyway, I used to start doing a song called "Lucy Mae Blues" by Frankie Lee Sims. "You See Me Coming, Go Get Your Rocking Chair," by Li'l Son Jackson. And then, about that time, Jimmy Reed came out with a song called "Baby, You Don't Have to Go," which was the first song that I ever played in a blues joint. My brother used to come get me, and I used to go up to the place called the Gold Dot, what it was back then. It later became the Glass Key, which was on Luella and, I believe, Harding Street or something like that. But anyway, I used to go in there; he used to get me in there. I was too young to get in then. There was a place up the street from there, maybe half a mile or less, called the Coconut Grove. And he took me up there one night, and there was a little band in there playing, and he kept pushing me to get my guitar and go up and sit in and sing with these guys. And so the first song that I sung—and this song was hot as a firecracker, then, Jimmy Reed's, I believe it was his first hit, first major hit, anyway, that went national—was "Baby, You Don't Have to Go." And I used to do that; I used to love that song. And I started playing. I only knew about two or three songs that I played well. That one I knew pretty well because I played it all the time. I got up and sang it, and you know, the crowd, people that were there, I mean, it was a joint. I mean, I won't call it a hole in the wall, but you know, it was nitty-gritty. And it wasn't truly what you think of being one of your nicer clubs. You know, the people were nice enough, but it was heavy-duty drinking and stuff like that, which was something I wasn't really used to. And women getting out and men getting out on the floor and dancing, and all this kind of stuff. So I was there during the whole course of the evening. I bet I must have done that "You Don't Have to Go" a half a dozen times, if not [more], and maybe one or two other songs, and that was about it. But these guys liked what I played, and they encouraged me, to say, "We want you to come back and play again." And I started sitting in, then, with them, and then the guy who owned the club was a good friend of my brother's, and he wanted me to play. In fact, his son, who's named David Lee Pearson, they ran around together. So it was Big David and Little David. And so, you know, it was my first gig, at this place called the Coconut Grove.

So I had been practicing on some songs and stuff, but I was a little nervous. I wasn't used to that, you know, and they were pushing me and pushing me to get out front, and to sing and all this kind of stuff. And I had a problem because singing, some things were a little simplistic and a little easy to do, especially country music. But playing blues was something different. And that kinda bothered me. I really didn't know the ins and outs of working with a group and rehearsing and all this stuff, and working out things and this, that, and the other. And it was just one of those kinds of things you're involved in at a very young age. So these guys came to pick me up. There was a drummer—well, both of them were drummers. Guy by the name of Lorenzo Bell, and he had a brother named Cornelius Bell. And Cornelius Bell was the better of the two, but Lorenzo was the one that I started out playing with. And I think they had a piano. I don't remember if they had a piano player or it was just drums and guitar. But anyway, they came to get me. That was on the east side of Fort Worth. The Gold Dot and the Coconut Grove were on the same side of town where I lived, because I used to live in the Butler Projects. But then my mother later moved, but it was still on the east side, to Eighteenth Street. And shortly after that, she moved over to 300 New York Street, in a garage apartment. So these guys had come over and were outside blowing for me to come down. And I went and hid under the bed. I didn't even come out. It was the first gig, but I was a no-show. They didn't get out or anything. They didn't know whether I was there or not. I talked to them later. I done forgot exactly what I said. My mother knew that I was supposed to play. She had been working, and she came home, and we were talking about it, and she told me, sat me down, and we had a nice, long talk. Say, the last thing in the world you ever want to do is tell somebody you're going to do something and don't do it. Say, you don't make commitments and then don't keep them. You show up whether you're able to do what you want to do or not. But if you've verbally committed yourself, you just don't do that and have people relying upon you and then you don't show up. And she said, if you didn't want to do it, then you should never have told them. And, you know, that old theory of hers, that mantra or whatever, if you can't do something right, do it well, then don't do it. And so I later got together with them, and we talked it out and so forth. And then we started over again, and I started playing over there on Fridays and Saturdays, I think. I think we rehearsed; I can't remember, that was so far back. We only played there like two or three times.

And then there was another friend of mine who was in high school with me, guy by the name of Billy Robbins, Billy Joe Robbins. But he went under the stage name of Billy Cole, which is the name he uses now professionally. And he was the one who introduced me, because he was playing over on Fourth Street, East Fourth Street, at a place called the Silver Dollar. And he'd been knocking them dead. Billy was a little more experienced. He'd started playing at a very early age. And he was playing clubs and a lot of other things a little bit before I was. And so he was a little bit more experienced with what he was doing. And he kept talking to me about coming over there, and so I went over there and sat in and played. Then he introduced me to the guy who owned the club. And he liked me, he liked what I did and everything, so next thing you know, I started playing with these guys. And I wasn't really having to do all the singing. There was another guy. Lord have mercy, I can't even think of his name. Oh, man. This is embarrassing. There was me and him, and Lorenzo Bell was the drummer. I was playing guitar. And this guy was the singer. I was playing electric guitar by then.

I got my first opportunity to record when I was playing at a place called the Penguin Club. By then, I was out of high school. I graduated in 1956, and I played all the way in my senior year at little joints and clubs on the weekend. And I did talent shows and all this kind of stuff. I had gained quite a bit of notoriety, popularity . . .

so I started playing some of these regular blues joints. And the people I was playing with were all professional musicians.

I was playing blues. I was playing in these clubs. These owners were white, as I said, but most of the places where I played, the owners were black. This was a rarity on this side of town. And so these people, this is what they did, and so they asked me to play, and I began to play for them, and they really liked what I played, liked what I did, so the owner took me from his club, which was a black club, over here on the south side, to a place out on Twenty-eighth Street called the Red Devil. The guy's first name was Ernest. And he owned a vending company also. They were playing there about three, four nights a week. And things began to go extremely well, and the band became very, very popular, because that was our first exposure in playing in a white club to an all-white audience. It was segregated back then.

We started there the latter part of December 1956, all the way through January, February, March, three or four months. The recording contract came later because Tommy Thomas, who became my manager, the guy who owned the club that I was playing called the Club 66, he had a partner. He was the one who took me to this Red Devil Club, and then the lady who became my manager had a club called the Penguin Club. They had been hearing a lot about me, decided to come over and listen and everything, and then had talked to him about me going over there to play. So he took me from the Red Devil to the Penguin Club, and I began to play there. I had been playing there approximately a year, almost, and then about that time, a guy by the name of Artie Glenn, who had a son by the name of Darrell Glenn, had recorded a song that Artie had written. This was a father-and-son combination. Darrell was the artist, and Artie Glenn was the father. And he wrote the song "Crying in the Chapel," I'm sure you've heard of that. It was a big hit. And rock 'n' roll was coming on like gangbusters, and Darrell was more or less considered a country, pop, Top 40 artist. And he was wanting to get into the rock 'n' roll scene. So he came to me because he felt like us doing a demo, which was really what it amounted to; we did a demo. And Artie paid us for the session, and he told me that if I had anything that I wanted to record, that if we had enough time left in the studio, then we could get it together and record it. Well, I recorded a demo. And one side of it was an instrumental called "Presley." The other side was a song called "That's the Way I Feel," which was a stammering, stuttering kind of a comedic type of song, where I'm just doing stammering and stuttering with the lyrics and all this kind of stuff, which attracted the producers, who eventually got interested enough to call Ernie and want me to come in and do a recording session. And it was just on the strength of that particular song. Keep in mind that was not a blues song. But all the time, I'm playing blues in these clubs. I'm playing Fats Domino and B. B. King and Jimmy Reed and Willie Mabon and Lloyd Price and Roscoe Gordon and whatever, Ray Charles and the whole nine yards.

Eleanor Smith had the Penguin Club. That was my manager. She was the one who came to hear me at the Red Devil. Well, the first recording I did was on Hamilton [Records]. The company was a subsidiary of Dot Records. Randy Woods was the guy, I understand, that owned Dot Records at the time. I never met the gentleman. The people that we were dealing with were Lee Hazelwood and Lester Seals, who were independent producers. And when Artie sent the demo out to them, he sent it to a number of other people. They liked it; they liked it well enough to say they wanted to get me in the studio to do some recording.

I did "That's the Way I Feel," and then I did "Oh, My Baby's Gone," on the back side of that, which was on Hamilton Records, and, boy, "Oh, My Baby's Gone" got a tremendous response on KWBC, which was the station I was telling you about, that three-format station that played country and played blues, and then they also played Latino music and so forth. They were interested in "That's the Way I Feel" because it was one of those kind of songs that's just a little different than the norm as far as the lyrics and the stammering and the stuttering and all this kind of stuff that I was doing. I did a lot of improvising with lyrics and with some of the songs I would sing, even though some of them could be blues songs, it just all depends. And doing things of that nature sort of attracted people to a lot of what I did; they liked the ad-libbing and all this kind of stuff. And they liked that. They released it on Hamilton, and it made its mark to a point to where they were interested in recording me again. But they didn't want to deal with having to split the royalties with Artie Glenn because I had a contract with him as one of my agents. After he had gotten the recording contract deal, he had all the publishing rights to all of my songs. Both of those songs that I released on Dot Records went to his publishing company and their publishing company, which was Greg Mark Music. There was a fifty-fifty split and they didn't want to deal with that anymore. So they contacted my manager, Eleanor Smith, and told her that the only way they would want to get me back in the studio again was, they would want full publishing rights to all of my songs. Artie went to her and told her, well, that's what they wanted, and he was glad to sell out to her, his part, which was something that he was literally given because of the fact he negotiated a record contract. Had it not been for him, and through his efforts, it never would have happened, at least when it did. And the contract with Lee Hazelwood and Lester Seals would not have happened at that time, may not have ever happened, because certainly we didn't know them. They were producers; they were producing people like Duane Eddy and Sanford Clark and all that. They were out in Phoenix, Arizona. Their offices were in Hollywood, California, but they came to produce stuff there because of the musicians and some of the artists that they used all the time. And then they got a lot of other artists from out of Phoenix, which was where audio recording studios were.

So Eleanor bought Artie out, I think, for a thousand or two thousand dollars; I forgot the exact amount, but she bought him out. And he relinquished rights to the publishing, gave them one hundred percent rights, so that set up the next deal to go into the recording studio, which was in '58. About a year had passed by then, and I think that song was recorded—well, the first song was recorded in early '58. Then, by the winter, December, somewhere along in there, either in late December of '58 or early January '59, I don't remember which. But anyway, we went back; I remember it was cold during that time, so it could have been late December or early January. We got three songs. I know "Red Sails in the Sunset" was one. And then—because that was one that they really, really liked—and then "Monkey's Uncle" was another. And then there was a third one that I had done. I don't know if that was "Silly Dilly Milly" or what the deal was, but I've forgotten now. One of them was never released at that time. But I do know "Red Sails" and "Monkey's Uncle" and another song, and then they needed a fourth song. And I had made some presentations of some other things that I had done and some recordings that I wanted to do, and they didn't particularly like them. So they said, "Well, let's sit down and think." Just sitting in the studio, just tinkling around on piano, and he says, "Try and think of another song because I don't like the ones you have." Which is what I did. I was at the studio, and I started plinking around with this "Linda Lu" thing. And Lee heard it and he looked at me through the window of the control room, and he came out there and asked me, "What's the name of that?" I told him that was this song I had written about a friend of mine's girlfriend, and I called it "Linda Lu." And he says, "I kind of like that. How does it go?" And I ran it down to him. He says, "Let's kind of go with that and see what we can get with it." And so we did, he liked it, we recorded it. I'm tempted to say the rest is history, almost, but that wasn't the case, because when the record came out, they were pushing "Red Sails in the Sunset," because they really liked "Red Sails in the Sunset." It was a good recording. I guess it's one of my favorites because I was playing piano on "Red Sails." A couple of songs in the studio during that period of time that I was recording for them, I played piano. One was "Justine," and the other was "Red Sails in the Sunset." And that was the first one. And so it got some decent play, you know, it was heard in certain areas. But the response just wasn't what they were looking for. And they felt like they wanted something that audience response would be greater and it would prompt them to decide whether it's a good record or it's going to be a fair record or a mediocre record or whatever. So right in the midst of what they were doing, they said, "Well, let's just turn it over and play 'Linda Lu.'" Which is what they did, right in the midst of while they were playing "Red Sails in the Sunset." And when they flipped it over and started playing "Linda Lu," I guess now I can say the rest is history, because it took off like a bat out of hell.

I have no idea how many copies were sold. I've been told—I mean, in order to get certified for a million copies, which is what I'm told by a number of people. I went through various changes regarding that. I'm in the midst of talking with some people now, again, regarding that.

"Linda Lu" was released three different times. The first time was in '59. Then the next time was in '61. And the next time was, I believe, '63, because I was out in California at the time, and Lee Hazelwood—well, they owned it. The first time was, of course, on Jamie. Then they re-released it again on Jamie, and then after their deal with Jamie had run its course, Lee Hazelwood—it could have stood for his name; it was a label called LHI, which was Lee Hazelwood, I assume. I was there on another recording date and some promotions and doing some tour stuff, and I always remained very close to them. And I went to see him, and we talked on the phone. I went up to his office, and he says, "We're releasing 'Linda Lu' again." I couldn't believe it. He showed me the record. It did it three times.

That song had the stuttering and the stammering, again. It was a mixture of blues, but the people who initially heard that song thought I was white because of my sound, voice-wise. And so, but the music that I was playing on the guitar, was blues, and it occurred I'd better repeat or redo that because back during those days, they used to have a slang for the black culture and the white culture. When black people referred to white boys playing music in just the general sense or general term—like the word they use now is *redneck* for cowboys, and this, that and the other—they had this slang that they used to use; they used to refer to them as "ofay boys." And I heard the term numerous times. Say, "Listen to that ofay boy play the blues," you know. Which they thought I was. And *ofay boy* was a term, a reference to white men or white boys. And that was one of the things that enabled that song to do as well as it did, because blues back then was not selling. The only thing that was selling was country music; but by far exceeding that was Top 40 and rock 'n' roll. And rock 'n' roll was coming on like gangbusters. You had people like Elvis and Jerry Lee Lewis and, of course, the late Johnny Cash and all of that. They were happening back in those scenes, among others. You had a lot of good R&B stuff being played.

Well, you know, people who have never met me, to this very day, think I'm white because that's just the way I sound. I don't have, as they tried to explain it to me, I don't have the diction of black; I don't speak the quote unquote Ebonics type sound. Of course, that's the new term being used now for a lot of things as far as in the black culture. But even back then, before that particular term was ever even thought about, was just that blacks had slang sounds that they used in terms of daily conversations or referencing other people or things of this nature, you know. And the way they sound, their wording, their diction, the terminology of certain things. But for whatever reason and how, because I'm the only one in my family, basically, that speaks in the manner that I do. I mean, my brother, Ladelle, he went to college and all of that, but his diction is totally different from mine. And how I came about the sound and how it happened, you know, I thank the good Lord for it because it was a blessing in disguise. But I have no explanation. I say somewhere down the road in my genes, there has to be a reason how it happened or whatever. But that's the way it happened with me in terms of what happened and particularly the recordings and things that I made. Because there was great acceptance and response to a lot of the things that I did. And it's all because of the sound that I generated in terms of my recordings and how I performed. Of course, when they went to see me perform, it was another different story. You know, it was accepted and all of that, but for a lot of people, I was a white boy playing the rock 'n' roll or blues whatever, and here's the black man, sounding like a white boy. It was truly, as I said, a blessing in disguise. I thank the good Lord for it on a daily basis.

I have no idea how many records I've made. Maybe, well, let's see. The only albums that I recorded here were three: *Texas Boogie Blues, Live at the Bluebird,* and *Welcome Back Linda Lu.* I had one over in England, which was a steal, a black-market album. It was titled *Ray Sharpe,* which [was named by] somebody with a hell of an enterprising idea because my music was very, very popular over there for whatever reason. See, I also got in this category of not only being a rock 'n' roll blues singer, but I also, with some of the lyrics and some of the songs that I did, got into this rockabilly area of music. And a lot of my songs were played. Some were recorded. I had a very good friend of mine by the name of Ronnie Dawson who used to do a lot of my stuff, and he was one who really sort of kicked some doors open and left them open, boy, for me until I got over there. We were good friends, became good friends, and I liked a lot of his stuff, music and stuff that he played. I guess you could say we had a mutual admiration for each other in terms of what we did. Ronnie was doing England and Sweden and Denmark and Copenhagen that I hadn't been. He'd been all over England and Ireland and just a number of places. Rockabilly music never had the base here that it had over there, for whatever reason. People just loved that Fifties stuff, and so it popularized my music in terms of that because of some of the music that I did. Some of it, of course, would not fit in the category of blues. It was either rock 'n' roll or it could be called rockabilly, not only because of the lyrics but the way it sounded, the instrumentations within the recordings, and so forth. And so I was very fortunate to be able to do that.

Well, man, blues is a lot of things. I mean, you know, you can have blues on the pop side, you can have blues in the blues R&B, you can have blues country. It's more than anything from a musical standpoint, it's just a feeling, you know, a feeling that you have, of expression that comes from within. It doesn't necessarily always have to be vocally done. It can be musically done. I love blues. I love all kinds of blues. First of all, I love all kinds of music. So I don't try to box myself in, in a category of seeing one type of music. I do the things I like, period. Like I was telling you, "Bojangles," for instance. "Bojangles," to me is a blues song because it tells a story, but it was what you call a Top 40 or a pop-type blues. It's a sad song. You listen to the lyrics of that song, man, at least I did. When I first heard it, when Sammy Davis was doing it, I liked it because of what he was doing. You know, there was a guy by the name of Bill "Bojangles" Robinson. I don't know if this had anything—I don't think, I don't know—that this had anything to do with Jerry Jeff Walker to write the song or not, or whether there was another Bojangles that he knew. But you know, telling the story of this man's life and what he did and how he did it, and how he lived, and what happened to him—you know, blues song. And just like Jimmy Reed, "Baby, You Don't Have to Go," that's a blues song. B. B. King, "Never Make Your Move Too Soon," it's just a variety. It's more or less a feel of lyrics, music, the combination, and from what you're feeling or thinking within yourself as far as other people's music or music you might write yourself. I've written a few blues songs, but not that many. But I just write songs according to feeling, not necessarily blues. I have generally done more blues by other artists than I have songs that I have written personally.

Man, there was one person who really influenced me early. Well, I'll tell you, that one person, man, who's now deceased who was a good friend of mine, bless his heart, Johnny "Guitar" Watson. Johnny was on my first tour. He came to see me. We became fast friends on my first tour in 1959. Johnny had been out there, man, at least two, three years, because I didn't realize it. I was reading some history on him, and they were saying he used to go under the name of Young Johnny Guitar Watson because he was around fifteen, sixteen, seventeen years old. He was still in high school. He done wrote and recorded and the whole nine yards, man. I remember hearing stuff from him in high school. So I was really surprised when he came to hear me play. We were on tour together, he and I and Dee Clark, B. B. King. B. B. King's another one that was an influence. I guess my greatest influences initially were Chuck Berry and Fats Domino. I love Fats Domino music. I play a lot of his songs. I used to. I learned how to play them. I had piano players who could not just copy or emulate the sound or the technique, you know, that he would do in a lot of his music. And some of it was just very simple. It was just a matter of rhythm, rhythmic sounds, and just listening to him and almost saying, you're not necessarily copying him note for note, to a degree. I don't know how to describe it. It's just a heck of a sound that he does when he's playing on piano. It's repetitious, like Chuck Berry, man; he's written a thousand songs, but basically, they all have something in common, the way he plays.

I've traveled some to Europe. England. My shows originally were rock 'n' roll shows. That was back in 1992. I played Germany. See, most of the people in Europe thought I was just, as that old saying goes, "Boy, you're a one-trick pony," I mean, in terms of the kind of music that I played. It was rock 'n' roll, and that's what they wanted to hear, which is what I did. But then I threw in some other things that I played, like Lloyd Price's "Lawdy Miss Clawdy," and I did some other things, blues things, that sort of got their attention, that I didn't just play all of the stuff that they had heard; there were other things, you know, there was another dimension in my repertoire musically—things that I did that people really liked and responded to. And through that, I got a booking the next time I went over there. I played London about three or four times. And one of the times that I went back, I played some rock 'n' roll clubs. And my last thing was a blues club called the One O One, which is right in the heart of London. And from that, I got the people from this blues magazine that comes out about three or four times a year.

One blues song that I've written, I've never recorded. And that was a song called "What Has Life to Offer Me?" That was written years ago, and I was thinking about rewriting it eventually, because I'm in the process of putting material together for a CD.

My interest and my enthusiasm [keeps me going], and what I'm doing. I guess if I ever lose that, then, there wouldn't be no sense in doing it anymore. I love music, period, and just not one kind of music. I love all kinds of music. So my interest is in that, and music is an ongoing thing, man, music is like, literally, especially performing, is like going to college or going to school, you know. And things are constantly changing until you never know it all. There's always something new and different to learn.

When you do this kind of stuff, and you do it for a living, as long as I have, it's the only kind of attitude to have, because if you don't have that kind of an attitude, you're missing the boat.

DELBERT McCLINTON

November 4, 1940– ; interview, 1987

DELBERT MCCLINTON, FORT WORTH, 1986.
PHOTOGRAPH BY ALAN GOVENAR.

I see my music going every which way. The reason I say that is because I never felt like it was confined. I never thought it was anything but what comes naturally. It's country music, R&B music, a combination of everything I've heard all my life. I've been influenced by everybody I ever heard, but I've never tried to copy anybody.

I have a book by John and Alan Lomax, and on the cover is a picture of the United States. By color code it shows musical influences from all over the world and all types. In Texas more of those colors come together than any other place. Going from coast to coast, from north to south, you just about have to come through some part of Texas.

Ever since I was a kid, I was always singing. I come from Lubbock, moved to Fort Worth in '51. I heard a lot of Hank Williams and Lefty Frizzell and Bob Wills, Patti Page. And I started realizing something from it when I had a particular uncle who really liked what I sang. He lived in Sweetwater, and he'd make a big deal out of it. I found out how easy it was to get money to go to the moving picture shows. I'd just sing him a couple of songs. I guess that's my first recollection that I could have a good time and see somebody else have a good time with it, and at the same time, get a little something for it. He liked me to sing "Hey Joe." That and "Folsom Prison Blues," which was the first song I learned to play guitar with.

I didn't get interested in blues until two or three years after I moved to Fort Worth in 1951. Actually, the way I got into it was I traded a kid I went to school with out of an old crystal radio set. I thought that a crystal radio was magic; to me, that tuning knob was bringing in music from out of space. And I lay in bed at night with that thing and pick[ed] up WDIA in Memphis, WLS in Chicago, and of course XERF across the border from Del Rio, Mexico. I started hearing blues stuff.

The first band I was in was during the heyday of rockabilly. We mixed in a lot of blues. We were called The Mellow Fellows. It wasn't much of a band. A whole bunch of us would get together, and we didn't know how to play. The drummer had a snare drum and a ride cymbal.

We played the "Big D Jamboree" on Jerry Lee Lewis's first night there. For the show, my drummer went out and bought a bass drum, a big old marching band bass drum. The band was myself, my brother, and a friend of his and his brother. There were fours guitars, no bass, a sax, and a drummer. None of us could really play, but we went over to the "Big D Jamboree" and signed autographs and all that stuff. From that day on, I have had my own band. It was the year Jerry Lee did "Crazy Arms," about '55 or '56.

Myself, the drummer, and the sax player went on from there and put together more of a real band. It was about the time I went to visit my aunt and uncle in Florida, and there was a motel there called the Starlight. Every Tuesday of the month they would have a talent contest, and on the last one of the month, the winners of the previous three weeks would go on. So my aunt rented me a guitar from a music store in Cocoa Beach. And I entered the contest, and I was there for a month, and I won singing "Goin' Steady," the old Tommy Sands song, and "That's All Right, Mama," the Elvis thing. That night, there was a woman in the audience who came up to me and said she was from Capitol Records and wanted me to send her a demo tape. Well, I thought, "This is it." So when I got back home we went in a studio in the basement of KFBJ radio and we cut "Mean Woman Blues" and the first song that I wrote, called "Who." 'Course, I haven't heard from that woman yet.

Right after that my drummer, sax player, and I put together a group called The Straitjackets. There have been so many names and so many bands since then. I don't know where that one ended and the next one started. But that's when we started playing blues.

We got into listening to KNOK. Man, that was a great station back in the mid-Fifties. I remember hearing "Honest I Do" come on the radio, and that's the first time I was ever really caught by someone playing harmonica. That was Jimmy Reed, and then shortly thereafter, we were the only white band that played at the old Skyliner Ballroom in Fort Worth on Blue Monday. It was black night out there, and we were the only white band playing on that. And one night Jimmy Reed was there on the show, and the next day I bought me a harmonica.

A little after that we went into a studio over on River Oaks and recorded an old Sonny Boy Williamson song, "Wake Up, Baby." And Jimmy Clemons, who was a deejay on KNOK, he booked a lot of shows. He played that record, "Blues at Sunrise," six o'clock in the morning. I'd be up to listen to it, and then he'd play our song "Wake Up, Baby." As far as I know we were the only white band back in those days that was on that radio station. It was mostly Little Milton, B. B. King, Jimmy Reed, Howlin' Wolf, all that stuff. The only time we'd be on the air would be at sunrise.

At that time we did some Sonny Boy Williamson, Elvis, ballads, Jerry Lee Lewis. Whatever we considered to be happening, we played. Back in those days, every guitar [player] around here went to play with Cornell Dupree at the White Sands Supper Club, an after-hours joint. Cornell lives in New York now. He's not more than four or five years older than me. I'm forty-seven.

Cornell Dupree and Ray Sharpe were the two people we went out to listen to. Ray is a dynamite guitar player, and he was, back then, very innovative and full of a lot of energy. Ray was the guy everybody went dancing to, doing the Push. He's always had his very unique style. He was doing country music, a vocal stylist, but also is a powerful and unique guitar player. Now, Cornell, he was called C. L., he had a different approach. He would sit up on a bar stool on the bandstand with his legs crossed, and just play his butt off.

Then there were the Duke/Peacock people that came through here, Junior Parker, Bobby Bland. They were always a package deal at the Skyliner. We did [Bland's] songs then, and I'm still doing "Turn On Your Love Light" in my show every night.

Sonny Boy Williamson used to work at a place called Jack's Place, out on the Mansfield Highway, right outside the Fort Worth city limits. It was a notorious place where kids could get in. He had a deal with the police out there. The neon sign [in front] was a big old jackass, and the unwritten law among everybody, all the kids, was that if the jackass wasn't kicking, there was going to be a raid. So it was a pretty safe place for young people to go.

We'd go out there and sometimes get to play with Jimmy Reed, Howlin' Wolf, Joe Tex, Sonny Boy Williamson. So when Sonny Boy came through here, we'd work out there with him Friday and Saturday. Sunday, we'd drive with him up to Lawton, Oklahoma, and play up there. We'd go out there and do fifteen or twenty minutes, and then Sonny Boy would come out. I learned a whole lot from those guys.

I remember one night they were having Buster Brown and Jimmy Reed, and hell, I was about nineteen. I was in the dressing room, sitting between those two guys with a brand new harp. I was going to learn me something. And they were passing a fifth of Old Granddad, and I was in the middle. I didn't drink, and I was hittin' it double. I never even saw the show, man.

We worked with Joe Hinton at the Tracer Club. It was one of those clubs that had telephones on every table, and on the wall, there was a diagram where you'd see some gal sitting at some table and you could call. It was a big hit around here. We were the house band out there for two years, and we worked with Joe Hinton, Barbara Lynn, T-Bone Walker. That was in the early 1960s. I always enjoyed playing in black clubs. I was learning, playing with people who were just magic to me. Freddie King was great, and he came out to the Tracer Club. He was a ball of fire, the hardest working guy I ever saw. He'd get up there and blow it all out.

The first recording we did of any consequence was a song that I wrote, "If You Really Want Me To, I'll Go." It came out on one of Major Bill Smith's labels around here. And it did so well around here that it was picked up on Smash. But Major Bill and one of the guys who worked with him got into a difference [of opinion] over who owned what. So the record ended up sittin' and dyin' on the floors of Big State distributor because Smash couldn't ever get any satisfaction from anybody.

Because of that record, The Straitjackets kind of busted up because the band that made the recording

DELBERT MCCLINTON, FORT WORTH, 1985.

had different people, and that caused some animosity. So the next band I had was called The Rondells, and we were kind of a big deal around here [in Fort Worth], and then that finally came apart. I stayed around and had any number of bands. Every week I'd call it something else. But finally everything turned to shit for me, my personal life, everything else, was chaos.

In 1970 I took off and went to California. A friend of mine, Glen Clark, was already out there. Well, he and I got to writing songs. We went to see a friend of ours that we met, Danny Moore, and T Bone Burnett. We did a "spec" thing at Paramount studio. This guy came by and heard us, Earl McGrath, and he had contacts at Atlantic. Earl had started his own label, called Clean Records, and we signed a deal with him. They never amounted to much, but they were good albums, *Delbert and Glen*, and *Subject to Change*. They were all originals and were very unique. Some of it was progressive country before its time. The players were all excellent. We got great critical acclaim but never really sold anything. After we did those things, Glen and I went our separate ways, not as friends, but musically.

Then I signed with ABC, and that very week everybody from coast to coast got fired, all the bigwigs. So nobody knew I was on the label for the first year. But I ended up doing three albums for them. I was going to be their Progressive Texan. The first one was *Victim of Life's Circumstances,* which is all songs that I wrote. The second one was *Genuine Cowhide,* which was some songs that I'd written, plus old R&B things that I love and want to do forever, like "Blue Monday," "Please, Please, Please" by James Brown, "Lipstick, Powder and Paint." After the third release, ABC went out of business. So I went with Capricorn. They had been big business with The Allman Brothers, but that was petering out. But I had two albums, *Second Wind* and *Love Rustler,* and within two weeks after *Love Rustler* was released, I had a song go into the *Billboard* Top 100. That week Capricorn declared bankruptcy, and all the telephones were disconnected.

So I did this thing with MSS Capitol, and I did an album called *The Jealous Kind* and had my first hit, "Givin' It Up for Your Love." And after the second album, *Playin' from the Heart,* Capitol went bust. I was going on forty years old and I was pretty disenchanted with the whole business, and I had a little bit of a drug problem. I gave up on recording. I'd had a lot of heartbreak. I started working the road, and since then I've done a pretty good job of cleaning myself up. In fact, I've done a damn good job. And I think it's starting to sound better than it ever has. I have a lot more stamina. Most of all, I feel real lucky that I had people to encourage me to go on, when I just wanted to forget about it. I moved back to Fort Worth about five years ago. Then I went through a divorce, which was just over two weeks ago. It was going on and on and has pretty much kept me from doing anything. I didn't want to do any record deals until I got that straightened out. Right now, I'm writing songs, putting a new band together. Next month we start serious rehearsals. I've a got lawyer in L.A. that's pitchin' some of this stuff around and is trying to get me the best record deal I can find. And I'm going back into the record business. I have had a couple of re-releases come out, and I did a guest appearance on the Roy Buchanan album that came out last year.

I'm going to stick with whatever sound feels right at the time. Lately, I've been writing stuff at the piano, and I haven't done too much of that, but it comes different than when I write on the guitar. I wouldn't begin to call my music traditional blues music, but there's no doubt there's a lot of influence there. I couldn't go through a day without playing a shuffle here and there. I don't know exactly what the next album will be. I'm moving to Nashville. I've written about five songs, and I'm still looking. I just don't want to put out a record, I want to put out something that I like. I've gone through a lot of band changes in the last few years. Working without a record deal is hard on musicians, a lot of it is just that, work. When you don't have a record out there happenin,' there's not much goin' on but the club circuit, and that will just wear them out. They drop like flies.

Bill Campbell is playing lead with me now. He's been dried out for two and half years, and he's a hard-playin' son of a bitch. He's the one who some say taught Jimmie Vaughan and Stevie Ray to play. He was from the early Antone's years in Austin. Right now, he and I are the mainstays of our operation. We're going to keep horns. It's not quite right if there's not two to five horns. It's hard to carry that many people around, but I'm going to have at least two horn players, tenor and trumpet. I'm playing piano, guitar, and I've just started playing harp again in the last year. I was getting away from it for a while, but I brought it back and it's feeling fresh.

I'm having a lot of fun, and I'm looking forward to the next year. I've a good attitude, and I've got a lot of things behind me that I really needed to get behind me. You might say I'm in the pink. Blues is reaching all the way down and expressing it. In that way blues and country are the same thing. It's about getting up in the morning and making it through the day and managing to go to sleep at night thinking you'll never be able to.

THE SAXOPHONE IN TEXAS BLUES

JOE HOUSTON, "ROCKIN' AT THE DRIVE IN," ACE 120.

INTRODUCTION

In 1987, in the Variant Zalen of the sprawling Congresgebouw that houses the North Sea Jazz Festival in The Hague, Netherlands, Joe Houston is making his first European appearance as a soloist in front of a Dutch rhythm and blues group called De Gigantjes. They have never played together before, though Rob Kruisman, tenor saxophonist for De Gigantjes, has studied Houston's vintage recordings on 78-rpm sides that are now available on European reissue albums. The general musical sophistication of De Gigantjes is impressive, but for the first few numbers there is a cultural collision in the sound. Then the raw strength of Joe Houston's tenor solo takes control, a surge of repetitive low notes that unexpectedly scream to a close.

Though mainly known as an instrumentalist, Joe Houston is equally exciting as a singer with a powerful, shouting voice. Well-groomed and well-mannered on stage, wearing dark glasses, he jolts his body as he plays and sings, jumping and twisting to emphasize every phrase. Houston embodies the soul and life blood of a style of performance that began in the 1940s and 1950s and had the raw energy of rock 'n' roll before the music spread to a white audience, and that now, thirty years later, is regaining popularity.

Joe Houston grew up with the honkers, the wild men of jazz, who broke open the standards of the day and defined the idiom of rhythm and blues. They played their tenor saxophones with abandon, relentlessly honking single notes, making sudden leaps to freak high tones, blowing low and dirty, igniting their audiences with crazed stage antics and crude sounds.

The basis of this kind of playing, Leroi Jones [Imamu Amiri Baraka] observes, is "the saxophone repeating the riff much past any useful musical context, continuing it until he and the crowd were thoroughly exhausted physically and emotionally. The point, it seemed, was to spend oneself with as much attention as possible, and also to make the instrument sound as unmusical, or as non-Western, as possible. It was almost as if the blues people were reacting against the softness and 'legitimacy' that had crept into black instrumental music with swing."

Honking was a music of dissociation from the smoothness of jazz and white popular song. Honking challenged the established order and, in so doing, responded to the abysmal conditions of postwar segregation and incipient racial tensions. For black musi-

DON WILKERSON, HOUSTON, 1964.
PHOTOGRAPH BY BENNY JOSEPH.

JOE HOUSTON, NORTH SEA JAZZ FESTIVAL, THE HAGUE, 1987.

cians, there were few opportunities for commercial success.

Discriminatory practices were embedded in all facets of the entertainment industry, from dressing rooms to radio broadcast and recording sessions. In honking and screeching tenor solos, musicians mocked expectations and created a sound that was more stylized than personal.

Lying on his back, kicking his feet in the air, blowing rowdy notes, the honker did more than simply express his personal feelings. Honking was a burlesque performance that separated jazz and rhythm and blues from the past, both musically and socially, and that ushered in the advent of rock 'n' roll.

By the time honking was introduced, several Texans had already achieved national recognition for their virtuosity on the saxophone. However, their style of playing was part of a larger southwestern tradition. Henry "Buster" Smith, a seminal alto saxophonist and mentor of Charlie "Bird" Parker, for example, started his career in Dallas in the early 1920s, but he emerged as a major stylist in the late 1920s and 1930s in Oklahoma City with The Blue Devils and in Kansas City with Bennie Moten and The Barons of Rhythm, which he founded with Bill "Count" Basie.[1]

Other Texan saxophonists who were highly influential during the 1930s and 1940s include tenor players Budd Johnson, Herschel Evans, and Buddy Tate. Johnson seldom led his own bands, but as a sideman, he was a common thread linking the large bands of the early and mid-1940s that were involved in the transition from swing to bebop: those of Earl Hines, Boyd Raeburn, Billy Eckstine, Woody Herman, and Dizzy Gillespie. Evans, with an intense vibrato at the end of his impassioned phrases, established a tradition for Texas tenor players of the 1940s, among them Illinois Jacquet and Arnett Cobb.[2] Tate was a cornerstone in the

1. Dave Oliphant, *Texan Jazz* (Austin: University of Texas Press, 1996), 112. "One of Buster Smith's compositions that was recorded by the [Basie] band is 'The Blues I Like to Hear,' from November 16, 1938, which [Gunther] Schuller considers an indication of 'how much further to the southwest Buster's Texas-based style was rooted . . . one cannot fail to note its distinctive sound and voice-leading, its 'crying,' blues-drenched harmonies. Clearly, it has a totally different feel: simple and uncomplicated, earthy low-down blues with a heavy rocking beat."

2. Ibid., 109.

JOE HOUSTON, "BLOW, JOE, BLOW," MACY'S RECORDINGS 5017-B.

JOE HOUSTON ORCHESTRA, "HOUSTON'S HOT HOUSE," MODERN RECORDS 1732.

Count Basie Band, and his playing embodied what jazz historian Dave Oliphant has described as "the identifiably Texas blues tradition of smeared notes falling off in a crying moan."[3]

Tate, when asked about the honkers after performing a set at North Sea Jazz Festival in 1987, said, "I didn't like it the first time I heard it, and I'm still skeptical. You can't hear the changes, it's too loud and distorted. The great rhythm and blues saxophonists had a more complicated sound: Louis Jordan, Big Jay McNeely, who was the first tenor to move off the bandstand into the audience, playing wild solos, standing on tables and sometimes honking with his back on the floor."

The style of Buddy Tate's tenor is more refined and introspective. The changes are deliberate and smooth, and strongly rooted in swing-era jazz, though he says he did play rhythm and blues with T-Bone Walker in 1933 and 1934. "It was in a place called the Big House, on the outskirts of Dallas, built by a gangster, who had us play dressed up in prison uniforms. T-Bone had a jazzier sound. I played a high-energy tenor, but it wasn't honking. The sound I was after told a story for T-Bone's guitar to follow. Honking was something else. It was more associated with Houston bands."

In Houston, Milt Larkin's big band was a breeding ground of Texas saxophone giants such as Arnett Cobb, Eddie Vinson, and Illinois Jacquet. In 1940 Jacquet was lured away by Lionel Hampton on the condition that he play tenor, but until that time Jacquet had only played clarinet, and sometimes soprano and alto saxophones. With Cobb's help Jacquet was soon playing tenor and went on to become an important stylist in the Lionel Hampton Orchestra, where he is credited with introducing honking in his 1942 solo on the recording "Flying Home." The success of this tune sparked a nationwide interest in honking. Even Jacquet's friend and teacher, Arnett Cobb, started to honk, but the life of honking in jazz was relatively short. In 1943 Jacquet left Lionel Hampton and was replaced by Arnett Cobb. Jacquet returned to more mainstream jazz, joining Cab Calloway and then Count Basie. Both Illinois Jacquet and Cobb, who were two of the great honkers of their generation, said that "honking is a gimmick, a novelty" and that they preferred straight-ahead big band jazz, where the saxophone solos could be developed with more subtlety.

The discography of the Texas tenor and alto saxophone stylists is complex and vast. It includes the work of Herschel Evans, Buddy Tate, Jesse Powell, Budd Johnson, Buster Smith, Illinois Jacquet, Arnett Cobb,

3. Ibid., 113.

Eddie Vinson, John Hardee, Aldophus Sneed, David "Fathead" Newman, James Clay, Henry Hayes, Grady Gaines, and King Curtis—some of the major Texas saxophone influences in modern jazz and blues.

As a musical instrument, the saxophone is voicelike, Jay Brakefield points out, making it a natural outgrowth of the blues singing tradition.[4] The legendary Ornette Coleman suggests that "the tenor [saxophone] is a rhythm instrument, and the best statements Negroes have made, of what their soul is, have been on tenor saxophone. . . . The tenor's got that thing, that honk, you can get to people with it. Sometimes you can be playing that tenor, and I'm telling you, the people want to jump across the rail. Especially that D flat blues. You can really reach their souls with that D flat blues."[5]

Coleman started off as a honker in Fort Worth rhythm and blues bands and later burst free from the constraints of conventional musical form. Others were doing the same. Coleman echoes the sentiments of his longtime friend Dewey Redman, and both credit the little-known, but profoundly influential tenor man Red Connor, who lived in Fort Worth and mentored younger players.

Perhaps, as Brakefield suggests, the quest for musical freedom by black musicians may be connected to the larger quest for civil rights that came out of World War II. All these musicians were breaking free of the patterned chord changes that had ruled blues, rhythm and blues, and swing, and finding other, freer ways to play. Some were accused of playing music without structure, but in reality they had found other, more complex structures beyond "the changes."

The enduring influence of honking, which constitutes only a small area in the overall history of the saxophone in Texas music, is evident in bebop, free jazz, and the white crossover to rhythm and blues and rock 'n' roll. Since the 1980s, honking has been repopularized by saxophone stylists, such as Mark Kazanoff in Austin and Johnny Reno in Fort Worth. In the playing of these musicians the rudiments of honking combine with modern techniques to create a contemporary music that embodies a regional sound. "What is generally considered the Texas sound," Dallas-based tenor player Jon

BUDDY TATE, NORTH SEA JAZZ FESTIVAL, THE HAGUE, 1987.
PHOTOGRAPH BY ALAN GOVENAR.

4. Telephone conversation with Jay Brakefield, August 11, 2004.

5. John Litweiler, *Ornette Coleman: A Harmolodic Life* (New York: W. Morrow, 1992).

(OPPOSITE) BUDDY TATE, 1960S.
COURTESY TEXAS AFRICAN AMERICAN PHOTOGRAPHY ARCHIVE.

HENRY "BUSTER" SMITH AND AN UNIDENTIFIED BLACK-FACED COMEDIAN, THE ROSE ROOM, DALLAS, 1940S. PHOTOGRAPH BY MARION BUTTS. COURTESY MARION BUTTS AND TEXAS AFRICAN AMERICAN PHOTOGRAPHY ARCHIVE.

Smith points out, "has its roots in the territory bands of the 1920s and 1930s and, historically, is more regional in nature. The axis between Louisiana and Texas, for example, is very important. I grew up in Lake Charles, but was raised in Texas and played with Johnny and Edgar Winter, but also with Delbert McClinton. Illinois Jacquet was from Boussard, Louisiana, but was tremendously influential not only in Texas, but nationwide."[6]

The saxophone has retained its basic presence as the cornerstone of rhythm and blues. The single-string runs of the electric guitar solos often follow the saxophone riffs and emulate the horn sounds. There is a call and response between the saxophone and the electric guitar that shapes the Texas style. The Texas saxophone sound, though diverse and regionally defined, is generally big with a relatively straightforward, melodic approach. How this is articulated empowers the solo and distinguishes the attack of the sound.

6. Interview with Jon Smith by Alan Govenar, October 18, 2004.

HENRY "BUSTER" SMITH

August 24, 1904–August 10, 1991; interview, 1982

HENRY "BUSTER" SMITH (LEFT), THE HEAT WAVES OF SWING WITH T-BONE WALKER, (3RD FROM LEFT), LOUISIANA, 1949. COURTESY SUMTER BRUTON.

I met Charlie Parker after I got to Kansas City. He was a slow reader, and he hung around me all the time. He liked my playing, said I was the king. And I'd tell him he was the king. So I hired him to play with me at Lucille's Paradise, and he followed me everywhere I'd go.

He got that name "Bird" because when he'd go home at night, he'd say, "I'm goin' to get my wife to cook me one of them yardbirds." And someone said, "What do you mean yardbirds?" He'd say, "One of them fowls, chickens." So they called him "Yardbird," then shortened it to "Bird."

They called me "Prof" because I was writin' some music. I'd write music every day. So Charlie Parker hung around me, stayed in my band. He wanted to do everything I did. I was like his daddy and he was like my son.

Jobs got a little scarce in Kansas City, and I cut my band down to eight pieces. I did that for about a year and then I said, "I'm going to New York." I told Charlie Parker to take care of the job until I sent for him. And I went to New York and stayed there seven months. So, while I was there, Charlie Parker done hoboed to New York to see what I was doing. He come there and didn't have no money, nothin.' He come to my house, where I was stayin,' and my wife and me let him stay in the bed in the daytime and we'd stay in it at night. I'd be writin' music during the day and my wife would be workin' at a restaurant. But she made him move because he never would pull his clothes off. So he got with Dizzy Gillespie and went over to Philadelphia. Then Jay McShann sent for him, had him come back to Kansas City and make some records. Next thing I know he's with Earl Hines and came back to New York by himself, gigged around. I was with Don Redman, but Charlie couldn't work with me. He wasn't particular about readin' nohow, liked to play a lot of solo horn. So he just stayed to himself all the time.

CHARLIE PARKER, LATE 1940S. COURTESY SUMTER BRUTON.

I wrote my biggest song, "One O'Clock Jump," in 1934. We were playin' at the old Reno Club, and Basie started things on the piano and said, "Take it, Prof, take it." He'd change keys. He started playin' the blues in F kind of fast. He said, "I'm gonna modulate the D flat and Prof, you set somethin.'" So I set them riffs and went to playin' and they liked it so much we had to play it three or four times a night. The name of it [at that time] was "Blue Ball."

So finally we went down to Little Rock and played a big colored club. They wanted us to play on the radio one night at the station there. We had thirty minutes to do, and the announcer says, "That number you play with all that jazz, is that that 'Blue Ball'? Well, I can't say that on the air with the kids and everybody listening. What name can you give it?"

I said, "I don't know."

So we set around there for ten or fifteen minutes, and said, "I tell you when to hit it, and we'll just call it 'One O'Clock Jump' since we're goin' to hit it at one."

I said, "That's all right with me." And that's the way it started.

Then when I got to New York in 1938, Basie was usin' the song as his theme song. I thought he kind of done me a dirty deal. I didn't know anything about copyrightin' it. I'll never forget, "Jus' don't sue me, Prof, and I'll record anything you write."

Then I wrote "Blues I Like to Hear," but I put it in D natural so he wouldn't be runnin' all over the piano because he couldn't play too much then in D natural. It was an uptown blues. I had someone offer me a hundred dollars for that score sheet, but my wife got ahold of it and it got destroyed somewhere. I can't find it. Basie said, God bless the dead, that "Blues I Like to Hear" was the greatest blues he ever had in his band.

Uptown blues has a little more power to it, plenty of reed chorus, and the brass fill in. I had the brass way up in the air and really did a good send-off.

I left New York in 1943. I seen what it was comin' to. I had my time, and I was ready to go home where a little time for hunting and fishing wasn't so hard to find. Back in Dallas, I had lots of bands [and influenced a lot of the young ones, like David "Fathead" Newman and others]. I did some writing, still do, arranging.

Jazz has more tricky stuff in it. Blues is a little more straight, making seventh chords all the time. That gives it that blues feel. That slow blues is what we call that cotton patch blues.

The blues was all around, growin' up, pickin' cotton up in Collin County. That's where I was born, 1904. I heard them work songs, church hymns. I tried that blues on my uncle's pump organ in Ennis, but my mother disapproved. I didn't get my first instrument until I was seventeen, a clarinet, for three dollars and fifty cents, bought in a pawnshop with money I earned in the cotton fields [seventy-five cents for every hundred pounds]. In the 1920s I got my first saxophone and was playin' around Deep Ellum, Central Track. Then The [Oklahoma City] Blue Devils came through and I left with them [Walter Page, Lester Young, Oran "Hot Lips" Page, Eddie Durham, Bill Basie, and Jimmy Rushing]. The Blue Devils went broke in 1932, and I joined The Benny Moten Band in Kansas City. We were playin' that jump blues, which was a cleaner sound [than that cotton patch blues]. I used to write a lot of blues built around that alto [saxophone]. I never did sing, always kept me a vocalist, either a woman or a man. I had four or five different boys that were with me in Kansas City.

Jump blues was more like jazz, but not as many notes. It's played with more of an up-tempo than slow blues. Slow blues was what you heard in the chock house. They'd be sellin' pig ankles, pig feet, pig ears, and they had a big tub full of chock with a dipper in it sittin' up on top of the piano. People drink as much as they want to. That's what you call a "Good Time House," homemade liquor, bootleg liquor. You hear that slow blues and there'd be fightin.'

I like that big band sound. I had to stop playin' alto when I lost my chops in 1959, but I'm still playin' some piano, took up that electric bass.

DAVID "FATHEAD" NEWMAN (L.) AND LEROY COOPER (WITH THE RAY CHARLES ORCHESTRA), LONDON, 1975. PHOTOGRAPH BY VAL WILMER.

HENRY "BUSTER" SMITH AND DAVID "FATHEAD" NEWMAN AT A DALLAS FOLK FESTIVAL REHEARSAL, 1986. PHOTOGRAPH BY ALAN GOVENAR.

EDDIE "CLEANHEAD" VINSON

December 19, 1917–July 2, 1988; interview, 1984

MILTON LARKIN ORCHESTRA WITH ARNETT COBB (3RD FROM RIGHT) AND EDDIE VINSON (2ND FROM RIGHT), HOUSTON, 1940S.
COURTESY SUMTER BRUTON.

Eddie "Cleanhead" Vinson performed professionally for more than fifty years. He was born in Houston in 1917 and grew up in a musical family. Both of his parents, Sam Vinson and Arnella Sessions, played the piano, but in high school Eddie had a friend who had an alto saxophone, and that became his instrument of choice. His parents bought him an alto, and he took lessons at Jack Yates High School, where he soon attracted the attention of local bandleaders.

Around 1935 Vinson joined Chester Boone's band, which also included T-Bone Walker. Then Vinson and Walker moved to Milton Larkin's territory band, joining Illinois Jacquet and his brother Russell, Arnett Cobb, Tom Archia, Cedric Haywood, and Bill Davis. They played at the College Inn in Kansas City and the Rhumboogie Club in Chicago. In addition to playing alto sax, Vinson became a featured vocalist.

In 1941 Vinson left The Milton Larkin Orchestra, which was then led by Floyd Ray while Larkin was in the military. Vinson joined The Cootie Williams Orchestra in Houston and made his first recordings on the Okeh label in 1942. These included "When My Baby Left Me" and "Stars at the Apollo."

His next recording session wasn't until 1944, when he played alto sax with The Cootie Williams Sextet and sang with Williams's orchestra on "Cherry Red" and "Things Ain't What They Used to Be," issued on the Majestic/Hit label. The Majestic/Hit recordings were followed by additional sessions with Cootie Williams on Capitol, but by 1945 Vinson had formed his own band

ARNETT COBB AND HIS DAUGHTER, CAPITOL RADIO JAZZ FESTIVAL, LONDON, 1979. PHOTOGRAPH BY VAL WILMER.

EDDIE VINSON, HOUSTON, 1950s. PHOTOGRAPH BY BENNY JOSEPH.

EDDIE VINSON SHAVING HIS HEAD, BERLIN, 1974.
PHOTOGRAPH BY VAL WILMER.

EDDIE "CLEANHEAD" VINSON, "HIGH CLASS BABY," MERCURY 8090.

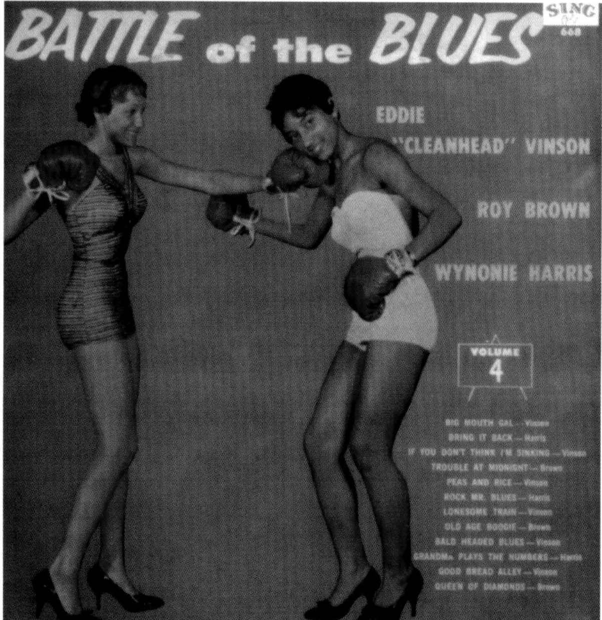

EDDIE "CLEANHEAD" VINSON, ROY BROWN, WYNONIE HARRIS, *BATTLE OF THE BLUES*, SING 668.
COURTESY TEXAS AFRICAN AMERICAN PHOTOGRAPHY ARCHIVE.

and signed with Mercury records. Between 1945 and 1947, Vinson produced some of his best work, including four instrumentals and twenty-six vocals, featuring remakes of "Cherry Red" and "Somebody," as well as new songs such as "Kidney Stew," "Cleanhead Blues," "Oil Man Blues," and "Lazy Gal Blues."

Vinson recorded on the King label from 1949 to 1952, then returned to Mercury in 1954. Since then his recordings have been sporadic, though he did front the Basie band in 1957 and worked with the Adderley brothers in 1961.

Over the years, Eddie Vinson built a solid reputation as an instrumentalist and singer with a wheezing vocal style. He has recorded both jazz and rhythm and blues, and has featured a wide array of musicians in his bands, including Tyree Glenn, Slide Hampton, Buddy Tate, John Coltrane, and Red Garland.

After his appearance with Johnny Otis at the Monterey Jazz Festival in 1970, Vinson was active on the festival circuit. He made numerous tours in Europe, working with foreign and American groups, and later recorded with Roomful of Blues.

Aside from his alto saxophone and vocal style, Eddie Vinson was known for his bald head, the origins of which he explained in a 1975 interview with Norbert Hess. "In those days, black boys used to try to keep their hair straight. So I put some of that stuff on my head one day, and it had so much lye in it, it ate my hair out. So by shaving it off rather than letting it grow back, I got a little attention. When I got bald, everybody wanted to feel it, play with it."

JEAN-BAPTISTE ILLINOIS JACQUET

October 31, 1922–July 22, 2004; interview, 2004

T-Bone Walker was a beautiful person. He was all of what the blues is all about, and he had an extension into jazz that no one that I can recall matched. I played with him, in his band in the early days. It was quite an experience with him.

I mean, it's two different highways—blues and jazz. Which one you want to take, you have a choice. It's like bullets. You have to have a jazz bullet and a blues bullet. It's according to which one you're going to use. You have to have them both.

T-Bone, I met in Los Angeles. And we worked at a little club in Watts, California, called The Brown Sisters. And it was one of the most exciting little clubs that you could have ever been involved with, with his group. And I can still hear things that we did together, and we called him Bone Walker. There was nothing like T-Bone. He was an individual that enjoyed what he did, and it was coming exactly from his spiritual soul.

The club was called The Brown Sisters. There were some ladies that were sisters. It was in Watts, California. And they finally built a big jazz club there, and then the big-name bands would go there to appear. But not at The Brown Sisters Club. The Brown Sisters Club was a little small club with about four or five pieces in there. T-Bone Walker was the leader, and I joined his band because we was all Texans and we loved each other, and there was a lot of creation going on that bandstand every night. You just couldn't believe what was happening.

When I was playing with T-Bone, we used to pack them in the club every night because he played jazz. It wasn't like Charlie Christian. But he played jazz, and he played what he felt. When he took a solo, it wasn't just like Blind Man Lemon or nothing like that, it was like you was here listening to an instrument, a saxophone. . . . He was different. He played guitar and it was almost like a conversation. Then he would sing. Like two people.

I was playing alto then. Now, I play any saxophone, anything got a reed on it. But I record with the alto and tenor and with the "Flying Home" solo, probably one of the greatest solos, if I have to say it, in the world. It created excitement that even Arnett Cobb, they all copied my solo. It just upset the world, all over Europe. It was a phenomenon, because they just couldn't believe that I was able to do that. But it was probably religious inclined, because this music is music that could be played anywhere, churches—it wouldn't make no difference where it was because you'd have to listen to it to realize that it was something that, just like eating a meal, and it clings to your body. It's a lot to talk about, this music. Jazz music is very biblical itself, you know. It's sort of like it never ends. You see, blues is sort of like the clink in the bottom of what you're walking on, but the blues have to be developed because the blues singers do the singing, and the instruments do the sound. And it's two different things.

Did you ever hear of a band called Alphonso Trent? They were one of the Territory bands. I was too young to play with him. I'm from Houston [born in Broussard, Louisiana], "Big H," they called it. Alphonso Trent went everywhere. Alphonso Trent was the Duke Ellington before Duke Ellington became Duke Ellington. He was the premier band there. And of course he had the musicians, probably the best musicians around, and he played at these big hotels where black people weren't allowed to even walk the sidewalk. I was born in 1922, so they were a little ahead of me in playing music. But we heard about them because it was quite a band, and the great record producer John Hammond spoke quite a bit about him, about Alphonso Trent, because he had a lot to do with Count Basie, you know. And so we learned a lot about that band, because it was a well-recognized band when I was growing up.

Buster Smith was one of the greats. One of the pioneers. I was too young to know him, too, but he certainly did leave a mark that will have a lot of depth in what we're talking about. And there was Buddy Tate from Sherman, Texas. And Herschel Evans. Herschel Evans was probably one of the most outstanding saxophone players ever. I would sort of like rate him with the late Coleman

Hawkins. And he came out of a band called Troy Floyd. And while I was in school, I did get a chance to hear that band. And they opened up a lot of doors. The youngsters' ears were right there on that band. And Texas had a lot of great musicians came out of that state.

I started with my brothers. I had three brothers, and we all were musicians. I was a tap dancer. Our father had a big band, and that's why we were interested in anything that came from Texas or any band. My father was Gilbert Jacquet, and he had a big band. I used to dance in the front of his band, as a tap dancer, so everything is in time, like everything you do, whether it's blues or—it's like cranking up a car. And what kind of motor you've got in there, in that car, under that hood. And it's the sound of the big band. And I came up dancing with my father's big band, so I knew about the rhythm. The rhythm was the whole thing. If you couldn't swing, it don't mean a thing. That's what Duke said; he so had it right.

I was a youngster three years old listening to this music, because you learn at an early age about this music because it makes you learn something besides robbing banks or anything like that because you have to have it in you. It's sort of like a gift from God. This music is very spiritual, and people don't know, really, how spiritual this music is and how gifted the musicians are and was in that day, because it will last forever, whatever they did. And that's why I've lasted as long as I've lasted, because this is born in you. You can't be taught that; that's just a gift.

I came up singing and dancing with my father's bands at three years old. And we used to play parties for people like Howard Hughes because my aunt took care of their homes. And they'd have those parties, and they'd have my father's band to come and play. I was three years old, and I would dance in the party. And I made quite a bit of money. I must have went to school with quite a bit of money in my pocket. But it comes from the ground floor, and it just develops, if it's cultivated. That's my career; it was cultivated from the ground floor, coming out of the family. Oh, everybody played, and that's what you did every day, just like you eat every day, that's what you eat, the music. And it becomes a natural thing, and it's still that way.

DON WILKERSON

July 31, 1932–July 18, 1986; interview, 1984

(L. TO R.) L. A. HILL, HENRY HAYES, V. WISER TURNER, HOUSTON, 1940S.

DON "LOW DOWN DIRTY" WILKERSON, LOS ANGELES, 1984.

As a kid I liked the blues. My mother was a piano player and I would hear her playing different tunes, and I'd hear different songs on the radio. My first knowledge of the blues was when "Uncle Sammy's Grab Bag" was on the radio in Houston. I'd listen to Basie, Jimmy Rushing, Joe Turner. They had all the blues artists on the program, and I would wait for that program every day. And as I grew older, I had the feeling for it and I started doing it professionally. The first time I ever performed was at the Eldorado Ballroom with Milt Larkin, one of the greatest bandleaders. I played alto, and then I worked different clubs around Houston, the Paradise Club for four years. Then a booking agent gave me forty-five one-nighters with Joe Turner.

Later T-Bone [Walker] came through and heard how we youngsters were doing, and we did thirty-one dates with T-Bone. I cried when he passed. I used to go by his convalescent home, not too far from here. Bone was a hell of an inspiration for all the musicians. I consider him the genius of the blues guitar. Charlie Christian was a good jazz guitarist, but he just didn't have the blues feeling that T-Bone had. Everything was mellow. He could stand there at the mike and it would flow out with perfect delivery.

After playing with T-Bone, my reputation continued to grow, and I've worked all over the country. I moved to California about 1960, but I still love Texas and I go back every year. And when I go back to Houston, I play with La La Wilson, Lester Williams, get in on whatever sessions come along. I play both jazz and blues. There isn't much difference for me. It's in the arrangements and the singing. If a musician cannot play blues, they can't play jazz. You have to have that feeling.

I wrote several blues, "My Baby Hiding from Me," "Low Down Dirty Shame, Parts 1 & 2," a shuffle blues with a backbeat. The blues is an expression of feeling. The meter is important, lyrics. It takes a lot of different things, you got eight-bar blues, twelve-bar blues, sixteen-bar blues, big band arrangements, ballads. When it comes down to it, blues is what matters most to me. Last week, I was playing behind Z. Z. Hill and he did "Down Home Blues," and it hit me so. I wasn't really supposed to take a solo on it, but I got up and I blew and that moved me. I thought this was the living end. Some kind of blues, it will make you do things you had no idea you could do on that horn.

HENRY HAYES

August 5, 1923– ; interview, 1987

My daddy bought me a clarinet when I was about fourteen years old, and I played in the Lincoln High School band in Dallas. I was brought up in Dallas. I'm sixty-four now, but I've lived in Houston for about forty years. In Dallas I studied private lessons under E. S. Jackson, who had big bands up around Chicago and New York and was at that time teaching in the school system. I studied the basics, and then I started to experiment with a little jazz, classical music. There used to be a fellow around named Shorty Clemons, and he used to help the younger musicians. Then there was Buster Smith, who had left for Kansas City, and he came home from New York when he was in his thirties. He was the man who taught Charlie Parker. I had a chance to listen to Buster after he came back to Dallas, and I ended up playing trumpet in his band. He was one of the greatest alto players that I ever heard, and he inspired me to take up saxophone.

I moved to Houston because I wanted to make it on my own. I landed with three dollars in my pocket, and I went over to see my friend Eddie Taylor, who had all the white clubs. I called him and asked him if he needed a sax player. He said, "No, but if you meet me on Main Street tonight and go out with me, I'll make it worth your while." And he liked my playing so well that he hired me. I started playing with him in the white clubs, and I was able to enroll in Texas Southern to finish my degree in music. So, I became a music teacher, thirty-two years in Dickinson, Texas, between here and Galveston.

I was a music instructor and played white clubs six nights a week, and played the matinee at the Tropicana, a black club, on Sunday. I met Albert Collins through Joe Hughes. He said, "Man, you got to hear Albert." So I made it over to see him, and he was great.

I had a friend that had a small record label [Kangaroo], and Joe brought him out. I said, "Albert, you got to cut that number 'The Freeze.'" And the first or second time we tried, that was it. Albert got his guitar, and I picked up a tenor, and together the band played what we felt.

In no time, everybody around the country started to imitate Albert. They even came out with a dance on Dick Clark [American Bandstand] called the Freeze. To me, "The Freeze" was a blues, but it was structured differently, with a kind of African beat.

My style of saxophone added something to it. If you listen to my playing, it's different, comes from gospel, a lot of feeling. There's the right amount of repetition, so that people can feel what they're hearing. It's simplified, not too complicated.

Honking is what I call gut playing, getting on one note and squealing. It's a gimmick, growls, riding. It was popular for a while, but I could put something more into my playing. The saxophone was the most popular solo instrument before the war [World War II], but then the guitar took over.

I used to record with a lot of the blues musicians around Houston, Joe Hughes. We tried Joe's "Ants in My Pants," "We Can't Go On This Way." And I wrote some of my own numbers, "All Alone Blues" and "Hayes' Boogie," which I recorded for the Mesner brothers on Aladdin in the early 1950s. They were looking for that Three Blazers sound.

I started Elmore Nixon off when I wrote "Alabama Blues." We went out to Don Robey and put it on his label. After the number came out, it became a southern hit. But Robey didn't want to use me too often because I knew too much about the business. He wanted these younger players, more inexperienced. So I only did one session with Robey.

I told Elmore, "Go ahead on and try without me," but he didn't make it, because he needed me to help him with the styling of his voice, his ideas. They put Roy Milton behind him, and nothing happened. So, I got Elmore off Peacock and I wrote to New York, and they sent someone to Houston and put us on Savoy records.

Elmore was a piano player and singer, started when he was sixteen years old, hanging around with me. We

traveled around after "Alabama Blues." We followed Lester Williams, who had a hit with "Wintertime Blues." We went to all the little towns in Louisiana and Texas. But then he decided he didn't need me, and that's when I started teaching school.

I always had to depend on someone else singing, but they seemed to always let me down. I'm doing a little singing now. Since retiring, I'm finally getting a chance to do what I always wanted to do, writing, trying to get an album out. I've written probably a hundred and fifty to two hundred numbers, but I've lost more than I can remember.

HELEN P. COLE, PRAIRIE VIEW A&M COLLEGE COEDS, 1940s. COURTESY TEXAS AFRICAN AMERICAN PHOTOGRAPHY ARCHIVE

DEWEY REDMAN

May 17, 1931–December 2, 2006; interview, 2004

I grew up in Fort Worth. The south side. I grew up in a segregated society, so, you know, it was—but we had a good community. . . . You didn't rebel; you just accepted things the way they were.

I was always interested in music. And at the age of about thirteen, I decided that I wanted to play an instrument. And the instrument I wanted to play was the trumpet because it only had three keys [values]. And I was discouraged from playing the trumpet and told that I must play the clarinet because my teacher was also the band director for a church band. And so he convinced me to start playing the clarinet, which was a good thing because from there, I went to the saxophone, when I was in college. And as it turned out, it was a good thing.

My father was named George Dewey Redman, and my mother's name was Odessa Wilson. My father worked on the railroad a lot, and then they split up when I was about eight or nine, and he went to California, where he proceeded to work on the railroad, you know, as a porter. And my mother continued working as a domestic.

My uncle had a record player. I used to stay with my mother, my aunt, and my uncle. And they had a record player, and they had music by Duke Ellington—that's a long time ago—and some other records, you know. But I remember Duke Ellington.

Well, when I was very young, there used to be a juke joint diagonally across the street from where I was living when I was born in Fort Worth. And I used to sit on my lawn and listen to, you know—they used to play the jukebox, you know, the nickel jukeboxes? I don't remember exactly because it's been so long ago, but I loved the music. And it was mostly just rhythm and blues, black music. And then, coming up, I listened to what everybody else listened to, which was like Amos Milburn, Ivory Joe Hunter, Jimmy Liggins, and Joe Liggins. In Fort Worth they had a place called the Rainbow Terrace. And it was a dance place, you know, and there were no concerts. And it was Buddy Johnson's big band, and Louis Jordan was big time, and there was also the alto player that Coltrane played with. Coltrane played in his band. But he was a very good saxophone player. I used to go to this Rainbow Terrace. I used to sneak in because I wasn't old enough, you know, to listen to all these people. My earliest memories of listening to live music.

When I was young, I used to slip into these places and listen to bands like the Buddy Johnson big band with his sister singing, Ella Johnson, Louis Jordan. Oh, yeah, T-Bone. Yeah, yeah, T-Bone, yeah. There's so many; it's been a long time, so I can't remember. Dallas [when I was growing up] was verboten. You didn't go to Dallas, I mean, why go to Dallas? I mean, you know, because actually, we had a great community in Fort Worth.

At that time, all the black kids had to go I. M. Terrell High School. And so Ornette [Coleman], even though he lived on a different side of town, we all went to the same high school, I. M. Terrell High School. I played in the marching concert band, but I wasn't really into jazz, you know, per se, until I went to college. But Ornette was already playing, you know, in the jazz sense.

A person who was very important to me is a relative of mine. I know he was my uncle because his name is Don Redman. And he was a famous composer and bandleader back in the Twenties and Thirties. He took over McKinney's Cotton Pickers. And I had seen the name, you know, Redman is an unusually spelled name. But when I saw a picture of him, he looked just like my father. And my father was short in stature. He was short in stature. And they were from the same place, in West Virginia, Piedmont. And so I just assumed when I saw a picture of him, I knew he was my relative, although I never got a chance to meet him. He passed in 1965, and I came to New York in 1967. But I know that he was a relative of mine.

I was a late bloomer. I just played in the church band. My first gig was in the church band. And then things progressed, and I went to college. I went to Prairie View A&M. And I was still playing clarinet at the time. And my first year at Prairie View, there was a trio with me and James Tatum, who was a piano player, who still lives in Detroit, and a couple of other people, a bass player and a singer. And then the second year, I joined The Prairie View Collegians. And I'm playing alto. And then the third year, the tenor player graduated, and they said, "Well, if you want to play in the Collegians again, you have to start playing tenor." And I said, "I don't want to play tenor." And they said, "Well, you have to play tenor if you want to stay in the band." And so that was the beginning of my tenor-playing career.

Well, I didn't go to the Jim Hotel until I was in college. And by then, it was on the way out, you know. It still was alive, but it wasn't as popular as it was, say, in the Forties, early Forties. It was one of *the* places to go in Fort Worth. And so, when I was in college, I remember one time there were a bunch of friends from college. We came to Fort Worth, and we went to the Jim Hotel, and of course it was still okay, but as a matter of fact, my mother didn't want me to go to places like that, so if I did go, I had to sneak in, you know, so I didn't go very much. I went to the Jim Hotel. It was, you know, a weekend joint, and it was lively.

But I remember when I used to go to the Rainbow Terrace, these guys like Big Jay McNeely, whoever, would have to go. You know, they would come from Dallas to Fort Worth, of course. But then the next gig might be in Lubbock or Odessa. Or if they were going east, the next gig after Dallas might be Longview or Tyler. Or if they were going south, the next gig might be in Houston or Austin. So they would crowd in this car and go to the next gig after the gig in Fort Worth because a lot of times, it would be a long way away. And on the Chitlin' Circuit, you know, one-nighters, it was very difficult. I could see that, you know, it was difficult. And I never really wanted to be a musician because I saw how they lived and, you know, it just wasn't a thing for me. I never entertained the thought of being a musician. Okay, and fifty years later, here I am in New York. You know what I'm saying? But I never liked what I saw, you know.

After college, I was drafted into the army, and I went to El Paso, and there I stayed for two years. And I met a wonderful trumpet player named Jerry Hunter, and I started playing in his band, you know, in El Paso, for almost the whole two years I was there. And he taught me a lot about music. And then when I came out of the army, I had already graduated from college, and I started teaching school. My first gig was in Plainview, Texas, in West Texas. And then, the next three years, I taught school in Bastrop, which is about thirty miles south of Austin. I was a fifth-grade homeroom teacher in Bastrop, and in the afternoon I had band, music classes. And on the weekends I would go to Austin and play in different bands, mostly rhythm-and-blues bands. And then I received a lot of compliments, and I was encouraged to go to New York. And then, in 1960, I went to California, on the way to New York, and stayed in Los Angeles because I wanted to find my father, who I hadn't seen in a long time. And on the way to New York, I was encouraged to go to San Francisco. I went to San Francisco for two weeks and stayed almost seven years.

I got a chance to play with T-Bone Walker in San Francisco. When I lived in San Francisco, there was a place called Bop City. It opened up at two o'clock in the morning until six, and you could go there. They always had a rhythm section, so when I was there in the Sixties, I used to go down there and play. And in the latter part, before I left to come to New York, they opened up another joint called Soulville. And they asked me would I like to have the band, same hours, two to six, and I said yes. And so I had the band, and a lot of people would just come in and sit in. Phineas Newborn. Redd Foxx used to come in and leave everybody with a stomachache. And I was in charge of the band. But at six o'clock in the morning, around the corner on Fillmore Street, was a place called the Blue Mirror. They'd open up at six o'clock in the morning. And the guy who was in charge of the band was T-Bone Walker. And I used to leave my gig and go around the corner. And one time I sat in, but usually, you know, I'd just sit there and listen to him, you know, and he played all his hits, you know, "Stormy Monday," and sometimes he would be sort of inebriated, you know. But he was still T-Bone, you know, the greatest.

Another guy I met in San Francisco was Roger Boykin [from Dallas]. He really helped me out when I was down. And we became good friends, and we played gigs together. And we've remained friends since the Sixties, although I don't see him much. From time to time, we speak on the phone.

When I was in El Paso, I played mainly with Jerry Hunter. It wasn't really a rhythm-and-blues band because we had a Mexican rhythm section. And then, when I would come back to Fort Worth, I would play in different bands, but they weren't exactly rhythm-and-blues bands. It was a little bit of jazz.

I've been told there's a Texas tenor sound. And there are a lot of great tenor players that came out of Texas, too numerous to name. But I've been told that I was the father of that, and so, you know, what can I say? I'm proud to be thought of as a Texas tenor player, of that genre.

Look at the great tenor players who have come out of Texas—Arnett Cobb. Illinois Jacquet, who I'm in touch with in New York. James Clay. Dave Newman. Red Connor was one of the best saxophone players I ever heard in my life. He was a Fort Worth guy. But he was a great player. And I didn't realize how great he was until I listened to John Coltrane and Dexter Gordon, etc. Red Connor was a great player. I heard him play many times, and he had charisma. I mean, he would be playing bebop and people were coming off the streets and listening to him. He was a Fort Worthian.

Red went to Los Angeles, I think, with one of the Ligginses. There was a Joe Liggins and Jimmy Liggins orchestra. And I think he recorded with them. But it was a blues band, you know. But I don't think he ever recorded jazz. But he was a great player.

I couldn't get rid of that Texas tenor sound if I wanted to. It's hard to define. I mean, it's there, whatever it is. We're putting together a booklet or a book on Fort Worth jazz musicians. It's in the ground floor stage, but we're going to do it. It's been an idea of mine for a long time because we had so many great known and unknown musicians who came from Fort Worth, and they've slowly gone, you know. For example, there was J. W. Carter, John Carter; there was Aurelius Simpio; he was a bass player. And he also was a writer. He was an author. He had a play on Broadway. He came to New York. He was a great bass player.

There was Julius Simpio. You ever heard of him? He rearranged and played in the World Saxophone Quartet for a long time. There was Charles Moffett, "Diddy" Moffett, who played with Ornette in the beginning. There's me, there's Ornette, there's Prince Lasha, I think he's in Oakland. There's Shannon Jackson, who's still in Fort Worth. Who else? I'm leaving out somebody. Thomas Reese, who is still in Fort Worth. Of course, Red Connor. James Jordan, who is at the New York State Council for the Arts, is from Fort Worth. He's a good friend of Ornette, and he's helping to get this book together. He's one of the few left, you know. And so, actually, we're trying to get money to fund this project, and like I said, it's on the ground floor now. And the last time I was in Fort Worth, we had a meeting, and we decided to get this thing off the ground for real. But there hasn't been much done. It seems that it's fallen into my hands, and I need to work on it more, but it's going to get done.

I've always been an individual. I've always approached the saxophone as me, as Dewey. I never tried to imitate John Coltrane or whoever. But it's always been the way I wanted to play. But I have to say that in my playing, I learned a long time ago that what I really wanted to do was have a good sound. And I have many guys that I admire for that, including Gene Ammons, Dexter Gordon, Big Jay McNeely, who was a rhythm-and-blues guy who used to come to Fort Worth, really a great saxophone player. What's his name, "Shotgun," the saxophone player? Junior Walker. Okay, he recorded a tune called "Shotgun." And Red Connor, and through the years I've always admired players who had what I thought was a good sound, so I've always concentrated on sound. That's my first objective, to get a good sound. And technique, you know, maybe. But there's technique in sound.

Well, in the first place, the music [of rhythm and blues and jazz] is different. There's no more rhythm and blues, per se, as we knew it when I was growing up. There's a different thing on the scene, hip-hop, and you rarely ever see a saxophone or any other instrument. And so the music has undergone a great transformation. As far as jazz is concerned, it has undergone a transformation, too, not as severe as popular music. And one of the geniuses of all of this is Ornette Coleman, who introduced whatever you want to call it, avant-garde, free playing, in New York, in 1959. And it was revolutionary/evolutionary.

Ornette Coleman is a genius. He's explained harmolodics to me, and he told me that I had it, but obviously, I guess, it's a combination of harmony and melody, you know, somewhere in there. If you ask Ornette—I think you'd have to ask him. If you listen to early Ornette recordings, you can hear the blues in his music.

Ornette has a recording studio in New York. I did a music video there. In 2002 I got a Guggenheim [fellowship] for music composition. And instead of just writing some music and turning it in, I decided to do a music video. I got some of my close friends and associates, and I did this video. It cost me a little more money than what they gave me, what the grant was, but I finally got it finished. And I did it at Harmolodic Studio, Ornette's studio, in Manhattan. And so, maybe one day when I come home, I'll bring it with me, and you can, you know, dig it.

These days I'm playing my compositions, mostly. I don't play in one style all night because it bores me. So I play a little bit of this, a little bit of avant-garde, a little bit of bebop, ballads, a little bit of blues. I have to play the blues because I'm from Texas, you know. And so, that's about it. I march to my own drummer.

I just completed a tour of Europe last month. I travel with a quartet. I use the same sidemen: John Menegon on bass, Mack Wilson on drums, and in Europe I use Rita Marcotulli on piano. It's a great band. We went to Italia, went to Rome. We went to France, the south of France. And we went to Austria. We went to Norway, and we went to Switzerland. And we went to Spain. As a matter of fact, this bombing in Madrid was on a Saturday, and we had a gig at a club in Madrid the following Monday, Tuesday, and Wednesday, which was a little bit strange, but we made it.

I see myself as a country boy from Texas trying to make it in the big city. I've been extremely lucky, you know, because like I told you before, I never intended to come to New York to stay, just to get it out of my system and then go back to Texas and teach school. I've been incredibly lucky, and maybe I've been at the right place at the right time because when I came to New York, I was like thirty-five years old, around thirty-five or thirty-six, something like that. And then, within a year of coming to New York—I came to New York in '67—within a year, I was playing with Ornette Coleman. How lucky can you get? He'd come out of his hiatuses. He and some other musicians used to sort of go into hiatuses, like Sonny Rollins. So I guess it was the right place at the right time. So, I've been here a long time, and I've had a chance to play with some of the best. And I know I have talent, but I never thought that I'd have survived this long in New York and gotten a chance to play with some of the best musicians in the world.

GRADY GAINES

May 14, 1934– ; interview, 1987

I was about twelve years old and I was a paperboy when we first moved to Houston from a little town called Waskom, Texas. Louis Jordan was real hot then, and I'd listen to him playing the saxophone, and that's who inspired me to get a saxophone. I got a paper route and started throwing papers for the *Houston Chronicle,* and I saved up enough money to buy me a saxophone. And I took lessons from a lady named Miss Punch, who lived a couple of blocks from us. Another guy who taught me a lot was R. P. Wallace. He lived third door from me on the same street in Fifth Ward.

From there I played the saxophone at E. L. Smith Junior High School, and there I met Calvin Owens. He was the student teacher. He would take over when the band director wasn't there. Calvin Owens taught me how to hold a saxophone mouthpiece, and he stayed with me for hours at a time until I got it together.

In senior high school the band director was Sammy Harris, and he taught me for a few years. During that period I had met Little Richard. He came to town with a group called The Tempo Toppers, and I played with that group for a while. That's how I first met Little Richard. We were working at the Club Matinee.

Little Richard did some recording for Don Robey at the Peacock Recording Company, where Joe Scott was the arranger, got everything together. From there, Little Richard decided to quit The Tempo Toppers, and he met Bumps Blackwell—that was his manager. They recorded "Tutti Frutti" in New Orleans, but Bumps lived in Los Angeles. They released "Tutti Frutti," and it was a real big hit for me. After that "Long Tall Sally," "Lucille." So Little Richard called me and asked me if I wanted to come on the road with him and lead his band for him. I told him I would, and I took another saxophone player with me; his name was Clifford Wirtz. Well, Clifford and I went to meet Little Richard in Washington, D.C., and from that night on we were gone. We did never look back from then on. We stayed with Little Richard up until the time he quit. We were with Little Richard from the last of '56, '57, '58.

GRADY GAINES
Steals the Show
from
LITTLE RICHARD
in the 1955 movie
"DON'T KNOCK THE ROCK"

GRADY GAINES AND LITTLE RICHARD, PUBLICITY PHOTOGRAPH FOR "DON'T KNOCK THE ROCK," 1955. COURTESY GRADY GAINES.

When he quit the business, we were on the Australia tour, and we stayed over there for about a month. We were on our way one day, we were on a bus on a ferry, and Little Richard said, "I'm quittin.' God's calling me and told me throw away all my jewelry." So he started pulling his rings off and getting ready to throw them overboard. So the other saxophone player grabbed him, and I jumped up to grab him. We tussled with him to

GRADY GAINES, HOUSTON, 1980s.

stop him, but he overpowered us and threw those rings, four or five diamond rings, in the ocean.

When we got back to America, Charles Sullivan, a promoter in San Francisco, had a lot of dates set up for Little Richard to play in Los Angeles and all up the coast, San Francisco, Portland, and even into Vancouver, B.C. But Little Richard quit, and we had to play those dates. That's when we named the band The Upsetters, and we had to play those dates on our own. We sent to Chicago and got Dee Clarke, who made "Raindrops" and several other hits, "Hey, Little Girl," and we got him and he took Little Richard's place. He had his own voice, but he could sound just like Little Richard.

We made those dates and the tour went over real well because the band was so powerful. We only had six pieces, no piano—guitar, bass, drums, and three saxophones, and the vocalist. We were good showmen.

After we got off of that tour, Charles Sullivan had some dates booked on Little Willie John, and Little Willie John didn't have a band. So we picked up Little Willie John and played the dates he had set up in the California area. Dee Clarke was still the vocalist for the band. We toured with Little Willie John and he wanted the band to play with him permanently, and we accepted it. We worked with Little Willie John for maybe four years through all his greatest hits, "Fever," "Talk to Me," "Leave My Kitten Alone," "Heartbreaks," "Let Them Talk If They Want To," "Unforgettable," a lot of them, some with the band, some with a studio band.

While we were working with Little Willie John, Sam Cooke got hot. He had been trying for a long time. He had three songs in the Top Ten, and Henry Wayne, the promoter from Atlanta, Georgia, contacted us, and we toured all through Georgia, Florida, the Carolinas. We even played dates in New York and New Jersey. He set up a little tour with Little Willie John and Sam Cooke. We played that tour, about twenty-five days, and after that, Sam Cooke talked with us, and he wanted us to come with him. We had a talk with Little Willie John and Sam together. We were all good friends.

We went with Sam and worked with him until the time of his death in '63 or '64. [Sam Cooke died December 11, 1964.] Then we took Sam's brother, L. C. Cooke, and toured the country for maybe a couple of years with him. After that things starts dying down. I came back home and formed me a band. I did real well recording a song, "Something on Your Mind," on John

Green's label. Then we released "Let Your Thing Hang Down" and "Midnight Sensation," and I kept that tape for about eight or ten years and then I released it myself on the Leo label about a year ago. It did real well and caused me to get a contract with the Black Top label for a new album. I use my brother, Roy Gaines, on guitar and vocals, Clarence Holliman on guitar, Teddy Reynolds on piano and vocals, Walter Joseph on the drums. My bass player is Michael Doggan; I use him on some of these things. I also had a bass player from New Orleans, Roy Lambert. He used to lead the band for Guitar Slim.

My brother Roy and I hadn't really played much together since we were little. He went out on the road with Roy Milton in 1956, I believe, and he's never lived in Houston since. He comes back, but he never stays for more than a few months. After Roy Milton, he went to New York and he stayed in New York, and that's where he ran into Chuck Willis. He helped Chuck put his band together.

Roy was more influenced by T-Bone Walker than anybody else. He liked Barney Kessel, but T-Bone was his main resource. T-Bone was great. I played his last Houston dates. He called me and asked me to put his band together. He was coming to La Bastille for a week down in Market Square. We played that date, and he went back to Los Angeles and died about a month later. T-Bone was an inspiration to everybody, whether they played guitar or whatever instrument.

Through experience my music has changed a little bit, but not too much. I quit playing for about five years in the Seventies because the only way I could make a decent living was to travel, but I didn't want to travel no more. So I stopped playing and got me a job working for United Airlines and also for Holiday Inn. I did real well with the jobs, but my friends, Elroy King, a blues singer around town, Milton Hopkins, a guitarist, and V. Wiser Turner, another saxophone player, they kept after me to start playing again. I had gotten to the point where I didn't play no more. They said I had too much going on my horn to give it up.

So I started with Milton Hopkins's group out to Etta's Lounge, Milton Hopkins and Julius Miller and The Blues Untouchables Band, and I played with them for about a year. That brought me into where I am right now with my band, Grady Gaines and The Real Thing. In this group I got Teddy Reynolds at the piano, Floyd Arseneux on trumpet, Michael Doggan on bass. I've got

GRADY GAINES, HOUSTON, 1980s.

GRADY GAINES, HOUSTON, 1980s.

two vocalists. One is Big Robert Smith, a real good blues rockin' singer. He tears the house up everywhere we go. He shouts, but he gets down and sings the blues, too. Our other singer is Joe Medwick, who wrote most of the Peacock hits for Bobby Blue Bland. He wrote "I'll Take Care of You," "That's What Love Is," I can't remember all of them. But he wrote a tune for me called "I Been Out There," and it tells about all the artists that I worked with. It's a rappin' thing, but it's hot.

At one time, a lot of people said I sounded like King Curtis, but King Curtis sort of got a lot of his style from me. He was from Fort Worth. When I played with Little Richard, when we did "Keep On Knockin,'" I did a lot of that chopping up of notes. He worked a show with me over at the Paramount Theater in Brooklyn with a big band. So he hung with me after the show, and before I knew anything, that yakkety-yak saxophone was out. He was doing it. I was working with Little Richard, and he stayed there in New York. So he made it with it.

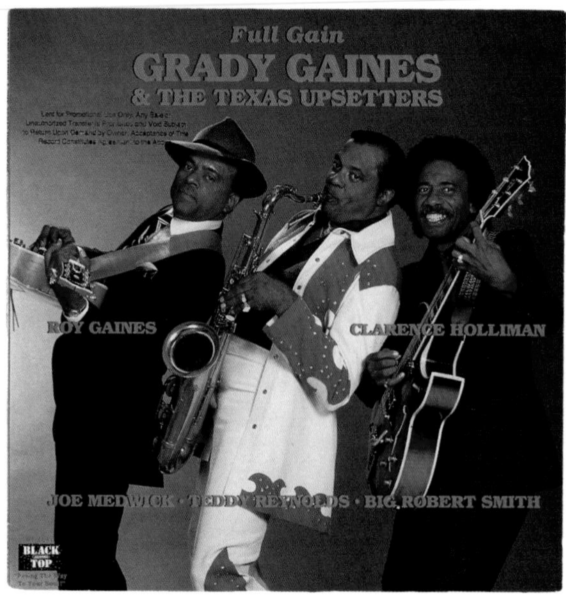

I love the blues, but I can play hot rock 'n' roll. I don't call my saxophone playing a real honking type. Some people might consider it that, but I don't try to play like nobody. I only play my own self.

I always keep a guitar close to me. The saxophone determines all the drive and rhythm with the guitar. Teddy [Reynolds] puts a lot of fire to it on piano. The saxophone in jazz is more like a singer, more out in front. In blues I can stand out in front with a guitar player, singer, or anybody else. I try to prove that to myself and to the audience. That's why I let both of my singers sing and do the best they can possibly do. Then I come up after them and see what kind of reaction I get from the people. I can do what a singer does by playing my horn.

Sometimes I even go out in the audience. We call that walking the floor, pleasing the people; where I play at now, they call it the Grand Finale. That means I have to walk that floor. If I don't do it, they're not satisfied. I seen Big Jay McNeely. He inspired both me and Albert Collins. We worked a show together. There were about ten acts together when I first saw Jay McNeely, and he inspired me to do a lot of walking. I had done it before, but I didn't do it as well until after I saw Jay.

Musically, I was influenced by Louis Jordan, Gene Ammons, Earl Bostic (I liked his highs). I don't sound like Gene Ammons, but I think about him when I'm playing, when I do my builds. A lot of my notes and feeling come from Louis Jordan. He was an alto player; I played alto too, but mainly tenor. Louis Jordan was my biggest influence—"Let the Good Times Roll."

I don't write out my music. I just play from feelings. I think I can get more out of it that way. In fact, I know I can.

GRADY GAINES & THE TEXAS UPSETTERS, *FULL GAIN*, BLACK TOP 1041.

MARK "KAZ" KAZANOFF

October 14, 1949–

TEXAS HORNS (L. TO R.) GARY SLECHTA, MARK "KAZ" KAZANOFF, JOHN MILLS. PHOTOGRAPH BY BOB DAEMMRICH.

I was born in Northampton, Massachusetts. My dad was an actor and director in the theater and ultimately a teacher as well. His name is Theodore Kazanoff. He's taught at several major universities around the country, and we moved around a lot when I was a kid because of that, so I lived in California twice, and I lived in Vermont, and I lived in Massachusetts, lived in New York City, lived on Long Island, lived near Pittsburgh for a while. So we moved around quite a bit when we were younger.

My father is Jewish and was actually bar-mitzvahed, but I never was really raised in any particular religion, and my mother was not particularly religious either. They both are fairly left-leaning in their politics, liberal Democrat or beyond.

Both of my parents are definitely blues and jazz fans. My mother's nickname is Lee. Oddly enough, when I was about eight or nine years old, she was attending Bennington College, and she started working part time for this guy named Stanley Edgar Hyman, who was a very well-known poet and teacher at Bennington College. And he also was one of the foremost collectors of jazz and blues records at the time. And she somehow got the job of collating all his records and tapes. So she brought home an endless supply of early blues and jazz, and started playing it in the house, and of course I listened to it. So that was really my education.

I took guitar lessons, believe it or not, I have to confess, when I was six and seven, and then I quit. I just decided I didn't want to play the guitar. So I didn't really take any more lessons for quite a while. I started playing the harmonica when I was eleven or twelve and pretty much taught myself how to do that. My mother happened to have the *Best of Little Walter* album lying around the house, so that proved to be fodder for me for a good three or four years of studying on the harmonica. And then I started playing with friends of mine and really just picked up stuff as I went along. I didn't really study music until I got to college. And even then, I was never much of a reader of music until I was in my mid-thirties and already playing saxophone for ten or twelve years.

The saxophone was very much an offshoot of my harmonica playing, originally. I played harmonica for a long time and wanted to play something that I could get all the chromatic notes on. And saxophone seemed to be a likely choice because it was also a reed instrument. So I kind of just haphazardly bought one and started playing it, and then about two weeks later, all of a sudden I was onstage playing it, so it became part of my musical personality pretty quickly.

I got my first horn when I was about twenty-two or twenty-three, but I didn't really seriously start playing it until I was about—I guess I was twenty-four, twenty-five, before I really began practicing it and playing in earnest.

I went to University of Chicago. I actually ended up studying music, both at the University of Chicago and in the city of Chicago. So I spent a lot of time in the clubs and bars listening to all kinds of blues stuff there. There were plenty of places to go, and lots and lots of friendly places to go, and at least three or four nights a week I was out in the bars, listening to music and eventually playing a little bit, too. So it was wonderful experience.

There were a lot of R&B guys. Of course, King Curtis was a big influence. But I was more influenced by the sort of jump R&B guys like the guys that were playing with Wynonie Harris, Allen Eager and Tom Archia and Hal Singer and that genre of players.

And of course a lot of the jazz guys were a big influence on me, too, especially Lester Young. To this day, I just absolutely love Lester Young. I can put him on and be in heaven for hours at any time. But I listened to everything from Count Basie-style to more modern jazz. My interests were pretty widespread, although the R&B influences were fairly typical . . . Louis Jordan, late Forties, early Fifties type sound.

When I really started playing the saxophone, I was in a band in Boston, and this was about 1973. It was a band called The Rhythm Rockers that was put together by me, Johnny Nicholas, David Maxwell, Frannie Christina, and Johnny Acerno, who was a bass player who's now living out in California. And that was pretty much my home band for three or four years at least after I had moved back to Boston from University of Chicago. I graduated in '73 from the University of Chicago. I started in '67, actually, so I was there for five years.

So we were playing a lot of blues, and I was listening to everything from Jimmy Forest to the more honkin' blues guys. I don't think I ever lost my love for that stuff. As time wore on, I started listening to more jazz, and I started playing more jazz. But I still really liked the R&B guys and focused a lot on their playing, and I've always liked the jazz guys that came out of the R&B world more. So, personally, that was kind of where my love was. But I really like listening to John Coltrane, too, for example. And Parker, of course, and so my interests were pretty widespread, I would say.

Johnny Nicholas himself turned me on to a lot of stuff. He's a guitar player and singer and harmonica player also. And he now lives in Texas. He moved here a year before I did, to the Austin area. In about '78, Johnny and I and several other, new members of The Rhythm

JOHNNY RENO (FORMERLY WITH THE JUKE JUMPERS), 1983. PHOTOGRAPH BY TRACY ANNE HART/THE HEIGHTS GALLERY.

Rockers came to Texas, and we spent about four months here in Austin, living on people's couches and sleeping on floors and kind of just playing around wherever we could get a gig. And then I went back to Boston and just kind of free-lanced up there for a while, and then I ended up playing with Sugar Ray and The Bluetones for a couple of years. Then I moved to Texas in '82. And when I moved here, I actually had already secured a gig with Marcia Ball through Frannie Christina, who at that time had moved to Texas as well, and he was playing with The Thunderbirds. And we kept in touch, and one day he said, "You know, Marcia Ball's looking for a sax player." And I said, "Hey, I'm moving to Texas." So, off I went.

Well, I had the preconception that every other guitar player in Texas was going to be playing T-Bone Walker and the kind of jump swing blues style that I loved so much. I thought it was going to be more prevalent in Texas than it was in Boston, and I actually found somewhat the opposite, that most of the guitar players in Texas were playing much more aggressive, loud blues. And so at first it was odd for me because I felt like I didn't fit in as well as maybe I thought I was going to. I think I had a mistaken idea about what Texas music was like, in a way, at that time, in the early Eighties in Austin.

At first, I think, it was kind of a shock for me. But on the other hand, I found a lot of amazing and great players to play with down here, including Marcia and her band and Denny Freeman and Angela Strehli and W. C. Clark. I mean, there were a lot of people down here who welcomed me with open arms but also were just great players and gave me a lot of opportunity to play.

After I left Marcia's band, in '84 or '85, I pretty much played at Antone's for months and months and months and years after that. And so, while it wasn't what I expected, what I found here was actually really wonderful. The music scene was great. The other thing was music in Boston was very compartmentalized. I mean, you had your jazz guys and you had your blues guys and you had your rock guys, and the social musical groups never intersected, hardly at all. And I found exactly the opposite to be true in Texas. I mean, there were jazz guys who were playing with blues guys, and there were *conjunto* Mexican guys who were playing with jazz guys. And it was much more of a loose, wide-open, fluid scene here, musically, and I really liked that. That felt very comfortable and real to me in a way that the Boston music scene didn't feel at all.

There were many of those [Duke/Peacock and big band] players still around in Houston. There was Henry Hayes, Grady Gaines, Calvin Owens. There was a whole bunch of people who were still around—but they had shifted. Their music had changed. The full horn sections, which were the hallmark of the Duke/Peacock sound, were just hard to put together because people weren't accustomed to playing them. A lot of the horn players had moved to California. Eddie Vinson was in California. Arnett Cobb was at the very end of his career. Milt Larkin still had a band, but it wasn't quite the orchestra that he had once had. Don Wilkerson was still around, but was playing with more jazz-oriented groups.

During the Eighties I started doing a lot more recording, both here in Austin for Clifford's Antone's Records and also in New Orleans for Blacktop Records. A lot of the Houston people ended up recording for Blacktop, so all of a sudden I was making a record a month or so, between Antone's and Blacktop. And that started in the early, mid-Eighties and just continued all the way through '92 or '93, when Blacktop finally folded up. But then, in the mid-Nineties, I had two kids. I'd already had one in the late Eighties. And so the focus of my life changed somewhat, and I wasn't sort of affiliated with any particular band or anything. I was kind of free-lancing and recording and producing. I started also producing more in the mid-Nineties, and that's kind of become another part of my musical personality, I guess, if you want to call it that, nowadays. Also, I started The Texas Horns and began doing some tours and some recording with that group.

I guess officially I put together The Texas Horns five or six years ago, but unofficially, the trumpet player and I had started doing gigs and sessions together earlier than that. I didn't actually start calling it The Texas Horns until maybe '98 or '99.

I started teaching privately way back in the Eighties, just individual students. And then I got invited to teach out here at a large private Episcopal school outside of Austin, St. Stephen's. It's a high school. So I started out here part time in 1992 and then full time in 1999. I teach music and music theory, and I run the jazz bands and have a couple of other duties out here.

I still play a lot of music and record and produce . . . I still love that early R&B sound. Well, if you look at the mid-Forties stuff, the saxophone, even in the smaller groups, was still the primary voice, you know, other than the vocal voice. And it wasn't really until you got into the Fifties that the guitar started to replace the saxophone as the primary voice in the instrumental ensemble. I think, honestly, it was a lot just a matter of volume. I mean, I think that guitar players came along with amplifiers and could play bigger halls and reach more people and be louder, and that was a lot of the reason why they took over.

The saxophone in T-Bone's actual bands was much more of an ensemble instrument, at least in the recordings that we have. Now, I never heard T-Bone live. Well, actually, I did hear T-Bone live, but it was much later in his career. So the saxophones were generally in an ensemble of two or three or four or I guess sometimes five horns, and occasional solos. And so, in that sense, they were somewhat subordinate to the guitar sound that T-Bone was getting.

DOWNBEAT MUSIC, DALLAS, 1984. PHOTOGRAPH BY ALAN GOVENAR.

When I first heard T-Bone, I didn't really know whether to think of him as a blues guy or a jazz guy. And I loved that. I mean, that was the kind of people that I liked listening to, was the people that seemed like they were kind of bridging both worlds, or they were part of both worlds. They were playing in both worlds, you know. Fathead Newman certainly was another example, to me, of somebody that could play jazz, but everything he played sounded really bluesy to me. And T-Bone was the same way.

Fathead was someone who was mentored by Buster Smith. I had the good fortune to meet up with Buster in Dallas. It was wonderful to meet him. I'd heard some of his early recordings from the Forties. And I looked at him and I said, "Are you the same Buster Smith?" It was kind of a shock to me, and then I realized, it had to be the same guy.

You look at a lot of the players who have become, in the contemporary world, more established in the jazz scene, like Fathead Newman, but clearly when they were playing in the Ray Charles band, it was that R&B sound. It's one of those chicken-or-the-egg things. I mean, were they playing R&B because they loved it, or were they playing R&B because they were playing in an R&B band? I don't know. They certainly were so good at what they did that in a way, it didn't matter. The solos that Fathead took with Ray Charles's band were some of the greatest solos ever played, as far as I'm concerned.

I don't think the Texas sound is quite as distinctive as some people think. If [for example] you compare Herschel Evans and Arnett Cobb and King Curtis, that's three pretty different sounds right there. And yet, everybody says there's three Texas tenors. I don't know. For my money, there's maybe less in common than a lot of people think between those sounds. It was more a regional sound, and I think the regional centers shifted as the years went by. It depends on what genre, too. If you're talking about western swing, it's a different thing. But certainly Kansas City was a center. Dallas was a center. Houston was a center. New Orleans was a center. You had peripheral stuff going on in a lot of different areas, but I think those were the four main areas. But even in a place like San Antonio, look at The West Side Horns. That's an impressive group of guys who came out of San Antonio. Rocky Morales—the saxophone player. I do gigs with him pretty regularly. He started playing in the early Sixties and played with Doug Sahm for a good part of Doug's life. Rocky was a huge influence on me. When I first heard Rocky, my jaw dropped. I thought he was just amazing. And I still do. I still absolutely love the way Rocky plays.

A lot of us say Illinois Jacquet was sort of the guy who spread a lot of that "honking" around. But I think maybe that was just because he was more out there than somebody like Frank "Floor Show" Culley. He was a honking R&B guy that not a lot of people heard about. I think he was from Oklahoma, actually, if I'm not mistaken. I'd have to go look it up, but I think he was from Oklahoma or maybe even Arkansas. But I'm pretty sure he was from Oklahoma and played around the central, southwest area quite a bit. I think he had his own band, but I'm not exactly sure. I just happened to hear him on a couple of fairly obscure R&B recordings. I think there's probably twenty-five, thirty, forty guys like that, sort of somewhat buried in the R&B woodwork there, that were as responsible for that kind of sort of honkin,' squeakin,' sort of trick saxophone sound as Illinois Jacquet ever was, but I think Jacquet kind of got more of the name for it because he was much more visible than a lot of those other guys were, nationally, and in the press as well. And of course of lot of people bad-mouthed Jacquet for playing that way, too. He got as many bad reviews as he got good ones.

Buddy Tate, he really didn't care for the honking sound. He was more of a pure guy, I mean more of a pure jazz player. But I mean, if you listen to somebody like Joe Houston, he certainly was playing that honkin' kind of stuff way as early as Illinois Jacquet or Hal Singer. So, I mean, there's plenty of guys around that you could point to. I don't think that there was any one guy that—at least, my impression is, it's not like there was one guy who sort of originated that honkin' R&B kind of sound. I don't think that there was. I mean, in the same way that there were other very important guitar players simultaneous to T-Bone.

The saxophone in R&B is very dance-oriented. I think the music, the bands that those late Forties, early Fifties players were playing in, they were dance bands. They were blues bands, dance bands that were playing in clubs. Well, it was a swing dance, jump dance, Lindy [Hop] kind of basic stuff. It was fairly up-tempo, but there was a ballad mixed in every three or four songs. I think a lot of it was kind of influenced, if you want, by popular music. I mean, you're always going to see a little bit of edge of pop songs and stuff seeping into your average R&B set. And yet, there was also a long history of blues and rhythm and blues that went into the music that people played in those bars and dance bands at that time.

The saxophone is like the human voice. But it depends on which saxophone you're talking about because the ranges change. The tenor is a little bit lower in range, maybe lower than some people's voices, but yeah, definitely, it's definitely a vocal instrument. And I think in that sense, it's part of that sort of trumpet-trombone tradition of jazz instrumental playing that's definitely influenced by vocal tradition. I don't think the saxophone ever had quite the thing like the trombone mute of Bubber Miley or that sort of stuff. The saxophone didn't ever have that level of unique vocal style of sound. But it was very much in that tradition, that same tradition that was influenced by vocals. And actually, that's one of the things that attracted me to R&B playing in general.

But more specifically, what I liked about the Texas or regional Southwest kind of playing, was that it was very melodic, not terribly concerned with busyness or the number of notes or lots of complicated chordal or arpeggiated interpretations of the chord changes or the songs. The Texas or Southwest sound is a more straightforward, simple, heartfelt statement. That's what I heard in that music and in those players. And certainly, I don't mean by that to say that it was melodically simple, because I think a lot of it was very melodically inventive and unique, but at the same time it wasn't terribly concerned with lots of notes or lots of scale patterns or kind of more sophisticated or up-tempo interpretations of chord changes or songs. Personally, I was a harmonica player before I was a saxophone player. And so the sense of making a melody or a melodic statement with a limited instrument that didn't even have all the notes on it, for me, spread into liking the saxophone players that played the same way, if you know what I mean.

The harmonica has the role of the saxophone in bands that don't have saxophones. When I started listening to Little Walter, I didn't realize at the time that what I was really listening to [in his phrasing] was a great tenor or alto saxophone player who happened to be playing the harmonica. Historically, too, I think there's a pretty good connection between him and J. T. Brown and some of the early Chicago guys that were playing saxophone. And Gene Ammons, of course. Little Walter was very aware of that sound and I think consciously tried to get a saxophone-like sound on the harmonica. And so I think I was drawn to that even before I was playing saxophone, way before I was playing saxophone. [The harmonica has been called the "Mississippi saxophone."] And, you know, it's a very chiseled kind of melodic way of playing. It's not haphazard. It's making a real strong melodic statement and a rhythmic statement. Charlie Parker was certainly an amazing saxophone player. But he also played a lot of notes, and I think there's sort of a tradition of R&B saxophone playing that doesn't involve quite as many notes that I'm attracted to.

I don't think blues is as regionally defined [today]. There are people all over the country who are playing that way. And especially, I think there were people from Texas or Louisiana who were playing that way who traveled, and people heard them all over the country, and so they'd start emulating their sound and their style. Most of the people that play in that style nowadays, I don't think—sound-wise, they don't sound like the R&B guys that I know that are still playing R&B. I mean, like Piccolo and myself and Beadle up in New England.

Gordon Beadle lives up in the Boston area and is a great young player. Greg Piccolo was always my hero. He played with Roomful of Blues for years and he was, to me, kind of a walking Illinois Jacquet and then some. And I still love Greg as much or more than any other saxophone player on the planet. He's just a fantastic player.

I saw Jacquet several times and just loved him, but I never got to play with him. Then, there's King Curtis. He was very much in that R&B sound that we're talking about, but I think he pioneered a kind of a more—and I hate to use this word—but sort of more of a pop sound for the saxophone. And I don't mean that derogatorily, at all. He had a beautiful saxophone sound that he really perfected in his recordings—the amount of reverb that he used and the kind of ensembles that were going on behind him. It was really a crossover kind of thing, you know, in a way that Fathead or even Grady Gaines never really achieved, even though they were on a lot of hits. But King Curtis, as a solo voice, I think he would have been a big pop star, you know, because I think he was able to take that R&B sound and translate it into very radio-friendly, very ear-friendly sound for people who were listening to pop music at the time.

And I absolutely loved Arnett Cobb. I got to hear him and play with him a couple of times, but if you go back and listen to his old recordings, that Texas sound, he was playing that sound as early or earlier than anybody else, earlier than Jacquet, right in there with Herschel Evans and the earliest kind of beat Texas sound, Arnett was there.

He had a rhythm style of playing, but at the same time, was very melodic but not complicated melodic. Fairly simple, fairly straightforward. Inventive, but not busy, kind of saxophone playing. His chord changes were very much based on early swing patterns, II–V patterns, fairly simple chord changes, although, you know, Arnett Cobb certainly played some sophisticated jazz tunes. His recording of "Ghost of a Chance" is still one of my favorite recordings ever of anything. So there was certainly the ability to play more complex, either Tin Pan Alley–type songs or original jazz compositions. But that was not the majority of his set on any given night. And as opposed to somebody like Parker or Coltrane, or someone like that, Arnett Cobb would be playing some blues, some fairly straightforward, simple, swing-type changes, where there might only be three or four or five changes in the song, and then a very simple bridge. He was a master at that simple style and certainly was quite able to play the more sophisticated style as well.

Fathead Newman was similar. He had that just wonderfully simple but right-to-the-point melodic kind of playing. Sometimes, actually, very much connected to the vocal melody. I don't have a particular tune in mind, but if you listen to Ray Charles, Fathead's solos sometimes are built around Ray's singing, the actual solo section is. But whether it was connected with the vocal melody or not, it still was a very simple, elegant way of creating a melodic improvisation over chord changes. Not terribly concerned with a complex interpretation of those chord changes, or, if you want, a substitution interpretation of the chord changes, but more creating a very beautiful, elegant, rhythmically intense interpretation or improvisation over those chord changes. And Fathead's rhythmic playing was just incredible to me, his sort of going back and forth between triplets and swing eighth notes and straight eighth notes. He was absolutely a master of that, and he had a beautiful sound, too. His saxophone sound was very recognizable and very lovely as far as saxophone sounds go, to my ear.

There's so much of that sound that I loved. Eddie Vinson was another. I had a chance to play with him a little bit in his later days. He had a ferocious alto sound—just great, monster sound, really strong and, you know, once again, very inventive. I remember reading somewhere that he could have been the next Charlie Parker or he could have been Charlie Parker reincarnated or something, and yet he chose to go in a sort of a simpler, earthier direction, maybe because he was also a singer; I don't know.

There's so many people—for example, I'm thinking about Johnny Hart from Louisiana, Blind John Hart. When I first came through Louisiana and Texas in '78 on that Rhythm Rockers trip, we ended up in a bar one night listening to, I guess it was Clifton Chenier, but Johnny Hart was playing with him, and as soon as I heard Johnny Hart, I almost fell down. I thought, "God, how many other guys are there like this?"—you know, [guys] nobody knows about, that are playing relatively small clubs in very regional bands.

Another one was Fats Jackson, who I ended up recording with. He was based in Atlanta. And I heard him on that same trip, in fact, '78, he came out to the club one night, all three hundred and something pounds of him, and just floored everybody in the club and floored me. We were friends ever since that day.

We're talking about the tip of the iceberg. And there were so many people back then. Then you look at the guys who were playing with, you know, the western swing bands in Oklahoma and Texas. I mean, there were some great saxophone players in those bands. I don't remember their names. But just listening to the recordings, I know there were some guys that could really play. Or even not to talk about the saxophone players, but the fiddle players and the guitar players. I got to hear Eldon Shamblin a lot, the guitar player that was with Bob Wills for years, and he was absolutely an amazing guitar player, melodically one of the most inventive players I ever heard in my life. And he played country music for most of his life.

Then, you think about the saxophone battles. Those went back into the Thirties. There's all those stories about the Basie band coming to town, and all the saxophone players and trumpet players coming out and jamming till seven o'clock in the morning or eight o'clock in the morning. I think that whole kind of cutting session notion—I always hated calling it cutting sessions, because I don't think that was really what they were about. They were about people getting together and playing because they loved to play, you know, and checking out the guy, the local tenor player or the local hot jazz player. The sense of cutting, I think writers have made too much out of that. My limited experience of that whole way of associating is that it's the oral vernacular of jazz. That's how you exchange ideas, and that's how you get better. It's not by reading something off the page or, you know, going and buying a transcription of a Charlie Parker solo. That's not how those guys got better and learned and associated. They associated by getting off the gig and going to a jam session at two o'clock in the morning. I mean, the whole pedagogical thing today is completely different. But back then, that was how people associated and how they learned and how they enjoyed themselves. That was their fun.

HOUSTON

ELDORADO BALLROOM, HOUSTON, 1940s; COURTESY MILTON LARKIN COLLECTION, METROPOLITAN RESEARCH CENTER, HOUSTON PUBLIC LIBRARY.

TAP DANCER, HOUSTON, 1940s. COURTESY MILTON LARKIN COLLECTION, METROPOLITAN RESEARCH CENTER, HOUSTON PUBLIC LIBRARY.

INTRODUCTON

In Harris County, which comprises Houston and its environs, the number of slaves increased from 905 in 1850 to 2,053 in 1860, and by 1870, the black population had tripled in size to 6,509. The population of the Fourth Ward grew after the Civil War, when freed slaves followed the San Felipe Road (present-day West Dallas Street) to Harris County. The Fourth Ward and its historic core, Freedmantown (or Freedmen's Town), was one of six political subdivisions carved out in the city's charter of 1839. Originally, the Fourth Ward was much larger than it is today, extending north to Congress Avenue, east to Main Street and south to the Rice University area, and encompassed a sizable portion of what is now downtown. In the 19th century, the San Felipe Road was a major route that connected the Brazos cotton plantations to downtown Houston, from which African Americans went to Shepherd Drive and settled along Buffalo Bayou. There, they erected small shanties and worshipped in brush arbors or in borrowed churches. Soon, they were joined by other ex-slaves from Texas and elsewhere across the South.

In 1868, the newly established Antioch Baptist Church selected Rev. Jack Yates as its first pastor. Yates, born a slave in Virginia, moved to Houston with his family in 1865 and purchased property in Freedmantown. The Edmund M. Gregory Elementary School, the first school for African Americans in Houston and perhaps in the state, opened in 1872. During the years of Reconstruction, the population of the Fourth Ward expanded so quickly that, as early as the 1870s, residents of Freedmantown began to move south into the adjacent Third Ward.[1]

African American churches, most notably the Antioch Baptist Church and the Trinity Methodist Church, were instrumental in the organization in 1869 of the Harris County Republican Club, one of the first integrated political organizations in Texas. In the 1880s, black civic leaders, after failing to attract Bishop College to the city, established Houston College in the Third Ward, but the campus was later moved to a three-acre

JOHNNY COPELAND AND KATHY WHITMIRE, MAYOR OF HOUSTON, JUNETEENTH BLUES FESTIVAL PROCLAMATION, EMANCIPATION PARK, HOUSTON, 1987. PHOTOGRAPH BY ALAN GOVENAR.

1. Ericka Schiche, "Rock of Ages: Four Homes and Eight Pastors Later, Historic Third Ward Church Receives Marker, *Houston Chronicle*, August 8, 2001, "This Week" section 1.

JOHNNY COPELAND, HOUSTON, 1970s. COURTESY CALVIN OWENS.

FOURTH WARD HIGH SCHOOL, HOUSTON, 1908. PHOTOGRAPH BY FRANK SCHLEUTER. METROPOLITAN RESEARCH CENTER, HOUSTON PUBLIC LIBRARY.

tract on the western edge of the Fourth Ward. Over the years, the Fourth Ward emerged as the center of African American business, attracting lawyers and physicians, who, in 1910, founded Houston's first black hospital.[2]

By the early years of the 20th century, living conditions in the Fourth Ward were overcrowded. Three-room shotgun houses were commonplace, in addition to the cramped T-shaped houses, L-shaped houses, and two-story tenements. Tensions over high rents and institutionalized racism intensified, and protests by African Americans escalated. In the summer of 1917, Houston was in the midst of a prohibition campaign. Those seeking to rid the city of alcohol ran a newspaper ad invoking the memory of a riot by black troops in Brownsville, Texas, in 1906. In July 1917, 654 black soldiers and eight white officers were dispatched to Houston and stationed on the outskirts of the city. Within weeks, the black soldiers were involved in a series of

2. Cary D. Wintz, "Fourth Ward, Houston," *Handbook of Texas* (Austin: Texas State Historical Association).

conflicts with white workmen, streetcar conductors, and police. Finally, after an alleged incident of brutality on August 23, about 100 of the black troops seized rifles and ammunition and marched along West Dallas and Andrew streets in the Fourth Ward, killing 14 whites and badly injuring eight others. After three hours of violence, the leader of the riot committed suicide. Sixty-three soldiers were court-martialed, and 13 were hanged in secret near San Antonio on December 11, 1917.

By the 1920s and '30s, officials in Houston estimated that the population density of the Fourth Ward was nearly six times higher than the citywide average. In 1928, C. F. Richardson, editor of the African American *Houston Informer*, wrote that the residents of the neighborhood could "stand in one house and hear the inmate in the adjacent house change his mind."[3]

VAUDEVILLE TROUPE, HOUSTON, 1925.
MILTON LARKIN COLLECTION.
COURTESY METROPOLITAN RESEARCH CENTER,
HOUSTON PUBLIC LIBRARY.

With the growth of Houston as a shipping and industrial center, the African American population increased rapidly. By 1920 there were an estimated 35,000 African Americans in Houston, and by 1940 the number had swelled to roughly 86,000. Houston's black community congregated in four segregated wards: the Third, Fourth, Fifth, and Sixth, each of which was known among musicians for the blues performers who lived and worked there. It was in the Third Ward that Sam "Lightnin'" Hopkins in the 1920s accompanied his cousin, Alger "Texas" Alexander, and where Hopkins returned in the 1940s to play on Dowling Street, sometimes accompanied by the barrelhouse pianist Buster Pickens. In the Fourth Ward was the "Santa Fe Group," a loosely knit association of blues pianists in the 1920s and '30s that included Robert Shaw, Black Boy Shine, Pinetop Burks, and Rob Cooper. They frequented the roadhouses along the Santa Fe railroad, playing a distinctive style of piano that combined elements of blues with the syncopation of ragtime. In the Fifth Ward there also were black pianists, but according to Robert Shaw, their style of performance was even more eclectic. Probably the most well known of these were members of the George W. Thomas family. The eldest child, George Thomas Jr., was born about 1885, followed by his sister Beulah, better known as classic blues singer Sippie Wallace, and brother, Hersal. Their style of piano playing involved more fully developed

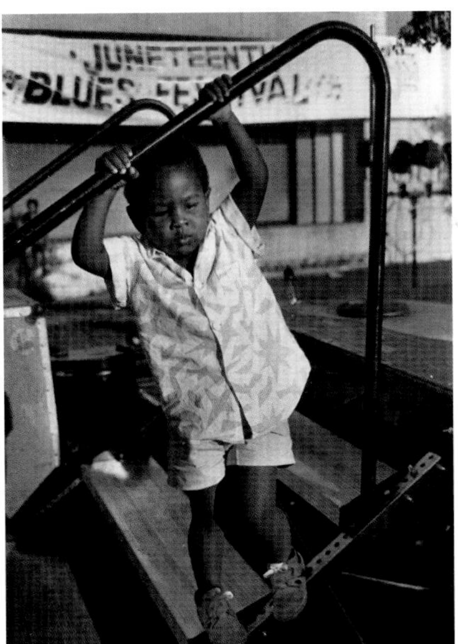

LEON HUGHES, JOE HUGHES'S GRANDSON, JUNETEENTH BLUES FESTIVAL, PROCLAMATION, EMANCIPATION PARK, HOUSTON, 1987.
PHOTOGRAPH BY ALAN GOVENAR.

3. Mike Snyder, "With Its Rich History, Fourth Ward Is Strong in Symbolism," *Houston Chronicle*, January 9, 2000 section A, 24.

AARON "T-BONE" WALKER, PUBLICITY PHOTOGRAPH, 1940S. COURTESY HELEN OAKLEY DANCE.

bass patterns than were used by the Santa Fe Group, and it integrated the influence of other performance styles that they acquired after moving from Houston to New Orleans and then to Chicago in the mid-1920s.

In Houston there were fewer opportunities for recording than in Dallas until after World War II, when several independent labels were started. The earliest to record blues was Gold Star, founded by Bill Quinn in 1946 as a hillbilly label to record Harry Choates. In 1947 Quinn decided to enter the race market by recording Sam "Lightnin'" Hopkins.

Hopkins, who began traveling and playing guitar with Texas Alexander in the late 1920s, never recorded with him. Hopkins was discovered by Mrs. Anne Cullum (also known as Lola Cullum), a talent scout and promoter for Aladdin Records in California who was then managing the career of Houston pianist Amos Milburn. Cullum had heard Hopkins playing with Alexander on Dowling Street in the Third Ward and made arrangements for both of them to accompany her on her next recording trip to California. But when she was preparing to leave, she found out that Alexander had just gotten out of prison, and she hired pianist/singer "Thunder" Smith to replace him. In California, according to one version of the story, Hopkins' finger work on the guitar was so fast that he was nicknamed Lightnin' by the recording engineer after he heard that the pianist's name was Thunder. On the Aladdin label, Hopkins recorded his first hit, "Katie Mae," which was followed by another hit, "Short-Haired Woman," released after a second trip to California. Cullum insisted that Hopkins tour on the so-called "Chitlin' Circuit," but Hopkins refused, preferring instead to stay in Houston. Out of frustration, Cullum made arrangements for Hopkins to record for the Houston-based Gold Star label, and between 1947 and1950, Hopkins cut 48 songs, which are some of his finest.[4] Although the sides recorded by Hopkins were successful, Bill Quinn was unable to keep him from recording for other labels, and in 1952, after the death of Harry Choates, Quinn ceased operations and sold or leased many of his masters to Saul Bihari.

By the early 1950s competition among independent record labels in Houston was intense. Macy's, Freedom, and Peacock (as well as Bob Shad's New York-based Sittin' In With label) were all involved in recording Houston area musicians, including Goree Carter, Lester Williams, Little Willie Littlefield, Peppermint Harris, Grady Gaines, and Big Walter Price. In addition, there were countless other African American blues, jazz, and gospel musicians who were active in Houston. They came largely from the segregated wards of Houston as well as from the surrounding areas of East Texas, the "Golden Triangle" (Beaumont, Orange, Port Arthur), and Louisiana.

Of the Houston-based independent labels, Peacock emerged as the most prominent. It was started in 1949 by Houston businessman Don Robey, who operated the Bronze Peacock club in the Fifth Ward. The Fifth Ward had been settled as early as 1866 by freed slaves. Today, it is located northeast of downtown, bounded by Buffalo Bayou on the south, Lockwood Drive on the east, Liberty Road on the north and Jensen Drive on the west. In the 1870s, approximately half the population was black (578) and half white, but by the 1920s, the Fifth Ward had become predominantly African American. In the 1920s, approximately 500 blacks of French and Spanish descent settled in an area of the Fifth Ward known as Frenchtown.

4. Lightnin' Hopkins, *The Gold Star Sessions*, vol. 1 (Arhoolie CD 330), liner notes by Chris Strachwitz and Lightnin' Hopkins, *The Gold Star Sessions*, vol. 3 (Arhoolie CD 337).

El Dorado

BALLROOM

"Featuring Houston's Top Jazz Personalities"

FRI JULY 5th

GUITAR SLIM

LLOYD LAMBERT

AND

ORCHESTRA

SAT JULY 6

JIMMIE REED

ETTA JAMES

CLIFTON CHENIER

GUITAR SLIM

JULY 8TH

CHARLES BROWN

RETURNS

Presale Tickets $1.25
At Door $1.50

CLARENCE FOSTER, BLACK-FACED COMEDIAN, LATE 1940S.
COURTESY MILTON LARKIN COLLECTION, METROPOLITAN RESEARCH CENTER, HOUSTON PUBLIC LIBRARY.

EL DORADO BALLROOM, *HOUSTON INFORMER* ADVERTISEMENT, JULY 6, 1957. COURTESY DALLAS BLUES SOCIETY.

DON ROBEY, HOUSTON, 1959. PHOTOGRAPH BY BENNY JOSEPH.

BELLS OF JOY SPIRITUAL SINGERS, PEACOCK RECORDS PUBLICITY PHOTOGAPH. COURTESY TEXAS AFRICAN AMERICAN PHOTOGRAPHY ARCHIVE.

BIG MAMA THORNTON, HOUSTON, 1950s. COURTESY TEXAS AFRICAN AMERICAN PHOTOGRAPHY ARCHIVE.

WILLIE MAE "BIG MAMA" THORNTON, "HOUND DOG," PEACOCK RECORDS 1612.

Black-owned businesses were concentrated on Lyons Avenue, including a funeral home, a theater, barbershops, and cafes. Other businesses developed in the 1930s, including printing plants, photography studios, and Club Matinee, called the "Cotton Club of the South." By 1947, when Robey opened the Bronze Peacock, Lyons Avenue in the Fifth Ward had a teeming nightlife.

Robey's headliner at the Bronze Peacock was Clarence "Gatemouth" Brown, whose impromptu performance of "Gatemouth Boogie" at the club after T-Bone Walker had became ill had made him a star. Robey wanted the Aladdin label to record Brown, but was having problems finalizing the contractual terms and decided to record Brown himself. Brown's recordings on the Peacock label did not sell well, but Robey was not deterred and actively sought out other singers and groups. In the early years of the Peacock label, Robey's biggest success was with gospel groups, such as the Five Blind Boys of Mississippi, Bells of Joy, Mighty Clouds of Joy, Dixie Hummingbirds, and Sensational Nightingales, but he continued to record rhythm and blues.

Robey was a well-known entrepreneur, born in Houston in 1903, and rumored, because of his light skin, to be a racial mix of Negro, Irish, and Jewish ancestry. Robey was a self-made man, tough and hard-nosed, known as a gambler and an aggressive businessman, and reputed to have pistol-toting bodyguards.

The first rhythm and blues singer with whom Robey made the charts was Marie Adams, whose song "I'm Gonna Play the Honky Tonks" was released in 1952. With this success, Robey acquired the Duke label in 1952 from disc jockey James Mattis in Memphis and began to represent and record the blues artists then under contract, including Bobby Bland, Johnny Ace, Larry Davis, Roscoe Gordon, and Little Junior Parker. In 1953, Big Mama Thornton's "Hound Dog" on the Peacock label reached No. 1 on *Billboard's* R&B charts. This was followed by a string of hits in the 1950s by Bobby Bland, Johnny Ace, Little Richard, and Johnny Otis, and, in the 1960s, by Joe Hinton and Roy Head, a white artist, whose "Treat Her Right," on Robey's newly established BackBeat label, went to No. 2 on the Billboard charts in 1965.

Much of Robey's success during the heyday of Peacock Records resulted from the horn-dominated arrangements of Joe Scott and the talented sidemen he assembled for the recording sessions. Pluma Davis, Hamp Simmons, Clarence Hollimon, Wayne Bennett,

JOE HINTON, HOUSTON, 1963. PHOTOGRAPH BY BENNY JOSEPH.

JOE HINTON, "FUNNY," BACK BEAT RECORDS UV 5086.

SAM "LIGHTNIN'" HOPKINS, HOUSTON, 1964.
PHOTOGRAPH BY CHRIS STRACHWITZ. COURTESY ARHOOLIE RECORDS.

LIGHTNIN' HOPKINS, "FAST LIFE WOMAN,"
GOLD STAR 665-A.

LIGHTNIN' HOPKINS, "EUROPEAN BLUES,"
GOLD STAR 665-B.

(OPPOSITE) WELDON "JUKE BOY" BONNER, REHEARSING AT ROYAL ALBERT HALL, LONDON, 1969. PHOTOGRAPH BY VAL WILMER.

Fender

WELDON "JUKE BOY" BONNER, ARHOOLIE 1045.

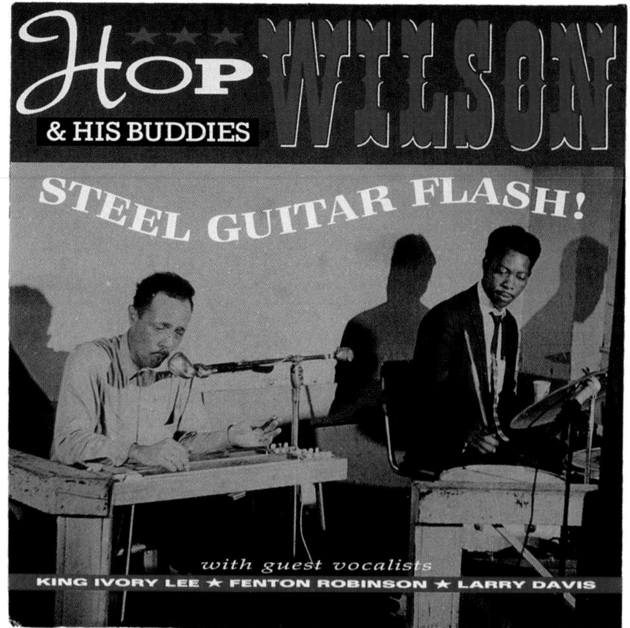

HOP WILSON & HIS BUDDIES, ACE 240.

SAM "LIGHTNIN'" HOPKINS, NEW ORLEANS JAZZ AND HERITAGE FESTIVAL, 1974. PHOTOGRAPH BY MICHAEL P. SMITH.

Johnny Brown, and Teddy Reynolds were among the core group of sidemen who worked regularly for Don Robey and helped to shape the distinctive Duke/Peacock sound.

Robey was both respected and feared because of his aggressiveness and violent temper. At the peak of his career, Robey had more than 100 individual and group recording artists under contract to his label, and over the course of one year he was known to use of the services of more than 500 studio musicians. Robey's business began to wane in the early 1960s, but benefited greatly from the British and European interest in the rhythm and blues. In 1973, however, when a court decision in litigation with Chess records went against him, Robey decided to sell recording and publishing interests in his four labels (Peacock, Duke, BackBeat and Songbird) to ABC/Dunhill, under the condition that he remain as a consultant, which he did until his death in 1975.

PROJECT ROW HOUSE, HOUSTON, 2004.
PHOTOGRAPH BY ALAN GOVENAR.

One of Robey's closest business associates was Evelyn Johnson, who not only worked with him at Peacock Records, but also managed the Buffalo Booking Agency, which brought the biggest rhythm and blues talents of the day to Houston. B. B. King was a regular visitor, performing before capacity audiences at the City Auditorium. T-Bone Walker was also frequently in Houston, and an emerging generation that was not recorded by Robey was coming of age: Johnny Copeland, Albert Collins, Johnny "Guitar" Watson, Joe Hughes, Clarence and Cal Green, and Pete Mayes. Living in the Third Ward within walking distance of each other's houses, they were the first generation of African American blues musicians to grow up listening to T-Bone Walker in live performances and on radio. When they got their first guitars, they imitated the T-Bone sound and eventually developed their own styles of performance. Playing at Club Matinee, Shady's Playhouse, and other nightspots in and around Houston, these artists slowly gained popularity in the black communities. They recorded for small labels in Houston and Los Angeles in the late 1950s and '60s,[5] but did not achieve widespread acclaim until

ELDORADO BALLROOM, HOUSTON, 2004.
PHOTOGRAPH BY ALAN GOVENAR.

5. For more information on some of the more obscure Houston blues recordings of the 1950s and 1960s, see *Houston Shuffle* (Krazy Kat 7425) and *Howling on Dowling* (Krazy Kat 7444). Featured performers include Ed Wiley, Blip Thompson, Clarence Samuels, Hubert Robinson, Conrad Johnson, Bill Hayes, Little "Guitar" Pickett and His Fabulous Rockin' Fenders, Clarence Green, Joe Hughes, Pete Mayes, Gene Vell, Tommy and The Derbys, and Earl Gilliam with Lucian Davis and His Orchestra.

they were discovered by a white American audience and by Europeans, who eagerly reissued their earlier recordings and offered them contracts and concert tours.

Concurrent with the growing popularity of blues abroad, festivals began to spring up around the United States, including San Francisco, Chicago, and many other places. In Houston Lanny Steele started the Juneteenth[6] Blues Festival, sponsored by SumArts, a community-oriented performing arts organization that he founded in 1967. The emphasis of the Juneteenth Festival was to recognize Houston-born blues artists in a series of free concerts with nationally known performers at Hermann Park's Miller Outdoor Theater and other Houston area parks. Each year the Festival selected a blues artist of the year who was honored in public ceremonies. Over the years, these included Sippie Wallace, Milton Larkin, Arnett Cobb, Clifton Chenier, Eddie Vinson, Gatemouth Brown, Albert Collins, and Johnny Copeland.

By the 1980s social and cultural conditions of Houston blues began to reflect a changed society, though there were lingering racial tensions and new problems posed by upward mobility and assimilation in the Texas post-boom economy. Rhythm and blues became a more integrated music, stylistically and culturally; black and white performers came together on stage to play a music that combined traditional and pop elements. However, concurrent with this, there remained a strong African American blues and jazz scene in the black communities of the Third, Fourth and Fifth wards. In addition to rhythm and blues, the Fifth Ward also became known for its zydeco, a highly syncopated Creole music brought by Louisiana migrants to the area. Zydeco has influenced Houston rhythm and blues, which, in turn, has also affected the gospel sound of singers, instrumentalists, and arrangers.

In the mid-1980s, European interest helped propel a revival of Houston blues. Musicians such as Joey Long, Jimmy "T-99" Nelson, Grady Gaines, Clarence Hollimon, Joe Hughes, Pete Mayes, Big Roger Collins, Milton Hopkins, Pops Overstreet, Clarence Green, Johnny Brown, Joe Medwick, Henry Hayes, Arnett Cobb, and Milton Larkin re-emerged with new material and international acclaim. Over the last two decades, there have been more than a hundred reissue albums of Houston blues by Ace Records, Flyright, Krazy Kat, and Charly in London, Mr. R&B and Route 66 in Sweden, Mina records in Japan, and Marcel Vos of Double Trouble records in the Netherlands. With the Grammy Award-winning success of Gatemouth Brown, Johnny Copeland, and Albert Collins, the demand has swelled for Houston shuffles, the big band beat, heartrending ballads, and hard-rocking rhythm and blues.

A New Century

The vitality of Houston blues endures. Project Row House, founded by Rick Lowe in 1993, has helped to revitalize the Fourth Ward, which had started to decline around 1940, as African Americans moved into the Third and Fifth wards. The building of San Felipe Courts (later Allen Parkway Village), a white housing project, hemmed in the neighborhood on its north side, and the construction of Interstate 45 cut off the area from downtown on the east. Still, the Fourth Ward continued as an important center of black business and cultural life into the 1960s, when many black homeowners left the neighborhood as integration opened other residential areas of the city. The population of the Fourth Ward declined from almost 17,000 in 1910 to fewer than 4,400 in 1980, with almost 50 percent of its residents living below the poverty level and only 5 percent owning their own homes.[7]

The idea for Project Row House originated through a series of discussions among a group of Houston's African American artists, who worked to renovate 22 shotgun-style houses to foster a positive creative presence in the community. Seven of the houses provide gallery space for Artist Installation Projects; one is devoted to performance art; seven are dedicated to a Young Mothers Residential Program; and the others are utilized for offices and education programs.

6. Juneteenth is a holiday in Texas that commemorates June 19, 1865, the day Texas African Americans learned of the Emancipation Proclamation, signed two years earlier. Freedmen and former slaves began observing the anniversary with picnics, speeches, and reminiscences in verse and song. For blacks in Houston and those elsewhere around Texas, Juneteenth still has great significance, and is not only a time of parties and concerts, but of offering respect to accomplishments of freedom in education, politics, economics, and social progress. However, it was not until 1979 that Juneteenth was officially recognized, when Gov. Bill Clements signed a law declaring June 19 "Emancipation Day," with ceremonies and community gatherings planned around the state.

7. Wintz, "Fourth Ward, Houston," 1142.

In 1999, a private donor gifted the Eldorado Ballroom to Project Row House. The Eldorado Ballroom, erected in 1938 in the Third Ward by Charles and Anna Dupree as an entertainment venue, had functioned as a fraternal gathering spot and community center until it closed in 1973. In its heyday, the Eldorado Ballroom featured the major rhythm and blues stars of the day: T-Bone Walker, Goree Carter, Lester Williams, Peppermint Harris, Little Junior Parker, B. B. King, Bobby Bland, and a long list of others. There were teen hops and social club dances that lasted late into the night. Carolyn Blanchard, a Third Ward native who sang with many of the bands, recalled that the Eldorado had a "social grace. . . . That was a time when family was family, communities were communities, respect was respect. During that era, the respect and dignity became this place. We went ballrooming. This was class and society at its best."[8]

KPFT blues disc jockey Mr. V said the Eldorado fulfilled a community need during the years of segregation. "We couldn't go places, couldn't go here, couldn't go there, so we made our own paradise. This was our paradise."[9]

8. Marty Racine, "The Original 'Golden Oldie,' The Eldorado Ballroom has been renovated and again celebrates African American history and Culture, *Houston Chronicle*, May 21, 2003, Houston section, 1.

9. Racine, "Original 'Golden Oldie,'" 1.

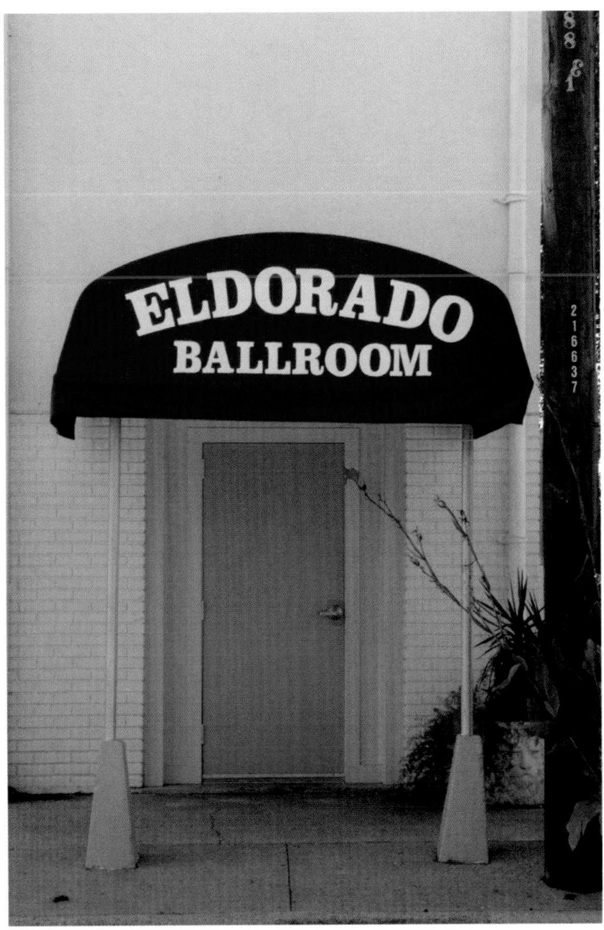

ELDORADO BALLROOM, HOUSTON, 2004.
PHOTOGRAPH BY ALAN GOVENAR.

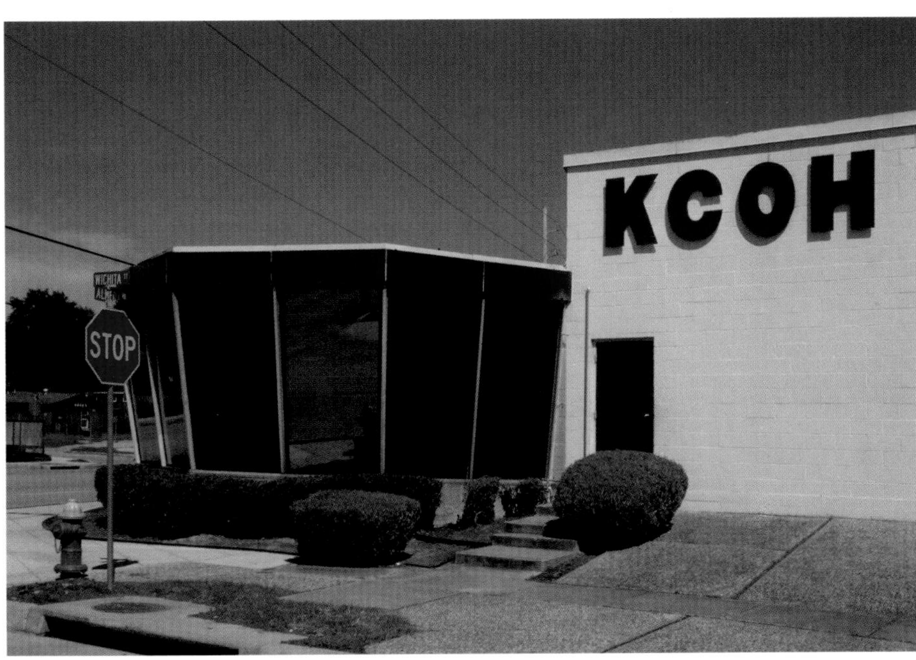

KCOH RADIO, HOUSTON, 2004. PHOTOGRAPH BY ALAN GOVENAR.

BOBBY "BLUE" BLAND, "I'LL TAKE CARE OF YOU," DUKE 314 .

CLARENCE "GATEMOUTH" BROWN, "SWINGIN' THE GATE," PEACOCK ACA 3937.

On May 17, 2003, after more than three years of fund raising and renovation, the Eldorado Ballroom reopened to the public. Since then, it has become a focal point for the historical and cultural preservation interests. Its mission, according to Lowe, is to "figure out the meaning of this place from a historical standpoint in order to design programming for the future," including concerts, a gallery space, and possibly a museum of African American history.[10]

Roger Wood and James Fraher's book, *Down in Houston: Bayou City Blues* (2003), has heightened public awareness of the scope of Houston blues, chronicling its development in a personalized text and photographs covering the period from1995 to 2002. My book *Meeting the Blues* (1988) explored an earlier period, when many of the blues artists I met in Houston were struggling to find work. During that time, I interviewed numerous Houston blues performers, produced the radio series *Traditional Music in Texas* and recorded three albums on Houston rhythm and blues for the Double Trouble label in the Netherlands, featuring Joe Hughes, Pete Mayes, Clarence Green, and Teddy Reynolds, among others. The following texts combine oral histories, narratives, and photographs from the 1980s with additional information and images compiled over the last decade.

10. Racine, "Original 'Golden Oldie,'" 1.

VICTORIA SPIVEY, *VICTORIA AND HER BLUES*, SPIVEY LP 1002. COURTESY TEXAS AFRICAN AMERICAN PHOTOGRAPHY ARCHIVE.

VICTORIA SPIVEY, HOUSTON, 1960s. COURTESY TEXAS AFRICAN AMERICAN PHOTOGRAPHY ARCHIVE

MILTON LARKIN

October 10, 1910–August 31, 1996; interview, 1984

HOME FROM THE WAR: MILTON LARKIN (6TH FROM RIGHT) HOUSTON, 1945. COURTESY MILTON LARKIN COLLECTION, METROPOLITAN RESEARCH CENTER, HOUSTON PUBLIC LIBRARY

My dad played violin, and my sister took it up. I wanted to play violin, but I liked so many instruments, I didn't know which one I wanted to play. When I was about ten or twelve years old, I saw a picture of Noble Sissle in a magazine, and I told my mother that I wanted to be a musician. I was born in 1910 in Navasota, but we moved to Houston in 1923. I started playing the trumpet, but I switched over to valve trombone after I went into the service. My mother didn't want me to play because she thought I'd get into trouble, but I showed her I was different.

A lot of musicians have gotten their start with me: Eddie Vinson, Tom Archia, Wild Bill Davis, Cedric Maywood. Illinois Jacquet played alto with me in one of my first bands, and then he switched to tenor with Lionel [Hampton]. I've had my own band since 1936. Arnett Cobb was another of the greats who played with me. We'd have saxophone battles; whoever had the chair next to Arnett would battle with him. That's what led to honking. It's in the phrasing, the repetition of notes, squealing.

The Texas sound has more feeling, melodic syncopation, and a different beat. You can hear it in Louis Jordan, even though he wasn't from Texas. Any time there's a Texas band, blues and jazz fit together.

In my early bands, I had a banjo in the rhythm section. Guitar started later, around the time of bass violin. At first there were tubas, no bass violin. Then the guitar came along, electric guitar. T-Bone played with me when he was in his early thirties, at Joe Louis's Rhumboogie Club in Chicago. I went for two weeks, and I ended up staying nine months. T-Bone would come in and go out on the road some of the time. T-Bone was wonderful. He was a picker; he used his fingers, sometimes with a pick. He was in my sixteen-piece band. He played blues and other things. There were five reeds, four rhythm, five saxophones, myself, and a vocalist. We were playing swing, big-foot swing, which is what I still play now.

After several one-record deals with small labels, I worked as a sideman on sessions, playing trombone or piano with Eddie "Lockjaw" Davis, Hal "Cornbread" Singer and Eddie "Cleanhead" Vinson. Around 1949 I cut some sides for Regal with Howard Biggs's Orchestra and two years later for Coral, with the former Erskine Hawkins sideman, piano player Ace Harris, whose band included Count Hastings on tenor. I was with my own vocal group, The X-Rays, but that didn't last that long.

In the 1960s I played at the Celebrity Club in New York. There were two rooms there. I played one room, and Buddy Tate played the other. Well, that lasted into the 1970s, and then I went back to Houston around the time I cut my album *Down Home Saturday Night* with a group I called Milt Larkin and His All Stars on my own Copasetic label. The record had Wild Bill Davis on organ, alto man Jimmy Tyler [from Boston], who played with Count Basie for many years, trumpeter Johnny Grimes [from Birmingham], and Johnny Copeland from Houston.

PLAYING CARDS ON THE ROAD: MILTON LARKIN (CENTER), 1950S. COURTESY MILTON LARKIN COLLECTION, METROPOLITAN RESEARCH CENTER, HOUSTON PUBLIC LIBRARY.

It seems like people are beginning to like what they're hearing of it again now. A lot of it's through the ear. It's playing chords that are more melodic, chords that will stick with a person. Well, you took that solo, you can hum the whole song. You appreciate what you hear.

I'm in a group now with the city called Get Involved Now, a nonprofit organization. I play for shut-ins. It don't matter what language they are, how old, they all react to music.

MILT LARKIN
and his
ALL STARS
Down Home
Saturday
Night
COPASETIC
933
STEREO

MILTON LARKIN AND HIS ALL STARS, *DOWN HOME SATURDAY NIGHT*, COPASETIC 933.

BEULAH "SIPPIE" WALLACE

November 1, 1898–November 1, 1986; interview by Christopher Brooks, 1985

Oh, yes, I knew them well [Ma Rainey, Bessie Smith, Ida Cox, and Alberta Hunter], but I never thought I was going to be a blues singer, because I was nothing but a gospel singer. At seven years old, I was the organist of my church. Instead of going to Sunday school classes, I would go up to the organ and start playing. The pastor said, "Let's give this child a music lesson, or lessons." So when Mama came in, they told Mama, "Sister Thomas, the members of this church have decided to give Beulah music lessons." Mama said, "Thank God." When Mama got home, she told my oldest brother what the church had decided to do and said, "George, why don't you give Beulah music lessons, so that'll help the church out." So he did, believing that I'd sing his songs and the church songs, too. . . . Mama died, and the city bought her property in Houston. I went to Chicago and lived there for about ten years because my brother George was there.

After Mama died, I thought my brother was going to take care of me, but my brother told me to get a husband—I never had any company. It caused me to look dumb—I didn't know what sex was, even after I was grown and married. Children today are born knowing what sex is.

After I made "George, George" [her first recording success, on the Okeh label], I had twenty-eight hits! That gave me a contract—so, when I got the contract, Clarence Williams wanted to play for me. He played one song for me [on Okeh]. Then my little brother, named Hersel, began playing for me. He was in Chicago at the time, with George. Hersel made about 150 records with me.

I wrote a song called "Special Delivery Blues." My husband, Matt, had gone to the army, and he told me he was going to send me a special [special delivery package]. He never did send me a special, so I wrote a special tune, and Louis Armstrong helped me to make the song a hit. I had King Oliver playing with me and Sidney Bechet, too. That's one of my greatest songs!

I talk—I tell a story behind every song and why I wrote it. I wrote a song about Adam and Eve. I said, "When God made man, He loved man. He loved man so, He made him in His own image. He told man he would never have to work because this garden would furnish food for him. He said, 'You can eat of all the fruit, don't touch the fruit tree in the middle of the garden.' While he was gone, Eve saw a snake near the tree. The snake said, 'Did I hear him say that if you eat that fruit, you would die? Don't believe that—you won't die, but you'll be as wise as God.' Well, God came back. He called, 'Adam—Adam! Adam!' Adam said, 'Here I am, Lord.'

"'Where art thou?'

"'I was naked, God, and I tried to hide myself.'

"He said, 'Who told you you were naked?'

"He said, 'Eve told me I was naked.'

"He said, 'For your disobedience, you shall earn your bread from the sweat of your brow. For Eve's disobedience, she will bear nine.' And so, he drove Adam and Eve out of the garden. And that's how we came to have the blues. Eve was the cause of it. Now, if that had been a man and did what God told him to do, we wouldn't have the blues. Since that day, everybody has had the blues."

I could sing the blues after the man I had started wanting liked everybody but me, so I sang the blues about the way the man treated me. When I sing the blues, I am talking about myself.

I'm a mighty tight woman, and there's nothing I fear. When I'm singing to the audience, I make them tell me how I'm doing. Say, "How am I doing?" Then, I tell the women something. I say, "Women, be wise, keep your mouth shut and don't advertise your man." Because I declare I'm going to take him away with me. I know that from experience.

Not a bit [of difference between gospel and blues]. I play for a church right now. I have an adult choir and a junior choir. I played last Sunday. You don't see any place in the Bible that says you'll go to hell if you sing the blues. If you can sing gospel, you can sing the blues.

SIPPIE WALLACE, NEW ORLEANS JAZZ AND HERITAGE FESTIVAL, 1985.
PHOTOGRAPH BY MICHAEL P. SMITH

He only thing that divides the blues from the gospel are the words. When you say "Lord" in gospel, in blues you say "Daddy."

Even now, they advertise the blues, but they won't advertise the gospel. When I got up there and sing the gospel, they will say, "Sippie, you ain't doing nothing but preaching." But I won't advertise it.

The music [gospel] uplifts me. I believe if I were dying and someone played:

Ain't you glad.
You've got good religion.
So glad
I've got good religion.
So glad
I've got good religion.
I've got good religion.
Asleep in His arms, but not in the grave.

I believe I would stop dying to hear that song sung. I love to sing.

BIG WALTER PRICE

August 2, 1914– ; interview, 1984

BIG WALTER PRICE, PEACOCK RECORDS/BUFFALO BOOKING AGENCY, PUBLICITY PHOTOGRAPH, 1950S. COURTESY TEXAS AFRICAN AMERICAN PHOTOGRAPHY ARCHIVE.

I go by Big Walter, the Thunderbird. No one ever calls me Big Walter. I was born in Gonzales, but I was raised in San Antonio, and I've been in Houston off and on since 1956. At that particular time I had a chance to get with a bigger record company. I started off with TNT, that's Texas and North Town. So, after talking with Mr. Don Robey, he told me that if I got my release from TNT, he would record me. TNT wasn't really too interested in blues anyway; they more or less recorded Spanish people. So that was a pretty big step for me, as far as rhythm and blues was concerned, because they didn't have rhythm and blues anyway. And they just wanted to get me started. I was recommended by the man they call Red River Dave. Red River Dave had a radio show on WAOI, Channel 4, out of San Antonio. So when I got on Channel 4, I got to record for TNT, and TNT recommended me to Peacock.

Rightfully, I'm seventy. There is a three-year difference than my birth certificate. So, we're talking about sixty-seven. It's not really true. But we have to go by what we know.

There was only one blues player in San Antonio at that particular time, and he moved out. That was Gatemouth Brown. He used to room with my auntie. So he was a roomer. He was a little ahead of me as far as Peacock was concerned. I started as a spiritual singer, The Lord of Wonders out of Michigan, and one day I was just hummin' a song when a friend of mine [who] was workin' with me on Texas-Pacific railway says, "As good a voice as you got, you should sing blues."

I says, "You got to be kiddin.'"

He says, "Try it anyway."

Well, he kept nagging me about it for a month and a half. He says, "If you don't get 'head on and start singin' the blues. . . . Your voice is beautiful."

"Me?" I says, "I singin' spirituals now."

And he says, "I'm not knockin' it, but I don't think you'll be too good in that field. You let somebody stay in that field like Sam Cooke." So I kind of laughed it off. I didn't think much about it, and then one day it kind of dawned on me. I'll try it. So they had a club in Fort Worth called the Zanzibar, and I came in one afternoon and I asked the lady, "Can I sing?" And she says, "Yes."

I says [to the band], "Can I sit in?"

And they said, "No."

So I went back and told her what they said and she said, "You tell them that if they don't let you sit in, they don't have a job." What that lady didn't realize [was] that I played in one key, and that was in C, and I played all night in C. I got the job.

I have had the question asked many times [how Texas piano is different from other styles], but it's really hard to explain. You have a music expert or lover, an arranger to answer that question for you. But as far as me, I couldn't answer that. You have to have feeling as well as sound, because if you don't feel what you're doing, there's no point in foolin' with it because you're not going to be able to get it over to the public if you don't feel it. You can't get it over to them. This is what I am saying. Of course, somebody else might have a different version of it.

The blues really tells a story, the past as well as the future. It depends what you got your mind on. Playing the blues will kind of prevent you from doing things; well, that's fine, but if blues is motivating you to do other things, then you ought to do something else.

The only change in the blues I play today, that I ease in differently than when I started, is the beat. The beat is different on certain songs, but some songs, that beat don't work regardless of how you do it. Blues is just blues, but the precious Lord may step the tempo up and put a different beat to it.

Louis Armstrong said there wasn't any difference between blues and jazz. When you're listening to jazz, you are listening to blues. You might have to slow it down or back it up; you still got it. The only little change in it is in the tempo. I just have to give it to you the way he gave it to me. I had a talk with him several years ago when he was down here and several people asked him that question, but when I got my own personal chance, he told me they were the same.

I perform myself and also with my own unit. That's how I made my European tour. I went over by myself. I got paid for thirty-eight dates. Thirty-seven were standing ovations. I don't know what happened to the other ones. The European audience is great. The European people, fans, great. They accept blues more than

BIG WALTER PRICE, "JUNIOR JUMPED IN," TNT 8005.

BIG WALTER PRICE, "CALLING MARGIE," TNT 8005.

BIG WALTER PRICE, HOUSTON, 1950s. COURTESY WALTER PRICE.

they do in the U.S.A. You'd have to talk to a European about that. They have records on blues artists we don't even have in the United States. Anything anybody ever did before, 98 percent, they have it. I met one German piano player who had won all of the high awards, and I asked why he doesn't play more, and a high official related to me, "Because he wasn't black. As far as playing piano, any type of instrument, but they walk over you like hot water, but they can't get the credit because they're not black."

I got a hundred and sixty-nine original songs, and three hundred instrumentals. I got fifty-two records on the market, and I'm credited in three different movies, and one of them is *Sugar Hill.* I played the role of the drunken preacher. That was a production out of Beverly Hills, California. I did a courtroom scene with Muhammad Ali, the Greatest. They didn't give me a talking part on that because at that time, I didn't have my license [union card]. My license hadn't come back. So I did an instrumental.

I got a lot of music that I almost done forgot. My albums are still available, but I couldn't tell you where to find them. They're collector items.

EVELYN JOHNSON

September 28, 1920–November 1, 2005; interview by Robert N. Simmons, 1972

James Mattis [of WDIA in Memphis] found Johnny Ace. He was one of the Beale Streeters. He had recorded him, had already made "My Song." But then it fell to our lot [because Don Robey purchased the Duke label] to record him from then on. Four of his big things, well, everything Johnny did for us was big. "Pledging My Love" was his last and biggest. He was a real giant at the beginning, a real giant at the end, and in between was smooth sailing. He was a natural and yet all day long you could find boys who could out-sing him. But they didn't have that certain something that he had. He was a very unassuming person. He would pick up a lyric, not read it, just look at it, and say, "I don't want to do it." "Why, Johnny?" and he'd say, "I don't want to do it. It's too many words." And he said very little. He played a lot, which is why he's dead. He was playing. He was no more aware of what happened, and that was the worst sight I ever seen. I hope never to see it again.

It was Christmas of 1954, in the City Auditorium that has been demolished and replaced by a fabulous building now. He'd just come off stage, singing. It was in the dressing room, sitting on the dresser, surrounded by people, friends and musicians, and playing with a little .22 revolver with one bullet in it. He had the very bad habit of pointin' that gun. He was playing with that gun—all of this is hearsay, but everybody says the same thing—Big Mama Thornton said to him, "You're always pointing that gun at somebody. I notice that you never point it at yourself." He pointed it at her and snapped, just constantly playing, and after a while he said, "I'm gonna point it at myself." And he put it to his temple. The bullet was there that time. And that little bullet made a small opening right there and his hair stood on end like horror movies. His brain oozed out of that little hole. He bled so immediately and so profusely until it was like a river. And it coagulated just that fast. He had a little smirky grin on his face and his expression was, "What I'd say?" When you looked at his face, you'd see, "What I'd say?" It was horrible! He was twenty-six years old.

DON ROBEY AND EVELYN JOHNSON, HOUSTON, 1960s. PHOTOGRAPH BY BENNY JOSEPH.

That was a very sad death, and another one was Joe Hinton who, I assure you, had untold talent. But very few people knew that he had had a very rare skin cancer. As a matter of fact, they wouldn't accept him in the clinic because they said they couldn't treat it. They said he was the first Negro that had been there with this particular disease. So they sent him to Boston because they were working on some treatment there. Once it hits the bloodstream, it's some form of leukemia. Now the name of it is twelve syllables. I can't remember it.

JIMMIE NELSON AND THE PETER RABBIT TRIO, "T-99 BLUES," RPM 325.

JIMMIE "T-99" NELSON, HOUSTON, 1950S, COURTESY JIMMY NELSON.

CLUB EBONY
4415 DOWLING at ROSEWOOD
"The Club That Brings Broadway To Houston"
FOR FREE RESERVATIONS - JA-2-3368
THE REGULAR FELLOWS SOCIAL CLUB
DANCE THURSDAY NITE
TWO BIG SHOWS
FRI, SAT AND SUN 10 AND 12 P M
FEATURING
AN ADDED ATTRACTION
Jimmy 'T ninty nine' Nelson
JEWEL (Teasin) BROWN
HOUSTON'S SWEETHEART OF SONG
DUTCH & DUTCHY
THE GREATEST
COMEDY AND DANCE TEAM
RON LA ROQUE and GAIL
THE DANCE-SATIONS - SAMPSON & DELILAH
I H SMALLEY'S BAND
EVERY MON "A FREE"
BLUE MONDAY PARTY - 3 P M UNTIL
FREE JAM SESSION
EVERY SUNDAY - 3 TO 7 P M
EVERY WEDNESDAY NIGHT - THE BIG BAND
AND MODERN JAZZ SEXTET
WE RENT CLUB - ANY NITE TO ORGANIZATIONS,
SOCIAL CLUBS OR PARTIES

JIMMY "T- 99" NELSON, CLUB EBONY, *HOUSTON INFORMER* ADVERTISEMENT, HOUSTON, 1950S. COURTESY DALLAS BLUES SOCIETY.

As often as he could, Joe went into seclusion for about three months. That was when the reaction was keloid-looking things, and they hit his face at that time. Now, he had lost his hair several times. But he would wear wigs. But when they hit his face, it was more than he could bear. It originally had been on his back and arms. He always wore long-sleeved shirts. I doubt that there were two people who had seen him other than the doctor and myself. His mother didn't even see him. But when they hit his face, he stayed inside with the shades drawn and wouldn't face anybody. So he was successful in kind of getting them off, and he had gone to work. He did a club engagement, and as soon as the club engagement had ended, he had to rush on up to Boston. As fate would have it, I was in New York when he was at his worst. So they called me and said he asked for me. I couldn't get any [transportation] out of New York until seven o'clock the next morning. They called me at four o'clock and told me, "Don't bother. He's gone." He held up all the way; his absolute decline didn't come until he went into the hospital. And he drove [himself] to the hospital. "Funny (How Time Slips Away)" was his biggest hit.

I booked Joe Hinton, B. B. King for nine years, Bobby

JIMMIE "T-99" NELSON, HOUSTON, 1950s.

COURTESY JIMMY NELSON.

JOHNNY ACE, PUBLICITY PHOTOGRAPH, 1950s.

JOHNNY ACE, THE BEALE STREETERS, "ACES WILD," DUKE 112.

JOHNNY ACE, THE BEALE STREETERS, "THE CLOCK," DUKE 112.

O.V. WRIGHT "I'D RATHER BE BLIND, CRIPPLED, AND CRAZY," BACK BEAT 45-628-A

O. V. WRIGHT, "PLEDGING MY LOVE," BACK BEAT ML 5242.

Bland, Junior Parker, Johnny Ace, Willie Mae Thornton, Lloyd Price, Little Richard from scratch, Little Richard and The Tempo Toppers, one of the most terrific male groups that there ever was. I had the Buffalo Booking Agency. That was just my thing. It started with Gatemouth Brown. I finally gave it up because it was very unrewarding. It was a tough row to hoe. However, I can boast that I kept their heads above water until their time came. When I first met B. B. King, he couldn't move to the next town. I wasn't even interested in a contract on him. But we had nine nice years together. I remember them. I don't know who else remembers, but I do, and the United States Treasury, they remember very well.

There were certain clubs I couldn't go into, couldn't get a foot in the door. But the acts [I booked] worked more than any other show on the road. Maybe for less money, but they were working for two reasons, not only for their living, but for mental stability. This was their life. So the more that they did, the better off they were. And they worked more than anybody [else] on the road. Every now and then we'd get a decent job here and there. We did the theaters. And that was the thing then, because at that time these people weren't going into these other clubs. Who was going to Tahoe? [No black entertainer] but Nat King Cole. You just didn't cross those lines, and you stayed in your own back yard.

When we first went into the record business, the record companies didn't want us in. It was unheard of that a Negro group would come through this way. There were only one or two [black-owned recording] companies, who had floundered around with a record now and next year. But we went into like, here we are, a record [company with a full catalog]. This was unheard of. Now, that stigma didn't last too long. Then we didn't grow to a competitive status except with product. So your product couldn't go any further than your internal situation could make it go. Then in later years we had the problem of the disk jockey; we couldn't get our records on the air. So you see, our problems came in stages.

So many of our records [Duke and Peacock] were ahead of the time. They're more popular now than they were then. This is the strength of our catalog. We've got a great "repeat catalog." All these dates they're bringing back now, rather than delete them. They are meeting the demand, and they are cutting the pirates off at the pass.

RILEY "B. B." KING

September 16, 1925– ; interview, 1985

LAWRENCE BURDINE, LEO LACHNER, B. B. KING, HOUSTON, LATE 1950s. PHOTOGRAPH BY BENNY JOSEPH.

In the white light of the stage of the Venetian Room, one night in 1985, the blues of B. B. King is larger than life. The institution of contemporary blues stands in the spotlight of hard-won success. To be a blues singer, B. B. King says, is "like having to be black twice," once by birth and then again by the music he performs.

The next day, in a suite at the Fairmont Hotel, B. B. King looks tired. Circulation problems in one of his legs have slowed him a little, but his face still radiates a dynamic energy, even behind sunglasses. He is wearing a yellow shirt with a tan suede sportcoat. Next to him

B. B. KING, HOUSTON, 1960S. PHOTOGRAPH BY BENNY JOSEPH, COURTESY TEXAS AFRICAN AMERICAN PHOTOGRAPHY ARCHIVE.

is a radio producer from Los Angeles who is planning a series of syndicated programs called the "B. B. King Blues Hour."

B. B. King stands up slowly and extends his hand, says, "It's a pleasure to meet you," and then motions me to a table off to the side. As he talks, the words seem timeless, spoken with sincerity. Being a blues legend begets a responsibility, which B. B. King accepts with dignity. He is as generous with conversation as time permits.

(OPPOSITE) B .B. KING, MONTREUX INTERNATIONAL JAZZ FESTIVAL, 1987. PHOTOGRAPH BY EDOUARD CURCHOD.

Our booking agent was in Houston. Buffalo Booking Agency. Evelyn Johnson used to book us. We used to spend a lot of time there, but I never did live there. Evelyn Johnson is a remarkable lady, one of the great women of her time. I don't think she gets enough recognition, because to me she was one of the pioneers, she helped a lot of people. Not only in the blues field, but jazz, soul, and rock as well.

She worked with Don Robey, who owned Peacock Records. I never did record for Robey, but I almost did, if the Bihari brothers didn't give me the money I wanted. Robey was just as fair as the rest of them that I ever worked for. I was very happy with the booking agency. I didn't see any difference between what they were doing and what all the other booking agencies and record companies were doing.

Eveyln booked us into white clubs, but that was not a lot of them, because at that time, in the 1950s and 1960s, I was not at the point what they call crossover. There were not a lot of white clubs that would have me. The crossover for me didn't happen until the latter part of 1968, early '69. It started with the song "The Thrill Is Gone."

My producer at that time was Bill Szymczyk. He was just starting on the scene, and his ideas reminded me of the old Bihari days. He wouldn't interfere with you while you were recording. There's a big mistake a lot of people make; they try to coach a guy and record him without letting him be himself. Don't misunderstand me. I know this was a different time, and some of us need coaching. I'm one, but only to a point. Make sure I say the word right, make sure I don't break a verb or something, but the sound, allow me to express me as I am. Let me play as I do. Don't say, "Sound like this person," or "Do you remember hearing the record so-and-so?" Well, that kind of attitude makes me not want to be on record because I like to be myself.

Bill Szymczyk was a young producer and he understood me, one of those types that bring out the best in you. They tell you when you're not close enough to the microphone, and say, "Would you please play that again?" With that kind of coaching, the artist is going to do his very best to be himself. That's the way it was, night we recorded "The Thrill Is Gone," one late night. I had Hugh McCracken on guitar, Herbie Lovell on drums. The bass player was Gerald Jemmott, and a keyboard player [Paul Harris].

I told Bill, "I've got this tune I've been carrying around for about eight years. Every time I record I've never been able to do exactly what I want with it, and this rhythm section is cookin'! I think that I want to try this!" He said, "Fine, go ahead." And we went into "The Thrill Is Gone," and man, it was just like hand-in-glove. It clicked for me, but not for him. So we finished about 2:30 in the morning. I said, "All right, we're gonna knock off." Bill said, "Fine." He thought it was a good session. But I knew it was a good session. So I said, "'The Thrill Is Gone' is that tune." All of my career, I'd never thought of Top 40, Top 20, like producers and record companies do. I think in terms of a good record. And I knew "The Thrill Is Gone" was a good record. So I said, "Man, think about it," but Bill wasn't too into it. I went to my apartment—we were in New York—and he went to his. About two hours later, I get a call and he's all excited, "Man, B! This is Bill Szymczyck!"

I said, "Yeah, Bill, what's happenin'?"

And he said, "Man, 'The Thrill Is Gone,' that's a song. That's a good record!"

"I agree."

"What do you think about adding some strings? I think strings will help it."

"Fine."

He said, "Man, that's a good pop record."

I didn't really think too much about it because I liked strings. So he got a guy called Bert DeCoteaux to do the strings. About three or four days later I went down to hear the strings being put on, and they did give it a different flavor from what began on record. I liked it, and when "The Thrill Is Gone" was released, my crossover began. It was soon after that The Rolling Stones invited me to tour with them.

My audience had started mixing before that, of course, but that really pushed it over the top. A lot of people heard me on that Rolling Stones tour that hadn't heard of me before. I remember once in Baltimore, one white lady came out, she had teenagers, who seemed to be impressed with what I did. She came up to me and asked, "Have you made any records?" I'd made a whole lot of albums. I don't remember how many I had in 1969, but I have about sixty-seven albums now.

When I first went to Europe, my first country was England. I remember when my group and I was getting off the airplane. For years they had tried to get me come over without a band, but I would never go, but this time it was good. I had my own group.

We came through customs and there were about 2,300 people waving American flags. Well, I knew that the Beatles had been over here, and everybody was crazy about the Beatles at the time. So I was thinking. Well, I don't know what was running through my head, but I had no idea these people were welcoming us to England. And as we walked through customs, everybody started hollering, " B. B.! B. B.!" By God, I was frightened. I almost turned around! But my manager was with me, and he said, "This is a greeting for you, B." And gosh, my hair was almost standing up on my head. I'd never seen anything like that before. Never, ever! I was actually like a superstar to them—at least, that's the way they treated me.

The first press conference I ever had was in London, and everybody wanted to know what I think. It was sort of weird. What difference does it make? Who wants to know? Everybody was so polite. We must have had reporters from most of the countries in Europe, and they had their photographers. My manager said, "A lot of this, whatever happens in London, will go throughout Europe." In other words, he was reminding me that if I didn't go over well there, it wouldn't go well anywhere else. That started it. Now, I've been all around the world two or three times.

One of the keys to being able to stay out there so long is playing to the audience. I wouldn't play in the Venetian Room what I would play across the street where you got a lot of teenagers. They're more conservative downstairs, even the young people that come down there. I like to keep it where I'm still doing blues, still being B. B. King, but that's the other side that I try to portray, a type of blues that can be humorous in some of it, and have feeling in some of it, kind of in between, not just hard-core blues. But if I go across the street where you got a disco atmosphere, I'll do "Big Boss Man," "Into the Night," and songs like that.

In the Longhorn Ballroom they have such a mixed audience there, even when it's full of all blacks. There's a mix among them. So I need to play different things. I'd do "Three O'Clock in the Morning," but I wouldn't do that in the Venetian Room because I feel the audience couldn't relate to it as well. But "Sweet Little Angel," they can. I'm the quarterback. I figure out the plays.

B. B. KING MURAL, THIRD WARD, HOUSTON, 1987.
PHOTOGRAPH BY ALAN GOVENAR.

What I do depends on the audience and who's on the bill with me. Any time I got to follow a female, any female, talented or not talented, or a teenager or a kid, it's murder. Most of my things are upbeat, and I don't shake my tail like a lot of guys do. You've got to start thinking about David and Goliath, and I'm David. You got to think how to maneuver your way in. So I try to think of myself as a guy with long rubber arms that I reach around the audience and try to make them dance with me, swing with me.

If I'm following Millie Jackson, I try something that's going to draw attention from the audience. The guys, they don't want to see you at all, but the ladies might be a little relieved, but you still got to give them something that's going to take their mind off what just happened.

When I used to do the early rock shows, the original rock/soul shows, where the kids didn't know me or think much about me, you'd have people there that didn't want to be associated with the blues, I would do things like "Sweet Sixteen" because there was a line, "Treat me mean, but I'll keep loving you just the same." See, I was living that while I'm on the stage, "But one of these days you're going to give a lot of money just to hear somebody call my name." I used to belt it out, because that's the way I used to feel on stage sometimes, because kids back in the early 1960s, they'd boo me. They heard Mom and Dad talk about me. So, when they heard blues—these were black kids—they didn't want to be associated with that at all.

Black kids weren't exposed properly to blues. Blues never had the presentation of rock or soul music. I remember once when a guy introduced me in Chicago. I was on a show that mixed jazz and blues, Sarah Vaughan, Dizzy Gillespie, and some people in rock, Jackie Wilson, I believe. So the emcee got right to the point when introducing other people—"Ladies and gentlemen, here's Sarah Vaughan, the lady of jazz"—but when he got to me, he said, "Ladies and gentlemen, you can bring out your turnip greens and black-eyed peas and cornbread because here's B. B. King. You can bring your watermelon out and your chitlins." That didn't flatter me a bit, but I went on with one block that he had set in front of me. I thought, well, I'm already a blues player, and the way he made me sound is like being black twice. I went on and worked as hard as I could, and afterwards I went over to the emcee and said, "You know, I like chitlins and cornbread, and eat watermelon, but I know a lot of blues players that don't. So why do you have to introduce me like that? You didn't do it to the rest of them."

This is the way kids have been presented the blues, like it's something that be thrown away and that you shouldn't be associated with it. They take a "that was then" attitude. Well, if you're black, probably so was your grandfather and your grandmother. They're still a part of you. I've tried to change things through my music, but I can't do it singlehanded. You need a family.

A lot of blues purists don't really dig me. There's an argument there. You know, I'm almost in the jungle by myself because blues purists say I'm not playing true blues, and jazz don't really claim me, nor soul. So, I'm just there.

CALVIN OWENS

April 23, 1929–February 21, 2008; interview, 2004

CALVIN OWENS, AGE 15, HOUSTON.
PHOTOGRAPH BY A. C. TEAL. COURTESY CALVIN OWENS.

CALVIN OWENS, HOUSTON, EARLY 1960S.
PHOTOGRAPH BY BENNY JOSEPH. COURTESY CALVIN OWENS.

I was born at Jeff Davis Hospital. I grew up in the Fifth Ward, on the north side. My mother was from New Orleans. My father was from Texas. My mother's name was Blanche Ware. And my father's name was Sam Owens.

Well, my mother, she was like a cleaning lady, worked in restaurants, and my father, he worked for the Southern Pacific Railroad. The story [on how I started playing music] goes, a cousin of mine's parents bought a horn for him. And, you know, we were kids together, so naturally, I wanted a horn, too. And my reason for choosing the trumpet was my mother was from New Orleans and she used to tell me stories about Louis Armstrong. So I grew up hearing stories about Louis Armstrong, so when I decided I wanted to play music, trumpet was my choice of instrument. My mother would tell me stories about him [Louis Armstrong] playing in New Orleans during her times. She was a young teenager.

I was in the high school band. I worked at a bowling alley, and I bought my first horn myself because my mom wasn't able to buy an instrument for me. And it was nobody but just my mom and I. My mom was a single parent. And so, I always had little jobs and stuff, so I saved up enough money to buy my first horn.

I went to Phillis Wheatley High School. I graduated in 1949. I was playing professionally even before I got out of high school. I think after about three years, I was playing professionally, if not sooner than that.

I was thirteen years old when I got my first horn. In my very early gigs I played with cats like Amos Milburn. And my first-ever time being in a recording studio was with Lightnin' Hopkins. I couldn't have been more than about fourteen, fifteen years old at that time. I played trumpet for Lightnin' Hopkins. We did a recording session. I don't know what ever happened to it. Well, I don't really know what Lightnin' was like, because I was too young. But then, I knew Lightnin.' I never really knew him personally, but he used to hang in the neighborhood when I was a kid. He used to hang out in the Fifth Ward, out there on Lyons Avenue. I have no idea [where the recording session was]. The only thing

CALVIN OWENS, HOUSTON, CA. 1985. COURTESY CALVIN OWENS.

I can remember about that recording, the man bought three or four bottles of whiskey, and everybody got to drinking and talking, and after everybody got to feeling good, the cat say, "Okay, let's record something." And I wasn't drinking at that time. That's been an awful long time ago.

I played with Amos Milburn in a place in the area called Acres Homes. And they had a little band out there. And Amos Milburn was the piano player. As a matter of fact, they had two piano players, Amos Milburn and James Francis. And R. P. Wallace was on saxophone, and Luther Taylor, I think, played drums or something like that. It was really my very first nightclub gig. That's in the north part of Houston. Amos Milburn was a beautiful cat. We remained friends throughout the years. He was a great guy. We played a lot of dates.

When I was coming up, every Saturday, I would go on my shoeshine route. I was a shoeshine boy. And I'd go drop my overalls off at the cleaners, so they would be starched and ironed when I come back from making my money shining shoes. You know, go to a movie that evening. And this particular night, I came out of the movie, there was a little band in front of the club, in front of the theater. It was a little vaudeville band. Leonard Duncan and The Harlem Revue. The instrumentation was drums, tuba, and trombone. So I asked them if they needed a trumpet player, and they said yes. So the guy told me to go get my horn, and I went home and got my horn. I have no idea what I was playing at that time because I don't think I really knew. I was maybe about fifteen, fourteen, fifteen years old, something like that. I knew how to play Harry James's "Backbeat Boogie," trumpet solo. That was about the only thing I knew at that time. But that was not the kind of music that they were playing. They played in theaters. But before they would start the show, the band would play on the outside to draw people in. It was just mainly like dancing girls, comedians, and tap dancers, and that kind of a thing. And then after that, I went on and I went out with another group like that called The Brownskin Models.

The Brownskin Models was a show that had been very successful on Broadway, I think, in the mid or late Thirties or early Forties or somewhere back in those days. And so, after Broadway, they just toured around the country. And I happened to get with that group.

I was about nineteen, eighteen, nineteen years old. With Leonard Duncan, we played black theaters, but with The Brownskin Models, we went all over the country.

Later on, I played behind T-Bone Walker. We had a four-horn section and rhythm section, like trumpet, trombone, tenor, and baritone. And I think I even played with him with one of my smaller groups, which was just two horns, trumpet, and saxophone, and a rhythm section. Jim Wynn and Maxwell Davis were the only two saxophone players that I know of.

With T-Bone, the horns were just a background for the guitar. Then there was also different styles, you know, like the question and the answer [call and response between the guitar and the horns]. Sometimes it was the saxophones, and sometimes with the trumpet. I'd solo, and the saxophone might solo. T-Bone was a very nice, pleasant man, easy to work with.

CALVIN OWENS AT HOME, HOUSTON, 2007.
PHOTOGRAPH BY ALAN GOVENAR.

CALVIN OWENS, BRUSSELS, 1990s. COURTESY CALVIN OWENS.

I hooked up with B. B. King in 1953. Well, I knew him before then because they were being booked out of Buffalo Booking Agency. And there was that Texas and Memphis, Houston and Memphis connection thing. So they were in town, and I was playing at the Eldorado Ballroom with Pluma Davis. We were the house band up there, and that was my first really great professional band to play with. And so, you're in the best band in town, so, that meant that you're one of the better musicians, and you're playing at the best club, where everybody goes. So there was a relationship you struck up with the cats coming to hear the band and stuff. So when they needed a trumpet player, they called. That was the first time.

I played at the Eldorado from 1950 to '53. And I was A&R director for Don Robey out there [at Peacock Records, for a short period], and I did an awful lot of recording. I played a lot of sessions. Don Robey was a great man. And to me, he was nothing like most people say that he is. I think that he was a very great and a very fair person. He sure gave a lot of people a lot of work. He really did. When he closed the doors, that work was missed—I mean, really, really, really bad—because nobody else was recording.

I guess I kind of grew up with that [big band sound] because the kind of stuff that I record today, that's where it is. As a matter of fact, we're in the studio finishing up an album right now. I was [just] listening to the final mixes of my newest CD. Sawdust Alley Productions. I have my own independent label, Sawdust Alley Records. Sawdust Alley Productions has been around for about twenty years. Sawdust Alley Records has been around maybe about fifteen years. I think I only did one CD under that label. Didn't anything happen with it, really. But we got very serious about it about fifteen years ago. After I left B. B.'s band in '84, I moved to Europe

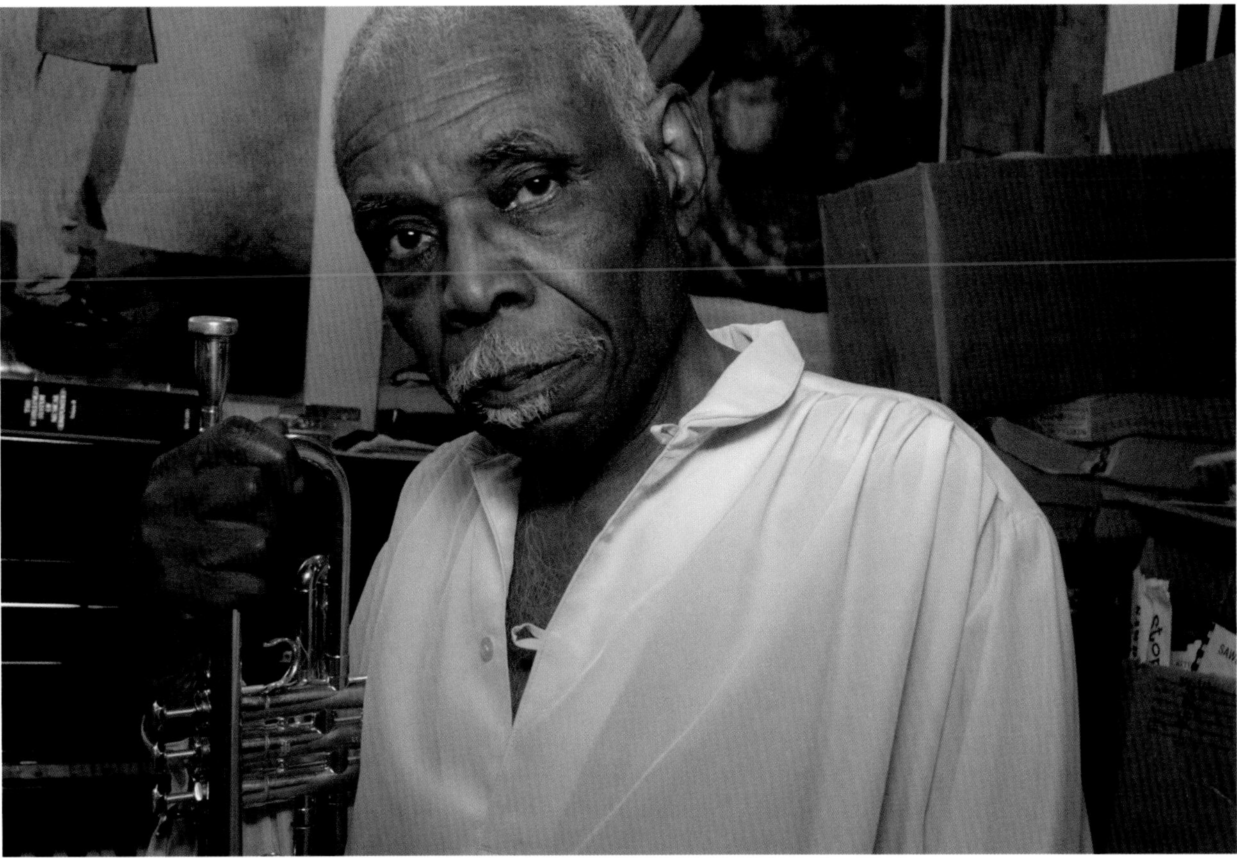

CALVIN OWENS AT HOME, HOUSTON, 2007. PHOTOGRAPH BY ALAN GOVENAR.

and put together an orchestra over there. I left B. B. in Brussels. I married a Belgian lady, and I moved to Belgium and lived there for about thirteen, fourteen years. And that's where I started working on my solo albums. Right now I think we got nine albums on the market.

Well, the first time I was with B. B., I was with him from '53 to '57. And then I went back to work with him in '78 until '84. When I left him the first time, I came back to Houston, went back to school for a little while. I got married, had to get a job, worked at Maxwell House Coffee Company for thirteen years. And woke up one morning and said I had enough of that. Of course, I had a recording contract and a producer's contract with the company that had licensed my very first 45. I think that was in 1969. My first 45 had the tunes "The Cat" and "Sawdust Alley." Two tunes. That was released in '69.

Well, when I started to work at Maxwell House, I was just working on the assembly line. And when I left Maxwell House, I was working in quality control. I was a quality control technician. But I went back with B. B.—oh, man, that's when I realized that I really had something going—because when I went back to work with B.B., it was to put a new band together for him. And I did that. And I had fifteen minutes to open the show every night. And I didn't play anything but original charts of my own, and people responded to them, really. Then I realized that I might have a little something going, so I started really dreaming then.

I use a full orchestra, even now. I have an eighteen-piece orchestra. When I record, it's with the eighteen-piece orchestra, plus strings. I'm trying to keep big band blues alive. Last year, I was nominated for the best blues horn player on the W. C. Handy Awards. I didn't win it, but I did get a nomination for it.

Every day I do some kind of writing. I'm also in school, studying composition at the community college here in Houston, out at the Town and Country campus. I get up early every day, and I get my practice in for the day. Might start writing in the morning, but my best time for writing is at night when everything is quietened down and the telephone is not ringing all over the place. You know, the activity of the day. After the activity of the day is over is my best time. It's something that you have to do every day, on a daily basis. And to have an eighteen-piece orchestra is always something to write, always. I had been writing all the charts up until this last album. Actually, the album before. But I've brought in other composers and arrangers, and I think the album's going to be—I mean, I know it's a great album. It's really a great album. It's called *The Calvin Owens Show.* Gloria Edwards is a vocalist in my band. My guitarist is Charles Davis. Charles Davis, and then another cat is doing some guitar fills. His name is Bert Wills. They're both white.

Blues is just good music, man. You know, I don't like the sad blues. It's just an emotion. When I write, I just don't sit down, just write anything. I try to put as much emotion and feeling into what I do. I don't know the difference from Texas blues and Mississippi blues myself. I really don't, man. I'm so involved. I grew up in the era with big band blues, and big bands used to come to town all the time, and they played blues, jazz, all kinds of stuff. So that's where my ears are, and that's where they've been all of my life: big band blues. And I try to make every tune that I write, you know, like every band, they have a tune that they showcase every night, right? So when I do my CDs, I try to do the CD with every tune on it, the tune of the night.

Musically speaking, my biggest influence was people like Duke Ellington and Count Basie and bands like Lucky Millinder, Erskine Hawkins, and, of course, like Dizzy Gillespie and Miles Davis. Blues musicians—well, those are my favorite people. Of course, I love B. B. King because we kind of grew up musically and I like the way that he plays.

What's happening today [matters to me now] and what you're going [to make] happen tomorrow. I'm a very big dreamer. And I'm an extremely hard worker. I've never worked this hard in my life, but I'm being driven. Trying to be better. Always learning. That's why I'm in school now. You've got to have that spark. You've got to have it, baby. You've got to have it. If you don't, you'll die.

HARRISON D. NELSON ("PEPPERMINT HARRIS")

July 17, 1925–March 19, 1999; interview, 1987

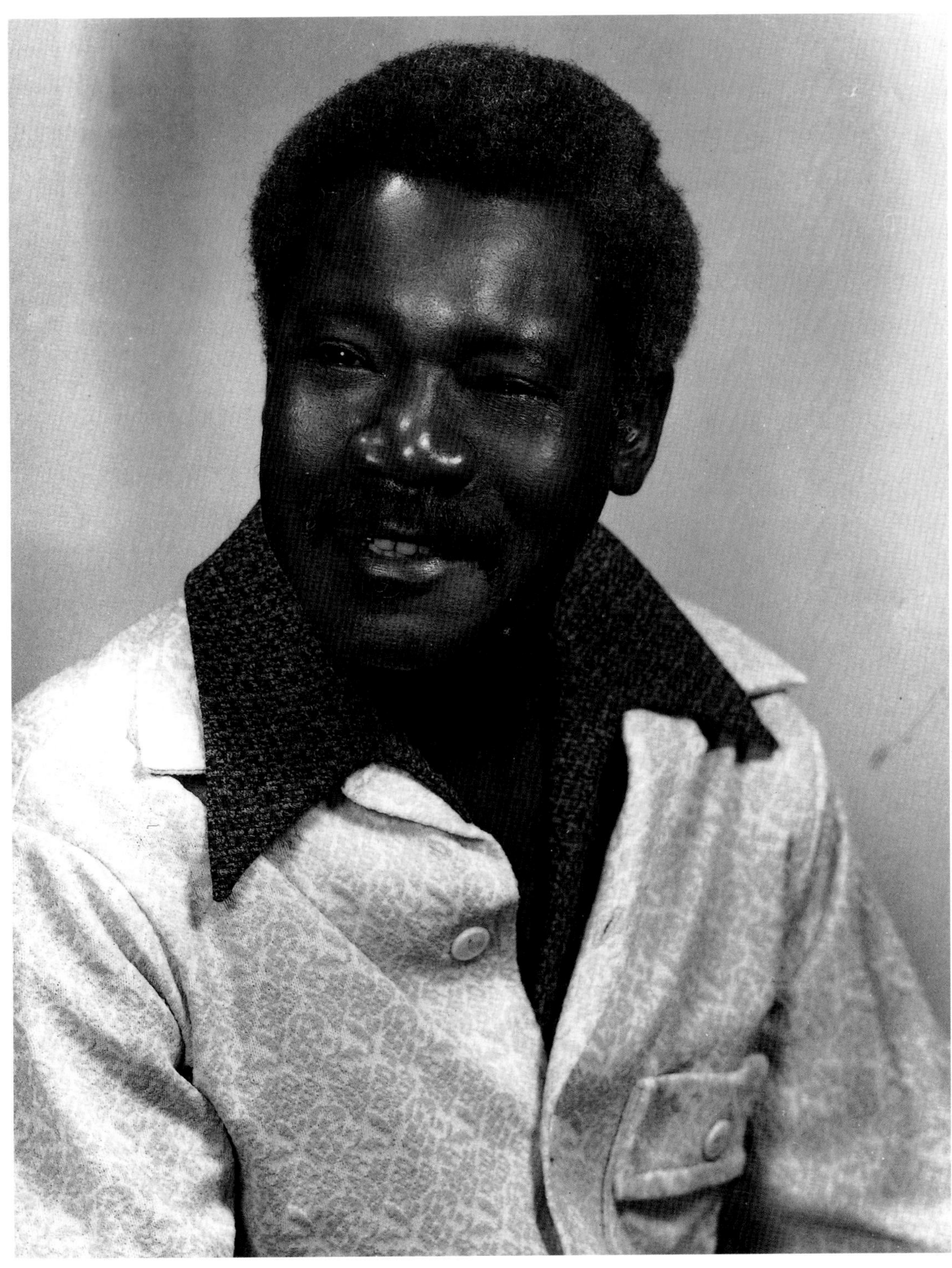

PEPPERMINT HARRIS, HOUSTON, 1960s. PHOTOGRAPH BY BENNY JOSEPH.

PEPPERMINT HARRIS, "RAINING IN MY HEART", SITTIN' IN WITH 2034.

I'm originally from Texarkana [Texas], and I've been playing blues professionally since 1947. "Peppermint" is just a moniker I made up. Everyone had one, so I got one, too. When I started, I wasn't doing this professionally. I just liked it. I went around with guys that played, and one night I went with some friends of mine to a studio. I was just going as a spectator, and that was when there was the [musicians' union] recording ban [1942–44]. So nobody was recording anything. There was a lot of bootlegging going on in Houston. As a matter of fact, there was only one studio, and I just went out there to fool around, and they asked me if I wanted to make a record. I had played a few gigs around town at the old Eldorado [Ballroom] and it seemed to me that it was just something to do.

I got the name Harris from the Sittin' In With label. They brought several of us in for an audition, and I was the last one they recorded. And when they edited the tapes, they found out I had the best songs, and they made it into a record. They knew they called me Peppermint, but they didn't know the last name. The confusion was because my first name was Harrison. So they just called me Peppermint Harris, and they released the record, and the name stayed with me.

I had bought my first guitar overseas. I was nineteen years old and I bought it from some guy aboard a ship in the South Pacific. I'm fifty-nine now, and I've lived in Houston off and on since 1943.

When I started playing the blues, the blues was as big as rock 'n' roll is today, maybe not as big, but it was the predominant music from the early 1940s on up to the late 1950s. Louis Jordan was the one who started the thing with small groups. Before then there were mostly big bands. Then there was Johnny Moore and The Three Blazers. But compared to today, the blues is basically the same, the same patterns, but the beat has changed to keep up with the times. The tempo is different. They might try to change the songs, but they keep the basic pattern. Look what the Rolling Stones did to Tampa Red songs, and what Elvis Presley did to Big Boy Crudup. They didn't change that much with rock 'n' roll. The people are different, but it was a continuation of the basic chords.

The blues is very complicated. You have the Mississippi blues, and they play quite a bit differently than people in Texas. It's a different sound. Take people like

T-Bone Walker, Lonnie Johnson, or Lightnin' Hopkins, Smokey Hogg. They are significantly different from B. B. King, Muddy Waters, Elmore James. They use the sliding effect. Elmore James put a cylinder on his finger, but B. B. King says he couldn't handle the cylinder. So he developed a style with his tremolo. Well, Texas bluesmen very seldom use that kind of sound. You can hear the whining in the guitars of people from the Delta. Even the Louisiana blues is different. The Texas bluesmen tend to pick more. They don't use as much tremolo. It's a subtle difference.

It's hard to compare T-Bone, because basically, he was a jazz guitarist. Like Charlie Christian, he brought the guitar to a different plateau than where it had previously been. At first, people only played rhythm guitar in bands. T-Bone, you might say, had a revelation, and he had a great impact on blues guitar and singing. He made the guitar into a lead instrument.

Every blues that I recorded I wrote myself, except for a couple of classic blues, like "Key to the Highway." I've done very few tunes that I didn't write myself, but everybody wants the blues singer to do some tunes by other people, like "Backwater Blues" and "Going Down Slow."

I don't write just blues. I write lyrics, and by the time they get to the arranger, there are a lot of changes made. There's a song now that Buddy Ace is doing called "Check It Out." The way I wrote it was a traditional blues, with basic changes, but Joe Hughes has changed to something else than I originally intended. That's the peculiar thing about the blues because it can easily be changed to fit another pattern. The form is changed, but the lyrics usually stays the same. [*Sings:*] "I kicked the habit of being a fool for you. I kicked the habit of being a fool for you. I was so hooked on you, baby that I don't care what you do." That's something that I wrote that Buddy Ace is doing on a new album, but you probably wouldn't recognize it. Buddy Ace is in Oakland, and the sound there gets more into urban blues. There's a different interpretation. There are a lot of Texans out there. They're the ones that brought the blues to California when they migrated there, while the people from Georgia, Mississippi, and the East Coast, they go to New York and Chicago. I think that probably the biggest blues place today is in Chicago because a lot of different singers have gone there, Jimmy Reed, Muddy Waters, Elmore James, John Lee Hooker, but there you have a melting pot of the blues and you hear all of them. But in California, you hear more of a Texas big band–influenced sound.

Several blues are improvised. My friend Percy Mayfield wrote songs on his way to the studio. A lot of times I'll be singing a song and there are so many different lyrics that will fit the music. I have forgotten lyrics, but because of the pattern of the music, I can always make something. Most of the records I made with Aladdin records were with jazz musicians, but they could play my blues. I've written maybe a thousand different tunes and recorded for more than fifteen different labels, between 1947 and 1984, and there hasn't been a year gone by that I didn't work with somebody. You can just imagine how many records that might involve, but in fact, I can't remember half the records I've done.

What I like best about the blues is the feeling. I compare it to country music, because probably just about every country record you hear can be applied to everyday life, what really happens. I think the blues is like a reporter. You're not making up anything when you write blues songs. You're writing about what you're doing. You're writing about society, and you're singing about the truth. It's nothing that you dream up. It fits any situation in a person's life. It's like when I was a kid, and I was seventeen years old, in Wichita, Kansas, alone, when I started singing, "Please write my mama and tell her what shape I'm in." That was the song "Going Down Slow." It hit me right away because this was happening to me. I have written songs about just about everything that happens in life, or relationships between man and woman, hard times, good times. The word *the blues* is just a label, but everything goes into it. I don't know where it ends. I pick up the guitar and start singing. The biggest song I ever had was "I Got Loaded," and I never intended it to be a song. There was a stigma on marijuana, so I changed it to a drinking song because drinking is more permissible, but the story is the same. In the early 1940s and 1950s they wouldn't let you record suggestive songs, but times have changed now. People say anything now.

LESTER WILLIAMS

June 24, 1920–November 13, 1990; interview, 1987

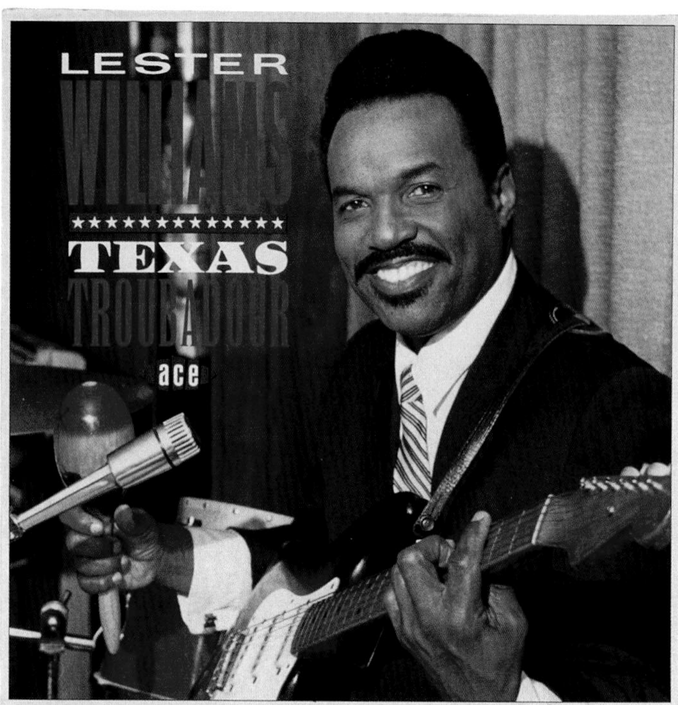

LESTER WILLIAMS, *TEXAS TROUBADOUR*, ACE 202.

I've been singing all my life, elementary school, high school, college, church choirs. I was born in Groveton, Texas, in 1920. As a boy we moved to Houston, and I remember hearing those records by Blind Lemon Jefferson and Lonnie Johnson.

After the war, I heard T-Bone Walker and liked that guitar sound. His phrasing and voicing was fantastic. He was my inspiration. I said to myself, "I could learn how to play guitar and pull in some of that money that T-Bone made." I had been singing with Ike Smalley's band at the Eldorado Ballroom, and I quit. I applied to the New England Conservatory of Music in Boston, and I went up there. Blues guitar was not in vogue, so I studied piano and voice. Then when I came back to Houston, I got myself a guitar and studied diligently for six or seven months. I had these songs in my head, and I made a couple of tapes of "Winter Time Blues." Before long I cut it as a record with a band I put together, and it took off. That was in 1949 on the Macy's label, produced by Steve Poncio. All of a sudden everyone wanted to hear Lester Williams play blues. Later, in the early 1950s, I went to Art Rupe's Specialty label, where I cut "I Can't Lose With The Stuff I Use," "Trying to Forget," "Lost Gal," and "If You Knew How Much I Love You."

It was my interest at that time to prove that a blues musician could have academic training and didn't have to be someone sitting on a stump. I didn't graduate from the New England Conservatory, but I did get my fundamental training there. And when I got home to Houston, I worked on my guitar and applied those principles. I started playing at Don Robey's Bronze Peacock. And I later cut a session for Robey on the Duke label in 1954, "Let's Do It" and "Crazy 'Bout You Baby." But I never did sign a contract with him, though his [Buffalo Booking] agency got me several different touring dates.

For me the blues is a way of telling a beautiful, lifelike story. It's like country music, about what someone has lived and knew. When I wrote "Winter Time Blues," my wife and daughter had gone to Los Angeles for the summer and I was going to Texas Southern University. Fall was coming, and the house became so lonely. I wrote asking her to come home, and this thought came into my head, "I'm walking down a track, winter time is coming and my baby has gone away. Ain't nobody's told me, but I believe she's gone to stay. I sure do get lonesome here by myself, but I guess I'll have to take it, can't use nobody else." I was a family man, and those were true lyrics. The neighbors were talking. "They don't think I can make it. That's what the neighbors said. Winter without your baby, you might as well be dead."

Blues can be just as sophisticated as any other form of music. I'm kind of an oddball entertainer. I don't drink or smoke. I don't fool with dope. I love my family, my wife, children, grandchildren. I'm a different kind of blues singer.

WILLIE MAE "BIG MAMA" THORNTON

December 11, 1926–July 25, 1984

Originally from Montgomery, Alabama, Willie Mae Thornton came to Houston in 1948 on a long southern tour as part of The Hot Harlem Revue. She liked the city so well that she decided to stay and try to further her career. A self-taught musician who sang and played drums and harmonica, she had already developed her own style by the time she arrived in Houston. In a short time, she got a job in Joe Fritz's band and was discovered at the Eldorado Ballroom by Don Robey, who signed her to a five-year exclusive contract and booked her into his club, the Bronze Peacock.

In early 1951 Robey took Thornton into ACA Studio with Joe Scott's band to produce her first records, "Mischievous Boogie" and "Partnership Blues." These were followed by "Let Your Tears Fall, Baby," which became successful enough that Robey had Evelyn Johnson book her on the road with B. B. King and Bill Harvey.

Johnny Otis, on tour in 1952 with his band in Houston, negotiated a contract with Robey under which Otis would record his band and vocalists in Los Angeles and send the masters to Houston for pressing on Robey's Peacock label. Thornton was included in the deal as a vocalist. Later that year, she recorded eight sides with the Johnny Otis band, including "Rock A Bye Baby" and "Hound Dog," which Robey did not release until 1953.

With the chart success of "Hound Dog," Robey added Thornton to his blues package show that included Bobby Bland, Junior Parker, and Johnny Ace.

In 1954, after the death of Johnny Ace, Thornton joined Otis's band and toured with it until 1955, when she returned to Houston to reunite with Bill Harvey. She recorded three sides with him and his band, featuring guitarist Roy Gaines.

In 1956, after her contract with Robey expired, Thornton left on a West Coast tour with Gatemouth Brown. She eventually settled in the San Francisco Bay area. In the 1960s she relocated to Los Angeles, where she recorded for several labels, including Sotoplay, Kent, Movin, Speed, and Galaxy.

WILLIE MAE "BIG MAMA" THORNTON, AUSTIN, 1969.
PHOTOGRAPH BY BURTON WILSON.

Horst Lippmann invited Thornton to appear with the American Folk Blues Festival in 1965 on a tour throughout Europe. In England, Chris Strachwitz of Arhoolie Records produced an album, *Big Mama in Europe,* that presented Willie Mae Thornton with Chicago musicians Buddy Guy, Walter Horton, and Freddy Below.

In the late 1960s and 1970s, Thornton appeared often at blues festivals and concerts, and released albums on Mercury, Pentagram, Buddah, Vanguard, and Crazy Cajun. Because of illness and heavy drinking, she dropped from 350 "Big Mama" pounds to a skeletal 95 pounds. She died embittered at not receiving the popular and financial success she deserved. The covers of her songs, most notably "Hound Dog" by Elvis Presley and "Ball and Chain" by Janis Joplin, were never as good as the originals but always outsold them: Willie Mae Thornton's versions of "Hound Dog" and "Ball and Chain" sold thousands, while Presley's and Joplin's versions sold millions.

JOHNNY BROWN

February 22, 1928–   ; interview, 1987

My father was a musician. He was a blues player; his name was Clarence Brown. He played the ol' natural blues—say, like the Lightnin' Hopkins type country blues—though he did play that bottleneck style. I tried it in my early years. To be honest with you, I don't play it anymore, but it wouldn't be a problem for me to play. It's a certain way you tune your guitar. You tune it in the key of E natural, and that leaves it open. Say, you take a person that doesn't know the guitar that well, they use what you call a clamp [capo]. They can move that clamp up and down the board, just like positions, and still get that same thing goin' on.

My name is John Reilly Brown; my professional name is Johnny Brown. I was born in Choctaw County, Mississippi. My father was blind, and we traveled around a lot. I was very young then. He worked at the railroad before he lost his sight, and [they gave] him this pass where he could travel around on the railroad for either half price or no ticket. My father was shot with buckshot, and then we traveled from place to place. I was playin' guitar and tambourine. We played little clubs; sometimes we played street corners. He never did any recording.

Let me tell you a little story. Okay? We used to play these things around Natchez, Mississippi, what they'd call the Pilgrimage Fair. They have these old Colonial homes; this is in the first part of the year, like April, May, and we used to play around those different homes for the tourists coming around. We'd play on the street and collect that money. And one time there was a producer from Hollywood that came there. This is a true story. My father had a dog that played guitar. Really, he would hold the guitar on his knee and he'd make the chords, and the dog would sit down and paw the strings with his paws. My father had a couple of little tunes he would sing, and the dog would paw the strings. So this producer came by and saw this. It was in the early Forties, and we got a letter from him to come to Charlottesville, Virginia. They were shootin' a movie and we had a little short in the movie, *Virginia*, with Sterling Hayden, Madeline Carroll, and, I think, Marie Wilson.

In 1946 I moved to Houston with my father. It was there that I met up with Amos Milburn and The Chickenshackers. I toured with them for a while and then went into the service, the army, from 1950 until 1953. Then I went back with Amos. Amos was gay, but easy to get along with. He recorded "Chickenshack Boogie," "Took a Long Time, Baby," "Operation Blues," "Two Steps from the Blues."

During the late Fifties I started working with Peacock Records and the Buffalo Booking Agency. I went on the road with Bobby Bland and Junior Parker during the years of "Wishing Well," "Further On Up the Road," "Cry, Cry, Cry."

I recorded with Peacock during 1959. Most of the recordings I did with Peacock were with Bobby Bland, Junior Parker, and for myself. I did [wrote] some tunes, "Two Steps from the Blues," "What Can I Do," "Screaming Please," "Suspense," "Snake Hips," "Red Pepper in Pie" [with Don Wilkerson]. Some of them weren't released.

I worked as a session musician just about every day, from 1959 through part of the Sixties. And during the time I [was] working in the studio, I was also traveling at the same time, mostly with Bobby Bland, Junior Parker, Buddy Ace, Joe Hinton. They had a package. We'd travel, then come back in and record, and then go back out. I played lead guitar.

Workin' with Don Robey I can't say was all good, but I can't say it was all bad. We did some good sessions. But as far as the touring part, it was an existence, but there was no big money in it. That was one of the problems. He was hard-nosed, but he was fair in his way. But he

AMOS MILBURN, "CHRISTMAS (COMES BUT ONCE A YEAR)," KING 45-K4913.

(OPPOSITE) JOHNNY BROWN, HOUSTON, 1960S. PHOTOGRAPH BY BENNY JOSEPH.

was a hard man to get that money from. As far as the studio part, he wasn't really in the sessions that much. He had this A&R man, Joe Scott, and to me he was a beautiful person to work with.

Robey had a certain sound that he wanted from particular people. Say, for instance, Bobby, Junior Parker, he had a particular sound he wanted from them, but I think more, he was just trying to get a good record out. Bobby was his most successful artist. Then Junior Parker. I played on "Look on Yonder Wall," "Annie Get Your Yo-Yo," and "Next Time You See Me." Clarence Hollimon worked on that, too.

Well, I came back to Houston in '63 off a tour, and decided to leave Peacock. I just played local and started working a day job; the first was for a delivery service, working for a uniform company. Did that for about three years, and then I became a shipping/receiving clerk for Memorial Baptist Hospital for about five years. Then I left that and was self-employed for a while, had a dump truck. Now, I work for MKI as a forklift operator. I still play. I got a four-piece band, guitar, keyboards, bass, and drums. I'm playin' the blues, doing some writing, too. But I haven't done any recording since the 1960s.

Charlie Christian was a big influence on my guitar playing. I never met him, but I remember his playing. This goes back to the time of my father, and there was a little cafe that had those records on the jukebox. But I like a variety of music. I play the basic sound I've always played. I do a little jazz, blues, C&W; we do it all. But the blues always kicks it off. What you call the real gut, man, straight-out gut. We do "Every Day I Have the Blues," some of Lowell Fulson's tunes like "So Long," and maybe "Next Time You See Me," "Look on Yonder Wall." I do Bobby's songs, but I don't do the vocalizing.

Now, I'm doing the things I've wanted to do, that I've always wanted to do with my instrument. The guitar that I'm playing now has these attachments, modules that you can plug in to get different sounds. But it still has the natural tone.

GOREE CARTER

December 31, 1930–December 29, 1990 ; interview, 1984

GOREE CARTER'S HOUSE, HOUSTON, 1984. PHOTOGRAPH BY ALAN GOVENAR.

GOREE CARTER AND JOE HUGHES, HOUSTON, 1984. PHOTOGRAPH BY ALAN GOVENAR.

I'm from Houston, the Fifth Ward area, 1310 Bayou. I've been playing the blues since about twelve years of age. I had a cousin that was going to California, and his daughter used to play guitar. He left his guitar with me. So I started pickin' on it. I couldn't get no help with it because there weren't too many guitarists around during that period of time.

I had a wind-up Victrola that I used to take out in the park. There were certain artists that I liked, and I'd listen to their music and I'd try to pick string by string. This is how I learnt because I had no teacher and no one to show me. So I would get along and play. Finally, I learned a few chords, listening. Then I went and bought a book, a chord book, and I started finding my chords from there. This is the only thing I had to go by.

I'm fifty-four now. Let the public be the judge. I can't judge myself because the public is the one who make you. The blues is a feeling that you have within yourself and other people. You see other people and you see yourself, too.

I figure it this way, every town has the blues, and I couldn't say whether California has its own blues, or Washington, whatever, New York. The blues is within a person and the life that you live, the things that you go through with. That goes with the richest or the poor.

Most of my records were my own songs. "Rock a While" was probably my most well-known piece, but I could call a lot of songs. I had one song that was even written for me, Johnny Copeland's "Working with My Baby." Most of my songs I wrote myself. Then I had a lot that I just tore up, and they were good songs. I tore them up because they wouldn't let me cut them. They said I was ahead of myself. So I destroyed them. If I can't perform them, then I'll do like Moses did with the Ten Commandments. Can't live by it, die by it.

I had to do what they tell me to do. I was young, didn't know anything about going out in the world. I had always just stayed at home. So I got to the studio and I had to do what they tell me to do. I don't have anything to go by anymore but what I feel. I sit there and sing. I

NATHANIEL "POPS" OVERSTREET, HOUSTON, 1985.
PHOTOGRAPH BY ALAN GOVENAR.

talk with people. They tell me their problems, and then I put mine in with it. And this is the blues, because as long you live, you're going to have a problem. So I listen to other people and I see people. I see myself in them. Some people are doing worse than myself. That helps me because a lot of times when you think you're really down, you're not. You look around you, there's always someone doing worse.

The blues is experience. What you know, you try to get out of, you know, if you're down, if you're in a hole and you want to crawl out of it. And once you get out, you want to stay out of it. Okay? So the blues comes from a person that had it hard, have lived this, plus he meets people that have the same problem. You see, you never walk alone with anything. It doesn't matter if you're rich or poor. Whatever life you live, there's always someone with you, and this is the music. You have all different fields of music, ballads or whatever you want to call it, or symphonic sounds or rock, but it all adds up in a way, speaking to the same thing. It's all about the world. Music is just life. Without music, I don't think the world would make it.

It's a biblical thing. The blues is a task in life, I mean, hard living. That's why the bluesman never died, because there was a foundation. It comes from hardship.

ALBERT COLLINS

October 1, 1932–November 24, 1993; interview, 1987

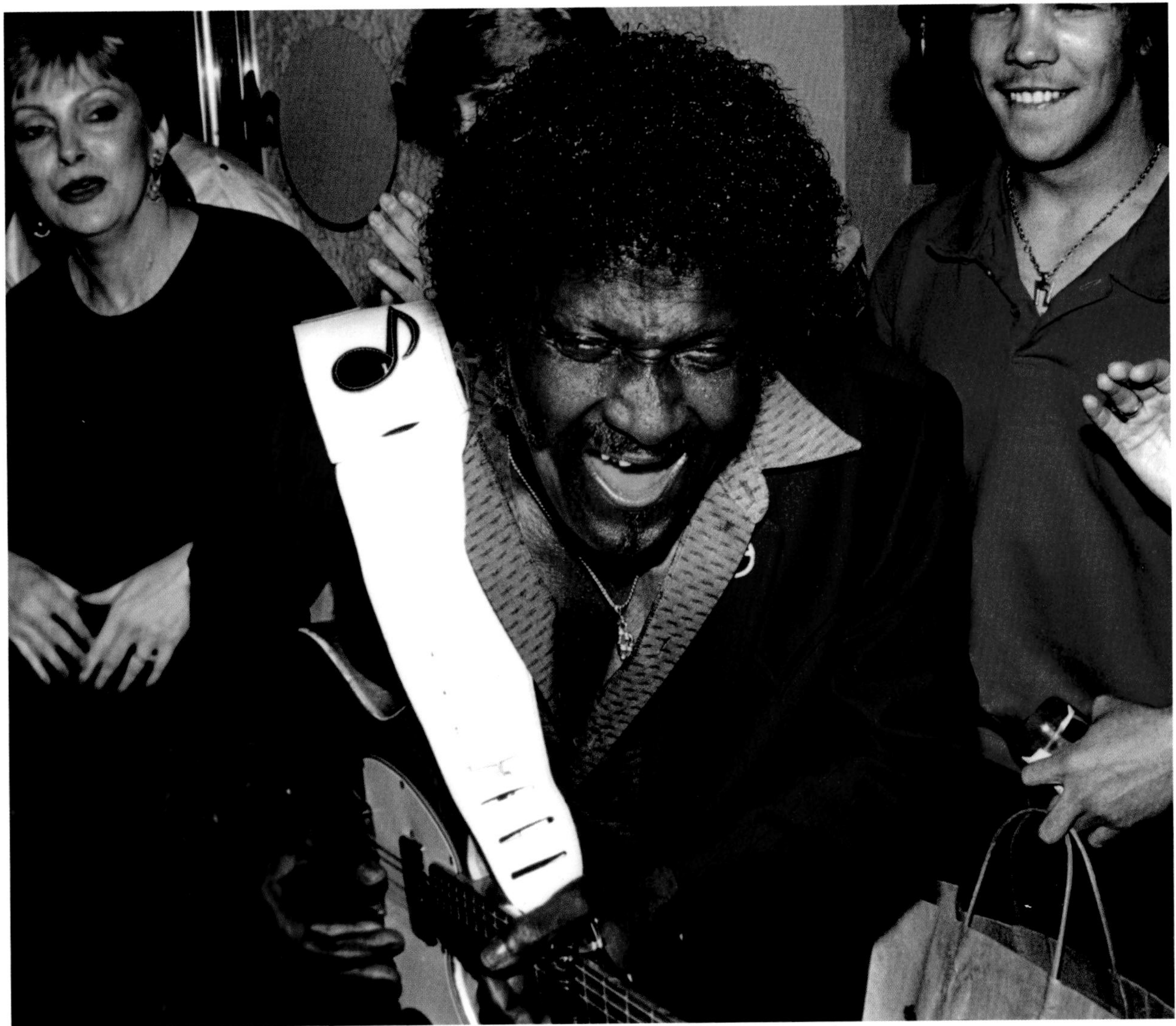

ALBERT COLLINS'S GUITAR WALK AT THE HARD ROCK CAFÉ, DALLAS, 1987. PHOTOGRAPH BY ALAN GOVENAR.

Spring 1987: The blues is the bus getting a flat tire on the way to Dallas outside Waxahachie, swinging through Texas in ten days with dates in Houston, Austin, San Antonio, Fort Worth, and Dallas. The bus is running hard, belching smoke. Albert Collins, 1987 Grammy Award winner, drives this bus with an understated determination. At age fifty-four he is going strong, but there are still obstacles, the most immediate of which is the flat tire. His sister, Marie, lives in Fort Worth, and

ALBERT COLLINS, HOUSTON, EARLY 1960S.
PHOTOGRAPH BY BENNY JOSEPH.

he knows he can take care of his engine problems there. It's getting to Dallas that's on his mind now, to the Hard Rock Cafe. He played the Hard Rock New York last year, and he's hoping to get dates soon at other locations in the burgeoning Hard Rock chain.

The sky brightens, and they find a mechanic who loves the blues. They get to Dallas early. In the parking lot off McKinney Avenue Albert begins to wind down. "The blues have never been better," he says with a calmness that belies the pressures of the day. He looks out the open door of the bus and nods. The lines in his face are drawn tight, but he seems to smile without showing his teeth as the crowd overflows from the Hard Rock steps onto the sidewalk.

"Today they know what they're listening to. They understand the music," Albert Collins says, "In the 1960s when white kids first started hearing blues, they didn't really know what it was. It sounded like rock 'n' roll but it wasn't. It took them awhile to figure out that blues is the root."

Inside the Hard Rock Dallas the memories of the past are everywhere. Vintage electric guitars line the domed ceiling of this self-proclaimed "Supreme Court of Rock 'n' Roll." Photographs of Jimi Hendrix, Mick Jagger, Buddy Holly, and more stars than you could ever count are mounted in gilded frames. A backlit glow emanates from a stained-glass portrait of Elvis Presley at the rear of the stage. Hard Rock Dallas is completely self-conscious, a shrine to popular culture since the advent of the electric guitar.

A man who says his name is Brick sits next to Albert Collins on the bus and laughs loudly, remembering his first meeting with Albert in the mid-1970s in Austin, in the days when Stevie Ray Vaughan, Jimmie Vaughan, and The Fabulous Thunderbirds were starting out.

A friend of Brick's comes onto the bus, and Brick keeps talking about the greatness of Albert Collins. They are interrupted by the unexpected arrival of Albert's nieces, Charlene and Darlene, who are the daughters of his sister in Fort Worth. Charlene and Darlene are twins, twenty-eight years old and bubbling with exuberance. Albert hasn't seen them for more than two years and his gestures are excited, though he doesn't say much. Darlene, who works as a kindergarten teacher, can't stop talking. Charlene is quiet and squeezes herself into a seat next to Brick with a smirk on her face.

A waitress comes to the door of the bus and asks if anyone wants a drink. Everyone orders a beer, except for Albert, who requests a tomato juice with lime. He stopped drinking four years ago, and says that he feels better than ever.

With Albert Collins's death in 1993, Texas blues lost one of its most prodigious performers. Collins wrung a unique tone from his Fender Telecaster. He played with his bare fingers, usually tuned the guitar to an F minor chord and used a capo to change keys. "I got the idea for the cap from Gatemouth Brown," Collins recalled. "I started without one, but I looked at Gatemouth and said, 'Man, you're using that choker.' We used to call it a choker. Now I can't play without one."

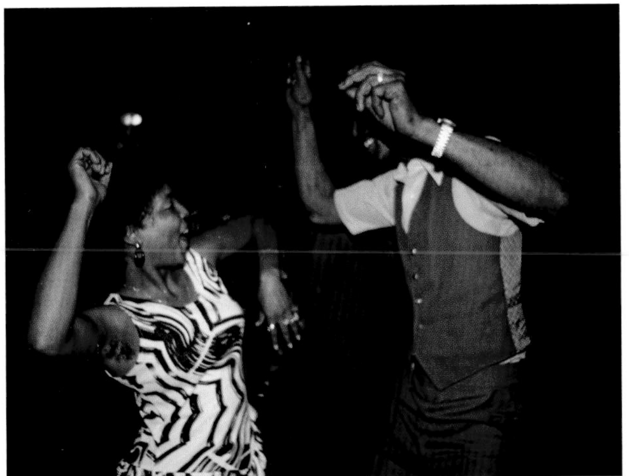

DANCERS, HOUSTON 1986. PHOTOGRAPH BY ALAN GOVENAR.

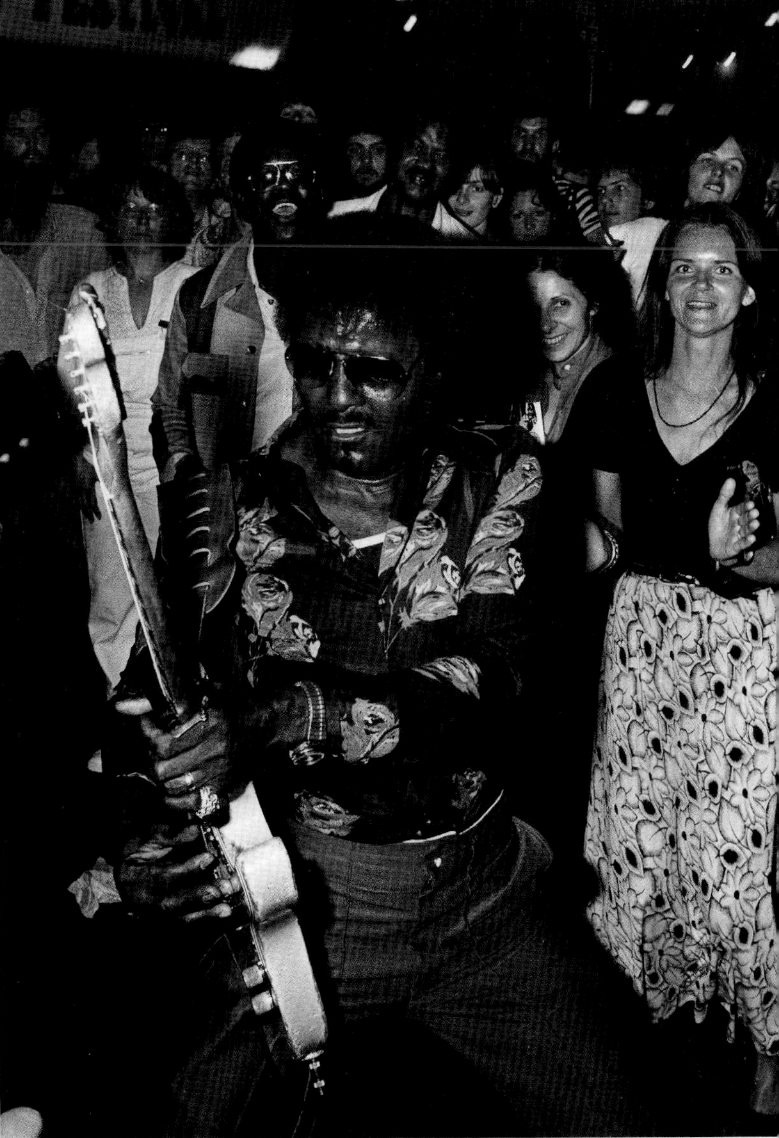

ALBERT COLLINS, STOCKHOLM, 1979.
PHOTOGRAPH BY ERIK LINDAHL. COURTESY TOMMY LÖFGREN.

Collins electrified audiences across the United States and abroad with his stinging guitar sound, often strutting with a fierce intensity through the crowd while continuing to play. His 1979 Alligator recording "Ice Pickin'" won the best blues album award from the Montreux Jazz Festival and was nominated for a Grammy. He won a W. C. Handy Award for best blues album for his 1983 recording *Don't Lose Your Cool* and shared Handy and Grammy awards with Robert Cray and Johnny Copeland for their 1985 collaboration *Showdown!* He even made a cameo appearance in the 1987 film *Adventures in Babysitting.*

Collins liked to credit the amp that he used as a major factor in making him unique. "I've been using a 100-watt Quad Reverb. I always put the volume all the way up on 10, treble on 10, middle on 10, and I don't use bass, intensity, or none of that. Reverb, I set at 4."

My mother was kin to all the Hopkins family. Lightnin' Hopkins is my cousin. When I was a kid, they had Saturday night fish fries out in the woods with kerosene lamps and lanterns. White folks used to think that when black people played that kind of music [blues], it was evil. I was born in Leona, Texas, about thirty miles out of Huntsville. It's twenty-three miles from Madisonville, Texas. But we didn't stay in Leona too long. I went to school there until I was about seven and then we left, went to another little town called Marquez, Texas. And when I was nine, we went to Houston, where I was raised up. I started playing guitar when I was twelve after hearing John Lee Hooker's "Boogie Chillen." The first guitar I had was acoustic, but soon after that I got an electric, an Epiphone. I played Epiphone all the way up to '52. That's when I got my first Fender.

I listened to T-Bone Walker, Guitar Slim—they were two of my favorites. Me and Johnny "Guitar" Watson and Johnny Copeland, we were raised up together in the Third Ward area. T-Bone was my favorite at that particular time, even before B. B., and there was

ALBERT COLLINS, NORTH SEA JAZZ FESTIVAL, THE HAGUE, 1974. PHOTOGRAPH BY ERIK LINDAHL. COURTESY TOMMY LÖFGREN.

ALBERT COLLINS' NIECE CHARLENE DANCING AT THE HARD ROCK CAFÉ, DALLAS 1987. PHOTOGRAPH BY ALAN GOVENAR.

Gatemouth Brown. I knew his family. Every little bit you hear helps.

I started playing the clubs in Houston in 1951, '52, signed with Buffalo Booking Agency, and Evelyn Johnson got me bookings around, though I never recorded for Peacock or Duke. My first group was Albert Collins and The Rhythm Rockers. The problem with Houston was that if you played a white club, the minute we got off the bandstand, we had to go to a little room, and we had to wait. Any time we wanted a drink, somebody would bring it in and give it to us. You couldn't leave that room. That was in the Fifties, early Sixties.

When we came along, I wanted to know about your race, you know, the other side. I wanted to express my feelings with somebody on how I felt, [to which the usual reaction was] "Okay, we know how you felt, boy. Hey man, he's black and we don't worry about that." What I'm saying, I'm talking about heart to heart, like we were trying to have a heart-to-heart talk. But you'd sit down and have argument to argument. This is something I always wanted. If I could just express it in my fingers, let them know how I feel.

I did my first recording of "The Freeze" in Houston with Henry Hayes. Henry Hayes was my teacher. He encouraged me to play. He played jazz, anything. He taught me a lot when other guys wouldn't help me. He taught me about timing. That's the reason I always had horn players when I started out. I had nine pieces. He taught me to listen to the big band sound.

There was a time I was into piano. I took piano lessons as a kid. I always liked piano. And I bought an organ one time, man, got ripped off when I was coming out of Port Arthur. I played down there a lot. I used to cut all of my records in Beaumont. It was Johnny Winter, Janis Joplin, we all hung out together for a long time. I was cuttin' for Big Bopper Enterprises. They named it after him after he got killed in the plane crash with Buddy Holly.

We cut a lot of stuff in Beaumont. Janis was with me when I cut "Frosty" in '62. She was just a kid. Janis didn't sing, she was just hangin' out. And I was with Johnny

Winter, when Edgar Winter was a little baby. Johnny was very young, about eighteen or nineteen or so. In 1980 Johnny and I did an album together at the New Morning Festival near Geneva, Switzerland.

I stayed in Houston until 1968, when I met up with Canned Heat. So they asked me about going to California. My first concert was at the Shrine Exposition in Los Angeles. They had me as a warm-up band. When I played the Fillmore West, Elvin Bishop helped me out with that. Buddy Miles, Elvin Bishop, B. B. King, we all did that show together. [Paul] Butterfield, Mike Bloomfield.

I did three albums with Empire. And then I went with Tumbleweed Records out of Denver, Colorado, in 1972. I figured I was on the track again, and all of a sudden they went out of business, so ABC-Dunhill picked my stuff up. Then I freelanced for four years, and a friend of mine, who I've known for several years, Dick Shurman, he introduced me to Alligator in 1978, and I've been with them since.

I really don't know what way my music's going to go now. The blues is really out here now, but I'm really afraid of what's going to happen. I just don't know. I've seen it happen, 1968, '69, '70, and first part of '72, it declined. See, what I'm trying to do now, I'm concentrating on music, but I'm studying to be in movies and to do commercials, trying to get something else to carry me along, just in case the blues get a little slow. I love playing. That's why I stopped drinking. I like my music so much that I get high off it.

Around 1953 I saw Jay McNeely, the saxophone player; he'd run out in the audience with his saxophone. So what I did, I said I can do this with the guitar, and I went out to Parker Music Company in Houston and said, "You all make me up a hundred-foot guitar cable." Everyone in the store looked at me and say this man has gone crazy. "What are you going to do with all this cord?" I say, "I'm going to play with it." So when I started doing that, it just caught on, and I've been doing it since. It makes the crowd feel closer to you. They have more fun.

I usually am out there ten months out of the year, but I have to get away from it for a little bit. I'm taking it a little easier. I'm getting a driver for my bus. But I like driving, I'm used to it. I used to drive a truck, done a lot of driving over the years, but you can't keep doing it.

Blues is my music. I don't want to get away from that. I just want to update my style. That's what we're talking about now, what to do with my next album. I used to listen to country music, jazz. There was a lot of jazz around Houston, Illinois Jacquet, Wynonie Harris. When I started out, my playing was different. I played without a capo. But after four or five years I met up with Gatemouth Brown, and that's what started me. Never did fool with a pick. When I started out, guitar wasn't supposed to be played with a pick. I don't know where

ALBERT COLLINS, HARD ROCK CAFÉ, DALLAS, 1982.
PHOTOGRAPH BY ALAN GOVENAR.

they got that from. I know they used thumb picks. Freddie King used to use a thumb pick. I could never use none of that. My fingers don't get sore until I'm off for a while, but it don't bother me. I pick with my thumb and first fingers, almost like playing a bass. I never did play many chords. I always wanted to be a lead player. I always had my own bands.

My style got the name of being something cold from a bass player who used to be with me, played upright bass. His name was [Donald] Cooks, out of Houston, and I played in Corpus Christi, Texas, one night, and we were on our way back to Houston and my windshield fogged up. He said, "Why don't you put your defrost on?" So I was just looking at the dashboard of the car, and later I cut me a tune called "Defrost." Down through the months, when I was cutting in Beaumont, they said, "Well, man, that will be your trademark. Just like something in the icebox." That's how I got the name, something cold, and in 1978 a bass player I had said, "Why don't you call the band The Icebreakers?" And that's what I did.

My wife writes a lot of my songs, Gwendolyn Collins. She wrote "Master Charge," "Conversation with Collins," "Give Me My Blues Song," "Lights On, Nobody Home," "I Got That Feeling." We collaborate pretty good. It's hard for an entertainer, traveling all the time; I don't have any kids. But my wife and I have been together for twenty-one years. I think that's a lot for an entertainer. When I first met my wife, she didn't listen to blues. She used to like that song "Tremble" on the other side of "Frosty." That's what got her into my kind of music. She's a nurse, but she's going into computers now.

My songs usually come to me just by listening to people, just going down the highway, something come across my mind. Sometimes, I just write it down on a piece of paper so I don't forget it. Then when I have time to relax and be at home, I'll finish a few words to it, and then she'll look at it. She might add a few words. That's how I did "Conversation with Collins." We were just sitting there talking. We got dressed and we were ready to go out, but we just sat there talking from nine in the evening until four o'clock in the morning. We didn't go anywhere.

See, a lot of people misinterpret that blues. They feel it's depressing music. It's kind of hard for some people to relate when you say blues. Some people don't want to hear it, but it's reality.

TEDDY REYNOLDS

1932–October 1, 1998; interview, 1987

I started to listen to people like Amos Milburn and Charles Brown. I loved their style of playing, and I just started playing by ear at first. Everybody said I sounded good. Then I had Joe Scott as a music teacher, and from there I started working in a studio for Mr. Don Robey. Joe Scott was the arranger, and he started teaching me chord structures and different things. I played behind a whole bunch of Peacock artists, Joe Hinton, Big Mama Thornton, Gatemouth Brown, all of them, but Joe Scott was the one that started me playing. I'm from Houston. I'm fifty-six, and I started working in the studio at sixteen, about 1948.

Don Robey was a wonderful man. He was good to the musicians. He loved us all. Once he wanted something done, he wanted it that way, and that was it. My close friend Joe Medwick, who wrote the songs for Bobby Bland, we'd get together. I'd be on piano, he'd come get me and say, "Hey, Teddy, I got some songs I want to put on tape. Let's go over to Mr. Robey." So we'd catch the bus and go over to Erastus and Lyons Avenue. Joe would hum the melody. He'd say, "Teddy, go like this here," and I'd sit at the piano and I'd play the melody along with him. and he would start putting the words to the song. From the arrangement he hummed to me, I took it on from there and put the songs on tape. Next time we hear them, it'd be Bobby Bland singing them, or Junior Parker.

The biggest sessions were Bobby's sessions. They were beautiful. That was the thrill of my life, to be able to put these patterns that Joe Scott had taught me behind Bobby Bland. Joe would put the sheet music, the chord structures, in front of me and tell me, "Teddy, put your own feeling into these chords." And I would play my own feeling, something from the heart. The blues is everything in my life, you know. By me having all these artists at my piano, I put all these styles together, and that's why I can change to any pattern you want. That's a gifted thing. You play the blues from your heart, you know that. I've been playing for more than forty years.

I went on the road with Bobby Bland, from 1957 to 1959. During that time we cut "Drivin' Wheel" and "Two Steps from the Blues," and "I Pity the Fool." Oh, there were so many during that time. Bobby was a very hot artist. Still is.

Mr. Robey had a package with Bobby Bland, Junior Parker, TNT Braggs, and Miss Eloise. One of the greatest shows you've ever seen. It was just beautiful, and the musicians were just great. Hamp Simmons on bass, Wayne Bennett on guitar, Joe Scott on trumpet, Pluma Davis on trombone, Melvin Jackson on trumpet. Jabo played drums, and I was on piano, and we had L. A. Hill, the boy who left home with me, on tenor. We had about three tenor players. We had such a big sound.

We'd all worked in the studio together; we'd been exposed to discipline. When you go into the studio, you have a creative mind. You create the lyrics like the singer is singing, and music is made to fit what he sings.

When an idea came to you, Don Robey would never get in the way, because he knew that when you'd straighten it out, it would fit those lyrics. Sometimes he'd look through the mirror in the studio, through the big glass mirror, and you'd see him with a big grin on his face. Yes, I know the old man was very satisfied. Joe [Scott] would get the musicians for the sound, that bunch of musicians for that sound. It would all blend in for the blues. Each musician played the blues, and though each might play it different ways, it was still the blues. Miss Evelyn Johnson was the producer, and we had Robert Evans, who played tenor and alto, and was also the engineer. But sometimes Joe [Scott] would engineer. He would tell the engineer what to bring up, what to bring down. He played trumpet, French horn, any brass. And he played a lot of piano, and that's where I got a lot of my knowledge at—Joe Scott.

We recorded records in the studio, and Mr. Robey pressed them in the back of the studio building. He had his own pressing company and everything. We just struck a groove, and whatever pattern fit what the artist was singing, we'd go on and cut. Next thing you know, the record was out there.

The only big thing I did live was with Bobby Bland and B. B. King together. That was a live thing in L. A. It was the first time Bobby and B. B. were together. I did the LP with them. I think it was in '72 or '73. That was great. I really loved that. James Brown and all of them were there at the session at Sunset Studios. It was live, and it was wonderful.

I also played with Gatemouth Brown, Nappy Brown, Percy Mayfield, Junior Parker. Junior liked to kid all the time, something like Johnny Ace. Junior played wonderful harmonica, and sang, man. I'll never forget when we did "Drivin' Wheel." It was a ball. Junior kidded with all the musicians, joked with them, tell them about their hair, and all different stuff. But he got serious when it got down to business.

We worked hard in the studio, but on weekends, we'd play in the clubs, Shady's Playhouse on Sampson and Simmons Street, Club Matinee. And people like Albert Collins, Johnny Copeland, they were youngsters, but they'd come around with their guitars. They didn't have electric guitars, and they'd come around and watch some of the professional guys and learn from them, and the other guitar players were glad to help them out. Now, today they're steppin' out with it.

ROY GAINES

August 12, 1937–   ; interview, 1989

ROY GAINES, NETHERLANDS, 1977.
PHOTOGRAPH BY SEM VAN GELDER.
COURTESY MARCEL VOS.

Roy Gaines was born in Waskom, Texas, and moved at age six with his family to Houston. He and his brother, the saxophonist Grady Gaines, grew up playing music. At an early age, Roy began playing piano in the style of Nat "King" Cole, but switched to guitar as a teenager, emulating the style of T-Bone Walker. In 1951, at the age of fourteen, he was asked to back up T-Bone on stage. He later moved to California to join Roy Milton's band.

During the heyday of Peacock Records in the 1950s and 1960s, Gaines worked often as a session musician and was featured on recordings by Big Mama Thornton, Junior Parker, and Bobby "Blue" Bland. In addition, he was invited to play sessions for Jimmy Rushing (1954), Coleman Hawkins (1957), and The Jazz Crusaders (1961).

In 1966 Gaines became part of Ray Charles's big band and while with that band wrote "No Use Cryin'" for Charles's hit album *Cryin' Time*. Over the years, he traveled frequently between Los Angeles and New York, where he worked with Chuck Willis. He also worked as a session musician and sideman with Aretha Franklin, Della Reese, Albert King, and T-Bone Walker. He toured Central and South America with The Supremes in 1976, and the United States with Diana Ross in 1977.

The Red Lightnin' label signed Gaines to record two solo albums in the early 1980s. His album *Gainelining* was critically acclaimed, but he did not record again until the 1990s, when he released *Lucille Work for Me* (1996), *Bluesman for Life* (1998), and *I Got the T-Bone Walker Blues* (1999). These recordings established Gaines as a master guitar stylist.

This is my dream. To have a symphony orchestra made of a blues rhythm section and a calypso rhythm section. And all these different forms of music I play with all these different rhythm sections to get the authentic sound. And of course, whenever I do an assignment, I come as authentic to it as I can, keeping my own part in it. I be as authentic to the music of whatever culture as I can. Otherwise I eat and sleep and live it for whatever period it takes to finish the assignment. But when I finish the assignment it's on paper, because I got my assignments wrote out. And all I have to do now is find the right financing or if I get lucky and I get into some money I'll bring in musicians and record my assignments. And hopefully find the right people that will take my assignments. And then with my classical background I could play some Bach, some nice things by Leadbelly, some folk things. I did that in Germany and it was really accepted because they didn't figure a blues singer could come out there and do Bach and Leadbelly at the same time. So I did Leadbelly, I opened the show, I did "Skip To My Lou," and I did song Bach did, not a song but Gavotte I and II, mixed together, 'cause they sound alike, and I was showin' them how if you're great, whatever you do is on the same level with whatever other greatness from another culture. Other words, cultures don't run from each other, they run to each other. I promised Bach when I was learning Bach that if I ever went to Germany, I would play some of his music, no matter what kind of tour I was on.

CLARENCE GREEN

1937–March 13, 1997 ; interview, 1987

CLARENCE GREEN, HOUSTON, 1960S. COURTESY CLARENCE GREEN.

My mother worked for a white lady who taught her how to play guitar. She always had a guitar around the house. My brother, Cal, and I—Cal was the guitar player for Hank Ballard and the Midnighters—but when we were little boys, we used to make guitars out of cigar boxes and little sticks stretched with screen wire that was on the frame of a window. And by my mother having the guitar around, we would slip in and pick it up. She finally let us have one with two or three strings on it, and we would bang, bang. My first guitar cost twelve dollars. It was a Stella. I started to strum on it in church, and it happened one night that I could play. Mama said, "Wait until we get home." And I picked up the guitar and showed her I could play. I was about ten years old. I've been playing ever since. I'm fifty-one; my brother is fifty. We're a year apart.

TEDDY REYNOLDS (PIANO) AND FRANK ROBINSON (DRUMS); CLARENCE GREEN RECORDING SESSION, HOUSTON, 1987. PHOTOGRAPH BY ALAN GOVENAR.

First I learned to play hillbilly. It was real popular. There weren't any black stations to hear much else. My mother worked for a disk jockey, and he found out that she had two sons that played guitar. We used to play church music on the radio. My brother broke away and went out first, and I came out after him. That's when we were swinging into the blues.

A young man found out that we lived over in Frenchtown [in Houston's Fifth Ward]. I was working at the Rice Hotel and decided to play an engagement at another place. We just had one guitar and a rub board. We called ourselves Blues for Two, and then we added drums and another guitar. We played big halls and clubs, different functions. But after a while we busted up. I kept playing and soon joined a group with Elmore Nixon and Dave Fisher at a club called the Silver Spur. And I left from there to play with Ted Taylor. He came through one night, and he needed a bass player. You know how sometimes guys get in bad shape and they want you to hold their instruments for a few dollars? He left his instrument with me, and I said, "I'm gonna take advantage of this." Most guitar players can play bass, and that's what I ended up doing with Ted Taylor. Later I formed my own band, The Cobras.

CAL GREEN WITH HIS ORCHESTRA. UNIVERSAL ATTRACTIONS, LOS ANGELES, 1960s. COURTESY CHARLIE LANGE.

I had the experience of working some with Chuck Berry. I went on the road with him and did a few engagements in Louisiana. And one night Fats Domino came in, and Mr. Berry's nephew, who was a guitar player, took sick, and I got to play on stage with Fats Domino. From artist to artist that I met, I got more knowledge about my box.

CLARENCE GREEN, HOUSTON, 1988. PHOTOGRAPH BY ALAN GOVENAR.

SITE OF THE AVALON GRILL, HOUSTON, 2007. PHOTOGRAPH BY ALAN GOVENAR.

MAXINE HOWARD, JUNETEENTH BLUES FESTIVAL, HOUSTON, 1987. PHOTOGRAPH BY ALAN GOVENAR.

JUNETEENTH BLUES FESTIVAL, HOUSTON 1987. PHOTOGRAPH BY ALAN GOVENAR.

In the early 1960s I worked with Don Robey, in the studio, more or less in the background. I was the rhythm guitar player on sessions behind Bobby "Blue" Bland, Little Junior Parker, Joe Hinton, and so many artists I can't remember. I had one record myself and had more in the hole that were never released. "Welfare Blues" was one of the tunes, and "Keep on Workin' Baby" was another. Some of the other ones I can't recall. The only one that was released was "Keep on Workin' Baby," and this other tune, I can't think of the name of it. It's been quite awhile. It was an experience for me. I really enjoyed it. I learned things about recording and mixing and what to listen for. But working for Robey was another thing. I won't go into that too much. He was a cold man. He just got mad at me one time, because I cut a song not exactly as he wanted. It was a tune that Roy Head had cut, and I was supposed to have done the thing over, and I didn't. I did one of my tunes, so, boom, it shot me out of the saddle with Robey. But other than that, everything was straight. I didn't have any problems with him.

My brother, Cal, worked on one session with me at Robey's studio. We did about six numbers, and he played on those. Mr. Clarence Hollimon couldn't make it. He was a guitar player that Robey used for recording. He never did any recording that was released under his name. He was a studio guitarist.

I never went out on the road too much. I did five or six engagements with Percy Mayfield, Z. Z. Hill, Little Richard, Sonny Boy Williamson, Johnny Nash. I think I was influenced by B. B. King, Gatemouth Brown, and also Barney Kessel, the jazz guitarist. I've done jazz things, sentimental things, whatever it took to satisfy the public. That's what I got off into. Now the blues is becoming more popular. So I jumped into that.

I think blues is taking off. People at first didn't understand the blues. A lot of people don't realize that the blues is not just playing music. You might get up one morning, and you're late for work. You jump in your car, and that rascal don't want to start up. You know how you just get frustrated and angry. And you got the blues! People had the blues all along but didn't know it. They thought it was just music. You're disturbed because your ol' lady done burnt up the bread or you forgot something that you left at home, and you got the blues. Sometimes you can't do nothing about it, so you just start humming or moaning or whatever. You might be like a man that's got a problem and he takes a drink. He's out for a while and gets back up when he's sober. The blues works on you the same way. You just keep playing the blues, and you get a release for a while. Next thing you know, you're singing more blues. The problems are always around, and it don't take much for you to have the blues now.

JOE HUGHES

September 29, 1937–May 20, 2003; interview, 1984

The blues is a derivative of spiritual music because it comes from suffering. When you're in a depressive mood and you play the blues, it's sort of relaxed. It's sort of like taking an aspirin, a tranquilizer or something. It helps relax you. It kind of lifts you up. It comes from the spiritual, the other feeling.

In the cotton fields all us Negroes—I say Negroes because that's what we were classified in those days—all they had was their music to ease the pain. Blues is nothing but a spiritual that uses the praises of love of another person instead of using God or Jesus or what have you. You use "I love you" or you refer to a person instead of the Creator. Basically, you express your inner feelings and the heart of life that you've led. The more suffering you had, the deeper your feeling is. Blues is emotions, like Goree Carter says, it doesn't matter if you're rich or poor, there's some point in life you're going to suffer. If you're suffering and you're rich, it might come from the feeling that you can't watch over your money. Somebody is trying to take your money away. Suffering is suffering. The feeling is the same. It's just that the poor man, all he has is his music for relieving his pain.

When I was coming up, a guy would work ten hours a day, and he was living for the weekend. The only time he had enough money, after he paid his bills and what have you, the money he had left over, he could go out and party Friday and Saturday night. And he more or less lived for the weekend. Just as long as the week made it seem worth it. Because, "Hey, we're waitin' to the weekend. So I can relax, so I can enjoy a little life." And you would basically relate to music that was something about you, about your problems, about your way of life, or maybe some lady broke your heart, and though you might not be in that situation now, you still like to relate to those issues, because your memory is what motivates you today, what you've been through. And you don't want to forget what you've been through, because if you forget what you've been through, you forget your knowledge, because this is where your knowledge come from.

JOE HUGHES, JUNETEENTH BLUES FESTIVAL, HOUSTON, 1987. PHOTOGRAPH BY ALAN GOVENAR.

JOE AND WILLIE MAE HUGHES WITH "T-BONE" AND VIDA LEE WALKER, HOUSTON, CA. 1965. COURTESY JOE HUGHES.

JOE HUGHES, "MOVIN' ON," ROLLIN' RECORDS RRC-601-45.

When I came up, T-Bone Walker was my biggest influence. I refer to him as the grandfather of the blues guitar, because he was one of the first to play with an electric instrument. T-Bone expressed his feelings through different melodies played on the electric guitar like no one else. As far as I'm concerned, he originated it, and after him, as far as Texas was concerned, was Gatemouth Brown.

I would relate to the both of them. And I learned the way that Goree did. I learnt by myself. I had always had a good ear for music. So I could hear you play something now, and I could play it, you know, just from the sound. And when I started, I would do Gatemouth, Lightnin' Hopkins. One of my favorite tunes was the original "Rock Me, Baby" which was done by Li'l Son Jackson. You know, B. B. later recorded it, but I loved the style of Li'l Son Jackson, the way he delivered it.

T-Bone was the main man I listened to, because we didn't have a Victrola, and my aunt had one, and she was crazy about T-Bone. So I'd go out to her house and start listening to T-Bone.

I'm forty-six now, but I started in the business young. At sixteen I was on the bandstand. When I was fourteen, I bought my first electric guitar with money I earned as a dishwasher. In 1953 I saw my first electric guitar in the hands of my backdoor neighbor, Johnny Watson, and six months later I was on the bandstand with a group I called The Dukes of Rhythm. In this band were James Johnson, Hubert Henderson, and another Third Ward neighbor, Johnny Copeland, whom I taught to play electric guitar song by song. Johnny left The Dukes of Rhythm in 1960, and in 1964 The Dukes of Rhythm disbanded, with me going on the road with Grady Gaines and The Upsetters (which was Little Richard's original band that stayed together after Little Richard left).

Early in 1965 I got to play at the Apollo Theater with T-Bone Walker (whom I had first met ten years earlier). Then I was hired as a sideman for Bobby "Blue" Bland, and in 1967 I left Bobby to work with Al "TNT" Braggs, who had also split from Bobby Bland and was touring with his own group. Over the next three years I worked on and off with Al, and in 1970 I took the job of lead guitarist for Julius Jones and The Rivieras.

Between 1971 and 1981, I worked with several Houston-area bands, including We Four, Soul Brothers, and The Music Good. Since then, I've been mainly developing my own music. In 1985 I was asked to co-headline with Johnny Copeland at Blues Estafette in Utrecht, Holland.

Now, today you have a mixed audience, but I'd say blues now has a bigger white audience than black because blacks have grown too accustomed to it. It's just like any other kind of music you listen to; if you've heard it all your life, then you want to reach out for something different.

The bluesman is like a preacher. He's delivering a message. He isn't going to tell you something you haven't heard. But he's told enough people that he's made an art form out of it.

PETER MAYES

1938– ; interview, 1984

PETER MAYES AND JOE HUGHES, HOUSTON, 1987. PHOTOGRAPH BY ALAN GOVENAR.

I've been playing the blues professionally for more than thirty years. I started when I was fourteen, and I'm forty-six now, but I've wanted to play since I was four years old. I remember hearing the sound of T-Bone Walker. I used to hook little strings on doorknobs and pick on them. That was the beginning, and from there I got a little Gene Autry guitar. My uncle bought it for me when I was about thirteen or fourteen, and within a few months I was playing blues well enough to compete in a school talent show. I played a couple of T-Bone Walker songs, "T-Bone Shuffle," and the other was "Blue Mood." And it went so well for me. Everybody liked it so well, I guess that's why I'm still playing blues. If it had gone bad, I might have quit at that point.

I was raised out in the country, and I listened to battery radios, and T-Bone Walker was the music I heard. That guitar stuck in my ear, and even today that sound stays in my work. No matter what happens, I always got some of it in me. It's just there. T-Bone Walker was the first man to play the amplified electric guitar as a lead instrument. He was the greatest. Next was my man B. B. and Gatemouth Brown, and on down the line. But when I heard T-Bone it would send chills over my body, even as a little boy, and it still does lots for me.

I grew up in Anahuac, Texas, between Houston and Beaumont, Texas, about sixty miles away, but actually where I lived was a little community outside Anahuac called Double Bayou. I was raised by my grandmother and grandfather, and they didn't think a whole lot of blues. They were religious people, and they were from the old school, and they liked that religious music, but never once did they ever try to stop me from doing what I wanted to do. I always admired that, and I still don't how they put up with me, practicing six or seven, maybe eight hours a day. They would fuss at me, and how they stood me making all that noise I will never know. I stayed at home and started practicing in the afternoon and continued on into the night. They never said anything bad about it. My uncle, Manuel Rivers, owned and operated the Double Bayou Dance Hall from 1947 to 1983. It was there that I first met Joe Hughes in the mid-1950s in a battle of the guitars that my uncle arranged.

When I was young, I did T-Bone Walker songs mostly, but since then I've also written my own blues, "Moving Out," "Crazy Woman," "Texas Jump," "I'm Ready," "The Word Is Out," "Peace," "Honeysucker," and others I can only think of when I'm playing. The blues is an expression of something that may have happened to you or to someone else. It could be good or it could be bad; sometimes it's sad. Where I was raised up in the country, the blues had to do with some depressing things in my life and other people's lives that I saw. That's the way I see it, but someone else might think of it another way.

There's a Texas style of blues that's played with a kind of modern sound and a whole lot of expression. It's not jazz, but it's not like the Delta. Texas blues has class and is played with deep feeling. For instance, I was playing in France in 1978 [touring with Bill Doggett], and Illinois Jacquet, he didn't really know me, but he heard the way I was playing, and he came up to me after that and he said, "I knew when I heard you, you had to be from Texas. I could tell by what you were putting in the music." Texas blues has a clean sound with a lot of feeling.

In 1954 I met T-Bone Walker at Walker's Drive-In in Barrett Station [near Houston] and got my first opportunity to play with T-Bone on stage after staring long and hard. And from that day on I played with T-Bone whenever he'd come into this area. Sometimes he'd play piano and sing, but I did his style on guitar. Even back in the Fifties I played in a lot of the smaller towns with T-Bone. It was fun. He was a real good musician, but he was easy to work with. He could help you so much, tell you things and he'd never make you look bad in front of an audience. But afterwards, he might tell you about the things you did wrong.

T-Bone told me that he was a banjo player and that's why he played with the guitar flat out in front of him. The way he came up with that style, he said that it wasn't something he tried out, but it just came out that way.

I moved to Houston in 1960. There was more work there. In the late Fifties I had played with Big Joe Turner, Percy Mayfield, and Lowell Fulson. From 1966 to 1970 I was the lead guitar for Junior Parker and got to record four sides with him for the Mercury label at Universal Studios in Chicago.

Today blues has a larger white audience. You see, they picked it up later, while the black people knew about it all the time. In Houston I work different clubs where the audience is about 90 percent white. It's mixed slightly. Oftentimes the white people who come to hear are there to just enjoy the music, while a black audience might come out just to be going somewhere. The blues is the truth. If you start doing blues and there's something about it that isn't true, there's no way for you to sell it to the people. If you're telling the truth, the people can feel it, but if you're telling a bunch of lies, it's not going to work too well. When I do the blues I'm at my best. The blues takes everything away, even bad feelings, even if I'm feeling bad. I have to be awfully sick to not make a gig. The blues makes me feel better because I'm getting totally involved in what I'm doing.

JOHNNY COPELAND

March 27, 1937–July 3, 1997; interview, 1984

JOHNNY COPELAND, SWEDEN, LATE 1970S. PHOTOGRAPH BY A. SVENSSON, COURTESY TOMMY LÖFGREN.

JOHNNY COPELAND, PUBLICITY PHOTOGRAPH, 1980S.
COURTESY ROBERT TURNER.

Driving to Navasota from Houstonwith Johnny Copland in 1987, the road is black, straight, and fast. Johnny and I were squeezed together in the back seat of Robert Turner's Cadillac. Next to Robert was Johnny's wife, Ethel. I was in the middle. On one side was Robert's wife and small baby; on the other was Johnny, his face still dripping sweat from the fervor of Juneteenth in Emancipation Park. Johnny was singing in a scat voice, "Turn the radio down and let's get going." I turned on the tape recorder and Johnny told me about his life and music. By the time we were done, he offered me introductions to Joe Hughes and other Houston blues artists. He recognized the need to document Texas blues at a time when its legacy in the rhythm and blues of the 1980s was still relatively unknown.

Johnny Copeland's career began to take off when he signed with Rounder Records in 1981. His debut album on Rounder, *Copeland Special*, won a Handy Award. *Showdown!* (his 1985 collaboration with Albert Collins and Robert Cray on Alligator Records) won both Handy and Grammy awards. It also was named a Blues Hall of Fame recording. His touring took him to Africa and ultimately led to two albums that fused African influences with American blues. He was known for his generosity and for giving completely of himself, whether playing to a packed house of blues fans or performing with an acoustic guitar for residents of a homeless shelter. Copeland had immense pride in his Texas roots and worked hard to bring recognition to the Houston blues scene.

Heart disease developed in the 1980s. Copeland suffered several heart attacks and ultimately underwent eight open-heart surgeries. He lived for twenty months using an experimental battery-powered pump. His last CD, *Jungle Swing*, was released on Verve, while he was awaiting a heart transplant. Copeland's manager, Holly Bullamore, was quoted as saying that the wait was so long because "they can't find a heart big enough for him."

A few months after the transplant, on New Year's Day, 1997, Copeland resumed performing. He died that July after surgery to repair damage to the donor heart. He was buried in Houston with his trademark guitar strap bearing the word *Texas* across his chest.

Copeland encouraged his daughter, Shemekia, to perform with him starting when she was twelve. By the end of his life, she was regularly opening his shows. She paid tribute to her father by including his composition "Ghetto Child" on her debut recording.

I thought the show tonight [June 19, 1987] was great. I liked the way Joe Hughes performed, and I liked the way I performed. I didn't have long enough, due to circumstances as they are, but maybe next year I'll get enough time. This is my third time at the Juneteenth Festival. It feels great coming home. You talk about these things everywhere, and you tell everybody about Houston, and to be accepted by your home in your own community like I was accepted tonight makes it great. Houston let me come home. I appreciate the honorable mayor being out and giving me my proclamation. And the kind words, telling me that I was one of the few that pushed that music from this area and that she was proud of me. That's a good feeling.

I'm from Haynesville, Louisiana, born in 1937, the son of sharecroppers on the Prentice Meadows Farm. When I was six months old, my parents split up and I moved with my mother to Magnolia, Arkansas, where I did not get to see much of my father. I got to see him one time, and I guess about six months later he died. And they gave me his guitar. When I went to see him, I heard a lot of playing. I spent two weeks down there. The night I got there, he took me along. I'd been around other guitar players. I stayed with another guitarist named Son Beal when my mother went to Michigan once. He played at home, but he loved music. He'd play all day long, all them old blues, and he even had a record player with records by Lightnin' Hopkins and Louis Jordan.

Blues right now is in all the colleges, all the elementary schools and junior high schools, I see where the kids are going to have a wider knowledge of blues, and they're going to be able to put songs with faces, songs with names. That's something that our generation hasn't been able to do.

I'd like to think that I've had my part in the blues coming back. I've been out there hammering my brains out trying to get it did. I like to think me and the other representatives out there like me are really doing something. That's what brought Texas blues back. The uprising is the Texas blues.

JOHNNY COPELAND AND JOE HUGHES, JUNETEENTH BLUES FESTIVAL, HOUSTON, 1987. PHOTOGRAPH BY ALAN GOVENAR.

It was a strange feeling going to Africa, because before going I only had knowledge that I was from Haynesville, Louisiana, down on Prentice Meadows Farm, to Third Ward, Houston, Texas. That was as far as my whole thing went. But in Africa I got to go past that in reality, and I went to a place where 80 percent of the blacks in America come from. And I traveled from country to country, and I saw the similarities among people. I left from Paris, and went into the Congo. The picture on the cover of the *Bringing It All Back Home* album was from that first day. There were two or three hundred musicians playing their music on the field, and they were dancing all on top of their houses, in the trees. You can't hear nothing but music, nothing but the beat, and it was like the whole world was moving, whole world shaking, and funny as it may seem, I kind of felt the effect the drums had had on our people, to make us want to dance and move. It transferred me to another frame of mind. You're not with yourself, you're right there with the music. It was like you were floating right into the music, and the energy level never changed at one point, it moved all the time, but it stayed in one place.

JOHNNY COPELAND, ROBERT CRAY, AND ALBERT COLLINS, PUBLICITY PHOTOGRAPH, 1980S. COURTESY ALLIGATOR RECORDS.

I got an African band together, and we played up and down the East Coast, ten countries, and we got great reviews in the *New York Times, Boston Globe, Washington Post,* but it was only a trial. We wanted to see if it could work; we had four African musicians, a guitar player, two horn players from the Cameroon, and a percussionist. They all came in from Paris [where they record].

Africa made me realize the worst thing we could have ever done was disband the music due to the fact our young people [in America] felt that it was a disgrace, the

JOHNNY COPELAND, AUSTIN, 1987. PHOTOGRAPH BY ALAN GOVENAR.

moan out of the people. We have to accept ourselves, we have to be who we are.

I travel to Europe about three times a year. I don't see much difference in audience. Blues audiences are really great. All of the settings are pretty much the same, and the faces, they are there to have a good time. That's one thing that the artist has in his favor every time [in Europe]. I like to work with that little edge. You got to look like you belong there, not like you're borrowing some time. If you can do that, you fare all right because that's what they come to see.

I'm always working on a new album. I'm always working on my material, but the business is another thing. Whenever they call and say it's time to cut another album, I'll be ready. I want to have a choice doing my material. I like to do 90 percent of my own. I'm writing all the time.

Life isn't nothing but one big song. It works out. I wrote a song for this show today, but I was afraid to do it. You know how you write something, and you say, "I'm not sure if this is what I want to do, or say," and then you go back to the drawing board. I worked hard on it, but I never did get away, I have to go back and do some more.

When I was in Spain, I was writing all the time. I would sound-check songs, and if I didn't feel what I wanted to feel, I didn't use it. As I go along, I do lots of research. Living in New York, Harlem is the greatest place to be, by yourself or around four million people. It's given me time to think about what the blues really is.

With my first album in 1981, though I had been working on the music all along from 1978 up, I realized, hey, this is a brand new world. Now we're dealing with a liberated woman, a lady that gets up every morning and goes to work and doesn't feel like she's mistreated about it. She goes home and helps pay all the bills. You can't put all the blame on her anymore. You have to balance it off. The blues had a tendency, if it talked about the lady, it tended to put the man on the top and the lady at the bottom. So I thought the blues could use a new message. I wanted to have the same feeling, but a better idea.

I'm helping people through my music. Blues is what happens in life; it's trying to be happy. That's what I want to bring in my music. The vibes of the music come from God. It's an inspiration. When you're making music, you can't make trouble. And if you do make music and trouble at the same time, it's turmoil.

I've been in New York twelve years. I was in Houston, and disco was moving. My friend Robert Turner, he lived up in New York and he kept telling me to come to New York. Well, he was in Houston in October 1975, and he said, "You got to go," and he picked me up and took me there. I got to New York and started looking around. I don't like this big old town, and he kept talking to me about the city, explaining things, he made it comfortable enough to sit there and try to work my music, made it so I didn't have to be rushing to where I wanted to be. I never felt the roughness of New York. He was okay there, and he helped me dearly. Through that, I was able to start doing things through the community in which I was living in Harlem, and started building from there. He tried to set everything up for me, and there we met Kenny Vangel and Danny Doyle. Then things started happening, the *Copeland Special* album with Rounder. Now, I've done four, [including] *Make My Home Where I Hang My Hat, Texas Twister,* and *Bringing It All Back Home.*

JOHNNY COPELAND, JUNETEENTH BLUES FESTIVAL, HOUSTON, 1987. PHOTOGRAPH BY ALAN GOVENAR.

Then last year, there was the Grammy album [*Showdown!*] with Albert Collins and Robert Cray. Albert and I have been friends for a long time [since growing up together in the Third Ward in Houston]. We've always talked about doing an album. We're like brothers. We work together out here with this Texas music because he feels the same way I feel. We love the same people, the same community. We have so much in common that when we meet up on the road, it's like a family, Stevie, The T-Birds, we all have a good relationship going toward trying to help each other and push each other forward. I did ten dates with Stevie Ray Vaughan on his Midwest tour last year. It was very comfortable. We hope to do more.

Robert Cray got involved because he was a pupil of Albert. He had been playing jazz on the guitar, and he got to hear Albert at his prom one night in 1971, I think, and that's where he fell in love with Albert. He wanted to play the same music, and he was lucky enough to do some things with Albert. I got a chance to meet Robert, out in Portland, with Albert later on. I thought he was great, a great little brother who's loyal to where he came from and where he's going. We had a wonderful time making that record together, though at first we were to use Gatemouth Brown on it, but the business got in the way.

When we were growing up, we all knew each other real well, and we knew Mr. Robey. He made Gatemouth Brown. Robert Turner used to work for Robey, take his records out on the road. Robey once lent us his truck, and we wrecked it. We said we were going to buy it and tour. So we did the weekend with the truck and the last night, it got wrecked, and we had to try to get it back to Houston before Mr. Robey knew. It was all messed up, but we were friends. Mr. Robey was a nice guy in that manner, down to earth, and real with anybody who was real with him.

I don't think he really understand the music business, because he come from an area where he was the only one [black person to own a record company], so he had to tie everything up as much as he could to deal with it. That was his business tactic. If he had given anybody any room to sue him, his business would have ended twenty years before he sold. He was trying to protect himself. I don't like the way he did it in a lot of ways, but I understand where he was coming from. He wasn't doing anything worse than anyone else in this business.

I met Robey when I was seventeen or eighteen. I did one session over there with Miss Lavelle, only one, under the direction of Clifton B. King. I did have one song, though, that got caught up with this stuff. Johnny "Guitar" Watson came into Houston and came by the club, Shady's Playhouse, where I was playing. It was 1956. He said he was going back to Los Angeles and try to get me a contract from somebody, and he went back and he got me a contract with an actor that had a label in California.

So he said, "I'm going to fix it so that you can stay in Houston and cut the record with my friend Don Robey." And sure enough, he called Don Robey and he told me to come out. I signed the papers, and he said, "Let's go looking for material. You have to choose the songs carefully."

I didn't know nothing about writing at the time, so I get my friend Joe Medwick, and we sit down one night after hours. We started writing a song called "Further On Up the Road." We finished the song that night, and Joe went out to the studio the next day to submit the song to Mr. Robey because that was what Mr. Robey told me to do. I said, "You take it out there. I'm not going with you," because at the time I was married and I had little kids, and my wife was working during the daytime. I was home with the kids, and it was hard for me to move around.

Well, when Joe got to the studio, Bobby was cutting an album, and they needed one more song, and that was it. I'm not identified on the record because Joe tied the song up with Don Robey, just as he did with every song. Joe sold Mr. Robey maybe five hundred songs, ten, fifteen dollars apiece, and he cut maybe five, but they were big hits. You understand what I'm saying.

I understand Joe Medwick is back, singing, sounding good. He's maybe five years older than me, maybe fifty-five years old. We all grew up together—Pete Mayes, Clarence Hollimon, who was a little ahead because his brother taught him. He taught the kid how to play all of Charles Brown, lick for lick. After Clarence reached twenty or twenty-one, he got to go out on the road with Charles Brown and stay with him until he retired. He was one of the great guitar players. He played all of Junior Parker's sessions, Bobby Bland. It was Clarence Hollimon or Johnny Brown. There was Milton Hopkins, who played with B. B. King. Then Wayne Bennett. There's so many good guitar players in Houston. Joe Hughes. I always felt that Joe was someone special. We played together in The Dukes of Rhythm.

I've always been a T-Bone Walker person. Joe Hughes was always into Gatemouth Brown, and we'd have guitar battles and fist battles, too, all kind of battles. Joe and I used to be on stage, and he'd say something I didn't like, and I'd say, "You better not step outside." Of course, he'd put the guitar down, and we'd go outside, and he'd say, "Say, it again!" And we'd fight, then go back inside and start playing again. We were just kids. It wasn't really a fight. It was playing around. We didn't have enough intelligence to know we were messing with these people's money. We were once locked up in Galveston for being on the streets too young, and we were at the jailhouse fighting.

I once got a chance to record with T-Bone Walker. It was in '66 or '67, for Huey P. Meaux. We did a lot of playing together, Club Matinee, Eldorado, all up through the counties outside of Houston. My guitar style was influenced by his, those hot, cuttin' licks, but it took me awhile to start to like my singing because I couldn't sing like everyone else. I always liked to go to church and sing. There's a little bit of that preacher in me on stage. You got to use everything you got.

BIRTHDAY CELEBRATION FOR GUITAR SLIM (RAYFIELD JACKSON), GUITARIST WITH THE CLARENCE GREEN BAND, HOUSTON, 1986. PHOTOGRAPH BY ALAN GOVENAR.

SONNY BOY TERRY, HOUSTON, 2000.
PHOTOGRAPHY BY WAYNE SADLER. COURTESY SONNY BOY TERRY.

SONNY BOY TERRY

September 8, 1959– ; interview, 2004

I come from a small factory town in Ohio, northwest Ohio, originally. It's called Vanwert. My father was a union meat cutter for A&P groceries. His name was Chalice, and my mother was named Jeanne. She was a bookkeeper at a fertilizer plant.

I started getting interested in blues in late high school. My friends played in bands, and I wanted to play with them. I thought about harmonica. My interest in harmonica, I guess, came from how good the blues stuff was. I started buying a bunch of blues records and just got hooked. I saw Luther Allison when I was fifteen. He opened for Kansas. I think he was on Motown Records at the time. That was somewhat inspirational. But really, starting to buy the Jimmy Reed records and Howlin' Wolf records, and so on and so forth. And then I started buying *Living Blues* magazines. I'd go to the music store, and I'd buy harmonicas and albums. And it made me want to go to the big city and play the blues with the old guys, the old black guys. You know, I come from a real modest, very modest, blue-collar upbringing, and it was either that or work in a factory, I think. I'd worked in a cheese factory and done some highway striping or whatever, just kind of nowhere jobs, after I got out of high school, and playing music kind of gave me a dream. And nobody where I'm from played blues, you know. I mean, it wasn't even thought of. There weren't really that many black people in my hometown or anything. But I wanted to come to the big city and play the blues with the old black guys. That was exactly what I wanted to do. And I had an opportunity to come to Houston in 1981. And I took it.

I got a job working at a steel plant, when I first moved down here, a little six-dollar-an-hour job. But it was enough to get me started down here. I was grinding weld spots off of truck body beds. So I did that for a while and then just took my time and started breaking in the music scene. You got to figure in 1981, the roots scene was really just starting to get popular. You had all the Texas bands. So I could go to Fitzgerald's and some of the clubs and just see Texas bands. So there was sort of a boom in blues. Stevie Ray Vaughan was breaking out big, and The Fabulous Thunderbirds were breaking out big. And I went and saw them. You know, for a harmonica player, that's quite an epiphany to see Kim Wilson, when you're still pretty young. I never saw anything like it before. And so I come to the big city, I was able to see all these guys. The Blasters and all the old blues guys were touring at that time. You could go see James Cotton and Paul Butterfield and different harp players from Austin. You got a chance to really study them and be part of it up close.

I got in a band about 1983. I roomed with Uncle John Turner, who used to be Johnny Winter's drummer. He and I were roommates for about six months or a year, and he kind of helped introduce me to the scene a lit-

SONNY BOY TERRY, HOUSTON, CA. 2001. COURTESY SONNY BOY TERRY.

tle bit more. And once I started hanging out with him, I started getting gigs. Before that, I couldn't buy a gig. And he really helped get me going. He sort of mentored me. I was real young. I didn't have any idea what I was getting myself into before I got down here. But slowly, I started breaking in, and I hooked up—I got in a band. We started opening for The Fabulous Thunderbirds and The Nighthawks, John Hammond Jr., Sir Douglas Quintet, Los Lobos, Robert Cray, people like that, and started playing all the rooms around town. Then in 1984 I joined Jerry Lightfoot's band, and Jerry had real strong connections in the black community in Houston. Teddy Reynolds played in his band at the time, and different fellows like that. And we would do shows playing with people like Trudy Lynn. We'd go out in the little black clubs and some of the little country black clubs and play gigs out there. And that kind of really developed me as far as my connection to the Houston blues scene. I was playing with all those guys, Teddy and Jerry and Big Walter, and all those guys. I had two different stints with Jerry. In the second one, we even did more gigs like that. Juneteenth Blues Festival, we were the host band, we'd back up different artists. And so I did that. I probably had a total of about four years with Jerry. And as time went, I hooked up with Kinney Abair, and Kinney Abair and I had kind of like a little Sonny Terry–Brownie McGhee duo. He did the Lightnin' Hopkins thing, and I played harmonica. It was a white-black kind of combination. We did real well for a while.

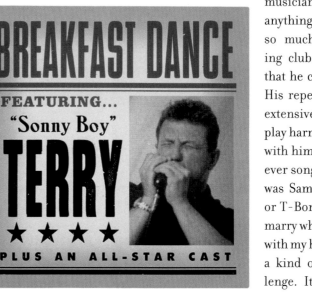

I played with Kinney Abair for a year and a half or two years, and we also did shows with Jimmy Dotson, who was from Louisiana—he was on Excello; he played drums with Silas Hogan. And he also played drums on some Slim Harpo sessions. And he was from that Baton Rouge group. And he lives here in Houston. He had recorded a bunch on Excello, and he's a really good bluesman from here in town, really fine bluesman. And he had that real Louisiana feel, good songwriter. But we'd do shows with him also, and we went to Europe with Jimmy, I believe twice. We played in Utrecht, Holland, and then we came back and did a little two-week tour. And Jimmy, he had a real deep history. So I hooked up with him, and I started doing some jobs with him, too. He lives in Humble, north of [Highway] 59, just right outside of Houston.

So then I hooked up with Joe "Guitar" Hughes. That was around 1990. It might have been a little later, around 1991. I played three and a half years with Joe. And I probably did about eight hundred gigs with Joe in my life. He was an extremely good musician. He could do all the T-Bone Walker, so he was a real sophisticated musician. And he could play anything, because he had had so much experience playing clubs here in Houston that he could play anything. His repertoire was just real extensive. And so I would play harmonica as a sideman with him, and overlay whatever song he had, whether it was Sam Cooke or Motown or T-Bone Walker. I'd try to marry whatever he was doing with my harmonica. So it was a kind of interesting challenge. It was real musical. Like, he'd play a lot of minor keys, so I'd have to play chords and backup, and horn lines, as well as regular straight blues style. It was really a good experience. We played all the time.

I went to Europe with Joe in, I think it was March of '93, and we recorded two albums. We recorded a studio album on the Munich label; it was called *Down, Depressed and Dangerous.* And we also did a live album, *Live in Brandenburg;* we recorded that live at a hall in Holland as a two-album set. So when I was in Europe, I made two records with Joe in the span of a week and a half or something. And so I had a great experience.

Then, Joe introduced me to Johnny Clyde Copeland. He was best friends with Johnny. And one Christmas, Johnny came home. He didn't bring his band; he just

BREAKFAST DANCE, FEATURING SONNY BOY TERRY PLUS AN ALL-STAR CAST, RADIOLA RECORDS RCC100.

brought Floyd Phillips, his piano player, who was also from Houston. Of course, they lived in Harlem, I guess, at the time, or New Jersey, or both, or something. And what happened was that we did a two-week tour with them. We played all these little gigs out in the Chitlin Circuit, I guess you'd call it. You know, all the little small towns like Bay City and Freeport and along the coast and everything. And Joe's band was Johnny's backup band. And we were doing different club dates and everything, and Johnny liked what I did on one of the songs called "Life's Rainbow (The Nature Song)," and he asked me if I wanted to come to Memphis. He goes, "Man, I want you to play harmonica on my next album." I thought it was real flattering, but I didn't know if he was serious or not. But Johnny was an extremely good man, real strong integrity type person, you know, real spiritual guy, and was putting out a good vibe and everything.

What we were doing was called breakfast dances. We were doing all-night gigs during the holidays, 2:00 A.M. to 6:00 A.M. gigs. They're called breakfast dances, and I thought it was really interesting. We were traveling around all these little Gulf Coast towns like Bay City and Freeport and heaven knows what. Traditionally around here, they do breakfast dances during the Christmas holidays. Christmas morning we played a 2:00 A.M. to 6:00 A.M. breakfast dance. Folks get all dressed up and go to the club, and they'd sell set-ups and things like that. They'd have a food buffet, like a soul food buffet, and folks would bring in their whiskey bottles; they'd put them in a paper sack and put them on the floor. I guess they couldn't be up on the table or something, by law. And we'd play shows like that during the Christmas holidays.

It's part of a tradition. I think Count Basie played those breakfast dances at the Rhumboogie. I think he even has an album out called *Barbecuin' and Breakfast Dances.* It's real common in different parts of the African American tradition. They might be Sunday mornings, say from 7:00 A.M. to 11:00 A.M., or 10:00 A.M. to 2:00 P.M., after church or something like that. So it's a big part of the African American tradition, I guess. It was pretty inspiring.

So Johnny [Copeland] liked what I was doing on one of his songs, "Life's Rainbow (The Nature Song)," and he asked me if I wanted to come to Memphis and record with him on his album. I thought it was really flattering that he asked, but I didn't know if he was serious or not. But come to find out that that spring, Joe Hughes called me up and asked me if I was ready to go to Memphis, to record on that album. And so we went to Memphis, stayed at the Peabody Hotel. It was for Johnny's album *Catch Up with the Blues.* It was recorded at Kiva Studios. I think Stevie Vaughan did some of his *In Step* record there.

Well, Gatemouth Brown was there, in at Johnny's session, and Lonnie Brooks, also known as Guitar Junior. Of course, Joe Hughes and Teenie Hodges, part of The Hodges Boys, which they're a big part of the Memphis music scene. And they did a lot of arranging and playing with Al Green and a lot of the Stax people and stuff. That's a pretty important family out of Memphis, the Hodges family. And so I got to meet all those people and hang out with them and get to know Gatemouth Brown firsthand. Of course, he can play about any instrument. He was back there showing the drummer how to play the drum parts and setting out the drums and all that. And him and Lonnie Brooks were going back and forth, going at it. Because Gatemouth's a real sophisticated musician, and Lonnie would say, "Man, every time I get on stage with you, you try to intimidate me." Because Gatemouth would start doing all fancy stuff, modulating keys, and throwing them off and everything, and the rest of that session, every now and then, Gatemouth Brown would look over at Lonnie Brooks with this kind of smirk, jokingly, you know, and he'd go, "Intimidate you, huh?" They kind of picked on him about it for the rest of the session, and that was pretty funny.

So I got to hang out with all these really old, really true music legends, firsthand, and it's incredible for a guy like me who wants to be part of this music so much. To have the opportunity to just sit there and absorb all of it was quite an experience for me. And I ended up doing three songs on that album, and it's a good record, a really fine record, and it's on Verve.

Well, after I left Joe Hughes's band in '96, I started my own band. At the time, I hadn't really had a lot of experience. I got a lot of experience knowing how to run a band by playing with Joe for so long, but I hadn't really sang full time in a band before. So it was a little rough going at first. I had everybody's support, and I had a lot of gigs and everything. Yeah, I've had my own band for over eight years now. It's called The Sonny Boy Terry Quartet. Right now, I have Eric Dane, guitar player. He plays slide and lead. And Bill Allison, who actually used to play guitar for me, plays bass with me now. Brian Scardino plays drums.

I think I very definitely have a Texas sound. I learned a long time ago, I'm real influenced by any and every guitar player, from Chicago to the old guys and the West Coast guys and such. But I realized that I kind of had to find my own sound, so I really got absorbed in the real Houston tradition. And so I really studied. I do a lot of Juke Boy Bonner songs. I sort of rave up Juke Boy Bonner songs, and Billy Bizor, who used to play harmonica with Lightnin' Hopkins. I kind of use him as an inspiration. And I also recorded—my last album was *Live at Miss Ann's Playpen.* I'm on the Doc Blues record label out of Austin. Little Ray Ybarra is on that album. I made sure he got his name on the front of the album, too.

The traditional Houston sound is kind of funny because back in the day, you had kind of two different paths. You had the Lightnin' Hopkins, Hop Wilson, and more of the crude, more rustic country-boy-goes-to-the-city type of blues. And then you had, of course, the Duke/Peacock sound, which was very sophisticated and everything. And through the years, because big bands are hard to make happen, and there are a lot of ice houses in Houston and a lot of small clubs, we kind of developed this sort of ice house blues type sound. Like in Fort Worth, in a lot of ways, they have this sort of Fort Worth jump blues sound. I guess that's a big part of it; I know that's not all, but as far as the clubs down here, and we take a lot of different elements from a lot of different genres to make it all work. You have a lot of working-class blues bands in Houston. There's more than that, but as far as the day-to-day music, as far as that goes in Houston, the guys that are out playing regular, a sound has sort of developed around here. You'll hear that on the Gulf Coast with people like Bert Wills and Benny Brasket. They're white, but they're real hard-core right along the Gulf Coast, super-hard-core musicians who came up playing all those real rough-and-tumble Ship Channel rooms and biker rooms and stuff like that. They're extremely good musicians. They can play about any instrument. They sing really well, and they write really well.

Well, for me, I've just got to have that rhythm that I play off of. For me, you've really got to be able to play a good, strong guitar for me to be able to do what I do. You've really got to be a pretty good guitar player because if you're just a so-so blues player—you've got to know a lot of different kinds of styles of blues, I guess, to do what I do. . . .

I play the lead—I think nowadays, you'll see almost every good harmonica player guy has a real strong lead guitarist, and it's a kind of a point-counterpoint. Because of the nature of the instrument, I'm not so sure it's always the best, unless maybe you're like Sonny Boy Williamson, the original, or something like that, to keep all the focus on the harmonica all night. I think it's good to have that contrast and another focus on the bandstand. It's kind of a call and response. I think it makes it more effective because when you go back to the harmonica, it makes it more effective, and I think it makes your band more entertaining.

The harmonica is definitely like the human voice. And you do voice through the harmonica in the same way you speak. You articulate. The way you voice through the harmonica, you hold your mouth and the way you move your tongue is much the same way as you're creating a language through those notes. And your tongue and the formation of your mouth is really almost exactly the way you would voice a language.

Harmonica, boy, you can bend them notes. You can bend those notes. Certain holes on the harmonica, you can bend down four steps. Like my B on my three-draw, I can bend it all the way down to an A flat. So you can take that note and just yank it down by drawing harder and get that big, fat, honkin' sound. And you learn a vibrato, that big, fat vibrato. And you can wail with it, too, so you go take that note, and you just go back and forth, that bend, and back and forth, and you just wail on that note. And so it's really, really good for blues. Much the same way a guitar player bends that note, bends those strings, harmonica is made ideally for doing the same thing.

Personally, blues became my life. It gave me something that I wouldn't have had otherwise, so discovering blues gave me sort of a mission and something that would give me happiness and a way to express myself. And from my very modest upbringing, my inspiration was to get out of working the factories and living a very mundane existence.

And I needed it. At the time, I didn't have a good school background. I didn't really have anything when I discovered the harmonica.

I always like to say my spirit brought me to Houston, because I couldn't have found a better place to learn. And so I just felt like there was some sort of divine guidance that actually took me here. And I don't know if other people see that in their lives. They see that in small or big ways, because I wouldn't have been wise enough or

THE MUSICIANS OF *BREAKFAST DANCE,* (FRONT ROW, L. TO R.), ALLISON FISHER, BENNY BRASKET, JIMMY ROSE, TERRY DRY, BILL ALLISON, KEVIN "SNIT" FITZPATRICK, (BACK ROW, L. TO R.) HARRY SHEPPARD, SONNY BOY TERRY, GRADY GAINES, JOE "GUITAR" HUGHES, PHIL MARQUEZ, ADAM BURCHFIELD, LITTLE RAY YBARRA.

smart enough to come here. I came down here wanting to get away from where I came from to play the blues, but I had no idea what an incredible blues scene there was in Texas at that time. I mean, I got the best experience in the world. And it was such a town. Like if I went to Chicago, I probably couldn't have got a gig and experience to play, but I was able to work my way into the scene and actually get real experience playing and developing my craft and developing my musicianship. I couldn't have found a more perfect place. If I went to Austin, it would have been too highly professional or something, and I probably wouldn't have been able to get experience that I needed, whereas here, I could work on it, develop it, play the small rooms, and build and develop something. And you could see and get all the experience, from the black clubs to the white clubs to the big shows, the high places, the low places. There is such a rich tradition here in Houston that I don't think a lot of people know about. Probably a little bit more nowadays, but boy, once upon a time, there wasn't. This is sort of the lost city of the blues in America.

I started the Houston Blues Society in 1993. I was president for three and a half years. There were six months before we had any kind of election, and I sort of ran it for four years. And my last year, we won a Keeping the Blues Alive Award, a W. C. Handy Keeping the Blues Alive Award for organization of the year. We did real good. We had a really good "blues in the schools" program. Dr. Joe Kotarba, he was professor of sociology at University of Houston, and he really did a good job because he knew how to work the bureaucracy. And so he would call magnet schools like the music schools in Fifth Ward and Third Ward. We'd go to Yates High. He helped us get little grants from the Cultural Arts Council. And we'd bring in people like Big Walter. Big Walter would play Yates High School, sit there at the piano and play the blues, and Jimmy Dotson and Milton Hopkins, and Kinney Abair. We'd have a real healthy mix. We tried to be real diverse about it. So that was really a big part of our organization, and it built a lot of credibility for us. We were really able to tie us in with the community a little bit more. We got a grant to go to different community centers like Cashmere Gardens and Acres Homes and Fifth Ward and Third Ward. It was really nice. And again, we were putting out a newsletter and promoting the organization. We were really bringing guys into the forefront. I think "T-99" Nelson told me he never played a white club in Houston before the Blues Society.

The Blues Society still does pretty good. They have a little videotaping thing at the Artery, which is another nonprofit. And every month they film and document and audio-record a different artist for archival reasons.

Today, there's not really any showcases here in town like there was. It's all spread out in the taverns, the neighborhood taverns and bars. You have the Big Easy in the Rice Village. A lot of blues guys play there, black and white; it's a good mix. That's about the biggest blues club, but most of it is all spread out, even in the black community. Of course, you have Etta's Lounge, and Grady Gaines still plays there on Sunday nights.

I never cheated this music in any way. Never in my life. And I always wanted to experience it the way it should be, and like these old guys, man, they've been parents to me, Grady Gaines and Joe Hughes and Pete Mayes and people like that. So for me, the blues has meant everything. It gave me a life. It gave me a chance to experience life in a much fuller way than I could have ever imagined.

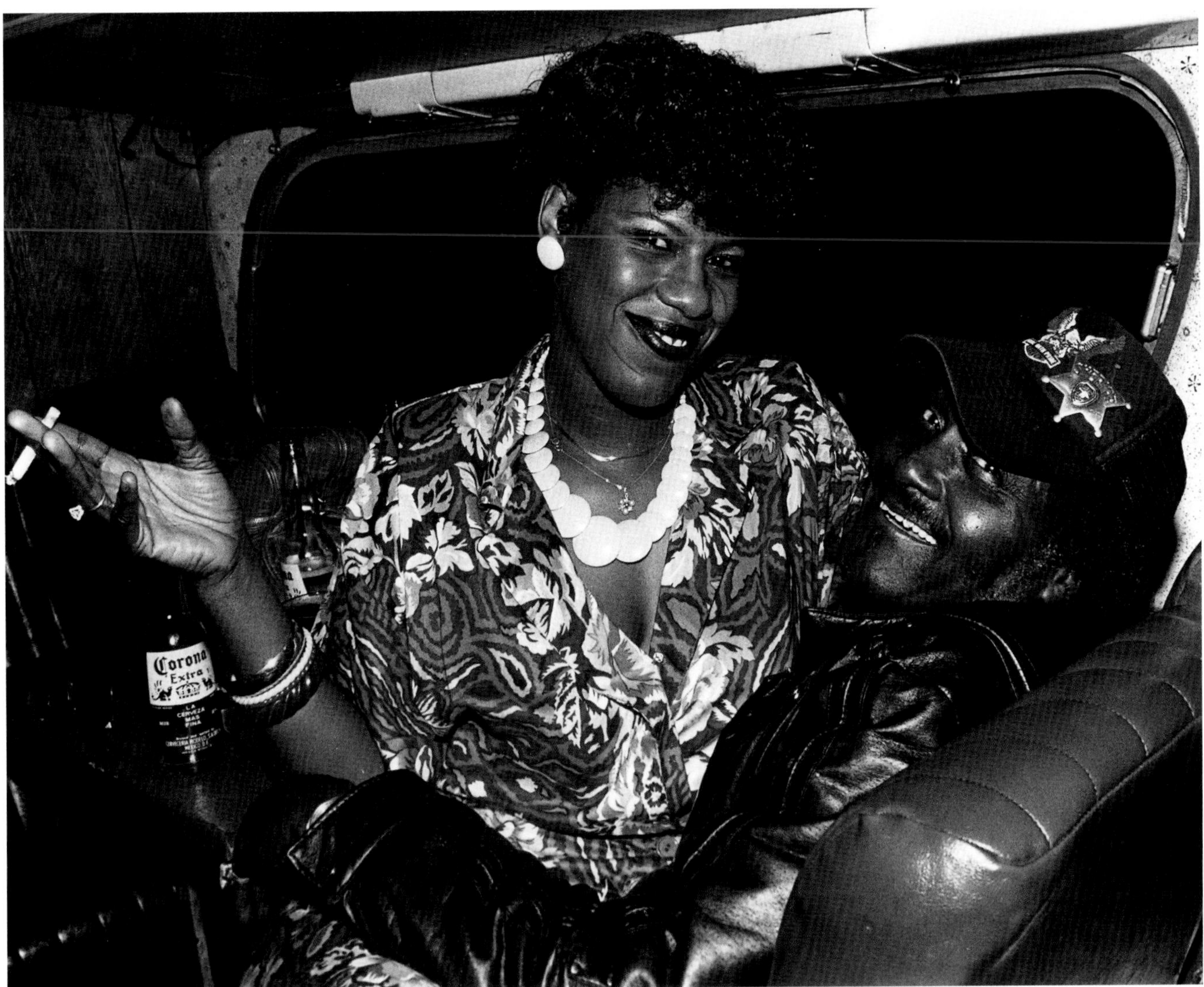

ALBERT COLLINS WITH HIS NIECE CHARLENE INSIDE TOUR BUS, DALLAS, 1987. PHOTOGRAPH BY ALAN GOVENAR.

GLORIA EDWARDS

November 1, 1936– ; interview, 2004

I grew up in Houston, Texas, in Fifth Ward, and I started off as a gospel singer first. My grandmother and my mother both were in the blues. Then my grandmother retired from that. And she raised me. And my mother, she continued in the music world as a blues and jazz singer for a few years.

My mother was Fronnie Smallwood, and my father was Albert Smallwood. My grandmother's name was Frankie Wallace, and she was a blues singer back in the minstrel days. She used to dance and sing in the minstrels. But she never talked about it with me; I only heard it from my mother and some other people. She didn't want to have anything to do with that kind of life anymore, so she didn't like to talk about it. But my uncle, he used to talk about it a lot, because Victoria Spivey was a cousin of hers, and I recalled as a little girl going to Galveston and going to this house in Galveston where they had a piano and they would be playing the piano and singing, and so I mentioned it to my Uncle Leroy once before he passed. His name was Leroy Green, and I told him, I said, "I have such vivid memories of going to that lady's house in Galveston, and Mama would be singing, my mother and everybody would be just having a good time and playing boogie-woogie piano." And he'd say, "Oh, that was at my cousin Victoria's house." And he started singing one of the songs, "That old blacksnake, done leadin' my rider." And then I remembered hearing that, "Lordy, Lord, hear me cryin,' that old blacksnake been leading my rider along." And so, that brought back great memories of that, you know, even though my grandmother didn't want to have nothing to do with that, and she didn't allow me to do it. She insisted on me taking voice lessons to sing classical, which I did in college, and she encouraged me to listen to big band music with Kay Starr and Ella Fitzgerald and Sarah Vaughan. She had all of those old albums like that. And I learned to sing a lot of the big band songs as a kid, just from listening to her music, and singing the stuff that she liked. Then during the time I was in high school, I used to sing with the high school big band, the regular performing and competing band, and I would sing some of the blues, but basically more of the ballads and standards and things like that.

I graduated Phillis Wheatley in 1955. And then I went to Mary Allen Baptist College in Crockett, Texas. And there, I had to put down my blues-singing days. So I had been slipping around doing some blues singing here in Houston before I went off to college, and I competed in some talent shows and things like that, and I won over at the Club Matinee in Fifth Ward, on Lyons. And I was hired to sing at eight dollars a night, my first paying gig. And so I had to slip to get over there with my brother and my daddy. They helped me get over there to do it. But once my grandmother found out, that was over. Then after I went off to college, I only studied classical music and show tunes; no more blues or jazz or rock 'n' roll. Then I met a girl at Mary Allen who was a sister to Joe Hughes. And we became very good friends, and we started visiting each other here in Houston to spend weekends and stuff together. I think her name was Ruby, but she's in a mental institution now; she's been in there quite awhile. She introduced me to Joe. So after I dropped out of college, then I started singing with him and Clarence Green, with Blues for Two, just two guitars and drum. Little Tiny played drums, and Joe played rhythm, and Clarence played lead. And then, after Joe left, Cal Green started playing guitar with them. And so, after that, I left them and had an opportunity to start singing over at the Club Matinee again with Pluma Davis. And I worked with Little Jimmy, a trumpet player. I'm trying to think who else I worked with over there—quite a few people. And then I went on the road with The Baxterettes, with Leo Baxter, and we did USO tours, stateside. And we did a lot of blues and R&B. Joe Hughes was in the band for a while. And then after that, I got married, stopped singing again. Then, after me and my first husband divorced, I started singing again. So, it's been an on-and-off thing with me, basically, with children, having babies and missed opportunities and all of that. I have four, two boys and two girls. And this marriage is number three. That's to Nelson Mills III; we've been together thirty-one years. He's the right one. He plays trumpet and arranges. He does just about all my arrangements, especially my big band stuff and the things that I do with Calvin Owens. I have a recent CD that we just completed with Calvin that will be released in October [2004].

Calvin Owens is keeping it alive. I think it's about fifteen, maybe sixteen of us.

Right now, it's just really difficult to find any gigs, especially with a group his size. There's just not any money out there. I do a lot of things on my own, independently, but basically more weddings, receptions, and things like that, but really nothing to just [jump] up and down about. Since I got back from overseas. I was in Indonesia in 2000 and Singapore, 2001, then I came home. And it's been too dangerous to go back out anymore.

I had my own group, Gloria Edwards and Tradition. It was just a rhythm section. In Indonesia, they hired the musicians there because they wouldn't allow us to bring any Americans into their country. So the musicians had to be all Islamic, you know, Muslim people. I got that gig through a lady named Alice Day, who lives in Switzerland. She was booking me at the time. And I went to Singapore to work there at the Westin Hotel. I was there with a group. The hotel actually hired the musicians, also, and my husband went with me as my keyboard player and trumpet player and arranger and all of that.

I would say that my idol in singing, more than anything, was Dinah Washington because of her versatility. And she was not only a tremendous blues singer, but she could also sing jazz and R&B and funk or whatever she wanted to do. So I always used her as my model from my early teens up until today, of being able to do anything, music-wise, at any time, and not limit it to just one specific type of music, you know. Now I'm not into this bump-te-bump, which I do need to listen to more because I have a daughter who sings that kind of stuff. And I really should show more appreciation for it, but I just can't get past some of the lyrics. I've never really been out to hear my daughter doing all the things that she can do. I've heard her do some of the things that she's very good at. Her name is Frankie Stevenson.

Oh, the blues is like the consummation to so many things. It helps you through your trials, and it helps you through your good times and your happy times. You've got so many different types and styles of blues, even though it's all based on the same chord progression. But the stories, you have just so many things that can help you and soothe you. You can sing a blues song when you're happy, and you can sing a blues song when you're sad. And it will console you and bring you around to being ready to accept things as they are, either take it or let it go, either way, it's all right with me. And that's the kind of attitude that the blues give to you because it all started off from the gospel and the camp songs. And then it progressed through the years after slavery. During the slave times, we would sing the blues according to what we heard in the fields, you know, about religion and spirituality. And then [after slavery] we, as blacks, had to suffer the consequences of decisions about where we would have housing and where the next meal was coming from, and then who your man is with. You know, everybody accepted the fact that you would not have any one man to yourself. You were always going to have to share with somebody else. And so songs were written about those things. . . . And then, killing him, and all the hard-luck songs and things like that.

Blues is different for a woman. Definitely. Because of the fact that we feel that we suffer a lot more than men. We have the suffering of worry about what's going to happen with the children and whether or not there's going to be food on the table for the children and whether or not there's going to be a roof over your head for you and the children. Whereas the men, they don't really have to worry about those things because the woman's always going to take care of that anyway. But it all falls back on the fact that we feel that we are the original sufferers. And men have been known to roam and ramble, but a woman, most of the time, we have to stay home. So what do you have to console you, other than your blues? Your blues and your gospel songs, those are the things. And that's why you find more women when you go inside of a church house, that you're going to find more women in there than you will the men, based on the fact that we're always seeking solace, not only through our Christianity, but we're also seeking solace just trying to find happiness here on earth. So it all boils down—you can go into a nightclub, you're going to find more women in there than you're going to find men because they're looking for happiness. They're just searching for a day, one night, one hour, of happiness, even if it's no more than just sitting with their friends and drinking and listening to the music and dancing and whatever, but they're looking for happiness, searching for that.

Blues is a spiritual music, because that's where it all started from. That was the beginning, before the work songs. That's how they started it out. It started from the old canons, you know, from the old camp songs that they were hearing, things like: "Didn't it rain, children, rain all night long, hallelujah. Didn't it, didn't it, didn't it, didn't it rain?" There you go. You know, it just all started from the same thing. It's just the difference between the lyrics and the difference between who you're expressing this particular emotion to. You can sing anything that you want to sing to the Lord because He rejoices in all music.

I don't remember how many different records I've worked on. I'm on more compilations than I'm aware of. The guy at In the Basement in the U.K., he sends me magazines from time to time, to let me know of compilations that he finds out about, you know. And I'm on so many compilations, I can't even number them all, but I have only had, of my own, just me independently on my own, I've only had one recording released, one album. And then later it became a CD, *The Soul Queen of Texas.*

I've been told when I lived in Kansas City that the people there claimed me because they say I could sing just like the Kansas City blues singers, you know. And then I have some CDs that I released on my own, my own CDs. I have *Gloria Sings Just Blues* and then *Gloria Edwards Sings Just Standards,* which are available here in Houston at Cactus. You can get them over there. And then, I'm on a recent compilation on Dialtone with Lavelle and Miss Candy. Miss Lavelle had a release on her own that is doing real well. She received several picks. She's older than me. But we all used to be on competitions and stuff back in the Fifties together, as good friends, and we're still good friends. I've always loved Lavelle, and especially her writing. Oh, she writes something like the lyrics, and the music is just unreal. She is just absolutely fantastic. We did a show, I think it was last year or maybe the earlier part of this year, over at the Project Rowhouse place over there at the Eldorado, the old Eldorado, and it was a fantastic show. It was just wonderful, all of us being together.

Some people say, "Well, I'm not going to sing the blues anymore because I'm a Christian now." But the Lord does not differentiate between your happiness and your sorrow. You can go to Him in sorrow, and any way that you go to Him, He's going to listen to your sorrow. And the same thing with your happiness. So, if I sing to Him that I've just found a man and I'm so happy I can jump and shout, He's going to be happy, too, because I'm happy. And that's what He wants us to do, is to rejoice. So, at one time, I had some problems with my faith and being able to differentiate, saying, "Well, I'm not going to sing the blues anymore because of the fact that now I'm a Christian." But that isn't true. That isn't necessary because He is not concerned about that. He is only concerned about what's in our heart. And He wants to know what's in your heart. So if you can't tell him what's in your heart, but you can sing to Him about what's in your heart: "Sometime I feel so bad, I want to lay my head on some lonesome railroad iron and let that 219 train ease my trouble in mind." And "Trouble in mind, I'm so blue." And you go through those things. But it's just that you can express the things that are deep inside your heart so much more with the blues than you can with anything other than gospel songs. Of course, with the gospel songs, you can always express, too, but more so with the blues because it's more about our life, the life that we live, the sorrow that we feel, the happiness that we share, either with another person or just with the Master. You can go to him any way you want to, and He's going to reach out and touch you.

LEE AUDREY ROBERTS (TRUDY LYNN)

August 9, 1947– ; interview, 2004

I was born in Houston. I grew up in the area called the Fifth Ward. It was super to me. I know there was a lot of blues going on, a lot of entertainers and clubs. I wasn't in clubs in the earlier days. But I was in high school, singing with the choirs and things like that.

My mother was a cosmetologist, which I was, too. Well, I still am. Mostly hair. And my daddy did just labor work. I just heard blues all my life. In the area where I was raised, there were a lot of cafes, and then we were listening to that local black radio station here, KYOK. And another one was KCOH. And just from listening to the radio and then hearing them big old glass records my parents had. Yeah, they went out. I remember when I was a little girl, my mother went to that concert where Johnny Ace shot himself, at City Auditorium. I was a little girl. But I remember it upset them.

I know my parents used to get up sometimes like late and go eat when they had this club here in Fifth Ward, Club Matinee. And it was a dinner club and a club and a hotel. It was where all the black entertainers went to stay when they would come to town. I think the hotel was the Dixon Hotel. It hooked right on to the Club Matinee, in the back.

I would have gotten my leg broke if I'd went up in there [to the Club Matinee]. But when I was going to junior high school, my mother had her place of business there in Fifth Ward, a beauty shop, and the junior high school that I went to was like on Lyons Avenue, so it was in like an angle distance across from it, so you couldn't help but see. I saw a lot of entertainers. Coming home from school, all the kids would walk through and just look to see who we could see, you know.

I graduated out of Phillis Wheatley there in Fifth Ward in '65. Coming out of high school, some of my gigging I did was with Leo Baxter and the big band here in Houston. And from there, I was with Clarence Green for a long stint, a good five or six years, I'm sure.

I was a vocalist for Clarence Green. He had a small band. As a matter of fact, back in those days, he was titled the best small blues band in Houston because he always kept him a good little snap. We had guitar, bass, drums, and two horns. That's what we had.

The horn players were Wilbur McFarland and Charlie Royal was on trumpet, flügelhorn, and trumpet. C. J. Turner was the drummer. Kazell Jenkins was on bass.

I never did any work with Don Robey over there, but I did have a chance to meet him because my kids' father used to do a lot of session work over there, at Don Robey's.

My kids' father is Ozell Roberts. He's a bass player here in Houston. He's my ex-husband. I never went to the sessions. Well, when I met Robey, to me, he was a perfect gentleman. I had my daughter, when she was a baby, there, and he played with the baby and talked to me, and that was just about it, you know. I didn't know that much about him, no more than just seeing him.

When I was coming up, I listened to ladies like LaVerne Baker, Fay Adams, Ruth Brown. Gigi was there when I first started; she was singing during shows. Her deejay name was Gigi, Gladys Hill. She was a deejay on KCOH. She was a blues singer, you know. She was good. And by being a deejay, which made people totally accept her, but as far as singing, she could. She was a good singer.

I characterize myself as a soul blues singer, because in the era I came up in, like the Sixties and Seventies, you had a lot of different types of music going through. So out of all this music, I did them all. Like with Clarence Green, we were the best little band in Houston, so and so, it was just like, everything that was on the radio that was tops, we were doing it, you know, Aretha Franklin, Etta James, everything, even country and western. So I had a chance to really just—I did all types of music, and I can still do all types. But I prefer soul blues.

I've worked with just about everybody in Houston. Really. I've worked with Clarence Hollimon, Calvin Owens, Leo Baxter. I've did things with Grady [Gaines]. I'm serious when I say everybody. Joe Hughes. Johnny Copeland. Wow, you name 'em, I'll claim 'em.

When I left Clarence, oh, Lord, I can't call the year—it

was in the Seventies. And I started venturing out from him, and I started doing shows. People never mention Ray Barnett, but Ray Barnett, I feel was like a mentor for entertainers here in Houston because he had so many clubs here in Houston. He had the Cinder Club, the Sands of Houston, the Casino Royale. Oh, my God, he had a whole lot of clubs. And all these clubs on the weekends had entertainment. And he really, to me, placed all the black musicians here into clubs, singing, you know. Ray Barnett. And I've read a lot of articles, but nobody ever mentions that man. And he played such a big role. Because being in his clubs was like being on top. He had the most beautiful black clubs here, and when he had the Cinder Club, there was a stage like in the middle of the floor, and when it'd be show time, the stage would rise up out of the floor. That was in Third Ward, on Dixie Drive. And this is where all the entertainers came. This is where I saw Etta, a lot of R&B singers. I saw Etta James there, Redd Foxx. Everybody was there at that Cinder Club.

Ray Barnett raised us all, so far as when you started getting paid a little bit. He wasn't paying no hell of a lot, but he was paying a little bit more than what it was when I first started. When I first started, we were making gigs like three, four, and five dollars a night.

I had one group we called The Winner's Choice. But usually when I had a band, it would be just Trudy Lynn and her band. A lot of times, I didn't even name bands with me. That way, you don't get caught if your band done left because one monkey don't stop no show. I never liked that. It was just me and my group, the Trudy Lynn show.

I got nine CDs out. Well, the last one was year before last. I started recording with Ichiban, since the Eighties. It's been two years since I've recorded, and we're getting ready to do some work now. But hey, I've been all over the world. I got with Ichiban through some of my musicians, and through Gary "B. B." Coleman. He's deceased. It's been about five, six, seven years, something like that. He was young. I know he had a problem with sugar [diabetes]. I think he had a heart attack.

Well, you know, Ichiban is no longer there. And most of the material I did was through Ichiban. I've been with Time Warner and with Rounder, different companies. But the majority of my recordings was with Ichiban. Ichiban was in Atlanta, Georgia.

I like a big band when I'm doing big shows, big concerts. Guitar, bass, keyboards, drums. And every now and then, horns. Most definitely, when I'm out doing the concerts, I have full bands with a full horn section, saxophone, trumpet, trombone. Well, a lot of times, like when I did the Chicago festival, sometimes I carry horn players out of Georgia, but I've also used like Chicago horns. You know, you go to different areas, and you just get with the union and just get the horn players, and they blow charts.

I represent Houston. I feel like my field is Houston. Chicago, they're driving, raunchy blues players, I mean, they drive, because I've worked with a lot of Chicago musicians, and I go to Europe a lot. There are more musicians that are from Chicago than from here, I'll put it like that. But I think most guitar players, they just sound different, to me. Houston is a dynamic type blues. It's like with a feel thing, they're singing it, you know. Just like I characterize myself as a soul blues singer. I'm not a crying, down, digging-in-my-head blues singer, shoot. I feel what I'm doing. When I do a show, I'm going to give you the whole theatrics that go with it so you can get what I'm talking about. Take, for instance, Johnny Brown. Now, he's doing good here. See, he's dominant, and then he's smooth, laid-back, you know what I'm saying? Kind of like T-Bone Walker. There you go, then. You ain't got to get out there and shake them legs to make somebody think you're playing that guitar. T-Bone Walker was all I heard when I was a kid. That was my dad's favorite, T-Bone Walker and Howlin' Wolf.

I think one of the first big-time recording people I met was Joe Hinton. And that's when he did "Funny (How Time Slips Away)." Wasn't that a beautiful song? He was a nice person, mannerable, quiet. I didn't know that much about him. I think he was before his time, I really do.

Well, I'm always doing something with music. I also write. Last CD I did, I wrote eight of the tunes that were on the CD. And in between with writing and in and out going working, that's about it. And then when I'm here, I spend time with my grandbabies, sometimes, my kids. I have three kids and four grandbabies.

I write about life in general, and sometimes I might hear just a phrase, somebody saying it. It'll just throw a click in me. And I like writing best early in the morning, when I get up. I'm usually up around about seven or eight. But usually when I get up, have a cup of coffee, sit down, smoke a cigarette. And if I'm off into it, I think I do better early.

One night I was out and I heard some fellows arguing, like dudes talking, messing around with one another, and a dude told me, "Well, I tell you, I don't want nothing from you but a whole lot of leave me alone," and I say, "Oh, Lord, that's it in a box."

I like little common things, everyday things that the average person does.

Altogether, I've written quite a few songs. I'll put it like that, quite a few. I wrote one called "Snatching It Back." How come you keep on snatching it back? Yeah, you give it up and then you take it back. What's going on? How come you keep on snatching it back? Blues is life. Life, life, life. There's another one I wrote, "No Deposit, No Return." And another one I wrote, "Turning the Same Old Corners." You know, sometimes in life, you have to catch yourself. You keep doing the same thing over and over and over, and you ain't going nowhere, just turning the same old corners each time, you know. Yeah. "Memories of You" is another one, which was the title of my live CD I just did.

Right now, I'm in the midst of shopping for a new label. I've been talking to quite a few people. And then, I don't know even if I want to go with somebody because I've been that route, and nowadays it's hard on anybody that's a musician, especially because of the almighty computer, throw the charley horse on everybody. People download you. They don't buy CDs, so I honestly feel like if you could do it yourself, do your own product, and sell it, you'd be better off. . . . I say, "You know, when you're in Rome, you have to do like the Romans. They got people out here bootlegging. I'm going to cut my own, put my own stuff out there and shoot some bootlegs out there, too, get that, too. That's the only way you're going to make it."

I think hip-hop is going to be here, because to me, it's a self-expression. A lot of people say it's just a fad; I don't think it is because people be making statements. I'm doing it now, but I feel like I did a long time ago. Yes, I was doing rapping a long time ago, back in the Sixties and Seventies. We used to do that "Dig my jive" stuff. We were just a little more morally with it, you know, wasn't just, boom, slap you in the face with it.

It's just that way, just like a boom, slap you in the face, and then, if you think about it, the way things are going on, nowadays, everything is so bold, it's best that they come out with it like that. You know what's in there and what the deal is. Some of it, I listen to, and it's cool because I have kids. But so far as sit down and listen, ain't no way, Jose.

I'll even go out and do some vocals for them. I ain't no rapper, you know what I'm saying? Well, there was a little group, well, they wasn't no rappers, just a young little group, I did a thing with them in Switzerland.

In Europe, they're different. They're very responsive. I hear a lot of entertainers say they like blues more. I think, even just like here in the States, people that like blues know where to go hear blues. So naturally, I feel like in Europe, it's the same thing. If that's what you like, that's what you go support, and that's what you come out for, you know.

The universal appeal of blues is the feeling. The feeling. The feeling and the stories, because everybody goes through the same old thing. And I was just telling my sister the other day, I said, "You know, I've been in the airport, I can just look at people now and tell where they are from, but we all go through the same thing. There's one God for us all." That's the way I look at it. You know, we're just different colors, different strokes, different folks, but we all got one God.

SHEMEKIA COPELAND

April 10, 1979– ; interview, 2003

SHEMEKIA COPELAND, CA. 2004. COURTESY ALLIGATOR RECORDS.

When I finally reach Shemekia Copeland, she is standing in the checkout line at K-Mart at Thirty-fourth and Broadway in New York City. The interview begins while she is waiting. After about ten minutes, she pays the cashier and tells me that she will stick around for a while, in the din of the people around her, and talk.

My father had a great presence about him. Everybody always asks me if I was born in Houston, but my father moved to New York in 1975. Of course, I was born in '79, and he was in New York for all that time.

I got into the music, just listening to it around the house. You know, my father just loved music so much, and he wasn't a big television guy or anything like that. So, growing up, all I heard was just him playing guitar around the house. And that was pretty much my life. And what a great one it was.

I sang with my father around the house, and then, of course, later on, he would play local gigs around the city and things like that, and I would go in and I would fit in with him. That's pretty much how I got started.

I went to elementary school and junior high school in New York City, in Manhattan. And then I went to high school in Teaneck, New Jersey. And I haven't gone to college.

You know, junior high school was great, because I was in a performing arts school. And I really enjoyed that, but when I got to high school, there was nothing like that happening for me, so it was really boring. And I was dealing with real issues at that point in my life, you know. I mean, extremely real issues. I was a very serious kid, and some people, the most important thing for them was what they were going to wear to prom. And I just couldn't dig that, I couldn't get into it. Yeah.

I started performing when I was maybe about sixteen or seventeen. I really don't know what "professional" means because some people say it means when you step out there for the first time. And others say it means when you start getting paid. So I don't necessarily know which one that is.

I guess I've been singing onstage in front of people since I was about sixteen. Oh, yeah, I traveled with my dad. We went all over the tri-state area. We went to the East and West Coasts. When I was younger, I went to Europe with him. We went to Spain twice. So I got to do a lot of traveling with my dad. Some of the best memories of my life, actually, was doing that.

Always, the New York shows were great, because my father was such a great performer. He had a lot of friends here in the New York area. I think I was influenced by his Texas sound, definitely. Anytime you're exposed to something—I was listening to that a lot growing up, so, yeah, I have some of those influences. But I'm a New York City chick, you know, so I have a lot of urban sound coming into my music.

I love calling what I do "contemporary," because you can do almost anything you want to do with a particular thing, but if you listen to it, you still know that it's blues-based. And that's my big thing. In my band I have four pieces: keyboards, guitar, drums, and bass. Everybody's from New York.

My guitar player is fifty years old, and Arthur's been around New York for years and just has a really great concept of what this music is supposed to sound like and everything. So he's just got a really, really cool, cool sound. His name is Arthur Nielson. And he can play anything, which is what's so cool about him.

Well, I've been off this month, which has been something completely different for me. It's been a long time since I've been off, so it's been very exciting, just being able to do like normal things, for a change.

I'm really doing well, you know. I can't complain. The state of the music industry right now is not that great, and it's just really cool that I'm still able to do well, even though the state of the music is not that great.

Everything is the blues for me. One of the statements that my father used to say was, "If it wasn't for the blues, I wouldn't weigh over ninety pounds." Which describes my life perfectly, because it's true, you know. It's fed me my whole life, and it's been my life. It moves me, in a way. I mean, I grew up in the middle of the hip-hop era in Harlem, so blues just has this certain thing that draws me to it, and I think a lot of it has to do with the fact that I'm an old soul, and I know that I've been here before. And I just end up taking things in, and I take that music in so much better, and I feel it so much. And I don't know what it is, but blues is just—uh!—you know. Blues is soul music, and country music—old country music, not the new stuff, yo! So I always say I'm living in the wrong time.

Did I like hip-hop? Yeah, yeah. I liked it a lot, you know, but it was just music, and a lot of it, for me, was just a lot of noise, and it was very rare for me to come across something that I thought sounded good or somebody who had a unique sound or a unique noise. Because, you know, the industry sucks right now; it's all about what you look like versus what you sound like. I was just talking about that today, you know? Now we live in a world of television and all that stuff. Years ago, it was just radio, so as long as you could sing, it was okay. And nobody cared what you looked like. Nowadays, we're living in a world where that's the most important thing, what you look like.

Every genre of music stole from blues, because blues is one of the oldest forms of music there is. So, of course, you'll find elements of hip-hop in blues, definitely—or elements of blues in hip-hop.

It's funny. I'm writing more and more. I find the longer I live, the more I have to say in my life, so I am writing more. For me, I don't sit down at a paper and think and wait for ideas to come out. I kind of just wait for an idea to come, and that's how my ideas come, laying in my van or just sitting around the house, whatever it is. But that's the way it happens for me.

I would say I've written and recorded about eight, seven or eight, of my own songs. But I have a lot of songs, of course, that I don't put on records. I like real subjects—anything that's like normal and stuff that you see and hear every day—because I want people to be able to relate to them.

One thing about European people is that they have a great respect for old things. And that's what I love about being there when I'm performing there and I'm working there. They really appreciate old things and old music, and that's why they appreciate blues so much—and jazz and music like that. They see it more as an art form. Whereas here, in America, it's all about what's the new thing that's out. There, no one cares about that—except the young people. I mean, I've been going there now for, I don't know, thirteen, fourteen years. And I'm seeing a change, you know. Techno's huge there for the young kids because they're always, you know, jumping up and down and moving and dancing, so I've seen that change. But they still have a real great respect for this music there.

Next, I'm going to be headed to, like, Buffalo and then down to Virginia, things like that. Going out to Chicago. I'm doing a little bit in November, but I'm off this month, and it's been great. Every now and then we'll play college campuses, but we don't do that that often. We play big clubs, you know, nice, big restaurants and theaters, too. We do a lot of things. Right now, there's a limitation in venues, so we're not playing a whole lot of venues anymore because there's not a whole lot of them left. Especially all the clubs. Clubs are closing down. So the state of music in general is not doing very well. But blues artists, we're used to suffering, so it's no thing for us because we're used to this being this way. It's always been this way for our music.

On every record that I've recorded, I recorded one of my father's songs. One of my favorites is "Ghetto Child." I recorded that on my first album. But my father had so many great songs, I can't even begin to tell you which ones I like. It's just ridiculous. He was such a great writer. He wrote like a country artist, and he played like a bluesman, and he sang like a soul singer. He had a great package.

I think he moved from Texas to New York because there wasn't anything going on down there. So he got the hell out of there. And I'm really glad he did. Yeah, most of the guys my dad grew up with, they're all gone. It's really sad, but you know, I'm here. And people come and they go. And it's sad, but I'm really glad to know that I'm keeping my father's legacy living. And I'll keep theirs living as well.

My biggest influences as a singer are O. V. Wright, Sam Cooke, Marvin Gaye, Joe Tex, a lot of males. Koko Taylor, Etta James, Ruth Brown. There are so many, I can't even tell you. Yeah, you know, I grew up listening to everybody. And I just take what I can take from all of them, and kind of made my own sound.

The music keeps me going, the fact that blues has always been a difficult genre of music to be in, and a lot of young black females, they're all singing hip-hop, R&B; nobody's singing blues. So I'm really proud to be called a blues singer, even though I'm a contemporary blues singer and I can sing anything. I'm proud to be doing blues, because I know how important this music is.

I think that blues has always had a black audience. The Chitlin Circuit was all black, you know. I couldn't go and perform on the Chitlin Circuit right now. No one would know who I was. But there's always been a big fan base of blacks who like blues music. But I think, now, I'm finding that a lot of young black men and women come out to my shows, and it's great. And it depends on where you are, you know. If I'm somewhere where there's no black people that live there, they're not going to be at the show. But if I go to D.C. or New York, you'll find a lot of young blacks out there.

Oh, I think that they [some young blacks] were taught to believe that blues was associated with the time in black people's lives that they don't really want to refer to. They think that it's all about slavery and picking cotton and the hard times. And that's why I do this, because I want them to know that blues is about good times, too. It's not just about the hard times. It's about life in general, you know what I mean? Blues, to me, is telling stories, and that's what I do. And a lot of them ain't, you know, "my man done left me" stories. There are fun ones, too. They're stories in general. But they associate it with a time in black people's lives where it wasn't so good. And their only way to get it out was—for years, I couldn't understand why—I would listen to old blues tunes and I would hear them talk about killing women and beating women and doing things to women. And it was just recently that I found out that a lot of those songs weren't talking about doing things to women; it was talking about doing things to their bosses and their slave owners and things like that. But they couldn't say that about them. They had to do it in code. They talk about, "I'm going to do this and do that" and da-da-da-da-da. But really, they were talking about what they would do to their bosses if they did this or if they did that. So they were actually very clever, you know. And the language has changed over the years, which is so cool. I mean, the average person on the street right now, if I played an old blues tune for them, they couldn't understand what they were saying. I was listening to some music in my car, and I was with some of my family members, and we were going somewhere. This song came on, and they were singing, "I don't want no woman if her hair ain't no longer than mine." And they were, "What the hell are they saying?" And basically, the guy was saying, "I don't want no woman if her hair ain't no longer than mine," but the way they said it. . . .

Yeah, you know what I'm saying? But if you listen to those guys sing it back then, you couldn't understand what the hell they were saying.

Gospel is the same kind of thing. They didn't want them to know how strong their faith was and how much they believed, because if they did, they would know that that gave them an extra power over them. So the stupider they thought you were, the better. But these people were very intelligent. And that's how I know powerful God is in my life right now, because they didn't know to read. They couldn't read the Bible. But they knew there was a higher power, which makes them, in my opinion, smarter than anyone else walking on the earth. Even if they don't have the book smarts. But their spiritual faith is what brought us this far. It's all connected for me.

I have my faith, and for me, my faith and my music are separate. When I'm singing, I'm a wild woman and you're a lucky man. That has nothing to do with my faith. So I keep them separate. Not everybody does, but that's how I do. Someday, I do believe that I will definitely do a gospel record, and I'll be singing for the Lord. But I won't stop singing my blues because my music is not the devil's music, which is how they referred to it. I'll never forget when Sam Cooke left the church. I said, "I'll never forget," like I was there. I feel like I was there. But when he left the church, and he was singing, "I love you, I love you, I love you, I love you, I love you, for sentimental reasons," they thought that that was the devil's music. So it's just unbelievable to me.

Yeah, I got to keep my Sundays open. I go to church every now and then. My aunt has a really great church in Yonkers that I try to get to. I love church, but my body has to be my temple because I can't always get there. And I'm probably more spiritual than half the people that go to church anyway.

I was raised Baptist. My father was great. There used to be times when he'd get home Sunday morning from working, and he'd get me dressed and take me to church. And I know he was exhausted, but when he could get there, he got there. And that's the way that I am. When I can get there, I get there. And when I can't, I just have church in my body, church with myself.

My mom's from North Carolina. Her name is Sandra Copeland. If it wasn't for my mother, I would not be singing, because my mom has a beautiful voice, a beautiful voice. She grew up singing soul music, and she also grew up working in the tobacco fields and picking cotton, which is why, until she met my father, she didn't give a crap about blues either because she associated it with the hard times. So that's how I was able to learn those things.

I live with my mom in Pennsylvania. My mother is my best friend. She's my roommate. We live in Lake

SHEMEKIA COPELAND, CA. 2004.
COURTESY ALLIGATOR RECORDS.

Harmony, Pennsylvania. It's pretty much in the country. It's a very peaceful place. I love it.

I guess I was about fifteen when I left the city. So, I've been out of the city for about ten years. First, I lived in Jersey, and now I've been living in the Poconos for about four years. We left before my father passed away. Well, right at the end, my mom had to go with him everywhere. So, for the last couple of years, you'd find my mother and I both there.

ZYDECO

ZYDECO CHA CHA LOUNGE, HOUSTON, 1986.

PHOTOGRAPH BY ALAN GOVENAR.

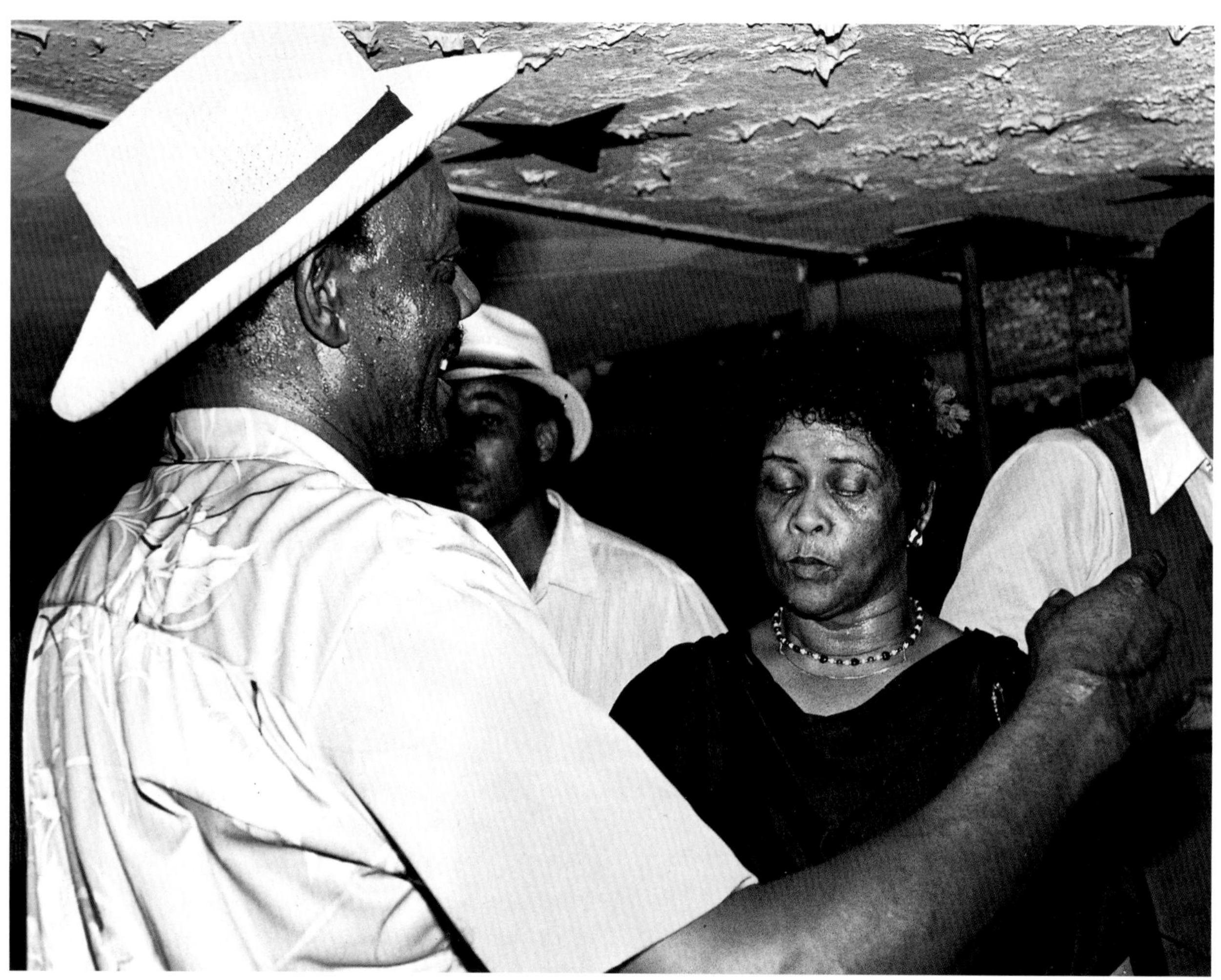

DANCERS AT THE ZYDECO CHA CHA LOUNGE, HOUSTON, 1986.
PHOTOGRAPH BY ALAN GOVENAR.

INTRODUCTION

In Houston's "Frenchtown" in the Fifth Ward area, the zydeco begins around 9:00 on weekend nights. The crowd is elbow-to-elbow, and the loud enthusiasm grows along with the syncopated rhythms of accordion, electric guitars, drums, and *frottoir*, or rub board. The rub board was invented in 1946 by Texaco refinery worker Willie Landry, a master welder/metal fabricator in Port Arthur, Texas, after being approached by two fellow Louisianans, Clifton Chenier and his brother, Cleveland.

Zydeco refers both to the highly syncopated songs and to the dance event itself. Literally, "zydeco" can be translated from Creole French as "snap beans." Although some critics and performers claim that the music derives its name from the line, "Les haricots sont pas sale," meaning, "the snap beans are not salted," folklorists John Minton and Mack McCormick suggest that the name derives from a common dance movement that involves holding closed wrists in front of the torso and then circling or flicking them in a motion that imitates someone snapping beans.[1]

The spelling of the word is also subject to some disagreement. In Houston the most common spelling on dance hall posters is *zydeco*, although alternate spellings, such as *zoddico*, *zordico*, or *zodeco*, are sometimes used.

There is general agreement, however, that zydeco originated among the Creoles of southwestern Louisiana and that the music combines the influences of Cajun accordion tunes and African American blues with Afro-Caribbean rhythms. In rural Louisiana the music was usually performed on a one-row button accordion and accompanied by rub board, angle iron triangle, or violin. With the migration of Creoles to urban areas such as Lake Charles and Houston, the more versatile piano accordion replaced the diatonic model. The rub board has been retained as a rhythm instrument, and the triangle and fiddle have been replaced by electric guitar, bass, drums, and sometimes keyboards and horns.

In Houston, zydeco was first played at house parties, but since the 1950s it has also been performed in clubs such as the Zydeco Cha Cha Lounge, the Silver Slipper Club, MJ's Place, and the legendary Continental Zydeco Ballroom on Collingsworth Avenue in the Fifth Ward, as well as at numerous black Catholic parish halls around the city. For many years, the Continental Zydeco Ballroom, which closed in 1997, hosted an annual birthday celebration for the "King of Zydeco," Clifton Chenier, on or around Juneteenth.

While the epicenter of Texas zydeco is Houston, the music is spread throughout Southeast Texas in the "Golden Triangle" (Beaumont, Port Arthur, and Orange), and in small towns such as Liberty, Dayton, Crosby, Double Bayou, Anahuac, and Raywood.

A. J. Walker Sr., for example, moved with his parents to Raywood from southwestern Louisiana. His father, Tom Walker, was a rodeo promoter in the region, and purchased forty acres outside of Raywood in 1941. There he and his son built the Circle 6 Ranch and he began hosting his own rodeos.[2] The Walkers built a dance hall adjacent to the rodeo arena, and local zydeco bands perform there on weekend nights.

The interest in zydeco has grown and paralleled the commercialization of Cajun culture and cuisine across the nation. There is even a website, www.zydecoevents.com, that advertises dances, concerts, instructional videos, and radio shows in Houston and the surrounding areas of Southeast Texas. My interviews with zydeco musicians in Texas span the period from the 1984 to 2007.[3]

1. For more information, see John Minton, "Houston Creoles and Zydeco: The Emergence of an African American Urban Popular Style," *American Music* 14 (1996), 480–526, and Roger Wood (with photography by James Fraher), *Texas Zydeco*, (Austin: University of Texas Press, 2006).

2. Alan Govenar, "A. J. Walker, Cowboy and Rodeo Organizer," in Sara R. Massey, ed., *Black Cowboys of Texas* (College Station: Texas A&M University Press, 2000), 291–300.

3. In 1994 I conducted extensive fieldwork for a public program, entitled "Preserving the Legacy: African American Cowboys in Texas," which I was organizing for the National Museum of American History, Smithsonian Institution. This program toured to the National Black Arts Festival in Atlanta and to Colorado College in Colorado Springs.

JOHN H. NOBLES

1902–1997; interview, 1985

JOHN "BONES" NOBLES, BEAUMONT, 1985.
PHOTOGRAPH BY ALAN GOVENAR.

I don't care how much rhythm we had. We didn't have no way to let it out. My dad was making fifty cents a day. Three dollars for six days. There wasn't no money to buy musical instruments. The only way for us to let our rhythm out was to find us some bones, but the fact is we didn't use bones at first. We cut our rulers at school at the six-inch mark and made us two little sticks to knock, and that would give us our vent.

Well, after a while, some of them boys got a little combo going, and I wanted to play with them. One boy had a Jew's harp, a rub board, and I was the bones player. See, I found this old cow, and the buzzard done cleaned him up and the weather had done cleaned him up and had done them bones white. I went and got me a saw and sawed me off some bones. That put me above them boys who only had sticks. They kept asking me, "Johnny, where'd you get them bones?" And I'd say, "A man done come through here from up the country and gave them to me."

I went out there and cut me a bunch of bushes and covered up that old cow so that they couldn't find it, and I was kind of unique. So they had to use me in that band.

I process these bones. I put a salve in them. It takes about two months to get a set of bones where they'll give you the right sound.

This white girl from Lamar College once stopped me and said, "Look there, Mr. Bones."

I say, "What you see?"

"Why is this [bone] white and that one here black?"

I say, "Why are you white and I'm black?"

So she say, "Go on with the show."

I didn't make them. That man put colors where he want them. Them bones were white when I got them. These bones were black. So the Good Master put color where he want it. I ain't got nothing to do with that. But the white and black ones have a different pitch. The black ones have a sharper pitch, keener. I play them both. Black and white get along mighty fine when I play them together. You hear that.

I can play myself or with a band. I played with Gatemouth Brown, Clifton Chenier, lots of bands. I like that zydeco beat. I always had a style of rhythm that was a little different from what they were puttin' down. You have to follow that beat.

I was a dancer, man. I could cut a rug, but arthritis took care of that. I can't do much dancin' now, but I got good rhythm in these bones. I'm eighty-five, born in a little place in Georgia in 1902, been in Beaumont since 1922. Back then everybody was either choppin' cotton or hoein' corn. But when that dance time come you put the hoe down. You put your hoe down, and everybody come to the dance. That's the way we had a lot of fun.

I learned to dance when I was shinin' shoes. It was a nickel for a shine, but it was two boys, one working against the other, one shining one shoe, the other shining the other, and the one that shined the best got the nickel. If he couldn't pop that rag and give you a hoodle-doodley, well, he didn't get nothing. I was the one who was going to get that nickel. I'd pop that rag and sound

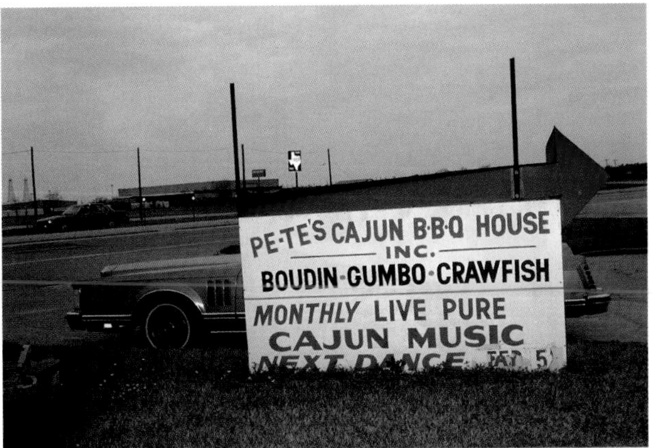

PE-TE'S CAJUN BBQ HOUSE, HOUSTON, 1986.
PHOTOGRAPH BY ALAN GOVENAR.

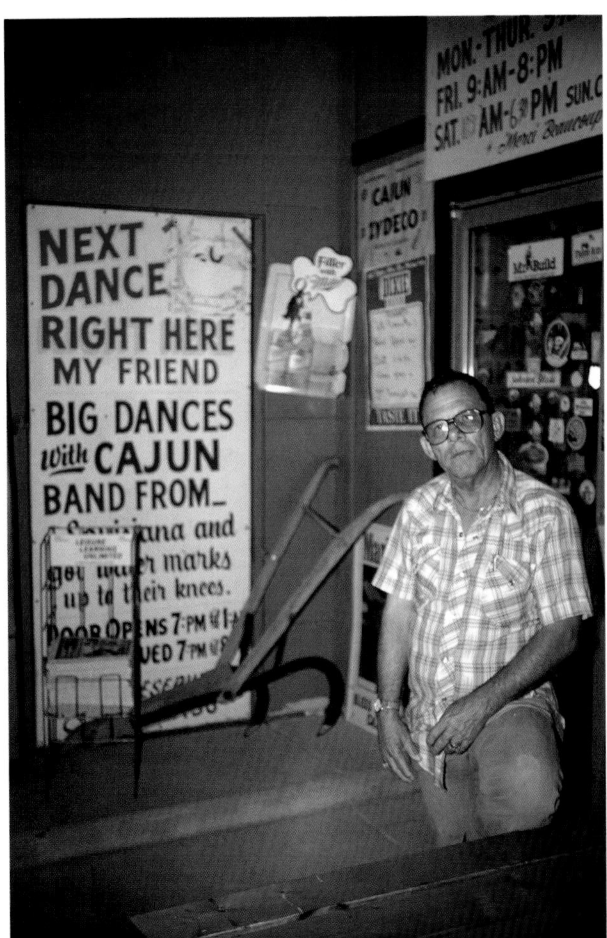

PE-TE (OWNER OF PE-TE'S CAJUN BBQ HOUSE), HOUSTON, 1986.
PHOTOGRAPH BY ALAN GOVENAR.

CLARENCE GALLIEN

(birth date unknown)–1989; interview, 1986

like a buck dancer.

When I came to Houston thirty-three years ago, Lonnie Mitchell was already playing for the Continental Lounge for five years. At that particular time the Continental Lounge was closed and was leased. So I approached the man who owned the building to start la la. He put me in touch with Lonnie Mitchell as reference for what kind of business he had. Lonnie Mitchell has played for at least thirty years at the Continental Lounge, but they didn't call it zydeco at that time; it was la la. They used to give different la la at the house or at a little cafe.

La la was a house dance when thirty, forty, fifty people get together and have a good time. The name changed from la la to zydeco when Clifton [Chenier] made the record "Les Haricots Son Pas Sale" ["The Snap Beans Are Not Salty"]. Clifton is the man who [gets] credit for changing the name. When he made that record, people would ask him what *haricots* means, and *haricots* is snap bean. And from then it was difficult to pronounce and spell the word, but now most around here spell it "zydeco." Clifton didn't really change the music that much, but any time anybody play the accordion, we call it a la la, a country la la.

When I came to Houston, I started a club, a country kind of club, in the early 1940s. But Clifton wasn't playing at that time. The other musicians would charge me a base price for a night dance, and after that, Clifton liked the music so much that the guy who was playing gave Clifton an accordion. Well, Clifton was playing so good that for some reason the guy took his accordion back. So Clifton's uncle, Bill Chenier, bought Clifton an accordion, and he went to playing. And before I knew it, he was number one in the zydeco business, and he's still number one. All the other guys that play, a lot of them copy Clifton's playing. But Clifton never played on anybody else's records but his own.

Now zydeco is one of the most popular [types of] music in Louisiana and Texas. If a club give a dance, or at a Catholic church, everybody will be at the zydeco. I have been helping to put zydeco in the churches for twenty years, and over those years they never had a misunderstanding. The people are like brothers, sisters, or friends. They go out to zydeco to enjoy themselves and have a good time. We never have a problem.

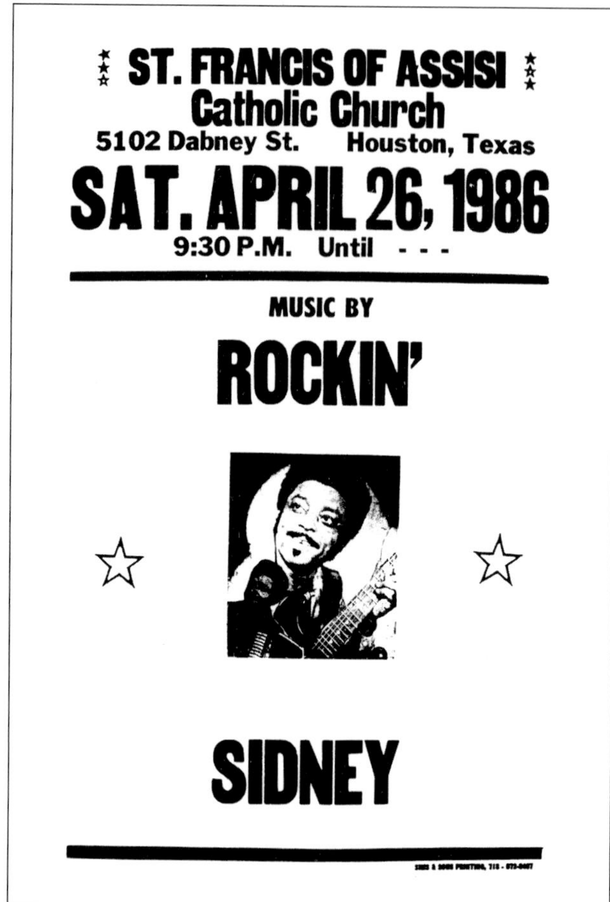

ROCKIN' SIDNEY POSTER, ST. FRANCIS OF ASSISI CATHOLIC CHURCH, HOUSTON, 1986. COURTESY JOHN MINTON.

When I first came to Houston I belonged to St. Nicholas Catholic Church in the Third Ward, and then I moved and we joined Our Mother of Mercy church. But I was told to transfer my membership to St. Francis of Assisi. So I decided that I would transfer thirty years ago. It was a settlement of whites, and I came over here and worked head and head with them in various bazaars. They used to tell me that, "One of these days we're going to give it over to you." I said, "That's no problem." And when they finally did that, we had a $250,000 debt in this parish. My pastor, Father Cumming, needed some means of raising money. We were only collecting $36,000 a year, and our expense was $52,000 a year because we had a school connected with the parish. So I told him that I want to give some entertainment, dance, zydeco, and he said, "Whatever you can do, please do it."

The first dance I had was a zydeco, and we paid the band $65. Well, we had a full house and we made money. Then the next month I got Clifton Chenier to play. At that time he was charging $125, and man, when he played there, everybody came of all walks of life, old people; now it's kind of mixed up with young. But then, all the old folks come because they wanted to dance the zydeco. Today, young folks participate in zydeco as much as the old.

The next band we got was a polka band, and I wasn't in favor of it. But they overruled me, and they went ahead and did it and came out eight dollars behind with the polka. From then on, we didn't substitute no other band but a zydeco band, and we've been successful. I go around and every place help promote the dances, and the other churches saw how great we was doing and started zydeco: St. Nicholas, St. Francis of Xavier, Our Lady Star of the Sea, St. Peter the Apostle, St. Gregory the Great, St. Anne, and others. We now got about twelve or thirteen churches that are giving zydeco in rotation, once a month, all churches. Some churches take it every other month, so that there isn't competition.

I retired from promoting the dances, but I still go out and advertise for my churches. I emcee just about anywhere I go at churches in Houston. I start the dance off at ten, and I emcee the dance.

The world is going for zydeco now, but it was never popularized on the radio until recently. We've been trying, and I'm so glad that somebody woke up for Creole cooking and zydeco. In San Antonio [at the Texas Folklife Festival] people were amazed. I love to cook. The ladies from the Altar Society make the gumbo at the dances. Of course, my wife is usually in there with them. I do the advertising and what I can to help out. I don't get paid anything. But I get a thrill out of this. I work with the senior citizens, I go and pick up bread for

ST. ANNE DeBEAUPRE
Catholic Church
2810 Link Rd. Houston, Texas
Between Airline And North Main
SAT. MAY 17, 1986
9:30 P.M. UNTIL ??
MUSIC BY
JOHN DELAFOSE

AND THE
EUNICE PLAYBOYS

JOHN DELAFOSE AND THE EUNICE PLAYBOYS POSTER, ST. ANNE DEBEAUPRE CATHOLIC CHURCH, HOUSTON, 1986. COURTESY JOHN MINTON.

ANDERSON MOSS

February 15, 1917– ; interview by John Minton, 1986

the needy. Whatever I do is no charge. I'm available.
I was raised in a place they call Mauriceville, Louisiana. And when I was about nine years old, they used to give them zydecos. It was close by where I lived. They had a big hall, they would give zydeco every two weeks. And I go down there, and I was too little to go inside because my mother and daddy was down there, I would stay on the outside, me and my sister and little brother. You see, they would dance, and we was looking. They had a fellow named Johnson play. He had a washboard, accordion, one beat the washboard and one played accordion. They didn't have nothing electric them days. And they had some little iron, they called, they call them *tite fer.* You know, just like you go on these ranches, when they ring that bell, that's what they do with it, they would whup them things, man. And there'd be three or four hundred people in that hall. And the people would be enjoying themselves. That's way back. The guy who was playing was named Johnson. And he wore a shoe, 15 1/2—big foot man, big man. But he pulled that thing. That'll go until about two o'clock at night, start about eight and go to two. That's every two weeks.

Now, they had another man they called, they would call Bidon. Bidon. He had a head about that long. But, brother, you talk about lay that stuff down, he laid it down. He played that accordion. Well, I know'd a whole lots of them would come down there and play in that hall. That's how I come to play accordion.

In 1927 we moved here in Houston. I went downtown and borrowed me an accordion. And I learned myself. Then I started playing. I learned, it didn't take me long. Because I come from down there. I knew how it'd go. And that's way I learned how to play. I'm seventy years old, now. I'm getting on seventy-one.

Nobody teach me to play it, learned myself. My mother and daddy, both of them was living, they used to laugh at me. But my daddy was a harp player, had a great big harp. I guess I took after him. And that's the way—zydeco! I come from the zydeco country. I knew a whole lot of musicians.

Amede Ardoin. Amede had a long head. Poor Amede, they finally killed him, they kill him. I don't know who did it. But that man, he was good. I was old enough to see him. Play good, man. He made records. It was good.

Then they had the Reynold boys. Joseph Reynolds, they call Zo Zo. They lived in Galveston, but they were raised up in my home. It was two brothers. They still living. Live up around Beaumont now. They was good, man. Well, that's during my time when I start playing. See, they had started playing before me, because they used to come out there and pick cotton for my grandpa, and they'd pull them accordions about four o'clock that evening, man. They was good. I know a lot of musicians.

When I come to Houston there was the fellow they call Willie Green. He's dead. He died a couple, three years ago. Yeah, heart trouble. He died. He was good. Willie Green! He played most in the Sixth Ward, back up in there. Well, I played in the First Ward, and Third Ward, Fifth Ward. I had this end covered. Yeah.

I had a washboard man. He died about a year and something ago. Cancer. And then I had a guitar man, just lately started with him, he died, they found him dead in his bed. High blood pressure kill him. He was good, man. And now I got to find me a guitar man; I'm gonna find one. So that's the way it goes.

They start adding, putting guitar, violin, horns, you know. Put all that in now. It wasn't like that when I was coming up. Like I got to go play a party, or play a dance, we were just two-man, a washboard man and accordion man. Now, for the last twenty years, they begin to put drum in. Go good with drums. Drum, washboard, accordion, guitar. Go good. Yeah.

Me and L. C. [Donatto] start about the time I would walk way from Third Ward to Fifth Ward, to save that dime. I'd go way down on Liberty Road, I was living way in Third Ward. I tell him, I say, "I got enough to play, now, you want to play some sets tonight?: He would tell me, "Okay, Moss," say, "I'll be there." Well, all his children was small, see. Say, "Okay. I can depend on you?"

SILVER SLIPPER DANCE, HOUSTON, 1986.
PHOTOGRAPH BY ALAN GOVENAR.

WILLIS PRUDHOMME AND THE ZYDECO EXPRESS POSTER, RAYWOOD, 1992.

I say, "Yeah. 'Cause," I says, "I got too much." I would play every night! And then I would work. You understand? Course, I got used to it, you know, playing after I found out the dope on it. But it wasn't no strain. I'd get up there an' play and drink me a couple of beers, and that's it! Drink that. And just feelin good, but I couldn't drink all that stuff that the people wanted to give me. Let it go by.

I know'd plenty musicians, where I come from. They had the Faulk boys. It was two brothers, one name was Ernest Faulk, and they had one named Boul. And man, they was good. But they all came from around where I was raised up. A place they called Mauriceville, Louisiana, that's where I was raised at. Not too far from Lafayette. Say, about twenty miles from Lafayette.

It's Creole music. That's all it is. They say you get old. I don't give up. I'll go play some. They call me, just so they pay me, I'll go. Man, I played all over River Oaks, all over River Oaks.

Lightnin' [Hopkins] was about the best bluesman they had around here. He was the best. I know Lightnin' from way back. Played blues, he could play zydeco too. Played zydeco. He was something else, man. He played, man, shit! Lightnin' took his time. You talk about play. Put that bottle right there, that little pint. He played that, don't let the people fool you, that Negro played. He knew what he was doing. You sit there and start drinking whiskey, he'd go to playing them damn blues, man, and you better wake up! He going to wake you up if you sleepy, if you tired, he going to wake you up. Lightnin' was good, man. He was about the best! Oh, they had 'em. Some over here, good ones here in Houston, but they wasn't good as Lightnin'! Lightnin' could sit down there an' start and make you a record right quick like that.

Zydeco in Texas and in Louisiana, it's all the same thing, don't let the people fool you. That zydeco music is cutting out everywhere now. Don't let the people fool you. They love it; even the whites like it too, because I play for those white people a long time. And they used to

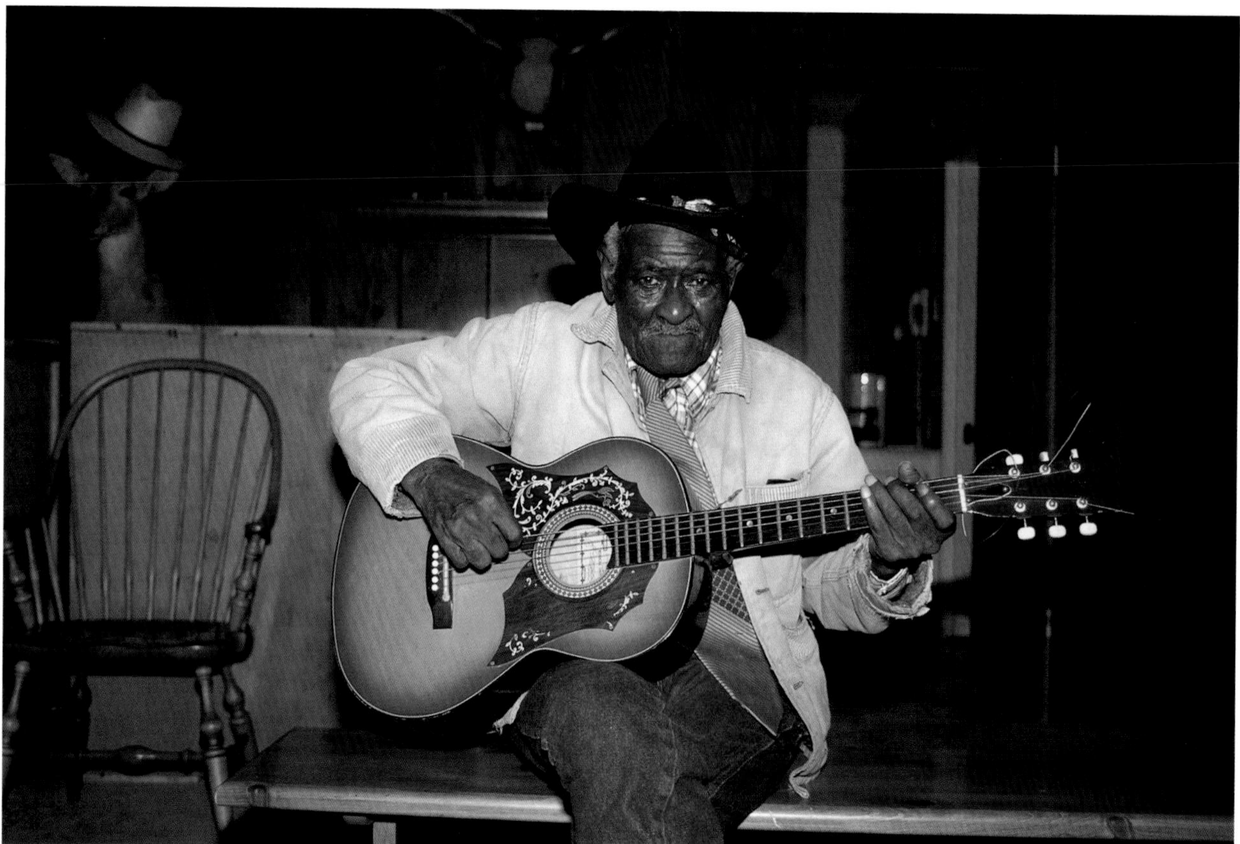

JAMES TISDOM, GOLIAD, 1994.

call it "swamp music," out there in River Oaks. All back there in River Oaks. I play out there at the River Oak Country Club, the richest club in Houston. I played at the club right behind River Oaks, kind of, back that-a-way. Big center they got there, I played there for them. And I play at the Warwick Hotel, I played at the Rice Hotel, and I played at, the old one, the Shamrock Hilton. They tore down, it closed down.

Back in the Twenties and Thirties, I used to play house dances, when I first started. When the "St. Louis Blues" come out and "Stormy Weather." Then they came out with "Black Gal." Them times. They used to give house dances. You pay a dime, a quarter, to come in. That lasts all night, brother. It like it is now. All night. And plenty of food to eat. Plenty to drink. And plenty pretty women. Yes, sir!

They had them little old wind-up [record players] back then. Put them records on the end of the row, you'll pick more cotton. I'll never forget that. Yeah, carry that thing, man, old folks would put them out there in the field, about four o'clock that evening, then turn that record on, wound it up. Shit! They'd pick more cotton. That time of the evening was cool. Cotton grows tall down in Louisiana, don't grow like it used to down home. Tall cotton, stand in the shade when you be picking. And they used to pick cotton by the moon, by the moon shining at night, they'd all go picking cotton. Sometimes people would pick maybe a couple bales of cotton that night. When the moon go in, everybody go to that house, that place of the fellow that giving it. Then they had a big dance in the house. Drink. A lot of good gumbo. Plenty food to eat. Dirty rice. Didn't cost that man nothing. But there, well, everybody got along in them days, wasn't there all this old shooting like it is going what you hear now that people killing themselves. It's just, uh, "I don't like you, uh, so-and-so." "Well, come on the outside, we going to have a little, we going to see which is the best man," then you could hear them fists pop! And then when they got through, they shake hands. You know. Everything was lovely. But then now all you hear is them boom, boom, boom, boom. But that's wrong, you know, killing your family. Oh, man. All these women hurt you, you going to go jump up and shoot a woman down, man? You just forget about that. And that's right!

Back there in Louisiana, my mother would get ready for the Mardi Gras. She'd have candy, food. See, they would come by droves. Sometimes maybe twenty-five or thirty men would drive up to your house, and they had all them masks on, they didn't know who they was, a lot of them was white and colored, they stopped there and they eat. It was dance, played [the dance], some of them, they had musicians with them, they play the music, they march for thirty minutes, they're gone! They go on down. That night, they'll have a great big dance. It's something else to see. But you don't see that no more, you go to New Orleans, Mardis Gras. But, man, they used to give Mardi Gras at home, down in the country! I was about this high. On horseback, man, pretty horse, had all them tails tied. Them horse dressed, man!

Things have changed down home, now, you see. The young got it. All them old people is about died out. Young people, it's all different. It ain't like it used to be. Young people, they like that zydeco. They got it down home. Every weekend they got something going down home, big zydeco. Every six, seven months they've got a new musician.

I was educated on that button accordion. I play at night, but the next day I couldn't raise them arms. That son-of-a-gun was killing me. You see, a triple note accordion you got to keep pumping. That pump and jerk. This here be all sore, now. I could, lots of times I have to play the next day. You have to put the accordion in my lap for me, I couldn't raise it up. So I left it alone, and I got me some piano notes. I got some more accordions. So I learned how to play both of them. They got a new kind there, I been watching on the TV, I'm gonna learn how to play that thing, I'm gonna buy me one. It's made flat like this. Hook it on your shoulder. I don't know what in the heck they call it, but that sound pretty. I heard some white boys play on the TV. I said, "I'm gonna get me one of them things one of these days, I'm gonna try it out." I was almost sure I could play it.

When I got to Houston, the first job I had was digging sewers. They didn't have no sewer. That darn is hard, thing is hard now, but way better than, way better than now. Well, they had plenty work, the ones wanted to work, but the price wasn't so high, but you made your food so cheap and rent. A house like this, it two-fifty a week. Now, go find one for two-fifty, man. Man, you got to pay or else!

We moved here in 1927. The crop in Louisiana went down to nothing. And so I had my two older brothers living here in Houston, they had good jobs. And so my mother came over here and my baby brother, and she seen how things was going over here, she come back home and told my daddy, says, it's the best thing to move to Houston; says, there's plenty of work, they's begging for men to work, see, we's were all big enough to work. So, we here. But I still go back and forth down home, I still got a lot of my people lives there. Four years, four years ago I retired. I was working out there in River Oaks. So—I thank the Lord, I can draw some of my money. You can make that money and when you get a certain age you can start drawing!

I made a record and I didn't get nothing out of it! They beat me out of it. Right here in town. I made four records. And so there's lots of people have asked me to make some, now. And with what happened to me the

CLEVELAND WALTERS

April 16, 1925– ; interview, 2004

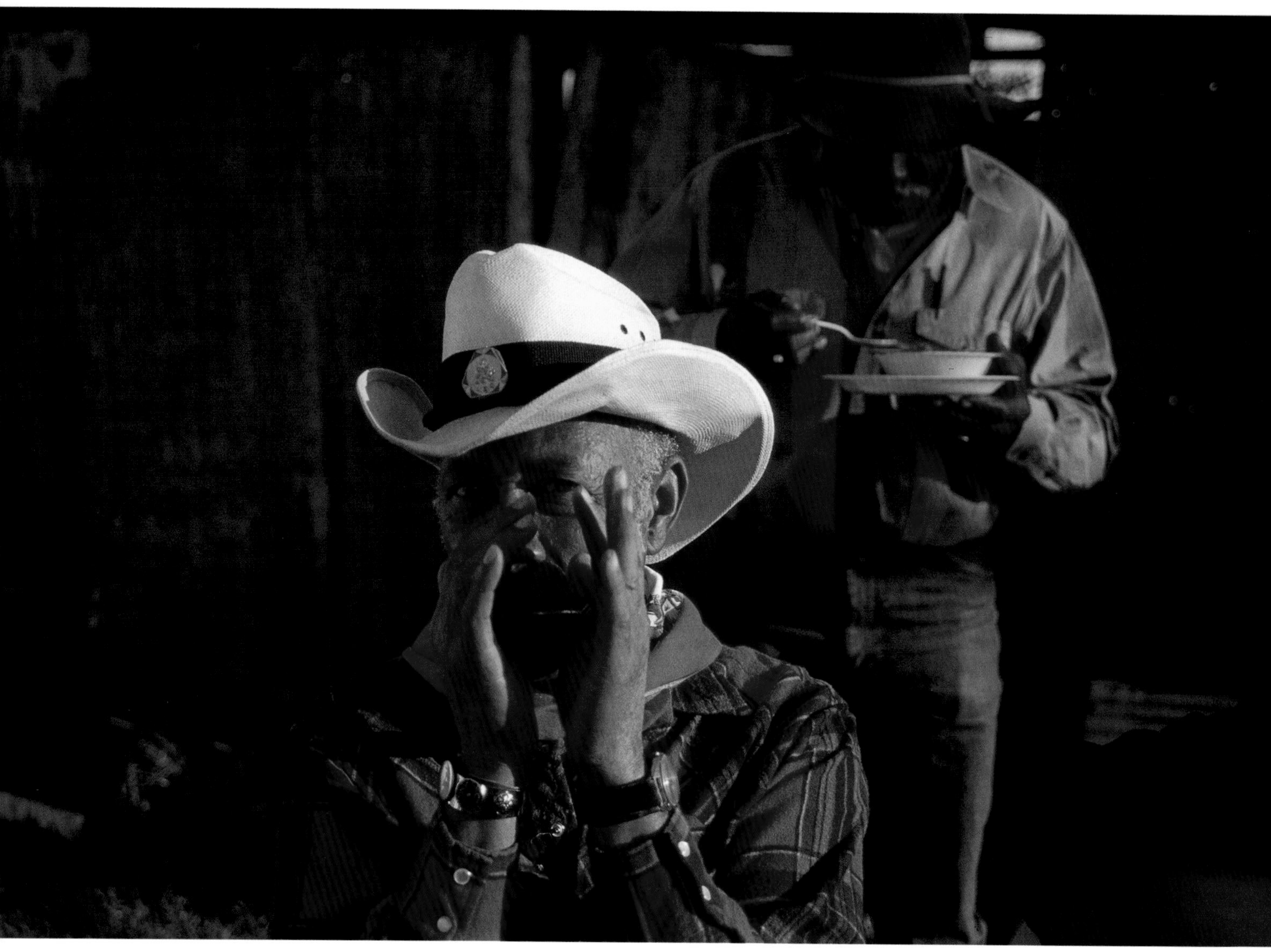

CLEVELAND WALTERS AND A. J. WALKER, CIRCLE 6 RANCH, 1996.
PHOTOGRAPH BY ALAN GOVENAR.

first time, I said, "Well, forget about records."

I was a kid when I started playing music. I was born in Ames, Texas. We were raised way back on the farm, so far back in the woods we just called it Foggy Bottoms. That's why a cowboy used to a carry a sidearm. When Christmastime come, you had two choices. I'd say I was four years old. You had to get a harmonica, a little ten-cents harmonica, or a little single-shot cap pistol, or an apple or an orange—not both. So I would always take the harmonica. And that's why I learned from there, from just a kid. I'd always keep one in my pocket. That's the best friend you could ever have, a harmonica. And I'd keep one in my pocket at all times. And that's how long I've been playing. And I still, sometimes the kids come, and even if I'm hurting and sick, they still want me to play a little bit for them. I got three or four harmonicas now that I keep.

My father was named Arthur Walters. And my mother was Sedonia Burt Walters. You can put *s* or *c*. Sometimes they said Cedonia. But I think it would be an *s*. That's what she used. They did just farm work. Well, when my father first came from Louisiana, he done some sharecropping, but we had our own place. Yeah, north of Ames, about three miles back in the woods. We had cattle, all kind of livestock. That's why we called it farming and ranching, not just farming. I still—after World War II, long in there, things started to change, and industries started coming in, and people started leaving off the farm. But after I got public work, I still kept livestock. I always did have livestock. So right now, my son-in-law got cows and horses. Right now I do a little gardening. I can't do much now; my health is bad. I'll be eighty years old my next birthday.

My father come from around the Crowley area [of Louisiana]. He had two families. I don't know what happened, him and his first wife, whoever the other family was, why they broke up. But he was a rice farmer there off from Crowley—they called it Esterwood, little place there, Esterwood—he was a rice farmer. And so, when he came from Louisiana down there, my mother come from around Abbeville and New Iberia area, where she came from. He rented a whole boxcar. When they came over here, they had everything in there, his wife and two kids, my two oldest sisters on my side, and his team and his tools, farm tools and everything. He had to sharecrop that year, and the next year, I think, he bought his own place. But two of my older siblings was born in Louisiana, and the others was born here in Texas. And all the other, the first children from his first family, was born in Louisiana, all them were born in Louisiana.

My brother and his dad [his name was Mansfield Walters] played music. His nickname was "Tebay." Everybody around here knew him by that; they didn't know his real name. I'm the youngest. My father had two families, and he had twenty-six children. And I'm

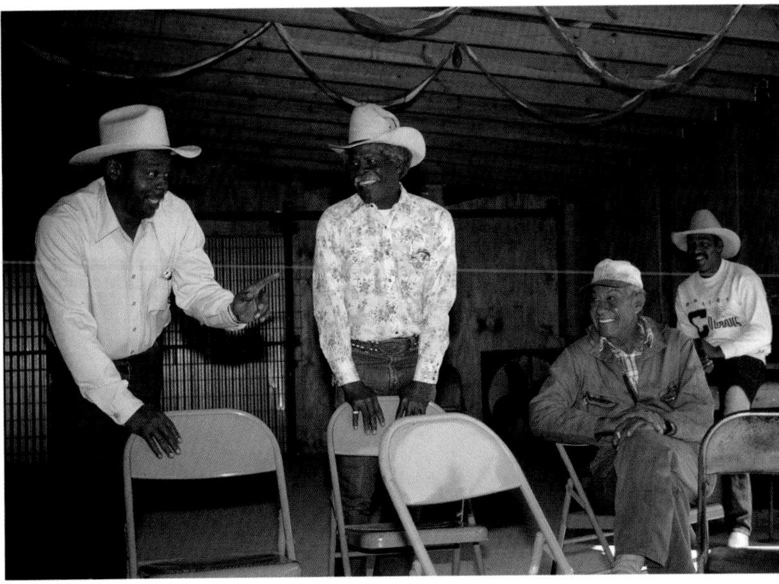

COWBOYS AT THE CIRCLE 6 RANCH, 1992. PHOTOGRAPH BY ALAN GOVENAR.

the twenty-sixth one, the last one. All of them is dead; I'm the only one left in the original Walters family. All of them gone but me.

My brother played accordion. He started when he was just a teenager, maybe fifteen, sixteen years old. He bought a little old Sears Roebuck single-note accordion. And he started from there, and then the white people used to get him to go play for them, and he started playing house dances. Really, he should have had a lot of recognition because he started way back, I guess before Clifton Chenier was ever born. He might have been fifteen years older than me.

Zydeco music, that's all we had, didn't have nothing else but that. Well, they just called it la la for a long time, at house dances, and then Clifton Chenier, he switched it over to zydeco. But for a long time, they just called it la la. We just played house dances and things like that, and my brother and me, we'd go all over. And later, just before he died, he got blind, and we'd go around. We had a real Cajun that played with us, Dominick Thibodeaux. So we'd go, we'd play for the church, we played everywhere. Thibodeaux's wife was bedridden, so I was working, so I would just go with them and give them the money, my brother and Thibodeaux.

Thibodeaux played a single-note accordion. That's what a lot of them young ones is coming back with now, coming back to that single-note. My brother, he left

OUR LADY STAR OF THE SEA
Catholic Church Hall
1401 Fidelity Rd. Houston, Texas
SAT. SEPT. 20, 1986
9:30 P.M. UNTIL 1:30 A.M.

Music By

BUCK WHEAT

AND HIS

IL'S SONT PARTIS BAND

Sims Printing 672-0467

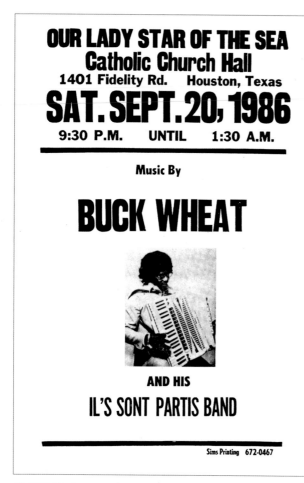

BUCK WHEAT AND HIS IL'S SONT PARTIS BAND POSTER, OUR LADY STAR OF THE SEA CATHOLIC CHURCH HALL, HOUSTON, 1986. COURTESY JOHN MINTON.

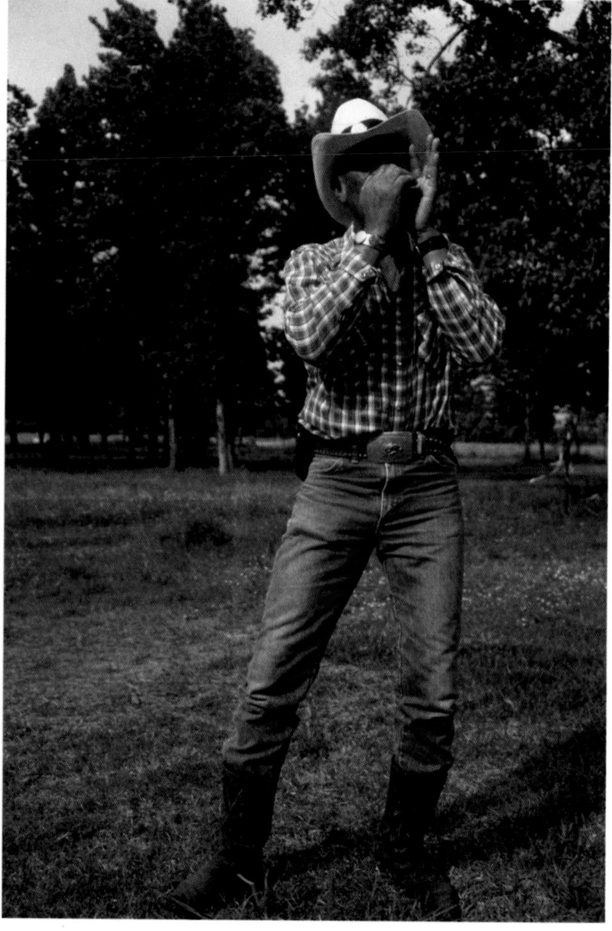

CLEVELAND WALTERS, CIRCLE 6 RANCH, 1996. PHOTOGRAPH BY ALAN GOVENAR.

from that and went to the double note, then he left from that and went to triple note. So, from time to time—it used to frustrate me all the time, by not buckling down to the accordion like I was supposed to. I was supposed to be one of the best, but I loved to dance a lot. I'm mostly an entertainer, more than anything, a musical entertainer, because we used to go all over. Sometimes, when my brother died, and all the other musicians died that used to play with me, I had to go by myself, so I had to bring all my instruments, my accordion and all that stuff, with me. And the people, I played for birthday parties, I played in the rest home, and everywhere. And they would help me. I had to go by myself, but I would play and then do some entertaining. I love to make people laugh and stuff like that. But the way I come up, there wasn't nothing else but that, way back in there.

Everyone in my family used to scold me all the time about not buckling down to it. But I used to do a lot of dancing, so after all of them, Lonnie Mitchell and all, a whole lot of them learned from him, come from him. And there was another one he learned from. I don't know if his right name was Joe Jackson. . . . Boozoo Chavis, that "Paper in the Shoe," that came from Joe—his nickname was Jesse—Joe Jesse Jackson. He couldn't read or write or nothing, but anyway, my brother went to Louisiana, brought him back over here to Texas, and he stayed on the farm awhile with us. And from there, when the war started, he got on with the Shell refinery. But he was the king of the accordion, that man there, he played a double note, and he taught my brother, and all those other accordion players got off the single note on the double note and learned all them different songs that Clifton Chenier first started playing. That came from him. He come from around Crowley, somewhere in there he came from. He was a cane cutter back in there. After Boozoo played—you know Boozoo got to be the king with the "Paper in the Shoe"—I talked to Boozoo about it, and come to find out that him and Joe used to cut cane together. That's why he learned that. And he plays it exactly like Joseph. He don't have all the words that Joseph had in it.

And there's one song, I don't know how Boozoo got it, but my brother did it first. "Baby, Do Right," you heard that? That was my brother's song. But he never did record.

They didn't have all that back in there. They just sang songs like that. It was bad they didn't have no kind of recognition. Those are the real original accordion players back in there. And I came up with them. I should have been one of the best, because they used to fuss at me, but I'd always want to dance and get on the board. I was the one used to rap behind them.

I was a dancer, man, some of everything—two-step, waltz. We finally got what they call the swing, swing your partner, because them old people didn't want that close dancing. They'd all be watching. You had to have some daylight between you and the girl back in them times. But I done two-steps, waltzes, and finally the swing came out.

House parties were for dancing, and they had food. When they said, "Ladies to the bar," well, then, you'd take the lady you were dancing with, and they had candy and popcorn balls and stuff like that, gumbo. You had to treat them to dance with them.

We had chicken and had guinea gumbo; they'd put all kind of different stuff in it, sauces and all that other stuff goes in it. Frenchmen put all kind of stuff in the gumbo. That's why they call it gumbo because it's so much mixed up, so many different ingredients in there. But we had a good time. . . . We had to put all the furniture in one room, you know, like the living room, where they dance, you take all the furniture out of there and put it in another room or outside on the porch or somewhere, till the next day, then put it back.

The house party would start after everybody get out of the field and get cleaned up. I guess it would start up around eight o'clock, something like that. Sometimes it would go to the wee hours in the morning. Then some of them had to go to church on top of that, then do their regular morning chores. We had to milk cows and stuff like that, do a lot of feeding. After you come from church, then you can go find a shade tree somewhere and sleep the rest of the evening. But all that had to be done regardless of how late you stayed up. You had to do your regular chores.

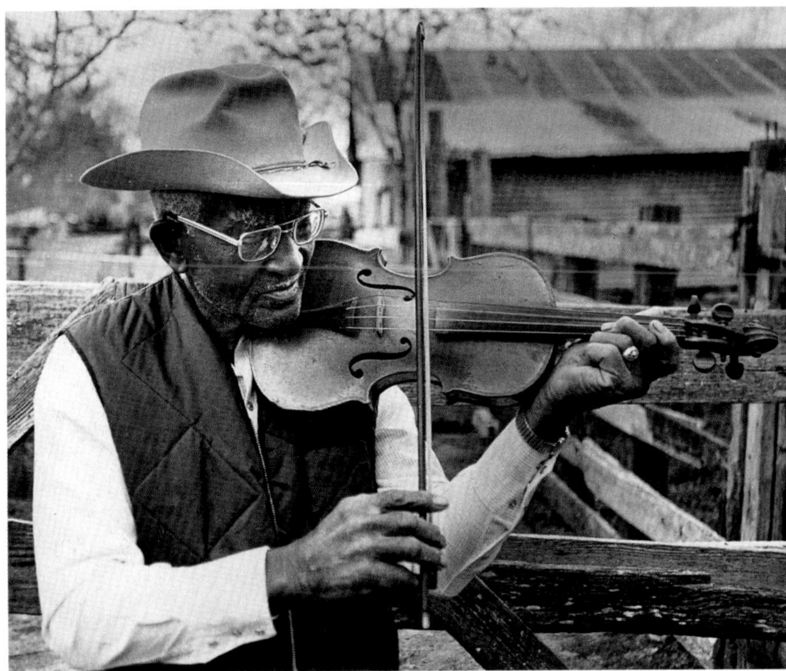

MANUEL RIVERS (OWNER OF THE DOUBLE BAYOU DANCE HALL AND UNCLE OF PETE MAYES), DOUBLE BAYOU, 1985. PHOTOGRAPH BY ALAN GOVENAR.

We had a creek behind our farm . . . and they made moonshine, what you call it, and that rotgut. What they call rotgut, they would drink it, too, but they mostly used it for medicine, because it was so bad. But they would drink that, and they would make a lot of different homemade wine, mulberry wine, muscatel wine, and then make brandy, peach brandy. But then they didn't throw those peelings and core away. Like pear trees and all that stuff, they'd make brandy out of that. That's some good stuff.

Maybe it cost a nickel or a dime back in them times, for a shot, a little, small glass, what they call a shot. But that moonshine, the old people, they didn't have to tell you twice, they'd tell you, you didn't drink that. You had to sip it. Sip or nip. A shot, you take a shot, wasn't going to be but that shot or two. You didn't want no more because you'd be out. So you had to learn to sip or nip just a little bit because it was so bad. You didn't just turn it up and drink it because somebody gonna pick you up [off the floor].

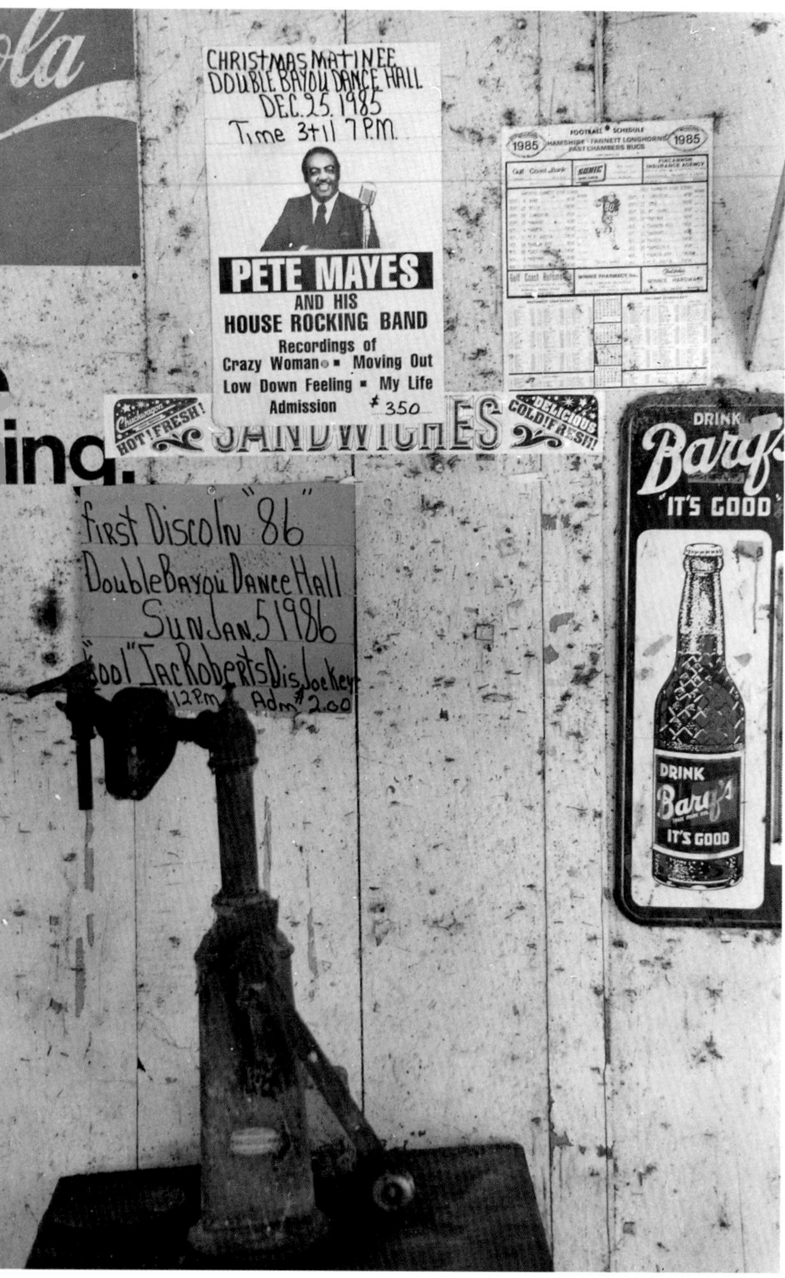

PETE MAYES POSTER, DOUBLE BAYOU, 1985.
PHOTOGRAPH BY ALAN GOVENAR.

I'll tell you a little tale about a man I used to work with. He say he got a job at a moonshine place, had to siphon from the vat, and he had a whole bunch of—instead of a half a pint, they'd call that a flask. A flask was smaller than a half a pint. You filled that, and a half a pint, and a pint, and quart, different sizes, and that was his job, to fill those things up. Say what happened, when the whiskey started coming, he started to drinking. When the man came, he was out and the whiskey running everywhere. So he lost his job. But that's the kind of stuff we was raised with—it was a long time before we could ever go to town to drink this whiskey they've got now and wine they got now. On the farm, we made all that stuff ourselves.

My brother used to go play for white people. They'd have house dances and things, but on the farm, we all got along just fine. We'd help each other, and it didn't make no difference. We got along like one big family—until you go to town. We had to go to Liberty for some reason. That's when you had to be careful, because some of them would beat black people up just for the fun of it. If you go, you had to be sure and have enough with you, three or four people at least, to keep from being beat up. But other than that, we got along good. According to whom you worked for, too, that had a whole lot to do with it because you worked for some of those rich people, it wasn't nobody going to touch you. Like the ranchers that I worked for, they called them the Rich brothers. They were just as rich as the name. And I didn't have to worry about it. All the people I worked for, other people didn't bother me. If they did, it was always another white man there to take it up. So discrimination was there, but we got along good. It was mostly in town, you understand what I'm saying?

They started playing zydeco in the churches, I think maybe in the Forties, when some of those accordion players started coming from Louisiana down here. And we had, like my brother, he and I—you know where Trinity Gardens? What they call it now is Fifth Ward. But Fifth Ward, it was named Frenchtown for a while. And down Trinity Gardens was nothing but trees. We used to play all on Saturday night and then take the pig trail to go to Fifth Ward for that Sunday. And that was back maybe in the late Thirties or late Forties, along in there.

Back when I was coming up, we would start—for instance, my brother, when none of them had a car, he'd load his musicians [into his car]. We had a guitar player and a bone man, and myself, mostly, because by me being the younger—my daddy died when I was three years old—so he would take me with him, promise my mother that he would take care of me. The main thing was to watch the equipment, the instruments and things in the car, until we get over there. You know where the Trinity River is. Well, on the east side of the Trinity River was a Philips 66 station there. He would stop there, and he'd play enough to get his car filled up with gas, and then we'd leave. We'd start at Dayton and go on all the way into Houston. And when we come back, we'd have enough money to make the rest of the week.

They would pay him so much, like the house dances, he'd stop at a house dance in Dayton when we'd leave that Philips 66 station, he had a dance to play in Dayton, a house dance. Then we'll go on up to play a little bit—might sometimes he wouldn't play the whole dance because might be another musician to come in. But we'd stop on the other side of Shelton, there's a little town there, and then we'd leave and go out to Houston around Trinity Gardens and Frenchtown, and then back. And around here were house dances, and we'd have birthday parties and little stuff like that.

Sometimes he had to play, according to if he go straight—say, he'd stop at Dayton, he had to play maybe four hours, and then we'd go on. Maybe if he'd play just two hours and then stop on the other side of Shelton two hours and then go on into Houston. Sometimes it'd be an accordion player already there, and they'll switch. So they'll go till wee hours in the morning, till three or four o'clock in the morning. But the other musicians would be gone, so sometimes they'd switch. He'd play three or four hours, and then another musician would come in and play until the wee hours in the morning.

Me and Lonnie [Mitchell] was just like brothers. He had cattle, too. I done a lot of his cattle work. South of Ames, just about maybe two miles south of Ames. He used to live maybe a quarter of a mile right north from me before he went to Houston.

And he was a good accordion player. He took [lessons] from this guy Joe Jesse and my brother. That's where he learned at. Joe Jesse Jackson. L. C. [Donatto]. That's where he learned at, too. Joe Jesse, they called him, he learned all of them how to play, and all those songs come from him. And Clifton Chenier, when they got to Barrett Station, they met, and he learned a lot from Joe. And Joe stayed with us on the farm till he got on with the Shell refinery. When he died, he died rich. Joe had two homes when he died. He got on with the Shell, and he bought a home there in Barrett, and then he bought another. He had two homes there in Barrett, and a lot of them guys learned from him. Bud King and all them. Joe was the king, but he couldn't read or write or nothing. During World War II, he got on in the labor department; he was a good laborer. He didn't have to read or write. And he kept on playing. I got to be his main board man. I don't care where he was playing at, when I would come up, he would get rid of the board man and put me on there. And when he retired, he wanted me to follow him. I told him no, I couldn't do that because I was still working and I had a family. I couldn't follow him. So, it wasn't long after he retired that he died, but we all learned all that from him. When he come back to Louisiana, must have been in the Thirties. I was one of his pallbearers at his funeral in Barrett. I didn't know he had two sons. That's the first time and the last time I saw them.

They [Joe Jesse Jackson's sons] were supposed to [be musicians]—he had bought one of them a brand-new accordion and everything, the amplifier and everything was blue. He was in the bed, on his last leg, when the wife called me to go over there. And one of the sons, I don't know which one, fell out of that. You know, just like Clifton Chenier's son, he's still got that old accordion. But so I don't know what Joseph's sons—I never heard from them, I never seen them. I was hoping I could talk to them and maybe get some pictures of him. When I met Boozoo Chavis, after he played in Dayton [Texas] and he played "Paper in the Shoe." And so I asked him if he knew Joe Jesse, and he said, yes, so he told me they used to cut cane together. And so I told him that was Joe's song. Of course, there's a lot words that Joe sung there in Creole and English. Boozoo just sung it in English, but Joe mixed it up. He'd mix up Creole and English in it. But Boozoo played it exactly like, the tune is exactly like Joe's.

I played the board. Well, back then, we had to use a regular rubbing board what they washed clothes with. And then we'd get a raggedy one that the side was coming off and just take the metal part. And with the metal, some of them wasn't nothing but a little brass; it didn't have much of a sound to it. And then they finally got the galvanized, which had a little bit of sound, and the little triangle thing, the little triangle iron. You could hold it on the end of your thumb. But that board, finally we got to where we'd take a piece of galvanized and make some ridges in it, and you hang it on your neck and let it swing. That's where you get the different sounds. You can let it swing in different ways and get the different sounds from it. And Clifton Chenier [and his brother, Cleveland] made the first one that you put around your shoulders.

The board that I got now, that you seen there, it look like the others, but there ain't no other one like that because that's made out of airplane steel, and it has a different sound from any board that I ever had. Some of them board men get aholt of it, they don't want to turn it loose. See, one of my sons was in the Air Force; I don't know how he got ahold of that, but I guess it was because they had these plane wrecks, and he brought it to me, and I went to Carlton Semien. He was an accordion player. We played a lot together, and he told me he knowed where there was a machine shop in McNair that might make one. So we brought that piece of metal over there, and the diagram, and a young man, he had never heard of nothing like that before. So after I told him what I wanted, I was standing right beside him, and he took a little piece of metal, and he bent it and started the ridges in it. I put a 3/8 [inch] ridge in there. I said no bigger than that, and no smaller. I wanted a 3/8 ridge. He said, "That's what you want?" I say yeah. So then he took this big piece. I made it long enough till I told him to stop. Then he wanted me to show him the sound of it. So he got two drill bits and I got two drill bits and showed him how it goes. And all the people in the shop came there and wanted to listen to all that. He had never heard of nothing like that or seen nothing like that before. But I got the only one that's made out of airplane steel. Way back there, they used to have them old rubbing boards. It was kind of a brass. And then they went to galvanized; it was a little bit better.

We'd put a hole, two holes in it, on each end, either end you wanted to use. The ridges would run crossways, so you put two holes in there. And then you put a string in there with a loop so you could adjust it. You know, if you wanted it to come down a little lower or higher, you could just slip in that loop and put a slip-knot in there. That's how you adjust it.

All of them accordion players in Texas, they want to put a little bit different sound and a little bit different rhythm in their music. I think Texas might have had a little bit different rhythm in it than Louisiana. A little more jazz and little more swing in it. Everyone would put their little touch on it. Like these young accordion players now, that ain't no real zydeco. They put so much, they want to put some of that rock music in there, and they mix it all up. And it's not the real zydeco sound.

I think some of it [zydeco] came from Africa. Some of it was fast. We used to call some of them the slow burners. That was real fast, breakdown. And then you could two-step. You could slow a two-step down, or you could do it a little bit faster, a fast two-step or a slow two-step. Same way with a waltz. They got to where you could speed a waltz up a little bit and play it slow. And finally, they got to where you could have a swing waltz. You could swing out on a waltz later on. But it was two ways for a waltz and two ways for a two-step, fast one or a slow one.

We used have a lot of zydeco in the churches. Well, we had the St. Francis of Xavier and St. Francis of Assisi. That was south of Houston, St. Francis Xavier, and St. Francis Assisi was right back in the main part of Houston. I don't remember which street. I've been there many times. There was Clarence Gallien [who used to book the church zydecos]. We used to have a lot of dances here in Ames, at our church, Mother of Mercy, used to give a lot of zydeco. Clarence Garlow played with us, too. Clarence Garlow, far as I know, I can say, he was a pretty nice fellow—interesting to be around, I'd say. He mixed it up. He'd play some zydeco. Ain't too many would play zydeco on a guitar.

We used to have that old hall not too far from here, Double Bayou Hall. I knew Pete Mayes. His uncle had that place. Every once in a while, they come back and play for free, just for old tradition. That old hall is still there. It's raggedy, but it's still there. They're keeping it for a landmark and history, historical. Every once in a while, I think once a year, every once in a while, they come back once a year now. Gather round and play.

Well, I done all kinds of work. We had to do some farm work, and we had to do some ranching. Wasn't nothing but farming and ranching back in them times. And from then on, I learned a whole lot: carpentering, and later on, I learned anything can be made with iron, I'll make it. Give me a cutting torch and a welding machine, I'll make it. And music. There's a whole lot of things I do. I done all the electrical work in my house, all that stuff. Me and my family—I had five boys, and those girls, there are two girls, they're just tough as those boys are. We didn't hire nobody for nothing. We done it all ourselves. It might've not been as good looking as the rest, but it was substantial. . . .

I got on with the state for twenty years. I run a machine beside the road, the main thing. But they could use me all the way around, any way they needed me, but one of my main jobs was welding, anything that needed to be fixed. They had other welders there, but when I fixed something, I had to find out the cause of it, why it broke. You had to fix the cause, and so, in other words, it would hold up better than some of the other men, and it didn't take me all day fooling around with it, because when they wanted me to do something, I would go ahead and do it and be back on my regular job. I learned different types of metal, to use different kinds of rods for different metals, build all kinds of things in there. We had one of the first machines that came out that had what they call an extension telescope. It was mounted on an International tractor with a little Wisconsin motor, and we used it to cut grass. I could reach out in all these ditches where the mowers couldn't get in at. I could reach in there and get it, and all beside the fence. Then, I got to where I made my own. I asked the boss man if I could take that—the first mower we got used to be on wheels. And then those things would ball up with dirt, and they wouldn't turn, and they had all that weight on it. So I asked him if I could take one of the old mowers and make my own mower that used some skids instead of those wheels. So he told me, well, he said, "Whichever way," because they know how good a welder I was. "Whatever you decide," say, "Go ahead." It took me maybe a day or so to make what I wanted, and I put it on skids instead of those wheels. And then I could open it up and start cutting bushes. And I got to where I could cut trees, anything from 2 inches, 3, up to 4 inches, I could cut them with that mower.

So, then, I'd go all over. I would leave here, I would go all the way up from Liberty to Montgomery County, west, and all out in the Cleveland area, north, and all over Liberty County with that mower. I wouldn't turn down nothing. It was bushes and trees and grass and everything with that mower; that was one my main jobs. And then when they needed me to do some welding, I would go ahead and do that. That was mostly repairing stuff. Sometimes they would just tell me what they wanted something to do, make some object, they'd tell me what they wanted me to do, and I would make it, and it would turn out successful. Then I would go back to my regular job. Sometime I had to go out and help the patch crew. I could drive trucks, front-end loader and all that. Anything they wanted me to do, I would do it. Even sweeping. Rainy days, my machine be down or something, couldn't get out there. "You doing that?" I say, "I'm here to work." I say, "It don't make no difference; I'm here to work." "Well, I ain't getting paid for that." I say, "It don't make no difference. Whatever the boss man tell me to do, that's what I'm going to do."

I been married, I think this year is fifty-eight years. To Grace Walters. She was a Roy, Grace Ann Roy. I thank the good Lord gave me something to match out. Building this house here, she done all the work inside. She can use a hammer and saw just good as I do. She's tough. That's where those girls get it from. I got two girls. They don't back off of nothing.

I just say my prayers morning and night, and if I take a noon nap, I say a prayer. And you got to believe before you can receive, you know that. When it come to the Holy Spirit and Jesus, you have to believe in Him. I don't farm but maybe a third of what I used to farm. I go out in the garden, and I still ride my bike. I'm known around—I'd ride my bike. That's when I had livestock. I rode my bike. One old bike, I rode fourteen years. I called it Old Reliable. Then when I retired, they went to Sears and bought me a brand-new one, the state bought me a brand-new one. And they fixed it up. That's what I ride now. Every morning, I ride that old bicycle. And I take enough rest. . . . And being eighty years old, I think if I'm ever going to be with the good Lord, now is the

ALPHONSE "LONNIE" MITCHELL

1925–September 18, 1995; interview by John Minton, 1986

time, and I use my common sense, and please Him. I was born in Liberty, Texas, and that's where I started playing. I learned, I could play good enough for dancing when I was eighteen. Early '50 I moved to Houston, and I didn't hear nothing about zydeco music for about a year after I moved here. Then I heard about a guy named Willie Green [who] was playing out in Sixth Ward. So that's when I went over there, played some, and a guy heard me, and they said, "If you get your music, I'll hire you to play." Now, I got started that way, and once—well, for about three years—I played every night but Wednesday night. And I do body painting, by the way, for the Cadillac people in Alvin. I play and go to work the next morning, have to be to work by seven-thirty. So that's how I got started playing. Yeah.

My mother and daddy are from Louisiana; one from Crowley and the other's from Estherwood, Louisiana. I'm the only one [who plays music]. There was ten of us. And I'm the only one out of ten that wanted to play music. The rest of them didn't want to fool with it. I just love music ever since I heard, you know, zydeco music. It was a guy in Houston, name of Joe Jesse, he was playing. My uncle lived in Raywood, a little town, and he would get that guy to play every other Saturday. My older brother and him was good friends, and he would come over there and spend the night with my brother and he showed me how to play the accordion, and I just started from there coming up. I was about twelve, I guess, something like that, when he first started coming to my mother's, and so my mother bought me one, and I just took up from there. By ear, that's right, most zydeco music back then was just by ear. You just make up your own song, and it work out all right. Clifton Chenier and I started here in Houston about the same time.

Zydeco music. It's different from other music. I don't know, it's some way or another, people just love that type of music, really love that type of music, and it's come up like that. Well, it's related, yeah, Cajun music, sure is. Just blacks play a little different. Yeah. Well, it related to blues, 'course it a little different from blues, but you can play blues on a zydeco. I don't know, zydeco music. It's related to blues, but a little different than the blues. Mostly blues is played with a guitar, and, course you can play blues on accordion if you know how. You know, just got to take it up, because I know I can play blues, whole lot of pieces of blues. And you know all the guys that play accordion, some of them can't and some of them can. Yeah, you can play a blues and play zydeco, and you play it in a different tone, but you can still play blues on the zydeco music. 'Course, they call it, when you play a blues with the accordion, they call it a "slow drag." Yeah, I play a whole lot of blues myself, but most people want that regular zydeco. Fast two-step, yeah. That's a fast two-step.

They can play guitar zydeco, because that guy [who] plays with me, he can play zydeco on that guitar. Whole lot of guys can play it. A special style. But most anything I can play, now, he and I been together about two years now. And he can play a zydeco piece on that guitar just like I play on my accordion. Right. [His name is] Sylvester Anderson. My bass man, we call him "Tiny." The boy on the bass guitar, his name is Roy. I just can't think of the last names. So we going good, real good on, you know, playing together.

Well, when I first playing zydeco, it was just a washboard. That's what they used, washboard, then. I played quite a few years just with a washboard. Yeah, Clifton did the same thing when he started, and a little bit later in the years, well, we got a drum, and the washboard, then got a lead guitar, and went on from there. Yeah, but I played about, I know, about eight, ten years just with a washboard. Yeah, because I used to play, when in Liberty there, I played, I didn't start using a drum and a guitar until I come here to Houston.

There ain't much difference [between zydeco in Houston and zydeco in Louisiana]. Most of the guys

(OPPOSITE) LONNIE MITCHELL, HOUSTON, 1985. PHOTOGRAPH BY ALAN GOVENAR.

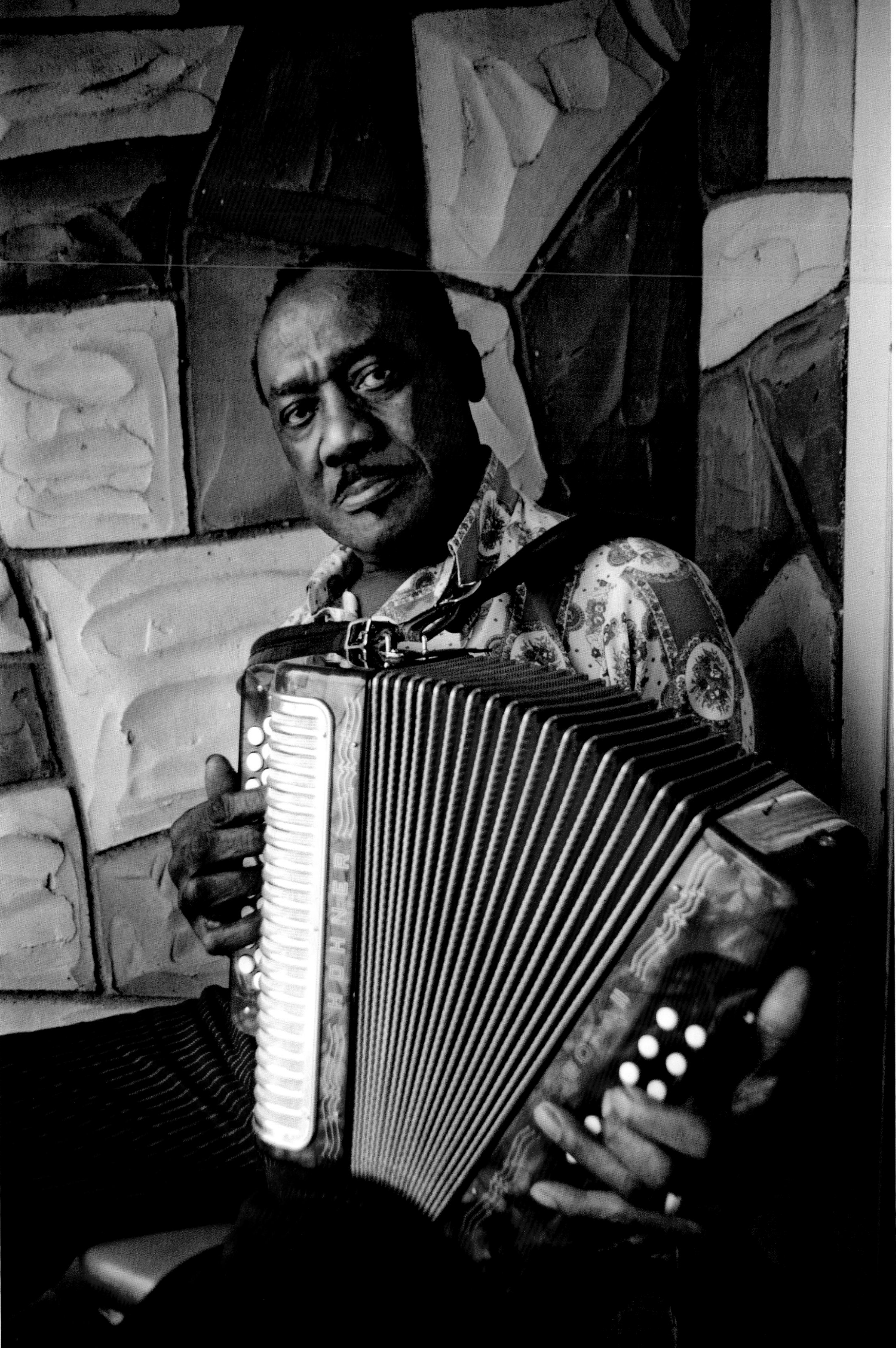
HOHNER

LONNIE MITCHELL POSTER,
CONTINENTAL LOUNGE, HOUSTON, 1987.
PHOTOGRAPH BY ALAN GOVENAR.

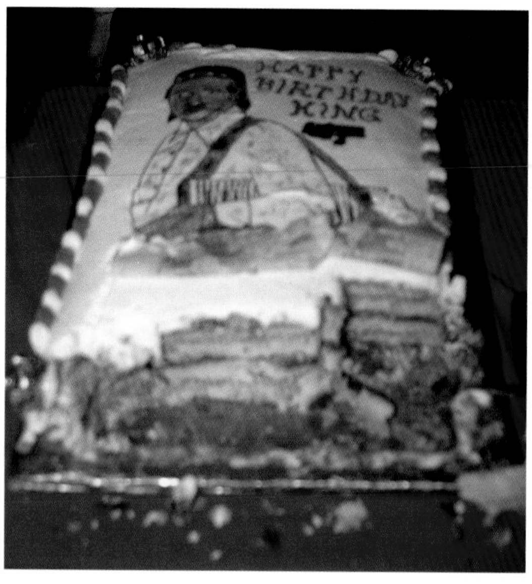

CLIFTON CHENIER'S BIRTHDAY CAKE, CONTINENTAL LOUNGE,
HOUSTON, JUNE 19,1987.
PHOTOGRAPH BY ALAN GOVENAR.

from Louisiana, they play more two-steps, fast pieces, than the people here in Houston, Texas. But now there's a whole lot of them come here from Louisiana and play, and they don't play all fast pieces. Only one guy just play most every piece a fast piece is John Delafose, that's all he play, is fast piece, mighty few slow pieces.

I don't care about playing no waltz. But all them other guys play waltzes. John Delafose, he play on the bandstand three and a half hours. He play about ten or twelve waltzes or more. Yeah, he love to play. Whole lot of these guys that go to dances from Louisiana, they like that waltz. But I don't, I don't care about playing that.

Willie Green was playing back then. Broussard was playing, and L. C. [Donatto] was playing. He came in the last part of the Fifties. And Anderson Moss! 'Course we played together many a night, and some night he wasn't playing, he'd come by me. When I wasn't playing, I'd go by him. He started almost the same time I did. He's a guy that liked to play almost all of his pieces fast.

I opened Mitchell's around the first part of '80. And ran it for five years. Old man Johnson had it first. And he passed away. Well, I was playing there before he passed. And when he passed away, his wife wanted me to take it over. And that's when I started playing over there and running the place, the dances, and playing my own dances too. Most everybody wanted to hear me play. I remember the time, if I would take off when Old Man Johnson had it, I take off, wife and I go somewhere. And I get back around ten, there'd be people standing around on the outside, because they don't want to hear nobody else but me. During them times, see, didn't have too many zydeco places. That place there was about the only place, large place, they had zydeco, and other little old, bitty places, they'd have zydeco every now and then. But here, over there they used to have it every Friday and Saturday and Sunday. And I played there many years, played there thirty years altogether.

Now, they call it the Continental Lounge. Used to be Mitchell's. I was there last night. Jabo played. I think this was special, this was a birthday party. The lady [who runs the place] called me, wanted me to come over there and play some.

Willie Green used to play in a place called Irene's Café. I never did play there. That's when I, before I started playing music, I never had heard about zydeco music in Houston. It was a small little old place, and I heard over the radio one night somebody's giving a birthday party. See, when my wife and I married, I promised I would quit playing music, and I stayed ten years before I started to play after I move here. She was born in the Baptist church and people don't go to dances. And so after we was here a while, she went to work at night, and

COWBOYS AT THE CIRCLE 6 RANCH RODEO, RAYWOOD, 1986. PHOTOGRAPH BY ALAN GOVENAR.

CIRCLE 6 RANCH, RAYWOOD, 1992. PHOTOGRAPH BY ALAN GOVENAR.

COWBOY AT THE CIRCLE 6 RANCH RODEO, RAYWOOD, 1986. PHOTOGRAPH BY ALAN GOVENAR.

she was off Wednesday. So this guy Willie Green wanted me to play a few pieces so he could hear how I play. And I could play real good, and so, a man come to me—his son had got killed, and he was playing music. He says, "Mitchell if you want to play," say, "I got a whole lot of places to play," small places. And he said, "I'll furnish you a little, all the music, and pay you half of the money what people can play for." I said, "Okay, I'll do it." I said, "But I got to talk to my wife." So we talked it over, and I told her, "Well, the nights you off, I won't play." And I was working for the Cadillac people then. So every Wednesday night when she was off, I wouldn't try to play nowhere. But otherwise, I played like, two or three years, every weeknight, and I worked doing paint and body work. When I was young, I don't know, maybe I was different from other guys. I never could feel like I was tired, you understand, I could work all day and all night. I had that much energy.

We mostly played at house parties and clubs like that. But then, I go to the Catholic churches. I think it started about in the Sixties, I don't remember. Everybody in the Sixties, they start giving dances in their church hall, and every church starts building a hall so they can give dances. Clifton [Chenier] and I was the only ones playing here in Houston. We was playing like little clubs during that time. And so they, all them churches, started building halls, and that's where it started at. They'd get mostly, get them bands from Louisiana. So it would be different. It was the funniest thing, people [from Louisiana], they don't play as good as people live in this town. But most of the people who would go to these dances are all French people from Louisiana. I remember a guy who lived in Galveston, and he would come to hear me every, every Friday, Saturday, and Sunday, drive all the way from Galveston. He just loved to dance. He was an old guy, and I mean he danced to damn near every piece we play. He really loved music. But he don't want to hear too much guitar! He want to hear just accordion mostly.

Adding guitar and drums changed zydeco. It makes it sound better. I don't know if I could play now with just a, a washboard. It'd have to be a mighty good one. You

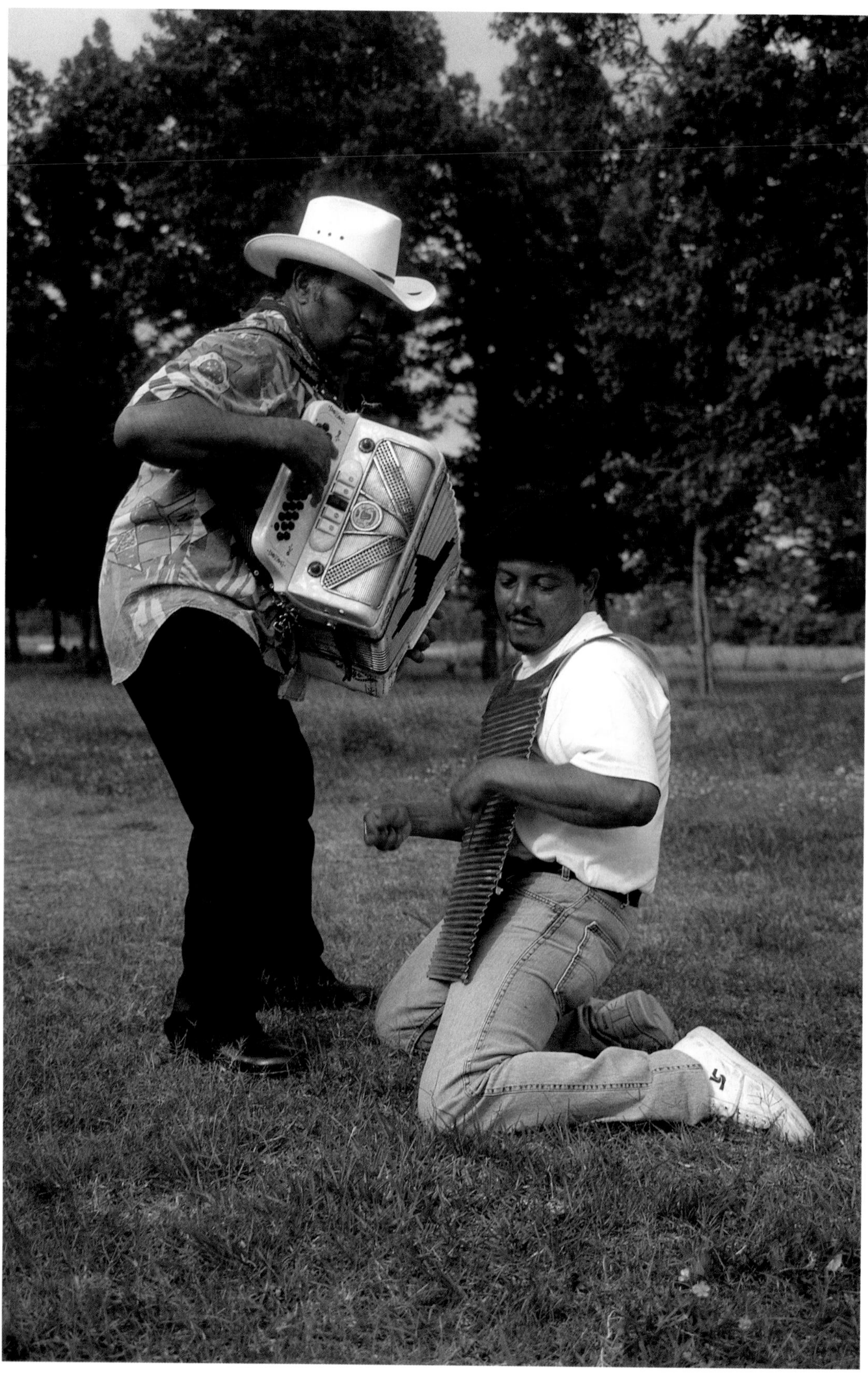

CIRCLE 6 RANCH ZYDECO, RAYWOOD, 1986.

PHOTOGRAPH BY ALAN GOVENAR.

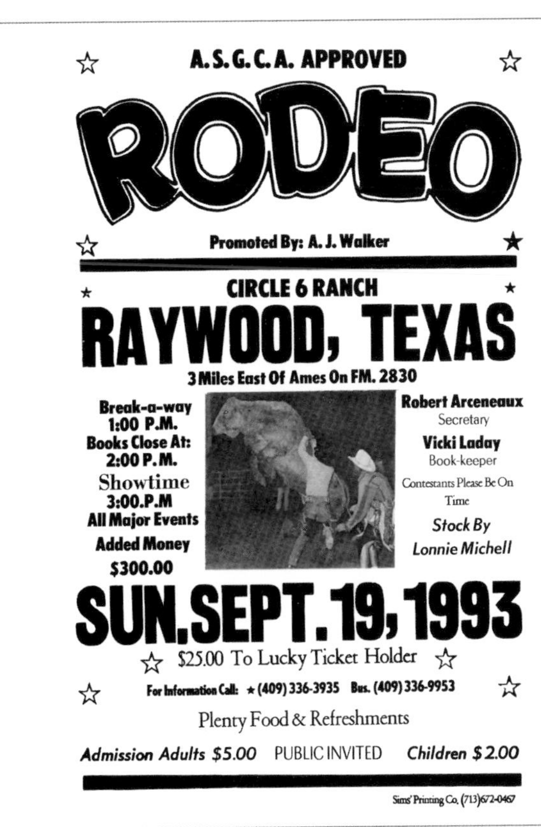

CIRCLE 6 RANCH RODEO POSTER, 1993.

DJ AT THE CIRCLE 6 RANCH, 1996.
PHOTOGRAPH BY ALAN GOVENAR.

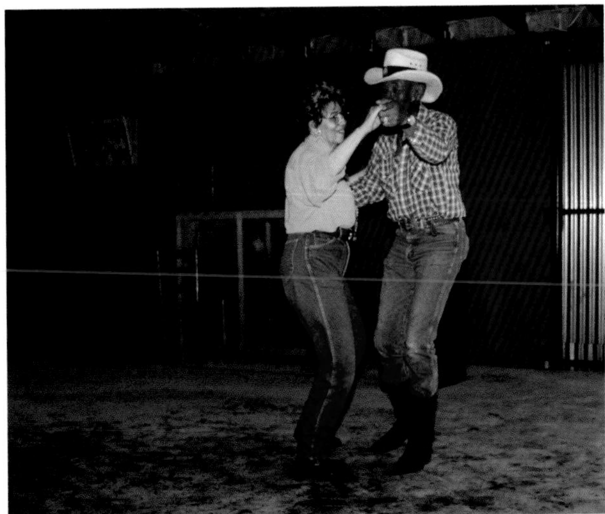

CLEVELAND WALTERS DANCING AT THE CIRCLE 6 RANCH.
PHOTOGRAPH BY ALAN GOVENAR.

can play [the accordion] the same way, but when you got guitar and drums and all that, it just give more pep to the music.

Clifton Chenier made the first zydeco record. Of course, we played here in Houston about three years without having a drum and stuff. And he just started, he decided he would try to make up a big band. Cut a record. He was a good player, he always was, play good, he always did. And he started up. And the first record he made was "Te Fe," they call it, yeah. He was singing French. And that's how he started. And from there he just keeps coming up, but now he's in awful bad shape. They had to cut one of his legs off.

After I moved to Houston for a while, I could go to the radio station, and they'd put me on the radio station. I cut one record, but it didn't go very well. There used to be a black guy name Don Robey. But that guy was crooked as a bad old snake. He'd tell you that record didn't go nowhere.

A guy's going to make me a tape. I'm going to take it to Ville Platte, Louisiana. I'm just having them make the tape for me. Rockin' Sidney says that's where he take all of his. And Clifton Chenier, same way. All these bands out of Houston, that's where they take it, they have these guy here make a tape, then take it over there and let him make the records. I never been there.

I been in music many years. They want to expect the accordion. They want to hear it more than they do the other guys. That's right, the accordion, he's the leader,

CLIFTON CHENIER

June 25, 1925–December 12, 1987; interview, 1986

MARGARET CHENIER AT HER HUSBAND'S BIRTHDAY PARTY, CONTINENTAL LOUNGE, HOUSTON, 1987. PHOTOGRAPH BY ALAN GOVENAR.

CLIFTON CHENIER BIRTHDAY PARTY, CONTINENTAL LOUNGE, HOUSTON, 1987. PHOTOGRAPH BY ALAN GOVENAR.

you're supposed to hear him.

When I was small, there was a lot of them around, playin' accordion. Zydeco was strong in '43, '44, with the old people, way back. They were playing back home. But it faded out. They'd zydeco in the houses in the old times, with the violin, accordion, and rub board. No drums. They just stopped it. It went out. I brought it back. A little of my style goes back, yeah, I keep that French in there, but they played more Cajun. I got that French, but I got a little rock in there, too. A lot of people used to laugh at me. They'd say the accordion couldn't make it, but then I had a hit in 1955, and that got them. They opened their eyes. I was way ahead of them.

I used to listen to B. B. King, Fats Domino, things like that, when I was learning. I listened to Fats a whole lot, and all those New Orleans piano players. Professor Longhair was one of 'em. Guys like that. The beat came from the religion people. My daddy was a musician, so I guess it rubbed off. Even in the little clubs, it seemed like everybody was playing rock in those days. Something just came to me. I said to myself that I wanted to change from that, and so I started playing rock with French music mixed in.

I learned to play in Lake Charles and in Texas, Houston mostly. My sister lives there. I never picked up an accordion until 1947, and after my uncle got me one, I kept it up and played around Lake Charles. I was working in the oil fields. When I was back on the farm, I wasn't playing at all. I remember when that song "The Honeydripper" came out. That was when—first record I learned how to play. I started from "Honeydripper" to "Caledonia." I was in the clubs by this time. Then I learned how to play boogie on the accordion. People didn't understand how the accordion could make those sounds. What I did was my own thing. Nobody showed me.

That zydeco music, people who don't know how to dance, it still gets them up on the floor. They got to dance. That zydeco's got the beat, but it's a pure country sound. We was country boys, and you never lose that

CLIFTON CHENIER, 1979. PHOTOGRAPH BY CHRIS STRACHWITZ. COURTESY ARHOOLIE RECORDS.

CLIFTON CHENIER, CONTINENTAL LOUNGE, HOUSTON, 1987. PHOTOGRAPH BY ALAN GOVENAR.

CLIFTON CHENIER, "AY-TETE FEE," SPECIALTY 552.

ASHTON SAVOY

October 29, 1928– ; interview, 1987

ASHTON SAVOY, SATURDAY AFTERNOON DANCE, PE-TE'S CAJUN BBQ HOUSE, HOUSTON, 1986. PHOTOGRAPH BY ALAN GOVENAR.

country feeling.

I've been playing since back in the Forties. My daddy used to be a violin player and guitar player, and I just took it up from him. I'm from Sunset, Louisiana, and back in them times he'd play that Louisiana music, blues, country, la la. My daddy could make that violin cry. My mama used to dance. They used to play it on the porch. I used to find that funny, but it was sounding good. My daddy started to teach me when I was seven or eight. He learned me a few chords on the guitar, but it wasn't really what I wanted to do. I was catching the blues on the radio, out of Nashville.

I started playing blues when I went on my own. I had an uncle in Chicago. He came out here one Christmas, and the day after New Year's he went back to Chicago, and he took me with him. I started at playing different places across the river where they had all them bands playing, Li'l Son Jackson, Bo Diddley. Then I started liking the blues, and I started playing blues.

My uncle had a club in Chicago called the Palomino, sixteen-, twenty-piece bands, that old jazz, back in the Forties, '46, '47. Louis Jordan, the big bands. I was about fourteen years old. That's where I got interested in music, but what I heard my daddy playing, that violin and guitar, it was back when there was Blind Lemon Jefferson and all that back yonder. It come a little bit ahead of my time, and I didn't like that kind of music. In Chicago, that music I really started liking. I bought me a little old guitar and amplifier. I started playing like that and catching on fast, T-Bone Walker, a little bit this and this. Lightnin' Hopkins, Jimmy Reed, I started playing their style.

I came to Texas in '62 and I'm not playing too much. It kind of got away from me for a little bit. I stopped playing for six, seven years, and then L. C. [Donatto] asked me if I wanted to get something together, me and him, and get some drummers and stuff like that. But when I first came to Houston, I had a bad band, about an eight-piece band; we were really jumpin.' I was playing then, but now I done forget a lot of what I was doing. Now, I'm playing something I can hold on to, but I used to be way up there.

I did a little recording, for Goldband, Eddie Shuler in Lake Charles, and J. D. Miller out of Crowley. I did some recording, "Down Mexico Way," "You Upset Me," and they said I sounded too much like Jimmy Reed and they didn't want to take too many chances. So I just quit recording then.

Zydeco in Texas is a little different than the way they play it in Louisiana. In Texas they're kind of mixing that zydeco up, but in Louisiana they play that natural zydeco—accordion, rub board, triangle, that's all they had back there. No drums, no bass, and they play on them wooden floors back out in the cotton fields, you hear that old accordion about five miles down the road. The accordion player and that rub board were over there in that corner just stomping the beat, pulling that 'cordion. And everybody started running, trying to get there, walking, on horseback, in the wagon filled with about twenty people. They had some bad accordion players who would play until they fall out. And then they'd put that accordion in the sack and go back home, wringing wet across the field. They call them the good old days, but I think the days now are better than they used to be. The music is different now. When they started coming to Texas, they put horns in it. When Clifton [Chenier] first used to play in Houston, he just had accordion and rub board, and then after that, in the Fifties, he started getting him some horns, bass, drums.

I met L. C. in Texas, and saw him playing around, and about five years ago he asked me if I wanted to play with him. I said, "Let me think about it," because I wasn't too familiar with that zydeco. So we had a little rehearsin' and we got together that little old group there. There's more blues in the zydeco now than what they had in Louisiana. The people today don't know how to dance that zydeco, they jumpin' that rock 'n' roll. With that zydeco you see a joker start in one corner, and when you look again he's in the next corner, kicking that dust up. The woman and the man know how to zydeco. The young folks today, they're just rock 'n' rollin.' Back in them days, they used to play them old waltzes and two-

ALCIDO "L. C." DONATTO SR.

March 11, 1932–July 7, 2002; interview, 1985

steps. Today they're mixing it with blues.

Up from where I live is called Frenchtown, off Liberty Road, the Frenchmen everywhere now. In this part of town there is probably as many French Creole as Texan people. I moved to Houston in 1944 and brought the same zydeco I heard when I was coming up. When you talk about adding saxophones and horns like they do now, that really is not zydeco. The real zydeco was accordion, violin, rub board, and an angle iron, a triangle. I've added a drum and guitar, but I have no horns because it does not go well with zydeco. Today we don't have violins, but it still fits in the Cajun music, early zydeco, like Canray Fontenot. I knew Alphonse Ardoin, and his son, Lawrence "Black" Ardoin. I was born in Opelousas in 1932, and I heard a lot of it when I was coming up, and I still love it. I love to look at the people having fun. I get a kick out of them dancing.

My wife only comes to listen to me if I'm playing at the Catholic hall, but she won't come to the cafés. When I'm not playing, I be working or I stay home and rest. I work a day job for the city of Houston. I do floor work; I'm figuring on retiring. I've done it for thirty-three years, but I'm continuing with my music, can't let that go by.

You can play blues on the accordion, but blues is blues and zydeco is zydeco. They think it's French if you play that accordion, but it's not, they're different. You have to play from your heart. And what makes it really good is when you get a full crowd of people. It makes you play better. I'm not a drinking man, can't be, especially if you're going to pull that accordion. It weighs 35 to 38 pounds. I have a bigger one at home, that weighs 40-some pounds, but now that I'm getting a little older, I want to get me something a little lighter.

Clifton [Chenier] [is still] playing, but not as much as he used to. He's done his part. I'm related to Clifton on my mother's side and my wife's side. We're double kin. I play mostly in the style of Clifton and like Joseph Riley, who taught me to play button accordion.

Willie Green—he's dead now—and I were the first two blacks to play zydeco here. When I did start off, it was very hard to make a living in Opelousas. I was only getting but four dollars a week, but soon after that time I was able to get about eight dollars a night in Houston. I knew how to work. Well, I, when I got here, I went to a little cafe, and Willie Green was playing, and I stood over at the bandstand. He said, "You know anything about this?" And I said, "Oh, a little bit." He said, "I'm going to let you try," and I got on there. Everybody was surprised—I was a small boy—and then one time, we were driving around on Christmas morning in Sixth Ward, playing that accordion, and somebody on a front porch banging on a guitar stopped us and went in the house and asked his wife if we could play some of that, and she said, "I'd like to hear it myself." And before you knew it, the yard was crowded. They stamped all the lady's flowers in the ground, but she didn't pay no attention to it. She said, "Forget about the flowers, you all." So Miss Irene heard us and came around and seen all the people in the yard. She said, "Come on over to the café." And we did; we're the first two blacks to play zydeco in Sixth Ward. That's how we got started.

Now I play piano accordion, too, but I still play button accordion, single-row French accordion, and a three-row button accordion, organ, piano. My mother used to play the French accordion. My father couldn't play nothin,' and he was real jealous that Mama could play. So I learned, got it in my blood from mother, and it's carried me a lot of places—Paris, France, Switzerland, El Paso, St. Louis, Chicago, Los Angeles. I have had a whole lot of fun. My mother and father never taught us how to talk French. The few words I do know, I learned it by listening to the records. By me being French Creole, it's not hard for me to say it, but I can't hold a conversation talking French.

We can play zydeco, rock 'n' roll, blues, and French. Zydeco you sing in French. We mix it up. They really went for it here, and they still do. There is lots of zydeco in Houston—Paul Richard, Jabo—but for the real zydeco you have to get with the old players like Lonnie Mitch-

L.C. DONATTO AT MJ'S PLACE, HOUSTON, 1986. PHOTOGRAPH BY ALAN GOVENAR.

ell, Anderson Moss, Vincent Frank. Anderson Moss, he's seventy, I'm gonna bring him my accordion, so he can play. I'm fifty-five, and I feel better than I did when I was young. I take better care of myself. I have fourteen living children, and I've been married thirty-five years. Sunday evening at the Silver Slipper, you have to get there real early if you want a seat, or even a standing

L. C. DONATTO JR.

(birth date unknown)– ; interview, 1986

L. C. DONATTO JR., MJ'S PLACE, HOUSE, HOUSTON, 1986.
PHOTOGRAPH BY ALAN GOVENAR.

place.

I've been playing zydeco since I was twelve or thirteen. I play rub board. It takes a lot of work, yes, indeed. It keeps the rhythm, and I'll be watching Dad all the time, watch his feet, checking him out. I love zydeco. I love everything about it. It's beautiful music. When I get off into it, that's where my mind is deep into the music. I sing sometimes behind Dad. Dad, Mom, I love doing it for them. I like to see them enjoy the music. I'm thirty-three, thirty-four in May.

It took awhile to learn the rub board, you know, with both hands, but then once I got on to it, I tried to put my own rhythm into it. I used forks; different people use different things, bottle openers, but I love to use the forks. A friend of Daddy's made my rub board, and he died, and Dad let me have it.

BEAUMONT, PORT ARTHUR, & ORANGE

Peacock
RECORDS
I'VE BEEN MISTREATED
Vocal by
Clarence "Gatemouth" Brown
His Guitar and Orchestra
1508-A

INTRODUCTION

The cities of Beaumont, Port Arthur, and Orange form what is called the "Golden Triangle" near the Gulf Coast of southeast Texas. It is an area of oil and sulfur production, as well as shipbuilding and rice and shrimp farming. It is also home to thousands of Cajuns—descendants of the French-speaking Acadians who entered Louisiana after being expelled by the British from what is now Nova Scotia, in the period from 1765 to 1800—and Creoles, people of mixed racial ancestry. Since the mid-nineteenth century, Cajuns, Creoles, and blacks have migrated from southwestern Louisiana to the Golden Triangle in search of jobs. The first draw was the lumber industry.

Beaumont is located in the northeast part of Jefferson County, an area where the black population increased steadily, from 269 in 1850 to around 1,200 in 1880. After the Civil War, freed slaves settled on the south side of Beaumont, along the Neches River waterfront. Later, another community formed on the north side. The south side was the business district, the north side more residential. The south side was largely self-contained, with cafes, stores and, by the 1940s, several nightclubs, including the Raven, the Chicken Shack, and Cheney's. The Raven was the premier club from the 1940s to the 1960s, and major performers such as T-Bone Walker were regulars there.

A similarly segregated black community grew up on the west side of Port Arthur, which is a younger town than Beaumont. Race relations have generally been less problematic in Port Arthur than in Beaumont. One factor may have been that the black population in Beaumont was larger and represented nearly half the overall population of Jefferson County. Living conditions were more crowded; tensions between whites and blacks escalated and resulted in a race riot in 1943 in Beaumont. Racial separation, however, did not extend as much to music as it did to housing, education, and health care.

With the migration of Creoles to urban areas, such as Lake Charles and Houston, the more versatile piano accordion replaced the diatonic model, and the instrumentation and styles of zydeco and associated forms of Cajun music evolved. For example, Allen Thibodeaux and The French Ramblers from Port Arthur added the pedal steel guitar to their otherwise traditional Cajun ensemble of guitar, accordion, fiddle, and triangle. In Houston, Cajun music was influenced by country and western; Creole music, by rhythm and blues. The assimilation of different musical traditions is apparent in the instrumentation and performance styles of both black and white musicians, such as Clarence Garlow, Long John Hunter, Tom Hunter, Janis Joplin, and Johnny Winter.

CLARENCE GARLOW

February 27, 1911–July 24, 1986; interview by Allan Turner, 1982

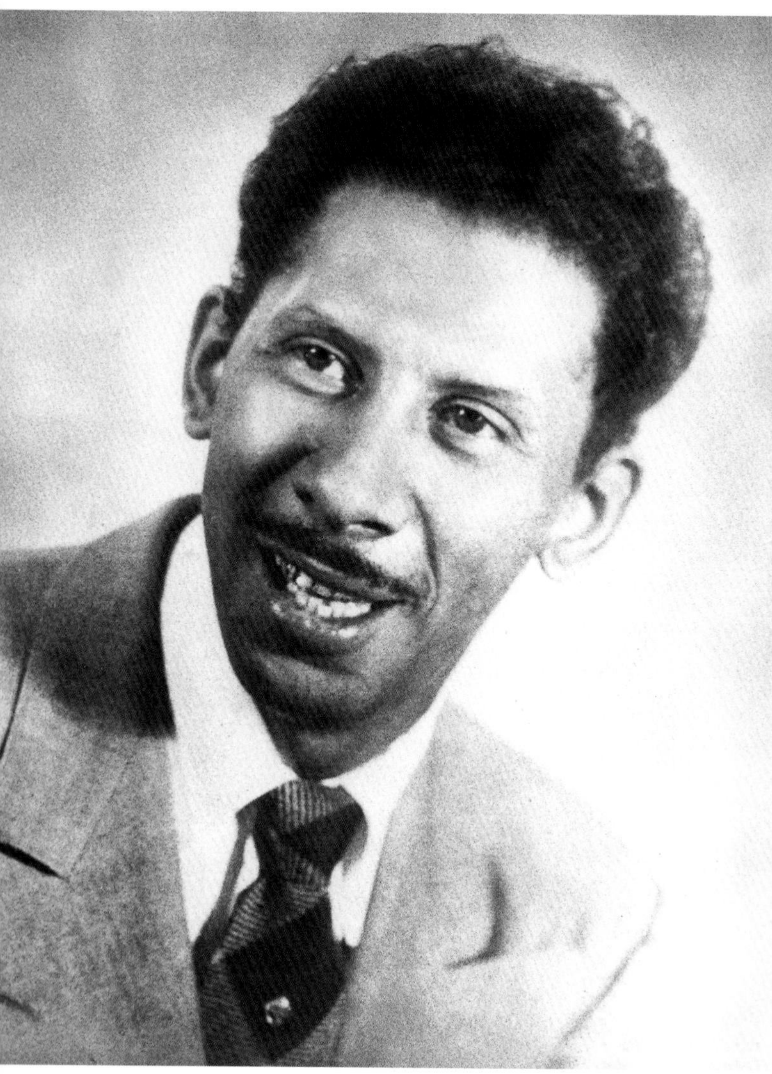

CLARENCE GARLOW, PUBLICITY PHOTOGRAPH. COURTESY CHARLIE LANGE.

I was born in Welch, Louisiana. It's about twenty-three miles east of Lake Charles. Of course, I was brought up here in Beaumont. We came here when I was five months old, and I've been here ever since.

My father was named Compton Garlow, and my mother was named Ophelia. And I'm an only child. They were from the Opelousas Territory. My father was mainly a longshoreman. I worked down on the docks, too, with him. I started at the age of sixteen. I worked down there sixteen years. I did that work until World War II. And then I became a letter carrier here. I delivered mail here eight years.

Well, I'd made some investments while I was at the Post Office Department, and some of my investments didn't pan out so well, and I kinda got busted. Left me big in debt, you know, I figured it would be about six or seven years paying my debts back out of my job. So I decided I was disgusted. I just resigned [from] the Post Office Department, picked up the guitar, went and joined the musicians' union. Picked up the guitar, organized a band, didn't know anything about music. I had the guys to tell me which way to go. And I learned to play on my bandstand. But in the first year, I had netted more money than I had grossed for the eight years carrying mail. So, therefore, I got completely out of debt in around a year's time, see. And then from there on, well, I mean, you know, it's never been no real big thing, but it's been pretty lucrative.

I remember when I was a kid, my daddy and them had kind of one of those things like what the Cajuns had. At that time, they didn't have drums, but my daddy would play the fiddle and strum on the guitar. And I had another uncle, he would play the bass. He had the big bass viol. And another uncle, he played the fiddle and strummed on the guitar. And they had a three-piece little thing. In those times, they didn't play nightclubs and halls; they'd have what you call those soirees in homes. And they'd have a bunch of fun out there, out in the country. So that was my daddy; however, he was never professional. They'd make a couple of bucks, but he was never really a real musician, just one of those kind that played the hoedown music.

Well, the music was not necessarily French. It was basically French and, can we say, country and western; I don't know how you'd classify it. Like, they'd play a thing like "Under the Double Eagle." They'd play "She'll

Be Coming around the Mountain When She Comes." And they'd play old "Sugar Blues" and "St. Louis Blues." And, yeah, breakdown. They'd play "Chicken Reel" and all that stuff.

Oh, I went along with my father. As a matter of fact, I was grown and they were still playing. We had just a lot of fun. Oh, I could rap on the guitar, but I didn't know over three chord changes. I wasn't a musician by a long way. I was inspired by T-Bone Walker. T-Bone would come here. I would love that guitar, especially. T-Bone would come down, and I met him and I'd get his records. And I bought the guitar, and I'd try to play the blues like him. I understand he's the father of the blues amplified guitar, the first one with the amplified guitar. And so I wanted to play like him. I tried and tried. Well, I guess eventually I've gotten this good.

T-Bone would play most likely at the Raven Club or the Harvest Club. Well, he played Houston a whole lot, at the [city] auditorium and the coliseum. He was big-time. And then, I met Ray Charles. We were good buddies. We were buddy-buddy. And I've tried to see Ray Charles several times, but I realize security is kinda tight; they wouldn't let me see him for several years. I had some tunes I wanted him to write for me. We were so close, he and I. I had a Cadillac car, and believe it not, he drove it. He must have driven ten blocks one way and maybe fifteen, twenty blocks the other way, brought it back. However, he did have one of his friends in there with him.

I was a fellow that always loved to meet people. Like I said, I was interested in learning this music. Like now, I know a lot of the artists. And I'm in good fellowship with them. However, I never was no great, great. I did luck up on a little popularity. Sometimes I wonder: if I would have had the confidence in myself, I guess, that I should have had, I could have gone a long way. But I didn't. When I'd have a big crowd of people there, it would shy me off. And the people would tell me, some of the musicians said, "Hey, man, they love you." And I would figure that's the bigger crowd that come to laugh at me because I thought they sensed that my timing was bad and all. And I had them captivated, but after we'd play awhile, showtime, and had them captivated, well, then, the boys would tell me, say, "Okay, boss man, go walk around the crowd awhile. Let us play awhile, because that's how you bug me. Let us get back in the groove, hit a groove." Well, by the time they'd get a good groove going, we'd jump it up. Somebody out there, "Let's bring him back on," so I'd come back on and say, "Well, they want to laugh at me some more."

It was in 1949 that I started my first band. It was called Clarence Garlow and His Band, after myself. At different times, I had different instrumentation. Sometimes I've had maybe eight or ten, twelve people up on the bandstand. Most times, my band was mostly five of us, see, because I found out that they didn't need no whole lot of people to make a whole lot of noise. Once you've got your little group tight, you didn't need no whole lot of fellows, and a whole lot of fellows make for less money. I have mostly used saxophone, one, maybe two saxophones, drummer, bass, and piano. In those days, you just had to have a piano. Most of the clubs had pianos. But they were usually bad pianos. We just had to make do with them. We'd play primarily dances. I had a circuit, more or less, within an area of Beaumont, around about, say, about 150-, 160-mile circuit. I could play the same places over again the very next week and still draw the crowds. I didn't have to lay out nowhere. I had it so that I just worked a circuit. I didn't have to worry about bookings, hardly, you know.

My main territory was around Opelousas and Lafayette, all in that area, St. Martinville, Abbeville, and all up in there. Well, I played New Orleans. But my saying New Orleans is when Fats Domino went into the big time. I went to work out under the Cate Agency, which was Fats Domino's agency, and then began filling out dates behind Fats. And the eastern Louisiana territory, northern end of Mississippi, and places around. And for some reason or other, didn't get no tomatoes and things chunked at me. And then I played on the West Coast, Los Angeles. I played all those places. I played Malibu. I played Ocean Park. I played Ventura, and oh, just any number of them.

I played more or less the T-Bone blues and rhythm. I made a record called "Bon Ton Roulez," but it's not a French record. Now I'm fixing to do another version of it, which I'm going to have, it's going to be some French in it, see, because the verses that I wrote in English, I sung in English, I'm doing it in French. I'm working up a deal now.

When I started out, I didn't necessarily have a circuit [I played] at that time. What happened, I had a bunch of

CLARENCE GARLOW, "BLUES AS YOU LIKE IT," MACY'S RECORDINGS 5001-A.

boys, and we would go here and yonder; I'd go here and yonder and get an engagement. . . . We could get two or three a week, you know; we could make a little money. Sometimes we were lucky to get one this week, or next.

One time I was in Houston fooling around, and I came by a place they called the Coconut Grove on Market Street or something like that. I stopped there awhile, and I was having a few drinks with some friends. Well, at that time they had a little blues band with the lead guitar up in the front. So I'm boozing a little bit, and my booze tell me, that conceit, you know, that I can play as good as him. I think I can beat him. So anyway, I asked him, "Hey, man, do you mind if I sit in with you?" "What you play?" I say, "Guitar." Guitar player say, "Yeah, man, here, play my guitar." Somehow or other, it spruced the thing up. I played several [songs]. One of the waiters come to me later on; he say, "Hey, fella, those people sitting at that table over there want to see you." I say, "Which table?" "Right there." I say, "Okay, soon as I finish this number, I'll be over there." So when I did, I walked over there. And they were white people, a lady and two men. And I walked over there, shook hands with them, [and they] asked me if I wanted to sit down and have a drink with them. I say, "Okay, I'll sit down and have a drink." And they asked me if I was recording. I told them no, I didn't record for anyone. "Would you like to record?" And I told the lady I didn't think I was good enough. She say, "Well, I've been listening to you quite awhile." She says, "My name is Leila Henry Macy." You know, that's the Macy, Macy record company. She said, "Well, you sound good enough for me. How about coming to my office tomorrow, and we'll talk about it?" Said, "Okay. Let's see if I'm interested."

I didn't know what it was all about. However, when I did set it up with them, and I went there with my boys, [I realized] you got to have something original. I don't know what I thought; I figured maybe somebody going, "Well, you learn this song," and do it. But we got in there. "You got something original?" I said, "Oh, yeah." Well, I had my drummer. He is a very well-renowned drummer, big as the band eventually, named Johnny Marshall. Call himself "Fast Stuff" Marshall. But he loved that Pan American beat, calypso. And you know how musicians clown? He was a younger clown with the drums. Calypso beat. And I'd tell him, "Johnny, cool it. Let me think. I've got to try to think. I'm trying to think of something to write." And I didn't know what in the world to do, but I figured I could do it. I had a lady piano player named Mildred Smith. She lives in Houston. And she started playing behind the piano, you know, da-da-da-da-da-doo-doo, da-da-datndoodoo," you know that old number? So she's fooling around with that, and then I looked around and they said, "We'll stop." And I said, "No, don't stop. Keep that up. Keep that beat you got, Johnny, right there." I said, "Mildred, just keep playing behind that." Well, I had a guy with me; he's dead now. He was a boy used to work around San Antonio, name was Wilmer Shakesnyder. He was a musician's musician, see. And he was with me, too. So, I told Shake and another boy with me, I said, "You guys set me some kind of a riff behind that; let me see something. Just set me a little riff on that thing." Da-da-da-da-da-da-da-da-doo-dah.Da-da-da-da-da-da-da-da-doo-dah. I say, "Okay, I'm going to try it on for size. Play it down six bars and break it, just follow me." Okay, so I wrote down there [sings], "Do you see me there, well, I ain't no fool. I watch my French, never been in school. You want to get somewhere in the Creole town, you stop and let me show you your way round. You let the bon ton roulez . . . Now don't you be no fool-eh. Let the bon ton roulez." You know what I mean. I got that down. Then I wrote my next verse, and I wrote my next verse. And the people say, "Oh, I like that. Oh, I like that." That was born right in the studio then, so we run it on down. And that's how "Bon Ton Roulez," how

I became known as Clarence "Bon Ton Roulez" Garlow, see, my record. And my record still go out; I've done it for three different labels. Macy's, Aladdin, and Goldband. Now I'm fixing to do it again for another label. I don't [know] which label it's going to be. It's going to be done with Cajun lyrics.

The Macy's record sold good. Well, I wouldn't say it was a hit, but it was a fair seller. In other words, what happened there, it gave me the shot in the arm. But me, well, my mother was very ill at the time. And me being an only child, as I said, my father's gone. Well, then, I didn't do any venturing too much. I wasn't getting too far away from home. But nevertheless, I went on, and then, when I did stop somewhere in there, I'd invest in different businesses. I've had nightclubs, grocery stores, cafes, motels . . . the Bon Ton Drive-in. And in the meantime, I became a disk jockey, radio KJET. Right here in Beaumont, see. And I was a disk jockey for a pretty good while.

I started the show on KJET. It was 'round about '54, '55. Then, I don't know, for some reason, later on, I got fired. I decided, well, I had ambition to become a radio engineer. So I went on through that and I became a radio engineer. You would see my engineer's license on the wall. So I've gone back to work at that same station as their engineer. And I worked as assistant engineer. I worked with them at that station, KJET, after they built a station out here, well, I was right there supervising. I was their assistant engineer eleven and a half months, and I was chief engineer three years.

I haven't been treated badly by no company that I know of. I do feel that I wasn't paid properly for my writing on the B. B. King records. My publishers, that I know of, received no royalties from his record company, and he's the only one who went on the chart with it. You're supposed to get some royalties off them. I got pretty good from other labels that I didn't even know the artist did it. And plus, I got my BMI, which was pretty nice. But I know from this particular B. B. King thing, I never got any royalties from them.

I don't know how many songs I've written. Maybe quite a few. Like I said, maybe if I hadn't been in a way disillusioned a lot of the time, maybe I'd have been further in the field. I don't know if it's a fact or not, I don't understand why, but I've had the recording companies tell me, "I like the way you write; I like your material." And sometimes I've brought good artists in there, with pretty voices, and tried to get them sessions, you know. And they'd ask me, "Why don't you do it?" I say, "I don't have the voice to do it." Say, well, "I can sell yours, but I can't sell. . . ." They told me in California, say, "Clarence, pretty voices are a dime a dozen. . . . I ain't got to eat your records." All of them told me, say, "We don't have to eat your records. . . . Now, you never got no big seller. One day you might get you one. But you never got no big thing where you made no money out of it." Now you take, for instance, like the "Bon Ton Roulez," well, I didn't get any money, a lot of it, for royalties, because, well, I was on the label myself and, for some reason or other, I don't know whether they did or not. See, when I did it, it wasn't published. And later on, I published through Eddie Shuler and that bunch over there [at Goldband]. But I never let that bother me. See, the way I understood it back in those days; I don't know how it goes now, but see, the session was always supposed to be on the artist. And whenever the artist would get any monies in front, if he did it on a royalty basis, well, advance royalties, see. Now you take, for instance, let's put it this way: Suppose I'm getting, say, two cents a side. A pretty good seller would be, maybe, say, a hundred thousand records. We're talking about four hundred dollars, maybe. All right, now. The session cost five hundred dollars. See what I mean? You still owe the band. But you got a hundred thousand records. I figure this way, that records has always been to me good advertisement. Like I told you, when that "Bon Ton Roulez" thing came out, every time I put out a record, it was another shot in the arm, see. When I was first going out there, say, making fifty or seventy-five or a hundred dollars a night, I got to the place—oh, I don't guess it went over a thousand, maybe once or twice. But it was always pretty much in the double zero thing, you know what I mean.

I had nightclubs. I had a place, right, called the Bon Ton Drive-in, back in the Fifties. Now, in '53 and '54 is when I was out in California. All right, now, in the meantime, Clifton Chenier used to have a little group, and they'd play for me every Monday and Thursday. I'd give them the door. Well, they charged fifty cents at the door, so they'd make a hundred or more dollars, you know. But I didn't play my place, see. See, I played on my circuit. I'd sit in with them sometimes when I was there. But when I got to California, I told you, on an adventure, and I knew this guy named Fulbright, who was working with other artists. He's a hustler. And I knew him well. And he's promoted a whole lot of people, got a lot of people going. So I was talking with him, and I told him, "Fulbright, you know what? I've got a guy back in Beaumont that I'd like you to hear, and maybe you can do him some good." He said, "Okay." I said, "He plays accordion. He plays my place. When I get back, I'm going to call you and have you hear him." And I set that up with him.

So, that particular night, Clifton Chenier was playing on my bandstand. And I called; my telephone booth was right there by the bandstand. I called Fulbright and said, "Here's the guy; I want you to listen to him." Fulbright say, "I'll be right down after him, Garlow. I'll be after him." And Fulbright came and got Clifton Chenier. So, when he came and got Clifton Chenier, he brought him up there. And when Clifton Chenier came back, well, I was using one of Clifton's cousins, one that was killed in an accident. I was using him and his little group. When Clifton came back, Clifton told me, say, "Well, now, look"; say, "I'm back, man. I want my job back. I've been playing here a long time. I want my job back. I want my job back, man." And I told him, "Cliff, you got a record. I think you're a little too big for the Bon Ton Drive-in. I think I'll work a deal and put you with the Bon Ton himself." "You mean playing with you?" I say, "Yeah. But I need a picture on you. You got any pictures?" "Yeah," he said. "I just had some pictures made." So he gave me the key to his house; he lived in Port Arthur. Gave me the key to his house. He said, "I won't be there. I'll be at work, but you go there." And he told me where to look. "Find some pictures; pick out the one you want." And I said, "Okay." So I did that, and he told me where to leave his keys. I did that and brought the picture on in.

Well, I had this placard made and everything, went to Houston and had it made. And had him with my band. So then I went out with him with my band, well, he had that record out, that was another shot I had in the arm. But I guess he must have played about fifteen or twenty engagements with me. And, for some reason or other—the poor fella's dead now; I won't call his name—but the guy I used to play for on my circuit, the man had to enlarge his place to accommodate people. But the man was telling him [Clifton], "Man, you don't need Garlow no more. The people like you now." Well, see, Clifton and I had a deal. We were going to pay the musicians off. "We won't talk about no expenses, just pay the musicians off. Whatever it costs for promotion, we'll pay that off, and you and I will split the rest down the middle." So, that night, for some reason or another, Clifton—I didn't know his mind went that way. So the very next day, at a Fourth of July thing we were playing in Crowley, Louisiana, well, when I got there—of course, I had a contract with that guy; I had booked that. And the guy asked me, "What's the matter with you and Cliff?" I said, "What's the matter with me and Cliff how?" He say, "Well, Cliff says that you're not with him anymore and to pay him." I said, "I don't know nothing about it." He say, "Well, look. Just act like you don't know nothing because, boy, we're going to have a crowd of people here." I said, "But if you want to pay Cliff, you pay Cliff." He said, "Well, I'm not no damned fool. I got a signed contract with you." I say, "Okay, well, that's up to you. You pay Cliff if you want to pay him. But I won't worry about it. I'll walk on." He said, "Man, you ain't going to walk off from me and come back and get your money. I'm going to pay you." I said, "Well, okay, pay me right in front of Cliff." So he say, "Well, that's strange. Cliff said to pay him, but don't pay him in front of you."

So, nevertheless, we played. Well, I noticed that for some reason or other, Cliff wanted to play the whole night. "Look, I got a lot of requests." But when the deal went down, Cliff was trying to get me to go back in that back room and settle up, but he kept fooling around. "Come on, Garlow; you ready?" So we goes on back there, and so he pays me off. But nevertheless, Cliff had me to know that we were no longer together. I said, "Okay, Cliff, if that's the way you feel about it. I'm glad I could get you going." But I said, "Cliff, this hurts, if that's the way you feel about it." "All right, then, I might excite somebody else. And you're not going to want to turn me loose."

I can be playing right now, and I'll sing something and rhyme it out right then and there, and it's strictly original because I'm making it up as I go. And that's just the way it is. Now, if I decide I want to write a number, I just stay with it awhile, and I write it. In other words, I just think about it. See, I wrote a number for my ex-wife. . . . I wrote a number for her that I never did. It's a beautiful thing. I never did do it because it's a personal thing and I don't have the voice to do it. I think I might have the music score somewhere. Shakesnyder wrote it all up for me. He loved that thing. He said, "Man, it's a pity you don't do this." I said, "Well, I don't have the voice to deliver it like I should." And I wrote that just thinking about it, you know what I mean? And I wrote another number that I did for Tony Keys called "All This Belongs to Me." Now, I wrote that while driving back from California, on the road. Somebody was in there with me. I had some paper, say, "You are to write as I tell you." And I'd drive along and write it. And it came out just beautiful, but Tony didn't do it like I wrote it for him. Tony's dead now. I was trying to make an artist out of him. But he didn't do it like I wrote it in the sense of the word, see what I mean? In other words, same as B. B. King didn't do my "Please Accept My Love" like I wanted him to do it, see. He turned it kind of bluesy, but he lost me a whole lot of people. However, he stayed on the chart with it. Same thing with Tony wanting to do all that variation of voice. Just like I wrote this "Route 90" and "Crawfishing." Now "Crawfishing" wasn't done the way that I wanted that done. It fell on its face. "Route 90," I believe, pretty much fell on its face. People like it when I play it on the bandstand, but I play it a little different. On those two records, I got some bad boys. I got name drummers, name bassmen, name saxophone players. I got name people on there. And they are driving it. I said, "That don't sell." And sure enough, it didn't.

A lot of times, I'm just singing. I'd play the guitar, maybe, in a solo. . . . See, what hurts me, I did "Crawfishin,'" and it didn't go nowhere. And the next week or so, right after "Crawfishin,'" here's another record that came out that went like everything, "Maybelline." And when I heard that "Maybelline" going, I said, "Hey, there go my 'Crawfishin.'" They got that riff, that background. . . . You remember "Maybelline," how it goes? "While motivatin' over the hill, I saw Maybelline in a Coupe de Ville." Watch this here: "Now you tell Judy, and I'll tell Jay to bring some chicken and a chocolate cake. Bring a little home brew to keep awake. Now hurry, hurry, for goodness' sake, 'cause Pierre's a-comin' and so is Sue. The crawfish is jumpin' in the big bayou. Bring some bait for the crawfish line; now bring your gal, and I'll bring mine. Crawfishin.'" You know what I mean? "That's 'Maybelline,' right in there. Lord. But mine got that old . . . plenty money when I play it on the bandstand. "Hey, man, play 'Crawfishin.'' Play 'Route 90.'" Now "Route 90," I wrote that, but the guy I had helping me, I gave him half of writer's credit, because he was helping me to get stuff in and helping me write the lead sheet and everything. And "Crawfishin.'" You might have heard of him, Leon Rene. See, he was the one that wrote "Capistrano." He and I wrote "When the Swallows Come Back to Capistrano." And I wrote a thing, "All This Belonged to Me."

Let's put it this way: I've never recorded anything that I was doing on the bandstand because I didn't think that I could sing good enough to cover anyone. So wasn't no point in me doing your record; I can't cover you. In other words, I sound bad trying to do your record. So what I'd do, I'd go ahead on and write my own. Now, then, I'll use the record, and if my record seem to move the public, well, that's great.

CLARENCE "GATEMOUTH" BROWN

April 18, 1924–September 10, 2005; interview, 1987

CLARENCE "GATEMOUTH" BROWN, NEW ORLEANS JAZZ AND HERITAGE FESTIVAL, 1979. PHOTOGRAPH BY MICHAEL P. SMITH.

In his room at the Hilton Hotel in Dallas, in June 1987, Gatemouth Brown is with his family: Yvonne, his wife of eight years, and their daughter, Renee. Yvonne, who is from Baton Rouge, recalls that she didn't know much about the blues until she heard Gatemouth in New Orleans and later met him by chance. Yvonne is warm and friendly, Renee is watching Saturday morning kid shows, and Gatemouth is uneasy. The presence of an interviewer seems to make him anxious, though he tries to be nonchalant. He leans back against the side of the full-length mirror across the from the bed and says, "The last man that interviewed me wrote a book. He called me at home and asked me questions for an hour and a half. And then when the book came out, I saw him in New York, and he asked me if I wanted to buy a copy. I don't do interviews anymore for books. I'm writing my own book."

When I show him my collection of unpublished Duke/Peacock photographs, Gatemouth grows more irritable. "Man, these are worth a million dollars," he says as he turns his head away. "What am I going to get out of this interview?" In a surly tone, he mutters, "Am I going to get a royalty?" Then he lowers his face and says nothing. The silence is deadening until he unexpectedly looks up and declares, "I feel like I've been crushed in a vise of bullshit. Call me tomorrow; maybe I'll feel like talking then. I'm not mad at you. It's just the way the system works."

I look at Gatemouth with a kind of disbelief, shaking my head and smiling. I leave the room quietly, saying, "Hope you feel better. I'll call you tomorrow. Maybe we can get together. I'll bring my daughter. She's the same age as Renee."

Later that night, in a long conversation with Jim Bateman, Gatemouth's manager and longtime friend, the source of the morning's conflict becomes perfectly clear. Without knowing it, I knew too much. The photographs of the 1950s Houston scene had an intensity that conjured up the past with an unforeseen power. Those were the years of Gatemouth's youth and national success as one of the hottest rhythm and blues sounds, but today there is little to show for it. The recordings have been bootlegged and reissued, and the publishing rights were innocently signed away to Don Robey, who often took or shared the authorship and publishing with an alias, Deadric Malone.

Gatemouth Brown's early recordings on Robey's Peacock label are classics. The electric guitar sound is modern: quick, single-string runs with a driving rhythm backed by tenor saxophone and trumpet. On some of the early sessions the horn section is enlarged to give a big band sound with swing-era solos in a call-and-response pattern with the electric guitar.

There are three important reissues of Gatemouth's earliest recordings, one on Rounder in the United States, and two on Ace in the United Kingdom. His first sessions appear on Ace and appropriately mark the beginning of Ace Records' multi-album reissue series of the Peacock and Duke catalogs originally owned by Don Robey. Together these reissues establish Gatemouth's stature in the history of rhythm and blues but bring little direct monetary benefit. The licenses are bought directly from the present owners of the original contracts, in which Gatemouth naively signed away virtually all the residual rights to his music. There is, however, some contention over the assignment of royalties, and in time, Jim Bateman hopes to help secure for Gatemouth some of the compensation to which he is entitled.

On the next day, Gatemouth is more relaxed. Jim Bateman has called and said that I was all right. I bring my daughter, Breea, and she and Renee go swimming and play together. Gatemouth and I sit by the side of the pool; Yvonne joins us and orders coffee. For the next hour Gatemouth recalls his life with a sincere tone, mocking his early inexperience with hoarse laughter, reminiscing about the past with a rambling clarity.

Gatemouth Brown was born in Vinton, Louisiana, but lived there for only three weeks before his family moved to Orange, Texas. His early musical influences were as various as the interests of his father, Clarence Brown Sr., who worked as an engineer for the Southern Pacific Railroad and played in a string band on weekends. He played fiddle, banjo, mandolin, and guitar at house parties, dances, and fish fries, performing, in the songster tradition, the popular country blues, zodico, and fiddle tunes of the day.

At age ten Gatemouth began playing the fiddle under the tutelage of his father, though he was also interested in the instruments played by his brothers, Bobby, a drummer, and James "Widemouth" Brown, a respected blues guitarist and vocalist. As a teenager Gatemouth worked as a drummer with Howard Spencer and His Gay Swingsters in Orange, and later went on the road

CLARENCE "GATEMOUTH" BROWN, HOUSTON, 1960S. PHOTOGRAPH BY BENNY JOSEPH.

with William M. Bimbo and His Brownskin Models. In a 1979 interview with Ray Topping, he recalled, "I was about sixteen or seventeen. I went all the way to Norfolk, Virginia. I worked at the Eldorado Club on Church Street in Norfolk. I played drums in a little house band until the outbreak of World War II."

After serving in the war, Gatemouth returned to Texas and joined Hort Hudge's twenty-three-piece orchestra at the Keyhole Club in San Antonio. After hearing of the success of T-Bone Walker at Don Robey's Bronze Peacock, Gatemouth began playing electric guitar in a style that challenged Walker's virtuosic abilities. His first encounter with T-Bone Walker was in Houston in the mid-1940s. He remembers the experience with a vivid clarity.

"I hitchhiked to Houston to see him and went into this club called the Bronze Peacock. He was the hottest stuff on guitar in Texas, but he was sick with a stomach ulcer, and he laid his guitar down on the stage and walked off to his dressing room. I got up and went up to the stage. No one knew I was a guitar player, but I just picked up T-Bone's guitar and started to play, inventing a little boogie—'My name is Gatemouth Brown. I just got in town. If you don't like my style, I won't hang around.' Well, they loved it, but T-Bone didn't. He came back out on stage and snatched away his guitar and told me that I was in big trouble if I ever fooled with his guitar again."

Don Robey, the owner of the Bronze Peacock, intervened, realizing Gatemouth Brown's raw ability to play in the style of T-Bone Walker, who by that time was quite successful. Robey bought Gatemouth a new Gibson electric guitar and some new tuxedos from a custom tailor on Dowling Street. Later he flew Gatemouth out to Los Angeles to sign a recording contract with Aladdin Records. In November 1947 four sides were recorded, including "Gatemouth Boogie" and "Guitar in My Hands." However, Robey was dissatisfied with the timetable and the promotion the records received and decided not to renew his contract after the first year.

Brown's recordings for Robey's Peacock label have an undeniable energy. His first sessions included at least three slow blues, though his rarest recording, "Ditch Diggin' Daddy," is still unavailable. His first song to achieve regional success was the up-tempo "Mary Is Fine." This motivated Robey to switch his recording operations to the ACA studios in Houston. Even then, as Gatemouth recalled in a 1983 interview with Dick Shurman, the conditions were much different than today.

"We had maybe one mike for the big band. That's when a man walked out and soloed. We had one mike for me to sing. They would put a mike out in front of my amp. . . . If everybody played and tried not to overplay, then everybody could be heard."

From 1949 to the mid-1950s Gatemouth regularly worked and cut standard four-song sessions. The Ace and Rounder reissues follow his development as a rhythm and blues stylist and show the importance of studio arrangements. The horn charts were put together by Bill Harvey, Joe Scott, and Pluma Davis, who also contributed heavily to the shaping of the overall sound.

Many of the individual session players, however, were selected by Gatemouth; they included two hometown friends, George Alexander on trumpet and Wilmer Shakesnyder on alto and tenor saxophone.

Gatemouth's music from the Peacock period combines slow blues, like his perennial "I've Been Mistreated," with up-tempo guitar instrumentals like "Ain't That Dandy" (which he still uses as a set opener and redid for his *One More Mile* album on the Rounder label). In addition, the early recordings included jump blues like "Okie Dokie Stomp"; the influential "Boogie Rambler"; reflective blues ballads like "Sad Hour," "Depression Blues," and "Mercy on Me"; and the intense vocal shuffle "Midnight Hour." Together, these recordings are considered some of Gatemouth Brown's best, though it is clear from talking to him that he has worked since then to develop a new sound that brings together his regional influences into what he calls a "true American music."

CLARENCE "GATEMOUTH" BROWN, "IT CAN NEVER BE THAT WAY," PEACOCK RECORDS1508 B.

I don't think that nobody alive put more into Peacock records than I. I suffered the growing pain. I went in there as a young child. It was an adventure to me. I think about money. I put trust in people. That's why today it's hard for me to trust anybody, and yet, I have to trust somebody. But who is this somebody? Sometimes it's the most wonderful people who do you wrong.

CLARENCE "GATEMOUTH" BROWN, "JUST BEFORE DAWN," PEACOCK RECORDS ACA 3936.

Robey was a gambler. The world knows that, but he had a friend in San Antonio, who I started dealing with before I met Robey. He did some gambling, but it wasn't the kind of thing Robey was into. He was more forceful. He got it all at once or nothing at all. That's the kind of man he was. I'm grateful for one thing. Everything that happened to me wrongfully worked out rightfully in the future. I'm doing real well today, thanks to him. For years, there was no one doing anything.

The problem with Robey was that he had a fictitious name, D. Malone, Deadric Malone, that claimed authorship to things he didn't write. It was a way to get the royalties. As time went by, it was clear my feelings for him deteriorated. I started out feeling like he was a father of mine. I respected him that much, and after I got in there, I considered Evelyn Johnson a mother figure of mine in business, meaning I would trust these people with my life, because I figured they would never do me wrong. Poor Evelyn, I feel sorry for her. She was caught up in the Robey web and couldn't get out of it. Me, I walked out of it.

I left in the early Sixties. I walked into his office and looked him right in the eye and said, "Look, Mr. Robey, I'm splittin.' Don't try to do anything to me." I went to freelancing around to different companies. For years I couldn't find a company. He had it so no one would record me. I don't know how many sides I recorded for Don Robey. A lot were never issued, and a lot got lost in

WILLARD MAYES (L.), T-BONE WALKER (CENTER), PETE MAYES (R.), CLUB RAVEN, BEAUMONT, 1960. COURTESY PETE MAYES.

the shuffle. Robey was a cold man. He sold the company and cut music away from his life. Then one night awhile later, Evelyn [Johnson] told me, he was up watching TV and got up, turned the set off, and dropped dead on the spot. I don't know how he had died, but he did. He turned the music off in his life.

I've been together with Jim Bateman since 1976. We've gone through so many ordeals that we made it. He's the cause of me getting some royalties today on some of my past records. I've done three albums with Rounder. They're all right. I don't really like record companies. Where I see my music going is where the modern blues player has never been able to go, to a vortex on the other side of Mars, beyond that. In order to get there, you have to suspend the G force. Then if you do that, you might a get a chance to stop in the twilight zone, a rest period, but the ultimate part of this trip is the nine giant steps. You got to go at supersonic speed to get there, and not many can get there. What I'm talking about is my idea of music. You listen to all of my records from the time I started to today. I don't go back and try to sound like I did ten years ago. I may take one of those tunes, but when it comes out to be heard again, it's another piece of music. I'm still growing. I won't stay in my place. I've heard this all my life. "Stay in your place." Well, where the hell is my place? I'm talking now about the prejudice in my life. You know what makes a good colored man? What is it? Stay in your place. My ideas go beyond music. I have the greatest love for the human race any man can ever have, but what burns me is to see one, just one, put himself up on a pedestal in front of a crowd of five thousand and say that he's good and I'm not.

My music is explanatory. I don't have a college education, but I've got sense. Texas is where I grew up, where I learned to play white country music, French music, and blues. The blues depends on what you're feeling, but it's also supposed to be an explanation. How can I tell you what I'm doing if I can't explain it? You heard what I did, but can you ever truly know if I don't tell you? Anything I do is an explanation; otherwise, it's a mystery. The idea is to make people feel better when they leave than when they come in. I try to record and create the positive ideas for the people around me, black and white. I don't want to make my audience feel guilty. Nobody owes me anything. But I'm a threat because I'm trying to tell the truth.

CLARENCE "GATEMOUTH" BROWN, HOUSTON, 1960S.
PHOTOGRAPH BY BENNY JOSEPH.

LONG JOHN HUNTER

July 13, 1931– ; interview, 2004

I was born in a little town in Louisiana. I moved to Texas in 1952. I don't know nothing about Louisiana. I grew up in Arkansas. I'm named after my daddy. I'm John Thurman Hunter Jr. And my mother's name was Marie Irene Hunter. Her maiden name was Fleake. Well, they all was born poor and sharecropping on farms everywhere they could find somebody that needed slavery.

My daddy played a little guitar. He liked Lightnin' Hopkins and Muddy Waters. But we wasn't allowed to mess with his guitar because, like I say, when we was in Arkansas, we knew nothing about nothing. My mother was a church person, but she wasn't like a solo singer. She'd sing along with the rest of the choir. I used to sing in the field, yeah, oh, plowing that mule, I did. But I never did sing blues music, because all the music that you heard in Arkansas was like Hank Snow or Hank Williams or something like that. I thought I was better than Bill Monroe singing "Blue Moon of Kentucky." Oh, I thought I could sing that, man, and I'd plow a mule to death singing that song, all day long. "Blue Moon of Kentucky."

I was real small when we moved from Louisiana to Arkansas, and we lived all over Arkansas, different farms. All of it was sharecropping. I started working when I was eight years old, in the field. I'd do whatever the next one would do, almost. When I was twelve years old, I was packing hundred-pound sacks of fertilizer as well as my daddy. And we never had nothing. I mean, that was just slave work, and all we got was a little food. About every three weeks, you could go to town and buy some groceries on the tab, and all that came out when the settle-up come in the fall. And we never cleared anything. We was always in the hole.

Living out in the country there in Arkansas was pretty tough. We always lived way, way back in the woods. There wasn't no houses beyond where we lived, for the most part. There was times when Santa Claus was supposed to come Christmas Eve, and I'd wake up Christmas Day, ain't nothing there, and my daddy would tell me, "Well, Santa Claus said he couldn't bring you nothing this time, but maybe he'll have something for you for New Year's." Well, that was the end of it, because it was just a matter that he didn't have no money and wasn't nothing, you know.

(OPPOSITE) LONG JOHN HUNTER, 1960S. COURTESY MARCEL VOS.

It was tough. I mean, I lived that life—I was twenty-three years old before I left the farm. And I'll tell you the saddest thing for me was, I was away from Arkansas forty-two years, and I went back, and some of the same guys that was growing up as I were, they're still in that area, and it's pitiful to see them, the way they look, man. They're not human. They don't know nothing about nothing, and they could have been me very well. I just got lucky. I've always been a mother's child. And a sawmill from Arkansas moved to a little town called Devers, Texas, between Dallas and Beaumont. And my daddy left Arkansas and moved down to Texas with that sawmill. And after, I don't know, about three weeks of being away from my mother, I told the man on the farm up there, "I'm going to see my mother." He didn't like it because I was working seven days a week on the farm. And I took off. I never will forget that bus ticket: four dollars and something I paid on Trailways to go from Arkansas to Beaumont, Texas.

I was living about a hundred miles south of Little Rock at that time. You ever heard of a town in Arkansas called Magnolia? That's pretty close to the Louisiana border. They grew cotton, corn, you name it. . . . Oh, my God. I mean, it was sad. I have some kind of a problem with that now. I mean, I don't never see colors until I have a problem with a white person. Then I remember all of the things that they used to call me as a child out there in them woods. It was sad. Sometimes when I be traveling, I have to go through Arkansas, and I tell whoever's driving, "Hurry up and get me through this," because I just hate it when I'm in Arkansas. I know that's crazy. As old as I am now, I should have done forgot about it, because I would imagine that the people that did me so bad, they're dead and gone now, but I still think about it.

My wife come with me to Texas. She's dead now. She died about four months ago. Her name was Ernestine. She was from Waldo, Arkansas, which is about six miles from where I lived. Moving to Texas was the best move I ever made in my life, to get away from Arkansas.

Well, when we got to Beaumont, I hadn't never seen nothing like that. They had a couple of buildings that was two-story buildings, and in Arkansas, you don't see nothing like that. I mean, you see an old, broken-down barn or an old, raggedy house, and that was about it. But getting to Beaumont, I got off the bus at eight o'clock in the morning, and I see these buildings. Wasn't no tall buildings, just something like two stories, maybe. And man, I'm telling you. It's a shame to be that green, don't know nothing about nothing. And I saw like four or five people walking down the street, on their way to some kind of work, and I just thought, "Man, where are all these people going this time of morning, at eight in the morning?" Five people. Because in Arkansas, you didn't see nobody because there was so much distance between where we lived and anybody else. And nobody had cars then. For a whole week, you might see one person walk by. And there wasn't nobody that you didn't know. Everybody that was out there, they knew you, for one reason or another.

So when I got to Beaumont, I got a job at a box factory. And I was making $47.50 a week, and man, that was a lot of money, a whole lot of money for me. I hadn't never seen that kind of money, because in Arkansas, if you had $2.00, that was a lot of money. That would last you six months, because you wasn't going nowhere to spend it.

I didn't start playing music until I was a grown man. That was after I got to Beaumont. The story is that I met some guys at this box factory I was working at, and one of them was kind of a musician. His name was Ervin Charles. And he was somewhat a little, small-time guitar player then. And after we worked together a couple of weeks, talking back and forth, where we come from and what we have done, he told me he play a little guitar every once in a while just for himself. And so, one Monday morning he came in and say, "Hey, man, B. B. King is coming to town Wednesday. You want to go?" I say, "Naw, I don't think so." "Aw, man, come on, let's go down and check him out." "No." He come in Tuesday with the same story. "Man, I told you B. B. gonna be here Wednesday [at the Raven]. You still ain't going?" I say, "Naw, I told you, man, I'm not going nowhere." So, come Wednesday, of the day of the dance of B. B. King, he comes in and say, "Well, today is the day; B. B. King'll be here tonight." And I say, "Man, I told you, I'm not going to see no B. B. King. I never heard of B. B. King." And I asked him how much it cost; after he done worried me for three days with that, I asked him how much it cost to go. He said, "A dollar and a half," and I like to had a fit. I said, "I'm not paying no dollar and a half to go see nobody, B. B. King, man." And he told me that if I would go see that show, that he'd pay my way, and he did. And that was the best dollar and a half ever been spent in my behalf, because I watched B. B. King play. As God is my witness, that was a Wednesday, and I couldn't rest after seeing B. B. King play that guitar, and women and everybody was screaming and hollering, that just worried me to death. And I knew from that what I was going to do. When I got my lunch break, I was going downtown and buy me a guitar, and I was going to learn how to play a guitar. And that's what I did. That was a Thursday. Friday, I played my first gig, made $2.50. And I've been trying to play ever since. Now that's the honest God truth. I've told this story a million times since then, and I guarantee you it's the same every time because from here to Christ, that's the way it happened.

My first guitar in my life was a Fender Telecaster. My father had played just some old scrapped-up guitar. He'd order an old guitar from, like, Sears Roebuck, out of a catalog or something. I think he was paying something like seven or eight dollars for those guitars. Just wasn't much of a guitar. I used to try to make me a guitar and nail baling wire up on a tree and put a snuff bottle down there for a bridge. That was my guitar. But I couldn't play any music that way.

I think that Fender cost about $165. I put $10 down and $5 a month. Once I got it, I didn't have any trouble playing it. In fact, I almost got arrested the Thursday night that I got it because I was living in apartments in Beaumont. And after I got off work, I was trying to learn how to play my guitar till about three in the morning. And the police came around. I guess somebody had called and said I was making too much noise. I had just bought a little old Fender amp. I don't know, it wasn't much, just enough to make sound.

Well, I just found me a sound that I liked on the guitar, and I played that all night long, just that one sound. I wasn't making no changes at all, just that one sound. And I just loved that sound, whatever it was. And that's how it was that I learned how to play guitar. And like I say, we played our first gig, which was a little club right behind where I was living, and made $2.50 apiece, and that's how I started. I just told myself I was going to learn to play a guitar. I had one song by B. B. that I liked to hear him sing, and I tried to do that, and it was a mess. I mean, it was sad. We just tried to play a couple of instrumental things that we thought we could play. It was bad. It was really bad. The guy [owner] knew me from knowing my daddy, and he said, "I ain't got nobody here tonight, and I can't pay you nothing, but if y'all want to play for the door, well, you're welcome." And that's how that came about. And we were so bad that we couldn't play with our face to the few little audience that we had. We played with our backs to them. It was called Randy's Place. It was all black. At that time, blacks and whites didn't get close to each other.

That was in 1953. Yeah, we just started playing. And you know, in two weeks' time—I know this sounds like lying—two weeks' time, we had more work than we could do. We all had day jobs at that time. And people went to calling from ever-which-a-way. It's really funny how it happened, but we had more work than we could keep up with, just in the matter of weeks. And I was named as Long John Hunter and The Hollywood Bearcats. Now, that was our stage name. We had two guitars and a drum. At one time, down in Houston, and all places like that, that was a big-time band at that time: two guitars and a drum.

We were just playing dance music, and part of it we'd know, and some of it, we was trying to play like B. B. King. And we had a song that I used to make a lot of money on, called "Two Trains Running," by Muddy Waters. And I made more money playing that song than I made for the work that I was doing.

Well, they say I was good And anybody I see that remembers a long time, they say, "I ain't going to let you get away without you singing that song to me, 'Two Trains Running,'" because I guess I had a good voice for that. I guess I did, really did.

One time, there was two or three people standing round, and we was talking about me being in the band. And I started off just as John Hunter. And somebody say, "You need a stage name, man." And one guy say, "Well, his name is John. Why don't we call him Big John?" Well, at that time, I was tall and slender. And another guy said, "No, that won't work because he's too skinny." And the other guy say, "What about Long John?" So I been Long John ever since 1953.

Not long after that, I recorded a little old thing at a radio station there in Beaumont called "Crazy Girl," and "She Used to Be My Woman," and man, that thing just caught on fire. I mean, every radio station in town was playing that record. And then this guy Don Robey, which was a big music man in Houston, called, and he was going to do big things for me. He got me under a contract for three years. And I never heard the record played no more. That was his way of getting me off the street because I was causing too much problems for the people that he was trying to promote. And this is another true story; that's the way it happened. I didn't get one day's work after I signed with—he had two labels, which was Peacock and Duke. Well, I signed for the Duke label.

After about two and a half years of that doing nothing, I went to Houston, got in my old car, and I say, "I'm going over there, and I'm going to get this straightened out." And I walked in his office. The secretary had to buzz you in to get you into his office. Well, I went there and say, "I want to speak to Mr. Robey." She say, "Do you have an appointment?" I said, "No, ma'am, I do not." She say,

LONG JOHN HUNTER, 1980S. COURTESY MARCEL VOS.

"Well, you can't speak to Mr. Robey today because he's busy." And I just kicked the gate in and went on in there where he was. And everybody told me, says, "Man, you risked your life because he's known to pull his gun and shoot people." But I just kicked the gate open and went and kicked his door open. I know that was wrong, but I did it, admittedly, I did it. I was going to get some kind of results out of him because after all that time, I had nothing, got no dates, no work dates or nothing out of it, and I just could see myself being locked down and couldn't do nothing. I was going to end it one way or the other. And that was a stupid way I did it, because, like I say, he'd been known to pull his pistol on people. Like Gatemouth Brown, that used to just be a natural for him to pistol-whip Gatemouth Brown. And I left and come on back to Beaumont and went to doing the same thing I was doing when they picked me up over there.

After a few years in the music, me and a guy called Philip Walker went to California, and I went to T-Bone's house. And he was a very nice man. We just sat down for a whole afternoon, just talking about a whole lot of nothing, you know. I used to play some of his music, but the only influence that really had me was B. B. King. And I could play just like B. B. King. Some guy came up one night and told me, say, "Man, I like the way you play. You play good music. But you sound like B. B. King." And that just pulled me down. I said, "I got to stop this." And from that day on, I started trying to be myself, be Long John Hunter.

I left Beaumont in '55 and went to Houston, and I started playing around over there with Albert Collins. And Gatemouth Brown had two brothers, one called Widemouth and the other one called Bigmouth. So I played in and around with them. I played Shady's Playhouse. I never played the Matinee, no. That was the big boys; that's where they hung around. I played the Eldorado one time. Sure did. I played three gigs with Lightnin.' That was a hard job because Lightnin' have no changes in his music. He'd hold one note for two hours. He was a nice guy. I mean, Lightnin' was himself. He'd be having them drinks and play that music, and people'd be screaming and hollering. So, he was good at what he did.

I started driving a lumber truck in Houston. At one time, I was doing like seven nights a week music and five and a half days work. It was tough, but I was young then. It didn't matter. I could do it. But I stayed in Houston about two years. Then somebody come by and say, "Man, y'all need to be in El Paso, Texas." Say, "Man, them people is jumping up there." And we loaded up the car the same day that we was told that and headed to El Paso. We got there Saturday evening, August 13, 1957, on a Saturday. And we played at a little club there called Claudel's Place. And the three of us, we made $40 apiece, passing the hat. Man, that was more money than we ever made. I had a drummer called Calvin Rose and a guitar player called Allen Price. We played together about three years. Then I took them to El Paso, and they went crazy because they couldn't stay away from them girls over there. They'd be late for work, wouldn't want to work, and I just said to hell with them. I had two Mexican guys wanted to learn how to play that music, and I guarantee, in two weeks, that was the best band I had in Juarez. I got two Mexicans from behind the bar. They was bartenders. The drummer was named Miguel. I've forgotten his last name. And the guitar player's name was Ralph. I'm terrible with names. I'm surprised that I remember their names, but I knew them so well and played with them so long. And I worked in Juarez ten years, a place called the Lobby. It was a packed house from eight o'clock till six, seven o'clock the next morning, every night, seven days a week. The first five years that I played over there, I worked seven nights a week, from eight o'clock to you say when the next day. Like on weekends, on Sunday morning, people'd been to Mass, and on their way back, and the sun be way up, we'd still be playing, still got a houseful of people. Just had to put them out and close the door. They wasn't going to leave. I never seen nothing like that. And all I know this day, I learned it in Juarez. I learned all I know today, I learned it in Juarez.

It was all kinds of people. Fort Bliss was right there. And, man, at that time, El Paso was closing up at twelve o'clock. Well, we'd already have a full house before El Paso closed up, but when El Paso closed up, and about that time, about twenty steps and you was across the bridge. You could be in Juarez. And when El Paso would close down, everybody in El Paso would be in Juarez, coming to that Lobby. That was something. Like I say again, if it didn't happen at the Lobby in Juarez, it didn't happen nowhere in the world. It was wild. I mean, it was crazy. They used to have to lock the doors, and they'd have a line two blocks long, waiting to get in there. But they'd close the door because they had too many people in there. They'd close the doors; if two left, they'd open the door and let two in.

I recorded "El Paso Rock" in Alamogordo, New Mexico, in 1960. Well, I recorded that thing about three times. I did it just as an instrumental once, and then I did two versions of singing. But that was the main thing; in every club I would play in, I would get a lot of requests: "Play 'El Paso Rock.'" I got pretty famous up in that area. I could go a couple of hundred miles out, but I just really started traveling about '92.

I stayed in El Paso thirty-three years. After a few years of doing other people's music, I started trying to write my own stuff, and I can't write no song sitting at home. I've got to ride. I can get in my car. As of today, if I ride thirty minutes down the road, a song just comes to me. I don't know why, but I cannot write a song sitting at home. I've got a whole bunch because I got four CDs on Alligator, and I got two more CDs, and all of the songs on all of my CDs, I had a couple of co-writers, and one of them just died here about a month ago. Tary Owens. He was the catalyst of getting me to Europe, in 1989. I got real famous over there because they like ugly musicians over there. And I fit that mode real good. And they like blues music. It's no other music like blues music in Europe, and I went over well over there. And I've been almost all over Europe in the last few years that I've been traveling. I've been everywhere.

I've lived in Phoenix about a year. I can stand the heat, but I can't stand cold, and it don't never freeze here. The reason why I'm here is because I usually travel about eight months a year, and where I go, like Canada and all that, I don't travel there in the wintertime. They sent me up there in the wintertime two years in a row, in January, and I say, "I'll never do it again," so I bowed out from traveling in the wintertime up in them New York and Boston and all them places like that.

I never drank or smoked in my life. And I'm seventy-two years old. In Juarez, Mexico, I could have been anything I wanted to be. I could have been a snitch. I could have been a dope dealer. I could have been anything I wanted to be. But I never, so help me God, I never in my life had nothing to drink or smoked cigarettes or gotten high or nothing like that. Well, you know, I like to play music, and I like to see people smile and enjoy what I do. That's my all-time high there, seeing people—I do a lot of crazy things that musicians say they don't know how I get away with it, but that's just my thing. Going out in the crowd, putting the guitar in women's lap. I make a lot of money sometimes doing that. Guys'll come up and tell me—to be honest with you, I had a guy in El Paso, I put the guitar in his wife's lap one night. And the next time I saw him, he say, "Man, here's twenty dollars. Every time I come here, I'm going to give you some money." I say, "Why?" "Because the best sex I ever had was after you put the guitar in my wife's lap. We went home, and we had sex, and that was the best we had. We've been together ten years," he say. Now, that's the honest-God truth. If it was a lie, he told me a lie, but every time he came through the door in El Paso, he'd always hand me from $20 to $50, say, "You know what your job is." And after awhile, I'd go around, put the guitar in her lap, five or six songs later, he'd say, "Well, I'll see you, Long John," and he'd laugh. And I don't think he ever told her what the deal was between him and I of that, but he'd tell me every time I would do that that she'd just freak out. I don't understand it because to me, that's nothing, but they like it. I try to figure out ways to kind of keep up with the times until they make requests to do a certain song that they've heard me play before, and then I'll play it like it was a long time ago. But I've always got different ways that I try to do things. You've got to stay fresh, because if you become stale, then you've done lost your touch.

Well, they tag me as a blues player, and I can play the blues. But I don't live by the blues. I live for happy music, and I think most blues music is sad music, in my thought. Somebody tried to tell me, "Oh, that's not so," but that's my thinking of blues music. It's sad music. Well, I don't particularly like playing sad music. I play what I call happy music, where people can laugh and dance and jump up and down and smile. That's the kind of music that I try to play to make people smile and sit back and watch and see some dumb thing that I do. I build myself on that kind of mentality.

TOM HUNTER

March 22, 1943– ; interview, 2004

I was born in Arkansas, and we moved up to Beaumont. My dad found a job in Beaumont, and we moved in 1951. He was a guitar player himself. His name was John Hunter Sr. My brother Long John is named after him. John is a junior. My dad never did play out anywhere; he just played around the house. And he'd lay the guitar down and walk out on the street somewhere, and I'd go in there and pick it up and plunk around on it a little bit. It was a Gibson hollow-body electric. And I still have that guitar today. Then we commenced to form a little band here and there, and eventually I joined up with a guy by the name of Christian White. I was a sophomore in high school, must have been 1960. And Barbara Lynn, the great Barbara Lynn, of "You'll Lose a Good Thing" fame, she was a singer, playing the guitar in the band with us at that time.

When I graduated high school, I went into the military, formed up some bands around in the different bases I was on. I was in the navy. After I got out of the service, I moved to El Paso to go to college, the University of Texas at El Paso, for a year and a half and played around up there with different bands. One of our bands backed Wilson Pickett. Me and my brother Long John, we played together over in Juarez, Mexico. He played at one club, and I played at another sometimes. He's twelve years older than I am. Now, he lives in Phoenix, Arizona. He was living in El Paso at the time. When I got out of the service, I moved out to El Paso and lived with him awhile. I got a job as a porter at the Federal Reserve Bank of El Paso. And the banker looked at my military record and saw how well I did in the military. And he called me in and told me, "No way you ought to be working as a porter." So he suggested I go to school out there, and I did. But I didn't graduate. The banker that suggested that moved off to Waco, and being young, I just drifted away from it. I was out there for two years. Then I moved back to Beaumont.

The Club Raven had all kinds of entertainment there. Nearly all of the big names came there: B. B. King, The Midnighters, The Five Royals, Etta James, you name it. They all came through there. That was one of the main stopping points. I was too young to actually get in, but they had a big fan in the window that turned real slowly, so we could look directly in at the stage from outside.

My brother was not really much of an influence on me, because for years, he was gone. He left Beaumont, I think, about 1959. And I just heard him play off and on. The first time I really got around to playing with him was 1966, when he was playing in El Paso. But by that time, my cap was set to play like Wayne Bennett. I met him when he was with Bobby Bland. They used to come to Beaumont at different clubs, and I always got a chance to hook up with him and shake his hand and talk with him. He was not a very outgoing type of guy. You'd talk to him for about a minute, then he was through with you. Now, I spent lots of time with Bobby Bland, talking to him, every time he came to Beaumont. In fact, Bobby Bland came to the Club Raven. And he was on his bus sleeping. The door was about half open, and I opened the door. His bodyguard told me, "Shut that damn door!" But Bobby Bland said, "That's okay; let him come on." I was a kid. Man, I sat there and I talked to Bobby Bland for about twenty minutes. His music was really popular at that time; it's always been popular. And, man, I was just thrilled to death to be sitting there with him on the bus. He was real friendly. And every time he's come back to Beaumont—I wrote for about seven or eight years for the local newspaper, the *Beaumont Enterprise*, and each time he would come to Beaumont or Lake Charles, I'd always go backstage or meet him on the bus and talk with him. I don't think he would know me from anybody else, but I have experienced talking with him on several occasions. I never met the Winter brothers, but I knew of them. I think the first recording, I used to try to play it. That's the first one I know of, "Blue Day Blues." I think Johnny and I are pretty close to the same age [Johnny was born February 23, 1944].

Well, to start with, we played a lot of what you might call rock 'n' roll. Not really that much blues at the time. I try not to play like anybody, but if I like to be told that I play like somebody, it really would be B. B. King, because he was one of my idols. But believe it or not, the first idol was the guy who used to play lead guitar with Bobby Bland, and that was Wayne Bennett. Yeah, that was my first influence, right there. I played a lot like him. And of course he took his style after T-Bone Walker. But I emulated Wayne Bennett more than anything. But I picked up a lot of B. B. King's stuff, and B. B. is my idol today. I've met him three times, but I'm sure he wouldn't know me. I never got a chance to play onstage with him. Oh, man, the guy's awesome. I just adore him.

I got two different kinds [of guitar] that I actually play. I've got a Gibson SG, and I also have a Fender semi-hollow body. It's a rare one; I bought it at a pawnshop. It's a good guitar. It's close to the thinline Telecaster, but it's got one F-hole at the top. I have a friend in Nederland at a big music shop, guy named Cecil, he got on his computer and tried to find out what it was and where it came from. All we know is that it's a Fender. I paid $300 for it about two years ago. It's black. I asked about the thinline Tele, and they said, no, it was not a thinline Tele. I haven't had anything done to it. It has a battery in the back for the preamps; I have to change that quite often.

Well, up until 1995, I worked at a Mobil Oil refinery. I took early retirement and really got into the music after that. In fact, I was a deejay for a number of years, playing blues on KALO radio out of Port Arthur, about eight years. And that was about as close as I came to playing at that time. But when I retired from the refinery, then I got more into it, like I am now.

I have several recordings out. In fact, we'd got this CD out now, Long John and I, called *One Foot in Texas*. And that CD is actually named after one of my songs. And it's recorded on the Doc Blues label out of Austin, Texas. The guy who owns it is a doctor—Dr. Jim Thompson. It is making pretty good progress. In the latest charts I've seen, it was number seven. It was recorded in Austin, at Orleans Studios. They tell me that Willie Nelson has recorded there. It's a big, beautiful studio—all digital.

My brother and I play live together on the album. We did some overdubbing. Mark Kazanoff and his horns, and Derek O'Brien, they came in later. But Long John and I recorded it live. He did his song; I did mine. We didn't do anything together. We played on each other's CDs, but he sang his song, and I sang mine. He has a very high-pitched voice, and I don't. I shout a lot more than he does. Yeah.

Well, my brother and I have played off and on from time to time. In fact, last time we played together was in Phoenix, Arizona, where he lives now. And they hooked us up when the CD first came out. And we played together there in May of this year. And that was the last time we hooked up. But we are getting ready to go to Europe for the Blues Estafette in November. And at the tail end of the Estafette, we're going to tie on to Spain and Portugal.

I've stayed in Beaumont all these years. Regrettably, yes. It's not my favorite place. I'd rather be somewhere else. Family was one of the main reasons I stayed. I was raising kids and had a good job and stuff like that. But now I'm ready to make a break. I don't know yet. I'm thinking about this area here, Dallas–Fort Worth. That would really be it. Beaumont is a good city, but there's not much there for a musician, a blues musician. And right now, Beaumont is so rock-oriented. Any club you go to, you can just look at the names of the bands that are playing there. Houston, I don't think there's a whole lot there. I think the competition is great there, but it just doesn't seem like there's a lot happening there right now. And I just kind of like the Dallas–Fort Worth area. It's where I would like to be. I haven't made an honest effort to get started, really. I like both Dallas and Fort Worth.

I've done covers, and I do covers all the time, but as far as recording, I like to do my own stuff. I get a better feel for what I'm doing if it's my own. If I do somebody else's as a cover on a recording, I will revamp it, kind of dramatically, to my own style. I like to write my own stuff. I write with my guitar. Sometimes I'll use a keyboard just for the ambient effects, to see what it would sound like. But mainly, it's on a guitar. I've got a little [recording] system I set up, a rhythm and stuff like that. I've just got the little four-track recorder there. I'm looking to going into that with the computer; I use the computer, but not for the music. I use it for business and anything else.

I hope I've kind of developed my own style, but I know lots of times, it's just something I picked up from B. B. Whatever I'm playing, I know this is one of B. B.'s licks, and I'm not ashamed when I do it. I love it, so I think that'll be with me. I've always got that feel that this is something that B. B. would do in this instance. And there's a lot of things he does that I never will be able to do, but some of the stuff, I just feel like this is applying B. B. King's licks here. Well, sometimes he makes a few little licks there that I think are his signature licks. I would have to do it constantly, and he does it without even thinking. His tone is beautiful. Very clear. In one of his interviews, he was asked what advice he would give to young musicians, aspiring to be professional musicians. B. B. said, "Listen to all types of music," which I did before I heard that advice. But he said, "Steal a little bit from each one." And if he said it, well, it sounds good to me. If I hear a guy with a beautiful lick, and I feel like I can incorporate it into my playing, I'll do it. B. B. said one of his greatest influences was Louis Armstrong on trumpet. And so he emulated the horn on the guitar.

In Beaumont [the racism has eased up]. It has eased tremendously. If you're there, you're used to it. But people who come there from other places—I've had white guys tell me, "Man, I don't see how you stay here." But it's something I'm not even noticing. You see it every day or whatever, and some things, you know you can't change, so you just do the best you can and go on about your business.

The ironic part, the strange part, about all that is that Port Arthur is roughly twenty miles from Beaumont. There's as much difference between Beaumont and Port Arthur racially as there is between daylight and dark. Port Arthur is a whole lot more relaxed. If you're okay, you're okay; don't give a damn what color you are. If you're not okay, you're not okay, regardless of what color you are. And we play over there sometimes at a little club not any bigger than this [Fort Worth hotel] lobby called Madelyn's in Port Arthur; on Saturday nights, there's just a big jam session. And shoot, everybody just packs in. If you can play, let's get up and play. You want to sing, come on up and sing. No problems. They had a club in Beaumont called Pearl Street Café. It was a blues club. It was a real nice club, had an upstairs balcony and all this type of stuff. It was an old building, but it was a renovated club. My band played there each Saturday night from the night they opened up in 2001 up until nineteen months later, when they closed down. We played there every Saturday night. Well, they opened up this old part of Beaumont only a block away, called Crockett Street Entertainment Center. And that kind of took away from what we were doing there. In fact, Jimmie Vaughan played at the Pearl Street Café. He brought his show there one night, sold the place out, packed it. . . .

I've sung gospel, and I'm into all styles of music. Man, I got enough country and western 45s to run a radio program for two months and never play the same song twice. And I love jazz, but I can't play it. I'm not a good jazz player. I like all styles of music. I even do some country music onstage at the club we play out in Baytown on Wednesday nights—well, this is not really country, but I did one song by The Eagles last Wednesday night. Got good reception. "Lying Eyes." I do a lot of Delta stuff, but I think a person could listen to me and tell that I am from Texas. I have the Texas influence. If you look at the tree, blues tree, you'd see where it would filter back down to T-Bone Walker and Lowell Fulson—of course, he was from Oklahoma, but still . . . a southwestern style.

In the heyday of Duke Records and Peacock, I was just a little too young. I was still in school, so I never did get a chance to meet Don Robey or see anything about the labels. All I did was hear about it.

Right now, believe it or not, I've got three in my band, Tom Hunter and The Hurricane Band: me, a bass player, and a drummer. And I've got this lady that sings with us, Miss Candy. One guy lives in Nederland, which is close. If I move, I'll have to get a new band; I doubt that they will come along. I got some good leads on musicians, and they told me that if I did get relocated to Dallas, that they would help me put a band together. One guy's got a recording studio at his house. He's got a club he calls the Attic upstairs at his house, where he has entertainment, and he said that we could use that anytime for rehearsals. So I've got pretty much a basic foundation of a band if I ever do get relocated up here.

I've been looking for a manager, agent, somebody to kind of help me out a little bit, help me get a little bit more into what I'm doing. Well, I'm trying to branch out now, especially since we've got this CD out, Long John and I, and just take it as far as I can, really. That's where I need somebody to point me in the right direction. In the last two years, I've played the South by Southwest music fest. And I've played another club or two around Austin, Jazz on Sixth Street. I've played Antone's. With this One Foot in Texas CD, we got good reviews in the *Blues Revue*, *Living Blues*, and *Down Beat*.

I'm always referred to as Long John's brother. If it helps, okay, but I'd rather be known for myself.

JOHNNY WINTER

February 23, 1944–   ; interview, 1987

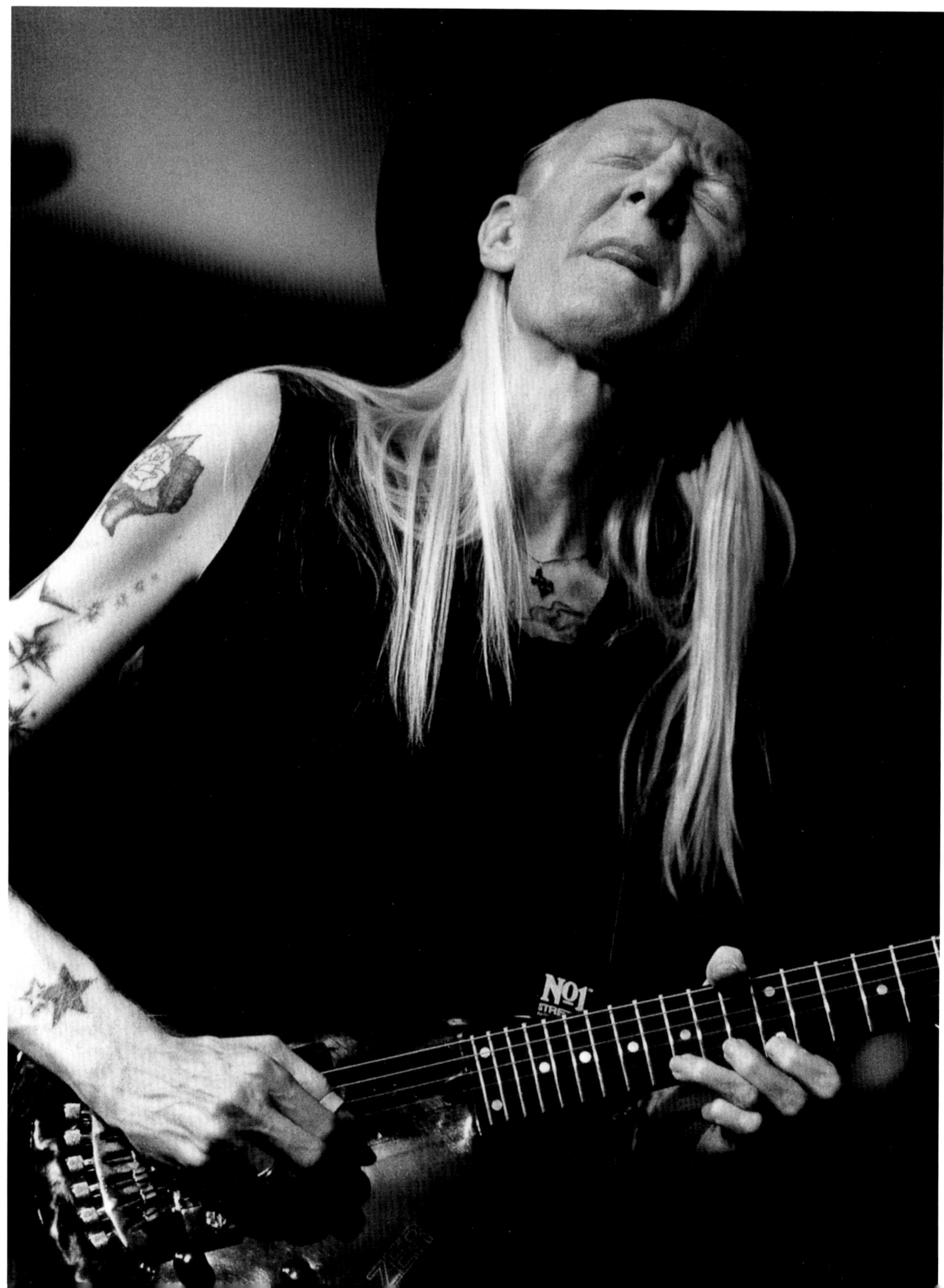

There were great radio stations that you could pick up around Beaumont from everywhere. There was one in Del Rio; it was actually an American station in Mexico. Wolfman Jack had a blues show, and there was someone before him called Dr. Jazzmo. There was a station in Shreveport, KWKH. Frank Page, I think, was the disk jockey. He had a show from Stan's Record Shop. There were a couple of stations from Nashville. WLAC had two record shows, and there was Ernie's Record Shop. Ernie's had Excello Records. Later on that night, there was Randy's Records. The good thing about those shows was that you could get the records if they weren't available. You could send in your five or six dollars around the South and get blues specials, great records, if you didn't know what you were doing. Literally, I bought every blues record that I could find. That's when I was still too young to go to the clubs myself, and there wasn't anybody else that was interested in that kind of thing that I knew of.

Later on there was a station in Beaumont, K-Jet. Clarence Garlow was a disk jockey, and at night he'd play a lot of his own records. When I got old enough, I'd go out to clubs and listen to him, but before that, through my teenage years, I just listened to radio.

After I started playing clubs, I met Joey Long. I was sixteen or seventeen and started going to Houston, playing all over Texas and Louisiana. I got to meet people myself. There were never very many color lines among the musicians, though in clubs there were some problems mixing on stage. In the white clubs it was a little scarier than the black clubs, but nothing ever happened. We survived.

I don't know where Joey learned to play. He was about ten or fifteen years older. He had been doing it longer, but he was definitely the first white guy that I was aware of that had been playing good blues. He opened for Fats Domino, B. B. King, and a lot of people. They'd come through, and he opened up for them. I think Huey Meaux managed him at that point, and he was bringing a lot of people in. He'd put Joey in with a lot of acts. Joey was really famous; we thought he was. In fact, I still go down and see Joey, and he still plays practically the same way. He's kind of hard, it's just getting him in the right mood.

JOHNNY WINTER, POSTER BY MICHAEL PRIEST; AUSTIN, 1978.
COURTESY CENTER FOR AMERICAN HISTORY, UNIVERSITY OF TEXAS.

I've never really thought there really was much of a Texas style. If anything really stands out, there are so many different influences in Texas guitar players. You just can't say they sound the same way. There's Lightnin' Hopkins, and how can you compare him with Blind Lemon Jefferson, or Hop Wilson? There's all that country and western and jazz influence. You can hear so many different styles of music down there. In fact, it's just forced on you. You're exposed to a lot more varied styles.

Over the years I've learned more technically, what makes different things and where the influences come from, why people sound the way they do, but my actual enjoyment of the music hasn't changed at all. Emotionally, I still feel the same way. At first, I didn't know ex-

(OPPOSITE) JOHNNY WINTER, SWEDEN, 1980S.
PHOTOGRAPH BY HANS EKESTANG. COURTESY TOMMY LÖFGREN.

JOHNNY WINTER, PUBLICITY PHOTOGRAPH, 1987.

actly why I was doing it. If I liked them, I learned them. If I didn't, I ignored them, but I didn't really know why. I've tried to find out.

I bought every record I could get my hands on, but I never said, "This is what I want to sound like." The Chicago people, I guess, were the people who impressed me the most, like Muddy Waters, Little Walter; those were the records that were coming out, that were new when I was first getting into it. Later on, I heard the earlier stuff as it came out, then I heard the Twenties and Thirties music, but the Chicago Fifties style, that and what was going on around Texas at that point—Bobby Bland, Junior Parker. Bobby "Blue" Bland had some great guitar players.

T-Bone Walker was probably my favorite of Texas people; even though I don't sound a whole lot like him, I probably learned more from him than anybody. The way he would change the meter to different songs. Start out in one meter and switch back. He'd play that big fat guitar with no feedback, so I don't have the same kind of tones that he did, the actual sound, but from his approach to playing I learned more than just about anybody. He was very good at switching the meter around on things. That appealed to me. B. B. said that he learned a lot from T-Bone, and most of the others I heard also listened to T-Bone. That's what I was trying to get to.

Then I heard Muddy Waters on the bottleneck style, and there wasn't anybody around that played that kind of stuff that I was aware of. I learned about that from records. I didn't have any idea of what that was at first. I thought it was steel guitar or something like that. I just learned it in little bits and pieces, and finally I think there were a couple of articles out that mentioned how they were doing it. I tried cutting a test tube off and playing with the crystal on my watch—different things that took me a long time to develop, because it wasn't really anything I did on the bandstand, something I just did for myself. I didn't start using that until the mid- to late 1960s.

I always thought that I was always more influenced by the music in Chicago and the Delta than the Texas music that was actually around me. Most of the records were from Chicago, electric versions of the Delta, Howlin' Wolf, Muddy Waters. It was always more primitive, more raw; I liked it a little better. It was something I had never heard. At the same time I started hearing rock 'n' roll, but blues was more of it, and I couldn't understand why I was the only kid that felt that. I didn't really think of myself as a Texas musician until later.

In the mid-1960s Roy Ames was doing some things with Don Robey, and he had talked to Don Robey about me. Then Bill Hall came out of the woodwork and said that he had bought my contract from Ken Ritter, and that scared Don Robey off. I only met Don Robey one time and talked to him for fifteen or twenty minutes. I recorded some stuff for Roy and Huey [Meaux], and both of them put out the same stuff at the same time. I was actually with Roy, but Roy was working with Huey, and both of them got the tapes from each other, and the music wasn't even well produced. They might have been Roy's, and he was just keeping them at Huey's.

I'm glad to be away from all of that. I had to move to New York to be closer to the management, the record companies, the booking agencies. Now I suppose I could live anywhere, but I have kind of grown to like New York. I feel I've reached a point where I want to continue exactly what I'm doing and, if possible, put it into a little more commercial format. I've tried to do that, but it's always very hard to do. I've talked to the people who work with Robert Cray. The part that's hard for me is coming up with material. I'm not that great a songwriter myself. There's a lot I've thrown away. Once in a while I'll come up with something I like, but I can't depend on that to happen. Doing remakes of the old stuff is fun, but I'd like to come up with some original songs that I like. That's what I want to do. I've had the same band for the last eight or ten years, John Paris, the bass and harmonica player, and Tom Compton, the drummer, for three or four years. I really love having a trio. With a small group, you don't have to work things out. I think it's more exciting that way.

I'm still playing my Gibson Firebird for my slide, and I'm using a Laser, designed by Mark [Erlewine] in Austin. I bought it because it was small, and I thought it would be a nice guitar to just practice on, and I was playing it through an amp. I didn't even play it through an amp for a couple of months after I had gotten it. Then when I was doing *Guitar Slinger*, I used it in the studio, and I've been using it since. It's a cheaply made guitar, but it sounds so good. I've been using the same one for three or four years now. I really bought it because I thought it would be easy to take on the plane. It's got a real nice sound. The thing I don't like about it is that it only has one pickup; the one pickup it's got is the one I generally don't use. The pickup out of the neck is the one I usually use. For my next record, he'll have a new one made.

When I was younger, I was afraid my blues would change. My brother, Edgar, would always try to get me to learn more chords. I was afraid that if I played the jazzy stuff he liked, I wouldn't be able to play mine. At this point, I don't think it makes much difference. If you don't want to use it, you don't have to. But when I was thirteen or fourteen I wasn't real sure of that. I was afraid that if I learned too much I wouldn't like my playing. I tended to like the guys that played more primitively. If they got too good, I didn't like them too much. We used to have gigantic arguments about this stuff, music and what was good, and what wasn't good. Edgar would agree with me on Ray Charles and Bobby Bland, but he wasn't real sure if they were more primitive or if they hit beats in the wrong places, like Lightnin' Hopkins, John Lee Hooker. He wasn't too sure about that kind of stuff at all. I was afraid I was going to learn too much. I love Edgar, I respect him, but our approaches are completely different. Now, I still have no interest to change my style all around. I just want to get better at what I do.

It's hard for me to say where blues stops and rock 'n' roll starts. I've always played both of them, and to me they're the same thing. The rhythm might be different. Writers have always wanted to put me in one particular category or another, and if you get out of that category,

HUEY MEAUX AND DAVE ALVIN, 1980S. PHOTOGRAPH BY TRACY HART.

JOHNNY WINTER, PUBLICITY PHOTOGRAPH, CA. 1976. COURTESY CENTER FOR AMERICAN HISTORY, UNIVERSITY OF TEXAS.

you're not real—things I never dreamed about and still don't make any sense to me. I missed that freedom to be able to do everything. I want every album to have a country song on it, a dance song; I like all that variety. I've done now about twenty-five albums, and they have their differences. But if you're going to have your audience out there, you can't confuse them with anything's that's too weird. But if you're playing a good Texas bar, they want to you to be able to play anything, a jazz song, you have to be able to play country, but you can slip in some rock 'n' roll here and there, blues. You can pretty much play all of it through the course of the night. Even Cajun music. That was an influence. Beaumont is so close to Louisiana.

Keith Ferguson was one of the first white guys I met who was into the blues, and he's been into all kind of things. He loves the Mexican music, he understands what they're saying and I don't. It doesn't mean as much. But he still plays blues. In Texas even the Mexicans played blues, in San Antonio and Austin. They played in white bands [Doug Sahm] and they played in their own [Sunny and the Sunglows, Charlie and the Jives, and The Chili Peppers]. But where I lived you could hear Cajun, and you might never hear Mexican music.

I like traveling, hearing as much I can, but if we did it all the time, I'd hate it. The way we do it, for about a month. At the first of the month, I can't wait to get out there, but at the end of the month, I'm real ready to come home, then having a couple of weeks or maybe as much as a month to be at home and away from the road completely. I wouldn't go out on a six-month tour for anything in the world. I did that for years and liked it, but now I couldn't live that way. I've been doing it this way for about the last fifteen years; keeps me healthier. When I'm off the road I like to hide, and New York is a great place to hide. Living on the Upper East Side, it's quiet, a little neighborhood, peaceful. It's a lot easier than a small town, where everyone would know when I got back. I want some time to explore other areas.

My interest in tattoos doesn't relate much to blues. I was just wanting to try something new. . . . Tattoos are a way of being different.

In that way, I suppose tattoos are like my blues. I still don't know exactly that my blues is any one thing. I used to feel bad about that, that there wasn't anything to fit into. Here I was from Texas, I was into the way people play in Chicago. The white players who have come along in the last twenty years from Texas probably have more in common than the people [black players] who have come before us. We all play the electric guitar and are maybe more influenced by the Chicago sound.

To me, blues is getting your feelings out. It's not a particularly fast thing; a lot of people think it's crying in your beer, let's all feel bad together, but it's really not that way at all. The blues has a lot of up songs, your experiences. Even if you're talking about the bad, you can feel better because you can relate to it. If it's done right, it should make you feel like you're sharing the experience. The music goes along with that, there's a lot of sevenths and ninths [chords], I can play the bluesy notes, sliding up and down, but it's hard to put into words. Every time I do a song, I do it differently, according to the way you feel. It's easy to communicate with other musicians that you've never played with, other blues players; you can usually play together and make it work out without pre-planning. There's a spontaneous part of it. It's a living music. It makes me feel good, whether I'm playing or listening to other people. That hasn't changed since the first day I heard it. One of the things that's fascinating to me is not quite understanding why I like it; it's mysterious, but whatever it is, it still works the same way on me. I don't feel good if I'm not playing, not hearing it; there's a real hole in my life. For me, blues is a necessity.

BARBARA LYNN

January 16, 1942–   ; interview, 1987

BARBARA LYNN, PUBLICITY PHOTOGRAPH, 1980S.

Elvis inspired me. I was playing piano then. I was a teenager then. I started piano when I was in grade school, but I was getting tired of that. Then I heard Elvis and decided I wanted to do something odd. I thought it would be odd for a lady to play guitar. My first guitar was an Arthur Murray ukulele that my mother went out and bought me for $9.95. Then they saw that Barbara could really do something, and they bought a solid body guitar, and then one you could plug into an amplifier, a Gibson. Now I play the Fender Squire.

Huey Meaux heard about me, a girl playing lefthanded guitar, at a place called Lou Ann's. I had an all-girl group called Bobbie Lynn and The Idols, and we did a lot of the Elvis tunes like "Jailhouse Rock," and I swung my instrument and we all wore pants. Joe Berry saw me sing and perform, and went back and told him about me. Mr. Meaux came to my home and asked my parents' permission to record me.

We recorded a song out of Houston called "Dina and Katrina." It didn't do very good until I recorded "If You Lose Me, You're Losin' a Good Thing." We recorded that in 1963, and that started it off. It took me to forty-some states; I've been overseas three or four times. I have really traveled with that one record. It was originally on the Starfire label, and then Jamie Records licensed it from Huey Meaux and thereafter it started blooming like a little flower—planted a little rose, and it kept going and going.

Around Beaumont and Houston there were lots of rhythm and blues singers: Gatemouth Brown, Guitar Slim, Ray Charles, Bobby Blue Bland, B. B. King, Junior Parker, O.V. Wright. I think my singing combines a lot of what I heard and brings together rhythm and blues with soul and a little pop now. I got ideas from other musicians. I observed and learned my own approach.

Some of the songs—"Until Then I'll Suffer," "You're Losin' Me," "Second Fiddle Girl," "Teenaged Blues"—I wrote these in the late 1950s, so by the time I got to perform them on stage, I was ready. My first LP was called *You'll Lose a Good Thing*, in the late part of 1963, and then I had *This Is Barbara Lynn* on Atlantic in the early 1970s.

I got to be on Dick Clark [TV show] twice. It was nice. Dick interviewed me, and I was finally looking at the blue-eyed man I had seen on TV for so long. This is when *American Bandstand* was in Philadelphia. Then I got married, and that slowed me down a little, and in the

PORT ARTHUR, 1986.
PHOTOGRAPH BY ALAN GOVENAR.

1970s not a whole lot happened. After the Atlantic release, it dropped off. I still had a band, and we played in Oklahoma, Louisiana, and Texas. After I got divorced, I was able to pursue my music more. My former husband was interfering with my career, and it was time to do something else. In 1978 I did my last record with Huey Meaux, *Movin' on a Groove*, but it didn't go well. After that I slowed down but have never stopped singing or writing, and am looking for new recording opportunities in Los Angeles. But I play sometimes at the Classic Club in Dallas and at Antone's in Austin. Clifford [Antone] says, "This is your club, baby," and whenever I'm there, I always feel at home. It's a warm feeling.

A lot of people say I started something, because it's so odd for a woman to be playing a guitar. I use a thumb pick, and I strum the strings with my first finger. I have a style all of my own. I can't play the way most guitarists do. If I get a title in mind, then I have to go right to my instrument, and then I work out the lyrics on the guitar. I have faith, patience, and determination that it will break again.

ALFONSO R. "LITTLE RAY" YBARRA

June 30, 1967– ; interview, 2004

LITTLE RAY YBARRA, BEAUMONT, CA. 1999. COURTESY RAY YBARRA.

A good buddy of mine in Louisiana, Gumbo Phil, started calling me Little Ray about fifteen years go. He's like, "Little Ray, Little Ray," because I always went by Ray because the name that I have is a Hispanic name. I'm half Hispanic. And growing up in southeast Louisiana and Texas, it was just kind of easier for me to go by Ray.

I was actually born in Amarillo, Texas, man, Potter County, and lived in Dallas on and off a lot of my life. My father still lives there. My father is Alfonso R. Ybarra, and my mother is Elaine. And her maiden name is Sibley. And she's from Louisiana originally. So I'm kind of a mixture of Mexican and Cajun.

Blues music I probably got into originally because of my mother, listening to Jimmy Reed and Slim Harpo and stuff like that on eight-track, man. As a kid, I always liked it a lot. And it's just that kind of stuff, man, it just kind of stays with you, I guess. I went through my period of playing rock 'n' roll and thinking maybe that I would be a rock 'n' roll star or something like that. But that never did work out, you know, so my true calling was the blues.

My mother got me a set of drums at a garage sale. We were living in Baton Rouge, Louisiana. And she just bought them because they were so cheap, and brought them home, and my brother actually got first shot at them, but he didn't really want to fool with them. He was kind of wanting to be a guitar player. And so I just started playing around with the drums, and kind of taught myself how to play the drums good enough to play with some different musicians and stuff. And it just kind of went from there. Then I found my true calling on guitar when I was about fifteen years old. And I've been doing it ever since.

My father owned a barbershop in Dallas for years, on the corner of Northwest Highway and Abrams. And my mother, she's done just about every kind of job you can imagine, everything from cleaning people's houses to working for an insurance company. You name it, man, my mom has done it. She's done waitressing, she's done convenience store clerk, nursing home, just about everything she had to do to pretty much make ends meet.

My folks split up when I was six years old. We had just built a new house there in Dallas, and I thought everything was great. But my father was the kind of a guy that likes to ramble around. And my mother divorced him. I have two half-sisters and one half-brother. I'm actually an only child from my father. I moved to Louisiana when my parents divorced. My mother, being from there, brought all of us kids back down there. She definitely has Cajun background, for sure. Her mother's side of the family was Cajun. And her father had a lot of Cherokee Indian—of course, everybody says that—and then, Irish descent, and stuff like that.

I was playing Cajun music before anything. I played in some different little bands around in Louisiana, just playing, actually, just traditional Cajun, just to be able to kind of play with some guys and play some gigs when I was about thirteen years old, thirteen, fourteen. Then, as far as playing in a band, playing guitar, I was probably about fifteen or sixteen, with just some local kids in the neighborhood that I grew up with there in Louisiana. And it's funny, in south Louisiana, it seems like everybody plays something. Everybody plays some kind of an instrument.

So I went from Cajun to rock 'n' roll to blues. What attracted me to blues? I would be hanging out with my rock 'n' roll friends, playing back in the early, mid-Eighties in Dallas, and I was always tinkering with the blues. And a lot of those guys would be like, "Man, that's what you play best. You ought to play blues, man." You know, I would actually have these guitar wizard guys want me to show them blues riffs. And so it just kind of stuck, man. Once a blues bug bit me, that was it, man!

I started playing guitar when I was about thirteen, fourteen years old. I started fooling with it. And I kind of taught myself, man. I never really took any formal lessons or anything. Actually, a guy that's really responsible for a lot of what I am today is one of my mother's boyfriends. He was a guitar player. And they never actually married. They lived together for a long time, and he had a nice Les Paul, and he would let me play that thing every once in a while and kind of show me some stuff. His name was Rick Francis. He's a native to Louisiana, south Louisiana. Really great slide player, man. Really good, you know, he just never done anything with it.

It was real natural, man for me to play blues. Real natural. I remember a guy awhile back in Houston. I was in a gig, and I was talking to this other guy, and this—I won't mention any names, but this guy was saying that he didn't think that a Mexican could play the blues until he heard me, being I'm half Hispanic. And I thought, man, that's really a shallow way to think. The blues is for everybody, man. I think that you can't just, you know, label it as black music. I think it's everybody's music. Of course, it started with black people, but I think that it's just for everybody. You know, any music—it's for all of us.

I'm starting to find out there's more people, Hispanic people, involved in the blues, like Sunny Ozuna. and I'm really proud of that. I think that it's a good thing, man. I know a lot of guys, like Doug Sahm, wanted to be a Chicano. And guys like The Fabulous Thunderbirds looked to a lot of Chicano guys to find out how to dress right. I'll tell you probably the biggest Hispanic blues player that I know of, that I've played with, on and off for the last four or five years, is Paul Orta. Great harmonica player from Port Arthur, Texas. I call him the Mexican Little Walter. Yeah, Paul's originally from Port Arthur. You've heard of Paul, I'm sure. Actually, Paul's back in France now. There's really nothing for Paul here in this area, Port Arthur. It's kind of a dead scene. I'm just lucky. I have a gig with a band in Houston. I play four nights a week over there, you know. There's not anything for a bluesman in this area, Port Arthur and Beaumont, anymore. It's kind of mainstream; all the good stuff is gone, man.

I met Paul Orta at a gig about 1995. We talked and everything, and he let me sit in. And he was really impressed. He was like, "Man, I didn't know there was any guys like you around here." You know? I said, "Yeah, I live here." And so then our paths crossed again in about '99, and we actually ended up touring Europe together and making some albums together, and we gigged together for about three years. He's been on and off over there in France for the last twenty years. He's hanging out in Paris right now. Paul's very, very well liked in France, man. The only thing that Paul's ever had any problem with was alcohol. That's why I left the band. Too much alcohol. I like to have fun, too, and I am a drinker, too, but I always try to make sure my show goes over first, and then if there's time to have some beers or whatever, that's fine. But you [first have] to play, man.

His band was called Paul Orta and The Kingpins. I think he still uses some kind of interpretation of that. I'm not sure exactly what he calls it. I mean, he plays over in Europe a lot now, and he uses whomever he can kind of get to play with him. Maybe it's something like Paul Orta and The International Kingpins or something now.

Right now I play with a cat, Sonny Boy Terry, out of Houston, another harmonica player. I use a lot of different guitars. I use a Stratocaster, of course, Telecaster, Les Paul, some Silvertones, Harmonys. I do some acoustic stuff. I do an occasional duo with Sonny Boy Terry, and I'll do acoustic with him. We do all kinds of stuff when we do that acoustic act. We'll do anything from Jimmy Reed, some Silas Hogan, some T-Bone Walker, just a big variety of stuff. Probably one of my favorite guitar players that I really enjoy listening to and trying to be like is Magic Sam. I like Magic Sam, and I like Freddie King a lot. And then, I like a lot of the more contemporary guys, too: Ronnie Earl and Anson Funderburgh and Derek O'Brien, Jimmie Vaughan. I know all those guys are great players, and they were very helpful with what I've done. I think what they're doing is really good. And it's very tasteful. I think that they kind of stay true to the way guys like Magic Sam and Freddie King played. They kind of just carry that tradition on, and that's kind of what I'm trying to do, too. But it's a tougher market than it is doing blues-rock. If you do blues-rock you can play probably five, six nights a week. But if you're more traditional-based, it's a little tougher. You have to pick your spots a lot better.

I've been on about seven CDs, and I'm working on a brand-new one right now as we speak. I'm hoping this new record really opens up some ideas. It's going to be a Little Ray and The Blues Sonics record, and I'm going to have Lazy Lester doing some vocals and harp with me, and a fellow by the name of Brian Templeton, sang with a band called The Radio Kings out of Boston, Mass., he's going to do some vocals, and maybe Paul Orta if Paul Orta comes back around in time. I don't know if he's going to be back from Europe, but I managed to become good friends with Lazy Lester, and that's been a great thing.

Lazy Lester, he's like me. That's why we hit it off so good, because we've both lived in Louisiana a long time, and Lester's just full of stories. He's a funny guy to be around, that's for sure. Lester lives in Detroit right now.

Well, I've learned that you don't have to show them everything you know the first song. You can kind of take your time. I try to play with as much feeling and soul as I can, and I don't think it's about how much you know, it's just how you use what you do know. And I try to stick to that format, and not try to be some hotshot. I think everybody has the blues at one time or another. It doesn't matter if you're a little girl or you're a sixty-five-year-old man, I mean, everybody's got the blues. And I think that I've been very blessed to be able to play the blues for people and be able to share that with them, and I think that, probably in a nutshell, I'm just glad that I'm able to do what I do, man, and play the blues like that. The blues is a feeling, it's an attitude, it's all of that rolled up into one. I mean, it's life lessons that come out in your music. And you've just got to put it out there and hope people like it.

I do Sonny Boy's regular gig, his electric and sometimes acoustic gig. And then I also do my own thing, Little Ray and The Blues Sonics, which is the CD I'm working on right now. And I do some gigs with that title also. We do a lot of swamp pop, a lot of traditional, a little bit of roots rock, and just stuff that I like to play. That's one thing fun about that band. I usually get to pick the material most of the time that we do. It's basically a three-piece with harmonica, drums, bass, guitar—a four-piece band. And occasionally, we do hire a piano player, just depending on how much the gig's going to pay, if we can afford to have that fifth member sometimes. Sometimes they require it; they want a piano player to be in the band, too, so I usually call Matt Farrell out of Austin. Great piano player. In my band, I have a guy, he's Hispanic, Joe Mendoza. He plays harmonica and sings. And then, on bass, I use a guy by the name of Paul Choate. And my drummer is a fellow by the name of Louis Reeves. And all these guys are kind of like veterans to this area. They've all played with just about everybody you can think of in this area through the years, and it's a great, great group of guys, man.

I moved here because my wife of seventeen years, which I love to death, has family here. And we moved here back in about 1992 and been here ever since. My wife is Robin Elizabeth Ybarra. The music scene ain't nothing what it used to be. We now have an Antone's here, but that's all it is, is a name. It's pretty much of a college-type scene, where they have a lot of these rock 'n' roll bands, and stuff like that. It's really not nowhere for a bluesman to play around here no more, man.

Most of the legacy is gone as far as cats. I mean, there's not really that many guys here. Me and possibly Tom Hunter, Long John Hunter's brother. There ain't many. Richard Earl. Have you heard of Richard Earl before? He's a black R&B singer, blues singer. He kicks up a little dust around here every once in a while, but not too much.

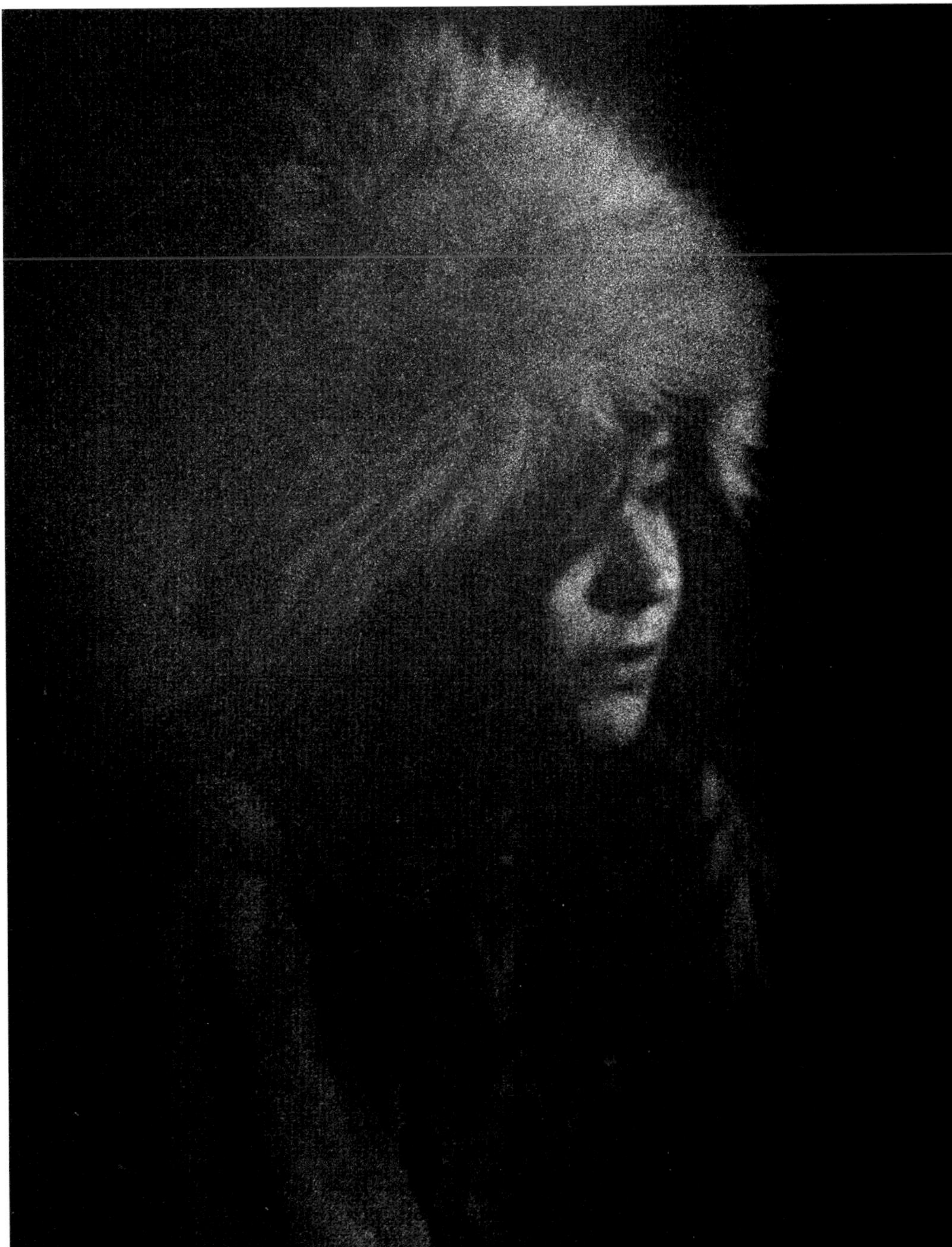

JANIS JOPLIN, THE MATRIX, SAN FRANCISCO, 1970. PHOTOGRAPH BY BURTON WILSON.

I want to mention a friend of mine, Ervin Charles. He's no longer with us. Ervin was playing that Texas blues right here in Beaumont in the Fifties, man. And I'll tell you what. When you listen to him, you hear Jimmie Vaughan and you hear all those guys. But Ervin to me was the real deal, man. I mean, I was very honored to be able to play with him before he died. He was black. I mean, he's had some write-ups in *Blues Access* and *Blues Revue*. When they showed pictures of Ervin back in the Fifties, man, and I'll tell you what, boy, he was the man around here. When B. B. and T-Bone and all them guys come through town, that's who they called for a band. He's on that record that Alligator put out, the *Lone Star Shootout*. He's on there with Lonnie Brooks, which all of those guys were like Ervin's students, man. Lonnie, Philip Walker, Long John Hunter—all of them used to go to see Ervin Charles's shows right here in Beaumont. They are all different places now, but you know, Guitar Junior's from Port Arthur. All those guys, really, to be honest with you, are from Louisiana. Guitar Junior? There's Lonnie Brooks. So was Ervin. Ervin was from Port Barre [Louisiana]. And see, all those guys moved over here. They were sharecroppers. And they moved over here to Texas because of the opportunity. You could make more money. You could go to work in a refinery. You had a lot more opportunity. Plus, they had a boppin' night scene, you know, nightclub scene, back in the Fifties and early Sixties.

I used to hear Ervin talk about places that he played at through the years. And at one time, he said, man, there were so many gigs around here for people playing blues and rhythm and blues and stuff, he said, you didn't have to go nowhere. And he said then all of that kind of just died off, and a lot of guys that were playing kind of moved away. I was playing with Ervin when he died, man. He had a tumor and went in the hospital and never came out. That was in 2000.

Ervin recorded a little bit of stuff here and there, but Ervin, when the scene started dying, he took a job as a truck driver and kind of gave the music up. He's one of the only ones that didn't go. All those other guys left, but Ervin stayed because he had a family and stuff. And I guess he just thought at the time, I'm not going to make it with my guitar. That's not going to feed my family, so I got to take a real job. And he did that for a long, long time, man, And then up until about, I'd say probably around the early Nineties, Ervin started getting out back playing again. And I was just fortunate to meet him. And he told me one time, he said, "Little Ray," he said, "you know, I'm so glad I met you, man, because you just really inspire me to want to do it more." And he said, "Nobody ever tell you you can't play the blues, man, because you're white and Hispanic, whatever," because he said, "I hear it. And you got it." And I'm like, "Ervin, that's the biggest compliment anybody's ever given me, man." Because I really looked up to his playing. He was a real Texas style, big time. He had that stinging, played with his fingers, kind of like Albert Collins. But I remember in a recording session, with me and him and Lazy Lester and Uncle John Turner, I was sitting there listening to Ervin cut a track, and I told Uncle John, I said, "Listen to that, boy." I said, "Man, he sounds like Jimmie Vaughan." And Uncle John looked at me and goes, "No. Jimmie Vaughan sounds like him." And I said, "You know what, you're right. You're right." He said, "I been knowing Ervin for years, Ray." And he said, "He's the real deal, man. Just nobody knows about him."

For my day job, I have a little painting and drywall business I do part time to make ends meet. And it's just enough. But it works out great because I kind of set my own hours, and if I need to do roadwork, which I'm going to be doing in August, I can do it.

When I first moved here to Vidor, my family was a little bit concerned for my safety because of me being Hispanic, with a Hispanic name. Playing black music, living in Vidor. I know, isn't that funny? But you know what, if these people only knew. Nobody's ever harassed me or any of my family. We've never had any trouble here, and I purchased a house. Actually, I kind of live out of town. I'm kind of in the country here between Vidor and Beaumont. I love my little place. It's real quiet.

This guy bought my CD and he found out I was from Vidor. And he lived in Vidor. He's like, "Man, you know, boy, I'm really proud, man, that you're from Vidor and you're playing this good music and stuff." And I said, "Well, that's great, man. I'm glad to hear that. I mean, I didn't really expect that from anybody, but I'm really glad that you like it."

I think that when it comes to playing blues music, or probably just about any music, for that matter, that there's no racial barriers. It doesn't matter, black, white, or whatever. If you got good chemistry playing with somebody, it makes for good music.

This is where it's at right here. That's one thing I can say is I'm proud to be a Texan, man, because I think we have the best music in the world. What makes Texas blues different is attitude. Attitude. If I could sum it up, I would say—of course, it's a sound, definitely. But I think that Texas guitar players are like, "Hey, man, get out of my way, baby, I'm here to lay it on you." And we do. It has that stinging, just that Texas sound. And it's been around for a long time, too. I know Stevie [Ray Vaughan] opened the doors for a lot of people, but if you go back and look, that sound has been here for a long time.

JOE JONAS

February 22, 1937– ; interview, 2003

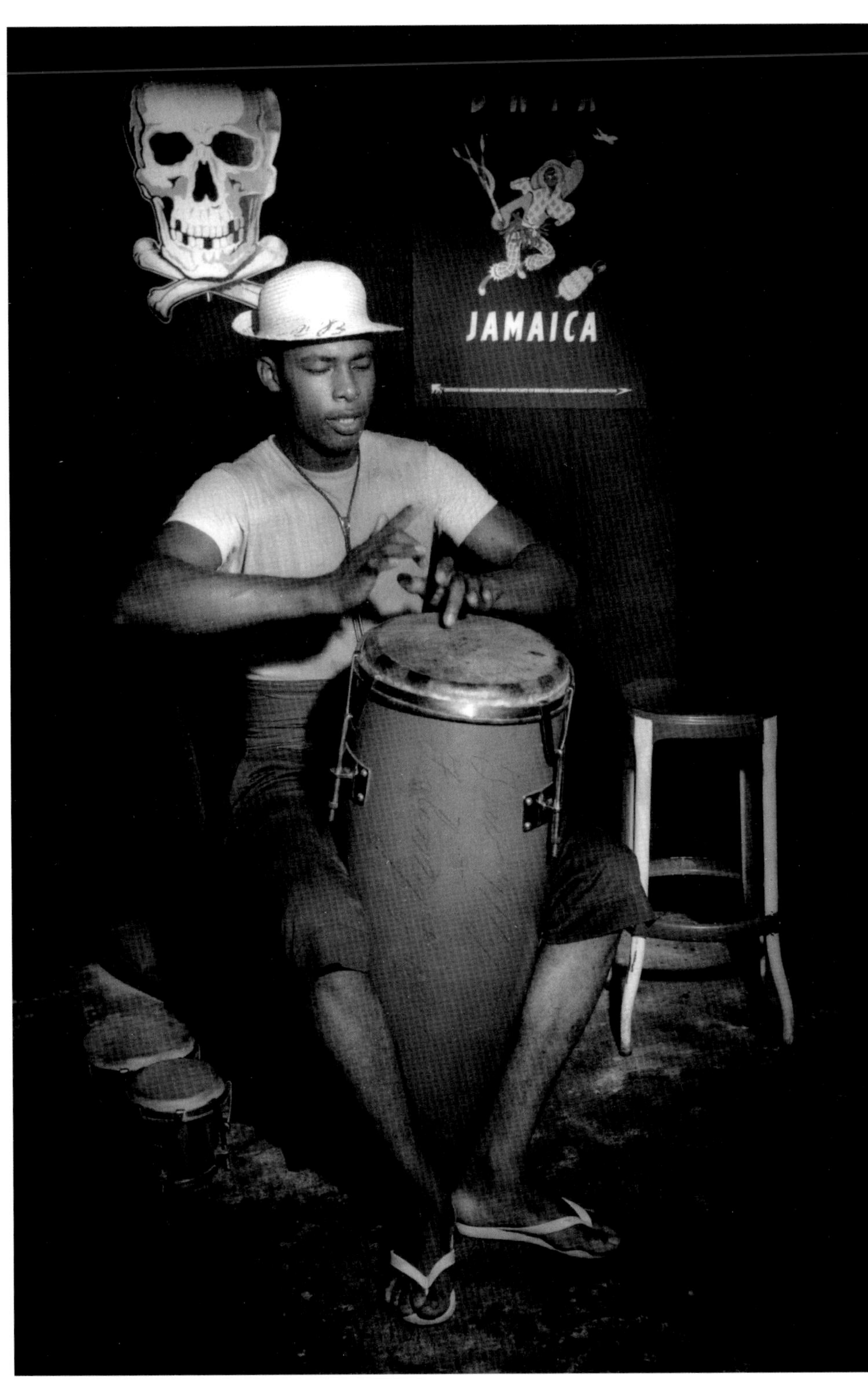

JOE JONAS, RON'S COFFEE HOUSE, DALLAS, 1958. COURTESY JOE JONAS.

JOE JONAS AND THE SOUL CREATORS (L. TO R., BENNY HUNTER, DRUMS, I. V. HUNTER, TRUMPET, WILFRED SIMS, TENOR SAX AND FLUTE, SQUEAKY, BASS, AND LITTLE RONNIE, KEYBOARD), DALLAS, 1963. COURTESY JOE JONAS.

I grew up in Beaumont, where I was born. My name was Joseph Jones, but I changed it later on. My mother's full name was Frances Glaston. My dad was Samuel Jones. My dad was a railroad man, Kansas City Southern Railroad.

Everything is just perfect when you're a kid. But when you get up into your teenage days, where you begin to really understand, it was good in spots and it was rough in other spots, because Beaumont is a very prejudiced town. Oh, man, some of the things that happened, like hiding from the Ku Klux Klans when they come riding. You get the sound of the chief of police announcing, "Hide! Get off the streets. The Ku Klux Klan is riding," stuff like that. I remember from when I was in junior high school, elementary school. You had to be careful where you went and what time—we had strict curfew from our parents, because so many things was happening back down in those years.

Music for me was a spiritual thing through church, like every other blues artist and every other musician. It started at church. And I found out that there were some music people in my family. Some I never met, like my dad's dad was a barrelhouse piano player up in Mississippi somewhere. But I never got a chance to meet him. I don't even know his name. My dad was born out of wedlock. And my mother's side of the family was Indian. So there's music abilities on that side of the family also. I guess I fell in the middle with blues, which my parents refused and really tried to beat out of me, to keep me from doing it. Out of eight living children—one brother died when I was about ten—I'm the only clubber musician in the family. And my dad tried to beat it out of me because I think he really thought I was going to be a carbon copy of his dad, who he never knew.

As a boy, I went to the Starlight Baptist Church, out on Beaufort Street down on the south side of Beaumont. And we had a bunch of kids that were in church, and we all went to school together, and we formed little groups in school. We sang in the choral group, and I was in the band, and we hooked up together, and we got to doing little things without our parents knowing it, until one of the good old people in the church heard us doing it in a nightclub, and that was taboo. That was butt-whipping times.

At that time, it [the music scene in Beaumont] was popping. It was good. The main club where we finally got a chance to get into was called the Raven. And it was owned by a man by the name of M. C. Carter. We all called him "Blue Buddy." He was a real dark man, and he owned the club, and we happened to be hanging around when there was nothing going on. Me and the piano player, Roosevelt Dixon, we said, "Man, let's see if we can get in." So he happened to let us in one night on the stage, and that's when it started. I think we both were both about twelve or fourteen years old.

There was all kinds [of musicians who played at the Raven]. Smokey Robinson came through. Ray Charles came through. Fats Domino came through. Big Joe Turner came through. T-Bone Walker came through. Guitar Slim. Oh, man, it was—in that little corner of Texas, it was hot. It was hot back then.

I grew up with Curly Mayes. Curly Mayes was T-Bone's daddy's cousin or uncle, one or the other. But we could not perform when anybody else was there. All we could do is hang outside the door and listen. But when there was no one there on a Friday or Saturday night, when they didn't have no band, we got a chance to get in there, just the two of us. It was just two of us at that time, Roosevelt on piano and me on harmonica and vocal.

I can remember one time, Sonny Boy Williamson came to Beaumont, and some kind of way he lost his harmonicas, and someone brought him my house to borrow a harmonica from me. And I asked Dad if could I go. I could not go, but I let my harmonica go on.

I went to Charlton Pallard High School and Carroll Street Elementary. They were both on the same lot, the elementary school and the high school. I went up to the eleventh grade. The schools was segregated. They were good schools. We had a lot of players, musicians, football players, teachers, came out of that school. It was a good school.

I ended up in Dallas. It was a situation that I was in down in Beaumont that my parents felt like I was going to end up getting locked up in jail or get dead, so they maneuvered between my oldest brother [and me] to get me out of there. And he said he was going to bring me down to the air base in Wichita Falls to work at the NCO Club, and then I can still go to school. And it happened, that's how I ended up in Dallas in 1955. It snowed. Dallas was locked down. He had to get back to the air base, so he left me with a friend of mine by the name of Robert Stoker, out in the Record Crossing, on old Harry Hines out there. That was before St. Paul [Hospital] or anything was built out there. And I stayed there until I found a job with Vick's Restaurant they had put up out there, off of Record Crossing, and that's how I got my toehold in Dallas. And he come back looking for me, he couldn't find me. I had made my way. And I wasn't even twenty-one then. Restaurant work is what I started doing in Dallas, at Vick's Restaurant. I started working the

JOE JONAS, DALLAS, 1984. COURTESY JOE JONAS.

kitchen, washing dishes, stocking, watching the stock come in, and stuff like that.

The music scene was just as hot in Dallas as it was down in Houston, Beaumont, Texas, anywhere else. It was hot. I managed to work my way into the music scene by singing. I did a lot of vocal work with a man that played piano, solo piano, up at one of the noted clubs, the Green Parrot. His name was Paul Monday. He's been dead quite some time now, and I would work with him whenever I could get up in the Thomas-Hall area. Then I would swing by the Zanzibar, the Ascot Room [formerly the Rose Room], and do vocal work and stuff like that until I got established to know the town. I used to walk the streets at night because I couldn't find a way to get back home. And Smith Hotel, they would give me things to do. And then I made it that way.

Paul Monday was with Peacock [Records]; he sure was. He was a mellow type guy. He was a real nice guy. He was a good musician, and you know, he took me under his wing, and I was able to get food to eat and a little chump change and stuff like that. His music was more jazz- and ballad-oriented. He played a lot of jazz and a lot of ballads. He was good.

I went through the Rose Room. I sang a couple of times at the Rose Room, but I didn't hang out there too much. The Green Parrot was on the corner of Thomas and Hall Street in the Fifties. You know, it was live. Like I say, you could walk the streets all night long, and somebody was out there, all night long.

I stayed in Dallas until 1957. I think I took sick in '57, and I went back to Beaumont and got well, then I came back to Dallas. And I've been in and out of Dallas ever since. The first time I married was in '60, here in Dallas, and my children were born, and I stayed here, on and off, until 1969, when I left and went to Riverside, California, and that's how I started my West Coast movements. I worked just around little small clubs. I had a chance to work with Pee Wee Crayton and Lowell Fulson and places down in Riverside, a little club down in Riverside. Wasn't nothing strictly happening in Riverside, it was just a small little town then.

In high school, I played upright bass and second trombone. And then, out of there, I built my first conga [drum] and started using my conga. And I had harmonica. When I hit Dallas, in the early Sixties, I met a guy by the name of Big Jack Dixon that had a group. I played trombone some with him, his group, and harmonica and vocal. Really, to say that I have an idol of a musician, I don't. I started at an early age, and I progressed to a style of my own. I always wanted to have a style of my own. I listened to a lot of musicians, a lot of vocals, a lot of singers, country and western and all. And I have my own style, which nobody has been able to label as sounding like anybody else. I sound like me, and they have tried—in the early Sixties, when I had the group The Soul Creators, I tried to get some contracts. I sounded, so they said, I sounded too much like Lou Rawls. Which was strange to me, because I don't think so, but United Artists was the one that told me that I sounded too much like Lou Rawls, so I didn't get anything out of that. So I really don't have an idol that I can say I practiced and just followed his footsteps or her footsteps all the way, no, I don't.

I remember Abe and Pappy's when I was in Dallas. It was on Elm Street. I remember Abe. It was like any other well-noted place, but you still had the prejudice stuff here, too. You had to be with a certain type character or person that knows somebody. You had to know somebody. It was a white club. But they had that big black mural on it. And they had a lot of black entertainment. But it wasn't mixed in the audience. We could not—even from my childhood days in Beaumont, Texas, Pappy's Showland, and places like that—you could not mix with the audience. You could not get off the stage to do anything. If you was dancing, you have a dance team, you do your show, you get off the band floor, you go to the kitchen, you go to the storeroom, or you go outside, either way, until it's time for your show again. That's just the way it was. And it made you really believe and know, if this is what you want to do, follow the rules, stick with it and build yourself. That's what I had to do. Well, it's not over. There's still some movements out there that still have a little bit of taboo as far as the color is. And I mean, a lot of people say it's over. It is not over.

Shorty Clemons [played at Abe and Pappy's]. He was a happy-go-lucky fellow. He had a good jazz-orientated, big-type blues band, and they played some Count Basie stuff, they played some ragtime blues stuff, and they was just good. They got the bigger, the better jobs, really, because they were so good. I think the last I remember Shorty having was a ten-piece. He was a bandleader. I don't remember Shorty even playing a full show. It was more like Lawrence Welk, you know. He played several different instruments, but the younger musicians were so strong and coming up. He put them together. [In his band] I think he had James Clay. I think Leroy Cooper. And several other people I can't remember. David Newman. Fathead was there, too. Yeah, Fathead and Red Calhoun. They were out of here, out of Dallas, out of these schools in Dallas, and they were good.

[Red Calhoun was a local bandleader, the main rival to Buster Smith. Red's band was in the film *Juke Joint.*] I met Buster in the Seventies when I came back. Buster was a good leader, and he helped a lot of the young musicians out of this town. He really helped them.

Yeah, Buster was good. Hey, man, you know, this town has turned out some hell of a musicians.

This is the first time that I have been able, since I got hurt, to do my music and nothing else but my music. I was a finish machinist, transformer machinist. And I got hit with pre-charge and blew out my right knee in '72, and that gave me sixteen years of down time. And they got it fixed, and it came out again on me in '95. I had to have another one [surgery] on the same knee. And then I had to have the left one done. So I've have had three total knee replacements and working for DISD here in Dallas, had a wreck and had C6 and C7 spine fused. I was driving a bus, plus I was a finish carpenter with them before I started driving the bus, and for special education students. And that's when the wreck occurred, in '87. So this is the first time I've been able to do just my music alone and nothing else.

JOE JONAS, DALLAS, 1963. COURTESY JOE JONAS.

Basically, I'm trying to hold it to the traditional blues and rhythm, rhythm and blues. I had my own band, but not anymore. I just released them about four years ago. It wasn't getting anywhere, and the people weren't concentrating into the music like I felt they should have. So I turned it over to a guitar player that was working with me, by the name of Ken Savage, who has The Best Kept Secret, and I told him if he kept the group together, and he needed a vocalist and frontman, I'd work for him. And this is how I've been working here for the last five years. In my act, there's the harmonica and vocals. I'm really doing the front line; I'm being the front person for his group whenever he needs me. And it's been pretty constant and pretty solid.

I have three CDs out now, plus three with Top Cat Records, plus Neil Ray Music I've been working with. I have three CDs out. They're not in the market anymore. The last one I done was last year with The Best Kept Secret. . . . And the other one that I did down in Huntsville four years ago through Charley's Guitar Shop; Ken Wheeler, he probably has some copies. They would not put them in the record stores; why, I don't know. They figured they could sell them across the stage and make more money. And I did *Hog Wild for the Blues* in the Nineties. It didn't go where I thought it was going because I didn't have the distribution, so I think I've run a total of seven CDs since the Eighties.

Blues has changed to more of a—if we want to go from the dance music, it's more rocky with the blues flavor, but it's more rock. Your guitars are the lead instrument, and as far as the lyrics are concerned, they've gone more open with lyrics. Now, talking about the women and the heads and the getting down and the going south and all that kind of stuff. And I recorded one called "Choke the Chicken," on the *Hog Wild for the Blues* CD. They won't touch it, but yet and still, the supposed-to-be-the-blues scene have taken where they're talking underneath the woman's clothes, the women are talking about what the man's got to get down and do for them, you know, stuff like that. Well, I wasn't brought up that way, so I have not really got off into that because it's not expressing the blues for what the blues is. It's expressing disappointments in love affairs and all that kind of crap, you know, I haven't been able to do. So I try to keep my sound more traditional.

Blues for me is an expression of the body and soul and the disappointments and the achievements that I have come through from 1937. That's what the blues is to me. Letting the people know, like when I recorded "Life Was Cold." It explains how it was when I worked in the country with my grandmother and them, hauling water, you know, from the well, slopping the hogs, and all the kind of stuff that you really did to see a major change in economics and everything else. But the blues music today does not express that.

When I write, I try to write some things that I have seen, some things that I have been through, that I know other people have been through, and to give the enjoyment of—hey, he overcame it, I can overcome it, too, and not hate and not drug out and stuff like that.

My music [keeps me going] and wanting to be around to see my great-grandkids raised and keep giving my experiences and my vocal music, which I tend to try to give with an emotional feeling that people can relate to. I hope if I can keep going, I will have that kind of legacy behind me. Money is not the object. That I can leave a good, clean legacy. I don't want to go out of this world as an addict or a druggie, or by doing bodily harm to someone, or someone doing bodily harm to me. I have seen too much of it in my lifetime. And I pray that I never go out that way, and this is one of the things that keep me doing the type music that I do.

God, you know, I really don't know how many songs I've written. I'd have to take inventory. I would have to take inventory because a lot of them, I lost a whole box. My last wife took lyrics, and I don't know where they are and, you know, I just lost.

Well, I wish it [my career] could be better, like everybody would like to be in the Top 40, you know, and above. But who knows, maybe we wasn't all meant to be. And so that's the way I try to live my life, but I'm still doing what I want to do, and that is my music. I'm still trying to get up as far as I can go. I'm still trying to get back where I can do some more traveling again in music. But it takes time, with the handicaps that have occurred, and I have, you know, I just have to be patient.

I had my own bands. Whoo! Okay. In Oakland, California, was The Shades of Rhythm. That was in the Seventies, in Oakland, California. Before then, here in Dallas, in 1963, I started The Soul Creators. And they went on through the Sixties. And from The Soul Creators was The Shades of Rhythms, up in Oakland, when I left Dallas. And then come back, I put together SST, Supersonic Transport. And then, we did The Ax Band, and from The Ax Band, I did The Wailers, Joe Jonas and The Wailers. So that's about five bands here in this town.

I've been to Europe, I've been to England, I've been to Germany and Greece. Yes, yes, I have. And I can truly say, from my age and the experience that I have been through in the music scene, they appreciate music and relate to the blues scene like we related to it, putting it out back in the Fifties. But if it wasn't for the teletypes and the computers, they would be in that same boat today. But they're very appreciative and they are very knowledgeable. They caused some musicians and caused some things that I had never read about. They read, and they listen. And they appreciate the blues. My type of blues was appreciated, and they appreciate other types of blues, like the Mike Morgans and the Stevie Ray Vaughans, and they appreciate that, too. But they really appreciate what we call the gutbucket, Chitlin Circuit blues.

THE MOVE TO CALIFORNIA

PERCY MAYFIELD, LOS ANGELES, 1943. COURTESY TINA MAYFIELD.

The Jim Wynn Package Featuring
T★BONE WALKER
AND HIS SHOW ★ PLUS DANCE
with BIG JIM WYNN
and his
GROOVE MASTERS
BAND
JIM WYNN
ANNA
LOUISE
T-BONE
WALKER JR.
AL GOODLOW
Management Reg. G. Marshall Agency P.O. Box 41004
Los Angeles 41, Calif. CLinton 5-0116

INTRODUCTION

(OPPOSITE) "THE JIM WYNN PACKAGE, FEATURING T-BONE WALKER," PROMOTIONAL POSTER. COURTESY CHARLIE LANGE.

The blues came to California via the thousands of African Americans who migrated from Texas, Louisiana, and Oklahoma. They were looking for work in the shipbuilding industry of Oakland and the oil refineries along the coast in Long Beach, Bakersfield, and other California cities. Census figures reveal that in 1930, there were only 81,000 blacks in the entire state of California; by 1950 the number had increased to more than a half-million. Some blacks settled in the San Fernando Valley to work on farms and in seasonal harvests, but the overwhelming majority was concentrated in the urban centers and lived in segregated areas of Oakland, Richmond, and Los Angeles. With this migration came numerous blues and jazz musicians who sought greater opportunities in the recording industry after World War II.

Many of the musicians who migrated from Texas to California had been encouraged by the success of T-Bone Walker. Walker came to California for the first time in 1935. He had been playing with Les Hite and decided to go on the road with his own band, managed by baritone player Big Jim Wynn. Though Walker had made his first recordings in Dallas in 1929 for Columbia, it was not until he went to California that his distinctive style coalesced. In Dallas, Walker had tried different instruments—guitar, piano, ukulele, and banjo—but in California he devoted himself to the electric guitar. He developed advanced harmonic chording and made inventive use of jazz-inflected arpeggios and fleet, single-string runs. In addition to introducing a new role for the electric guitar in rhythm and blues, he defined a performance style, playing the guitar while he did splits or swung the instrument behind his head or back or suggestively thrust it through his legs.

The contemporaries of T-Bone Walker who moved to California were influenced by his playing and performance style, but they also brought together distinctive regional traditions. The music that grew out of the Texas-to-California migration fused current styles with regional musical traditions that included country blues, boogie-woogie, and jazz. This fusion developed into what Arnold Shaw has characterized as the "murmuring, gentle ballad style" of bluesmen like Charles Brown, Ivory Joe Hunter, Percy Mayfield, and Amos Milburn. The musicians left Texas but maintained strong contacts there, especially in Houston.

Amos Milburn was from Houston; Percy Mayfield was from Minton, Louisiana, but spent time in Houston regularly, as did Charles Brown, from Texas City, and Ivory Joe Hunter, from Kirbyville. They combined the boogie-woogie blues piano and big band swing sounds of Texas with the blues-inflected ballad style of the popular singers of the day—Cecil Gant, The Ink Spots—and the crooning of Nat "King" Cole.

Lowell Fulson, Smokey Hogg, Pee Wee Crayton, and L. C. Robinson were guitarists who in one way or another emulated the style of T-Bone Walker and added yet another dimension to the eclectic California sound. Fulson, who grew up in Atoka, Oklahoma, worked with Texas Alexander for three years and moved to Texas in 1940. In 1942 he was drafted and stationed in California, where he settled after the war. He met Bob Geddins, originally from Marlin, Texas, in Oakland. Geddins had started a record label and cut two sides with Fulson, "Come Back Baby" and "Three O'Clock Blues," both of which had success on the charts. This success sparked Fulson's career and launched Geddins's Big Town label. Geddins would become an important producer of the Texas style of rhythm and blues in California.

In contrast to Lowell Fulson's smooth, ballad-inflected sound, Pee Wee Crayton, who moved from Austin to San Francisco, had a style more in keeping with that of T-Bone Walker, John Collins, and Kenny Burrell. Smokey Hogg was a country blues singer from rural Cushing, Texas. L. C. Robinson, from Brenham, was influenced by country fiddling, blues, and western swing.

In California in the 1950s and 1960s, the Texas-based regional styles were reshaped by the recording companies, including Aladdin, Modern, RPM, Imperial, Specialty, and numerous independent labels. The California sound brought together black musicians and white producers who were committed to creating new music that was geared toward mass-market distribution and radio. The success of Texas musicians in the Los Angeles and San Francisco areas spread nationally and had great impact on the development of rock 'n' roll and other popular music in America.

Although many of the first generation of Texas-born, California-based blues performers have died in recent years, it is clear that their legacy has become the musical threshold of the next generation. Performers as varied as Sonny Rhodes, Frankie Lee, Dave Alexander, Roy Gaines, Cal Green, Johnny Watson, Floyd Dixon, Buddy Ace, and Katie Webster, while integrating various musical influences, all retained elements of their Texas heritage in their performance styles.

BOB GEDDINS

1913–February 16, 1991; interview by Shirley Moore and Pat Monaco, 1987

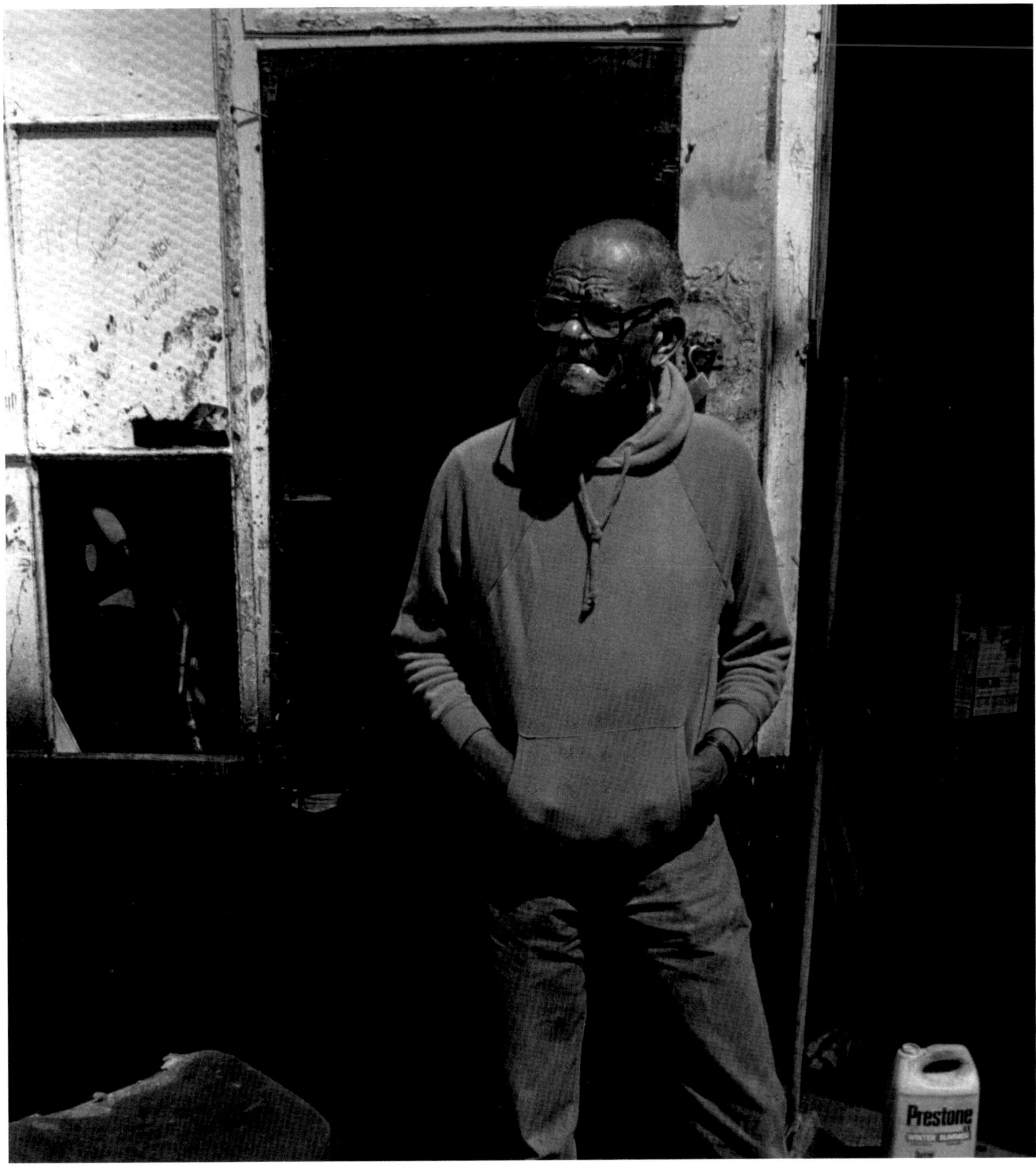

BOB GEDDINS IN FRONT OF HIS SHOP, OAKLAND, 1983.
PHOTOGRAPH BY PAT MONACO.

I started a record company in 1945. It was called Big Town Recordings, at Eighth and Chestnut in Oakland, but it wasn't much more than a double garage. It was a nice-looking building, and the building next door is where I put my first pressing company.

We didn't have a tape recorder. We had a disk machine; the needle cut the voice right into an acetate disk. You sang to a microphone, and the needle would go around and make a groove. Then we took that acetate and had it processed. You put it in a copper tank, and copper would build up on them lines so thick that you could peel it off and have a plate. At that time I had to get them processed in Los Angeles, and then later on we got our own processor. We were making 78s. You had to put them on a wheel and spin them, grind the edges.

I had a guy running the day shift, a guy running the midnight shift. We pressed twenty-four hours a day. The press in them days, you could only press one record at a time, take about a minute to make a record, so you know about how many we got in twenty-four hours.

I'd rehearse the bands for a week or two. Then I'd take them to the studio. I was using KSFO in San Francisco. I made my first big record over there with The Rising Star Gospel Singers and the song "If Jesus Had to Pray, What about Me?" Church records and blues records are similar. They'd have a mournful tone and sound. The same people [who bought the church records] got them blues, too. I'd find the singers. I'd go to the clubs, the churches. I went to clubs in Richmond, all blues, Jimmy McCracklin, Lowell Fulson, Jimmie Wilson [who sang "Tin Pan Alley"]. All of the clubs wanted them. I put out the records, and they were promoted on the radio. The record shops all around would call me up looking for the records, and there'd be a line waiting for those records to be pressed. Scotty's Records in San Francisco. That was a big place, on Third Street. That's where all the black people went to get their music. Scotty was a white man, but he had all the records. Most of them sold for $1.08 with the tax. We'd sell them to the stores for about 60 cents apiece. I took them around myself in my car. I'd load about a thousand and go all over San Francisco and Oakland. On a weekend, I'd take a trailer and go to Los Angeles. I'd sell all of them. I'd sell one distributor in Los Angeles about five thousand records.

There was a lot of blues around Oakland, Los Angeles, and Richmond in those years, 1940s, 1950s. It attracted the working people who worked in the shipyards. A lot of them were like me, came from Texas. They'd get together and dance in them little clubs, doin' "Walk The Dog," "The Chicken," all kinds of dances.

I remember them old [Texas] singers, like Petey Wheatstraw, Blind Lemon Jefferson, Texas Alexander. I've seen all those guys. They'd play in the little towns with that big old acoustic guitar. They came to the town where I lived, Marlin, Texas. That's where I was born in Texas, in 1913. They'd come up to the black part of town. All of them would come through. But I moved to California in 1933, and I've been here since.

I've worked in the recording business, and [after The Rising Star Gospel Singers' hit] I didn't have to advertise. If you're a company and you put out one good record, everybody in the neighborhood is going to come to you. When I had my studio, people were coming all day long. I'd have to turn them down. They'd want me to listen to them. Some of them didn't have nothing, but some of them were pretty good. Sugar Pie De Santo, the first day he came to me, we made a hit record, named "I Want To Know" [in 1960]. And there were others, "Tin Pan Alley" by Jimmie Wilson [who was from Dallas], "The Gamble" by Ray Agee, "The Thrill Is Gone" by Roy Hawkins, and songs by K. C. Douglas, Jimmy McCracklin, Juke Boy Bonner, and Lowell Fulson. Some of them were from Texas: Jimmie Wilson was from Dallas, Mercy Dee Walton from Waco, L. C. Robinson, and Juke Boy Bonner. He was from Texas. I recorded him first, and then I let Chris [Strachwitz] have him.

Blues has always been popular in the South. That's all they bought. That's what the jukebox played. And when these guys come out here, they were lonesome for the blues. We had a record shop, and they were coming asking for blues. "Got any blues?" "Got any blues?" And we were selling Cab Calloway and Louis Jordan. That's what gave me my idea. I had put the spiritual out, and I saw all them people there, and I switched to the blues. Nobody else had that blues. So I got a record manufacturing plant, cost me about, at that time, $10,000. And my mother's husband and a preacher next door with the church and another boy had to give me about $1,500 apiece. That preacher liked me. I was in the Baptist church. And I had a little money too, that I saved from that religious record that tore up the country. So I got that record company, and it took off from there [with several labels, including Big Town, Art-Tone, Cavatone, Down Town, Irma, Plaid, and Rhythm, producing and

BOB GEDDINS, OAKLAND, 1987. PHOTOGRAPH BY PAT MONACO.

leasing masters in the 1940s and 1950s to the major West Coast labels—Aladdin, Swingtime, Modern, Specialty, Imperial, and Fantasy—as well as to Checker in Chicago].

I took those records once to Texas, stayed eleven months, selling records on the road. I carried samples, about two thousand records, with me, different ones. I'd go to El Paso, stay about a week or two weeks, and I'd move from there, Big Spring two weeks, Austin, Texas, two weeks. I'd go to every record shop and jukebox, and they would take all of them. I'd send the orders back to California, and they'd ship them out. I'd got those records known all over Texas.

In the 1960s the blues started to go down, and I got into electronics, repairing radios, televisions, and car radiators part time. I had some big records, but the whole demand wasn't as great as it was. The radio stations was the fault. They wouldn't play the blues, but I stayed with it.

LOWELL FULSON

March 31, 1921–March 6, 1999; interview, 1984

LOWELL FULSON, OAKLAND, 1984. PHOTOGRAPH BY ALAN GOVENAR.

My first singing was done in churches, for picnics and socials. I was brought up around Oklahoma, born 1921. They had outdoor picnics. I'm part Indian, Choctaw. My grandfather was a good fiddler. My father used to play second for him on the guitar, but I lost my father when I was a small boy. One of my uncles played a guitar; another played mandolin. I started playing when I was very young. They didn't have anything more than guitars and violins, harmonica. In 1939 I worked in a string band for a while in Ada, Oklahoma—Dan Wright and his string band. I couldn't get the blues feel for the type of music they were playing. So Texas Alexander came through there, and he wanted a guitar player. So he heard me. He started singing a few songs when I started plucking on the guitar behind him. And I went on a trip with him to Texas. First, we started out in western Oklahoma and played Saturday-night fish fries and whatever else they had going on. They'd cut the nickelodeon if they thought you sounded pretty good. They let you play there, and then they passed the hat around, take up a little collection. There were no nightclubs at that time to play this kind of music, but the people had fun. Sometimes there'd be an old beat-up piano and somebody would bang on that while we played. We'd sing and play, and people danced. Cats paid pretty much money to hear them old blues. We'd make ten or twelve dollars and split it up, and why, that was a week's work.

I moved on in Gainesville, Texas, in 1941, and got a job as a fry cook, still playing my guitar every Saturday night at the country ball. They wanted to hear something other than that nickelodeon, and a guy with a loud voice, that was good. They'd give me three or four dollars and all the tips I could make. I mostly did it for my recreation. Cat was going to pay me to play, I was going to play anyway. I made up my own blues; "West Texas Blues" was the first one I made up. "Sitting here wondering if a matchbox would hold my clothes." It was a bunch of verses added together. Some called it "West Texas Blues." Others called it "South Texas Blues." It depended on where you made it.

The blues is a song a guy made up to himself the way he was feeling at the time. He had the blues. So the song matched the feeling that he had. In Texas the blues is different. It's in the fingering of the strings, the tones, the moans and the groans. Texas blues singers seem to hold notes longer than other singers. They've got more

LOWELL FULSON, "LONESOME CHRISTMAS," HOLLYWOOD RECORDS 577-242 A-X.

LOWELL FULSON, "SINNER'S PRAYER," SWING TIME 237-A.

spiritual-type delivery to the blues than they do in other parts of the country.

T-Bone Walker made the electric guitar popular with "Bobby Sox Baby" in 1943. He brought the guitar player into demand. I came to California the same year, but I was in uniform. I was in the service. I saw T-Bone here. He was the first to really play electric guitar. I saw Charlie Christian back in Oklahoma, but he was more a jazz player and played what I called a modern blues, where T-Bone played swing blues. There was a difference. T-Bone made blues his style, and Charlie Christian went with Benny Goodman. T-Bone came to California.

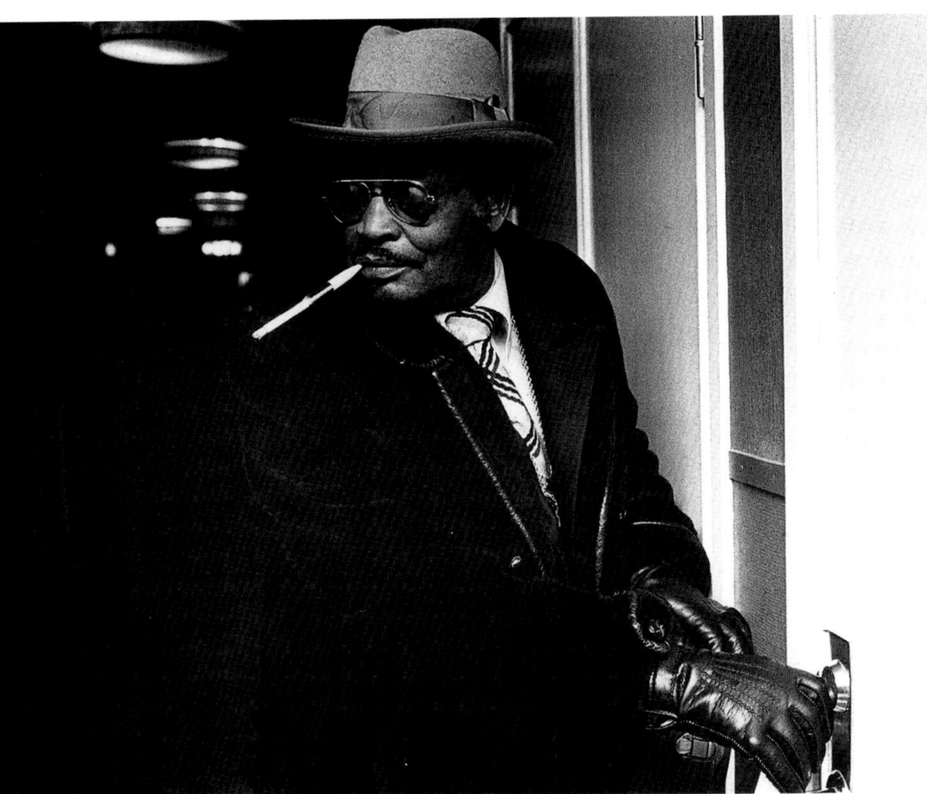

LOWELL FULSON, SWEDEN, 1980. PHOTOGRAPH BY ERIK LINDAHL. COURTESY TOMMY LÖFGREN.

LOWELL FULSON AND HIS WIFE, OAKLAND, 1982. PHOTOGRAPH BY PAT MONACO.

In those years was when blues was big in Los Angeles, but now it's quieted down. It has a bigger audience in Europe. Next time I play is in Switzerland, and then in London. I've played in France and Spain, Germany, Belgium, several places, all over, full houses and enjoyable sets.

Blues you can play a lot of different ways: you can sing ballads, mournful, play it shoutin' it, play a kind of rock style, dancing type. So we play it all kind of ways in Europe, and they find it entertaining. I go as a single, and they furnish bands. I rehearse with the fellows, or I send them a tape and they get it down before I come over and get to work. I don't have a band anymore. I move around mostly by plane, and the dates are too far apart, and I don't have a hit record. But there's more audience in Europe than in the States. It's mostly a white audience. They've taken a liking to the music. A lot of blacks want to listen to something else and think maybe that they've even heard the blues all their life, they want something new.

Personally, there's nothing I enjoy better than a good blues; if it's done right, it tells a good story if the music is put with it properly. I've lost track of all the songs I've written, I think, close to one hundred. Some are about me, but a lot are about other folks. If they were all about me, I'd be in pretty bad shape. You see a lot of things in travel. You see what other people do, whether it's good or bad, joyful. I've seen guys sing blues and cry like they were singing a spiritual. The blues will touch the soul. You'll feel it. It's looking like your hair is going to stand up on your head. Then you're getting into the blues.

CONNIE CURTIS "PEE WEE" CRAYTON

December 18, 1914–June 15, 1985; interview by Dick Shurman, 1982

(*Living Blues*, no. 67)

PEE WEE CRAYTON, 1940S. COURTESY ESTHER CRAYTON.

Pee Wee Crayton's long and vast influence on postwar blues has been extensively documented, including a lengthy two-part feature in *Living Blues* nos. 56 and 57. He recorded for around forty years, beginning with some obscure efforts as a bandleader and as a sideman for Ivory Joe Hunter and Turner Willis in the Bay area. He achieved his renown on the Bihari family's Los Angeles–based Modern Records, where he turned out classics like "Blues after Hours" and "Texas Hop." Under the tutelage of T-Bone Walker and John Collins, and the spell of Charlie Christian's records, he developed a guitar style that mixed jazzy single-note lines, wide bends, fancy picking, and some of the biggest, prettiest chords ever waxed by a blues player. He readily admitted that in the early days, his repertoire was very limited and his voice was light, but in his prime and right up to his death in 1985, he was a confident, accomplished musician and entertainer.

PEE WEE CRAYTON, PUBLICITY PHOTOGRAPH, 1950S. COURTESY ESTHER CRAYTON.

Within a decade of his success on Modern, he was starving in Detroit, where he managed to befriend and influence jazz great Kenny Burrell. When he made it back to L.A., he found work as a truck driver and stayed with it until his retirement around twenty years later. But he never left music behind.

Pee Wee left his mark on modern blues guitar, and he got to savor some acclaim. After being somewhat maligned by country and Delta blues lovers in 1960s blues journals, he made a notable 1970 appearance at Monterey with Johnny Otis that resulted in a Vanguard album. Besides making subsequent new recordings, he was able to see the bulk of his early work reissued in the United States, England, and Japan. He played as a sideman with Big Joe Turner, Sarah Vaughan, and Roy Brown. He was interviewed frequently, and his graciousness is partly shown in the never-ending stream of vintage photographs he provided to accompany the resulting articles. In general, he was able to spend his last years knowing that his family was fairly secure in their comfortable duplex, while he worked some pleasant musical engagements and played a lot of golf.

There's much to be said in Praise of Pee Wee's musical legacy. He left a substantial body of records behind, and memories of a lot of exciting performances. He was a master of those haunting after-hours mood pieces, aggressive blues vocals like "The Telephone Is Ringing," rhythm and blues pieces like "Treat Her Right" or "Down Home Blues," and poignant blues ballads. Probably the best place to start appreciating his available recordings would be the two reissues from England on Ace, which contain the bulk of the songs Crayton released on the Modern label.

John Collins taught me to play with all four fingers. Before that I only played with three, like T-Bone Walker. But John says, "Play with four fingers and you'll get prettier chords." So he showed me how with all four fingers. Many of my friends are jazz guitarists.

Kenny Burrell and I are very good friends. He's a jazz

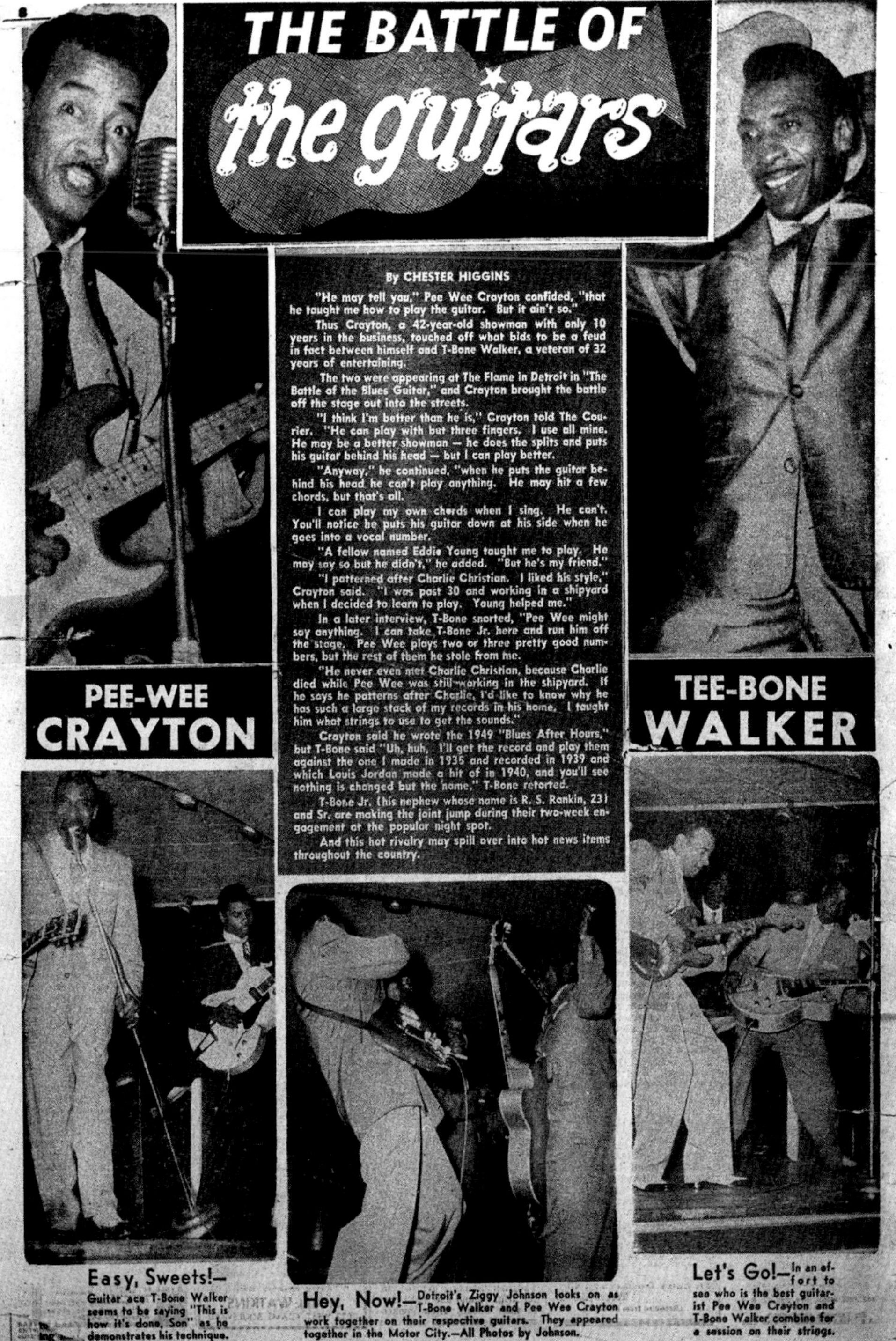

THE BATTLE OF the guitars

By CHESTER HIGGINS

"He may tell you," Pee Wee Crayton confided, "that he taught me how to play the guitar. But it ain't so."

Thus Crayton, a 42-year-old showman with only 10 years in the business, touched off what bids to be a feud in fact between himself and T-Bone Walker, a veteran of 32 years of entertaining.

The two were appearing at The Flame in Detroit in "The Battle of the Blues Guitar," and Crayton brought the battle off the stage out into the streets.

"I think I'm better than he is," Crayton told The Courier. "He can play with but three fingers. I use all mine. He may be a better showman — he does the splits and puts his guitar behind his head — but I can play better.

"Anyway," he continued, "when he puts the guitar behind his head he can't play anything. He may hit a few chords, but that's all.

I can play my own chords when I sing. He can't. You'll notice he puts his guitar down at his side when he goes into a vocal number.

"A fellow named Eddie Young taught me to play. He may say so but he didn't," he added. "But he's my friend."

"I patterned after Charlie Christian. I liked his style," Crayton said. "I was past 30 and working in a shipyard when I decided to learn to play. Young helped me."

In a later interview, T-Bone snorted, "Pee Wee might say anything. I can take T-Bone Jr. here and run him off the stage. Pee Wee plays two or three pretty good numbers, but the rest of them he stole from me.

"He never even met Charlie Christian, because Charlie died while Pee Wee was still working in the shipyard. If he says he patterns after Charlie, I'd like to know why he has such a large stack of my records in his home. I taught him what strings to use to get the sounds."

Crayton said he wrote the 1949 "Blues After Hours," but T-Bone said "Uh, huh, I'll get the record and play them against the one I made in 1935 and recorded in 1939 and which Louis Jordan made a hit of in 1940, and you'll see nothing is changed but the name," T-Bone retorted.

T-Bone Jr. (his nephew whose name is R. S. Rankin, 23) and Sr. are making the joint jump during their two-week engagement at the popular night spot.

And this hot rivalry may spill over into hot news items throughout the country.

PEE-WEE CRAYTON

TEE-BONE WALKER

Easy, Sweets!— Guitar ace T-Bone Walker seems to be saying "This is how it's done, Son" as he demonstrates his technique.

Hey, Now!—Detroit's Ziggy Johnson looks on as T-Bone Walker and Pee Wee Crayton work together on their respective guitars. They appeared together in the Motor City.—All Photos by Johnson.

Let's Go!—In an effort to see who is the best guitarist Pee Wee Crayton and T-Bone Walker combine for a session on their strings.

"THE BATTLE OF THE GUITARS," PEE WEE CRAYTON AND T-BONE WALKER, *PITTSBURGH COURIER*, 1956. COURTESY ESTHER CRAYTON.

guitarist, but he has what you might call a bluesy sound. I do a couple of his tunes, but I'm not a jazz guitarist. I'm a blues singer.

I sang with a gospel quartet years ago when I was real, real young, but that didn't influence me to start to singing the blues. Lot of the blues singers [in Texas] said that they started singin' blues because they were singin' the gospel end of church. Well, some of it is true. Some of it is not. I think it's just making up something, if you're not doing it. I used to sing in the choir and I used to have a quartet, but that didn't influence me to singing the blues.

PEE WEE CRAYTON, PUBLICITY PHOTOGRAPH, 1950S.
COURTESY ESTHER CRAYTON.

I don't think that a bluesman is like a preacher. Sometimes guys can relate to different things that they do and feel they can be a preacher. Some of the Baptist preachers years ago would put their hand up in the air, holler a holy tune. They said that was a way of preaching.

When I get ready to play, I can't plan out a show. I might play one song one way this time, and the next time I play it, I play it altogether different. Every guitar player has got a trait, and mine is hitting the high notes, followed by some of mine. It's like my song "The Telephone Is Ringing." But if I wanted to sound like B. B. [King], I would go like this. It all depends on what you want to do, the audience, the groove that you're in at that time, how the band is sounding. That's the way my playing comes out.

If I'm doing a show, I get to walking through the audience. I pick up different ideas, vibes from different people. I'll be at one table and I'll feel like this way, and I get to another table and something else will come to me. It just changes. I never try to outplay anybody just to make anybody look bad.

Some guitar players never talk about their influences, but me, I like them all: Albert King, Albert Collins; Muddy Waters and I were good friends. There's T-Bone, Lowell Fulson, B. B. King, Freddie King, Earl King, bunches of Kings. There were a couple songs that Roy Brown did that I really liked. He had a real high voice. You know, the thing that he put out, "The cold ground is my home tonight," something like that, and "I heard you were at the good rockin' tonight"—those are the kind of things that I liked to do. He was a good showman. We worked together on several jobs, like Percy Mayfield. He and I were the very best of friends, just close as T-Bone and I was. He wasn't a guitar player, but he was just a blues singer, and we were very close. He had a nickname for everybody and he called me "Wee Wee," called Lowell Fulson "Cherokee," but he was a wonderful person. I loved him.

I met Elvis Presley when he first started learning how to play guitar. He came to hear me play in Memphis, Tennessee. He was a little bitty boy. He said that I was one of his idols at that time. He came to hear me play, and I talked to him. We were in the dressing room together, but then he skyrocketed to the top.

PEE WEE CRAYTON, "AFTER HOURS BOOGIE," 4 STAR 1304.

PEE WEE CRAYTON, "THE BOP HOP," MODERN RECORDS 90-675A.

For a lot of musicians, there's professional jealousy, but for me, I'm not jealous of anybody. I love all the musicians, the singers: Wynonie Harris, Jimmy Witherspoon, Big Joe Turner, Arthur Prysock, and his brother, Red, who used to play tenor in my band.

Kim Wilson, he's a harmonica player. He's with The Thunderbirds now in Austin. Well, he lived in California for a while. I used to play with him. I taught him how to sing the blues. There are lots of musicians, white boys, these days that are out of sight.

The blues reaches people in different ways. There's one song by Jackie Wilson, "Don't Keep Doggin' Me Around." Well, you know, some woman feels likes she's mistreated, that's the blues. They [women] like the blues like that. And when you start doing them kind of songs and everybody getting too carried away and getting happy about it, I'm ready to quit singing and go in the dressing room. There's probably going to be a fight. So, I get away from that. I like to try to play, to set aside the crowd, keep them happy. I like to get the audience to be involved with my show, let them participate in it, too. It's better like that. You have more fun. When somebody else is helping you sing or applaud, keeping the beat for you, it's nice. It's just one of them things.

The blues will always be around. It will never die. It's something that will always be here. Disco is about to fade out. Blues is the basic foundation of the music.

PERCY MAYFIELD

August 12, 1920–August 11, 1984; interview by Dick Shurman, 1981

(*Living Blues,* no. 50)

Percy Mayfield was a distinctive vocalist and performer whose songs have been borrowed by people as diverse as Robert Nighthawk and Dale Evans, from Lovie Lee to Shirley Scott and Junior Parker. He was an exclusive songwriter for Ray Charles and B. B. King, and was a major rhythm and blues stylist whose musical roots were in Texas.

In an interview in the book *Urban Blues*, B. B. King told Charles Keil that Percy Mayfield could "put a song over better than anybody." And despite his narrow vocal range, exacerbated by tonsil removal and his terrible 1952 car crash, he made effective low-key use of "growls," bent and choked notes and phrases, and nuances picked up mainly from the smooth big band singers he followed during his youth. His words were full of dryness (even the ones about liquor), irony, and earthly acceptance of man's condition. He was first and foremost a blues balladeer, and his songs were often thirty-two bars.

Physically slight, he was neither a producer nor an onstage instrumentalist. He has been described as "the poet laureate of the blues." His songs and positive messages have strong religious roots. A frequently mouthed credo, as he told Dick Shurman in a January 1980 interview, was, "Acknowledge God in all thy doings," and he explained his role this way: "I'm a poet, and my gift is love."

Mayfield's parents had musical and performing inclinations, but he left early to hobo, hustle, and do odd jobs. Born in Louisiana, he spent time in Houston regularly before his 1942 move to Los Angeles, and started a family in Texas. He spent most of his time between tours in Houston, L.A., Louisiana, or Chicago. He began his professional ambitions as a songwriter. But when he took "Two Years of Torture" to Supreme Records for Jimmy Witherspoon, he was induced to sing it himself and was backed with a superb studio group led by Maxwell Davis and veteran Texas/California guitarist Chuck Norris. The rights to the record were passed around, and John Dolphin pushed it successfully on the West Coast. His next session was for Specialty, in 1950, and it magnified his success on a national scale through

PERCY MAYFIELD, LOS ANGELES, 1943. COURTESY TINA MAYFIELD.

JERRY WHITE'S RECORD SHOP, CENTRAL AVENUE, LOS ANGELES, 1984. PHOTOGRAPH BY ALAN GOVENAR.

"Please Send Me Someone to Love/Strange Things Happening." He rode the popularity of those and subsequent releases through most of the 1950s, though his auto accident disfigured him and set him back for a while. At the end of the decade, after a series of attempts to retain Specialty's momentum on other labels, he began a five-year contract as a private writer for Ray Charles. Some of Mayfield's greatest recordings also appeared on Ray's Tangerine label.

A lull through the late 1960s in Chicago was punctuated by an obscure but excellent album on Brunswick, then a deal with Stroud Productions that generated three RCA albums. After the last was released in 1971, times remained all too quiet for one of the great figures of popular music of his and future generations. He made an unplanned, unadvertised appearance on one song of a live Bobby Womack LP. He paid for a session with instrumental and production help from Johnny "Guitar" Watson that was sold to Atlantic, and did twelve more

PERCY MAYFIELD, "THE RIVER'S INVITATION," SPECIALTY XSP-451.

tracks out of his pocket in 1979. Not only did he have to pay for his own sessions the last ten years, but it's safe to say that today the best known musical Mayfield is Curtis. Meanwhile, covers of Percy's songs continue from all sorts of expected and unexpected sources.

He divided his own recording into his "career" (sustained relationships with attention to quality and promotion) and "hustles." The former group includes the hit version of "Two Years of Torture"; his long affiliation with Art Rupe and Specialty, which produced thirty-four issued songs and a "Best of . . ." album; his work with Tangerine (two albums, twenty-three songs released); and the trio of RCA LPs. The Brunswick deal put together by E. Rodney Jones is borderline. The "hustles" include a session for GruVTone that may be his first recording (Percy was forgetful and confusing, but his reminiscences were cleaned up during the editing of these conversations); one coupling each on Chess, Cash, 7 Arts, and Atlantic; two on Imperial; and a 78 of two early compositions on Selective by Dallas Red. His pre-Specialty blues and jump gave little hint that a prayer in ballad form would top the charts for him next. Specialty also kept the blues mood going, with songs like "Lost Love" (also known as "Baby Please"), "Life Is Suicide," "River's Invitation," "Hopeless," "I Dare You Baby," "Lost Mind," "Bachelor Blues," "I Need Love So Bad," and "Memory Pain" (usually called "Serve Me Right to Suffer" when it's covered), and bittersweet offerings like "You Don't Exist No More."

VIDA LEE WALKER AND AARON "T-BONE" WALKER, CHICAGO, 1942. COURTESY HELEN OAKLEY DANCE.

The Chess, Cash, and 7 Arts recordings are worth finding but made little impact; nor did the Imperials, though they allow interesting comparison to B. B.'s first treatment of "My Reward." There was also some association with Don Robey in Houston, since Percy's first Tangerine recording, "Never No More," has some of the Duke customary credits. The Ray Charles tie-up yielded the classic *My Jug and I* album; a second compilation, *Brought Blues*; and other excellent singles. Meanwhile, he was writing hits for Ray like "Hit The Road Jack/ Danger Zone," "But on the Other Hand Baby"/"Hide nor Hair," "At the Club," and brilliant, lesser known releases like "Something's Wrong"/"My Baby Don't Dig

PERCY MAYFIELD, PUBLICITY PHOTOGRAPH, 1940S. COURTESY CHARLIE LANGE.

Me." Ray's bluesy *Crying Time* LP deserves finding and/or dusting off to hear Percy's pennings, "We Don't See Eye to Eye" and "You're in for a Big Surprise." Percy's Brunswick LP, *Walkin' on a Tightrope*, contains the basic blues feel one would expect from a Chicago production with prominent guitar by Wayne Bennett; the songs and performances more than make up for murky sound. RCA put out mixed bags as blues, ballads, novelties, and inspirational messages attempted to keep up with tastes without much visible success. The Atlantic 45 lives on mostly through Johnny Watson's 1979 cover on his DJM LP Love Jones.

The best Percy Mayfield compilations are on reissue albums: *My Heart Is Always Singing Sad Songs* (Ace), *The Voice Within* (Route 66), and *The Best of Percy Mayfield* (Specialty).

JOHNNY "GUITAR" WATSON, PUBLICITY PHOTOGRAPH, 1950S. COURTESY TEXAS AFRICAN AMERICAN PHOTOGRAPHY ARCHIVE.

Well, my native home was in Louisiana. I was born in Minton, Louisiana, right there in that hot sun. Leo. Now, I got quite a bit of pride, you know. And there's nothing that I'm really tryin' to outdo nobody on, it's really just me, you know. Yeah, that's the way it is. You see, we had a big farm about seven miles out of town. And I came to

PERCY MAYFIELD, ELI'S MILE HIGH CLUB, OAKLAND, 1984. PHOTOGRAPH BY PAT MONACO.

PERCY MAYFIELD WITH BOBBY MURRAY, SACRAMENTO BLUES FESTIVAL, 1984. PHOTOGRAPH BY PAT MONACO.

California in '42. I was properly raised in Houston. See, I went everywhere. But I never did anything like show business around there before I came to L.A.

I just wanted to be a songwriter. You see, I been singin' all my life; when I was a boy growin' up, I was singin' in choirs and things like that, you know. And I never— when I came back to L.A., after I came to L.A. to live, I just looked forward to just pennin' for artists in the background. I like to hunt and fish, and I just wanted to be in the background and be a star-maker. But the cat would only accept it if I would sing 'em, you know. And that's the reason I really got started. And after I got a taste of it, I loved it, 'cause I love the people.

I was supposed to be the co-writer for our recordin' company, for our talent club with singers and dancers and all those people. I was in the Al-Muzart Talent Club. I don't know what the name means; it already had the name when I came into the club. There was about twenty or thirty of us in it. Monroe Tucker was the biggest name, and George Comeau, he was the trumpet player. And everybody was talented in it.

I couldn't refuse that cat [at Supreme Records] when he accepted mine, 'cause it was a Mexican girl, Ida Bravo, was at our club, and she had a tune called "How Wrong Can a Good Man Be," and I just put a melody to that. I couldn't refuse because I'd be lettin' them down,

Well, it's courtin,' man. Now if the melody comes first, you see, then I have to make the words marry it. And if the words—sometimes the words and melody come together. Most of my style, and when I'm singin' sadness, started from pain, you know. But after I got set in my ways as to find out what my title or my talent was, I could sell more sadness than joy. You see, 'cause there's more sadness in the world than there is joy. However, that don't mean that I got to live as sad as I sell. You see, you got have somethin' for that mass. Now, along about

PERCY MAYFIELD, "PLEASE SEND ME SOMEONE TO LOVE," SPECIALTY 775 A.

see. So I recorded "Two Years of Torture/Half Awoke" (Supreme 1543, Swing Time 258), "How Wrong Can a Good Man Be," and another melody (Supreme 1549, Swing Time 262).

What a lot of people considered my style, which I got acquainted with now over the years—when it first started on me, they let me know they dug it. Actually, I'd be runnin' out of breath. There's that "Baby, pleeeease." You know what I'm sayin'? Then I'd sing, "Baby please." Then I found out that that was my style through the public. So I started bendin' most of my notes on the blues. And so it just comes out natural 'cause evidently it must have been my style, you know. But it was forced on me.

I just created it, tryin' to be a little bit different from anybody else. So I wouldn't have so many followers, you know what I'm tryin' to say. Now, on ballads, I don't mind. But on the blues, you got so many blues singers out there that if you want to stand out, you got be a little bit different. But what I mean by being myself, I laugh a lot. You know, I grunt or bend notes or somethin' like that. But it's all comin' natural. If the band is kickin,' then they can kick out a lot of new material on me. 'Cause I just create as I go along.

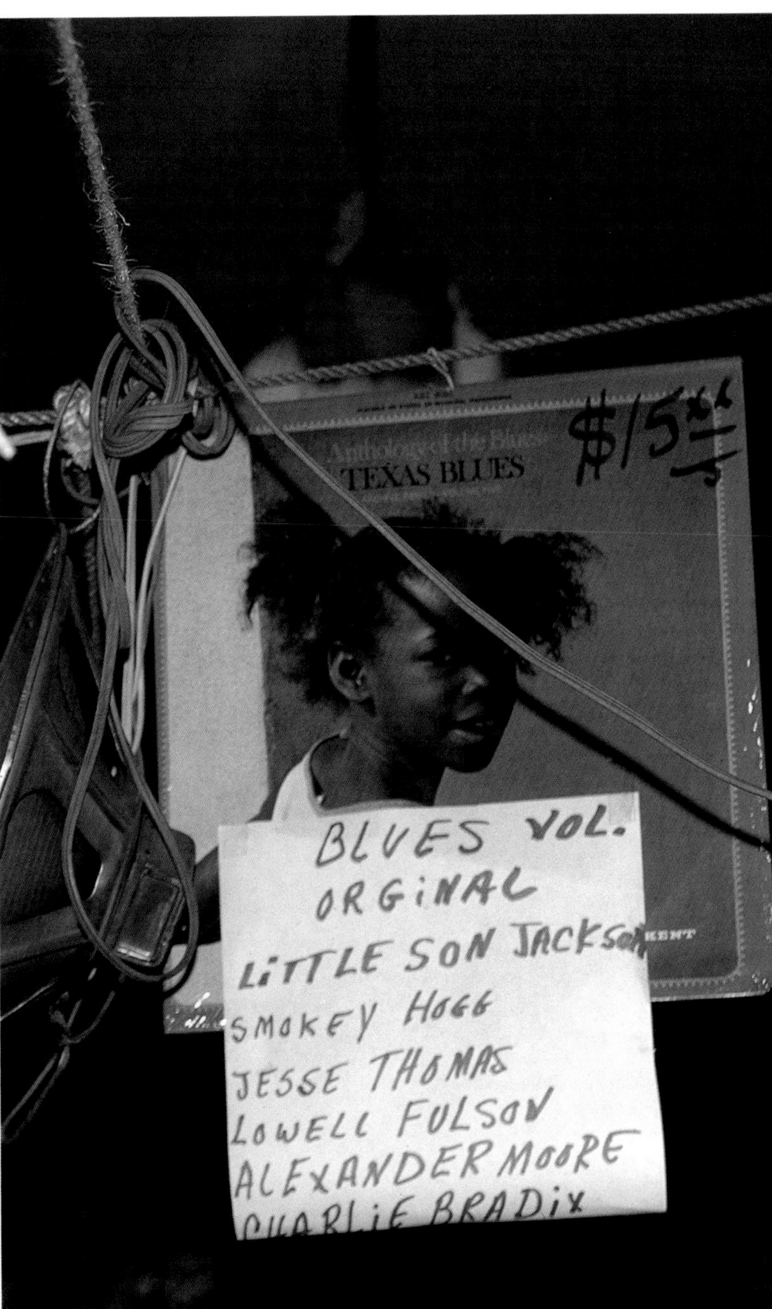

JERRY WHITE'S RECORD SHOP, CENTRAL AVENUE, LOS ANGELES, 1984. PHOTOGRAPH BY ALAN GOVENAR.

ABOVE: TINA MAYFIELD (PERCY'S WIDOW) AND VIDA LEE WALKER (T-BONE'S WIDOW), LOS ANGELES, 1987. PHOTOGRAPH BY PAT MONACO.

BELOW: TINA MAYFIELD AT PERCY'S PIANO, LOS ANGELES, 1987. PHOTOGRAPH BY PAT MONACO.

intermission, after intermission when the booze has started soakin' in, they want blues or sadness. Well, it can be a blues straight or a blues ballad, see, like that. But novelties, like from the time you hit the bandstand till midnight, like that [snaps fingers], jumpin,' it ain't like that. So it's just a twin thing with me. I gotta do what I feel, you know, I gotta write it as I hear it and see it.

Oh, man, I just love the people and I love to travel. It's no particular one strong point. I mean it's universal. I just wanna tour one more time, but I could have me somethin' new. I don't. I wouldn't go out there now. They can't hardly pay me enough to make the tour 'cause I'd be second or third or be on a bill. So-and-so and such-and such plus or also Percy Mayfield. Well, I got too much pride. Maybe—it look like to me that I'm just being given a handout. I like to be featured too, you know what I mean. So I'd have to have them somethin,' I wanna have somethin' new out there for them, you see. That's the reason I don't cater to one particular incident. I cater to the universal. I don't know how else to put it, man. I just wanna go, go, go. I used to say in my slogans that "the world is my playground, I'm at home everywhere I go." Well, that's because of what I believe in. It made me a poet, and my gift is love. And I love people, and there ain't no two ways about that. And to travel across the country, you know—to see the old faces and the old places that I ain't seen in a long time and sing to them, and then have something to offer. That's my highlight.

MERCY DEE, "ONE ROOM COUNTRY SHACK," SPECIALTY XSP-458.

NEW YEAR'S EVE, ELI'S MILE HIGH CLUB, OAKLAND, 1983.
PHOTOGRAPH BY PAT MONACO.

CHARLES BROWN

September 13, 1922–January 21, 1999; interview by Tom Mazzolini, 1976

(*Living Blues*, no. 27)

Charles Brown, like many of his contemporaries, lapsed into obscurity in the 1960s but experienced a career renaissance in the late 1980s. He opened for Bonnie Raitt on her 1990 tour and continued performing and recording for the rest of his life, often with younger musicians such as Raitt, Dr. John, and singer Maria Muldaur.

In his last years, too, Brown received overdue recognition. He was awarded the Rhythm and Blues Foundation's Lifetime Achievement Award in 1989 and the National Endowment for the Arts' National Heritage Fellowship in 1997. He died a few days after a tribute concert in San Francisco and two months before his induction into the Rock and Roll Hall of Fame.

Well, during my stay in Texas, my high school days, one of the teachers who taught chemistry and physics, Mr. James, had what you called little one-night stands on the beachfront out there with these nice white clubs, and this was just a little extra money to be made, and at that time I was a good reader in music because I was taking classical piano. He had a lot of guys who couldn't read, so he said, "Charles, I want you to come out here and learn this music that we play." And I went out on the beach with him, and I was satisfied with what I was doing because I was making a little money, and at that time, if you were making eighteen dollars a week, you were making good money. That was when I was first introduced into this type of music—"Stardust," beautiful tunes like that, standard tunes, "Beer Barrel Polka." I stayed out there until I got the gist of the music. This

CHARLES BROWN, WASHINGTON, D.C., 1997. PHOTOGRAPH BY STUART BRININ. COURTESY NATIONAL COUNCIL FOR THE TRADITIONAL ARTS.

was in, oh, I won't tell you when, it was a long time ago, but that was starting me into this music because my grandmother really didn't want me to play that type of music because I was playing in the church. She was a devout Christian woman. So I went on and played.

At that time, a guy who sang so well, Pha Terrell with Andy Kirk, I was always enthused with his singing. I just thought he sang so lovely and so beautifully, and I just wanted to sing like that. Then here comes The Ink Spots with this high type of singing, and everybody was trying to sing like that. Fats Waller, with his kidding and things like that, we called it comedy singing, and we would try to pattern after those records, but I figured that wasn't my style. I liked the sweeter things like "No Greater Love" and "What I Feel for You," and I was influenced, really, by this Pha Terrell.

When I went to college after finishing high school, I got into the college band. They asked me to sing only one number, "Big Fat Mama," which was a risqué number, and they would go wild over that. That was the only type of singing I did at that time. After I finished school, I got a job as a teacher there in Baytown, Texas.

[I attended] Prairie View State College, forty-five miles northwest of Houston. Majored in chemistry with a mathematics minor. In fact, I had two minors: math and education. Everybody ventured into teaching because that's all we knew at that time: when you finish college, you teach school. But we did take chemistry because at that time the war was raging and they said chemistry and the chemical industry was very prosperous.

I taught school in Baytown. Mr. Archer, he was the principal, he wanted me to teach because he liked my personality. He said, "Charles, you'll do well with children because you have a beautiful personality." I went down there, but I didn't like it because we were paid twenty-two dollars a week. You had to go to church, you had to pay your room rent out of that, and when I got through I don't think I had five dollars left. So I had to find something else. I heard they had these jobs in chemistry, and you could take a civil service examination. So I took this examination and made 96, which was a very high grade as a junior chemist. Washington, D.C., sent for me to come to one of the plants. I had a choice of Pine Bluff, Arkansas, Arsenal, or the one in Maryland. So I chose Pine Bluff because it was close to Texas, but I didn't want to go too far. I was a junior chemist there. I stayed there for six or seven months. Then I wanted to transfer, but the war was raging. and you had to register for the service and they classified me 1A. Then they asked me if I had asthma when I was young, and they wouldn't let me go. After that, I thought I'd go to California and make a new life.

CHARLES BROWN, LATE 1940S.
COURTESY TEXAS AFRICAN AMERICAN PHOTOGRAPHY ARCHIVE.

Berkeley, California, they had a research laboratory there called Western Research. They transferred me there because I had asked for a civil service transfer. I don't know what happened, but the job was taken, and I got another job and registered at school there to get a master's degree. And I think I stayed there about three months when I said this wasn't it, because everybody wanted some piano players, and I got a job working a little place out there in the International House, that was out near Chinatown, playing the piano. I worked there as an added attraction.

That was 1943 and into '44; that was the year I went to Los Angeles. My uncle had a church there, and he asked me to start playing for this church and he would give me money on Sunday. So I started playing in church. I didn't like that too well because it wasn't enough money. Then I got a job with the Broadway Department Store as an elevator operator, and I heard about an amateur show down at the Lincoln Theater on Central Avenue, and on Thursday nights they were giving away twenty-five dollars for the first prize. At that time, "Boogie Woogie on the St. Louis Blues" by Earl Hines was very popular, and I went down there and won first prize. When I played this number they had a fit; then I turned around and played the "Warsaw Concerto," and they didn't expect that. You know, here's this guy from Texas, and they gave me a week's work at the Lincoln Theater. So that was the start of Charles Brown, in the pit band at the Lincoln Theater.

Ivie Anderson, who used to sing with Duke Ellington, her husband came to the Broadway Department Store. I was working two jobs. He asked me to come over and work for him, and I started playing for people as dinner music at Ivie's Chicken Shack. I stayed there until I made a lot of money. Then she said she had to go to Mexico, and I wasn't satisfied with forty-two dollars a week, so I left and I didn't have any work at all. I quit the theater because they didn't pay enough money, but I had saved up my money and I went to Sugar Hill, which was in one of the most fabulous sections of Los Angeles. Ethel Waters lived there, Ben Carter, who was a great comedian. Man Tan Moreland was right around the corner. Nat "King" Cole, Noble Sissle, all of them living over there. When I moved up there, Johnny Moore came looking for me; he had heard about this piano player that won an amateur contest. He had lost his piano player, and he came to me to replace him, and he wanted to hear me play. I played for him, and he said, "Well, you'll be the right thing for us. We have an audition out in Beverly Hills at the Talk of the Town. If you can make it, we can use you. It pays $600 a week." I went with him and rehearsed. Our theme song was "Warsaw Concerto," trio playing those heavy classics, and "Holiday for Strings." So we practiced up. Then he said, "Do you sing?"

I said, "No, I don't sing."

He said, "Well, you got to sing."

So we practiced up for about two weeks before the audition. This was in 1944, and in September we went to the auditorium, and they had about twenty trios, and we figured we didn't have a chance at all. Then we came up there, and these guys had done their stuff, and the guy was asking questions: "Can you play this type of number?" So when we got up there, we had it together. When we opened with "Warsaw Concerto," and went into our theme, the man said, "When could you open?" We said, "Next week," and we had the job. Jon Hall, the movie star, and Martha Raye would come out there every night, and Tommy Dorsey.

Martha Raye and Ben Blue wanted me to play for their parties up in Coldwater Canyon. So a guy called Johnny Shadrack and I, he'd sing, we did a duet, and they'd give us $300 for every party. So we had it made, and all the movie stars just loved me. Then we started working out on Hollywood Boulevard, the Swing Club, which was one of the great clubs at that time. They had Eddie Heywood, Cee Pee Johnson, Harry "The Hipster" Gibson, and others. Frankie Laine, he was working out of Billy Berg's, and he started coming over. He said, "I want to sing like a spook; I'm trying to develop a style," and he was trying to sing like Nat "King" Cole, too. I was singing in an exaggerated style: "To spend one night with you." That was my type of thing, and Frankie Laine took that type of style, but it didn't come out in him, so he had a style of his own.

We made our first recording [for Atlas Records] with Frankie Laine, called "Melancholy Madelaine." I was on one side with "Tell Me You'll Wait for Me," the same number Ray Charles did in his *Genius of Ray Charles* album, that I wrote with Oscar Moore. So then Frankie Laine took this record out to Mercury Records, and they signed him up. He was made after that.

After we made the first record with Frankie Laine, Johnny Moore was the type of guy who wanted to always see that his trio always got over, so he wanted to make some records of the trio. Well, we were singing "Driftin' Blues," and all the people were going wild over "Driftin' Blues" during the war, but we had never made a recording out of it.

We liked to go to the races and to the horses, and Johnny said, "Look, I know Mother Davis over here on Forty-sixth Street. Let's go over and see her because she can give us some numbers to play at the races and they'll come in." When we went over there, I told Johnny, "I don't believe in it," but I sat out in the car, and she had a lot of people out there waiting for her. Johnny went in there, and she said, "Bring that fellow out in the car in here. I want to read him because I see something about him." So Johnny came out there and got me and brought me into this house. And she prayed this prayer, and I didn't want to go. It looked like the hair rose on my head, and she said, "I see where you're going to sign a contract in twenty-four hours; it's going to take you across the country. And this fellow has a magnet. I'm going to tell you something: If you stay with me, you will be successful. Listen to what I tell you." And we were listening, and she said, "I know you come here to play the horses, and I'm going to give you a horse tomorrow." I think she said the fourth race, a horse named Lovely Millie. I'll never forget it, number seven. She said, "Don't ever come here with this gambling no more." Johnny was glad; he didn't want to hear no more. All he wanted was this horse.

We went out there with our little money, about eighteen dollars between us, and put it on that horse, and that horse came in and paid ninety-something dollars. We went back to work. We had a little job at the Copa

CHARLES BROWN AND RUTH BROWN, STOCKHOLM, 1980. PHOTOGRAPH BY ERIK LINDAHL. COURTESY SCANDINAVIAN BLUES ASSOCIATION.

CHARLES BROWN, 1970S. COURTESY TOM MAZZOLINI.

Club, and clubs were going very late during the war, and about 2:45, a knock was on the door, and we looked through the door, and a guy had a satchel. It was Sammy Goldberg and Eddie Mesner, and Sammy said, "I want to hear this 'Driftin' Blues' that Johnny Moore's playing and Charles Brown is singing." He told us to play it and then asked us to sign a contract to make it for $800. So John said, "Is that all you got?" He said, "Yeah. If the record does good, I'll give you more. I'll give you a piece of the action in the company." It was the biggest mistake we ever made in our lives.

So when "Driftin' Blues" came out—we made it in '45 for Philo Records, which later became Aladdin—the other side was "Groovy"; everything was cute then. And they put "Driftin' Blues" on the jukebox, and we'd go from one jukebox to another to hear it because we wanted to know what we sounded like. And the jukebox operators in New York sent for us to come to New York. Then we had to get us an agent. So Johnny Moore went out to the William Morris Agency and they signed us up. Sammy Davis, Count Basie, and Pearl Bailey were the only black acts they had signed, and we were the next one. They told us they could get us right into New York, but the Apollo Theater wouldn't take us because we weren't strong enough. So they booked us at the Renaissance Casino on a one-night stand with Luis Russell's band. Nat "King" Cole introduced us, lemme tell you. The Apollo Theater had Buddy Johnson and Ella Johnson in a showdown there. They had to call the fire department; this place was packed. You get on Seventh Avenue, and the Apollo didn't have nobody in it; we had all the people. So Schiffman came down. He was the big boss of the Apollo; he owned it. He talked to us at intermission and asked us if we'd be interested in working for him. He asked us, "Would you take $1,200 for the first week?" He said, "If you do good that first week, the sky is the limit."

So when the Blazers opened the Apollo Theater, the band had to play a theme song, which was "Air Mail Special," that was our getting-on-stage number. And you had to run out there and get to the piano and get everything ready, and boom! You had to be quick. People came up to the stage screamin' and hollerin' when we did "So Long" and "Moonrise." They'd be crying, "Don't sing it no more. Do you love me? Do you love me?" Billy Eckstine came up there, and Jackie "Moms" Mabley was on the bill; she was doing a single then, and we went over really terrific. And we had our own show, and Johnny Moore hired Buddy Rich. We had Buddy Rich go to all the theaters with us.

We toured from '46 to '48, and when Oscar [Moore] left King Cole, we added him, because Johnny [Moore] was very sick. So I had to go on as Johnny Moore because the people heard the singing, and they thought Johnny Moore was the singer. They didn't look on the corner of the record and see "Charles Brown, vocal." In those years, the records said, "Johnny Moore's Three Blazers." It was his trio, but I was still the singer and the piano player. Then when we broke up in '48, there were a lot of misunderstandings about money.

So when I started on my own, I quite naturally had to get a recording company, and I got Aladdin back. When I left Johnny Moore, we cut a first record, "Get Yourself Another Fool," and everybody thought I was telling Johnny Moore this, [and] it made a big hit. I was getting big then. I was getting to be the number-one rhythm and blues artist, and I could hire anybody I wanted with the show. All the other acts that came into the office, like Ruth Brown, they would try to get them on the road with me, ask me if I'd take them, to introduce them at fifty dollars per night. That's what she was getting, but when she made her first round she went up to $450 a night, she did so good. She did "Mama, He Treats Your Daughter Mean."

Then I took The Dominoes, The Clovers, and Ray Charles. Ray Charles was working for me because I was the number-one R&B artist. They booked him with my band, and we made our rounds: Chicago; Lima, Ohio; Somerset, New Jersey; on around. We didn't go to New York. We went to little towns.

I had a good band. I took all the young guys that never had a chance: Boogie Daniels, Clifford Solomon, Walter Henry [who played with Johnny Otis]. And I had my cousin, who sings now. None of these people had played anywhere. I groomed them in how to play. Freddie Simon, of course, he's dead now, but all these people were just beginning. But now they all play with great bands. On guitar I had Wayne Bennett. He was with Amos [Milburn], but Wayne Bennett played with both of us. After him I had Jesse Irvin, who's my cousin, who's in L.A. now. He made "Black Night" and all the best of them. I had about seven pieces and a manager.

When we would go out to play these places, people would ask, "Why don't you sound like that in person?" See, now, on the records, it really disgusts me because the records never show what I really could do. Because when you heard the records, you heard a little plink-plink piano, a very simple guitar, a simple bass, plain singing. We didn't venture out. We had a style, and that's what people knew us by. I didn't venture out to take a lot of solos, just enough to make the record. The people would say, "Charles, why don't you play more? Why don't you sing more to show yourself?" I said, "No, I'm satisfied." Then when we went in person with the band, we sounded ten times better than the records. We even tried to get Eddie Mesner to record us like we sounded [live], but he said, "No, since you made money with a trio the way you sound, that's the way we want it, because that's what the people buy."

I stayed with Aladdin until 1952. Then we had a big run-in about royalties. I never got any royalty checks. They wanted to buy you Cadillacs but never give you royalty checks. I wanted an accounting of my royalties and what I had accumulated, and because I asked them for an accounting, they tried to put me in jail. I sued them, but I got only $8,000, but I could have got $100,000. Then, for suing them, they put me on the shelf, and I couldn't sign with nobody for about a year or two. I figure [I did] two hundred sides at least for Aladdin, and they have some stuff they never released. Beautiful numbers. Aladdin had a fire before they sold out to United Artists, and it burned up a lot of the masters.

I didn't sign with nobody after I got released from Aladdin. I just freelanced. I went back to Exclusive Records. We had a short-term contract before Aladdin Records. We did "New Orleans Blues," "Merry Christmas Baby," "Lost in the Night," "My Silent Love," "You Are My First Love."

IVORY JOE HUNTER

November 10, 1914–November 8, 1974

IVORY JOE HUNTER, PUBLICITY PHOTOGRAPH.
COURTESY HANS KRAMER.

Ivory Joe Hunter was originally from Kirbyville, Texas, about 135 miles northeast of Houston. His most vivid memories of his childhood were of his mother, who sang spirituals and organized her family of eleven boys and girls into a choir. The family moved to Port Arthur, where Hunter quit school after the eighth grade to begin working as a professional musician. As a teenager, Hunter had his own radio show on KFDM in Beaumont and became known as "Rambling Fingers" because of his abilities on the piano. In 1936 he settled in Houston, but left in the early 1940s to pursue opportunities in California.

IVORY JOE HUNTER, "DON'T BE NO FOOL-FOOL," KING 4183B.

IVORY JOE HUNTER AND HIS BAND,
"HIGH COST, LOW PAY BLUES," PACIFIC 630.

IVORY JOE HUNTER AND HIS BAND, "BLUES AT MIDNIGHT," PACIFIC 630.

In 1945 Hunter launched Ivory Records in Oakland, but his venture was short-lived due to wartime restrictions on shellac. He did, however, produce one successful record, a Leroy Carr ballad, "Blues at Sunrise," that he later recorded on the Dot label. Johnny Moore and The Three Blazers was the session band on Hunter's early recordings. Through his association with Moore, he met and worked with Charles Brown, whose vocal and piano style shaped his own.

On stage, Ivory Joe Hunter fronted a basic rhythm and blues band: piano, bass, drums, and tenor saxophone. In his recordings he combined blues and boogie with a pop-ballad orientation. After his Ivory label folded, he started Pacific Records and issued "Grieving Blues," "Heavy Hearted Blues," and jump tunes like "Boogie in the Basement." In addition, he recorded for the Excelsior, 4 Star, and King labels, but did not attain widespread success until he signed with MGM Records in 1949. His two original ballads, "I Need You So" and "I Almost Lost My Mind," ranked high on the *Billboard* charts.

In 1956 Hunter moved to the Atlantic label and achieved gold record status with "Since I Met You, Baby," and later had a hit with another of his songs, "Empty Arms." These songs were released at a time when young, white rock musicians were covering black recordings, and the music was receiving greater exposure and popularity. To make the most of this crossover audience, Hunter began performing country songs, spirituals, and pop ballads, in addition to blues. Before his death, he was honored with a special program of his songs at the Grand Ole Opry in Nashville.

LLOYD GLENN

November 21, 1909–May 23, 1985; text by Dick Shurman, 1986

(*Living Blues*, no. 68)

Lloyd Glenn had a style shaped by the sounds he heard in his San Antonio childhood from his father and friends, and the early boogie-woogie kings like Pinetop Smith, Meade Lux Lewis, and their cohorts. Jimmy Yancey's influence is strongly felt on Glenn's best known record, "Old Time Shuffle." Lloyd was self-effacing about the development of his characteristic harmonies and block chords; he said he worked them out because he "didn't have the reach." Instead of just playing rolling or boogie-type bass lines, which he left to a bassist, he liked to use his left hand more rhythmically and play frequent octaves. He also liked to play guitar-style intervals and use the volume pedal to make the piano ring like a guitar.

In 1928 Lloyd began working with Territory bands, including those of trumpeter T. Holder, with whom Lloyd first visited California in 1931, and Boots (Douglas) & His Buddies. In 1942 he moved to Los Angeles because his wife's parents were in California. He felt that what "West Cost blues style" there was existed because "migration brought the blues here." While working as a packer and a lifter in an aircraft plant during World War II, he began playing piano around town, and things began falling into place during a twin piano engagement with Walter Johnson on Western Avenue.

Once Lloyd's own career took off, it included arranging and playing piano on some of the best records by T-Bone Walker (including his original "Stormy Monday"), Lowell Fulson, and B. B. King, plus others like Gene Phillips, Jesse Thomas, Harmonica Slim, Big Joe Turner, and Gatemouth Brown. His own releases, usually on

LLOYD GLENN, "SLEIGH RIDE," HOLLYWOOD RECORDS 1021

LEFT: BUDDY ACE, HOUSTON, 1960S. PHOTOGRAPH BY BENNY JOSEPH. RIGHT: BUDDY ACE, OAKLAND, 1983. PHOTOGRAPH BY PAT MONACO.

DAVE ALEXANDER, IMAM OMAR SHARIF, OAKLAND, 1980S. PHOTOGRAPH BY PAT MONACO.

Aladdin, Imperial, or Jack Lauderdale's Swing Time and associated labels, were widely popular and influential, and have been internationally reissued on Stockholm (along with new recordings), Polydor, and Oldie Blues. In the last decade of his life he made albums in France for Black and Blue, including one co-billed with Gatemouth Brown and one of Tiny Grimes's finest. He also appeared at the 1982 San Francisco Blues Festival and toured with Big Joe Turner. Glenn put a strong stamp on many of B. B. King's Kent and ABC records, and was reunited on record with T-Bone Walker, and became, along with Charles Brown, one of the top pacesetters of West Coast blues piano.

With all of Lloyd's experience and versatility, he observed, "I've been playing music for a pretty good while, and I found out blues will move you faster than anything else. I don't care what kind of blues—somebody will listen." He helped the artists he worked with make some of their very best records; his influence on the playing of countless piano players is incalculable.

FLOYD DIXON

February 8, 1929–July 26, 2006; interview by Tom Mazzolini, 1975

(*Living Blues,* no. 23)

FLOYD DIXON, PUBLICITY PHOTOGRAPH. COURTESY HANS KRAMER.

The role Floyd Dixon has played in the evolution of the West Coast blues scene has long been overlooked. With his very first recording of "Dallas Blues," Dixon gained national prominence and had some big hits from 1949 to 1952. His smooth delivery and sophisticated piano style enabled him to join such talents as Amos Milburn, Ray Charles, and Roy Brown on the national charts and on the cross-country touring circuit.

He settled in Los Angeles in 1963 to a relatively inactive musical life. Dixon worked out of Los Angeles through the early 1970s. He could be found playing in Riverside or Pomona, California, and in Venice or over in Santa Monica and Bakersfield in the Central California Valley.

Rumors about Floyd Dixon have traveled in West Coast blues circles for many years. Some had him living in and performing in Texas, which was true to some extent, but that Floyd Dixon, it turned out, was an imposter. Other stories, which had him living in the Central Valley, were closer to the truth, but the fact was, Dixon was living in Hollywood. In 1973 he was living with the disk jockey Wolfman Jack and also was doing work unrelated to music.

Dick Shurman and Jim O'Neal (*Living Blues,* no. 23) commented that "Floyd Dixon showed impeccable piano technique, fabulous timing (especially on slow blues), and a voice like a foghorn—a surprise for one associated with such a supposedly subdued style of blues singing. Like so many Texas bluesmen, his nonconformist style was never fully accepted by the West Coast recording establishment, and he never won the recognition accorded to other West Coast pianists, such as Roy Hawkins, Little Willie Littlefield, and Amos Milburn. Dave Alexander (from Marshall, Texas) was right when he told Floyd, 'People don't usually sit in here, but I got to let you—you're one of the great cats.'"

I got into music when I came to Los Angeles. I heard a record by Amos Milburn, "Money Hustlin' Woman," and a record by Charles Brown, and I decided I want to sing. But Louis Jordan was my favorite artist at the time, you know "G.I. Jive," "Choo, Choo, Ch'boogie" and all that kinda stuff. So I started playing the piano—I didn't have one but would go to school and kinda practice and learned how to play and studied a little harmony. I went to an amateur hour, and I won first prize at the Million Dollar Theater when Johnny Moore and The Three

Blazers was there. And I left there and went to the Barrelhouse and won first prize there. Johnny Otis was co-owner there. He thought that I sounded very good and told me I ought to start recording. So then I went out to the Bihari brothers, and I didn't intend to record, but a guitar player named Tiny Webb was there and a bass player, and I asked them would they run over a couple with me. I brought a tune called "Dallas Blues," and I didn't know they was recording it in the back, and so they said "Listen to it back." So when Jules Bihari and Saul [Bihari] played it back for me, they said, "We would like to put it out." And I was shocked! They wrote me out a check for just doing those couple of tunes and asked me if I was in the union and I said no, and they gave me the money to go join that day.

Those were on Modern. They were put out in three weeks, and about six weeks, "Dallas Blues" was number two in *Billboard*. Well, I didn't know anything about *Billboard* and *Cashbox*, and he said it'll be number one in a couple of more weeks, and that surprised me because I didn't think it was nowhere but in California. But then I got letters from my home and Dallas and Shreveport and different places, saying, "I heard your record and was wonderin' if you's the same one," because everybody called me "Skeet," a lot of people didn't know my name was Floyd. And that was a thrill to me.

I was seventeen, well, right at eighteen, because it was a month before I be eighteen. This was in 1948, right at 1949. I was born in Marshall, Texas, February 8, 1929. I would play whenever I could. I took one music lesson from a fellow named Julius Hayward, but he beat my hands so much with a ruler that I didn't care to take no more lessons. So I stopped at one lesson there.

AMOS MILBURN

April 1, 1927–January 3, 1980; interview by Norbert Hess, 1979

(*Living Blues,* no. 45/46)

When I was a young boy about five years old, my parents rented a piano for my eldest sister's wedding. The following morning, they told me I went to play the piano and did "Jingle Bells." My father said, "We better keep this piano and get him lessons." I took only very few lessons; I was too fast for music. I said, "Just let me play, teach me the keys; I'll go ahead and play the song." It sounds stupid, but it carried me through. So I get a little older, and I start to listen to the jukeboxes and local taverns from the outside, 'cause I couldn't go in. They played so loud, you could hear them on the outside, and I remember hearing Billie Holiday, Louis Jordan, and I could go back and copy. I had a brother that influenced me with the old standards, "Body and Soul," "Stardust." I found out, when I went to New York later, that if you couldn't play those numbers, you couldn't get into the union, you wasn't a musician.

[Milburn joined the Navy in 1942, at age fifteen. After three and a half years overseas, he returned to Houston in 1945.] After leaving, I decided I would get a little band; we played all around the little towns around Houston and suburbs. Finally, somebody heard me. Mrs. Lola Cullum offered me to come to rehearse at her house. She had a big baby grand piano, and that was something new to me, after playing in these little joints, you know. I recorded "After Midnite," and she took me to Los Angeles on this train. We submitted the number to Modern Records; they refused it. Well, they didn't actually refuse it, but they offered me so little money till she refused it. She said we heard of another company that had Charles Brown. At that time, they were the Philo Record Company, what was made at Aladdin. At the time the president of Aladdin, Eddie Mesner, was at the hospital. So my manager [Cullum] took the record and a record player and took it up to the hospital and let him hear. And he told his brother Leo, the vice president of the company: "Sign him up right now, he's good. I like him!" And that started it all.

The first session took place September 12, 1946, and Milburn stayed with Aladdin for twelve years, recording about 125 numbers, until the company went out of business. Most were arranged by the famous Maxwell Davis, who blew the sax solos. During the late Fifties, the company released two albums on Aladdin and one on a subsidiary label, Score. Another album followed after Aladdin was bought by Imperial. Milburn's first record, "After Midnite," sold over 50,000 copies, and in 1959 he was *Billboard's* best-selling R&B artist.

Milburn's "Bad, Bad Whiskey" reached number one in *Billboard's* R&B charts in November 1950, and he continued to use either a happy-go-lucky enthusiasm or a sad, almost crying, voice on other drinking songs, such as "Just One More Drink," "Thinking and Drinking," "Let Me Go Home, Whiskey," "One Scotch, One Bourbon and One Beer," "Good, Good Whiskey," "Vicious, Vicious Vodka," and "Rum and Coca-Cola."

In the late 1970s, five labels reissued albums of Milburn's early Aladdin material, among them United Artists (USA), Riverboat (France), and Route 66 (Sweden).

(OPPOSITE) AMOS MILBURN, PUBLICITY PHOTOGRAPH.
COURTESY HANS KRAMER

L. C. "GOOD ROCKIN'" ROBINSON

May 15, 1915–September 26, 1976; interview by Tom Mazzolini, 1975

(*Living Blues*, no. 22)

Louis Charles "Good Rockin'" Robinson is one of the most dynamic artists to have emerged from the San Francisco/Oakland blues scene. An energetic performer who earned his nickname from his rocking music and showmanship, Robinson entertained San Francisco Bay area audiences for over three decades.

In 1940 he arrived in San Francisco from Texas. An older brother, A. C. Robinson, was already in San Francisco, and the two joined forces as they had years earlier in Texas and formed the first of many Robinson groups on the West Coast. L. C. Robinson was deeply influenced by the western swing bands that had emerged in Texas by the 1930s. Consequently, his style of blues offered a unique combination of violin, Hawaiian steel, and guitar. A. C. was adept at the harmonica and bass, often playing both instruments simultaneously, and the Robinson brothers were backed from the beginning by drummer Teddy Winston, a veteran of numerous big bands of the late Twenties and Thirties.

Although the 1940s and early 1950s would prove to be prolific years for the recording of modern blues, they were essentially empty years for L. C. Robinson. For the most part, record companies on the West Coast were focusing their attention on such stylists as Amos Milburn, Floyd Dixon, and Lowell Fulson, thus limiting the rough-edged blues of L. C. to just a few recordings.

In 1957 A. C. Robinson quit the blues to devote his activities to the church and its music. He joined the Pentecostal Temple Church of Christ in San Francisco, where he became a deacon and singer. Aided by his wife on piano, A. C. Robinson recorded a few gospel sides for Golden Soul Records, performing in a blues harmonica style. His voice is similar to Clifton Chenier's.

During his active blues days, however, A. C. played alongside such West Coast notables as Louis Jordan, Ivory Joe Hunter, T-Bone Walker and Jimmy Witherspoon. He claimed his harmonica style was different from most. "I can play with anybody," he said. "Take Sonny Boy Williamson, for instance, he always needed a piano, but I can play with anything, even a twenty-piece orchestra."

(OPPOSITE)

L. C. ROBINSON, PUBLICITY PHOTOGRAPH, 1970S.

COURTESY TOM MAZZOLINI.

L.C. Robinson remained musically active. Beyond a doubt, he was the hardest working bluesman in Oakland and recorded three albums between the late 1960s and early 1970s. His band varied from job to job, but included as many as two horns, guitar, bass, piano, and drums. Veteran Teddy Winston was Robinson's regular drummer, while Dr. Wild Willie Moore or Candyman McGuirt filled in on piano. Richmond saxophonist C. L. Jones was another regular, while the remainder of the band was more transient.

I was born in Brenham, Texas; that's sixty miles outside of Austin. I was born on a farm, and we used to give country dances. Quite naturally, we was small, my brother and I, and my daddy hired two brothers to play out in the country there; one played guitar and the other played violin. And I noticed the one playing guitar, and I told my brother, I said, "I can play like him!" He said, "Why don't you try, then?" Well, we didn't have a guitar. My sister went to a country fair and she won one, that's the old hollow-body with the hole in the middle, and she brought it back and gave it to us. And in about a week my brother was playing the harmonica, and he said, "I thought you could play like that fellow was playing the other night." And it come up to me how he made a G-chord, "Blues in the Bottom" and "Tiger Rag."

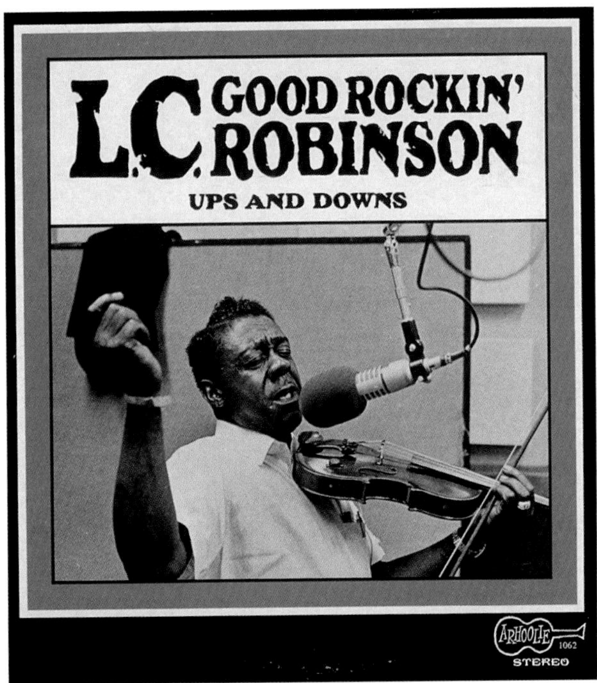

L. C. ROBINSON, *UPS AND DOWNS*, ARHOOLIE 1062.

Then I had a brother-in-law played bottleneck guitar. He was Blind Willie Johnson. He used to come stay with us two, three nights, and he'd sit there and play that guitar, religious songs, and I was watching him with that bottle on there and started out playing like that too. But I was playing blues. Yes, some of Lonnie Johnson blues, you know, and I would play with the bottle on there. I used to keep a turpentine bottle in my pocket, they was smaller, and I would play like that. And finally I got up in age, and we went to playing different places, my brother and I. We got a little better and better every time we played, and so we decided to move to Temple, Texas, in 1934. That was near Brenham, ninety-five miles from there. My brother was there first, and he came back and got me out there with him. I was quite young and got around there and got to playin.' We hooked up with The Three Hot Brown Boys at that time and went on the air. We just about had the town sewed up. At 4:15 in the evening people would beat it home to hear that program on KTEM, Temple. We stayed on the air three or maybe two and a half, three years broadcasting.

We played every evening, but on weekends we'd play dances out in the country somewhere, in town; we always had somewhere to play. On Saturday evening we'd play at an ice cream parlor called Marshall's, out in the front. That's when I met Clyde Barrow and Bonnie. They drove up in a green '34 Ford. I had one just like it. He called me to the car and asked me, "Can you all play 'Sittin' on Top of the World'?"

I said, "Oh, sure," and he gave me twenty-five silver dollars, playing with them in his hand. He handed them to me. "Tell him to play it!" And my brother really blowed that harp because twenty-five dollars in them days was a lot of money. And he sat in the car, he and Miss Parker, and Barrow had on this big white hat, and she was bare-headed. Her hair was cut real short, dark like yours. Finally, she put her hat on, and he begged for me to come back to the car again. He gave me twenty dollars and said, "Wait a minute." I looked around at him, he said, "You know who I am?" I said, "No, sir." I just thought he was just an ordinary cowboy because where we was playin' they showed nothing but western pictures there. I said, "No, I don't." He said, "My name is Clyde Barrow and this is Bonnie Parker." I thought she was another man the way she had her hair cut, and she had a machine gun laying across her lap. They both had on two pistols. He said to me, "Where's the police around here?" I said, "I don't know." Finally, he gave us twenty more dollars and took off and went due south, and brother, he left there in a hurry, too. And about twenty minutes later, the police came around, looking at my car and saying, "Did you see a car like that?" I said, "Yeah, he just went over the hill," and they took off. They didn't want to see them.

I learned [to play guitar] by watching. When I was in Temple, I came into contact with a lot of western music, which I used to play a lot. Such as Bob Wills, Milton Brown, which was a great favorite of mine. The Brownies. Jay Maynard, Bill Monroe, Joe and Bill Callahan,

A. C. ROBINSON (BROTHER OF L. C. ROBINSON), 1976.
PHOTOGRAPH BY PAUL KOHL, COURTESY TOM MAZZOLINI.

The Sunshine Boys. I knew all of them boys. I picked up the steel mostly from seeing Leon McAuliffe. He was with Bob Wills. I learned lots from him. He played my style. He was a good steel man.

And I liked Bob's style of playing the violin. He was a good blues violin player in his way. He had another lead violin with him. I don't know what became of him. His name was Louie Turner. He was the best in the business on the violin. But for blues I would take Milton Brown. He got killed in a car wreck. I liked the set-up he had, you know, and he had a terrific piano player they called Papa Calhoun, and I loved the way they played. My brother and I, we used to play a lot of western music, and I didn't change until I got to California. And for a long time I played western music on Howard Street here in San Francisco.

[In] 1940, I come here. My brother was already here [in California]. He sent for me to come out here. I hitchhiked into Abilene around 1935, and the only thing I had was a fiddle. I worked there in a cleaners until I bought me a guitar. I left there and come here in 1940 and stayed in San Francisco for twenty-some years. I finally organized me a band here called The Three Hot Brown Boys, and then I changed the name to The Combo Boys, and so now I've changed the name to The California Blues Band.

CLARENCE EDWARD "SONNY RHODES" SMITH

November 3, 1940– ; interview, 1984

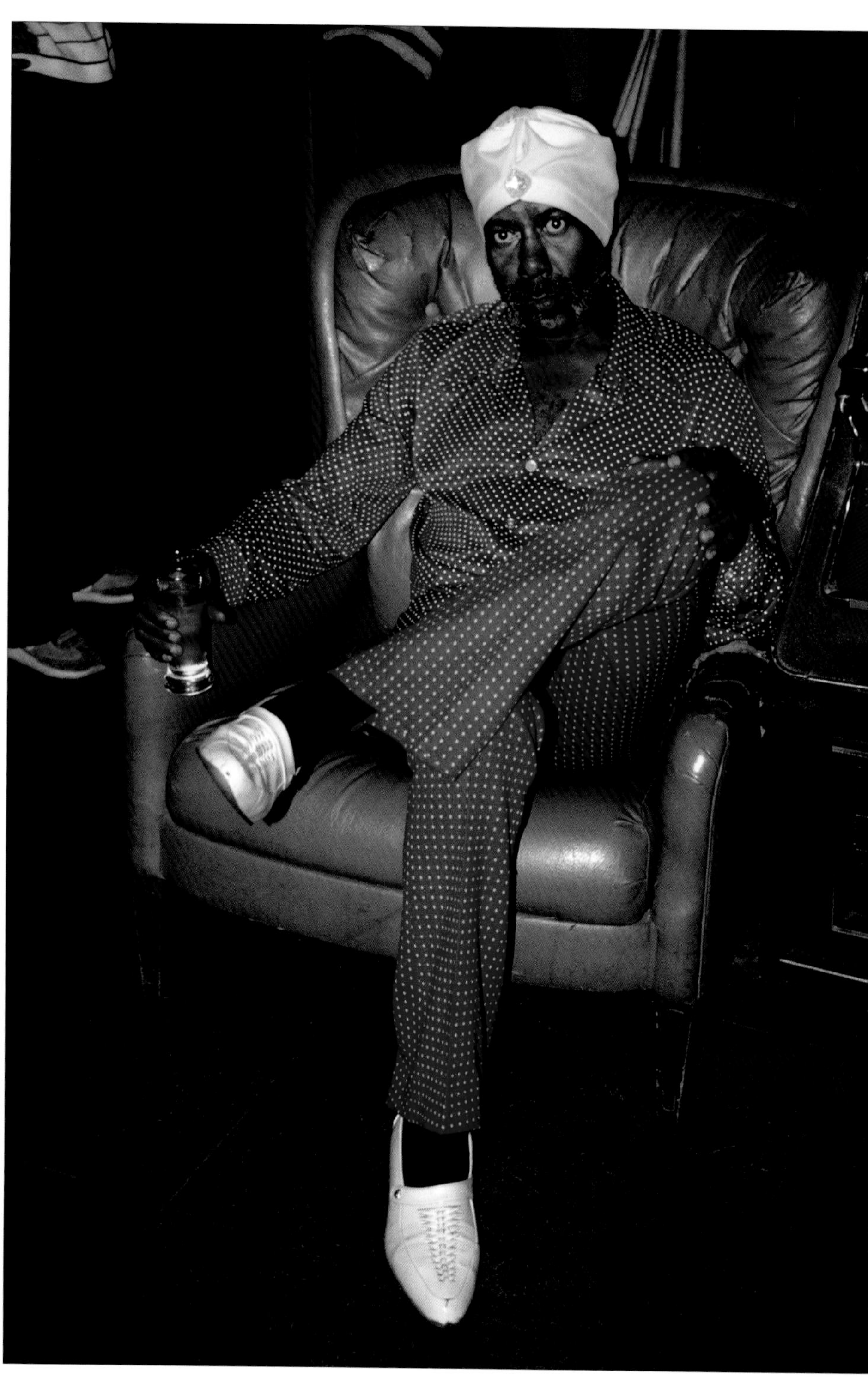

SONNY RHODES AT ELI'S MILE HIGH CLUB, OAKLAND, 1984. PHOTOGRAPH BY ALAN GOVENAR.

On an evening in 1984, ladies' night at Eli's Mile High Club in Oakland starts up slowly. There is a small sign at the door that says "Wednesday Night, Ladies Free," but the ladies don't show up until after 9:30 P.M. The audience is a mix of blacks and whites. By 10:00 P.M., Sonny Rhodes and The Texas Twisters take the stage. Sonny Rhodes wears his trademark turban, wrapped tightly around his head and pinned by a large costume gem. He sits in front of the band, his cherry red lap steel guitar stretched across his thighs, and above the twanging sounds, he wails, "I loved a woman, but she got cancer from smoking cigarettes. I tried to discourage her, but she never heard a word I said. She woke up coughin.' She thought she had a cold, but after years of smokin' cigarettes, her lungs were about to fold."

The crowd is sparse, but the enthusiasm grows with the intensity of the music. On any given night, the stars of San Francisco Bay area blues can be found at Eli's in the audience or performing on stage—Frankie Lee, Buddy Ace, Maxine Howard. There is an earnestness in the voice of Sonny Rhodes when he says, "The blues have haunted me. The blues have comforted me. It makes me feel good. The blues is just like a religion. It's something you can take out and preach to someone. Just like a preacher prepares for his Sunday sermon, I prepare for my nightly sermon that I have to go out and play for the people who come in."

I'm Clarence Edward Smith, also known as Sonny Rhodes, the disciple of the blues, guitar player, singer, songwriter from Smithville, Texas, born in 1940. I've been living in California since 1963. I've been playing since I been out here. 'Course I haven't that many jobs, but in the back of my mind, playing the blues is my first priority that I went out and went for.

DANCER AT ELI'S MILE HIGH CLUB, OAKLAND, 1984.
PHOTOGRAPH BY ALAN GOVENAR.

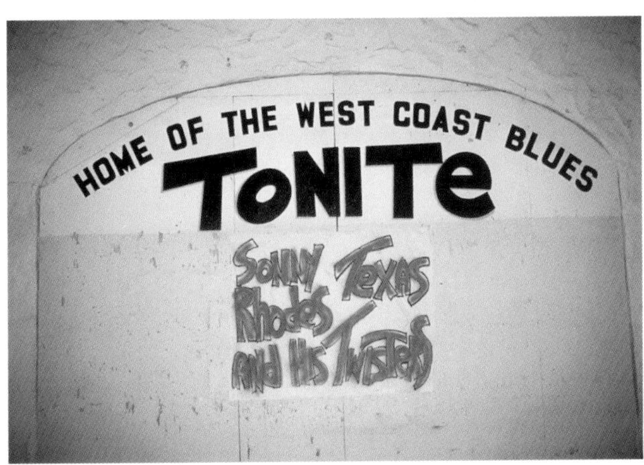

ELI'S MILE HIGH CLUB, OAKLAND, 1984.
PHOTOGRAPH BY ALAN GOVENAR.

I play a 1954 Music Master. It is probably one of the best guitars. I have three. A Gibson ES325, a rare one. I also have a thirty-year-old Hawaiian steel guitar that was made, of all places, in Japan.

In Texas there was this guy that played with Jimmy Heap and The Melody Masters, he had a slide guitar. He was probably a little [more] modern than mine. The instrument sounded so beautiful. I didn't know who I could take that instrument to and ask them to show me how to play it. Living in racist Texas, you couldn't go up and ask no white how to play nothing. You asked yourself. So I just concentrated on playing the guitar and bass, and when I got to California, there was a man I met [several] years ago. His name was L. C. "Good Rockin'" Robinson. He was an old Texan, and he was playing the Hawaiian lap steel. And I played with him and was able to observe what he was doing.

I finally got myself a Hawaiian lap steel about eleven years ago, and I've been playing ever since. It has become standard procedure with the Sonny Rhodes performance to see the electric guitar and the Hawaiian lap steel.

L. C. Robinson, when he was living in Texas, before he moved to California, he was playing the lap steel. He was from East Texas. Also, there was an old man in Houston. They called him Hop Wilson. He was a nice slide player. He just died in 1980. When we were down in Houston, he played quite a bit of slide. I guess, along with myself and Freddy Roulette, we are the only slide players that play the blues here in California. I'm probably playing the most blues on the slide guitar. I adapted the Elmore James style, and I adapted the way of individually picking the strings. Mine is tuned to an open E chord, striking it from the E first to the E sixth when you got a complete chord. I use a Stevens bar, which I grab and use to make and change my chords, and take out and play a solo I want to play while I'm singing.

It wasn't until I came to Austin, from Smithville, as a youngster, that I really got to listen and understand the blues. Only the fortunate ones had radios, and enough money to put in the nickelodeons to listen to the blues. At this point in the late 1940s and early 1950s I wasn't able to go out to the nightclubs, I was too young. Only thing I could do was partially hear something from behind the tin walls of the beer joints and beer halls.

In Austin, the woman who raised me—my mom and dad died at an early age—this lady had a machine, they called it a Victrola. It was a record player, but it was before electricity. It was something that you wound up and you put the record on and you had this horn and it would play. So, when my mom had company, I was the one who would sit near the Victrola; my job was to keep the Victrola from winding down. It kept the party happy, kept everything live, and I got to listen to a lot of records by T-Bone Walker, Blind Lemon Jefferson, Memphis Minnie, Bessie Smith, a whole bunch of people I listened to. And finally I got to the point, by playing

SONNY RHODES AT ELI'S MILE HIGH CLUB, OAKLAND, 1984. PHOTOGRAPH BY PAT MONACO.

SONNY RHODES AND LITTLE FRANKIE LEE, OAKLAND, 1983. PHOTOGRAPH BY PAT MONACO.

all these records, that I could duplicate the sounds that I heard. That put me into a vast identification with the blues. Everything else I heard didn't move me like the blues did.

I continued to sing and play this way until I got good at it, and I said, "This is what I'm going to do. I'm going to be a guitar player or blues singer." I went out and tried very hard to do that. I can look over my life and see some of the things I did right and some that I did wrong. If I were to do it all over again, I don't see one thing I would change because it's given me the momentum of the blues. Sometimes you have to work at things a little harder, if you don't have things to begin with. I'm still working at it, and I'll continue to work at it.

When I first started out, the critics compared my singing to T-Bone Walker, Junior Parker, and Percy Mayfield, but as the blues evolved in me, I became my own style, what is truly me. I came to California because I thought there were better opportunities for black bluesmen. I had a hard time in Austin. The biggest outlet for blues in Texas was the Houston-based Duke records. They always had such an abundance of artists that I found it difficult at the time to try to crack that barrier. So I had to change environments and get into a new place, and continue to keep my cultural province within me. I had to get out where somebody else could hear me. So I came to California, and I guess I kicked it around for about a year and a half before I was able to get my first 45 out on a label that was a subsidiary of Fantasy at the time. I put a record out called "Forever and a Day." From that record, it got into the audition hands of the people of Fantasy/Galaxy in San Francisco. They sent out contracts for me to do another recording for the Galaxy people. That was in 1965. I did another recording, but economically it wasn't feasible. I look back at it as an experience. I was just a young blues artist. I figure whatever was took from me, I could regain it, if I had enough longevity to hack it.

There were several Texas bluesmen in California: Johnny "Guitar" Watson, Lowell Fulson, Philip Walker, who was originally from Louisiana but was raised in Texas. I'd say there were probably at least thirty or forty blues musicians from Texas out here. My drummer, trumpet player, and my bass player are from Texas. I have one guitar player from London, but I tell everyone he's from London, Texas.

For me, T-Bone Walker was the ultimate, as far as guitar playing was concerned. He could make the strings say exactly what he just got through singing in lyrics. I found that he was able to answer himself. That's a characteristic of just about all Texas guitar players. Whatever they said lyrically, they could come back and say it instrumentally. It might not be in the same tone, but you can find a direct link to what they just got through singing.

The style of Texas blues depends on the region and culture from which the musicians came. You take an Otis Rush up against a T-Bone Walker. They're both excellent guitar players, but it wouldn't sound the same. There is a distinct characterization of Texas guitar, having the ability to repeat the lyric with your fingers on the guitar.

Blues is truth. Blues is about something that actually happened, in other words, being able to see why things exist, being able to look at someone and turn your head away and say, why not. The blues is a state of mind that is brought about by an unfortunate situation that could arise from self-pity or shame, or heartache.

My audience in California is mainly the young, intellectual, hippie white kids that come out and like to hear it because they can understand it. We have people come in that are black who are over thirty-five. I find them very receptive to what we're doing. Younger blacks tend to be more into the commercial music, but I think that in time, as this so-called fad music dissipates, people will come back to the music of truth and start all over again.

Both blues and the spiritual have soul. One calls on the good Lord to help them find a way, and they do this with abundance, and the black blues music don't always call on the Lord. They will tell you about the situation and speak optimistically that it will get better. For me, the blues is a religion. It makes feel good. It makes me happy to sing blues and look up at an audience that is responsive. If it's enlightening you, then it's enlightening them, too. I feel like a preacher. Any time you take a message to someone. That's the primary goal. My audience is my congregation. My guitar is my pulpit, and my heart and my mind are my vows. Somewhere in the Bible, it says praise Him with singing, dancing, and instruments. So I look at all of that. The blues and the spiritual has the ability to penetrate the mind and the heart, because the person who wrote it has had the experience. When I sing, I think I talk. There's a message in the music and in your voice.

LITTLE FRANKIE LEE

1941– ; interview, 1984

LITTLE FRANKIE LEE, HOUSTON, 1960S. PHOTOGRAPH BY BENNY JOSEPH.

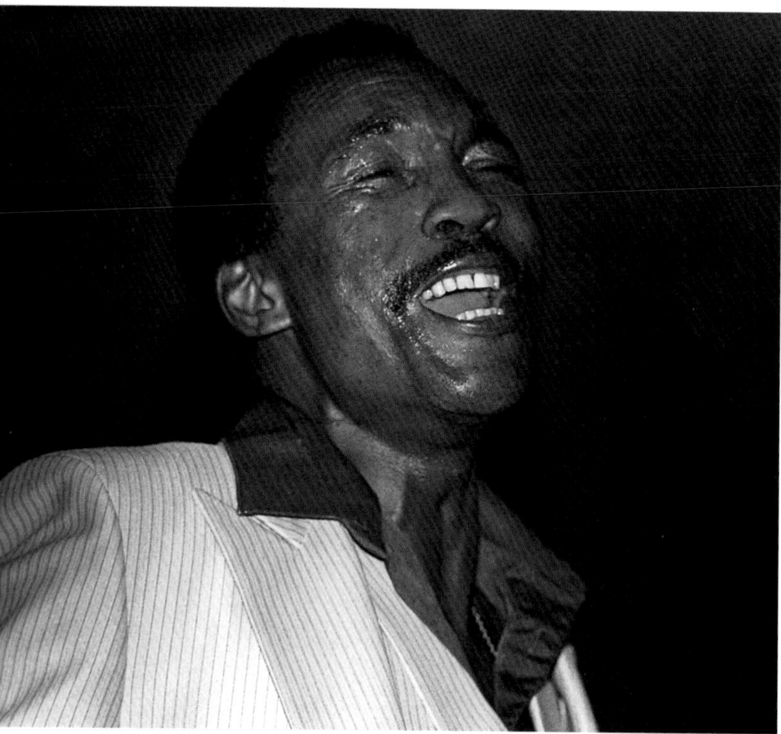

LITTLE FRANKIE LEE, OAKLAND, 1982. PHOTOGRAPH BY PAT MONACO.

My full name by birth is Frankie Lee Jones. I also go by the name of Little Frankie Lee, my stage name. I was born in Mart, Texas, eighteen miles east of Waco, Texas, and I'm forty-three years of age, raised up in St. Mary's Baptist Church, and graduated from Anderson High School.

I've been in California since 1968, the Oakland Bay area since 1973. The whole while I've been out here, I've been in the music field, blues, what we call soul-gospel blues.

I sung gospel for a while back in Texas, at home. After I did my first recording on the Duke/Peacock label in 1963, then I stopped singing gospel and started doing R&B, and I've been doing it ever since. I have a new LP on the Hightone label, premiering it at the Monterey Jazz Festival, and hopefully, we'll take off from there.

I don't know how I got started singing blues. I was singing gospel in the church, and one day I found myself singing blues. I always loved blues, but I wasn't allowed to sing blues in my home because in the church, as I was raised up, the blues was devil music. During that time blues was down music, and if you grew up in the church, the only time a person would let the pressure release of blues come out was when they were drunk, and all the people in the church could hear down the street was B. B. King, Jimmy Reed, Howling Wolf, or Muddy Waters, every record they were playing. After I found out years later that blues was an upper for me, my attitude changed.

I don't play an instrument. I was more influenced by singers, Reverend C. L. Franklin, Sam Cooke, Little Willie John, Bobby Bland, Ted Taylor. I'm not a writer, so, I have to depend on others. I have Miles Grayson, Jimmie Lewis, and Dennis Walker. I don't know if they're from Texas, but they have the Texas influence. They wrote songs for Ray Charles, Z. Z. Hill, Little Johnny Taylor.

There were so many different blues artists we had to listen to in the late 1940s and 1950s. I dug all of it, country western, gospel. I just found myself singing blues. In 1963 I made my first record, as I said, on the Duke/Peacock label, "Full-Time Love," which was the answer to Little Johnny Taylor's "Part-Time Love." And the song took off, and I got deep into it. Then we had a follow-up, "Taxi Blues," on the same label. I was around all the people I admired, the people I wanted to be with and see perform. I was in the middle of them. It was like a dream come true. There were Big Mama Thornton, Johnny Ace, Bobby Bland, Ted Taylor, Al Braggs, Gatemouth Brown, Little Junior Parker, O.V. Wright, James Davis, Joe Hinton. At the time I came along, Peacock was the gospel label and Duke was R&B. There were only two blues acts on Peacock, Al Braggs and myself, and then they started branching out with Songbird, Backbeat, and Sureshot labels.

I left Texas in 1965 with Albert Collins, and we stayed on the road touring for five or six years. I made one other record on the Peacock label, which was "Hello, Mr. Blues," because by this time the relationship between Frankie Lee and Duke/Peacock had kind of turned sour. Mr. Robey had no plans of renewing my contract by releasing another record. Just before Mr. Robey died, they sold everything to ABC, and then MCA bought it from ABC. So I kind of drifted around for a while. Then, in 1974 or '75, my cousin Johnny Guitar Watson and I were company-shopping, and I landed a contract with Elko records. Johnny Watson produced the session for me, and we did a few things together. Now, I'm on the Hightone label.

I love the blues. It lifts me up. When I have the blues,

and I have the blues every day, I can talk about it or I can sing and release this pressure, and I feel like a brand new person. Nowadays, people are starting to get more into blues. It used to be a few years ago, my kids wouldn't listen to blues. It was all about disco, rock, or whatever, but now it's blues. This makes me know that the younger generation is getting more into blues than they have been. They're beginning to feel that the blues can lift them up, rather than keep them down.

Blues and gospel have so much in common. If you were to listen to a gospel record and just take the lyrics away, you might have a blues instrumental. The main difference is the change in the lyrics. They both come up together, and they both send a message. The blues is a way of talking about problems, just like gospel. The blues is a religion. Once you have been spiritualized, you feel better. When the blues is delivered from the stage, you've touched someone out there because you're talking about everyday life. By the end of the evening, if someone tells you that they understand, that they've relieved that pressure, then you've accomplished what you set out to do.

Every day that you wake up, you have the blues for some reason or another. It's all the time that you have marital problems, but you have got to wake up and go to work. So you put yourself in the frame of mind that this is what you got to deal with today. This is reality, and blues is reality. It's something you got to tackle. It's life and success.

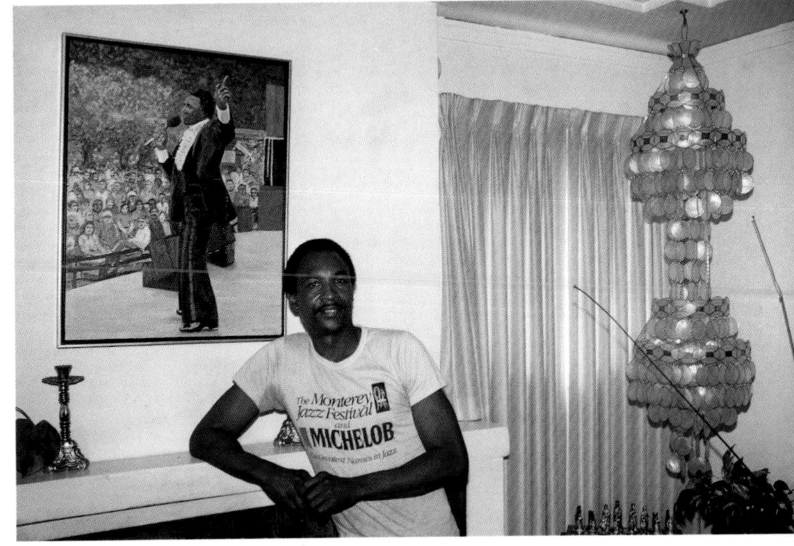

LITTLE FRANKIE LEE AT HOME, OAKLAND, CALIFORNIA, 1984. PHOTOGRAPH BY ALAN GOVENAR.

ELI'S MILE HIGH CLUB, OAKLAND, 1982. PHOTOGRAPH BY PAT MONACO.

KATIE WEBSTER

January 11, 1936–September 9, 1999; interview, 1987

KATIE WEBSTER, NEW ORLEANS JAZZ AND HERITAGE FESTIVAL, 1984. PHOTOGRAPH BY MICHAEL P. SMITH.

I'm from a state where they have many great musicians, Texas. I mix it. I have a little bit of everything in my style. I don't just do blues. I do country and western, gospel. My dad was a minister and my mother was a missionary and a classically trained pianist. We had a piano, but my mother said we couldn't play any blues, R&B, or jazz on that piano. It was gospel in the mornin,' gospel in the evenin,' gospel at supper time.

My father was from Chicago. When he was a little boy, he heard sidewalk musicians and hung around the clubs. I'm excited to come to Chicago to be near where he played in the speakeasies when his father would go out and gamble and stuff. And my grandmother would send my dad with my grandfather to keep him from doing wrong. My father was maybe ten, eleven, twelve years old and playing the blues in these places. They would get dimes and nickels in this little cup, like a spittoon or something for him. He played ragtime piano. Later he went into the ministry. That was one reason I really wanted to come here [to Chicago], because my father was raised in this area.

Amos Milburn and Little Willie Littlefield were friends of my family. Most of the guys I knew were guitar players. Like Juke Boy Bonner, I played a lot on his records. I created my own style. The only person I ever copied in my life was my father. I copied his left hand. He had a very dominant left hand on the piano. If I could play heavy like my father with my left hand, then I could always improvise with my right hand. So I kind of created my own style.

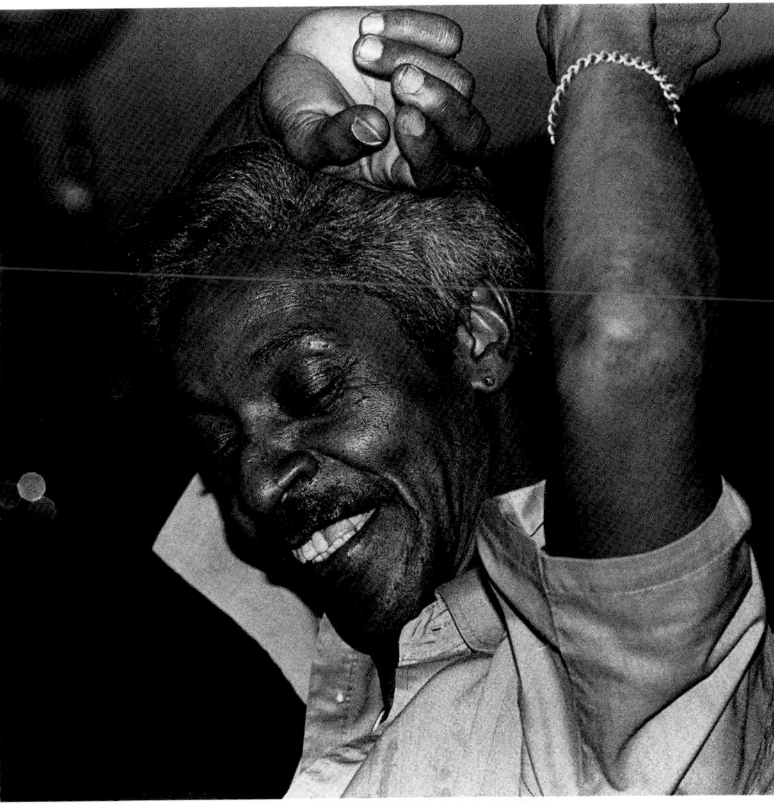

ELI'S MILE HIGH CLUB, OAKLAND, 1982. PHOTOGRAPH BY PAT MONACO.

ESTHER PHILLIPS, LONDON, CA. 1980. PHOTOGRAPH BY VAL WILMER.

I loved Dinah Washington, Ella Fitzgerald, Sarah Vaughan. I heard Sippie Wallace and Helen Humes sing, but the piano players that were really my favorites—Hazel Scott, Dorothy Donegan—I liked their styles, but I put what I felt with what I heard from my father and came up with my own style.

At age fifteen I knew seven hundred and fifty songs. Now I know over three thousand. I'm forty-seven. I haven't changed my style, but my repertoire is broader. I did more ballads when I was younger because I was just getting into the field. I was into the soul music scene more. I toured with Sam and Dave, and Otis Redding and James Brown. So I was more into the soul thing than the blues. I always loved them blues. In the late 1950s I played with Ashton Savoy and Lazy Lester at Goldband records. Then I recorded with Juke Boy Bonner and other people, and slowly I got 'way from blues, but in the last twelve years I've gotten back into it.

There's a demand for the blues because so many blues artists have passed away. The younger people don't want

KATIE WEBSTER, MONTREUX INTERNATIONAL JAZZ FESTIVAL, 1987. PHOTOGRAPH BY EDOUARD CURCHOD.

to be classified as blues artists, or even affiliated with the blues. They just want to be known as rock singers. I'm just classified as a versatile artist because I do everything. Pop, R&B, soul, gospel, country and western. I love country and western because it's closely related in theory to the blues.

I live in Oakland, California, now. But I'm in Europe nine months a year, touring. I'm going to Japan in July. I'm going to Montreux in Switzerland, Antibes in France. In Europe, they know if they don't get there at a particular time, they won't get another chance. They really love the music in Europe. And they know more about you than you know yourself. The day you were born, your grandparents' names, how many records you've played on. I don't know some of this, you know! Storms don't keep them away. They sit out with their umbrellas. They really appreciate the music. They're so happy that you're there!

I play for my audience, for their feelings. As long as they're enjoying themselves, time doesn't bother me. You know, like some people watch their watches to see how long they've been on stage. I could never do this. My manager has to wave a flag, say, hey, it's time to come off, and I ignore him and keep playing. Once I'm into it, I'm into it.

KATIE WEBSTER, CHICAGO BLUES FESTIVAL, 1987. PHOTOGRAPH BY ALAN GOVENAR.

SAN ANTONIO, CORPUS CHRISTI, & THE RIO GRANDE VALLEY

DOOLEY JORDAN BAND WITH BLUES SINGER CLAYTIE POLK (FAR LEFT), SAN ANTONIO, 1930S. COURTESY MARIELLEN SHEPPHARD.

BEER

INTRODUCTION

(OPPOSITE) DOUG SAHM, LOS ANGELES, CA. 1973.
PHOTOGRAPH BY ERIC WEHNER.

Since the 1970s, the music of the Texas-Mexico border region has attracted both critical and popular acclaim. This music, which is usually called Tex-Mex, Chicano, or Tejano, is unique in that it brings together Mexican norteño music and American country and western, blues, rhythm and blues, and rock 'n' roll. The increasing popularity of this music is due in part to the recent upsurge in ethnic pride among Mexican Americans, but it also builds on a long musical history. Adrian Trevino, a classically trained musician from Corpus Christi who performed with Sunny and The Sunliners in the 1960s, says that there were isolated Mexican American groups playing blues and jazz as early at the 1930s. Knocky Parker, a piano player with The Light Crust Doughboys, described western swing as a mixture of "Mexican mariachi music from the south with jazz and country strains coming in from the east."

While San Antonio was not known as a center of African American music, many blues players, including Robert Johnson (1936) recorded there. In the 1930s, The Dooley Jordan Band featured blues singers Cora Estell Woods and Claytie Polk, and in the 1940s and 1950s, T-Bone Walker often performed in the city. New Orleans–born trumpet player Don Albert (Don Albert Dominique) moved to San Antonio in the late 1930s to work as a civil service employee, and later became a local promoter for traveling bands. In the early 1940s he opened his own club named Don's Keyhole in San Antonio and began booking national jazz acts. During this period, interest in blues and jazz grew significantly among Mexican Americans in San Antonio and the Rio Grande Valley. Sunny and The Sunglows (formerly The Sunliners), Vincent Cantu and The Rockin' Dominoes, The Chili Peppers, and Charlie and The Jives were among the most popular Tex-Mex groups of the day.

In the late 1940s Arnaldo Ramirez established Falcon Records in McAllen and introduced Alegres de Teran and Freddy Fender. The success of Falcon Records sparked the formation of other small Texas independent labels; Corona in San Antonio; Ideal and Norco in San Benito; Duncan and Talent Scout in Harlingen; El Pato and Bego in McAllen. In Dallas, Johnny Gonzalez started Elzarape Music and promoted Little Joe (Hernandez) and His Latinaires.

During this period, musicians of Mexican ancestry integrated traditional music with music that was not specifically Mexican. Vikki Carr and Freddy Fender

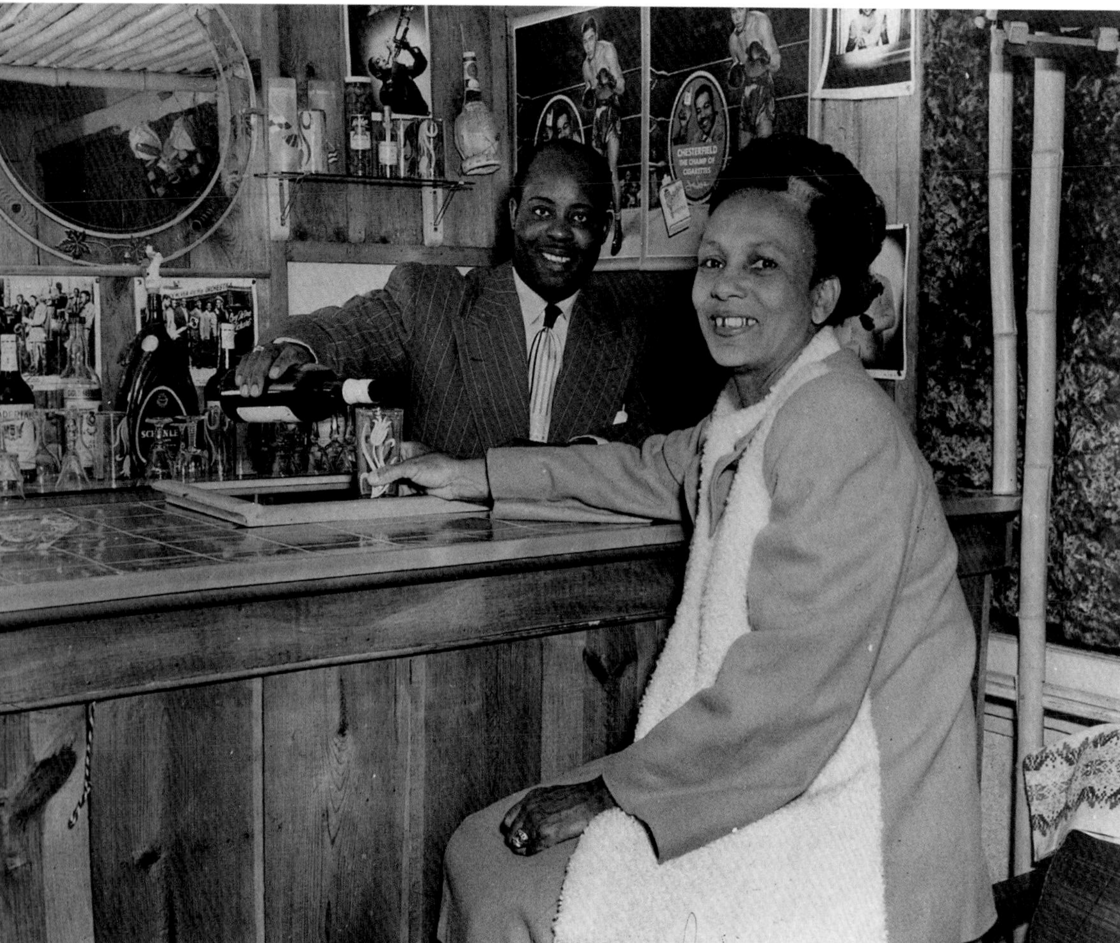

CLAYTIE POLK, ZEBRA ROOM, TUCSON, ARIZONA, CA. 1948. PHOTOGRAPH COURTESY MARI-ELLEN SHEPPHARD.

dropped their family names so as not to be stereotyped as "Mexican" in the U.S. market. Vikki Carr sang pop ballads, while Freddy Fender recorded blues, country, rhythm and blues, and rock.

Freddy Fender's real name is Baldemar Huerta; "Fender" comes from the electric guitar he played. He was born in 1936 in San Benito, the birthplace of the legendary accordionist Narciso Martinez. The musical interests Fender formed during his teenage years were, however, influenced more by popular radio than by norteño and Tex-Mex music. He listened to the Nashville stations and followed the country singers and steel guitar players. In the field camps of black farmworkers, he heard records by Muddy Waters, Elmore James, and T-Bone Walker, and then later, while in the Marines, he

CORA ESTELL WOODS, SAN ANTONIO BLUES SINGER, 1940S. PHOTOGRAPH BY MARTIN PEARL, COURTESY MARIELLEN SHEPPHARD.

learned about the music of Elvis Presley and the rhythm and blues of Fats Domino and Bobby "Blue" Bland.

The hard-won success of Freddy Fender exemplifies the aspirations and the struggles of many Mexican Americans of his generation. For more than fifteen years, he searched for the right sound and recorded for numerous small Texas labels and for national labels such as Imperial and Argo, a subsidiary of Chess. With his rhythm and blues–styled song "Wasted Days and Wasted Nights," Freddy Fender gained some national attention in 1959, but in 1960 he was arrested in Louisiana and convicted of marijuana possession. He spent two years in Angola prison. When he was released, he worked five days each week as a farmworker and performed only on weekends. It was not until 1974, when he met Houston producer Huey Meaux, that Fender's musical career began to take shape. In 1975 Meaux persuaded Fender to release the song "Before the Next Teardrop Falls," which quickly became an enormous success on both the pop and country charts and established Freddy Fender as a singer of national stature.

Huey Meaux worked as a producer and promoter for more than two decades and has recorded a varied group of Texas and Louisiana musicians on his own labels (currently Starflite and Crazy Cajun). In addition to his success with Freddy Fender, Meaux has been instrumental in helping Doug Sahm and other Texas musicians achieve national prominence.

Doug Sahm grew up in San Antonio, where he absorbed many of the same musical influences as Freddy Fender in San Benito. As a teenager, Sahm put together the first white rhythm and blues band in San Antonio and featured west side tenor man Eracleo "Rocky" Morales. Sahm recorded for small San Antonio labels (Harlem and Renner) from 1958 to 1964, when he signed with Huey Meaux's Tribe label. Meaux transformed the image of Doug Sahm and promoted him nationally as part of a British-style group called The Sir Douglas Quintet.

In the 1970s Doug Sahm returned to Texas from California and resumed playing a Mexican-influenced sound, working with South Texas musicians, such as keyboard player Augie Meyers, drummer John Perez, sax man Rocky Morales, and accordionist Flaco Jimenez. The blending of musical influences in Sahm's performance style reflects the cultural diversity of Texas and the important interplay of Mexican music with country, rock, and rhythm and blues. Contemporary Mexican American music combines these influences to create a distinctive sound that in the 1980s was popularized by Esteban "Steve" Jordan and Los Lobos, and has gained an international audience.

BONGO JOE (B. NOVEMBER 28, 1923, HAYNES, FLORIDA; D. SAN ANTONIO, DECEMBER 19, 1999), SAN ANTONIO STREET MUSICIAN, POET, AND DRUMMER. NEW ORLEANS JAZZ AND HERITAGE FESTIVAL, 1978. PHOTOGRAPH BY MICHAEL P. SMITH.

MARIELLEN SHEPPHARD

interview, 1984

Well, I'll tell it like it is. I was sneaking off on maid's night out [in San Antonio]. So I was up there as close as I could get, and T-Bone comes out in his white suit with big diamond rings. He comes out there and strikes up his guitar, v-room, r-room. Oh, Mister T-Bone! He couldn't even get through the first song before the purses started flyin' with everyone goin', "Play my song, Mister T-Bone!" Then they started goin', "Take all my money!" and he was so cool, but then after he got hot, he put that guitar behind his head. Then he'd really start to pluckin.' He'd turn around and swing. And then everything went: shoes, rings, bracelets, everything. Honey, he'd play them blues all night long. But sometimes the men got mad at the girls for throwing their money and purses or whatever else they could get on stage. T-Bone would back out and start playin' again, and they threw anything they could get loose.

ILDEFONSO "SUNNY" OZUNA

September 8, 1943– ; interview, 2003

SUNNY OZUNA, AUGUSTIN RAMIREZ, CARLOS GUZMAN, AND FREDDIE MARTINEZ, CA. 2001. COURTESY FREDDIE RECORDS.

I believe my dad passed on at the age of fifty-seven. My real dad, who I never got to meet. His name was Jose Frank, Joe Frank, Ozuna. I never got to meet him. I think they did separate, and when my mom came to the United States, her mom was a U.S. citizen somehow, or got them over there somehow. And then of course she met my stepdad, who rose me up.

I was kind of like too small to realize what was going on, but I can imagine that it must have been hard for them, with that many kids, getting them through school and dressing them and all that. You know how that is.

My mom's name is Isabelle Rodriguez. My stepdad's name is John—Juan, actually, Spanish—but Juan Rodriguez. My mom and my dad both had the family of the times, which was ten, eleven kids, so they both had two jobs. My dad worked at a hospital from 5:30 in the morning to around 5:30 in the afternoon. At 6:00 P.M., he'd go in, work for a restaurant at night. He'd come home, say, 11:00, 12:00 at night and do it again the next day. So he did two jobs. And so did my mom, because families were pretty big back then. And of course, you know, to support all those kids and get them through school and all that, you can imagine.

My mom was from Mexico, but my dad was not. My dad was a U.S. citizen. I take that back; my parents were both from over there, but when I came into the picture, my stepfather was the one that actually rose me up. He actually took on the responsibility of all the kids already made.

My folks didn't encourage me much to do what I wanted, when I wanted to do it, because the education and the schooling and all that was more important to them, as Mexican Americans. I went to a school called Burbank High School here in San Antonio. My grade school was Charles Graebner.

I thought I was a good student, but kind of noisy because I was writing a lot of songs, banging on the desk and stuff. I spent a lot of time in the office. But it was just not really on purpose; I think it was just something trying to get out, even back then, I think, and they kind of tolerated me until they couldn't anymore, and then I'd wind up in the office. And I went through the same changes in high school.

I didn't really play music when I was a kid. I did a lot of yelling in the shower that people had to put up with, like I said, coming from a large family. I must have started singing around fourteen, fifteen. What's really interesting is that my mom had this one radio program that she would not miss, religiously, a musical-oriented program that came on at eleven o'clock on the radio. And she would listen to that program—I mean, the day would not be complete [otherwise]. It was just music. I have no idea. I've never asked. But I just got this from her, and she said that when I was born, it was exactly at eleven o'clock. I would think it was on Spanish radio. I would think so. But I really didn't pursue it that much more, other than the story just kind of stayed with me.

Actually, I was about eighteen when I first started playing music. Around nineteen is when things really started to happen, because that was right around my graduation year. We had been kind of playing with wanting to do this for years before, because we got to the point of the school hops and doing the different little school talent shows and things like that.

In the late Fifties is when we started playing. We were just basically playing high school—they used to be called sock hops—at the school. After school was over, they'd have like a little dance in the gym. And the sock hop idea came in because you couldn't wear shoes inside the gym because they didn't want you to scratch up the floor. So, needless to say, it smelled very interesting. But that was the thing at the time. From there, we just started playing around the small little cities around here, and it kind of started taking shape. We didn't know that we would be on the beginning end of what would be known as Tejano music today because it didn't have a label. We didn't know what we were building, either. Since we started playing the rock 'n' roll of the day, we started applying Spanish words to a lot of the same licks that we were using for rock 'n' roll—not necessarily the up-tempo things, but the more slower, medium-beat songs—and started to develop something. Like I say, we didn't have a title for it. So it was kind of weird the first few years. But eventually, it got to a point where they called it Chicano music, for lack of another label. And so, then, of course, we wanted to record. I used to hang out at a little recreation park after school that a lot of the kids went to. It had tennis and all kinds of games and everything to keep us busy. And there was this one gentleman named Randy Garibay who used to come and pound on the piano. He kids me about it now, because I used to just stand there and watch him do this one song. I used to bug him for the same song every day I was there. "Hey, play this one; play this one!" And it happened to be the song "Talk to Me." It not only was a number-one hit in the nation for me; it took me to *American Bandstand*, Dick Clark's show, and did this whole thing off this one song. And, of course, that was the first song that I wanted to record, hopefully, someday, if I was to be able to do something. So we went to the recording studio. We recorded that song. That thing took off. By this time, I'm coming out of high school. In that same year, that thing just takes off bigger and bigger and bigger, and we start to actually branch out from the little cities around San Antonio, finding a place where we can perform and do this kind of music.

So through the years it's grown and grown and grown, whereas we kept recording and recording and recording. Forty-two years later, I have seventy-four different productions that we've done, from albums to CDs. As we speak, I'm recording four CDs at one time. I'm doing a country, a gospel, a Tejano, and an English oldies that just came out this week. I'm recording with Freddie Records out of Corpus Christi. And I'm going back and forth, during the week, back to Corpus, and working on these four projects and trying to get to my weekend jobs. So I'm more of a weekend warrior as far as the performances are concerned, but during the week for right now, all four projects are keeping me busy.

We originally started our first group as Sunny and The Sunglows. And we kept that for about four and a half years. When I graduated high school in '63, a major company was trying to pick me up as a solo artist, and I kept telling the guys, "You know, this is not what we planned on. We wanted to do something as a group." They didn't buy it, and so I decided, well, you know, I'd better go on and do something else, since they weren't buying the idea that I wanted to pursue as far as the group was concerned. So I went to Houston and picked up a group that was already shaping there, called The Rocking Vs, like the letter V, and I picked them up and named them the first Sunliner group. And from about that time, all this time, "Talk to Me" started to take off. And Huey Meaux is a record producer that has had a lot of luck picking up things like Freddy Fender's "Wasted Days and Wasted Nights," "Raindrops Keep Falling on My Head," "Rock the Boat," the Hughes Corporation. He had a lot of local Texas artists that had taken off at one time or another, and he helped to get their songs to a number-one spot. So Huey got ahold of us, and of course he was interested in "Talk to Me." He ran with "Talk to Me," and he was actually the one that got us the *American Bandstand* and the whole thing when it got to that level. "Talk to Me" started to become a hit in '63. I'd say from about '63 on. Right around '63, February '63. And when we did the *American Bandstand*, it was about as high as it was going to go.

The only taste [of discrimination] I got was after I got on the road a little bit, there was still some left, that I didn't really notice myself. But we had an older guy who was playing drums that actually came up with the idea of getting it together and doing something, when we started going into the Tejano field of it. His name was Manuel Guerra. He's now a record producer here in San Antonio.

We basically started off as a little rock 'n' roll group. And when Manuel came up with the idea, he was playing for a much larger orchestra, kind of a Benny Goodman–type orchestra, already doing the Spanish lyrics and stuff like that, something that didn't even have a title, either. They didn't realize what they were doing. What we attempted to do when Tejano was born, we took basically his ideas of what they were doing with, say, fifteen, sixteen, seventeen people, and we were going to be doing that with five and six people.

I was a typical teenager then, so I was listening to Elvis and The Beatles and Fats Domino and whoever was coming along, down the pipeline of the Dick Clark show, never in my dreams thinking that I was going to be able to appear on that show.

You know, we didn't really think that much about [playing rhythm and blues], but we were, because of the time. We were just so into what was going on at the time that we didn't really realize what we were doing. Tejano music wound up being a mixture of four or five different things that, when you go to our performance, you get to experience a little bit of everything instead of going to see a group that's going to be doing rock all night long.

Well, when we first went into starting our very first groups, not knowingly, we were playing R&B because a lot of those songs, even though it wasn't that identified to us, we were just kind of falling into place. We realized that a lot of the rhythm and blues fit in with what people would classify in the state of Texas as oldies. So, being that we were actually coming through the line of oldies and not realizing that—to us, it was just, "Wow, did you hear this on the radio?"—before we knew it, we went

SUNNY AND THE SUNLINERS, *TALK TO ME*, TEAR DROP RECORDS LPM 2000.

and took that thing out and actually started performing it at our jobs that we were doing.

I didn't get that deep into blues, but a lot of the black artists that were coming along the pipeline, because of us being young kids, we were just kind of falling into—we had better results with a lot of the R&B that was being played hot on the radio or that was coming down the pipeline at the time, at our performances, so that's why we pursued that. Oh, your Manhattans, a lot of your doo-wop groups. We weren't as deep, for example, as the B. B. Kings and down in there. We were doing a lot of the black doo-wop groups that were coming along.

As a matter of fact, I got to work with a lot of them [Peacock recording artists] because of [the success of my song] "Talk to Me." To us, it was real exciting because they were some of the guys like Bobby Bland; "Don't Cry No More" was kind of a big thing for us. We used to play it. And to realize that one day we were going to be able to get the chance to perform at the same place where he was going to perform. And Junior Walker and a lot of these guys. When Huey Meaux got the Dick Clark thing for me, right after that, there were a lot of gigs that were coming along where a lot of these people were like in the packages they are now, where you have seven, eight, nine artists in one performance. You get hooked up into that, and then you take out that job, and you to meet a lot of these people and work with them.

I didn't really get to meet Bobby Bland that much, other than I was aware of his music. And I was excited because, you know, we eventually got with our band to where I think the biggest band that we've had ourselves was maybe around ten people. And so, being a young man at the time, we figured, wow, it'd be good to get there one time, and because of his "Don't Cry No More," of course, we wanted to see what he was going to do with a huge band. He had a pretty large band. So we got to see him perform and see what it would be nice to go to someday, which we actually got a chance to do that also.

At one time, I had a full horn section. We had four saxophones, two trumpets, a trombone, and then, of course, the rhythm section, which is another four people. The rhythm section was bass, guitar, drums, and keyboard.

Well, you know, I kind of came in through the door

about the time—not to talk less of anybody else, but I came in right around the time of Fats Domino and James Brown. So I don't do any of their music anymore. I used to when I was a lot younger. I don't do any of their stuff now, but I loved what they were both doing and the direction they were taking, and I kind of learned from what they were doing and tried to model some of their habits to build my business for the last forty-two years.

Even James Brown didn't have an orchestra that big when he first started. I mean, that didn't come till later, when he got terribly on fire. But Bobby "Blue" Bland, he started with that big orchestra. I mean, it was awesome, man. For us, it was something that we thought we would never be able to really afford and to actually record with a group that size and actually travel [with] that many people on the road. But our time with it was just a fun time.

I grew up on the South Side of San Antonio. And the people that I'm talking to you about are basically raised on the West Side. But since the South Side is also predominantly Hispanic, you know, they were into all their oldies. So you take your oldies from the South Side and the West Side. The East Side is our black side of town, and the northeast, where I live now, used to, back in the day, be all white. So your oldies and the radio station was more or less catering to your South Side and your West Side.

I listened to black music mostly because of the radio. Well, those stations don't exist here now. But as I was growing up, there was Joe Anthony, KMAC, that was strictly black, and we got a lot of our tunes out of there. Through the years, as we were growing up, we were staying on top of everything he had, and he stayed on top of the newest, newest things happening. Joe Anthony passed on, and the station has gone under for a number of years now.

I didn't get that much of a chance [ever to go see live black music] because my career was moving pretty fast. Like I said, when I saw that it was going to be hard for us to maintain the level of one "Talk to Me" after another—because we found that that industry was very, very competitive. And all of a sudden, I wake up one day and I'm in the same category with Elvis Presley and The Beatles and Fats Domino and all these guys that could come back and do one after another, one after another, one after another. And so, my door opened up to Tejano in such a big way that I never dropped my oldies. As a matter of fact, I was telling you that I just finished my new oldies CD, just out this week. It's called *Mostly Sunny, Going Back in Crime*. . . . And you'll hear a lot of black influences in there because, I mean, the song calls for that. For example, we just redid a song by James and Bobby Purefoy called "I'm Your Puppet." And we have it on there, too, and when you hear it, you say, "Wow!"

We realized that trying to stay in the white market was going to be pretty much of an impossibility for us unless we were lucky to pop more "Talk to Mes." "Talk to Me" made the mark of an oldie. There's a song called "Smile, and I'll Cry Later" that got that same mark. And one that's called "Put Me in Jail" that got the same mark. So the gigs that even now today that I go do, again with this eight, nine other artists, is because of those songs. And I basically come into those shows, do those three songs, and I'm done. It's not a whole-night performance. But, for example, the one that I was just on, they had Santana, they had Rosie and The Originals, they had The Escorts, The Duprees, The Moments, myself. And I really don't belong there because I'm not black, but because my tunes did so well, up and down the coast of California, the Pacific Concert Group that does all these shows just called me up and says, "Hey, man, we've got this; are you available?" . . . And I usually wind up working with—I mean, Rosie is kind of an exception, and so is Santana, but I can't say that it's always, always black, but there's a few that got through. Like the guy from The Champs is not black. The guys from "Land of a Thousand Dances" are not black. And a lot of these guys—we even went to do a concert one time at the Greek Theater, presented by Budweiser, where they had all Latin stars that had these hits, and I was blown away, because a lot of those people—I was surprised at the hit songs that I was listening to, thinking that they were actually black, because that's the way they sounded. And that's what actually got my "Talk to Me." I went through the first, oh, seven, eight years of my career, people thinking I was black because of the recording.

They actually thought I was black, and they didn't realize that I wasn't until I walked on. But by then, I was already booked, and I actually just did my end of the job, what I was supposed to do. And I got a lot of return jobs when they found out I wasn't—it was kind of a novelty because they actually expected a black artist to come on and do the tune.

When I started out, I was doing a small group trip. Having the big band was just kind of like some impossible dream. Everything we were going to get there, it was through Tejano doing as well as it did; that opened the door for us to be able to afford the big band and do the big ideas that come with it and the big recordings.

We had a station on the Hispanic end at the time I was coming up that was called the "Triple T Show." And it was young kids from school that were playing the up-to-date songs for us as kids. And so, with them on one side, and KMAC on the other, and us starting to already move around and play around as far as the performances, and then the *American Bandstand* thing came, and we realized as young kids that we had the time between "Talk to Me," "Smile Now, Cry Later," "Put Me in Jail," "Golly Gee," "The One That's Hurting Is You," and the list goes on and on. I never let that part of my life go.

Right now I've been writing country for a year. I have no interest in country. But as a writer, I have no choice. I was just kind of stacking some songs. Then this Freddie record company out of Corpus says, "Man, you know we've been wanting to do an oldies thing for a long time. Are you up for it?" And I said, "Yeah, sure, I'd love to go back in the studio and do something." And he just put up a $2.5 million facility there in Corpus. So I was anxious to see what his studio was like. It is totally incredible.... But then, as we started working—and we were basically concentrating on the English one at the time because that's all we had talked about—he said, "Oh, by the way, man, you know we've been doing little projects here and there on gospel. How would like to have a gospel CD? You wrote some songs for us for a gospel release. Why don't you just add a few more, and then we'll release your own. And what have you been doing with those country songs you told me you had?" And I said, "Well, let me show you. I brought my guitar. Look, let me just play a few." He says, "Look, you know what, man, you're just going to have to do all of it." So finish one, go to the next one. Finish one, go to the next one. Like that. And we'll finish up with the Tejano because it's going to take us a lot more work, and so I put the hardest one at the end. But all this time, the reason I never let the oldie thing go is because I still go quite a bit back and forth to the coast, West Coast, to do these shows. And as a matter of fact, we got one coming October 25 here in San Antonio, where we're going to have Eddie Holman, "Hey There, Lonely Girl"; Bobby Lewis, "I Couldn't Sleep at All Last Night"; Lew Christi, "Lightning Strikes." Rosie's coming in on this one, "Angel Baby."

Lord, I've written a ton of songs, man. I'll probably never get around to producing everything, but being that, like, a pile of them just are going right now on country, and then, some of the English things that you'll hear, I wrote some of those.

I write both in Spanish and in English. Being bilingual, we got that. We got that kind of covered there, which is really nice. I'd say I've written at least a couple of hundred songs, yeah.

You get an idea, and then you can't seem to let it go. It's so many different experiences, actually, because some come real quick, like it was waiting on you to wake up so it could just feed everything to you. And sometimes you'll pick them up as you're getting up in the morning. And then, you just kind of stick with it for two or three hours, and it's done. Some are done real quick. Some ideas—on one of my country songs, I heard someone say, "You give cheating a bad name." And wow! It stops you right there, and you say, "Wait a minute. Wait a minute. Something here." And then you take "You give cheating a bad name," and you kind of put it at the top of the page. And then you start letting your mind just wander: Where could you possibly go? For example, I got another one that I wrote on this one called "Who Was That?" This musician wakes up in the morning in a typical musician condition, which is really weird, because I got no business writing a song like that. I don't drink or smoke. But what happens, he gets up in the morning and he's got all these aches and all these things that he knows he sexually went through the night before. But he don't remember. He remembers there was a woman involved, and he remembers that he met this girl but doesn't remember her name or anything and is going through the song saying, "Man, who was that? This happened to me and left the traces and the signs behind of whatever happened to me. I don't know who that was, but I sure hope she hurries back." Because he doesn't remember where he picked her up, probably at the performance or something. And you let your mind wander. You just let your mind wander, and you start seeing—I call it painting a picture. I take a title, and then I let my mind wander a little bit, wherever it's going to take me, and then you start painting the picture without too much of one color or the other, and just kind of start painting the picture till the whole song is my idea of a picture. And it works!

I've written quite a few *corridos*, as a matter of fact. Tejano was going to be a blend of—when you got to the performance, and you were going to see a Tejano act, you were going to hear a little bit of country, a little bit of rock, a little bit of your *corridos*, a little bit of what we call an everyday love, boy-girl polka. And then in Tejano, you have your branches just like you do in country. You have your up-tempo numbers, you got your cry-on-my-shoulder type songs, and boy-love-girl situations, and there's a million places you can go in the country field. The Hispanic stuff is kind of like that, too. Of course, so's your rock. But for some reason, it just seems to be a little more predominant in what we do.

I have used an accordion from time to time because, see, when we were coming up in Tejano, oh my God, we tried every adaptation of instruments. After a while, we really lost it in just trying to come up and see—we opened a floodgate to what artists that are in Tejano now, which are probably around, maybe, I'd say four or five hundred artists, maybe, that are out there that are existing with what we originally built in the pioneer days of Tejano music

Tejano is a very current thing, because there are now twenty-four-hour Tejano radio stations across the country. And it was just something, that Tejano—I have no idea how they put that [word] together. Of course, some of it is because the beginning part of the word, I think it's maybe a split between Texas and Chicano or Texas and Mexicano or whatever, the "ano" on the end, the Tex because of the end. When I first began, they used to call it "Chicano music." Then it went to "Tex-Mex." "Who are these guys who are coming to Oklahoma or to New York or wherever?" And it's a Tex-Mex group. Oh, okay, well, they identify with what Tex-Mex was because that was the thing. So now, through the years, it has been changing until it seems like the last thing that it's going to possibly be is "Tejano" for that type of music.

You know, growing up, norteño music didn't really interest me that much because what we were doing was kind of a slice of our own, and being young kids, and we were dealing with a little more electronic instruments, it didn't really catch our ear. We classified it as music that was playing in what we call cantinas, which are your bars, your barrio bars, and little places that were supposed to be rinky-dink places. What we were trying to do, what we were building, even in our younger years, was to take it to a little higher class. We were going to get out of the bars and go into nightclubs and ballrooms.

We didn't listen from the point of being interested over it, but we did listen because of ideas that they were doing. They were like the school before us, and we needed direction. And were we listening as far as wanting to do it? No, but in getting ideas from them to create, to adapt to what we were doing, with our type of instruments, was what actually opened the door for Tejano, believe it or not. And now, when we stepped from there into the modern day, the accordion being for Tejano what the steel guitar became for country.

The electric guitar and all that stuff are still being used. When I get to the level of this Tejano thing that I'm going to put out, I go and I have all my things that I'm usually using on the road to do my performances. But I better add accordion here and there, on the different songs, even if it's just a taste, in certain places, or it's not going to get played on your Tejano stations.

It's kind of a tip of my hat acknowledging the tradition. Exactly. That's why I made the comparison with trying to put out a country song without a steel guitar and you're going to have a hell of a time getting it played. I mean, it can be done, I'm sure. But it goes there. It goes there. Whatever you want to do is fine; just don't leave out the steel guitar.

I was very influential with all of them [pachucos and the zoot suit era] because that's where your oldies, for San Antonio and for the state of Texas, that's where all your oldies come from. We have, not to offend anybody, but we got what we called "white boy oldies." And your black and Hispanic oldies are the same ones. . . . There's like white oldies, and like your Hispanic and your black were the doo-wop groups, and everything that came kind of off R&B, the way we were raised. So we touched all the poor side of town, all your 'chucs, which is usually where they're at, where they're living. And that actually got my career going locally. It got it going because we were catering to the radio station that first started working with, that really helped me a lot, was catering to that side of town and to that market. That is KEBA.

We have tried to do crossovers. I am not that crazy about doing it anymore, but it was nice because music made it possible—like, for example, Rene Rene had these bilingual hits called "Angelito" and "Mucho Que Te Quero." "Angelito" got him to *American Bandstand*. But it's strange, but being that he is bilingual, and he should have stayed over here with the South Siders and West Siders and that type of market, or more into the Tejano, here's this guy doing Dick Clark's *American Bandstand*, which was really strange. So, talk about crossing cultures and things like that. And mine, too. Like I said, they actually thought I was black, but once I got there and they found I was Hispanic, I mean, the thing just got great for me.

I'm not a good guitar player, but I play enough to be able to follow myself when I'm getting to this point of creating something or writing something, enough to follow myself and where I'm going and what I want to do with it. Then, when I get to the point of doing the musical arrangement or to get to the point of recording, I can guide the guys: "Okay, I hear this; I hear that." And then I let each one that knows what they're doing in their own instrument put things together for us until we paint this picture.

I've got an acoustical guitar, a Giovanni that I saw one time when I used to have money. I saw it on a TV program: Jose Feliciano was playing it on TV on the *Tonight* show, and I set out to get me one. And so it's an acoustic guitar that I use here. And then I have a little Fender Stratocaster that I mess with as far as electric. But only for myself. I don't perform with it or anything like that.

I've done it for forty-two years, and at this point in my life, I think I'm doing it out of habit and out of liking and loving what I do. It's really strange, because you can imagine how interesting it is for me if this coming weekend, for example, I've got four groups across the country now. Instead of dragging mine like I did at the beginning part of my life, this other way now, I use the one that's the closest to where I'm going to go. So, for example, I just did San Bernardino and all that. Well, I used the closest one that I have to that particular job. But the exciting part is that I'm an oldie-but-goodie artist for that weekend only. Then the following week, I'm using a group called Ariso out of Houston to do my performance in Houston. But I'm a Tejano artist there. Now, I get onto some of these norteño shows that you were talking about because maybe a Tex-Mex or Tejano tune is getting played on a norteño station. Now we have Tejano stations 24/7 and we have norteño stations playing 24/7.

I've got a group called Grupo Aldaco out of East Lansing, Michigan. I've got a group called Tobias Rene out of Denver. I've got a group called Latin Express out of Fort Worth and Dallas. We have a group called Sierra out of the Valley. In California, we use the one out of the Valley, believe it or not; we fly them out. Yes, out of the Rio Grande Valley. We have a thing—this late in the game, we got together four guys from my school. We're called old school in Tejano now. And old school, we got together just four friends. And one of them that did very, very, very well that has the recording studio, he's Freddie Martinez.

Well, as we were growing up and being competitive with one another to try to stay alive, these guys became rivals, all these guys—not only to outperform them on the show, but to outperform them, not realizing that we were kind of using each other so that no one lets weeds grow around his legs. So what happened is that whoever was doing, say, one of my competitors was doing better, well, I'm going to work that much harder because I've got a copy of the last recording he had out. And, of course, if I get a bigger record and I got more airplay, and that excitement's out there, it was who can stay the hottest the longest. And, of course, that was going to show in your performances and your gigs, jobs that you went to. So, anyway, here Freddie wakes up one day and wants to do something, a project with four of our rivals of that time. Myself, Carlos Guzman, Augustin Ramirez.

At one time, we are playing this kind of R&B, doo-wop. Of course, now they want to do this—the project they wanted to do was in Tejano. And he wanted to do it just for old times' sake . . . and he kidded around about a Grammy. "Ah, yeah, yeah, sure, sure. This late in the game, sure." So we went ahead and did the project. We got nominated for the Grammy, believe it or not. And so we went out there to the show, the whole bunch and all that. And we didn't pick it up. But all of a sudden, because of the project, everybody in our market, from the old-school market, wanted to see all these guys again. So here we are for about a year, going from town to town, town to town, and then all of a sudden, Fred says, "Well, you know what, man? This is not really what I wanted to do," because he is doing so well with his business. He produces a lot of norteño groups, is what he really does.

And one of his biggest norteño groups is what's keeping the company alive. His name is Ramon Ayala . . . he plays accordion. And so Fred says, "Well, you know, let's just do this one more time." And so, just because I don't want to get out here and travel, the money was good and all that, and the performances. We were really just getting to a lot of people that we hadn't seen for years, and the places are getting packed, and all this, and it's all fun and nice and everything. But this wasn't the idea. You know, we wanted to kind of, this late in our careers, each one of us get a Grammy.

For this project, it's only been the last couple of years that we did this. So we did another one and got nominated again, and we actually picked up the forty-third annual Grammy, two years ago. The best Tejano album. Took all four of us to get it. None of us ever got it on our own.

It's been fun. It really has been fun. But you know, I never let go of that R&B thing in me, because not only do I still keep writing in that vein, but like, for example, I had written a couple more tunes that I just kind of had sitting here, and when Freddie called, before we talked about the four projects, he was calling about coming down there and doing another English thing. But he wanted to revamp with all the new technologies. There are some new things called pro tools in the recording studio. And this is what this guy has in his place now. And he said, "Man, I'm curious as to what you can do with these pro tools. I just want to update everything." He's got a pretty large catalog. So, just to put it in the catalog, man, for posterity and all that. And I said, "Well, that's good. That's good, Fred. Okay, well, let's do it. I'm up for it." So I went ahead and dragged the songs that I had written. He said, "What do you want to do?" And I said, "Well, I tell you what I'd like to do, Fred, because we're going to deal with pirates and all this, and it doesn't seem like we're ever going to beat these guys. So, if nothing else, let's get them to come steal from us." He said, "I don't want to walk over your idea." He wanted to revamp twelve songs that I had already done. And I said, "Look, let's revamp and bring up to date with the new technology and new arrangements on half of it, on half the CD, and then on the other six, give me some room where I can try something new that I've written and something that I've wanted to record for a long time that I didn't think I was going to record." And he thought it was a much better idea. So we split it down the middle. We're revamping six that we had done, your typical "Talk to Me," "Smile Now, Cry Later," "Put Me in Jail," some of those, we updated on the first six. And then we added six new ones with new ideas, and maybe we'll pop something, even if we're in the oldies stations, is what we're trying to get to happen.

You know, we started very simple, because of lack of money. And then we got, believe it or not—you're never going to believe this—we actually got to a point when we got to the pretty much largest orchestra that we had, where we were changing outfits twice a day, and they actually thought it was a different band coming on. We wouldn't let anybody see. I mean, it got to be a big thing for us to come in and perform one way and then change to something else. I was up to date with the *Gentleman's Quarterly* magazine. And I would get these outfits that were a little too far-fetched or weren't really going to happen for another two or three years, for everyone to be able to buy. And I would stay on top of that for my group. And I had a tailor that used to outfit some pretty big people that wound up here. His name is Danny Praspena. . . . He wound up here, and about that time, we crossed roads, him and I, and became good buddies. So, I would have him outfit my group completely, from head to toe, and he kept us ahead all the time, all the time, all the time, with all the new things that I was finding off of *Gentleman's Quarterly*. So, by the time something hit the market, and they'd say, "Oh, man, you've got to see these suits, man, we got to get us some, check this out, man, this is the newest thing." He said, "No, man, Sunny's been wearing that for a couple of years, man." But everybody seemed to have noticed that during that time; it's that extra little oomph that you put in whatever it is that you do, right? And it kept us ahead; I mean, people would just come see what the hell we were wearing. And of course, the performance helped a lot and all that, and excitement and all this, right? And then, of course, I guess you know all about the battle of the bands.

Okay, battle of the bands was, as you're performing and as you're getting up there with whatever it is that you're doing, with your particular band or whatever, where we come from, we would get these battles of the bands, where we would perform with someone else that thought they were as good as we were or one of these guys. It was the same people I kept telling you that were our rivals. And so, those guys would wind up on the same card with us. And of course, it was, you know, who was going to outplay who.

We had these band battles all over, actually. I mean, this thing really got out of hand. There was a place called the Pan American Ballroom in Houston. And there was a club called Club Westerner in Victoria. And in San Antonio, we had the HemisFair grounds here, when it got real big about that time, where everybody was focusing on coming to see the Tower of the Americas and everything from all over the world. Well, we were doing dances there on those grounds, at the HemisFair grounds. And we were doing some of these things where we would, you know, try to have these battles of the bands, wherever we thought we were going to draw real big, or that it might be interesting to do something there. City coliseums, ballrooms, that type of thing. A lot of these towns have—the biggest thing in the little town is actually the ballroom. So we would play something and then put a couple of competitors with us. We'd all try to outplay each other, right?

The battle of the bands was almost a going thing. It kind of started between Little Joe and I. And we were doing it in the big, major cities. The word got out, and so. . . . Joe has never gotten that lucky with the R&B and rocking sound. One time in his career, a major company went all out and spent a ton of money on his first English album, and nothing came off of there. But you can't beat him at his game, though. His songs are everything of the highest quality that we wanted to do with Tejano, but a lot of mine are not cantina-type bar songs. A lot of mine are a lot of boy-girl situations, and "You broke my heart" and "What am I going to do now?" and kind of like your country, cry with a bottle in your hand. And Joe's was more of a barroom-type song, and man, that's all he needs to do. It's all he needs to do. We're good friends, and he had always wanted to be able to accomplish what we did, and that was one thing that he always wanted, was to at least pop one that he could walk around with a "Talk to Me," "Smile Now, Cry Later," or something. And it wasn't meant for him. . . .

A thing I didn't tell you about all these guys that wound up being rivals was that we got to work together on the same stage many, many nights. For example, Little Joe and myself were some of the biggest, biggest draws that our market ever had. But it would depend on how we marketed, how we promoted it, and what location and what city, so you could have a huge crowd and stuff. I was lucky that I got to work with all these people because my career lasted so long. A lot of the guys that were doing real well, that we thought were going to be here a long time and phased out, well, I did work with them while they were here, while they were hot, because we wanted to always have a good combination that would make a good draw. If they thought Joe and Sunny were the hottest things, well, that's the draw you want to get.

Gosh, you can imagine, in forty-two years, I've done quite a few. Some of the biggest guys that were my competitors wound up putting the place—for example, that HemisFair grounds that I was telling you about—it's so huge that they could put their equipment clear on the other side of the ballroom, and I was clear on the other side. And I don't know if you know about polkas. You know, they dance these polkas. Well, if you've got a couple of circles, it might be a little too much. It was so long. And you would try to get all the way around that circle, come back to where we were, the ones that were playing. And then, when our set was over, the other group was at the other end, ready to go on, so they wouldn't lose anything. By the time I set up and tried to tell them it was my last tune and took it out, the other guy was ready to go on the opposite side of the building. Now, the most going thing among all these groups is to set up one good set of sound where you don't lose time tearing down. To think that I'm going to be putting my stuff up and perform and tear it down so that he can put his up is completely out of the question, because it would take two or three hours to set up his stuff. So we would get together usually, like a lot of your country stars, down and just say, "Hey, man, what's your system like?" or, "No, man, I've heard your system is better; let's just go and use your system if it's cool with you." "No, that's fine." So we'd make sure we got a good level of one system, and the only thing that changes would be the performers. And it worked out a lot better.

A majority of the artists that came out of Corpus came through Freddie. All the guys. And there's a pretty long list of people that came through there. But they were recording with Freddie. The rest of the artists basically recorded out of their own hometowns, the way we did . . . . Okay, Little Joe has his own recording studio in Temple, and he was producing his stuff out of there. I never had my studio, but this Manuel Guerra I told you about always had a recording studio here. So we would always record there. His recording studio was called Amen Recording Studio. He records strictly gospel now.

Teardrop was a record company, it was run by two partners: a guy named Foy Lee and Huey Meaux. Huey Meaux was the first record producer that had big number-one hits out of the state of Texas. Huey would find them. You didn't know you really had one. He saw the potential and would pop it for you. But Huey is now in the penitentiary.

But Huey and B. J. Thomas, "Raindrops Keep Falling on My Head," Freddie Fender's "Wasted Days, Wasted Nights," the Hughes Corporation, "Rock the Boat," the list just goes on and on. Huey had the ability to see a small fire before it got big. He'd capitalize on it and take it to the number-one status.

Freddie Fender is out of the Valley. I know him pretty well because of Freddie. Yeah, he was doing quite a bit of that R&B, doo-wop. "Wasted Days and Wasted Nights," "A Man Can Cry"—I'd say he had maybe three or four big ones that Freddie tapped into. But he tried country a little bit, and here recently, he's doing a lot of these Indian casinos. But actually, he used to go on to do a lot of the *Tonight Show* things. But he was doing them with "Wasted Days and Wasted Nights," some of the little R&B stuff that did help him. That's actually what got him there.

[Selena is another artist who has] passed on now, but she came in at a time where she was part of the new kids that took over after this old school. And of course she had that tragic death, but she was on her way to do some very interesting things, and she was kind of young. I got to work with her quite a bit. She was out of Corpus. A small story real quick: Freddie actually recorded her very, very first tunes. And then she took off with another company. Her dad used to be a musician from my school. His name is Abraham Quintanilla. He used to be with a group called The Dinos. It was a Tejano doo-wop group. And they never really did much. They pretty much kicked around the Corpus area, and when they finally gave up, he realized what he had. And then, he became the manager for Selena. And Freddie was the first guy they went to, to try to get her recorded. I did quite a few gigs with Selena. I did practically all the major cities at one item or another. We did Houston, Austin, Fort Worth, Dallas. We worked San Antonio.

I grew up four boys from two marriages, two in each, and when they [the marriages] didn't work because of my traveling and being so much out of pocket and stuff, basically, I raised up the kids on my own. I'm on my last little boy now.

When I do use my group that I can slap together to do something locally, my oldest boy is my drummer. And my second one down is my keyboard player. My oldest is David Sunny Ozuna. And then the second one down is Rudy Sunny Ozuna. And the third one—I guess I don't have to tell you—the third one is Jarrell Sunny Ozuna. And then the last one is Eric Sunny Ozuna. I'm just now finishing with Eric. He's seventeen. I'm going to have him like one more year, and off you go. And I'm done. Actually, they all got a taste in their own way. The oldest one, he's my sound man now, but he's my drummer also. My second one down is my keyboard player. The third and the fourth took trumpet in school, but they both dropped it. They loved it, and they were doing very well, but they just dropped it. The third one has gone on to gymnastics. He's doing real good with gymnastics. And the little one, I don't know where he's going yet. I'm trying to find a place for him now. It's working out. Yeah, it was tough, with all the traveling and stuff.

It's been good. I was lucky. I don't know how that happened, man. I blame it on the fact that my mom and dad, they didn't drink or smoke. And they kind of looked at it as a bad thing, and they put it in our minds it was a bad thing. And having such a large family, I guess, basically, we all bought it. So it never affected me one way or the other, and you think I should have known that it was okay once I got into the business and saw it around me 24/7, but it just never, never got to me. I never needed it, and I was too busy, I guess, being just hyper and a workaholic and all that and liking what I do. My time is pretty much full, almost every day, just as it is now, when it should be a lot more quiet. Yeah, the Lord's been very, very good to me.

ADRIAN TREVINO

interview, 1987

I came at rhythm and blues music in a way by default. In 1964 I joined a group called the Rockin' Ravens in Corpus Christi, Texas. I was going to Delmar College to get a degree in music. I had heard *conjunto norteño* music in my background, when I was growing up in the Valley in a little town, eight miles northeast of Harlingen, six miles north of San Benito, and thirty miles northwest of Brownsville. I'm forty-four now, and I heard a lot of *norteño* with accordion, or with a violin, guitar, and bajo sexto. But in 1964 I was coming in at the tail end of Chicano combo type of thing, rhythm, bass, lead guitar, and drummer. Those types of groups were fading, and the groups that were coming in were rhythm guitar, bass guitar, lead guitar, and drums, plus one or two saxophones. Previously, we were imitating bands like Chuck Berry. Whatever was happening in the Anglo market in the East we were imitating because we were having problems with identity, even me. We had a kind of follow-the-leader syndrome. If the top Chicano band does it, then every other Chicano band does it, too.

When the Chicano bands started to add saxophones and organs, that's what we did in The Rockin' Ravens. We had one tenor and one alto. I was playing electric bass. We would go to high school sock hops and play entirely in English. We did some B. B. King, and others by Bobby "Blue" Bland when he recorded in Houston, Texas. We heard the Duke and Peacock recordings, but we did it our way. Put yourself in a high school hop, and you don't do anything else but English, the blues, the top hits, rock 'n' roll, doo-wop music, and the whole works. The ironic thing about it was that once an Anglo came up and said, "Can you play a polka?" We said, "We only know one or two," and he said, "That's okay. That'll do." Usually, a polka was a "Rancho Grande" or "Jalisco," and that was it.

There have always been Chicano bands doing other kinds of music. In the late 1800s some were doing ragtime and jazz in Texas. These are the unknown heroes. I wish I had the money and time to go interview some of them, like Beto Garcia. He was a jazz performer; he played saxophone.

Henry Cuesta, one of the top saxophone and clarinet players of the 1950s—you're not going to believe this, but he's with Lawrence Welk. He's from Corpus Christi. One time when I interviewed him, I asked why such a great musician that you are, why are you playing Lawrence Welk and those simple tunes? And he said, "Well, they pay you ten grand a week to play these tunes. Yes, I would, and I signed up."

The biggest Chicano R&B band was Sunny and The Sunglows. The first album that they did, all of the musicians were on the front cover, and somewhere along the line, Sunny thought, "It's my thing, not your thing." That's why none of the musicians have been given enough credit. And we kind of feel bad about that, but what the heck, he was paying us $150 a week. Anyway, Sunny felt that the musicians are there and you're getting paid to do a job, rehearse in the morning and then again in the afternoon. In the morning we went over the music and in the afternoon we practiced dance steps. So everything we went up there and played, we did synchronized movements to the music. We all had tuxedos.

I started playing with Sunny in 1965, but it only lasted a month and a half. I couldn't take it any more. The musicians were workers. Sunny is still around today, but he's lost his voice. He can only talk to you in a whisper. He never really had a band. Sunny hired musicians and told you what to do. That was it. He gave us the charts, and we memorized them. Or sometimes we listened to the records of Bobby "Blue" Bland or Junior Parker, and we imitated that.

We were doing a second job of rhythm and blues, but we were playing it pretty well. We played high school dances, community dances. Of course, the saxophone had also been used in *orquesta* music at the turn of the century. The Union and Pacific railroad company had a band, and all the Mexicans played trumpets, saxophones, trombones, and what not. There were also community bands that had professors who had come from Mexico and set up shop. They taught people how to read and write, and talk music. The professores would teach you to play an instrument and read music. He was a jack-of-all-trades, and he was very well educated and held in very high esteem. There wasn't much money that circulated around South Texas, but he was provided for. So from the late 1800s on there have been Mexican and Chicano bands with horns in them, even if sometimes they were just pickup bands that played for a special occasion, eight or ten or twenty musicians. They were all Hispanics.

There weren't any mixed bands until the 1950s. There were record companies, Falcon Records, which had been started in the late 1940s in McAllen. And there were others in San Antonio—TNT, Harlem, Ebony, Cobra, Renner. There were Johnny Olen, Rickie Aguary, Mando and The Chili Peppers (Charlie Alvarado, Vince Cantu, Little Jesse, Sonny Ace). Then some of the bands had Anglos—The Lyrics and Denny Ezba's Goldens, who later were called BFBSA (Best Fucking Band in San Antonio). From this band came Mike Nesmith and Augie Meyers, who later played with Doug Sahm and the Sir Douglas Quintet, that featured the saxophone of Rocky Morales.

Aside from these bands, a lot of conjunto norteño bands played some blues, but if the audience doesn't like it, the music doesn't survive. Some of the low riders were into R&B and early rock 'n' roll, and they still are. Some of the low rider musicians who I have interviewed say, "Conjunto norteño is my dance music, my mom's music, but R&B is the cruising music." The slower tunes were for cruising. The best cruising, your music follows your heartbeat, which I think is about seventy-two beats per minute. So R&B is perfect when it's about sixty beats per minute, because the motors often go at sixty cycles. It all fits together.

To me, the blues meant you had a black vocalist and a good band backing it up. The blues was a way to transcend the [cultural] barrier. The R&B music that I came closest to was in the 1950s. I was a low rider, had a 1947 Mercury. R&B was the music of civil rights, and we listened to it on the radio. It was hard for us to pick up a blues. Bobby Bland's "Love and affection, a heart so true, I'm yours for the asking" was one of our favorites. The radio stations played it over and over. Sometimes we bought the records. We liked the sound, the rhythm and tempo. The lead guitar players wanted to learn those riffs, to be another B. B. King. My friend Phillipe Garza was one of those rare guitar players. He moved to Corpus Christi and joined a black band called Boo and The Trojans. He played with them because he wanted to learn it. For the first month or so, he said, "They were telling me the chords over and over," and he got it down. He was fantastic. In a way it was easier for the lead guitar player. For the singer it was harder. But there are still Chicano bands playing rhythm and blues. It's a way to experiment, to improve technique.

BALDEMAR "FREDDY FENDER" HUERTA

June 4, 1937–October 14, 2006; interview, 2004

FREDDY FENDER, (BALDEMAR HUERTA), EARLY 1960S. COURTESY IDEAL/ARHOOLIE RECORDS.

I started hearing that sort of stomping black kind of music from a border station in Acuña, Villa Cuña, Coahuila, with Dr. Jazzmo. He would come in, well, around one, two, three in the morning, and he would play Elmore James and Screamin' Jay Hawkins and all those Mississippi type of blues, guitar type of blues, harmonica type of blues, the kind of music circa, maybe, from the late 1940s and early 1950s. Later on, as the years went by, I developed a taste for the vocal type of blues that came in around 1952, '53—The Moonglows and The Penguins, The Nutmegs. . . . By then, I was in Japan then, in the Marine Corps, and I heard these songs. And eventually rhythm and blues started to dominate with the wah-wah groups and the sha-na-nas and stuff like that—not Sha Na Na as a group, but that kind of music, actually, until Motown and all that. It practically ended with The Beatles and the British invasion, which would have been, I think, around '63 or '64.

The fact is that even though my first exposure to music was Mexican American, or Mexican—I was right across the border. I was born and raised around Brownsville, Harlingen, and San Benito, and McAllen, all that—so the airwaves would come in from Mexico. But also the airwaves, like the program I told you, in Villa Cuña, Coahuila, Mexico, it's around Del Rio. XERF, Coahuila. Oh, man, that was 50,000—50,000 watts—and I don't know about nowadays, but it dominated the airwaves. There was one station, the one I'm talking about, and there was another one coming out of somewhere in Tennessee, promoting, you know, different medications and all that, or pomades, or whatever.

I remember the music of T-Bone Walker, Little Milton, of course, Ray Charles. I heard Ray Charles in '54. I still do "I've Got a Woman" myself. I love to do his songs. To me, he's definitely one of the very, very few elite geniuses, a man for all seasons. That would cover, I mean, any artist that has such an awesome, awesome talent. To me, he was a great, great entertainer. He was a natural.

Now, of course, it wasn't long before I got exposed to the jukeboxes. I could go into a beer joint, or whatever, and I started hearing people singing the blues, you know, like Sam Cooke. And I heard The Drifters and that "I'm Gonna Sit Right Down and Write Myself a Letter." And that guy, Little Willie John, he used to do a song called, it went something like: "When you're sincere, da, da, I love you." He was such a great singer.

Novedades!
Discos IDEAL
SIEMPRE CON LOS
ULTIMOS EXITOS
THE LATEST HITS
in Mexican Music

DISCOS IDEAL, CATALOGUE PAGE. COURTESY IDEAL/ ARHOOLIE RECORDS.

45 RPM — LISTA NO. 200 — JULIO 1965

 **MARCELO NOYOLA**

___45–2271 QUE MANERA DE PERDER — RANCHERA
LONE STAR BEER — POLKA

 **ELIGIO ESCOBAR**

___45–2273 MEDIA VIDA — RANCHERA
CUAL DE LOS DOS — RANCHERA

 **WALLY GONZALEZ Y SU CONJUNTO**

___45–2274 VIEJOS CAMINOS — RANCHERA
TRAIGO UNA PENA — RANCHERA

 **VALERIO LONGORIA Y SU CONJUNTO**

___45–2275 ADIOS MUCHACHOS — CANCION–TANGO
NO VUELVO AMAR — RANCHERA

★ **NARCISO MARTINEZ Y SU CONJUNTO**
"El Huracan Del Valle"

___45–2276 MUCHACHOS ALEGRES — POLKA
LA BELLA ITALIA — POLKA

 **FREDDIE FENDER**

___45–2277 ERES PARA MI — BALADA
YA ME VOY — ROCK

 **CARLOS MIRANDA Y SU CONJUNTO**

___45–2279 FRUTA PODRIDA — RANCHERA
PUÑALADA TRAPERA — RANCHERA

 **PEPE MALDONADO**

___45–2280 EL CORTON — RANCHERA
POR FIN ADIOS — RANCHERA

___45–2272 MUJERCITA ENCANTADORA — RANCHERA
REGRESA PRONTO — RANCHERA
RAMON PIÑON

___45–2270 PALOMA NEGRA — CAN.–POLKA
LOS INTOCABLES — POLKA
OSCAR MARTINEZ

___45–2269 MI ULTIMA PARRANDA — RANCHERA
QUIZA ALGUN DIA — RANCHERA
TONY DE LA ROSA

___45–2268 QUE SOFOCON — RANCHERA
DEBES VOLVER — RANCHERA
CONJUNTO BERNAL

___45–2267 ENCUENTRO — RANCHERA
QUE TE IMPORTA — BOLERO
CONJ. CADENA Y FITO FLORES

___45–2266 YA LO PAGARAS CON DIOS — RANCHERA
AMOR PERDIDO — BOLERO
ISIDRO LOPEZ

___45–2265 PA' QUE ME DICES COSAS — RANCHERA
LA RAFAELITA — CORRIDO
LYDIA MENDOZA

___45–2264 MADRECITA QUERIDA — RANCHERA
NO PUEDO QUERERTE — RANCHERA
ELIGIO ESCOBAR

WRITE — WIRE OR PHONE YOUR ORDER TO
RIO GRANDE MUSIC CO.
P. O. BOX 861 — PHONE EXpress 9-1471
SAN BENITO, TEXAS

7/15

FREDDY FENDER, (BALDEMAR HUERTA), EARLY 1960S. COURTESY IDEAL/ARHOOLIE RECORDS.

Later on, I used to listen to the blues that used to come around at Antone's and *Austin City Limits*. And they had great blues singers. Rhythm and blues, to me, is a kind of a slow song that does not have the same changes of the regular blues. Let's say you're in E, and then you go to A, then E, then B, and those are the chords you use all the time, like in "St. Louis Blues" or the Jimmy Reed kind of stuff. These sort of songs are the melody, you know? Songs like the ones Della Reese used to do. She sang like a man, with a very heavy voice: "Don't you know I have fallen in love with you?" I mean, those songs were immortal. She had another song that she did on the *Ed Sullivan Show* for seven straight weeks, man, the same song, she was so hot. And to me, rhythm and blues has always taken precedence and top priority over a kind of bubblegum type of rock 'n' roll that came in the Fifties. You know, the bubblegum type of the teenage singers, "Out on the Beach," and all that. I'm talking about very significant songs.

I think the appeal of blues had to do with the way your life was going or whatever your dreams were or whatever the reality was, plus what was not real and you were wishing it was. You know? What you just wished would happen. Let's say that this girl, or vice versa with a girl and a guy, you know, things go wrong and you wish it would have gone right, and then you can fantasize about what would have happened. Or let's say that you get the situation—this girl left, right? But you start coming out with imagination that maybe, let's say, right before she left, you said something, or things were so different, that she never left you, so you ended up with her, and you're happier now because she didn't leave in your mind, even though she probably left and got kids and married and all that. But music is a dream that people that are living their lives can hitchhike a ride on, like a dream, and fantasize on the story behind a song—which rhythm and blues, to me, is the perfect melodious song to come out with something like that because it's slow and at the same time soothing, and at the same time, it's very hip. It's almost a rock 'n' roll in slow motion.

Well, that's what it is. It gives you the same thrill that you would get choosing "Hound Dog," but you're listening to something serious that's messing with your heart, and you feel whatever it is, poignancy or even resentment, whatever feelings, emotional feelings, are coming out, negatives or positives, these songs will bring it out, and rhythm and blues has always done that.

FREDDY FENDER (BALDEMAR HUERTA), INTERPRETA EL ROCK! IDEAL ILP-136. COURTESY IDEAL/ARHOOLIE RECORDS.

FREDDY FENDER, EARLY 1960S. COURTESY IDEAL/ARHOOLIE RECORDS.

I still sing rhythm and blues. One of my songs is "Out of Sight, Out of Mind": "Out of sight, out of mind, so the story goes." And there "There is something on your mind," you know. It's got rock 'n' roll, and it's got that rhythm and blues thing. It's got that Fats Domino type of "Blueberry Hill."

One time they had a write-up on *Billboard* on [my song] "Wasted Days and Wasted Nights," and they described the song as—the beat, they called it a bastard type of rock 'n' roll or rhythm and blues. You know what I mean? But why they called it "bastard" is because I would say that in the area of Louisiana and Texas, you had this. And that's what mine had. That's what "Blueberry Hill" had. That's what Rod Bernard had in "Lonely Days and Lonely Nights." Texas rhythm and blues had that thing: "Breaking up is hard to do." You know. They called it a bastard type of rhythm and blues and rock 'n' roll. But I call it the old triplet, Fats Domino type of music, that you can hear that in Louisiana, Mississippi, and Texas. You don't hear it anymore. But you know, "Wasted Days and Nights" has been a song that fortunately has brought me a lot of recognition from Nashville.

So, even before "Next Teardrop Falls," which is my first hit—it's got a little bit of rhythm and blues in it.

Well, see, I started recording in Spanish first. Yeah, my first one was a song called "Holy One." I changed the words into Spanish, but later on, it became number one in New Orleans, San Antonio, it became number one on KTSA when KTSA was playing rock 'n' roll, rhythm and blues. It became number one on KLIF in Dallas. So, yeah, my first song that I wrote when I was in the Marine Corps—I wrote it in '55, and I got to record it in '57—in Spanish, "Ay Amor," but about a year later I recorded it as "Holy One," having nothing to do with religion; in Spanish, you can actually use the name "Holy One," and it's not sacrilegious. It's cool, you know. It's just the way you feel, that that person is so holy, but "holy" human-wise, not "holy" heaven-wise. Do you understand? And I would say yes, my first song was rhythm and blues. And it was "Ay Amor" or "Holy One." The disc jockeys wouldn't play it; some of them wouldn't play it because of the name "Holy One," so we changed it to "Only One." It came out on Falcon Records in the spring of '57.

I think I've written at least about ten blues songs. "Louisiana Blues." I wrote that one, recorded it. That was about 1960. And it's out on a record. I don't know if it's on Argo. I've written—hell, I've written a bunch of them, man.

I still like listening to blues. Stevie Ray Vaughan. He was just a badass, man. He is a good representative of what is the white side of blues. You know, the only thing that's white is his skin. His heart is black as the goddamn ace of spades when it comes to music. He came out with some beautiful black music, man. And let's face it, you know, who are we going to credit blues to, you know? You can go back to a lot of singers of different races, but the blacks, seems to me like they dominated it. It's a natural thing.

FREDDY FENDER, EARLY 1960S.
COURTESY IDEAL/ARHOOLIE RECORDS.

I have a taste for different kinds of music. For a while I was hung up on Brubeck, in the mid-Fifties, Paul Desmond on the alto saxophone, Chico Hamilton, these are all jazz musicians. I don't even listen to them anymore. I lost interest. But they were some bad musicians. Stan Getz and "The Girl from Ipanema," "Take Five." I think I love anything that moves.

I just got a Grammy in 2002, for *La Musica de Baldemar Huerta*, which is a bunch of boleros with sort of Los Panchos type and guitars. But I also have mariachi-type background. I did "Before the Next Teardrop Falls," as an added bonus on it.

I just hate the idea that I would like only one kind of music. I would hate that, you know. Now, subconsciously, I probably like one kind of music only, but it hasn't dawned on me yet. Yeah, I like to think that I like everything, but maybe it's not like that; who knows? Who knows? We'll find out someday.

AUSTIN

JUNETEENTH, AUSTIN, 1900. COURTESY TARY OWENS AND AUSTIN HISTORY CENTER.

INTRODUCTION

Austin was slower to develop as a blues recording center than Dallas or Houston, although there is a long history of blues in Central Texas. The late researcher Tary Owens believed that in the Austin area the country fiddle may have had its strongest influence in Texas on the development of early blues.[1] Oral accounts and music he collected in the mid-1960s corroborated evidence found in WPA slave narratives, suggesting that there were black fiddlers in Central and East Texas as early as the mid-nineteenth century.[2] His field recordings of Teodar Jackson (Austin), Tommy Wright (Luling), and the Nelson Brothers (Cameron) display a distinctive blues sound in the bending and slurring of notes, while also integrating white country tunes and fiddle styles.

Jazz guitarist Eddie Durham, born in 1906, recalled that his father was a fiddler in San Marcos, south of Austin, and that there were "a lot of black fiddlers who played at dances, for both blacks and whites. The audience was, of course, segregated, but the music overlapped." Gatemouth Brown (Orange), Mance Lipscomb (Navasota), and T. D. Bell (Austin) substantiate this with their own individual experiences in Texas, growing up with fathers who were fiddlers and played blues, country, and "whatever that was called for." Essentially, black fiddlers were part of the eclectic songster tradition, which was also prominent among guitarists and is evident in the varied dance rhythms in the performance styles of Mance Lipscomb and Hosea Hargrove.

In addition to guitar and fiddle, the piano clearly was popular as a blues instrument. It offered different stylistic possibilities and integrated the influences of ragtime, boogie, and stride. By the end of the 1930s there were many itinerant black piano players in Texas. Actively performing in the central area of the state were Roosevelt Thomas Williams and Charlie Dillard (Bastrop), Johnny Simmons (Hempstead), Mercy Dee Walton (Waco), and Robert Shaw and Lavada Durst (Austin). Although there are limited available recordings of these musicians, oral accounts attest to the stylistic variations among them.

1. Steve McVicker, "Tary Owens, 60, Texas Bluesman," *Houston Chronicle*, October 3, 2003, 28.

2. John Minton, "West African Fiddles in Deep East Texas," in *Juneteenth Texas: Essays in African American Folklore*, edited by Francis E. Abernethy, Patrick B. Mullen, and Alan B. Govenar (Denton: University of North Texas Press, 1996), 295.

Robert Shaw had been part of what was generally called the Houston, or Santa Fe, group, who played their characteristic fast, syncopated piano blues in the juke joints and barrelhouses along the Santa Fe railroad line. He settled in Austin in the 1930s, and it was there that he met Lavada Durst and taught him to play piano blues. The performance style of Mercy Dee Walton was different and derived more from the boogie-woogie techniques that he learned from Son Brewster and Pinetop Shorty in Waco. Mercy Dee Walton moved to California in the 1940s and performed in the jump band of Big Jay McNeely, while Robert Shaw and Lavada Durst stayed in Austin and remained solo players.

In the late 1940s Lavada Durst became the first black deejay in Austin, on KVET radio, and was known as Dr. Hepcat because he spoke in jive on the air. On his show, which continued into the 1960s, Durst played big band jazz and blues and promoted regional performers on Texas-based recording labels such as Duke/Peaccock, Freedom, and Macy's from Houston, and TNT, Harlem, Cobra, and Renner, from San Antonio.

T-Bone Walker made numerous tours around Texas and became an important influence on those he met and with whom he performed as a guest soloist on stage. In the Austin and San Antonio areas of Central Texas, Walker had great impact upon local musicians, including Dooley Jordan, Jewell Simmons, and T. D. Bell.

T. D. Bell was born in 1923 in the Belltown community of Lee County, Texas. His grandfather played mandolin, and his uncle played guitar, but as a small boy of seven and eight, Bell played banjo, which he "put down" at eleven or twelve. Then, as a soldier, he was inspired by the music of T-Bone Walker. When he was discharged from the military, he bought an acoustic guitar, but soon traded it in for an "electric with a small amplifier." In an interview he recalled, "After I heard T-Bone live in Temple [Texas], I had to get it. I'd stay up late at night practicing, keeping the neighbors and

FREDDIE KING/MANCE LIPSCOMB, POSTER BY JIM FRANKLIN, AUSTIN, 1970. COURTESY CENTER FOR AMERICAN HISTORY, UNIVERSITY OF TEXAS.

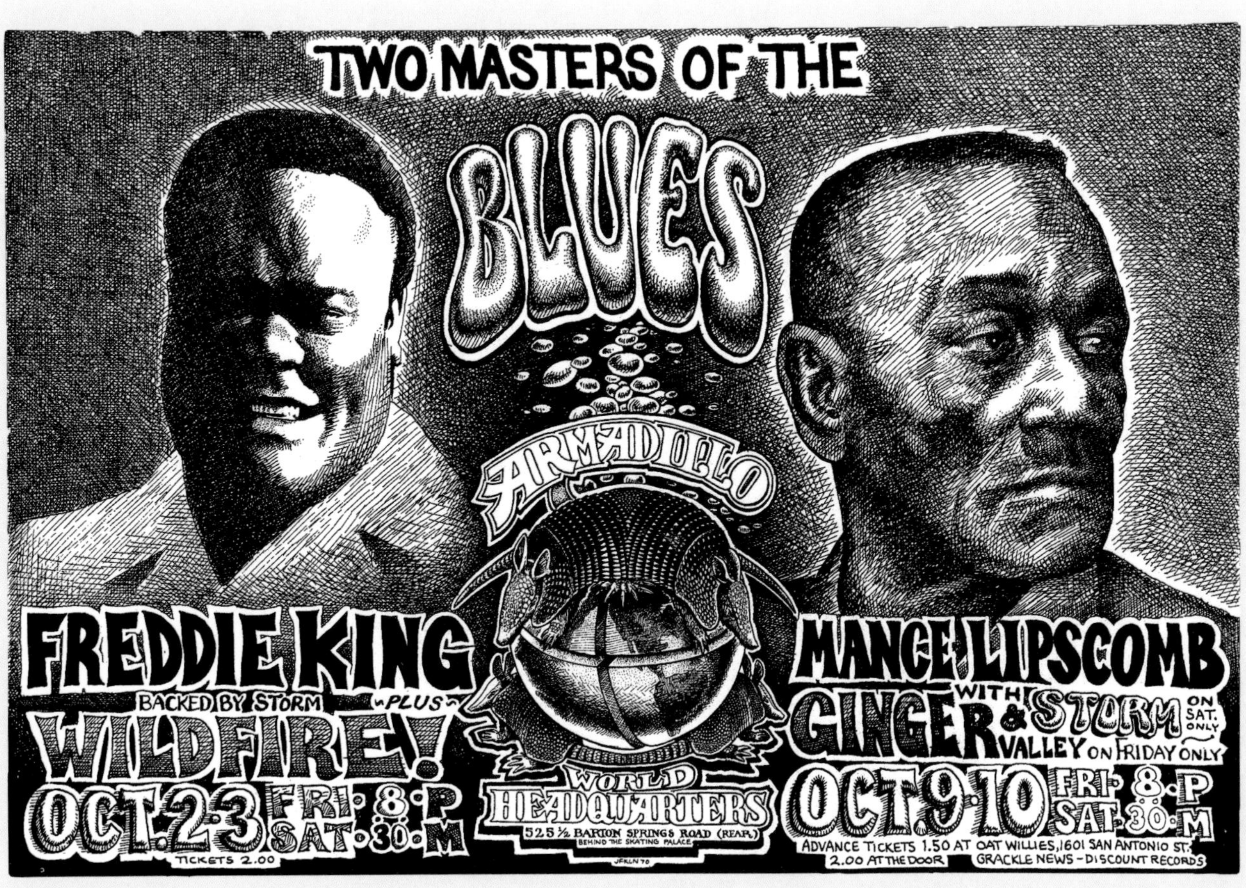

MANCE LIPSCOMB, AUSTIN, 1967. PHOTOGRAPH BY BURTON WILSON.

family awake. Then in 1949 Johnny Holmes asked me if I wanted to come to Austin to play in his club, the Victory Grill, which he had opened on V-E Day, 1945. And I agreed."

Johnny Holmes began his career as a blues promoter in 1932, as a high school student in Bastrop, Texas, when he booked pianist Grey Ghost (R. T. Williams) and others to play a high school benefit. In addition to owning the Victory Grill, he operated clubs in Midland, Odessa, and Big Spring, booking major blues acts all over Texas, including B. B. King, James Brown, Freddie King, and Bobby "Blue" Bland.

At the Victory Grill, T. D. Bell and The Cadillacs became the house band, playing T-Bone Walker hits, such as "Bobby Sox Baby" and other popular tunes of the day. T. D. Bell and The Cadillacs were the opening act for B. B. King, Big Mama Thornton, and Bobby "Blue" Bland, who got his start at the Victory Grill by winning talent contests that Holmes held there.

In the 1960s, during the civil rights movement, white students from the University of Texas began to go to some of the black clubs on East 11th Street, including Charlie's Playhouse. These young people included Tary Owens, who was at the time a student in the folklore program at the university, as well as Bob Simmons, Gilbert Shelton, and Martha Hartzog, all of whom have been involved in documenting blues since the time they first heard T. D. Bell and The Cadillacs (Erbie Bowser on piano, Little Herman Reese on drums, Walter Shaw on saxophone, Alvin Hennington on piano, and Willie Sampson on vocals).

T. D. Bell was an important influence on black musicians (Herbert Hubbard and W. C. Clark), but was also an inspiration to early white players, such as Bill Campbell. In the early 1950s Bell met Herbert "Blues Boy" Hubbard near his hometown of Rockdale, Texas. He was playing in a small band and living in a rooming house. Bell recalled, "He was using a clamp [a capo], and I taught him to play without it. He listened to my playing, and I helped him."

In 1955 Bell was introduced to W. C. Clark in a talent show at the Victory Grill. Clark was from the area and at the time played electric bass, but switched to lead guitar with the influence of Bell. In the 1960s Bell stopped performing to work full time building a trucking business. Over the years, with the growing interest in the history of rhythm and blues, Bell reemerged as a performer. In 1987 he participated in the Texas Blues Reunion, organized by Tary Owens and supported in part by Johnny Holmes's Victory Grill.

W. C. Clark has been active as a bluesman since the1960s and has performed with his own group and in bands with Angela Strehli and Stevie Ray Vaughan. In the 1960s and 1970s the interest in rhythm and blues waned in East Austin and was revived by a white audience at the Vulcan Gas Company, Armadillo World Headquarters, Soap Creek Saloon, and Antone's.

Opened on July 15, 1975, by Clifford Antone in a leased space on Sixth Street, Antone's has continued to be one of the preeminent Austin blues clubs. Antone himself moved to Austin in 1969 from Port Arthur. He was introduced to blues by the black men who worked in his father's liquor store and who brought him to the Golden Triangle juke joints that line Highway 80. Later Antone frequented the small clubs along the Sabine River bottoms that featured blues: the Texas Pelican Club, the Sparkle Paradise, Big Oaks, and Lou Ann's. In Austin Antone had intended to study law at the University of Texas, but instead pursued his interest in the music he loved most.

Over the years Antone's has featured an impressive array of blues artists: Clifton Chenier, Sunnyland Slim, Muddy Waters, Howlin' Wolf, Eddie Taylor, Hubert Sumlin, Jimmy Rogers, James Cotton, B. B. King, Bobby Bland, Barbara Lynn, Albert Collins, Pee Wee Crayton, Johnny Copeland, Pinetop Perkins, Grey Ghost, T. D. Bell, W. C. Clark, Angela Stehli, Stevie Ray Vaughan, Jimmie Vaughan, Kim Wilson, The Fabulous Thunderbirds, Omar and The Howlers, and others. For more than two decades, Antone's has created an environment that fosters vital interactions among musicians and audiences. As singer and deejay Paul Ray points out, "Antone's has been more than a club, it's been a home to the blues, where white and black performers could jam and learn from each other."

During the blues revival of the 1980s, Antone expanded his business to include a record store across from his club, which he had moved from its Sixth Street home to a new location on Guadalupe Street. In 1986 Antone's established a record label; its first release was the EP *Stranger Blues* by Angela Strehli. This was followed by the last recording of Chicago guitar great Eddie Taylor; a Grammy-nominated album by James Cotton (Muddy Waters's and Howlin' Wolf's harp player); an anthology of live anniversary recordings that featured everyone from Albert Collins to Otis Rush; and a string of albums and CDs featuring Matt "Guitar" Murphy, Jimmy Rogers, and Memphis Slim. In time, Antone began to cultivate more Austin-area talent, including Sue Foley, Lou Ann Barton, Omar and The Howlers, Doyle Bramhall, Kim Wilson, Doyle Bramball II, and Steve James, while continuing to record Chicago bluesmen such as Snooky Pryor, San Antonio bandleader Doug Sahm, Houston veterans Lavelle White and Pete Mayes, and Louisiana zydeco great Boozoo Chavis.

In August 2000 a company called the Texas Music Group announced its launch as an Austin-based independent record company releasing the music from Texas and points beyond. The Ryko-distributed label builds on the success of Austin's two most prominent independent labels of the 1990s—Antone's Records and Watermelon Records—to create a new, dynamic, and multifaceted record company. Texas Music Group has three labels under its umbrella: Antone's Records, focusing primarily on contemporary blues; Lone Star Records, devoted to roots country acts and singer-songwriters from Texas and elsewhere; and Tres Mojitos Records, a new label that will mine the rich musical heritage of Cuba and showcase Cuban music of today. Inaugural album releases from the Texas Music Group included Texas rhythm and blues singer and guitarist Barbara Lynn's *Hot Night Tonight*; pianist Pinetop Perkins's *Live, Volume 1*; and *Cliff's Picks*, an anthology of blues from the Antone's legacy chosen by Clifford Antone.

Though Austin blues has clearly shifted to a predominantly white audience, there has been a resurgence of interest in the black community. In the 1980s efforts to restore the Victory Grill and a block of East Eleventh Street helped revitalize African American businesses in East Austin. Antone's Records relocated its offices to the east side in 1994.

Historically, East Austin has had the greatest concentration of African Americans in the city. The black population of Travis County increased significantly, from 791 in 1850 to 4,467 in 1870. African Americans were scattered primarily in the rural areas surrounding Austin, but by the early 1900s city leaders moved

BLUES BOY HUBBARD, AUSTIN, 1950S. COURTESY TARY OWENS AND H. L. HUBBARD.

ALAN GOVENAR RECORDING ALFRED "SNUFF" JOHNSON, RICHARDSON, 1993. PHOTOGRAPH BY BREEA GOVENAR.

to create a "Negro District" in East Austin. Segregation of blacks and whites persisted, despite a two-month boycott organized by blacks to protest a 1906 ordinance requiring separate compartments on public transportation. In the mid-twentieth century Austin was still segregated in housing, restaurants, hotels, parks, hospitals, schools, and public institutions. In 1940 the number of blacks had reached 14,861, but their proportion of the total population was just 17 percent. In 1956 the University of Texas became the first major university in the South to admit blacks, and in the early 1960s student protests led to the integration of restaurants and other public accommodations. The first African American won a school board seat in 1968, and an African American was elected to a citywide council seat in 1971. Gradually, between the 1950s and 1980s, black leaders mounted a sustained effort to dismantle segregation.

Lavada Durst ("Dr. Hepcat"), who had recorded for Peacock Records in the 1950s, remarked that rhythm and blues was popular in East Austin in the late 1940s and 1950s, but that his community was more "churchgoing." Durst himself abandoned his career as a blues pianist and singer to devote himself to his church as an assistant pastor. But in the 1980s he was rediscovered as a blues performer. When asked to perform, he commented that the perception of blues in the black community had changed. "I don't play where people are smoking or drinking," he said, "but I do like educational programs at schools, colleges, and community programs. It's not the music of the devil if it's not doing any harm."

In Austin the identity of the blues has become a focal point of social and cultural change and has reflected the more eclectic, international dispositions of contemporary blues styles. Stevie Ray Vaughan, for example, saw himself as rooted in the legacy of Texas music, but he also was heavily influenced by British rock 'n' roll; B. B. King; the Mississippi Delta blues; the gritty, small-band Chicago sound; and the recordings of Muddy Waters and Jimmy Reed, among others. In many ways, the regional character of Texas blues has been transformed.

ALFRED "SNUFF" JOHNSON

August 10, 1913–January 18, 2000; interview, 1993

ALFRED "SNUFF" JOHNSON, RICHARDSON, TEXAS 1993. PHOTOGRAPH BY ALAN GOVENAR.

The fishing poles clustered together near a framed reproduction of *The Last Supper* in Alfred "Snuff" Johnson's cluttered apartment on Manor Road in Austin speak without words about the man and his music. At age eighty, Johnson likes to reflect about the quality of his life, musing, "It must be some awful good things I've done for the Lord to keep me here."

Over the years Johnson has opted to perform primarily for his family and friends instead of pursuing a career in music. He was brought to my attention by Charles Devitalis, an Austin mechanic, who met Johnson in the mid-1970s. Devitalis recalls, "I had a small garage in East Austin and was tinkering with an old Gibson one day when a black man in his late fifties walked in. I was startled a bit and asked what I could do for him. He replied that if I had any scrap metal, he would haul it off for me. Then he asked me what I was doing with the Gibson. He said, 'Let me see that,' and lifted it from my hands." From that day on, Devitalis and Johnson became friends, and because Johnson couldn't read or write, Devitalis acted informally as his adviser. After rejecting a recording offer from an Austin producer, Devitalis contacted me, and I invited Johnson to perform at the Dallas Museum of Art in 1989.

About a year later, after several attempts to record Johnson in Austin, I bought him a bus ticket to Dallas, where I produced a CD entitled *Black Cowboy Blues and Church Songs*. With assistance from my daughter, Breea, I recorded Johnson at the Announcer's Booth Studio in Richardson. The setting was sparse but intimate. The three of us sat about four feet apart, and once the music commenced, we seldom talked, moved in the stillness of the afternoon to a different time in a distant place.

Johnson learned about music by listening and watching. "Everybody sang the blues in them days," he says, "Black cowboys sang blues. They didn't sing cowboy songs. They sang them blues and some church songs. All of my people played some. My daddy was a fiddler, and he played blues on the fiddle. My uncle played guitar all the time. I couldn't get to play too much, because I wasn't over twelve or thirteen years old. That's when they gave me the nickname 'Snuff' because I started using snuff around that time."

The influence of Mance Lipscomb is apparent in Johnson's playing, especially in his use of a strong thumb on the bass strings, almost like the drum in a dance tune. Many of the songs Johnson performs are

ALFRED "SNUFF" JOHNSON AT HOME, AUSTIN, 1993. PHOTOGRAPH BY ALAN GOVENAR.

remembered in bits and pieces and combine traditional lyrics with those he improvises as he goes along. He sings with a deep, almost moaning tone, accompanying himself on guitar and sometimes humming. Overall, Johnson's memory of his songs is inexact. His versions of "Hey, Little Girl" and "The Good Book Told Me," for example, are essentially guitar instrumentals that incorporate humming with the repetition of what seems to be a truncated lyric of a longer song that might have been forgotten or never learned. When asked about these, he says that "blues" of this kind were sung by people at leisure and at work. "They sang the blues when they were sitting or walking, sometimes when they were herding cattle or riding down the road. The blues comes from worries, and to sing the blues gives relief."

American music specialist Kip Lornell suggests that in some respects Johnson's performance style is reminiscent of the black, southern banjo/song/string band tradition that could be found throughout the South, but especially in the southeastern United States during the teens and 1920s, and perhaps even earlier. Moreover, many of the lyrics in Johnson's blues or blueslike songs, such as "Good Morning Blues," consist of recompositions of familiar tunes.

Johnson's religious singing is largely indicative of the post–gospel camp meeting era. Such well-known gospel hymns as "Old Time Religion" and "Going Back to Jesus" typify the songs of the period from roughly the 1870s to the early twentieth century. In addition to gospel hymns, Johnson draws upon the earlier African American spiritual tradition.

In the 1950s and 1960s Johnson played around Austin on an informal basis, sitting in and jamming for free, but he didn't start playing professionally until the late 1980s when he was asked to perform at Antone's and the Continental Club.

I was born at Cedar Creek [in Bastrop County, Texas]. I was raised up there until I went into the service, 1941. I was working on a ranch out between Bastrop and Elroy, out there on Mr. Yost's ranch. I did horseback riding, taking care of cattle, farming. I was herding cattle, about a thousand head. It was a little better than 3,000 acres in that ranch. I'd work on the ranch awhile, and then I'd work on the farm awhile.

We started off riding horses when I was a little kid. See, what happened after my mother and father were getting up in age, before my mother passed, they give me to the Yosts. They give me to them. And so they just had me a little place built out there for me to stay. And they'd feed me, you know, shoe me and clothe me. I was around about thirteen or fourteen when they give me away. And I went to work on one of Mr. Yost's ranches when I was about fifteen years old. It was near Manchaca.

Them cowboys, they sang blues. They didn't sing cowboy songs. They sang blues. They ride and they shout them blues. Fiddlers played blues too. All through the country now, if you go down in there, you hear the coloreds singing. They're singing blues. Well, there's not too many left . . . once in a while you might run into some of them. See, the older people was doing more blues, they done gone.

The people that owned that ranch wasn't no black family. His name was Olsen Yost. He was just about the first millionaire in this county there. My mother and dad gave me to him. They owed him some money, and them giving me to him paid that off. They was getting up in age. Well, there was fourteen of us. But, in other words, they gave me to him, and I stayed up there with him until I got ready to go into the service.

I went to the army, got trained in Wilmington, North Carolina. Then, see, I was in the South Pacific. First, they sent me to New Caledonia, then to Saipan, and that's where I had to stay until they transferred me back to the United States. I came out in 1945. And after I came back, I worked some for them, and then I told them one day, I want to go and try something different. I moved to Austin. I've been here ever since.

So, I'm thankful. It must be some good things I did both ways. In Christian life, and through sinning life, it must be some awful good things I've done for the Lord to keep me here.

I got to playing guitar on account all of my people can play some parts of music. My daddy was a fiddler. He played blues. My uncle played guitar all the time. And they would take up in the country. I couldn't get to play too much, cause I wasn't over twelve or thirteen years old. They'd let me pick it up once in a while. And I'd be paying attention to what he [my uncle] was doing, how he was playing. And I would get to play a little bit. And then, it would probably be a week or two weeks before I would get a chance to pick up another one. But I kept it in my mind what he was doing, and I wanted to be a guitar picker and play the way he did.

So after I went into the service, I got to play a little bit more because they have, you know, many music positions in the service. And I'd go down and play when we had time off. And then when I came out of the service, I started playing for the church. 'Cause I was a Christian anyway then, just like I am now. I started to play for the church and finally I became a deacon.

My daddy's name was Frank Johnson, and my mother was named Uma. Her [given] name was Pearl Lee, but they called her Uma. My mother passed away in 1925. My dad didn't pass until 1954. My uncle was Will Johnson. He stayed down there at Cedar Creek. And we'd always go to the country ball, because he'd always have one. And I'd get a chance to go by some time and play on his guitar at the house. He'd let me play. But my dad, he didn't have any guitar. He only had a fiddle.

Those country balls was good. The people wasn't like they is now. The people would associate with one another. Maybe they have a country ball over to this place, maybe they have a country ball over to another place. That was every Friday and Saturday at night. They'd have just fiddle and guitar, and no drums. No piano. They would play country music, blues, just like we play. Oh, Lord, they'd have some of all kinds of songs—"Blues in the Bottle," "Goin' Downtown," "Black Gal," and "Bumblebee." It was sort of like Mance Lipscomb, his playing and going on.

I didn't know Mance personally. I met him a few times. And then he would be playing. He mostly went on horseback or in the wagon all the time. I guess I was about fourteen or fifteen years old. He was well known all around through Cedar Creek, Bastrop, Elgin, Taylor, La Grange. He used to use that real strong thumb on the bass strings. Almost like the drum in a dance tune. That's the way I do. When I be playing, I carry my bass with me. You can't find too many guitar pickers who can play and carry a bass, carry their own bass. You don't find that now.

They'd play different dance tunes. It was a little bit different. At the white dances, they played different songs. But at the colored dances, they'd just come out singing the blues like I do. A lot different than the way they was playing back then.

I picked for a good many of these guys around here, if they gonna play the blues. If they go to the jazz and this rock 'n'roll, I don't go for that. I been working on that electric guitar . . . that [acoustic] guitar with a pickup.

Got the whole lot in there. All the other time I been using acoustic.

I started picking at the church with the acoustic. And then, from then on, I come on with the religious songs that I generally plays. See, you got to time yourself in playing music. You got to have yourself in time with your music and your singing, and that's the most important thing there is.

I always played by myself. I do a lot of humming with my singing. That makes it come on better with you. In other words, while you're humming, it's giving you the thoughts what verses to place in with your music with your singing. That's what that's for.

You can't get up and play before an audience, like if they just pull me up there. You can't feel no ways skittish, no way fear what you're doing, because you already have it in mind what you're going to do and how it's going to be done.

I started by playing house parties. They would donate money. I play thirty to forty-five minutes. Then, I'd be through. Some of them would dance, and some of them would just want to sit and listen. They'd get out there, you know, slow drag and dance. They wouldn't get out there hopping and jumping and picking and kicking. They wouldn't do that. They just slow dance, mile-long, slow dance.

In church, I'd play with the sermon. See, just like people get up there and play while the people are singing, you know, according to what they're singing. I play guitar.

My wife's name is Jessie Mae. She was Jessie Mae Wilson. We been married about twelve years. But we was raised up together in Bastrop County.

My first wife, she's still living. But see, thing about it, you can't stay with someone you can't stay with. You don't stay with something that don't want to stay with you. So the best way out of that is the easiest way. She go her way and I go mine. She don't bother me and I don't bother her.

Life is built up on humility and the quality behind it. What I mean about that there, it got to the point that it's either the woman don't want the man in her life, or the man don't want the woman in his life. See, it's kind of a hard pill to take. It's dissatisfaction both ways. If you don't get away, you don't get on out, then that brings on trouble. I'm not a troublemaker. I have something else to think about. See, we're born in this world to live happy. We're not born in this world to go through hard tribulations. We born in this world by ourself. See, this is my third wife. I ain't staying with no one if I can't get along with her, and I don't want one to stay with me if she can't get along with me. I got thirteen children, but not one of them play music. They ain't got time.

You see, a lot of people can avoid things if they try. There's no such thing as "I can't." 'Cause you can. When I came to Austin, I started working construction. And then I started service station work. I did that for a while. Then I started to working for Mayflower Moving Company. I had done quit playing music. But I was always staying in practice my own self, playing. But I started getting back into music about four or five years ago.

I went to a shop to get my car fixed up, and the man who ran the shop, he [Charles Devitalis] would always work on my car. And I went in there one day, and he always kept guitars down there. He had two guitars down there, and I picked up one of them, and he said, "Can you play that there?" "I can play it a little bit," I told him. "Hit down on it!" So I hit down on it, and it wasn't before long I was playing regular.

In the Seventies, along about 1976 or 1977, the doctor retired me from work. My back got hurt. You know, lifting on them pianos and all that kind of business. One of them slipped as we was going up the stairways with it, and it caught between the catty-corner of it, just got me in the back.

I just sit around the house and play. Listen to myself. Just sing in church. You get to studying different songs, and different ones will come to you.

What keeps me going is, well, I guess, by the hopes of the good Lord about me. Taking care of myself the best that I can and just staying out of trouble. That's what keeps me going. I was never shy or nothing going up on the stage.

ROBERT SHAW

August 9, 1908–May 16, 1985; interview, 1984

ROBERT SHAW AT HOME, AUSTIN, 1984.
PHOTOGRAPH BY ALAN GOVENAR.

I've been playing the blues all my life. Sometimes I forget it. Sometimes it be six months before I remember a song. My mama bought a piano when I was little boy. She got a baby grand, "Steinway" printed on the bottom. That's the real thing.

In the early 1930s I was around Kansas City and Oklahoma City. I hardly fooled with bands. There was too much static with that money. With some people, alcohol gets the best of them. I don't know why. I always thought I could take care of myself better than anybody. There's one piano player, he could have two or three drinks of liquor and he'd misuse everybody, himself, too. He just couldn't stand that whiskey. I found that in the black and the white, some people can't handle the alcohol.

Blues is history and your actions down through life. It tells a story, and it tell it like it is, and that gets an individual. There's going to be something in this song that's going to run his mind back. Some of them can't stand it. Music is a fun and enjoyment type of thing, and some people can't stand fun. They get out of line, and there are a lot of people that enjoy music to the highest.

A whole lot of sacred music is timed on jazzy timing now. Because of blues, all of them sing the blues, they're changing the sacred style. It's according to what the individual thinks. I sing in church. I go to the Ebenezer Baptist down here. They have sacred music in all kind of ways.

You know, at one time, street people used to pattern after the society people, and now it's been changed around. The society people pattern after the street people. Some people make harm out of nothing. . . .

I've written several tunes, about six or eight or ten blues. You got to get it timed so it will work. You can't put too many words in a verse. You may be short, 6 and 8 and 2/4 timing. When you write the words, it has to be right. It's just like we talkin,' but you got to know how to time it. Now, we can run out of time on a subject, but you can't have too many words in the next sentence:

I'm gonna get me another woman
Who's going to be nice and kind.
I'm gonna get me another woman
Who's going to be nice and kind to me.
Lord, I'm going and I'm going back
To my old-time used-to-be.
I'm gonna get drunk, baby,
And I ain't goin' to drink no more.
I'm gonna get drunk, baby,
And I ain't goin' to drink no more.
I can't love you, baby,
You don't treat me good no more.
I can't love you, baby,
You don't treat me good no more.

I wrote that in the late 1920s. I used to play at house parties. Another song was called "Santa Fe"—I played on the Santa Fe line—it sounds like this:

I ain't goin' to tell nobody
What the Santa Fe done to me,
Carried away my good girl,
Come back and got my old-time used-to-be.

My way of seeing it. My music really hasn't changed. I can go to a music festival where they got 2,500, 3,000 people, I get my part from the people. I played in Berlin, Rotterdam, I was in Europe in '71 and about a year and a half ago [1982].

The blues makes you get your mind to think about both ways, for and against. What I mean, if I have a friend, it'll make me think if I mistreated him or mistreated myself. That's the way those things work. The blues is a two-way proposition. It will either make you think that you were wrong or your friend did something to you that wasn't right, or he was right. You get yourself hung up if you don't watch yourself. You sometimes wrong. You can't be right all the time. That's what the blues do to you.

There are a lot less piano players around these days. They're gone, the ones where I'm from in the city of Houston and Fort Bend County. There was one boy, Harold Holiday, but they call him "Shine," and he was something else. Peg Leg was a piano player, but he liked to shoot dice. In the Thirties they had places outside the city limits called roadhouses. Women would get mad because their husbands would go down there. Friday and Saturday nights, they were something else, depending on what kind of place it was, would [affect] what kind of music was played. We were youngsters in those days. There were piano players like myself and others. There'd be a lot of musicians. People came from Houston, Galveston, Bay City, Richmond, Sugar Land, all of them surrounding cities; that's not half of them. People would come and do their sportin' work, dancin,' and women made up.

Some people like emotions in music. Them that drink heavy, they like it slow. The blues is a hard music to play. There's so many frictions to it.

LAVELLE WHITE

interview, 2004

MISS LAVELLE, PUBLICITY PHOTOGRAPH, 1950s.

I was born July 3. I don't ever tell the year. I was born in Jackson, Mississippi, and I stayed in Louisiana, too, when I was a kid, but Mississippi most of all. I was born in Jackson and lived in a place called Hollandale, Mississippi; Greenville, Mississippi; all back up in there.

My dad was named Roosevelt White. My mother's name was Melissa Hampton. And I was the last kid, and she wasn't married to my dad. It was terrible in Mississippi. Very racist. Well, it was just like . . . my brothers, they couldn't go to school. They had to work year round. They wouldn't let them go to school and get no education and all that stuff.

My dad and my mom and all my brothers were sharecroppers. That's what we did for a living. When I was about seven or eight years old, I had to be in the cotton field picking cotton and hoeing cotton and being with my mother and all that. It was tough down there.

When I was about thirteen or fourteen years old, I came to Houston to live with my brother, Jake Lloyd. He lived in the Heights. And I'd just slip out of the house and go to clubs and try to sing. I was singing spirituals in Mississippi. My mother played piano in the Baptist church.

I was about sixteen in Houston when I started singing blues music. I used to go to these nightclubs and see the other artists, and it come to be natural because I was round where Gatemouth Brown and them was. I used to slip off and go to their dances and stuff, Johnny Ace and all those people. I went to some of the old clubs like Club Matinee, Eldorado.

I thought Houston was all right up to a point, till later on. I had a lot of help there with friends. In other words, I taught myself how to sing. God and me, you know, taught myself how to sing. Then, Johnny Copeland took me to [Don] Robey and I recorded for Duke Records. I had written a song, "If I Could Be with You." I recorded that, and then I recorded one by Joe Medwick, "Yes, I've Been Crying," and then I did "My Love Is So High," then I did "Teenage Love," all of those. I was with Robey for a long time. I had to wait my contract out.

After I recorded for Duke, Evelyn Johnson used to book me. And then I went into Atlanta, Georgia, to Henry Winn, and Henry Winn booked me out like with The Drifters and all the people, James Brown, Gene Chandler, Jerry Butler, and The Isley Brothers and just a whole bunch of people. I do a lot of stuff with Bobby Womack. I mean, I know some of the big-time people. I've worked on some of the big cards with the big people.

I done forgot how long. It's been so long ago, I can't remember all that stuff way back there because I have a lot of new things on my mind. The world is going so fast, I can't live in the past. It's a lot of people want to live in the past. I do not want to live in the past. I want to live in the future, because that's why I'm singing like I am now and doing different things because blues is not going to get you nowhere, not now. I still do blues a little bit, not too much. The blues for me is things like "Tin Pan Alley," like I recorded, and things like that, and "Mississippi, My Home," that I wrote and recorded. That's blues.

Well, I had to keep doing it [singing the blues] because it was in that phase. I stay in the phase of music. When the phase of it go out, I slack up doing it. And I think every artist ought to do that. When the phase go out of something, you still going to be in that same old bag. I'm doing funk and soul and stuff now. I got a couple of blues things on my new CD. I did the thing by Van Morrison, *Into the Mystic*. The name of the CD is *Into the Mystic*. It's on Antone's label.

Right now, I'm touring some here and there. Not a whole lot, because I don't think anybody is because of the terrorists. It's just too much happening to do a whole lot of touring like overseas, because that's where usually all of artists go, but now it's kind of skeptical.

I been staying in Austin for about thirty, thirty-five years off and on. I moved back to Austin about seven or eight years ago now. I was brought here because Ronnie Nemore was booking me then, and he wanted me to move here to be booked, and they wanted me to do another CD. Back then, I sang at Antone's once or twice. I don't sing at Antone's at all now. I don't hang, you know.

The memorable thing for me is getting recorded and getting some CDs out. And working with my own band and working with people that's really easy to work with. There's a lot of different artists that I work with that were really accommodating, and a lot of club owners. It's exciting, and I like to work at this club, Saxon Pub. I like that club here. It's on South Lamar, and it is really a great little club. And I like everybody there, the

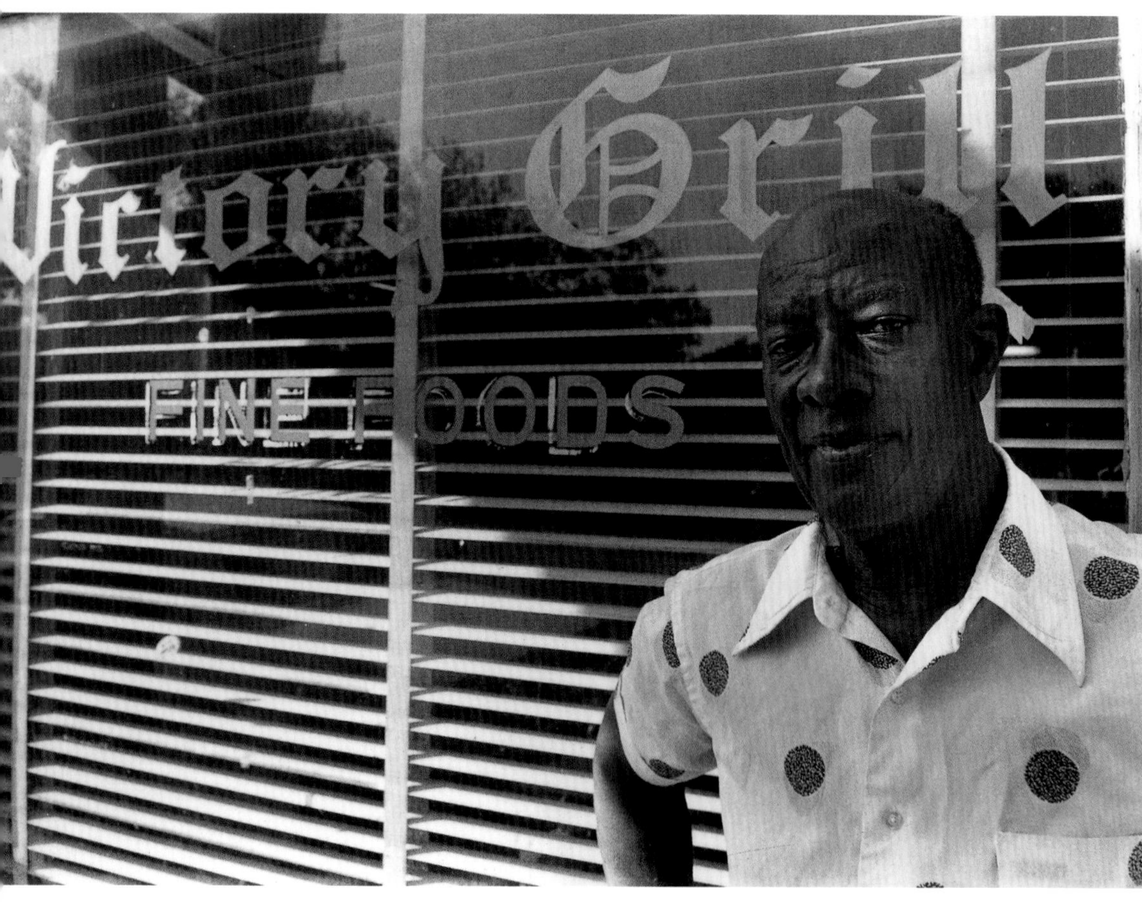

JOHNNY HOLMES, VICTORY GRILL, AUSTIN, 1987. PHOTOGRAPH BY ALAN GOVENAR.

JOHNNY COPELAND (GUITAR), CONTINENTAL CLUB, AUSTIN, 1984. PHOTOGRAPH BY ALAN GOVENAR.

people that own it, the people that work. Everybody's nice there.

In my band, I have two guitars, bass, and drums. I have a funk and soul band. It's a rap band, and I have like two blacks and one Argentine and one Hispanic. And the name of the band is The El Men.

Well, rap is a form of blues, some of it. But some of it is discriminating to the ladies, and to the guys themselves. But a lot of rap I like, when it come to the dancing rap and talking about people ought to get together and do this and do that and the other. I don't favor them cursing and talking about women and killing up one another. I don't favor that. But I love all the rap kids and the rappers, I love all of them, because I love all music. I love opera, big symphonies. I love classic, I love country and western. I love all music. I love waltz music. I love Hispanic music. I love Japanese. I love Brazilian. I love all of it. There's music in everything that I see and look at. I can look right here now at my window and write a song.

Writing is a thing that you have inside of you. It's the soul of a person. It's the mind. It's the beauty. It's the beauty of the world. It's the beauty of yourself, the beauty within you, that makes you write. It's a touch from God. God gives you that gift. He gives you a gift for everything. He gives you a gift to write, you know? And he gives me a gift to sing and write songs and sing to people and make them happy.

My style of singing? I wouldn't know how to categorize it right now, but I know it's different, very different. It's different from anybody else's, and if you haven't heard my new CD, I did one with Gloria [Edwards] and them that's all about [the terrorist attacks of] 9/11 and "Flight 449." This is the kind of stuff I'm doing, mostly. Not too much blues, no shuffles, and—you see, that kind of stuff that's all right in these honky-tonks where you can make $150 or $200. Because that's all you're going to make. And that's the only kind of joints you're going to play in if you sing nothing but blues. They can get a blues show together with every blues artist in Austin and Houston, it's not going to make too much money. I know that. And blues is over for right now. Now, it might come back in a different figure, okay? Yeah, because when I was young, everybody was doing it. See, I didn't really all the time do blues. I did rhythm and blues mostly. Which is songs like The Drifters, like that. And that's like that rhythm and blues.

T-Bone Walker was rough. Yeah, I liked T-Bone Walker. I didn't know him. But I did meet Howlin' Wolf, when I was about twelve years old. I went to one of his dances in Mississippi. People danced the Funky Butt.

T. D. BELL, AUSTIN, 1953. COURTESY TARY OWENS AND TYLER BELL.

They were doing the swing thing in the Fifties and early Sixties. And then it come on down and got off into disco thing. And I like some of that disco, too. Then, they was doing like the Gene Chandler, the Swim.

The older I get, the better I try to get. I try to get closer to God, get stronger in every way and love people more in every way, every day, and God is teaching me how to love. He's teaching me how to be. He taught me how to act and how to cope. Most of all is learning how to cope. You know, I counseled for a while, too. It's learning how to cope with the situations that's not working too good for you. You've got to cope with the bad before you get to the good.

God keeps me strong. I think I'm going in the studio with The Bells of Joy, with Marcia Ball, and I think Bobby Rush, and do a thing on Eddie Scott's label again like I did with Gloria [Edwards] and them, but it'll be with these other people. It'll be in November, I think. It'll be spiritual, though.

Blues is mostly a downer, like you would say, "I'm hurtin' from my head to my toes." Who wants to be in pain? Dig it. Check that. I ain't trying to run the blues down or do anything, because I was born with it. We are where it came from, you know what I mean? But it is a downer. And most people want to hear it, I guess, because they be down. But I want to hear something to bring me up, bring the world up, okay? I want to bring up the world.

LAVADA DURST

January 19, 1913–October 31, 1995; interview, 1984

LAVADA DURST, BERKELEY, 1990. PHOTOGRAPH BY ALAN GOVENAR.

I worked as a disk jockey for about fifteen years, from the middle of the Forties to the late Fifties. I can't recall exactly. I was the first black deejay in Texas and in a lot of states. If you were black, you had to get back. The radio station was the white man's property only. If you delivered mail, you had to deliver it at the back door. But I broke that color line due to the fact that there were some powerful white men in that day. They owned that station, KVET, John Connally, that bunch. Connally was the one who spearheaded it. Of course, his political career was on the line, letting the black on the radio station. But I think they hit a gold mine, because the station became very popular, one of the most listened-to stations in this area. To stay on the air, they had to be different than the other boys; that's why I let them know the black jive talk that we were talking on the East Side, the youngsters at that time. That's the reason they call me "Dr. Hepcat."

I played rhythm and blues, down-home blues, upstate rhythms, T-Bone Walker. I used Duke Ellington's "Things Ain't What They Used to Be" as the theme song, and I went out with blues. I played Lionel Hampton and those Duke and Peacock records. Big Mama Thornton, Gatemouth Brown.

I recorded one of my first records on Peacock. That was "Hattie Green." That was a blues, while I was a deejay. And I wrote a spiritual song, "Let's Talk about Jesus," and it sold over a million copies, and I didn't get a dime. It was recorded by a group of Austin singers, The Bells of Joy. I gave them that name, and they practiced over at my house. One of the fellas won't say that I wrote the song because I was in the blues business and people might not like it. So I didn't get any royalty from the lyrics, anything. That's it. I don't think I've lost anything.

There's a man in my soul
That keep me free from sin.
My whole life had been changed
Since Jesus moved in.

Some of the fellas who say they wrote the song are still around here today. I've written a lot of other songs, "Hepcat's Boogie," "I Cried All Night." The tunes kind of slip me because "I Cried All Night" was put on the label here in Austin, called Uptown, and I got screwed out of that because I was just a goody-goody, but I haven't lost a thing about it. I'm still in possession of my faculties and still can maneuver my fingers and I still can sing good and I still got a chance.

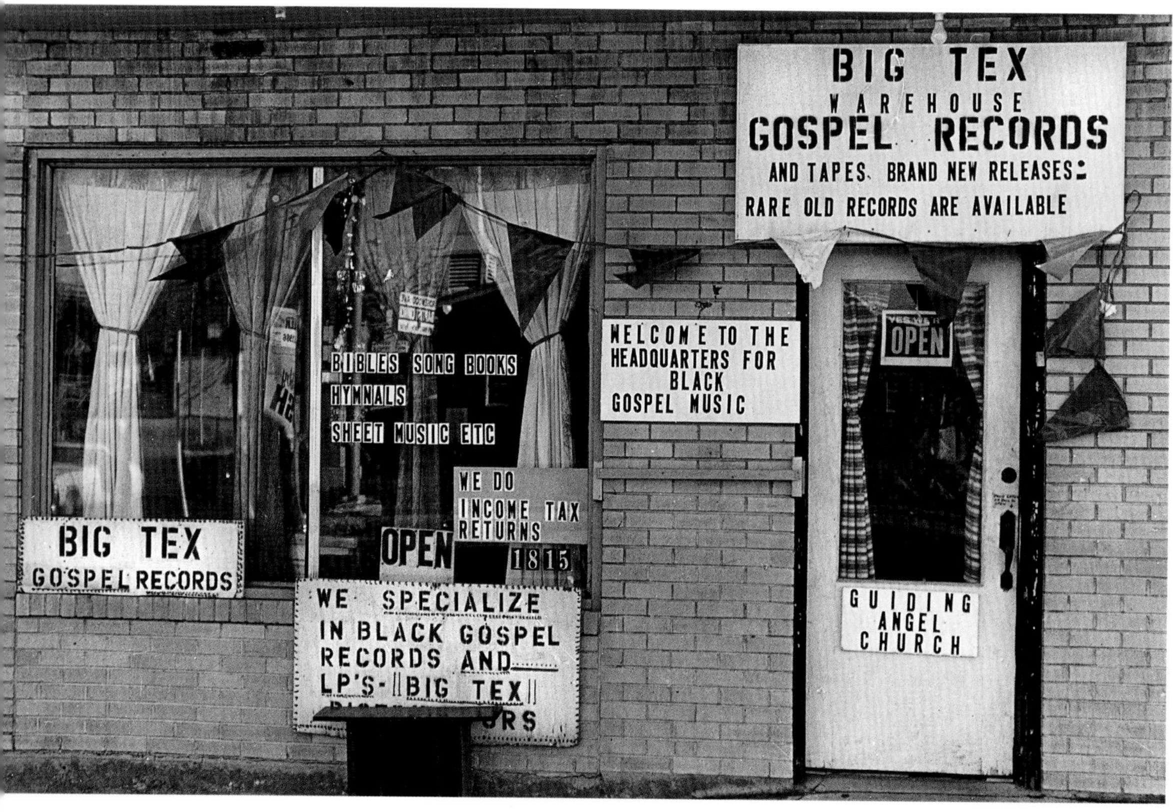

BIG TEX GOSPEL RECORDS, EAST AUSTIN, 1985. PHOTOGRAPH BY ALAN GOVENAR.

"THE JIVES OF DR. HEPCAT" (LAVADA DURST), 1300 KVET, AUSTIN, 1953.

I can improvise, and I can write blues. I sing some traditional blues like "Piggly Wiggly Blues." You know there used to be a grocery store back there. "My name is Piggly Wiggly, I got groceries on my shelf." That's a traditional blues. Robert Shaw used to sing that blues a lot. I've got several blues that I do. I'm the master of "Hattie Green," "How Long," "Black Gal," a number of those blues tunes. Recently, I've written "Blues in Trouble" and "I Need My Baby," "I Got Something to Tell You," and one or two more I can't recall on the spur of the moment.

My thoughts are traditional. My music didn't pick up that modern beat. My songs are traditional blues, born of the fact of black communities that had names like Froggy Bottom, Stick Town, Guy Town, Buttermilk Flats, Sugar Hill, different black communities with their peculiar lifestyles, their loves, their dislikes, their differences, their songs, and what not. When you're in the middle of that environment, you had to sing the blues. You couldn't get no jobs. If you went to town to get a job, the law had a way of picking you up and saying you were a vagrant. So, if you couldn't get a job you would play your piano or your guitar and sing the blues, but things always work out in due time. Sing where I want to go, to eat where I want to, drink where I want to, no more shoes with holes in the bottom of them. I feel like I'm braggin' because I'm wearing Florsheims and suits and things with no patches in them. When you look back, I think we've come a mighty long ways.

The music hasn't changed. It's blues with that Texas boogie beat. A Texas piano player has got a beat that's different than other piano players. We have a boogie beat and it just has a riff. Other blues players, they play the blues, don't get me wrong, but you can tell a Texas piano player whenever you hear him.

The blues is a way of expressing your feelings about the hard times and the troubles. A lot of blues songs, especially those down here in the South. If you listen real close, you find out a lot about the black experience:

I'm just sitting here wondering,
Lord, what's going to become of me?
I'm just sitting here wondering
What's going to become of me?
I've been a bad man,
Lord, I didn't intend to be.
My baby left me,
She did not say one word.
My baby left me,
She did not say one word.
Ain't nothing I done,
Something the poor girl heard.
That's all right, baby,
That's all right for you.
All right, baby,
That's all right for you,
Someday I'm going to be lucky,

THE BELLS of JOY
SPIRITUAL SINGERS

Be up to date like you.
I'm leaving, baby,
I don't got no business here.
I'm leaving, baby,
I don't got no business here.
Because the people in Austin
Sure don't feel my care
You know, sometimes the blues
Moves in like midnight showers of rain
I'm sitting here wondering
If my baby will ever come back home.
Sitting here wondering
If my baby will ever come back home.
I don't know if you know how
I'm all alone
I'm gonna leave your town.
I ain't coming back no more
I'm gonna leave your town
I ain't coming back no more
Oh, baby, baby, darling
Hang a crepe on your door
If anybody should happen to ask you
Who composed this song,
If anybody should happen to ask you
Who composed this song,
Just tell them Dr. Hepcat been here,
Poor boy is gone

I wrote that song; a lot of times you make up those songs and the music that go along. You sing them according to your feelings. If you feel blue, you sing blue. If you feel happy, then you play a happy tune. I learned to play blues by being surrounded by blues players that come here, especially Robert Shaw and different ones. I just like that blues beat. It sort of, like I say, expresses the black experience. The blues seems to be an outlet for your pent-up feelings, your frustrations. Blues is a mighty fine way to let it all hang out.

I'm an associate minister at the Olivet Baptist Church. I'm very proud of my position as a minister, and I feel that my experiences out in the world have helped me to relate to people now because I know what's happening. . . . I know what to tell them because I have seen it all. I have experienced a lot of it. Every good and perfect gift come from God. If it's good and perfect, and you don't do any harm, there's no devil in it [blues]. It says in the Bible, "Make a joyful noise unto the Lord, all you lands. Serve the Lord with gladness. Come before His presence with singing. Know ye that He is God and that it is He that has made us that way ourselves. We are His people and the sheep of His pasture. Enter His gates with thanksgiving and enter His courts with praise. Be thankful unto Him. Bless His name. The Lord is good, mercy is everlasting. Truth endureth to all generations." That means you and I, too. So there's no harm when you feel you want to hit a blues tune—as long as it's not harming my neighbor or hurting anybody, I can play blues all night long. Blues is a way of expressing your inner feeling, a soothing balm to your feelings, just like medicine is to a sore. Blues will satisfy you. Blues will make you cry, laugh, shout. The best time to play the blues is late at night, early in the morning. That's the time when everything falls all right.

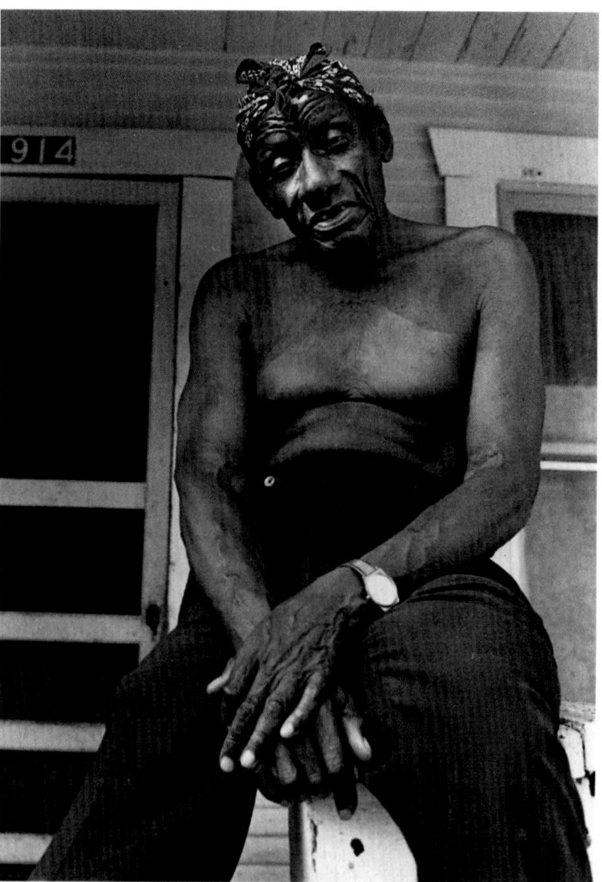

R. T. WILLIAMS, AUSTIN 1987. PHOTOGRAPH BY ALAN GOVENAR.

W. C. CLARK

November 16, 1939–   ; interview, 2003

W. C. CLARK, PUBLICITY PHOTOGRAPH, CA. 2004. COURTESY ALLIGATOR RECORDS.

My mother and my sisters sang, and my grandmother. I had been in the church a lot, around a lot of singing there. But I wasn't listening to blues because my mother was from the old church order, and most times we got to hear blues was when my stepfather would play it on the radio. So I'd listen to it then. But I was playing other music before I got into the blues, gospel. And my cousin out in Phoenix, Arizona, they call him "Big Pete Person," from Austin, Texas, he's L. P. Person. He was already playing the blues, and I was hanging around with him and trying to learn. And at the same time, there were guys in St. John's, where I was raised, that would go out in the fields, make campfires, sit around and play the blues on guitars and harmonicas, violins. And I would hang in there with them as long as I could, till they run me home. Then I finally learned enough to sit in on one of my cousin Big Pete's gigs as a bass player. And that was the first time I ever got into the blues, playing with bands.

When I started playing [blues], I listened to T-Bone Walker, Guitar Slim, Fats Domino, Amos Milburn, Little Milton, B. B. King and other guys. A lot of us started around the same time, like Albert Collins and people like that. Albert King. Those are my blues influences. My jazz influences were Kenny Burrell, back then, Kenny Burrell, Joe Pass, up into George Benson and people like that. My country influence was, oh, Hank Williams, people like that back at that time.

I'm from Austin, but St. John's is the historical Austin, I mean on the north end of Austin. It's an addition; it's a neighborhood. There's a little history behind it. It was founded by the black Baptist church, and it helped people out so people had homes and places to live with the church. They were able to buy land and houses and things like that, and they named it St. John's. And I was just raised right in that neighborhood.

My mother's maiden name was Richardson, Ida May Richardson. She married and became a Clark. My mother's mother and father were Idella Richardson and Wes Richardson. My daddy's name was Curly B. Clark. My name is Wesley Curly. But, see, my mother remarried. We lived with my stepfather, who was a carpenter. My dad was a mechanic, had his own garage, so I was lucky enough to learn enough of both to be able to survive when I didn't have enough gigs to make any money or when I was just learning how to get into the business. I used to work as a car mechanic.

My stepfather was named Cedric Shelby. So my mother, when she remarried, she was a Shelby. She died last Tuesday. She was eighty-seven years old, and the doctor said there wasn't too much they could do for her, just keep her comfortable and let her go. So she laid and talked, and one day she just took a deep breath, and that was it.

When I was growing up, I'd listen to my grandmother and my mother. While they were cooking or washing or working the fields, or whatever, I would always hear—those sounds. And those sounds were always kind of embedded in my soul when I was able to start being around these guys who were playing the blues in the

LOWELL FULSON, ARMADILLO WORLD HEADQUARTERS, 1972.
PHOTOGRAPH BY BURTON WILSON.

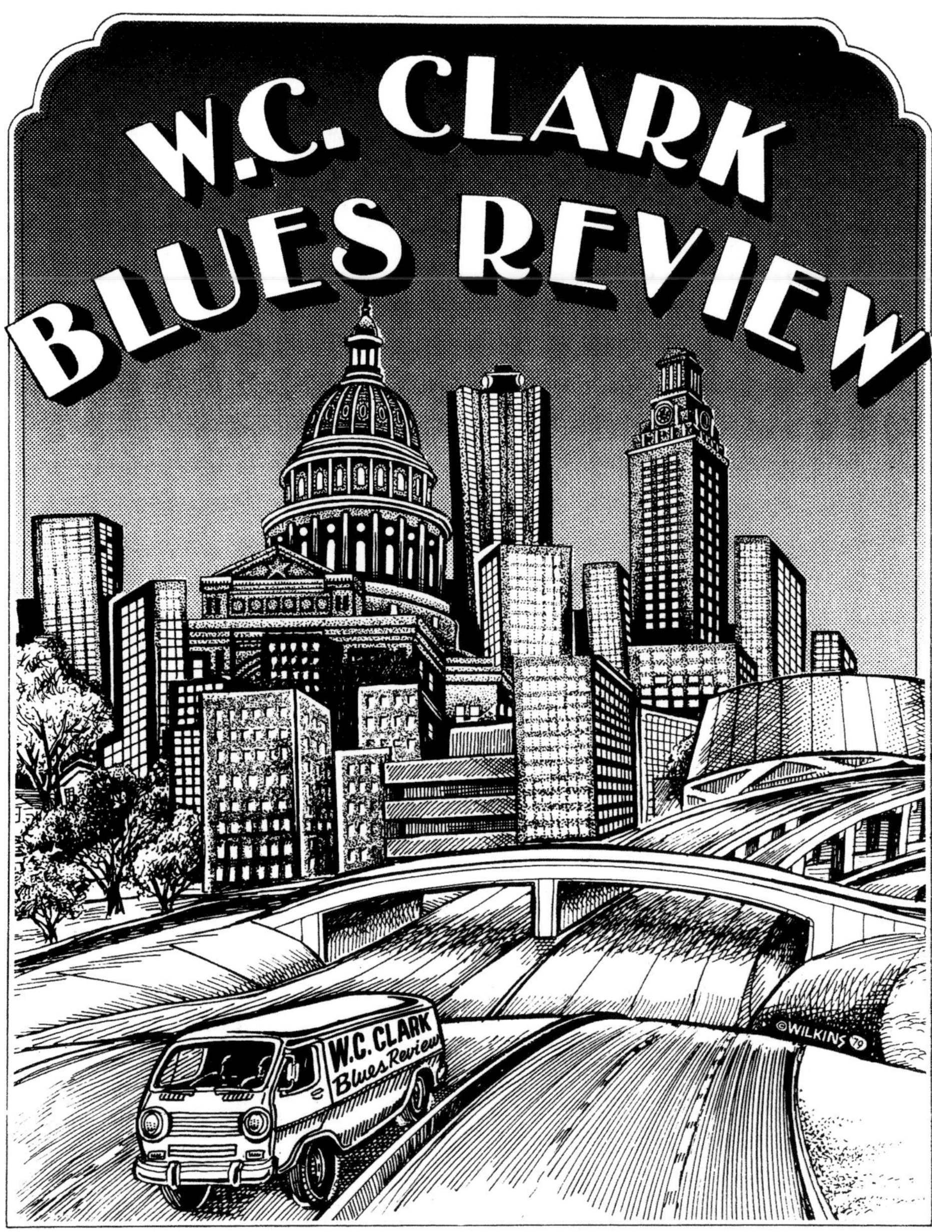

"W. C. CLARK BLUES REVIEW," POSTER BY DALE WILKINS, AUSTIN, 1979. COURTESY CENTER FOR AMERICAN HISTORY, UNIVERSITY OF TEXAS.

field and stuff. They had guitars and harmonicas, and whatever chance I'd get, I'd get around those guys and let them show me something. I finally learned enough to start playing with a quartet. Well, I bought a little old guitar; the brand was Stella. And I started playing around with quartets and stuff like that, and I got good enough to get with a quartet that had a nice professional guitar that they gave me to keep. And when that happened, there was a cafe there in St. John's, in my neighborhood, where you could hear T-Bone Walker and B. B. King and those people. And I would go and sit up by the jukebox and learn as much as I could then. It was just a little cafe where you could buy a hamburger, listen to some music and buy soft drinks. People danced in there. Oh, back then, they'd swing, a lot of foot movement and maybe that line dance they used to call the Slop or something like that.

My first gig, Big Pete had to do something else, and I played for him. I was seventeen then. But that was my first. To get into it professionally and study, I was nineteen, nineteen and a half, something like that. I played my first gig at the Victory Grill in Austin, Texas.

As I say, my mom, she was from the old order; she didn't go to clubs, listen to the blues, and stuff like that—only gospel. My stepfather did; he'd come around and hear me play different places where I'd be playing around Austin. He'd come around every once in a while.

In those days the Victory Grill was crammed tight with people all the time, in the daytime and at night. They had food up front, music in the back, bands all week long. At the Victory Grill, I heard T. D. Bell, Erbie Bowser. He was a keyboard player, and T. D. Bell was a guitar player. The whole street, Eleventh Street, during the time, there was as many as six or seven bands playing right there, in that little spot. So the street was crowded.

The Victory Grill is about five miles north of St. John's. St. John's wasn't in the country, but it was almost there. It was right on the edge, in the suburbs, right on the edge. . . .

So when we started playing professional, we played the Victory Grill about three nights a week. And Eleventh Street was busy, too, so there was after-hours [business] going on till three or four in the morning, so on Friday and Saturday—I'd play the Victory Grill, say, Monday and maybe Friday and Saturday, maybe even one other day. But then on Friday and Saturday nights, afterwards, we'd go and play from, say, 1:00 to 3:30 up on First Street, at a place called Good Daddy's. And that was an after-hours place. So all this was going on, I guess, when I was about twenty-one, twenty-three years old.

I started making records about '81, '82. I started saving my money, working on cars, playing as much as I could. I was working for the State Health Department. I had a position out there; I was working at the Rabies Section. And I would work from eight to five; I would get off, and I would play in the evening, and sometimes I would drive a cab an hour or two just to save money. And I finally got enough money to produce—I was executive producer and music producer of my album—I wrote all the parts, all the lyrics, all the music, arranged everything, paid for it myself, and did my first album about '83. It was called *Something for Everybody*.

But before that LP, me and Stevie [Ray Vaughan] and all the guys kind of playing around Austin were affiliated with a recording studio called Whole Sound. And we did a 45. Stevie was with The Cobras during the time. And "Rough Edges," done on that 45, is one of the songs that was on my first CD. Stevie was playing guitar on it. I played bass on it.

W. C. CLARK, PUBLICITY PHOTOGRAPH, CA. 2004. COURTESY ALLIGATOR RECORDS.

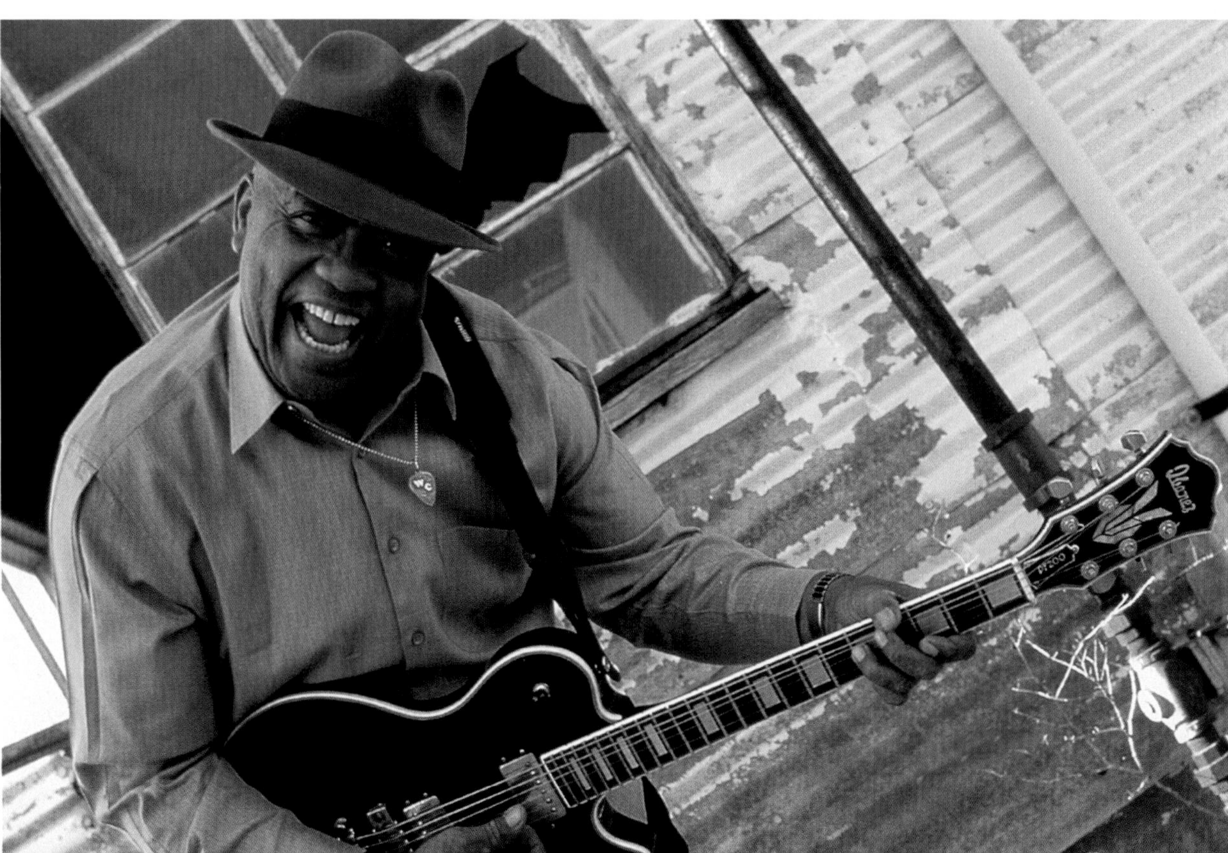

Well, see, that [playing with Stevie] was a little boost for me then, because I knew where he was trying to go, and I was already familiar with it. And the boost, the energy, coming from his playing, and me being excited about playing bass again, which I hadn't played for a while after playing guitar. Well, when we started out playing, from the very beginning, it was good. And we had been playing with each other off and on before we came together as a band anyway. He'd come sit in with me, or I'd sit in with them when he was playing with The Cobras, or we'd put together a little gig to go play somewhere or something. But then, I learned something from him, too, because during that time, I was working. He came down to McMorris Ford, where I was a mechanic. And he'd come down, and say, "Man, you shouldn't have all that grease under your fingernails, man, look how you're treating your hands." You know, he'd talk to me, and we'd laugh about it and stuff. I finally quit, and we started rehearsing, and we formed Triple Threat. And from then on, it was just like stuff going on all the time for all the while we were together, and I think the reason we named it Triple Threat is because I was a bandleader and Mike Kindred was a bandleader, and Stevie was becoming one, so that was the three threats. And eventually, it happened that way. Mike went on and did his own, and I did mine. But we never really lost touch with each other or anything like that. We still would play with each other every once in a while. In fact, you know, me and Stevie did that *Austin City Limits* video together. Actually, that was my fiftieth birthday. And since I had been affiliated with all these people down through the years, what I called the Movement—Jimmie [Vaughan], Kim Wilson, Angela Strehli, Denny Freeman, and everybody. Well, see, all those people who were involved there, they got all those people together for my birthday. But what they did, they edited out the birthday song and that exposure. But see, I didn't have enough momentum in my business to pull it off. Only Stevie had that much power during that time.

Well, after Triple Threat, I formed my group called Southern Feeling. That was Angela Strehli and Denny Freeman, Derek O'Brien, and Alex Maples. We played around for a while, and we did some tapes for Jerry Wexler, Atlantic Records, but our presentation was a little bit weak during the time, so we made an agreement to do something else in the future. That didn't happen. After that, then I joined Stevie with Triple Threat, and I played bass with him. And we played around for a few years. That's when I formed W. C. Clark Blues Review. And I had been playing there for a while, and Hammond Scott from Black Top Records, he had people that had been coming to him about me. He finally came to Austin, and they were sitting out in the audience taking notes at my gig, and at the end of the night, he had already figured out what songs he wanted me to record and all this stuff, so we went into that process, or project, and we did the first CD. It was called *Heart of Gold.* Then, I did three more CDs on Black Top, and this last one is on Alligator.

Alligator's been real good. You know, everybody's kind of hurting a little bit because of the economy and stuff, and the blues scene is a little bit weak. People are not buying very many CDs right now, nothing compared to like it was.

For me, it's hard to put my blues into one category, say "blues" and just forget about it, or "rhythm and blues." I can't do that because, see, what I feel when it comes to blues, you can go down to the bottom, you can go all the way down to the gutbucket bottom with blues and the feel. I get that same feeling that I get from listening to that from listening to, let's say, Johnnie Taylor or Al Green. I get the same feeling, but the energy is different. The feeling is the same. So, that's kind of like the way I feel about the blues and any kind of stuff I do, I feel the same about it. I'm just familiar with the energy that's in it that I can tap into, and I use those different songs to boost my energy or the audience's energy. But regardless of what song I'm singing, I feel the same.

Over the years, my audience has changed. From blacks and a few whites to whites and a few blacks. And that's really the truth. The young black generation is coming along now, but I tell you, all over the United States, the only young black I've met doing it—well, he's not so young now—was Gary Clark, in Austin. I think he may be sixteen or seventeen. I think when he first came to Austin and came to sit in with me at the Top of the Mark, he was around fourteen, maybe thirteen, something like that.

I'll tell you, all over the United States, I've met little young white players—young, fourteen[-year-old] harmonica players, guitar players, twelve years old. And a young audience is growing up with these players. And that's the future right there, regardless of what color is playing the blues, it's going to be there, young audience and young players, and that's going to be another generation of—I say it that way because I feel like I've been through at least two of them already.

My guitar, I traded up. I did a centerfold for Ibanez, and I got three free guitars made to my choice from Ibanez. I play those a lot. But I also play a Fender. It's a Strat. But it's a Strat Elite. My bass is a Fender Precision. I play a little bit of jazz, a little country, a little blues, all kind of mixed up in there together, B. B. King, Albert Collins, a little Freddie King in there, a little George Benson. But I have to admit, I play a rhythm style that I don't see very many other guitar players playing. In order for me to be able to sing and play both at the same time, and play my rhythm strong enough for me to survive my singing and everything, I've learned how to play it like that. And since I was a bass player, too, from the very beginning, my thumb was already trained. So I just added one other finger, sometimes two more fingers—sometimes I play with three fingers, sometimes two—with my rhythm. But I have to say that I believe that my lead style, picking little parts out of everybody, I did come up with my own little style of playing. But it came from what I heard and what I learned by listening and stuff like that.

I'm playing a lot of dates these days. I go out to the West Coast. Like, we'll go to the four corners of the United States, and then we'll go to the middle, and we just kind of alternate like that every year. I end up going up into Colorado at ski time because there's a lot of music going on at that time in Steamboat Springs and Vail, Colorado. Denver, I've played clubs there. But we just go from state to state, playing. It's not like we stay out there all the time. We might go out four or five times a year, from three weeks to a month at a time. The rest of the time, we're around home. In my band right now, I have keyboard, sax (sax player also plays harmonica), guitar, drums, bass. It's a big sound.

I've had a couple of chances to go to Europe, but we just never did. . . .

I guess one of the greatest things I've done the last couple of years is the Chicago Blues Festival. That's the biggest festival I've played. I've played a lot of festivals all over California and Canada, but that Chicago one, there was just people everywhere, it was a big, huge one. But I do enjoy playing festivals. I mean, it's not that I would take sides, I'd rather play clubs than festivals or vice versa, it's just play festivals for a while and play clubs for a while, they're both okay. But in the clubs, the people are right there; you're close to people, just like everybody's involved.

I think I tell myself that my playing in life, I'm reaching into emotional issues or something. And whatever it is, I don't think I'll ever reach it, but it gives me a reason to keep going. And I guess one of the reasons music is so important in that sense to me is because I never quit learning. I never get to the end of knowledge. That keeps me going.

I'm still active in my church. St. John College Height Baptist Church. I'm still going to the same church I went to as a child. I sang at my mother's funeral Thursday, a song called "Ask and It Shall Be Given." I've written other religious songs. I haven't put them on record or anything. Sometimes around here, I've got my own little obscure studio, and I get a notion, I'll play the bass part and the guitar part, put down the piano chords, and use maybe a drum machine, and then I will sing the lead part and all the backup parts and do the whole thing.

It don't matter if you think you are a good person or if you think you are a bad person, you're still going to receive ups and downs. You're going to receive aches and pains. And that feeling is tied to the thoughts. I'll say the thinking and pain both at the same time, eventually you have to admit, "I can't do this, and I can't do that." So you have to lay there and take the pain. Well, when you do that, even if it's physical pain or just heartache, then you give in, that's when the blues opens the door and comes on in, right there. And when it does, you can hear somebody on the radio go, "Oh, baby, you don't have to go." Well, that person's baby might not be leaving him or her, but just the spirit in that sound affects him or her so much so, because it's the same thing, it's pain. Just by hearing that will help this person over here. That's one of the reasons I always say blues is not sad, blues is happy; it makes you feel happy, not sad. If a person goes out and hears a good blues band and they feel sad, that's themselves making themselves feel that way, not the music.

ANGELA STREHLI

November 22, 1945– ; interview, 1987

ANGELA STREHLI, AUSTIN, 1985. PHOTOGRAPH BY SUSAN ANTONE.

Curiosity led me down the path to the blues. I heard blues on the radio to begin with and didn't know how to find it or what to call it or anything like that. Then I began the long process of educating myself. There weren't that many people to talk to. I'd hear some Shreveport station, something like that, late at night. I had to find out what was going on.

I went to Chicago in 1966. I had been in college at Carleton College in Minnesota, but I just went crazy because there were no black people at all, and I realized that I was in the wrong environment. I worked that summer as a YWCA worker in San Antonio's West Side and used to go to black churches. I loved the gospel music and different cultures of San Antonio. My father was a professor of Spanish at Texas Tech and was invited to teach in Argentina for the summer when I was sixteen. Well, we all went, and it was there that I first heard *musica folklorica*. In San Antonio these interests combined with what I liked about black music. But I also listened to *corridos*, *rancheras*, and *musica tropical*.

While I was working for the YWCA, I got a chance to go to Chicago for a conference and wanted to hear some blues. I knew people who would not take me to clubs I wanted to go to. They thought I was crazy. I said, "Okay, I don't care." So I went alone to see some of the people I had only heard on records. In the three days I was there, I listened to blues all over Chicago's South and West Sides. I saw Howlin' Wolf on New Year's Eve at his club, Sylvio's. I saw Buddy Guy, Muddy Waters, who at that time had Otis Spann playing the piano in his band. Muddy Waters was actually kind of hard up, and he asked me if he could borrow some money. All he knew was that I was some little white girl from Texas who loved blues. So he said, "Well, have you got about $300 you can loan me?" He was very serious.

At that time I wasn't playing anything, just piddling around with a harmonica. Then I wanted to play bass. I never wanted to be a singer. But people made me start singing. I grew up in Lubbock. There was a lot of good music there at different times (Joe Ely, Butch Hancock, Jimmie Dale Gilmore, Terry Allen, Delbert McClinton). You sort of had to make your own entertainment. In high school there was a folk music club, and Jimmie and Butch Hancock played there. John Denver wasn't from Lubbock, but he was there at that time.

I left Lubbock in '64, as soon as I was out of high school. I'm forty-one and I feel good. When I got into

JFKLN 72
FREDDIE KING
FREDA and the FIREDOGS
8:30 May 19
ARMADILLO WORLD HDQRS. 525 BARTON SPRINGS ROAD
ADVANCE TICKETS 2.50 AT OATWILLIES / DISCOUNT RECORDS / DISC RECORDS (HIGHLAND MALL)
477-0146

blues, the folk blues was dying down, and rock music was bringin' rhythm and blues back in. Anyway, after I went to Chicago I became more interested in playing music myself. The following summer I went to San Francisco with a band from Austin called Lord Greystoke and The Southern Fliers. We rehearsed a couple of times, but never played a gig. So I got a job in a black record store on Divisadero Street. Then at the end of the summer I moved back to Austin to finish college in psychology and sociology.

In Austin I met Lewis Cowdrey, and we started up a little band called The Fabulous Rockets, an integrated band, mixed blacks and whites. Then we had a band called Sunnyland Special. In the late Sixties there wasn't much blues here, so we moved out to southern California. We came back and cut my first record with Lewis. My side was "Do Something for Yourself" and Lewis's was "My Backscratcher." California got to be too much. It was '68 or '69, and we came back to Austin. I got a chance to be in a twelve-piece soul band with James Polk [who now plays organ with Ray Charles]. This was a great experience to have. For most of the time, it was all black, except me. It made me really shape up and see if

(ABOVE) ANGELA STREHLI AT ANTONE'S, AUSTIN, 1984. PHOTOGRAPH BY SUSAN ANTONE.
(BELOW) MARCIA BALL, PUBLICITY PHOTOGRAPH, CA. 2004. COURTESY ALLIGATOR RECORDS.

MARCIA BALL (L.) AND ANGELA STREHLI (R.) HOUSTON, 1986. PHOTOGRAPH BY TRACY ANNE HART/THE HEIGHTS GALLERY.
(OPPOSITE) "FREDDIE KING/FREDA[MARCIA BALL] AND THE FIREDOGS," POSTER BY JIM FRANKLIN, AUSTIN, 1972. COURTESY CENTER FOR AMERICAN HISTORY, UNIVERSITY OF TEXAS.

ANTONE'S CLUB PORTRAIT, AUSTIN, LATE 1970S. PHOTOGRAPH BY GREG STEPHENS, COURTESY PAUL AND DIANA RAY.

STORM: LEWIS COWDREY (HARMONICA, VOCALS), FREDDIE WALDEN (DRUMS), JIMMIE VAUGHAN (GUITAR), PAUL RAY (BASS), MIKE KINDRED (PIANO), AUSTIN, 1972. COURTESY PAUL AND DIANA RAY.

I was really a singer. There were some tough audiences, but it lasted a couple of years.

After that I had a good band with Denny Freeman and W. C. Clark, called Southern Feeling, and we traveled around and that carried me to 1975 when I felt I was kind of in a rut. I had done all my homework. I had had my experience performing for a wide variety of audiences. I felt it was time to start writing and contributing something back to the idiom. I wanted to do something with some of my other influences in Latin music and Mexican, gospel.

My influences as a singer have been Tina Turner, her

energy, but mainly I liked the low-down blues guys that didn't have beautiful voices, J. B. Hutto, Frankie Lee Sims, Dr. Ross, Etta James, Big Mama Thornton, who I got to know a little bit out on the West Coast. Magic Sam was a real favorite of mine. I still cry for him.

In 1975 Antone's was starting up on Sixth Street, and I gave up having a band. I worked at Antone's doing the sound, being a kind of stage manager, and I had the opportunity to sing with everybody who came through. I didn't always get on stage, but I knew I could if I wanted to. I did get out on the road a little bit, with the Cobras, who needed a singer to take Paul Ray's place. Paul was having problems with his throat.

The band I have was started 1981, '82, after Antone's moved from Sixth Street to North Austin. I had a little time to go into the studio and finally decided to get serious. Our newest member is Mark Kazanoff, who was touring with Marcia Ball. I had two guitar players, David Murray and Denny Freeman, and when Marcia started her new band she needed a guitar player. So she got David and I got Kaz. He kind of brings together both the Texas and Chicago sounds, playing both tenor saxophone and harmonica. The sax and other instruments are a real inspiration to my singing. My vocals often follow the saxophone and interact with the guitar.

Over the last three years we've gotten very tight. Derek O'Brien has been in and out of so many of my bands, but technically he's not in it now. Denny Freeman is the lead guitar, but he left for a while to work with Lou Ann Barton. The other members of my band are Pat Whitefield on bass and George Rains on drums and percussion.

We do some of the obscure music we've always loved, like Etta James's "I'd Rather Go Blind." To be able to sing like that is a kind of goal. A lot of the kids that come out to hear us never heard the older stuff, and it's new music for them. Otherwise, original material is where it's at. Some of my original songs are blues, but some don't come out that way. Songs like "Your Sweetness" and "Take It from Me" obviously have other strong influences, Latin things, country and western.

Being from Texas there's so much to be proud of. You have to be good because look at who you're following. All of the great bands, western swing, jazz, blues, Mexican music. There's so much to live up to, and I think that's why the musicianship in Texas is what it has been. Musicians have always gotten along, but the society has been slow to catch up. It's a little discouraging. Ironically, black people have been cut off from their musical heritage, or have cut themselves off. Radio plays a big part in that. The social strides of the 1960s made blacks look in another direction. Blues was being dropped by a lot of blacks when white kids were getting into it. I don't completely know why. Maybe if I could fully understand it, it wouldn't be so appealing. To me, there's a sound in blues that goes beyond anything you can explain in words. It's something so deep inside that you have to be drawn to it. It's a pure feeling. All it takes is one note, one sound, and that's it. That's the intensity that I strive for in my style. Straightforwardness. I like a wide-open, uncomplicated sound. The fun part is the story, the expression, the poetry. Blues has its own language. It's not like everyday speech, but it's about everyday life.

THE FABULOUS THUNDERBIRDS

THE FABULOUS THUNDERBIRDS, *GIRLS GO WILD*, TACOMA RECORDS 1979.

JOHN CROUCH (interview, 1987)

I just like that old Thunderbird rhythm myself. I come to as many of the shows as I can. You can dance to it. It's got a good beat. It doesn't sound like a bunch of bees in a jug. You know what I mean? Of course, I didn't know one rock 'n' roller from another until my daughter, Connie, started running around with Jimmie [Vaughan] and The Thunderbirds. Then the more I was around them, the better I liked them.

We always liked Jimmie. But we've known Stevie [Ray Vaughan] longer than Jimmie. Stevie used to come to the house all the time. We had a little party room upstairs, and Stevie would come up there and play his guitar. Some one else would bring an electric organ, another would have drums, and they'd have a little party up there.

MARTHA VAUGHAN (interview, 1987)

A friend and co-worker of my husband's gave [our son] Jimmie an old guitar, which I believe had three strings on it. And they were working out of town. So the next weekend when they came home, my husband Jim picked out a couple of songs, and he said, "Well, that's pretty good. I'll just take it and get it fixed for you." It had holes in it. It was all beat up. So we took it and got it fixed for him, got it strung, and that was it. It was just like he had played all of his life. He picked it up and started playing.

Well, we were so busy watching Jim that little brother Stevie got pushed aside sometimes, but I do remember him getting a Sears & Roebuck guitar for Christmas. We didn't pay much attention to him, and then all of a sudden he was playing, too. I can remember him practicing a lot in his bedroom. No one was home but me, and I could hear him singing. He was working on it as often as he could.

I always liked their music. So it was never very hard to support what they were doing. Before Big Jim got sick, we used to dance to it. It was something we could dance to.

When I hear them play, I'll say, I believe I like this one best. Then another song will come on the record, and I say I like that the best. I like them all.

(OPPOSITE) JIMMIE VAUGHAN, HOUSTON, 1983.
PHOTOGRAPH BY TRACY ANNE HART/THE HEIGHTS GALLERY.

JIMMIE VAUGHAN

(March 20, 1951– ; interview, 1987)

When I first moved to Austin, I was about nineteen. I was working construction with this guy. He was the construction boss; he was the foreman, and me and Denny Freeman were working for him. And he said, "Hey," when he found out we could play. "I'm going to get you all some gigs in small towns"—Bastrop, little places I don't even remember the names. And we would go and play these little bitty places that you didn't know they existed. And they would say, "Here comes Little Freddie King" and I'd play Freddie King instrumentals. It was a lot of fun, but a little scary, too.

When I lived in Dallas, the blues scene happened at the Empire Room, the Forest Avenue Club. I saw Freddie King, Lowell Fulson, T-Bone Walker, Little Milton, B. B. King, Albert Collins. Two people I really wished I had gotten to see, if I had known better when I was fifteen or sixteen, are Li'l Son Jackson and Frankie Lee Sims. I met him [Sims] one time when I was playing in Freddie King's band in Houston. And he started singing "Lucy Mae."

JIMMIE VAUGHAN (L.), KIM WILSON (R.), HOUSTON, 1982. PHOTOGRAPH BY TRACY ANNE HART/THE HEIGHTS GALLERY.

KIM WILSON (L.) AND JIMMIE VAUGHAN (R.), HOUSTON, 1982.
PHOTOGRAPH BY TRACY ANNE HART/THE HEIGHTS GALLERY.

Dallas might have been segregated, but I didn't think about that. I just wanted to hear the music. They didn't say anything about me.

I love blues the best, rock 'n' roll, rhythm and blues, country and western. I like good music, comes in a lot of shapes and sizes. I like music with feeling, with soul; it doesn't matter what is. I really like the songs of Mercy Baby; he was the drummer with Frankie Lee Sims. We did one of his songs, "Marked Deck," on our first album.

I like to think that when I play the guitar it sounds like Dallas. That's where I learned everything, and all the people I saw were playing here. I suppose it's a crazy way of putting it. I heard everyone that influenced me, either live or on the radio, KNOK or "Kat's Karavan" on WRR. However, [my brother] Stevie and I grew up all over the South. I went to first grade in Jackson, Mississippi. Then we moved to Shreveport, Spring Hill, Baton Rouge, Arkansas. When we were kids, blues was the music everywhere. On both sides of our family, folks played guitars, but never really did anything. We sort of liked Dallas, but I couldn't get a gig. So I went to Austin with my friends; we knew about a bunch of hippie joints where I knew we could get a job playing blues.

In my style I borrowed a lot of things, Freddie King, B. B. King, Lightnin' Hopkins, T-Bone Walker. I may have my own approach, but it's a Texas guitar sound. If I can make people aware of them, it's only a small part of what they've done for me. It wasn't for them, there wouldn't be me. It's a black music. I think what really helped us go over was that we're a blues band that plays rock 'n' roll. We've always tried to play the fun part up and make the people like it. There have always been a lot of white bands doing this with blues, around Dallas, Houston, Austin. Joey Long is one of my heroes. He's an expert. Keith Ferguson, who used to be our bass player, was from Houston, he knew all about Joey Long. He's now with The Tailgators. Another white blues band I used to like around Dallas were The Nitecaps. They had a regional hit called "Wine, Wine, Wine," which was actually a Li'l Son Jackson song. The white crossover happened a lot earlier than when these English guys, like The Rolling Stones, got into blues. Of course, they turned it around, but there were white bands back in the 1930s, 1940s, 1950s that were playing blues, but not too many people thought about it like that.

JIMMIE VAUGHAN, ARLINGTON, 1987. PHOTOGRAPH BY ALAN GOVENAR.

KIM WILSON (January 12, 1951– ; interview, 1987)

I started into blues kind of late, seventeen or eighteen years old. Some friends of mine in school turned me on to this kind of music. I played the horn when I was a young kid, about eight years old. There was time in the middle there that I didn't want to practice. So I kind of quit it. Then these people turned me on to this blues stuff, and I picked up a harmonica, and that was it. I was in a band a month later, and have been in bands ever since then. I was born in Detroit, but musically I grew up in California, moved there in 1960, and then via other places, I moved to Texas in late 1974. I moved to Austin, and I've been there ever since.

In California I played with Lowell Fulson, and Lowell had this guy, guitar player, named Mark Pollock. He was from Texas, and he told me about Austin. I was playing with all these greats in California—Pee Wee Crayton, Lowell Fulson, Luther Tucker, John Lee Hooker—and I was only making ten or fifteen dollars a night. I called to Austin, and they said nothing was really happening. So I moved to Minneapolis, and then about a year later Mark's friend Shirley called and said she wanted me to work in some kind of music business. Well, I got a round-trip ticket to Austin and met Jimmie [Vaughan]. I met him at a place called Alexander's. It was kind of a rib joint, and it was a Sunday matinee. Jimmie was playing in a band called Storm, and Stevie [Vaughan] asked if I could sit in, and they said no. So, Stevie, Doyle [Bramhall], and I got up during the break and played, and the crowd went crazy over it. I went up and shook Jimmie's hand, and about a month later I got a call from Jimmie and he offered me a job. About a month or two later, I gave notice and moved to Austin.

DOYLE BRAMHALL II, CA. 2002. PHOTOGRAPH BY DON O.

Nobody really taught me anything. I played a lot with George Smith in California, and he really helped me out. Then there was James Cotton, Little Walter, of course. I would play, and I'd say, "Is that right?" and they'd go "Yeah." I learned a lot of lessons from guitar players, like Lowell Fulson, who'd tell me I was overplaying, don't play all the time, very choice information. My playing improved real fast. I was a singer first, but I learned to play harmonica quickly. I would say there weren't too many white people that influenced me. My dad did; he was a singer on the radio, with Danny Thomas, for a little bit.

When I first started singing blues, I liked Otis Rush. A lot of people requested Otis Rush, and then Bobby Bland. People compared my style to his. I don't see how, but they do. Also, I got into people like Junior Parker, singers. I was better with vibrato, and after that I kind of developed my own style. The doctor said I may get better, but I'll never get well.

We do our music our way. We're not forsaking any of our teachers. You got to resign yourself to the fact that you can't do like anybody else but you, and that's it. Why try? I'd say we're going more toward songs than solos. It's not that we don't solo on harmonica and guitar. We think more about singles. We're doing more ballads. There's more balance, a little bit of everything we have. We remade "How Do You Spell Love" because the audience reaction was so good. With Dave Edmunds as producer, he's making us sound more like us.

Up on stage we're on our own. We try to have a pure sound. We have the instruments we want, and we've learned how to play to the back row, to reach everyone in the audience.

JIMMIE VAUGHAN (L.), STEVIE RAY VAUGHAN (R.), BACKSTAGE, AUSTIN OPERA HOUSE, 1984. PHOTOGRAPH BY TRACY ANNE HART/THE HEIGHTS GALLERY.

JIMMIE VAUGHAN AND STEVIE RAY VAUGHAN, AUSTIN, 1985. PHOTOGRAPH BY ANDREW LANG. COURTESY CENTER FOR AMERICAN HISTORY, UNIVERSITY OF TEXAS.

DOYLE BRAMHALL III

February 17, 1949– ; interview by Jay Brakefield, 2001

DOYLE BRAMHALL III AND CHARLIE SEXTON, AUSTIN, MAY 2005. PHOTOGRAPH BY TRACY ANNE HART/THE HEIGHTS GALLERY.

A lot of times, people confuse wanting to have that big, polished hit, and they forget about the career. When I first started playing music, my twin brother and I, Dale, we both sang when we were kids, and I remember growing up in Dallas and singing when we were about five years old at family gatherings. And I never thought, "Oh, boy, I can't wait to have a video on MTV." There was none of that. I didn't know anything about the music business or anything, and I had an uncle—Uncle Lloyd, who was a great harmonica player, chromatic player. He was in several bands in Dallas, some of the big bands. He was a harmonica player. And he was always coming over. Every time he'd come over, he'd bring us both harmonicas, and my brother would always play it. For some reason, I never picked it up. I had a drawer full of harmonicas I never used. But he was a great player, so there was that influence. My mother played a little piano.

In the late Fifties, early Sixties, [my brother] Ronnie had a blues club. They were definitely ahead of their time. I look back on it now. There were about four or five guys from Irving High School. They would rotate every week and be at our house. The next week would be at T. C.'s house. The next week would be at Larry's house. So about every sixth week, they would come to our house. And my brother Dale and I, we were too young to get in. They weren't about to let kid brothers in there to listen to it. But we'd always sit outside the door. They'd play Lightnin' Slim, and Muddy Waters and B. B. and all the Kings and Juniors. It was just great. And there was always music going on even before that with my parents, my sister, and my aunt. My mother loved to dance, so when we were very young, they were always dancing. There was always music. And I thought everybody grew up like that, with music around. Of course, later on, I found out that some people had no clue about music.

My brother and I were born in Methodist Hospital in Dallas. And actually, my parents lived in West Dallas, over in what was called Cement City. Off Singleton. Yeah, there was Trinity Portland Cement and Lone Star Cement Company. And a lot of my family worked at Trinity Portland. My father, that's where he worked his whole life. And so, when we were born, we lived in West Dallas. My dad wanted to get out of there. And so both of

DOYLE BRAMHALL III AND CHARLIE SEXTON, HOUSTON, FEBRUARY 2005. PHOTOGRAPH BY TRACY ANNE HART/ THE HEIGHTS GALLERY.

THE ARCANGELS: DOYLE BRAMHALL III AND CHARLIE SEXTON, CONTINENTAL CLUB, HOUSTON, 2005.
PHOTOGRAPH BY TRACY ANNE HART/THE HEIGHTS GALLERY.

my parents were just really hard-working parents. And they just had a vision of, "I just want to get my kids out of here." And so we moved to Irving in about '55.

My mother always worked at grocery stores, and there was a place on Singleton Boulevard called Friendly Foodland. And I remember when I was real young, my brother and I would go down there and just hang out. There were Mexicans and blacks and whites, and just everybody was always running into different people. And it was real interesting, because in the meat market, the guy would have a little radio, and he'd be playing country and western. And then, over the little PA thing inside the main store was like, KLIF or whatever, that was playing more the pop music of the day or whatever. And then, in the back rooms, on one side, there'd be blues music, and on the other side, there'd be Mexican music. I was always listening to a mix; I had a lot of that in my life at an early age.

I started playing drums, I guess, when I was about ten or eleven, even younger. I remember my parents, especially my dad, saying, "Put the fork and spoon down," because I was always beating on glasses and plates and stuff like that. And so, finally, I talked about maybe getting a drum set and whatever, but when The Beatles were on *Ed Sullivan*—I think they were on for three weeks in a row—and the first week they were on, like the day after, I was just like, "Dad, I've got to have some drums, please. Get me some drums." So we went over to McCord Music in downtown Dallas, and I got me a Ludwig bass drum and a Slingerland ride tom and a Gretch floor tom and whatever. But anyway, the next week, when The Beatles were on, I had my drum set set up in front of the TV. And it was real interesting, because about seven months later, I was in my first band.

People kept saying, "You ought to take some lessons." So I went in, and I just—I was in too big a hurry. I didn't want to do any flamadiddles or paradiddles or any of that stuff. After about two weeks, I took a record—I can't remember what record it was—and said, "I want to play like this." And he said, "Here's the way I teach." And I said, "But I don't want to do that." So anyway, I just went home. I had a friend that played drums in school, and he had a drum kit. He showed me a few things, and I just kept playing. And then, my brother, we had a couple of friends at Irving High School that were also just starting out, and we just got together and starting playing in the living rooms and stuff. I remember my first gig, somebody had a party, and we set up in their living room. It was about an 8-by-10-foot living room, little bitty house, and I remember having just a great time.

Where we lived in Irving, there was a Teen A-Go-Go. We had a creek; across the street from us, there were houses, but behind that, there was a creek. And across that was the Irving Community Center in Senter Park. Of course, my brother and his buddies would go down there. That building is still there. Upstairs, they had plate glass windows, so if you were standing outside, you could see in. And I just remember, my brother and

I would sneak out, and cross over the dam, and get up in there. I think, really, the first time, before even the Beatle thing happened, I remember specifically, The Nitecaps used to play there. My brother and them, they all went. But Dale and I snuck out and went over there, and I just remember [how we] looked up. They had the bandstand set up against one of the side windows, so you could see. You could see all the people going in and dancing. I remember standing out there and going, "That's what I want to do." And so we'd be sitting at home on the front porch. You could hear them playing "Wine, Wine, Wine" and "Thunderbird" and all that. So, really, that was probably the first time I thought, "That's what I want to do, right there."

The first band I was in was called The Cobras. Paul Ray and The Cobras, from Austin. The first rendition of The Cobras was Stevie [Ray Vaughan], Paul Ray, Denny Freeman, and myself. And I think we rehearsed for a few weeks, but we never actually played. But that's where The Cobras started. We were all sitting around in a circle and going, "Well, time for a name." So everybody went around the room. I think Paul said, "Okay, what's the first band you ever played in?" And it went around the horn, and I said, "The Cobras." And it was like, "Okay, that's it." But I don't think we ever played any gigs. Of course, Denny and Paul kept it going, and Stevie and I, I think during that period of time, it was right after The Nightcrawlers had broken up. Not too many people know this, but Stevie and I went out and played with Doug Sahm for about two months. Doug asked Stevie to play guitar, and Stevie said, "Well, I will if Doyle can play drums." And they already had a drummer. And so it ended up, for a while there, with double drums and Stevie.

I remember coming up here. I think it was Fannie Ann's. They would book bands for five days at a time. And, I don't remember, I know we played Austin a couple of times. That was '74, right after The Nightcrawlers broke up, which was the end of '73. We had just gotten back from Hollywood and recorded an album with Marc Benno. It never came out. But that was Stevie and myself and Benno and a guy named Billy Etheridge that played keyboards. And Tommy McClure on bass. I was in The Cobras first, and then these guys—they were older—I think I was sixteen. I went out with a friend of mine that was actually playing drums with these guys from West Texas, Levelland. And they were called The Nitrons. And the lead singer of that band, his name was Tommy Latham. And he actually lives in Fort Worth, still. I was sixteen; I think they were all twenty-three or something. I thought, "Man, these guys are old." But they were really good, and Tommy sang a lot of Roy Orbison stuff, and he sounded just like him, or close. And so I went out to this VFW hall with this friend that was playing drums with them. And after the gig, they were going to do one more. He said, "Why don't you get up and play drums?" "Uh-uh, I couldn't do that." I was scared to death. So anyway, I finally got up, and after the gig was over, they came over to me and asked me if I wanted to play drums for them. I don't think I ever talked to that drummer, ever again.

They were playing over at Lou Ann's at the time, in Dallas, at Greenville and Lovers, I think. It was such a great place, back in the Forties and Fifties, everybody played there: big bands and Jimmy Smith, and all the local bands would play there. If you were anybody and came through Dallas, you probably played Lou Ann's. So anyway, the way it was laid out, there was a big room. When the main band would take a break, there was a smaller room that the other band would start in. And there's where The Nitrons were playing, in the smaller room. And one night we were playing Lou Ann's, and these guys called The Chessmen were playing in the main room. At the time, I only sang two songs. I sang "Gloria" and "Satisfaction." And they happened to hear me one night and came up to me and asked me if I'd like to play drums with them. I mean, they were like big, to me, at the time. They were playing and making good money and whatever, so I jumped in on that. And we were together about two years, and we cut two or three singles. Actually one of them was called "I Need You There." And there was a deejay in Dallas named Jimmy Rabbit, on KLIF. We had a kind of regional hit with that. One time he came up to me and he said, "Doyle, what time do you get to school?" And I said, "Oh, about a quarter of eight."

So for two weeks after that, about a quarter of eight, I'd pull up in the parking lot. I mean, I barely had my license. But pull up in the parking lot, and he would play that song on the radio. And so, about the first two or three days, people were going, "Hey, I heard this song on the radio. It was your band." And I'd say, "Yeah." So anyway, after about a week, the word got out, and I'd pull up in the parking lot, and there'd be people standing outside with their car radios on. And then after about two weeks, there were quite a few people. And I was, "I like this." All the girls started coming over. And I went, "I think I'm doing the right thing." I already liked playing, so: "I kinda dig this. I didn't know this came with the territory." And we were together about two years, and one of the guitar players that we had, Robert Patton, he and Tommy Carter were the two guys that came from Midland-Odessa that started The Chessmen. And they both lived in Denton, and they went to North Texas State. A lot of musicians lived up there at the time, Don Henley and just a ton of musicians lived in Denton. Seemed like musicians back then, they got together more or something, so we'd all hang out with each other. But Robert Patton was pledging for this fraternity at North Texas, and he really didn't drink. But of course they were going to do their hazing thing. And they got him to drink, and they went to White Rock Lake, and they got on this small sailboat. And it was storming and just terrible weather. And he was sitting at the back, and a wave caught it and he hit his head on the back and drowned. It was just terrible. They found him about a week later. And we were like, "Oh, God, can we go on? Robert would want us to go on." So we held auditions, and this was in '66. And one of the players that came out to audition was Jimmie [Vaughan]. So that's where we first hooked up. There was a guitar player, Johnny Peebles. I think he's started getting back out and playing the last few years. Just a really fine guitar player. And he lived in DeSoto, but he was from Oak Cliff. And at the time, he was our second guitar player in The Chessmen. And he said, "Well, I know this kid that's fifteen, named Jimmie Vaughan." So he came out, and of course, after about one song, we hired him. But that's the first time I met Jimmie. He was fifteen; I was right at seventeen. And Stevie was twelve.

I didn't even know Jimmie had a brother, because he never talked about him. And what I would do—Jimmie didn't have a license. And either Johnny would go by and pick up Jimmie for the gig, or I would drive from Irving and pick him up. And usually, I would just pull up and honk the horn, and he'd come out. I guess about three

(L. TO R.) ROBIN SYLER, DOYLE BRAMHALL II, AND ALEX NAPIER, THE CAVE, DALLAS, 1979. PHOTOGRAPH BY ANN STAUTBERG.

or four months went by, and I pulled up and honked, and Jimmie walked out on the front porch and waved me to come in. So anyway, I went in and sat on the couch, and he went from the back of the house to the kitchen. When he walked in the kitchen, I heard this guitar playing going on in the bedroom the other way, and I went, "Well, couldn't be Jimmie because he's in the kitchen." So I walked back, and the door was open just a couple of inches. And I peeked in, and there was this little kid sitting on the floor with his legs crossed, playing "Jeff's Boogie," that Jeff Beck tune. And he looked up and stopped playing and he goes, "Hi. I'm Stevie." I said, "Hi, Stevie. I'm Doyle. Don't stop playing." So he kept playing a little bit, and Jimmie came over and went, "Let's go! Let's go!" So that was the first time I ever met Stevie. He had this huge, wonderful smile on his face that I'll never forget.

I know he was always trying to play Jimmie's guitar, and Jimmie didn't want him to. I think Stevie was playing a three-quarter-neck Gibson. I think; I'm not sure what it was. But I know it wasn't the regular scale guitar. It was like a three-quarter-neck something. But that was the first time I ever met Stevie. Yeah, there was definitely something there. And within a matter of a couple of years, it was like, "Stevie's band's playing here." And a few years went by, and I really had never heard his band, but I went out and heard them one night somewhere in Oak Cliff, and I was just like, "God," you know. I mean, here were two guys in the same family that could play the way they played. And so The Chessmen broke up, and Jimmie went to California with some guys. I think he lived in Oakland for about eight or nine months. And I was playing with another band in Dallas, and Jimmie came back from California and said, "Let's start another band." So we put together

(L. TO R.) DOYLE BRAMHALL III, CLIFFORD ANTONE, AND CHARLIE SEXTON, BACKSTAGE AT ANTONE'S, 2005. PHOTOGRAPH BY TRACY ANNE HART/THE HEIGHTS GALLERY.

this band that was called Texas Storm. And it was Jimmie on guitar, and Stevie played bass, and Phil Campbell played drums, and I sang. I'm sorry, before that, we started a band that was called Texas. And we played the Cellar for about a year or so. That was me and Jimmie. And then, Texas broke up, and Texas Storm formed, and that was with Stevie on bass.

I just sang in Storm. Well, in Texas, I just sang, too. Phil Campbell also played drums in that band. And we went out of town for a few gigs here and there, but we mainly played the Cellar, and I think at the time, about seven or eight months. They had a place in Houston and Fort Worth and Dallas. And it was a deal, like, it started at nine; it wasn't over till three in the morning. So there were like four or five bands that played. And the thing about it is, say, you played from nine to ten, you wouldn't go back on until two. You got to hear a lot of music. And Bugs Henderson was one of the bands that played. That's the first time I ever met Bugs. It was right downtown right across the street from the old KLIF. A lot of bands played there, and it was a real racist place. They had a sign over the door that said, "No coloreds allowed." And there were these huge black guys; they wanted to come in. And I just remember a big, huge fight. I mean, all of a sudden from the back room, these bouncers came running out that I never even knew were there. It was a mess. And I was like, "This is fucking weird." And like I said, growing up in West Dallas, I never saw any of that. I think after that incident, for a couple of reasons, we just decided to leave. But we played the one in Dallas with Bugs and the one in Fort Worth was Dusty Hill with Z. Z., and Rocky, his brother, and then Frank Beard, the drummer with Z. Z. They were playing at the Fort Worth Cellar. And I went to grade school and junior high with Frank. We were like the two drummers at Irving. He was in the rival band. But that's where a bunch of us met back then. During the Chessmen period, we would play down in Houston. It was an under-eighteen club, and we would play down there quite a bit. It was the first time The Moving Sidewalks would share the bill with The Chessmen, and that was Billy Gibbons.

Rocky was in a band called American Blues; that was the band that played the Cellar in Fort Worth. That was Rocky and Dusty and Frank. Well, Rocky's still that loud. Great player. We would play at Louann's in The Chessmen, and one of the bands that would play there once in a while was The American Blues. And that was the first time we met Dusty and Rocky. And then we'd go to Houston, and they were going to Houston and playing, too, so that's where they hooked up with Billy. But we would share bills with The Moving Sidewalks. All these players from back then, we were always running into each other because there weren't a whole lot of players. There weren't a whole lot of touring bands. There was just a handful that would tour around Texas, unlike today. And we'd go to Austin. I guess the first time I ever played in Austin was in '65. And the fraternities down there is what—there were no clubs, really, in Austin, but the fraternities and sororities would hire bands. And so that's the first time I ever met Doug and a lot of people from Lubbock and San Antonio and Houston, was when we started going to play at these fraternity parties.

Stevie and I played with Doug Sahm. It was during the period of time when that *Mendocino* album came out, so we were doing most of the songs off that album. "She's about a Mover." I think Augie Meyers showed up every once in a while, but like I said, it just didn't last very long, and at the time, it was not a good period for any of us, really. We were more interested in how drunk and stoned we could get. But that didn't last very long. And I just remember after a couple weeks of playing, we hadn't been paid. I think we played about eight or nine gigs. He ended up giving us half the money. But he was notorious for that. We get together now, we talk about Doug. I love Doug. But we get together and talk about Doug, and it's like, "Did he owe you any money?" "Well, yeah, of course he did." But Doug was a champion. He was behind so much of the music, and you couldn't have a better guy in your corner. He'd talk about you all over the world. He was a great guy; he just didn't like to pay. He had one of the greatest blues bands. He'd play Antone's and just knock your socks off.

In 1975 I left Austin and came back to Dallas. And when I came back up here, I kind of retreated from everything. I just kind of stayed to myself for a while and tried my best not to abuse everything that came my way. [In] '75, I played a few gigs. I played with Lightnin' Hopkins for a while. And a couple other acts that would come through town. And then I hooked up with Anson. I think Anson and I lived together for six or seven months. And we just played a few gigs here and there. I went back down to Houston and played with Rocky Hill for a while in the late Seventies. And then when I came back up here, I met Robin Syler and Alex Napier, and we started a band called The Millionaires. We were playing a club in Dallas called The Cave. I think Fannie Ann's was right down from the Cave. Stevie would come up quite a bit and play Fannie Ann's, and on break, I'd either go see Stevie, or we always stayed in touch. The Millionaires lasted from New Year's to New Year's—one year, that's all we could stand.

I think because it was so intense, that was right at the end of my drinking/drugging days. And it was so intense because we would see how many pitchers of beer we could drink in one night. So the bartender was always coming up to the bandstand and going, "Y'all got to give up some of those pitchers, because we don't have any for the customers." I'd look down, and I'd have like six pitchers next to my drum kit. It was just nuts. And then in '79 is when I decided I'd had enough. A number of things pointed in that direction, and I knew that I'd already lost one family to drinking and drugging, and I had met the woman I'm still with today, Barbara Logan. And I was about to lose her. And I just went, "Either get sober or do yourself a favor and get out of this world or whatever." So I got sober. I haven't had a drink since '79. I went back out about '83 for about a year off and on because I wasn't finished with pills and coke. I've been sober since '86, completely sober. That time around, Stevie sobered up a couple of months before I did; I think he sobered up in November of '85. We were always supporting each other because we'd already been through so much together. It's kinda like, okay, we did our thing together, we played our music, went to the extremes of everything, and then we had another chance. So we grabbed it.

Stevie was really into recovery. Well, Stevie was that kind of guy. No matter if he was playing or [if the issue was] his sobriety or shopping for shoes, or whatever, Stevie was totally into it, which was just—being around him just made you feel good. Even when we were fucked up, he was always funny. I always say if Stevie hadn't been a musician, he'd have been a comedian. He loved life and music and people. The bus would be pulling off, and Stevie would still be signing autographs. We'd have to jump off the bus and physically carry him to the bus. So that was always great to see, that he just loved being around people.

It was just awful when Stevie died. For a few weeks—well, even longer—I don't even remember. I was in shock. I remember I was living in Fort Worth at the time. My stepson came in and said, "You've got a bunch of messages on your answering machine." You know, I slept in late. So this was about noon, I guess, and I get up, and a few minutes after I'm up, Barbara walks in the front door, and she's just crying. I said, "What is going on?" Just before she walked in, I had pushed the answering machine. And nobody said anything except, "I am so sorry." And at the time, I thought it was my son because he was around and he was having some problems. So immediately, I thought it was Doyle. And I said, "What is going on here?" And Barbara said, "Well, they think that Stevie was on a helicopter and was killed." It was just awful. And having to go through that week was just terrible. But I look on it now, and I have such great memories. And of course his music is there, and for me, it was like a personal thing with Stevie. He was like a brother to me. I knew Stevie as Stevie. There wasn't any Stevie Ray; it was just Stevie. And he happened to be able to play and sing, too. He was just the sweetest, sweetest guy; had a heart as big as Texas, and being around him was so wonderful, but he was so into whatever he was into. And it was like, if I ever didn't want to drag my butt out of bed, Stevie'd be like, "Let's go! Let's go! Let's go! Come on! Come on!" So he was always that kind of an influence. "Okay, let's go! What are you doing?" A lot of energy, a lot of passion. It was just a really difficult time, but we had a lot of good times together and did hook up. We had written once before; back in The Nightcrawlers, we wrote "Dirty Pool." And so we'd been writing together and, of course, playing off and on together, but during the time when Stevie was doing *Soul to Soul*, I had a couple of demo songs, "Change It" and "Looking Out the Window." And Stevie was in Austin, and he was moving at the time outside of Austin, out in the country. They were in preproduction, and he called me and said, "I've got this song called 'Ain't Gonna Give Up on Love.' And I'd like for you to come down and help me see what we can do to it, help me write it."

So I went to this studio where they were rehearsing, and we worked on it for about a day and a half and just never could connect on it. But I had this tape in this little bag I had, and we went back over to his house, and he had like the Ryder truck, or U-Haul or whatever. We were loading up boxes; you know, I was helping him move. And he had this tape player sitting downstairs, and of course, then, I was like, "I've got these songs, but I never played them for anybody, because I thought people would look at me and go, 'Well, they suck.'" Except for "Dirty Pool," I didn't have any songs, and I thought, "Well, I'd better do something here," because we were down to pretty much our last box. And he was going to grab the tape player, so I just put the tape in, and "Change It" played, and he stopped and dropped the box and said, "What's that?" I said, "Well, it's a song I wrote called 'Change It.'" He goes, "I want to do that." And the next song was "Looking Out the Window," and he goes, "I want to do that one." And then "Too Sorry" was on there, a song that I put on my *Bird Nest* album, and he said, "I'd like to do that one, but every time I sing it, I lie." So anyway, he ended up doing "Change It" and "Looking Out the Window," and of course, immediately we got writing songs. And he would call me before a project. Usually he'd call me two weeks before he was supposed to go in the studio, like cramming for exams. But that's the way it worked for us. We'd get together for two weeks, five or six days a week, for about ten or twelve hours, and just go for it.

Playing with Lightnin' Hopkins was probably one of the greatest experiences I ever had because you know Lightnin'—I mean, he didn't really have any structure of songs. He would stop and start whenever he stopped and started. And so you were constantly on your toes, which to me was the greatest school you could go to because you would just challenge yourself every night. You'd have to just watch him, and he was so funny. For some reason, he never attacked me, but he was always stopping the show and saying to the audience, "Me and this bass player gotta get it together," or, "Me and this keyboard player gotta get it together." And I was, like, every night, going, "Please, don't point me out!" He was like real intense on getting it right.

Offstage, he was the man. You did it Lightnin's way, or you didn't do it any way. I mean, he was nice, but you do anything around him he didn't like, and you were out of there. I remember one night, we were playing the Granada Theater several nights. I went backstage, and we were just sitting around. It was just me and Lightnin,' and he goes, "Doyle, you know how I got my name Lightnin'?" And I'd already heard several stories. I just went, "No." And he goes, "I was sitting on my front porch, and lightnin' hit me." That was the story he told me. He had about six of them. I just went, "All right. I like that."

Over the years, going to Antone's or just being up here, being around Freddie King—I first met Freddie King in The Chessmen back in '66 or '65. There was a club in Dallas that The Chessmen played for about one summer. And then there was a club down the street called the Players' Lounge. That's where a lot of the musicians would get together and hang out. And one day a bunch of us were in there, and I looked over, and there was this big guy sitting at the bar. And they said, "Man, that's Freddie King." So I went up and introduced myself. I got to play with Freddie a few gigs here and there, which was fun, of course. That's the beauty of being around for thirty-some-odd years. You meet a lot of different people and hopefully share the stage with some of them. So I got to play with Freddie and Lightnin' and Mance Lipscomb and Otis Rush and these guys I'd idolized. You're up there playing, going, "That's Otis Rush!"

Mance hardly ever used a drummer. But there were a couple of gigs that he played. Of course, you sure didn't play loud. But he had a piano player, and he would have a drummer. And so, I just did a few dates with him. I don't know how often he did that. But I remember the first time I ever saw him, he had a drummer. I just remember Mance playing acoustic. He was a sweet man. Going from Lightnin' to him was like night and day.

Mark Pollock—I guess it was during the Marc Benno and The Nightcrawlers time period, when we went out to do the album for A&M Records in Hollywood, Mark was playing with Lowell Fulson. And he was living with Lowell. He was living in the basement of Lowell's house, and across the street was one of Ray Charles's houses, in Watts. And I went over there a couple of times and hung out. We were over there one day, and Lowell goes, "We're going to play some cards this afternoon. Whoever wants to join in." I said, "I don't want to play," and Mark said, "No, I don't want to play." Freddie King comes over, and he's got a bunch of Freddie King albums. And so we sat there. Lowell called his Cadillac, instead of "Cadillac Brougham," he called it a "Browham Wood." He said, "Mark, go up to the liquor store and get me some whiskey in my Browham Wood." So we went up there and got some, and we came back and sat there. It was so funny because there were Freddie and Lowell and a couple of Lowell's friends, and they were all playing cards all day. And they were sitting there, and of course, starting out, Lowell had his album on, playing something. And he'd get up and go to the bathroom, and Freddie'd walk over and take it off and put his on. They did that all day. And then that night, we got to go to Whiskey A-Go-Go and see Freddie play. Just a great show. I always liked that: "When's he going to leave again so I can put mine on?"

But like I said, it's just been so great to have a chance to see all these great blues players and to have an opportunity to play with them is just a dream come true. It seems like there was a level of playing that was kind of an unspoken word, that people used to—when you'd hear players play—for me, up until about ten years ago, or whatever—there was just a level it seemed like you had to play before you would want to go out and play in front of somebody. And nowadays, like I said earlier, the bar is lowered, and now if you can play three chords and look good, you have a band. But that just wasn't the way it was back then. Nowadays, a lot of people like to stick everything they know in one song. And it's not what you play. If you can't stick everything in one song, don't stick it.

What I've always tried to play for, is play for the song. Okay, you got a bass player, you got a keyboard player, you got a guitar player. You got a drummer; you got horns, whatever you have. I always sit back and try to listen to what they're doing, and if I feel something, then I'll put it in there. But I don't want to walk over everybody, and so many times, these days, you'll hear a band, and before the singer stops singing, the guitar player's already started playing again. It's like they're not in it for the team, they're in it just for themselves. That's not the way I grew up. To me, it's about the song, and that's how I approach producing. I have to like whatever I accept, like working with Marcia Ball or Chris Duarte or Indigenous. Those are the three projects I've done in the last year and a half. I have to like what I'm going to do, number one. I try to convey the song and what's best for the song.

As a producer, I'm involved in different ways. It depends. Like with Indigenous, there wasn't any preproduction, and they had a few songs already written and a few ideas. But basically, we just all got together, and it pretty much just happened during the time we were recording. Mato and I would get together, and we would write some stuff. Indigenous is an American Indian band from South Dakota, they gave me a call and said, "We'd love for you to produce our next record." I think it was late '98, early '99. At first I said, "I don't know if I can do this because I had a lot of other things going on." They just kept being persistent, and finally, I said, "Well, why don't I come up to Minnesota?" They were recording at a studio outside of St. Paul. So I thought, "Well, I'll just go up there for a few days and see what's going on." And after the first day, I was like, "I can't not do this." It's really interesting. I tell people, "American Indian band," and they go, "Oh, that's real interesting," and they say, "Well, what kind of music do they play?" "Well, it's rhythm and blues." "What?" But they're young; I think Mato is the oldest; I think he's twenty-six. The drummer, female, sister—two brothers, a sister, and a cousin. And they're a blues-rock band, but they've been getting quite a bit of publicity.

When I starting working with Chris Duarte, he already had all his songs. And I had always been involved as a musician and never on the side of the business. So that's something that I've been learning the last year and a half or so. I just want to go in and deal with the music. It's like, "Well, if you're going to be producer, you're going to have to deal with the record label." So you deal with all that, which is real interesting, because I had never done that before. So you learn the business side, too, who's going to come in, getting players together, and kind of being the go-between for the artists, and just trying to anticipate what the artists might want. I try to make things as comfortable as I can. I just think that's so important, because I've been around so many players that take themselves so serious. And it's like, "Wait a minute," you know. I mean, I look at music; when I'm playing, it is what I do for a living, and it is my business. And I believe in being very professional. But I also believe in having a good time with it. I know what it's like being so serious that you can't get outside of yourself. I went through that period in the early Seventies. Of course, I never hardly had any fun, either. I was too serious. We thought we had to live the blues to play it, make situations up: The drunker I get, the more I throw up, that means I've got the blues more than you do. And that was kind of the attitude back then, which is just ridiculous, but for whatever reason, I had to go through that.

I'm committed to do Joe Kubek's next CD. It looks like we're going to do it in January. And then, I've been approached by two other artists; I can't say who now, but two other artists that want to talk with me about their next CDs. I'm just kind of starting back; I think I have four dates through the end of the year. I'm trying to balance it out to where if a project comes along as far as producing, and it's something I really feel good about, I'll do. But I also would like to play thirty or forty dates a year. I've been relatively inactive for a while. The only gigs I really ever played were with my son. My son, Doyle III, is doing great. He's clean and sober now.

I didn't play too much for a while. That was kind of during the period when we were building the house. And I had some health problems, too, that I was dealing with. I was diagnosed with hepatitis C. And right now, I'm fine, but there were a couple of years there that—with hepatitis C, it's different for everybody, but one of the things is that you're just tired constantly. Just getting out of bed, for a while there, was tough. Now, I know a lot of people who have it, and my hat's off to them, because I know a lot of people that get up and go to work every day and have it, and I don't know how they do it. But it's a disease that's starting to get quite a bit of attention. In the era that we grew up, I found out there's probably something I did in the Sixties that's been laying dormant all these years. But about four and a half years ago, it popped its ugly head up.

We live now about ten miles south of Alpine, so we're pretty secluded. It really came down to in Wimberley, we thought about staying there, being close to Central Texas and Austin and Dallas–Fort Worth. But in order to do that, we were going to have to sink quite a bit of money into the house. We thought, "Well, if we're going to do that, why don't we just build?" And we had been going to Alpine or Big Bend. Barbara and I both are from Texas, and we'd never been down there. So about seven years ago, we went down there and just totally fell in love with, number one, no humidity—hardly any. When it came down to it, when we decided to look for some land and go ahead and build, one of the main things was humidity.

It really doesn't matter where I live. It's not like I have to be somewhere every week. When I play, I usually go out for a week or two weeks or whatever the time. To be able to write songs down here in Alpine. It's about eight or nine hours from Dallas. It's just beautiful down here. I feel like I've always lived here. It's quiet, like going back in time for me.

STEVIE RAY VAUGHAN

October 3, 1954–August 27, 1990; interview, 1987

Looking back, Stevie Ray Vaughan's death seems all the more poignant because his influence continues to resound in contemporary blues. Vaughan was at the forefront in the growth of rock-influenced blues that has blurred regional differences. Blues has become an international music that transcends cultural boundaries. Had Vaughan lived, his music would have continued to evolve.

Back in 1987, it seemed that Stevie Ray Vaughan had a new profile. He appeared calmer, more self-assured with his status as one of the reigning masters of blues/rock guitar. His single-string runs were as graceful as T-Bone Walker's or as biting as Jimi Hendrix's. He would pull out every sound he could find, bending the strings, twisting the guitar behind his back, showing every note in the gestures of his tightly drawn face. His performance was neater, perhaps slicker in the shuffles, faster, playing the distortion into his music with piercing notes. After a year of divorce, drug problems, and the death of his father, Stevie Ray Vaughan had adjusted to a new way of life.

OMAR DYKES WITH OMAR AND THE HOWLERS, HOUSTON, 1987.
PHOTOGRAPH BY TRACY ANNE HART/THE HEIGHTS GALLERY.

I don't think that my attitude [toward blues] has changed that much, only in the sense that I've got more knowledge of what I've been listening to all along. That really hasn't changed a lot. I've always really liked the music for what it is, and just try to grow with what I do with it.

Rhythm and blues and rock 'n' roll were my first interests. Before I got to playing, when I was seven or eight years old, you might pick out songs on the radio that aren't too hip. My brother, Jimmie, was bringing home records, Muddy Waters, B. B. King, T-Bone Walker, Buddy Guy, Howlin' Wolf, and at the same bringing home British blues boom records, Rolling Stones, Bluesbreakers, groups like that, and of course, the Beatles stuff started hittin' it. I was real fortunate because I was able to hear both sides of it, the originals and the remakes. It was a lot of fun. That's the influence. All of the people I was getting to listen to as the originals were the same people that The Stones, Clapton, and others were listening to. That's the way I heard it, with less restrictions about being a purist [bringing the Chicago small band approach together with the Texas guitar sound].

That Texas guitar sound is a good thing. I've never known what that means other than in some ways it's a little rougher and sometimes a little smooth, kind of mishmash. It's a big place. As far as I know there's a kind of a hard line, an attitude about it, more than anything. I guess that's one thing about all the players I listened to. It was all kind of, not necessarily this is the only way to do it, but this is how it's done. There wasn't any joking around about it. They might be funny songs, but the approach to the playing, it was right to the point.

I never saw T-Bone Walker live, but lots of times on record. But my biggest influence has been my brother, Jimmie, because of probably all the other influences he made it possible for me to have. Those people included Freddie King, B. B. King, Albert King, Lonnie Mack. The first record I ever bought was Lonnie Mack's "Wham," the first one I ever bought for myself. But there was Freddie, B. B., and Albert, Buddy Guy, Hubert Sumlin. Hubert is still one of the wildest guitar players I ever heard, without a doubt. Of course, from Hendrix I heard all these different influences that I couldn't put a finger on. Bo Diddley, Albert Collins. This is 1966 or '67 that Jimmie first brought home a Hendrix record.

(OPPOSITE) STEVIE RAY VAUGHAN, HOUSTON, 1983.
PHOTOGRAPH BY TRACY ANNE HART/THE HEIGHTS GALLERY.

STEVIE RAY VAUGHAN AND JOE ELY, HOUSTON, 1984. PHOTOGRAPH BY TRACY ANNE HART/THE HEIGHTS GALLERY.

After I heard that, then as I went along, I'd hear all these other people. I could pick this piece out of Hendrix's sound, and say this must have come . . . and go on and look at it from there.

Sometimes it's just the way I heard it. All these different people that I heard at different periods of time, and they all seem to fit together to me. So whatever comes to mind, whatever style, whether I'm in tune or not, sometimes. Most of the time it's just putting everything into play. You know, there's all sorts of things that go on at different times. Believe me, my thoughts are a lot more in a flow these days than they were a year ago or more. A year ago or so, it was everything flying around at once. I couldn't grab ahold of anything, but some good music came out when I took the time to slow down enough to see it.

It can get a little strange without having a new record out. To be out on the road, promoting a live record, we keep being expected to play these same songs. It's gotten to the point where I don't play "Cold Shot," or this one or that one. There's invariably somebody saying, "God damn, I came to see you, mainly to play that song." So, can't really win for losin' in that respect. If there's a time limit, we play as many songs as we can and try to have fun with it. We never have a song list when we go on stage. It's pretty much what comes to mind, and there's some nights we play more off-the-wall things than others. Sometimes it just seems that the right thing to do is to play familiar songs, but we're less and less doing that. We're trying to take the pressure out of the situation. Besides all the original stuff we plan to work on, and the stuff we're working on anyway, we're just thinking about in the meantime, just working a bunch of songs we always wanted to play, and go play some clubs, just have fun. To hell with all the pressure, and just try them out and see what happens. Out of what comes from just having fun, whether it's our new songs or songs we've always liked, out of that is going to come a lot of new original stuff just from the excitement of playing new things. I've realized that any time that there is a block to write, any time there is anything that blocks that fun of it, you need to just go back to square one, start off like a bunch of guys that want to get together and play some music that we like, and go from there.

Lately I've gotten my record player back, some of my records. I listen to KKDA a lot. I listen to old Bobby Bland, Albert Collins, Johnny "Guitar" Watson. I've been listening a lot of Buddy Guy, B. B., the same people I've always listened to. It's like I've just found them, a newborn kid, remembering all these feelings I used to have. Now that I'm sober, it's all something just vague in the past. Oh, that's where I came from.

We're planning to co-produce our new record [with the passing of John Hammond] with someone who will be a kind of backboard for us, someone to bounce things off of. When they see us going in a direction, going in and making it easy for us to do that, by pulling it out a little bit, by pulling out stops that we might not think of. When we go in, we want to know exactly what we want to do, which might mean finishing a couple of songs in the studio, which is what we do anyway.

I had a lot of fun working with John Hammond. It may not have been as much fun for the engineer. A lot of times the engineer is only involved in the technical end of recording and they really don't understand old school, where the performance is the most important

STEVIE RAY VAUGHAN, HOUSTON, 1983. PHOTOGRAPH BY TRACY ANNE HART/THE HEIGHTS GALLERY.

thing, what clicks while you're playing. If there's some rough spots, those can be worked out if you want to go out doing that way. However, a lot of times an engineer-type producer or someone who is an engineer and wants to be a producer becomes a lot more difficult to work with. John Hammond was mainly—all the knowledge he had, all the things he'd seen made you want to play from your heart, and just play good music. John Hammond wasn't there for the session for *Texas Flood*, but we had him in mind. My thoughts during each track was that if this is the last record, I want to make the best I can do. And we only had a day and a half to do the tracks. "Texas Flood" was the last song we did, and they said, "That's all the time you got." But we had ten songs, and that's what we needed.

John Hammond came to the sessions for *Couldn't Stand the Weather*. He was there for that. For me, he was easy to work with, for the band, everyone, as far as I know. It was the engineer that had some difficulty with John. We would leave the track alone as much as possible and rework it.

On *Soul to Soul*, I played drums on that. So that was done quite a bit differently. The engineers did not want us to play the song at that speed. So he didn't want to turn on the recorder or anything. What ended up happening, we waited until he took a nap, and we had his assistant run the recorder for us. Tommy [Shannon] played bass, and I played drums, and we just did a long deal. I kind of mouthed the words at him, so we would know where we were. We actually played it slower, and on record we sped the tape up, from C to D. The whole thing was fun to do. Even though it wasn't an actual live performance, it had that vitality. Then I went back and put a guitar part on it. Then the keyboard player did it, and I sang it. That was really the only stacked one we did, but it doesn't sound stacked at all. The beat is like an old Duke shuffle, kind of a backward shuffle, when the drums were used backwards. The actual rhythm of it is backwards.

I really liked Fenton Robinson's guitar on the Duke recordings, especially with Larry Davis. And the guitar on the Bobby Bland, they were heavily produced,

PAUL RAY AND THE COBRAS: JOE SUBLETT (SAXOPHONE), PAUL RAY (VOCALS), DENNY FREEMAN (GUITAR), STEVIE RAY VAUGHAN (GUITAR), RODNEY CRAIG (DRUMS), AL NAPIER (BASS), AUSTIN, 1976. COURTESY PAUL AND DIANA RAY.

STEVIE RAY VAUGHAN, ANTONE'S POSTER, 1982. COURTESY CENTER FOR AMERICAN HISTORY, UNIVERSITY OF TEXAS.

but there's something that sticks up in your face, even though it's smooth. There's a lot of deep friendship in the music, a lot of people just coming together and making some good records. It's the kind of thing we had at Antone's. Clifford got the idea to start the club, and everybody wanted to be the house band there. Everyone was claiming to be the house band that week, but we were all friends. You see, everybody was changing bands every three to six months. Every time anybody felt stale, they'd go hook up with somebody else. It kept us real fresh, and then when everybody found a good, solid combination, musicians stayed together two or three years, and then they would shift it a little more. Well, The Thunderbirds had the same musicians for eight years. Now, it's twelve or thirteen years since they started, and I think they have really found a combination they like. It's the same with us [Double Trouble], we stayed together. I got back together with Tommy. Tommy and I have played together on and off since 1969. I met him in Dallas, the night that he quit Johnny Winter. He was on his way to California to play with another band called Krackerjack. And they came by The Fog on Lemmon Avenue, and it was time of year that he had met Johnny at the same place, almost to the day, three years earlier. The night he quit, I was at The Fog. I was fourteen, and Tommy was the only guy in the band that would talk to me. Everybody else was too hip, I don't know. I was a fourteen-year-old fart. That was the second part of my first club gig. We had an eleven-horn band. We were doing some things off the radio and some things we had heard on record. We sort of had a big band—put it this way, we had a lot of people in the band.

I like to play in a lot of different ways. With just a drummer, you don't have worry about changes. I like to play with a trio, and trade with a keyboard player, and use a big horn section as well, two drummers sometimes, if they can work together. Joe Sublett played saxes on "Little Sister" and "Looking Out the Window," and we had another horn player on "Stang's Swang," on "Couldn't Stand the Weather." Other than that there isn't much horn playing on there, though I'd like to record with a big horn section, four or five or six horns. I love to dodge horns. I like to stand in the middle of a semicircle and play. I follow the horns, and they follow me. I love to play solos with the horns blasting and play in between them.

STEVIE RAY VAUGHAN, HOUSTON, 1987.
PHOTOGRAPH BY TRACY ANNE HART/THE HEIGHTS GALLERY.

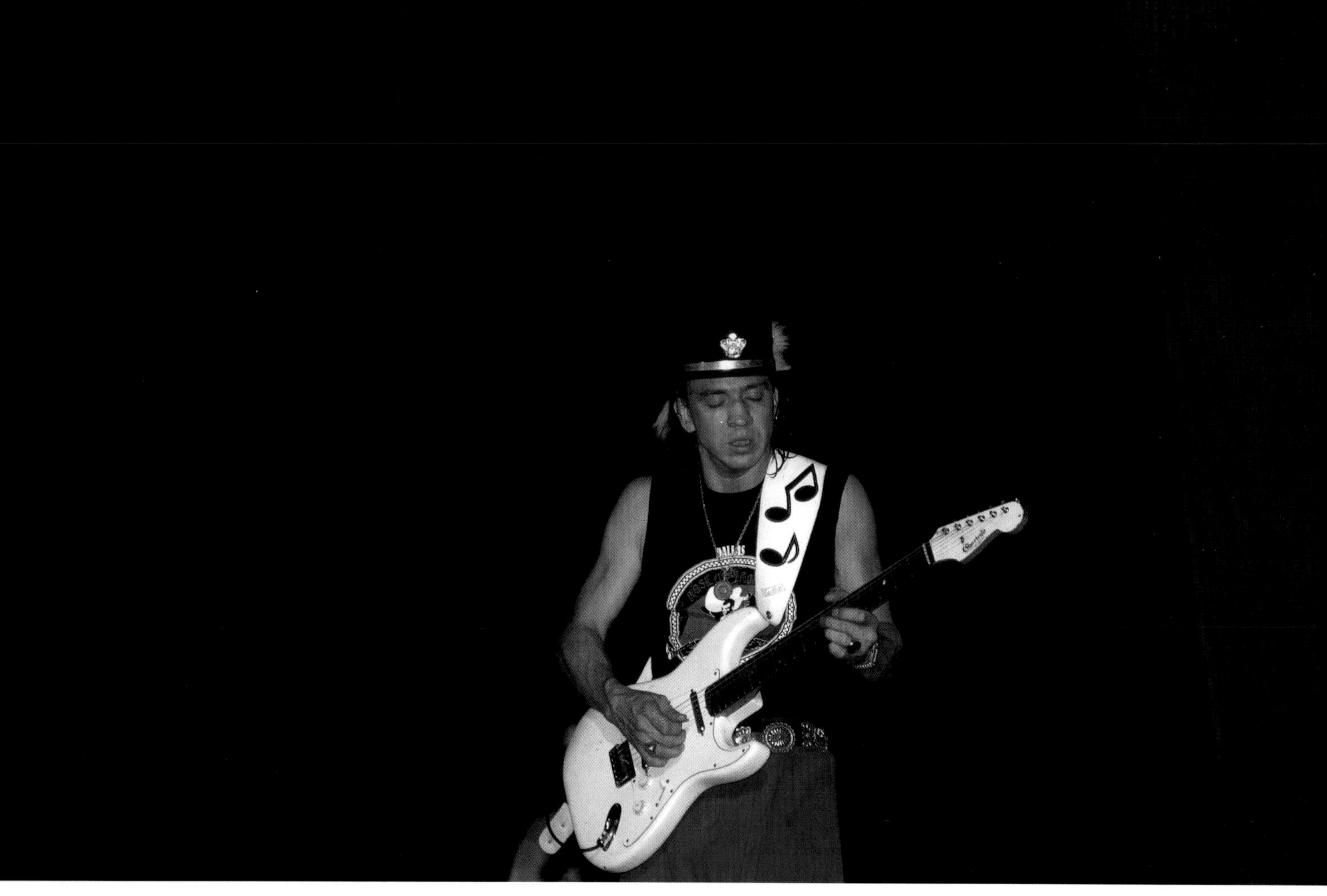

STEVIE RAY VAUGHAN, ARLINGTON, TEXAS, 1987.
PHOTOGRAPH BY ALAN GOVENAR.
(OPPOSITE) STEVIE RAY VAUGHAN, ARLINGTON, TEXAS, 1987.
PHOTOGRAPH BY ALAN GOVENAR.

My phone message is a bad recording of "Soul Scratch," the Bobby Bland instrumental. It's that Duke big band blues sound. And I like the drums, not necessarily how they're done in the mix, but how they sounded, just the drums themselves on the record. It was bright, and didn't sound like they were playing loud. It was just there, not like the New Orleans backbeat sound, but I like that, too.

The blues doesn't have to be three chords, or two or one. It doesn't have to be a lot of passing changes. It can be any of those combinations, or notes. What I'm thinking about writing, I don't think I'll be writing any "Everybody Go Out and Get High" songs in the future. The blues is just it in the first place, whether it does it by getting you mad in the first place, and then you get over it, or if it's relating to somebody else's story that's

the same as yours, or worse than yours, so that you don't feel so bad. Or it's a happy song. It doesn't matter. It's all soothing anyway. It's to help somebody's emotions. That's what it is. I hope I'm helping other people with my music. It helps me, makes me feel better. The blues gets me going. I have to wind back down.

My brother's guitar style is more poised than mine. I play like I'm breaking out of jail. I get excited and I can't stop. I don't really know how long my solos are going to be, but I try to bring them to a point without being redundant. When it stops being fun, it's time to be doing something else. Sometimes when you do something over and over, the meaner it gets.

One of the most memorable performances was Carnegie Hall. We had Jimmie and I on guitar, George Rains, and Chris Layton on drums, Tommy Shannon playing bass, Roomful of Blues horn section. Angela Strehli was there; it was the day after my birthday, October 4. There are so many that were a lot of fun. That's the main reason for doing it. If it's really just a job, then what are we doing?

I want to do an album with Jimmie. It's not too often that we get to play together. Usually, if we do, I'm sitting in with his band, or he's sitting in with mine. We are all supportive of each other. I'm very fortunate that way. It's something that I missed for a long time, because I was runnin' from everything. It takes a person a long time to get out of old habits. The rehabilitation program made me realize a lot of things, about people and places and things. The main thing I found with the problem was low self-esteem and a huge ego at the same time. No middle ground. That's what happens when someone is insecure, unless you can get by feeling sorry

STEVIE RAY VAUGHAN, NEW ORLEANS JAZZ AND HERITAGE FESTIVAL, 1981. PHOTOGRAPH BY MICHAEL P. SMITH.

for yourself. Sometimes that works, too. When you find yourself in a place that you can't stop drinking and you can't keep going, either, that's a pretty rough place to be. That's where I was, and at the same time, things I care about were quickly going out the window, those cares, not necessarily just material things. I was in a position where I could have hired somebody to baby-sit me, and buy the drugs, and buy me this and buy me that. Have them carry it for me, and if they got busted—"Oops!" I could have done that, but I chose not to do that. Both Tommy and I went into the treatment program. Now the whole band is clean. Rees and Chris aren't alcoholics, though us alcoholics sometimes resent the fact that other people can drink, but that's the trap. You have to deal with those feelings.

I think my playing makes more sense [now]. I listen to old live performances; we record every night. There are a lot of new things I really like. A lot of tones that I had no I idea how I got. A lot of things connected; fortunately, my addiction to alcohol and drugs hadn't taken away everything that I cared about, but it was fast becoming where those things were dying, because I was dying inside. Now, I can choose to live.

I'm just trying to take it as it comes along; all four of my records have gone gold in the last year. The next one, we just have to take our time and not try to top the other ones, but to make the best record we can. It's a matter of not paying attention to the other pressure. It's there, but what good does it do? We're planning to do club dates, maybe not advertise for a while.

Now, it's okay when there's blank spots. You know, I used to be scared to death of blank spots, and sometimes they still scare me. Sometimes you have to clean out the refrigerator before you put some food inside.

LIST OF ILLUSTRATIONS

ELECTRIFYING THE BLUES

DALLAS

FORT WORTH

SAXOPHONE

HOUSTON

ZYDECO

BEAUMONT, PORT ARTHUR, AND ORANGE

CALIFORNIA

SAN ANTONIO, CORPUS, RIO GRANDE VALLEY

AUSTIN

SELECTED DISCOGRAPHY

The two standard discographies that cover the history of blues recordings are *Recording the Blues* by Robert Dixon and John Godrich (New York: Stein and Day, 1970), and *Blues Records: 1943–1970* by Mike Leadbitter and Neil Slaven (2d ed., 2 vols. [London: Record Information Services, 1987]). More current releases and reissues by British, Dutch, German, Japanese, French, and Scandinavian labels are reviewed regularly in *Living Blues* (United States), *Juke Blues*, and *Blues and Rhythm* (England), *Jefferson* (Sweden), *BN* (Finland), *Blues Life* (Germany), *Block* (The Netherlands), and *IL Blues* (Italy). The following discography is a select list of Texas blues artists and available recordings on CD. For more information on reissue and contemporary recordings of Texas blues, try the following Web sites:

www.arhoolie.com
www.alligator.com
www.rounder.com
www.tower.com
www.document-records.com
www.docarts.com
www.acerecords.co.uk
www.rhinorecords.com

Johnny Ace
Johnny Ace Memorial Album. MCA Records 31183.

Alger "Texas" Alexander
Texas Alexander Vol. 1, 1927–1928. Document 2001.
Texas Alexander Vol. 2, 1928–1930. Document 2002.
Texas Alexander Vol. 3, 1930–1950. Document 2003.

Dave Alexander
Boogie Woogie Riot. Arhoolie 526.

Marcia Ball
Presumed Innocent. Alligator 4879.
So Many Rivers. Alligator 4891.
Blues House. Rounder 3131.
Hot Tamale Baby, Rounder 3095.

Black Ace (B. K. Turner)
I'm the Boss Card in Your Hand. Arhoolie 374.

Black Ace & Oscar Woods
Texas Slide Guitars, Complete Recorded Works, 1930–1938. Document 5143.

Bobby "Blue" Bland
Blues at Midnight. Malaco 7512.
Two Steps from the Blues. Remaster. MCA Records 112516.
Blues and Ballads. MCA Records 11977.
Greatest Hits, Vol. 1. MCA Records 11783.
Greatest Hits, Vol. 2. MCA Records 11809.
The "3B" Blues Boy. Ace 302.
The Voice. Ace 323.

Little Joe Blue
The Very Best of Little Joe Blue. Collectables 5744.

Weldon "Juke Boy" Bonner
Ghetto Poet. Arhoolie 9040.
Life Gave Me a Dirty Deal. Arhoolie 375.

Charles Brown
Drifting and Dreaming. Ace 589.
One More for the Road. Alligator 4771.
Charles Brown, 1944–1945. Classics Jazz (France) 894.
Charles Brown, 1946–1947. Classics Jazz (France) 1272.
Charles Brown, 1947–1948. Classics Jazz (France) 1147.
Charles Brown, 1948–1949. Classics Jazz (France) 1270.
Charles Brown, 1949–1951. Classics Jazz (France) 1272.

Clarence "Gatemouth" Brown
The Original Peacock Recordings. Rounder 2039.
One More Mile. Rounder 2034.
Real Life. Rounder 2054.
Pressure Cooker. Alligator 4745.
Standing My Ground. Alligator 4779.
No Looking Back. Alligator 4804.
Alright Again! Rounder 2028.
Okie Dokie Stomp. Blueseye 9622.
One More Mile. Rounder 2034.
Real Life. Rounder 2054.
Texas Swing. Rounder 11527.

Texas Johnny Brown
Nothin' But the Truth. Choctaw Creek Records 00012.

Sumter Bruton & Michael Price
Swingmasters Revue, Vol. 2. Aristokraft Records 7805.

Goree Carter
The Complete Recordings Vol. 1, 1949–1951. Blue Moon 6027.

Goree Carter, Lester Williams
The Complete Recordings Vol. 2, 1950–1954. Blue Moon 6036.

Cilfton Chenier
60 Minutes with the King of Zydeco. Arhoolie 301.
The Best of Clifton Chenier. Arhoolie 474.
Bogalusa Boogie. Arhoolie 347.

Bon Ton Roulet. Arhoolie 345.
I'm Here. Alligator 4729.

Charlie Christian
The Genius of Charlie Christian. Columbia/Legacy 065564.

W. C. Clark
From Austin with Soul. Alligator 4884.

Arnett Cobb
Story-Wild Man of Tenor Sax, 1943–1947. EPM (France) 159422.
Texas Sax. Aim Records 1302.
Movin' Right Along. Original Jazz Classics 1074.
Arnett Blows for 1300. Delmark 471.

Albert Collins
Ice Pickin'. Alligator 4713.
Frostbite. Alligator 4719.
Frozen Alive. 4725.
Don't Lose Your Cool. Alligator 4730.
Live in Japan. 4733.
Cold Snap. Alligator 4752.
Deluxe Edition. Alligator 601.

Albert Collins, Johnny Copeland, and Robert Cray
Showdown. Alligator 4743.

Johnny Copeland
Ain't Nothin' But a Party, Recorded Live. Rounder 2055.
Boom, Boom. Rounder 2060.
Bringin' It All Back Home. Rounder 2050.
Honky Tonkin'. Bullseye Blues 9621.
Make My Home Where I Hang My Hat. Rounder 2030.
Texas Twister. Rounder11504.
When the Rain Starts Fallin'. Rounder 11515.

Shemekia Copeland
Turn Up the Heat. Alligator 4857.
Wicked. Alligator 4875.
Talking to Strangers. 4887.

Pee Wee Crayton
Blues Guitar Magic. Ace 767.
The Modern Legacy. Ace 632.
Things I Used To Do. Ace 6566.

King Curtis
Hot Sax, Cool Licks. Ace 757.
Old Gold/Doing The Dixie Twist. Ace 614.
Trouble in Mind. Ace 512.
Trouble In Mind/Party Time. Ace 545.

Carl Davis and Dallas Jamboree Band, Dallas String Band, William McCoy, Will Day, Frenchy's String Band, Jake Jones and The Gold Front Boys
Texas Black Country Dance Music, 1927–1935. Document 5162.

Floyd Dixon
Cow Town Blues. Ace 740.
Wake Up and Live! Alligator 4841.

Robert Ealey
Turn Out the Lights. Black Top 1133.

Gloria Edwards
Texas Soul Sisters. Dialtone 009.

Hershel Evans, Illinois Jacquet, Hot Lips Page, Eddie Durham, Count Basie
Count Basie: One O'Clock Jump. Living Era 299.

Fabulous Thunderbirds
Girls Go Wild. Remaster. Benchmark 8002.
What's the Word. Remaster. Benchmark 8003.
Butt Rockin'. Remaster. Benchmark 8004.
T-Bird Rhythm. Remaster. Benchmark 8005.
Tacos Deluxe. Benchmark 8006.
Wrap It Up. Sony Music Special Products 24202.

Freddy Fender
Interpreta El Rock! Arhoolie 9039.
Eddie Con Los Shades: Rock 'n Roll. Arhoolie 9038.
Best of Freddy Fender. Aim Records 3007.
Greatest Hits. Columbia River Entertainment Group 191050.

Lowell Fulson
My First Recordings. Arhoolie 443.
Black Nights: The Early Kent Sessions. Ace 804.
The Final Kent Years. Ace 831.
The Tramp Years. Ace 755.
Tramp/Soul. Ace 339.

Anson Funderburgh and The Rockets
Which Way Is Texas. Bullseye Blues 9619.
Change in My Pocket. Bullseye Blues 9573.

Grady Gaines
Essential Texas Blues. House of Blues 1286.
Blues Sax Power. Easydisc 367047.

Roy Gaines
New Frontier Lover. Severn Records 0008.
In the House: Live at Lucerne, Vol. 4. Crosscut (Germany) 11074.
Gainelining, Roy Gaines with Crusaders Crew. P-Vine 8161.

Clarence Garlow
Zydeco: The Early Years, 1961–1962. Arhoolie 307.

Lloyd Glenn

Merry Christmas Baby. King Records 5018.

Lloyd Glenn, 1947–1950. Classics Jazz (France) 5016.

Lloyd Glenn, 1951–1952. Classics Jazz (France) 5069.

Lillian Glinn

Complete Recorded Works in Chronological Order. Document 5184.

Clarence Green

Guitar Crying the Blues. Double Trouble (Netherlands) 3022.

Peppermint Harris

Lonesome As I Can Be: The Jewel Recordings. Westside Records 909.

Texas on My Mind. Aim Records 8001.

Penthouse in the Ghetto. M.I.L. Multimedia 3033.

Z. Z. Hill

The Down Home Soul of Z. Z. Hill. Ace 099.

Z. Z. Hill, Freddie Hill

The Brand New Z. Z. Hill/Friend. Ace 532.

Smokey Hogg

Deep Ellum Rambler. Ace 780.

Midnight Blues. Ace 1019.

Serve It to the Right. Ace 866.

Sam "Lightnin'" Hopkins

The Best of Lightning Hopkins. Arhoolie 499.

The Gold Star Sessions—Vol. 1. Arhoolie 330.

The Gold Star Sessions—Vol. 2. Arhoolie 337.

Lightnin'! Arhoolie 390.

Po' Lightnin'. Arhoolie 403.

*The Texas Blues.*Arhoolie 302.

The Hopkins Brothers

Texas Country Blues. Arhoolie 340.

Bee Houston

The Hustler. Arhoolie 9008.

Joe Houston

Rockin' at the Drive In. Ace 994.

Joe Houston Blows Crazy. Ace 772.

Joe Hughes

Texas Guitar Slinger. Bullseye Blues 9568.

Ivory Joe Hunter

I Almost Lost My Mind, 1945–1950. EPM (France) 159992.

Jumpin' at the Dew Drop. Aim Records 1305.

Blues at Midnight. M.I.L. Multimedia 3038.

Long John Hunter

Ride with Me. Alligator 4861.

Swinging from the Rafters. Alligator 4853.

Border Town Legend. Alligator 4839.

Ooh Wee Pretty Baby. Norton 270.

Long John Hunter, Tom Hunter

One Foot in Texas. Doc Blues 6805.

Melvin "L'il Son" Jackson

Blues Come to Texas. Arhoolie 409.

Illinois Jacquet

Illinois Jacquet, 1951–1952. Classics Jazz (France) 1376.

The Illinois Jacquet Story [Box]. Proper Records (UK) 49.

Jacquet a la Carte. Ocium Records (Spain) 25.

Swing's the Thing. Universal/Verve 2003.

Blind Lemon Jefferson

Complete Recorded Works in Chronological Order, Vol. 1, 1925–1926. Document 5017.

Complete Recorded Works in Chronological Order, Vol. 2, 1927. Document 5018.

Complete Recorded Works in Chronological Order, Vol. 3, 1928. Document 5019.

Complete Recorded Works in Chronological Order, Vol. 4, 1929. Document 5020.

Alfred "Snuff" Johnson

Black Cowboy Blues and Church Songs. Documentary Arts 1001.

Blind Willie Johnson

The Complete Blind Willie Johnson. Columbia/Legacy 52835.

Coley Jones, "Bo" Jones, Little Hat Jones, Willie Reed, Oak Cliff "T-Bone" Walker

The Complete Recorded Works, 1927–1935. Document 5161.

Tu Tu Jones

I'm for Real. JSP 2112.

B. B. King

Blues in My Heart. Ace 996.

The Modern Recordings, 1950–51. Ace 835.

The RPM Hits, 1951–1957. Ace 712.

The Vintage Years. Ace ABOXCD 8.

Freddie King

Hide Away: The Best of Freddy King. Rhino 71510.

Clyde Langford

Paper Plate Blues. Documentary Arts 1008.

Huddie "Leadbelly" Ledbetter

Midnight Special—The Library of Congress Recordings, Vol. 1. Rounder 1044.

Gwine Dig a Hole to Put the Devil In—The Library of Congress Recordings, Vol. 2. Rounder 1045.

Let It Shine on Me—The Library of Congress Recordings, Vol. 3. Rounder 1046.

The Titanic—The Library of Congress Recordings, Vol. 4. Rounder 1047.
Nobody Knows The Trouble I've Seen—The Library of Congress Recordings, Vol. 5. Rounder 1048.
Go Down Old Hannah—The Library of Congress Recordings, Vol. 6. Rounder 1049.
Lead Belly's Last Sessions. Smithsonian Folkways 40068/71.

Mance Lipscomb
Captain, Captain. Arhoolie 465.
Live! At the Cabale. Arhoolie 482.
Texas Blues Guitar. Arhoolie 001.
Texas Country Blues. Arhoolie 9026.
Texas Songster. Arhoolie 306.
You Got to Reap What You Sow. Arhoolie 39.

Mance Lipscomb, Clifton Chenier, Lightnin' Hopkins
Live! At the 1966 Berkeley Blues Festival. Arhoolie 484.

Little Willie Littlefield
Going Back to Kay Cee. Ace 503.
Kat on the Keys. Ace 736.

Joey Long
Anthology. Blues Factory 47029.

Barbara Lynn
Hot Night Tonight. Texas Music Group/Lone Star Records 47.
Live in Japan. Vivid Sound 3044/5.
So Good. Bullesye Blues 9540.

Osceola Mays
Spirituals and Poems. Documentary Arts 1006.

Pete Mayes
For Pete's Sake. Texas Music Group/Lone Star Records 40.

Percy Mayfield
Poet of the Blues. Specialty Records 7001.
Memory Pain. Specialty Records 7027.
Hit the Road Again. Timeless Records 170.

Delbert McClinton
Live from Austin. Alligator 4773.
Delbert McClinton Live. New West Records 6048.
Second Wind/Keeper of the Flame. Raven Records (Australia) 133.
20th Century Masters: The Millennium, Delbert McClinton. MCA Nashville 0000309.

Joe Medwick
I'm an After Hour Man: The Crazy Cajun Recordings. Edsel (UK) 632.

Amos Milburn
Amos Milburn, 1947. Classics Jazz (France) 5047.
Amos Milburn, 1948–1949. Classics Jazz (France) 5077.
The Chicken Shack Boogie Man. Proper Records (UK) 102.
Bad Bad Whiskey. EPM (France) 160022.

Lillian Miller, Hattie Hudson, Gertrude Perkins, Ida May Mack, Bobbie Cadillac
Texas Girls: The Complete Recorded Works. Document 5163.

Alex Moore
From North Dallas to the East Side. Arhoolie 408.
Wiggle Tail: Original, Eccentric, Legendary and Lascivious Piano Playing and Stories. Rounder 2091.

Mike Morgan
Raw and Ready. Black Top 1051.
Full Moon over Dallas. Black Top 1080.
Texas Man. Severn 0014.

Mike Morgan, Jim Suhler
Let the Dogs Run. Black Top 1106.

Bill Neely
Texas Law and Justice. Arhoolie 496.

Jimmy "T-99" Nelson
Cry Hard Luck: The RPM and Kent Recordings 1951–61. Ace 228.
Rockin' and Shoutin' the Blues. Bullseye Blues 9593.

Sunny Ozuna
Mostly Sunny: Going Back in Crime. Freddie Records 2085.
Underground Oldies, Vol. 4. I.T.P. Records 8904.
30 Grandes Exitos. Freddie Records 2033.

Junior Parker
Way Back Home. Connoisseur Records 291.
Mercury Recordings. Collectables 5624.

Esther Phillips
The Home Is Where the Hatred Is. Raven Music 174.

Sammy Price
Sammy Price and The Blues Singers, Vol. 1, 1938–1941. Document 5667.
Sammy Price and The Blues Singers, Vol. 2. Document 5668.
Sammy Price, 1942–1945. Classics Jazz (France) 696.
Sammy Price, 1942–1945. Classics Jazz (France) 1083.

Dewey Redman
Choices. Enja 7073.
Musics. Original Jazz Classics 1860.
School Work. Mons Records (Germany) 875877.

Sonny Rhodes
A Good Day to Sing and Play the Blues. Stony Plain (Canada) 1273.
Blue Diamond. Stony Plain (Canada) 1257.
Out of Control. Kingsnake 031.
The Blues Is My Best Friend. Kingsnake 22.
Just Blues. Evidence 26060.

L. C. "Good Rockin'" Robinson
Mojo in My Hand. Arhoolie 453.
Doug Sahm
Juke Box Music/Last Real Texas Blues Band. Texas Music Group/Lone Star Records 61.
Son of San Antonio: The Roots of Sir Douglas. Music Club Records 50181.
San Antonio Rock: The Harlem Recordings 1957–1961. Norton 274.
Best of Doug Sahm and Friends. Rhino Records 71032.
Barou Sall, Massiren Drame, Boukounta Ndiaye
The Hoddu, Xalam and Gambere of Senegal: Griot Roots of the American Banjo. Documentary Arts 1004.
John T. Samples Sr., Virginia Peoples, Robert Berry, Jack Wislon, Cleveland Walters Jr.
Hallelujah Jubilee: East Texas Black Harmonica Players and Their Songs. Documentary Arts 1003.
Ray Sharpe
Linda Lu. Bear Family.
Robert Shaw
The Ma Grinder. Arhoolie 377.
Frankie Lee Sims
Lucy Mae Blues. Specialty Records 7022.
Texas Country Blues 1948–1951. Flyright (UK) 941.
Henry "Buster" Smith
The Legendary Buster Smith. Koch Jazz 8523.
Alto Sax Story, 1937–1950. Jazz Archives (France) 159972.
J. T. "Funny Papa" Smith
Complete Recorded Works in Chronological Order, 1930–1931. Document 6016.
Victoria Spivey, Lonnie Johnson
Idle Hours. Ace 518.
Angela Strehli
Blonde and Blue. Rounder 613127.
Deja Blue. House of Blues 1399.
Soul Shake. Texas Music Group/Lone Star Records 6.
Sonny Boy Terry
Breakfast Dance. Radiola Records RCC100.
Sonny Boy Terry, Little Ray Ybarra
Live at Miss Ann's Playpen. Doc Blues 6807.
Henry "Ragtime Texas" Thomas
Texas Worried Blues: The Complete Recorded Works 1927–1929. Yazoo 1080/1.
Willard "Ramblin'" Thomas
Ramblin' Thomas and The Dallas Blues Singers, Complete Recorded Works 1928–1932. Document 5107.
Big Mama Thornton
Ball and Chain. Arhoolie 305.
Jimmie Vaughan
Out There. Epic 67653.
Strange Pleasure. Epic 757202.
A Tribute to Stevie Ray Vaughan. Epic 67599.
The Essential Jimmie Vaughan. Legacy Recordings 86425.
Do You Get the Blues. Artemis Records 91.
Stevie Ray Vaughan
In the Beginning. Epic 53168.
Texas Flood. Legacy Recordings 65870.
Couldn't Stand the Weather. Epic 65871.
In Step. Epic 65874.
Soul to Soul. Epic 67599.
Live at Montreux 1982 and 1985. 86151.
The Sky Is Crying. 47390.
The Essential Stevie Ray Vaughan and Double Trouble. Epic 86243.
Eddie "Cleanhead" Vinson and Etta James
Blues in the Night, Vol. 1: The Early Show. Ace 9467.
The Late Show. Ace 9655.
Aaron "T-Bone" Walker
T-Bone Shuffle. Culture Press 1007.
T-Bone Blues. Rhino 08020.
Blues Masters: The Very Best of T-Bone Walker. Rhino 79894.
T-Bone Walker. Atlantic Jazz 8020.
The Complete Imperial Recordings, 1950–54. Definitive (Spain) 11259.
Beulah "Sipple" Wallace
Complete Recorded Works, Vol. 1, 1923–1925. Document 5399.
Complete Recorded Works, Vol. 2, 1925–1945. Document 5400.
Mercy Dee (Walton)
Troublesome Mind. Arhoolie 369.
Johnny "Guitar" Watson
Blues Masters: The Very Best of Johnny "Guitar" Watson. Rhino Records 75702.
Katie Webster
I Know That's Right. Arhoolie 393.
No Foolin'! Alligator 4803.
Swamp Boogie Queen. Alligator 4766.
Two-fisted Mama. Alligator 4777.
Hop Wilson
Hop Wilson and His Buddies. Ace 240.

U. P. Wilson
The Best of the Texas Blues Guitar Tornado. JSP 808.
Boogie Boy. JSP 255.
Whirlwind. JSP 277.
This Is U.P. Wilson. JSP 266.

Johnny Winter
Guitar Slinger. Alligator 4735.
Serious Business. Alligator 4742.
Third Degree. Alligator 4748.

Little Ray Ybarra, The Blues Sonics
Hot Rod Blues. Great Blues Recordings 79901–2.

SELECTED BIBLIOGRAPHY

Abrahams, Roger D. *Singing the Master: The Emergence of African American Culture in the Plantation South.* New York: Pantheon Books, 1992.

Albertson, Chris. *Bessie.* New York: Stein and Day, 1982.

Alyn, Glen. *I Say Me for a Parable: The Oral Autobiography of Mance Lipscomb, Texas Bluesman.* New York: Da Capo Press, 1994.

Bastin, Bruce. *Red River Blues.* Urbana: University of Illinois Press, 1986.

Broadbent, Peter. *Charlie Christian: Solo Flight—The Seminal Electric Guitarist.*

Blayden on Tyne, U.K.: Ashley Mark Publishing, 1997.

Charters, Samuel B. *The Country Blues.* New York: Da Capo Press, 1975.

Conway, Cecilia. *African Banjo Echoes in Appalachia: A Study of Folk Traditions.* Knoxville: University of Tennessee Press, 1995.

Dance, Helen Oakley. *Stormy Monday: The T-Bone Walker Story.* Baton Rouge: Louisiana State University Press, 1987.

Davidson, Chandler. *Biracial Politics.* Baton Rouge: Louisiana State University Press, 1972.

Dixon, Robert, and John Godrich, *Recording the Blues, 1902–1943.* New York: Stein and Day, 1970.

Evans, David. *Big Road Blues.* Berkeley: University of California Press, 1981.

Filene, Benjamin. *Public Memory and American Roots Music.* Chapel Hill: University of North Carolina Press, 2000.

Gart, Galen, and Roy C. Ames. "Taking My Chances: Don Robey and the Bronze Peacock." *Blues and Rhythm,* May 1989, 4–6.

Gart, Galen, and Roy C. Ames, with contributions by Ray Funk, Bob Bowman, and David Booth. *Duke/Peacock Records: An Illustrated History and Discography.* Milford, N.H.: Nickel Publications, 1990.

Ginell, Cary. *Milton Brown and the Founding of Western Swing.* Urbana: University of Illinois Press, 1994.

Govenar, Alan. *Meeting the Blues.* Dallas: Taylor Publishing, 1988.

Govenar, Alan. *Living Texas Blues.* Dallas: Dallas Museum of Art, 1985.

Govenar, Alan. *Osceola: Memoirs of a Sharecropper's Daughter.* New York: Hyperion, 2000.

Govenar, Alan. *Untold Glory: African Americans in Pursuit of Freedom Opportunity, and Achievement.* New York: Doubleday/Harlem Moon, 2007.

Govenar, Alan, Francis E. Abernethy, and Patrick Mullen, eds. *Juneteenth Texas: Essays in African-American Folklore.* Denton: University of North Texas Press, 1996.

Govenar, Alan, and Jay F. Brakefield. *Deep Ellum and Central Track: Where the Black and White Worlds of Dallas Converged.* Denton: University of North Texas Press, 1998.

Govenar, Alan, and Benny Joseph. *The Early Years of Rhythm and Blues.* Altglen, Penn.: Schiffer Publishing, 2004.

Guralnick, Peter. *Lost Highway.* New York: Vintage Books, 1982.

Harris, Sheldon. *Blues Who's Who.* New York: Da Capo Press, 1983.

Harrison, Daphne Duval. *Black Pearls: Blues Queens of the 1920s.* New Brunswick, N.J.: Rutgers University Press, 1988.

Heilbut, Tony. *The Gospel Sound.* New York: Simon and Schuster, 1971.

Herzhaft, Gerard. *Le Blues.* Paris: Presses Universitaires de France, 1981.

Herzhaft, Gerard. *Encyclopedia of the Blues.* Fayetteville: University of Arkansas Press, 1992.

Hofstein, Francis. *Le Rhythm and Blues.* Paris: Presses Universitaires de France, 1991.

Jones, Leroi (Imamu A. Baraka). *Blues People.* New York: Morrow, 1963.

Keil, Charles. *Urban Blues.* Chicago: University of Chicago Press, 1966.

Kupik, Gerhard. *Africa and the Blues.* Jackson: University Press of Mississippi, 1999.

Ledbitter, Michael. *Nothing But the Blues.* New York: Oak Publications, 1971.

Ledbitter, Michael, and Neil Slaven. *Blues Records, 1943–1970,* 2d ed. Vols. 1 and 2. London: Record Information Services, 1987.

Levine, Lawrence W. *Black Culture and Black Consciousness.* Oxford: Oxford University Press, 1977.

Living Blues, nos. 1–86. Oxford, Mississippi: Center for the Study of Southern Culture, University of Mississippi, 1970–1989.

Lomax, John A. *Adventures of a Ballad Hunter.* New York: Macmillan, 1947.

Oliphant, Dave. *Texan Jazz.* Austin: University of Texas Press, 1996.

Oliver, Paul. *Blues Off the Record.* New York: Da Capo Press, 1984.

Oliver, Paul. *Conversation with the Blues.* Cambridge: Cambridge University Press, 1997.

Oliver, Paul. *Songsters and Saints.* Cambridge: Cambridge University Press, 1984.

Palmer, Robert. *Deep Blues.* New York: Viking Press, 1981.

Pearson, Barry Lee. *Sounds So Good to Me.* Philadelphia: University of Pennsylvania Press, 1984.

Porterfield, Nolan. *Last Cavalier: The Life and Times of John A. Lomax, 1867–1948.* Urbana: University of Illinois Press, 1996.

Price, Sammy. *What Do They Want? A Jazz Autobiography.* Urbana: University of Illinois Press, 1990.

Russell, Ross. *Jazz Style in Kansas City and the Southwest.* Berkeley: University of California Press, 1971.

Salem, James M. *The Late Great Johnny Ace and the Transition from Rhythm and Blues to Rock 'n' Roll.* Urbana: University of Illinois Press, 1999.

Shaw, Arnold. *Honkers and Shouters.* New York: Collier Books, 1978.

Titon, Jeff Todd. *Early Downhome Blues.* Urbana: University of Illinois Press, 1979.

Wilkinson, Christopher. *Jazz on the Road: Don Albert's Musical Life.* Berkeley: University of California Press, 2001.

Wolfe, Charles, and Kip Lornell. *The Life and Legend of Leadbelly.* New York: HarperCollins, 1992.

Wood, Roger. *Down in Houston: Bayou City Blues.* Photography by James Fraher. Austin: University of Texas Press, 2003.

Wood, Roger. *Texas Zydeco.* Photography by James Fraher. Austin: University of Texas Press, 2006.

INDEX

* Note: Page references in **bold** indicate primary treatment of subjects. Page references in *italics* indicate photographs and illustrations. Page references including "n" denote material found in the notes.